Cranston's Consumers a...

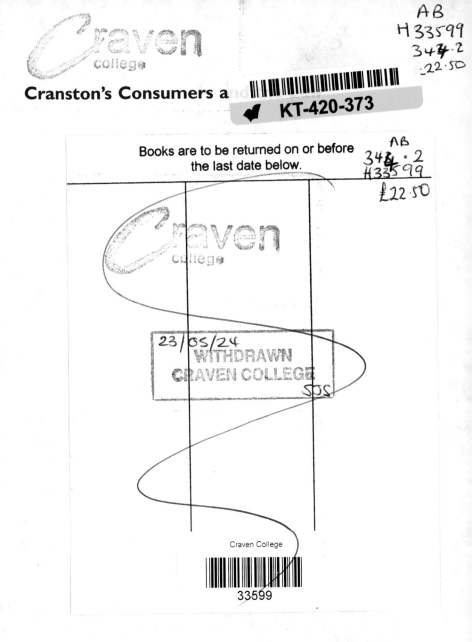

Books are to be returned on or before
the last date below.

Law in Context

Editors: William Twining (University College London) and
Christopher McCrudden (Lincoln College, Oxford)

Ashworth: *Sentencing and Criminal Justice*
Barton & Douglas: *Law and Parenthood*
Bercusson: *European Labour Law*
Birkinshaw: *Freedom of Information: The Law, the Practice and the Ideal*
Cane: *Atiyah's Accidents, Compensation and the Law*
Collins: *The Law of Contract*
Cranston: *Legal Foundations of the Welfare State*
Davies & Freedland: *Labour Law: Text and Materials*
Detmold: *Courts and Administrators: A Study of Jurisprudence*
Doggett: *Marriage, Wife-Beating and the Law in Victorian England*
Dummett & Nicol: *Subjects, Citizens, Aliens and Others: Nationality and Immigration Law*
Elworthy & Holder: *Environmental Protection: Text and Materials*
Fortin: *Children's Rights and the Developing Law*
Goodrich: *Languages of Law*
Hadden: *Company Law and Capitalism*
Harlow & Rawlings: *Law and Administration*
Harris: *An Introduction to Law*
Lacey & Wells: *Reconstructing Criminal Law: Text and Materials*
Lewis: *Choice and the Legal Order: Rising above Politics*
Moffat: *Trusts Law: Text and Materials*
Norrie: *Crime, Reason and History*
Oliver & Drewry: *The Law and Parliament*
Oliver: *Common Values and the Public-Private Divide*
Page & Fergusson: *Investor Protection*
Palmer & Roberts: *Dispute Processes – ADR and the Primary Forms of Decision Making*
Picciotto: *International Business Transaction*
Ramsay: *Consumer Protection: Text and Materials*
Richardson: *Law, Process and Custody*
Snyder: *New Directions in European Community Law*
Stapleton: *Product Liability*
Turpin: *British Government and the Constitution: Text, Cases and Materials*
Twining & Anderson: *Analysis of Evidence*
Twining & Miers: *How to do Things with Rules*
Ward: *A Critical Introduction to European Law*
Zander: *Cases and Materials on the English Legal System*

Cranston's Consumers and the Law

Third Edition

Colin Scott and Julia Black

Butterworths
London Edinburgh Dublin
2000

United Kingdom	Butterworths, a Division of Reed Elsevier (UK) Ltd, Halsbury House, 35 Chancery Lane, LONDON WC2A 1EL and 4 Hill Street, EDINBURGH EH2 3JZ
Australia	Butterworths, a Division of Reed International Books Australia Pty Ltd, CHATSWOOD, New South Wales
Canada	Butterworths Canada Ltd, MARKHAM, Ontario
Hong Kong	Butterworths Asia (Hong Kong), HONG KONG
India	Butterworths Asia, NEW DELHI
Ireland	Butterworth (Ireland) Ltd, DUBLIN
Malaysia	Malayan Law Journal Sdn Bhd, KUALA LUMPUR
New Zealand	Butterworths of New Zealand Ltd, WELLINGTON
Singapore	Butterworths Asia, SINGAPORE
South Africa	Butterworths Publishers (Pty) Ltd, DURBAN
USA	Lexis Law Publishing, CHARLOTTESVILLE, Virginia

ISBN 0 406 98802 1

Printed and bound in Great Britain by
Butler & Tanner Ltd, Frome and London

Visit Butterworths LEXIS *direct* at: http://www.butterworths.com

Preface to the Third Edition

It is sixteen years since the last edition of *Cranston's Consumers and the Law* appeared. We have retained the objectives of earlier editions—to provide a contextual and critical account of the consumer law of England and Wales with extensive comparison with solutions adopted in other jurisdictions. We have substantially retained the structure of earlier editions also, though we have removed the chapter on title, risk and performance and replaced it with a full chapter on services. Ross Cranston has no responsibility for any of the views expressed in the book, and we take entire responsibility for the text.

It is a tribute to Ross Cranston's vision that though nearly every aspect of legal doctrine analysed in this book has changed since the previous edition, the original structure and analysis continue to illuminate the topics. Ross was an early observer of such important phenomena as selective enforcement and self-regulation in the consumer domain, even though he was an advocate of neither. He believed passionately in strong public regulation as the basis for effective consumer protection and this was the primary basis for his critical approach both to the private law and self-regulation and to critics of public regulation.

We share Ross's interest in regulation—in different ways we would each claim it is our main field and we have both been closely involved in the development of graduate teaching and research in regulation at LSE. However, our own researches and understanding of the broader literature on regulation have led us to diverge to a certain extent from Ross's views on the respective merits of public regulation, self-regulation and private law. The contemporary emphasis of regulation research on institutional design is to find ways to mix a wide variety of instruments so as to promote development of and compliance with appropriate norms. We have followed this approach in examining regulation (broadly defined) in the consumer domain.

We noted above that major doctrinal changes have occurred in the field of consumer law over the last sixteen years. There have been at least four major sources of reform. Firstly, the Law Commission made recommendations for reform of the law relating to sale of goods and privity, implemented by the Sale and Supply of Goods Act 1994 and the Law of Contract (Rights of Third Parties) Act 1999. Secondly, membership of the European Community has enabled the UK to participate in wider processes of consumer law reform with the consequent obligation to implement EC law in the UK. The importance of EC law in the consumer domain was hardly apparent at the time of the publication of the last edition. Now it is obvious that EC law is central to many developments. Major examples of such EC-inspired legislation include the Consumer Protection Act 1987 Part I (which introduced strict liability for producers of defective products), the Control of Misleading Advertisements Regulation 1988, the General Product Safety Regulations 1994 and the Unfair Terms in Consumer Contracts Regulations 1994 and 1999. There are numerous other examples discussed in the book, and other important EC measures such as the Injunctions Directive 1998 and the Consumer Guarantees Directive 1999 await UK implementation. Notwithstanding the importance of EC norms in the shaping of contemporary UK consumer law, it should be noted that we have taken the view that the history and institutions of EC consumer law and policy are substantially outside the scope of this work.

A third source of law reform is direct government initiative. While the Conservative governments in power from 1979–1997 were not noted for their enthusiasm for consumer law measures, they were responsible for important reforms on product safety and misleading price indications (introduced in Parts II and III of the Consumer Protection Act 1987 respectively), the Food Safety Act 1990 (parts of which implemented EC legislation) and for major new regulatory regimes in the areas of financial services (first under the Financial Services Act 1986, and now displaced by a Labour measure, the Financial Services and Markets Act 2000) and utilities services (currently undergoing major legislative reform).

The Labour government elected in May 1997 has committed itself to substantial reform of consumer law (in the 1999 White Paper *Modern Markets, Confident Consumers*) and to a number of related areas (including utilities and financial services regulation, noted above, and the Competition Act 1998). Consequently at the time of writing we are in the midst of major and welcome legislative reform. Some new measures have already been introduced, such as the creation of the Foods Standards Agency by the Food Standards Act 1999, and the reforms of utilities and financial services regulation mentioned above. New legislation is planned to reform the Trade Descriptions Act 1968 to align the principles relating to services with those applying to goods and to strengthen the capacities of the

iconient world
the world
of physical spaces.

Office of Fair Trading to approve codes of practice and to secure injunctions against unfair trading practices. New powers are proposed also for the Secretary of State to criminalize unfair trading practices by statutory instrument and for local trading standards departments to enforce the provisions of the Fair Trading Act 1973 which relate to unfair trading practices. New independent consumer councils are to be established for the telecommunications, water and postal services and the existing Gas Consumers Council is to be replaced by an energy consumer council for gas and electricity. The final chapter provides an early evaluation of this work of reform.

A fourth source of law reform is the activity of the courts. Perhaps the most important area of judicial activism affecting consumers is in the field of professional negligence, where the House of Lords, having pulled away from the possibility of recovery in negligence for pure economic loss (in *Caparo v Dickman* and *Murphy v Brentwood District Council* in particular), subsequently surprised commentators by treating more generously third party beneficiaries to a will (*White v Jones*) and house purchasers adversely affected by a negligent survey (*Smith v Bush*). The density of the legislation in the consumer domain arguably gives to judges rather less scope for the development of judicial policy than might be true in other areas. This notwithstanding, the Court of Appeal played an important role in the development of the interpretation of the Trade Descriptions Act 1968, and more recently the House of Lords has occasionally had to consider consumer statutes, as in *Warwickshire County Council v Johnson* (clarifying the obvious, that employees were not to be prosecuted for pricing offences under s 20(1) of the Consumer Protection Act 1987) and *Dimond v Lovell* (a decision with very wide implications that a car hire agreement where payment was deferred was a consumer credit agreement under the Consumer Credit Act 1974, and invalid if not complying with the Act's requirements). Furthermore the importance of EC legislation gives to Community courts an important interpretive role, as with the effective neutering by the European Court of Justice (in *Commission v United Kingdom*) of the contentious wording of the state of the art defence in Part I of the Consumer Protection Act 1987.

Colin Scott would like to record the intellectual debt he owes to Iain Ramsay who taught him consumer law at Osgoode Hall Law School and to the discussions he has had with many consumer law students at the University of Warwick and the London School of Economics over the last ten years. We thank our colleague Joe Jacob for his assistance in getting to grips with the new Civil Procedure Rules introduced in April 1999. We are endebted to Ross Cranston for his support and encouragement. Julia Black revised and updated Chapters 1 and 12 and contributed the sections on financial services in Chapters 6 and 9. Colin Scott revised and updated

Chapters 2, 4 and 6, wrote Chapters 5 and 10 and took responsibility for the overall editing and updating of the work. The concluding chapter of was written jointly by Colin Scott and Julia Black.

Colin Scott
Julia Black

July 2000

Cranston's Consumers and the Law on the internet

An internet home page has been established for readers of this book. This home page has two main purposes:

- firstly, it provides links to website containing important primary sources such as codes, consultation documents and reports which are not always easily accessible in law libraries;
- secondly it will be used to provide periodic updating information on key developments in law and policy.

The first update will appear in January 2001, with further updates in April and October.

To access the website go to the Butterworths academic home page—**www.butterworths.com/academic** and click on the *Cranston* link. You will be asked for a password. Please enter the password 'breadandale'.

Contents

CHAPTER 9

The provision of information   337

CHAPTER 10

Product standards: regulating for consumer health and safety   377

Table of statutes

References in this Table are to page number. Where a page number is in **bold** this indicates that the Act is set out in part or in full.

Trade Descriptions Act 1968–*contd*
s 16 349
  20 .... 326, 327
  23 327
  24 333
      (1) 329, 332, 334
  35 520
  54 418
  57, 58 418
  60 418
Trade Descriptions Act 1972 349
Trade Union and Labour Relations
    (Consolidation) Act 1992
s 219–221 21
Trading Schemes Act 1996 411

Unfair Contracts Terms Act
    1977 .... 9, 79, 88,
                        89, 148, 155,
                        157, 178, 180,
                        222, 227, 523
s 1(1) 85
  2 414
    (1) 85, 152
    (2) 85, 152, 199
  3 .... 85, 102
  4 86
  5 .... 85, 177
  6 .... 84, 154, 179, 414
    (2), (3) 8
  7 414
    (2) 199
    (3A) 85
  8 151
    (1) 85
  10 86
  11(1) 87
    (2)–(4) 88
  13 164
    (1) 86
    (2) 87
  27(2) 86
Sch 2 87
Unsolicited Goods and Services Act
    1971
s 1 426
  2, 3A 427
Unsolicited Goods and Services Act
    1975
s 1 426
  2, 3A 427

PAGE

Water Act 1989 463
Water Industry Act 1991 463
s 28 20
  30 223
  30A 224
  38 .... 224, 226
  86A 223
  95 224
  150A 224
Water Resources Act 1991 463
Weights and Measures Act 1878 . 324
Weights and Measures Act
    1985 .... 324, 355
s 22(3)(b) 348
  28(1) **323**
  45(1)(a) 348
    (3) 348
  48 347

AUSTRALIA
Cigarettes (Labelling) Act 1972 .. 344
Consumer Affairs Act 1972
s 20A 428
Contracts Review Act 1980
s 7–9 99
Sch 1 99
Packages Act 1969–72
s 26, 37 348
Trade Practices Act 1974 418
s 4(1) 8
  56(1) 317
    (2), (3) 318
  74(2) 203
    (3) 8
  80A 65
  82 336
  84(2) 334

CANADA
British Columbia
Class Proceedings Act 1995 133
Ontario
Class Proceedings Act 132
s 1(1) 128
  31(1) 128

GERMANY
Standard Contract Terms Act
    1976 90

List of cases

H

I

J

X

Y

Z

Decisions of the European Court of Justice are listed below numerically. These decisions are also included in the preceding alphabetical list.

Chapter 1

Introduction: the context of consumer protection

1   PROBLEMS FACING CONSUMERS

Do you trust a secondhand car salesman to give you the correct information about a car? Is the medicine that you have just bought going to have any effect? Does your builder really know what he's doing? Do mobile phones emit brain-scrambling airwaves? Is that low fat chocolate bar really low in fat? Did you pay the right price for your stereo or the extended warranty you just bought with it? Do you have any idea what the right price would be?

Consumer law and consumer regulation are ostensibly aimed at providing consumers with protection from, and rights against, producers and suppliers of goods and services. But how necessary are those measures? To what extent are consumers disadvantaged? And how should we see the consumer, and, more fundamentally, consumption itself? In many debates on the need for consumer protection, particularly economic debates, consumers are posited as sovereign economic actors, with stable preferences that have been formulated rationally and autonomously, and who have the potential to exercise power in the economic system by their purchasing choices, so ensuring that producers and suppliers respond to meet those preferences. In this model, it is the role of consumer protection to enable those choices to be made more efficiently.

Others question both the model of consumer sovereignty and the desirability of assisting or encouraging consumption. In 1958, JK Galbraith argued that rather than the consumer determining the pattern of production, it was the producers and suppliers of goods and services that controlled consumer demand. Advertising, marketing, packaging, market research all serve to shift the decision of what to consume from the consumer to the producer. As for fulfilling consumer's wants or needs:

'[p]roduction only fills the void that it has itself created'.[1] This 'dependence effect' means that if production is to increase, wants must effectively be contrived.[2]

> The fact that wants can be synthesised by advertising, catalysed by salesmanship, and shaped by the discrete manipulations of the persuaders shows that they are not very urgent. A man who is hungry need never be told of his need for food.[3]

Producers are not alone in creating consumer desires, however, Galbraith argues. The urge to consume is fathered by a value system which places great emphasis on the ability to produce, and which thus evaluates people by what they consume.[4] Others have taken the theme of social construction much further, and argued that rather than seeing the process in terms of individual needs being created for individual products, what is produced by society is a system of needs and an overall propensity to consume.[5] In this view consumption is in affluent societies based not on needs and enjoyment but on complex codes in which what an individual consumer buys indicates their social class and status. Consumption is for communicating at once social affiliation and social demarcation. What you consume signifies to others the type of person you are and your social position. Consumption is a system of values, which encompass the value of production, but also social integration and differentiation. Consumption, or more particularly, the language of consumption, the language of what different commodities signify, is furthermore a system which has to be learnt: 'the consumer society is also the society of learning to consume, of social training in consumption'.[6] The perspective from which such arguments would view consumer law and policy is a less comfortable one: that in facilitating consumption such policies simply serve to enhance the dependence effect, and to encourage the pathologies to which consumption can lead.

It is probably fair to say that it is a modified consumer sovereignty view that informs much of the post-war development of consumer law and policy in the UK and underlies current government thinking, as it engages in processes of reform. The opening statement of the 1999 White Paper on

---

1. JK Galbraith *The Affluent Society* (Andre Deutsch, 4th edn, 1984) p 127 and generally Chapter 11.
2. JK Galbraith *The Affluent Society* p 133.
3. JK Galbraith *The Affluent Society* p 131.
4. JK Galbraith *The Affluent Society* p 129.
5. J Baudrillard *The Consumer Society: Myths and Structures* (Sage Publications, transl 1998; Editions Denoel, 1970), especially Chapter 5.
6. J Baudrillard *The Consumer Society: Myths and Structures* p 81.

consumer law states '[c]onfident consumers, making informed decisions in modern, competitive markets, promote the development of innovative, good value products.'[7] Consumer policy is focused on redressing consumer detriment. Defining detriment is not a straightforward task, however. It has been defined in part as the difference in purchasing decisions that consumers make on the basis of information that is available, and decisions they would have made with further information that they could usefully obtain and assimilate.[8] The principal government body responsible for consumer issues, the Office of Fair Trading (OFT), is engaged in a process of determining how detriment may be further defined and measured, for example defining it in terms of lost welfare,[9] and of identifying indicators of detriment in terms of costs of complaining both financially and in terms of emotional stress.[10]

One indication of detriment is the number of complaints that are made. Between 78.5 million and 93.1 million complaints were made by consumers in 1999.[11] Just over half of those complaints concerned the quality of products or services, the second largest category (15%) related to selling techniques or misinformation, and 10% concerned problems in obtaining redress.[12] Given that only 29% of consumers complain, this is likely to be an underestimation of the level of dissatisfaction experienced.[13] In 65% of cases, the reason given for not complaining was that the person felt it would not do any good.[14] Indeed, of those that did complain, only 36% reported that they were very satisfied or quite satisfied with the outcome, as opposed to 43% who stated they were either very dissatisfied or quite dissatisfied.[15] Complaining is also expensive. The total estimated cost of all complaints in 1999 was between £5.6 billion and £11 billion. Taking the mid-range measurement of £8.3 billion, the OFT calculated that this represented 1.5% of total household consumer expenditure, or £180 per adult per annum.[16]

---

[7] DTI *Modern Markets: Confident Consumers* (Cm 4410 (1999)).
[8] London Economics, *Consumer Detriment under Conditions of Imperfect Information*, OFT Research Paper 11 (HMSO, 1997).
[9] R Vaughan, *Distributional Issues in Welfare Assessment and Consumer Affairs Policy*, Appendix to OFT, *Vulnerable Consumers and Financial Services* (HMSO, 1999).
[10] *Consumer Detriment*, OFT 296, February 2000.
[11] *Consumer Detriment*, OFT 296, February 2000.
[12] *Consumer Detriment*, OFT 296, February 2000, Table 5.2.
[13] Consumers' Association *Handled with Care? Consumer Complaints 1991–1997* p 8 (1997 figures); the number was down from 49% in 1994.
[14] Consumers' Association, *Handled with Care? Consumer Complaints 1991–1997* p 13.
[15] OFT, *Consumer Detriment,* Table 7.1. Similar results were found by the Consumers' Association, *Handled with Care,* p 17.
[16] OFT *Consumer Detriment* para 6.17.

However consumer dissatisfaction only measures those instances where consumers are aware or think that they have cause to complain. As a gauge of the extent to which consumers are disadvantaged by producers or suppliers, it is a very approximate measurement. Not only might consumers not take the trouble to complain, but for reasons that are explored below they might not be aware that they have cause to do so. The problem is exacerbated in the case of taking legal action, for not only are the costs significantly higher than for making a complaint to the company concerned, but two-thirds of people are not aware of their legal rights.[17]

2   VULNERABLE CONSUMERS

The problems that consumers face in the market are not the same for all consumers and can fall most heavily on vulnerable consumers, in particular on low income consumers. Research published by the Office of Fair Trading (OFT) in 1998 identified seven categories of vulnerable consumer: those on low income, the unemployed, those suffering long-term illness or disability, those with low levels of educational attainment, members of ethnic minorities, older people and the young.[18] The categories are not mutually exclusive, and a key common characteristic of the members of those groups was low income.[19] The report found that those who were members of the potentially vulnerable groups were likely to be on low income, and four-fifths of those on low incomes were in one or more of those groups.[20] Consumer protection is thus not just a middle class issue. Instead, as Caplovitz noted in the 1960s in *The Poor Pay More*, it is a matter of vital importance for the less well off members of society.[1] Their interests are somewhat different, however, from what has been conventionally regarded as the main concern of consumer protection. There is still the need that the products and services they buy should be

[17]   DTI *Modern Markets: Confident Consumers*, Cm 4410 (The Stationery Office, 1999), para 1.5.
[18]   OFT *Vulnerable Consumer Groups: Quantification and Analysis,* Research Paper 15 (Ramil Burden (OFT, 1998)).
[19]   Very low income is defined by the OFT as those whose income is between £4,000–£7,000 per year, low income as those households whose income is between £5,000 and £8,000 per year (within that the amounts vary with the type of household, eg single lone pensioner, lone parents, couples with children): OFT *Vulnerable Consumer Groups: Quantification and Analysis,* Research Paper 15 (Ramil Burden (OFT, 1998)).
[20]   OFT *Vulnerable Consumer Groups: Quantification and Analysis,* Research Paper 15 (Ramil Burden (OFT, 1998)).
[1]   David Caplovitz *The Poor Pay More* (Free Press, 1963).

satisfactory and provide value for money, 'but the fuel bill rather than the faulty washing machine is ... symbolic of the central consumer issue' for low income consumers.[2]

The welfare impact of consumer detriment is also greater on those with lower incomes (a loss of £10 per week is more significant to someone with a weekly income of £100 than it is to someone with a weekly income of £1,000).[3] So overpaying for goods or services has more of an impact on those with low incomes than on those with higher incomes. Those on lower incomes also tend to pay more for what they purchase. One report suggested that prices for the goods in shops in lower income neighbourhoods in the UK were up to 60% above the average price for such goods in supermarkets.[4] Access to supermarkets or other larger stores may be difficult for many people on low incomes due to poor provision of public transport, and levels of car ownership being low.[5] Other factors may also enter, such as the non-availability of credit facilities in stores outside the area. Further the lack of financial resources or storage facilities may necessitate the constant purchase of small quantities, which can be more expensive.

A further difficulty which low income consumers face is financial exclusion. The issue of financial exclusion is one that has only recently arrived on the public agenda, and the issue is of such topicality that even the British Banker's Association has become involved in studies on exclusion of low income and ethnic minority groups from access to basic financial services.[6] The government has been considering how the rules surrounding credit unions could be altered to increase their role in providing

---

2   David Caplovitz *The Poor Pay More*. See also Social Exclusion Unit *Bringing Britain Together: A National Strategy for Neighbourhood Renewal* (Cm 4045 (1998)) para 1.27; NCC *For Richer, For Poorer* (1975) pp 9–14; David Piachaud *Do the Poor Pay More?* Poverty Research Series 3 (Child Poverty Action Group, 1974) p 5. Alisdair Aird 'Goods and Services' in Frances Williams (ed) *Why the Poor Pay More?* (NCC, 1977) pp 14–15. See generally Alan R Andreasen *The Disadvantaged Consumer* (Free Press, 1975); Ronald Sackville *Law and Poverty in Australia* (AGPS, 1975) Chapter 4.

3   See further F Cowell and K Gardiner *Welfare Weights,* OFT Research Paper 20 (January 2000).

4   Social Exclusion Unit, *Bringing Britain Together: A National Strategy for Neighbourhood Renewal* (Cm 4045 (1998)) para 1.27.

5   Frances Williams *Why the Poor Pay More?* (NCC, 1977).

6   The BBA, the DTI and the Commission for Racial Equality launched a joint project on the difficulties faced by ethnic minority businesses in the UK, particularly in relation to obtaining finance and business support. The two year project is due to start in 2000. Also starting from 2000 the BBA is to provide an Annual Community Involvement Report on promoting enterprise in deprived areas: BBA Briefing Point, 2 November 1999.

credit to those on low incomes.[7] It appointed a review of the competitiveness of the banking industry under Don Cruickshank,[8] and the OFT has recently completed a survey on the access that vulnerable consumers have to basic financial services.[9] Basic financial services are identified as bank or building society accounts, home contents insurance, short-term credit and long-term savings.[10] 38% of those on very low incomes, and 24% of those on low incomes do not have a bank or building society account; over 50% of both groups have no credit. For the majority of those without bank accounts or credit facilities, the reason given was that they preferred to budget using cash,[11] although there is reason to think that in some cases lack of an account may be an imposed choice: banks refuse around 25% of applications made.[12] Whilst a preference for cash may in some circumstances be understandable, relying solely on cash does pose several disadvantages. Only 12% of employees are paid in cash; having a bank account can thus in effect be a condition of employment.[13] Further, a number of goods are cheaper if bought over the telephone, or if paid for by direct debit. The government's Green Paper on utility regulation showed that gas consumers who settle their accounts on direct debit pay an average of 12% less than those who use pre-payment meters and 7% less than those paid on receipt of a quarterly bill; the figures for electricity were 8% and 3% respectively. Of those using pre-payment meters, over 50% were on incomes of £12,000 per year or less.[14]

[7]   HM Treasury *Taskforce Report: Credit Unions of the Future* (November 1999).
[8]   Review of Banking Services in the UK, *Banking Review: Interim Report* (1999); *Competition in UK Banking* (March 2000).
[9]   *Vulnerable Consumers and Financial Services, The Report of the Director General's Inquiry* (OFT, 1999).
[10]   *Vulnerable Consumers and Financial Services, The Report of the Director General's Inquiry,* p 19.
[11]   OFT *Vulnerable Consumers and Financial Services, Appendix 4—The Consumer Survey,* p 4.
[12]   OFT *Vulnerable Consumers and Financial Services: The Report of the Director General's Enquiry,* p 25
[13]   OFT *Vulnerable Consumers and Financial Services: The Report of the Director General's Enquiry,* p 20.
[14]   OFT *Vulnerable Consumers and Financial Services: The Report of the Director General's Enquiry* and DTI *A Fair Deal for Consumers: Modernising the Framework for Utility Regulation* (HMSO, 1998).
[15]   Though, following the second Cruickshank report (noted above) the banks have reached a voluntary agreement not to charge their own customers a 'disloyalty fee' and to make any charges levied on users of their own atms known prior to completion of the transaction. Cruickshank additionally envisaged the development of atms by a wide range of commercial actors (such as petrol stations and post offices) other than banks. The development of charging for use

Table 1: Use of financial services by low income consumers*

Financial service	Very low incomes	Low incomes
Bank/building society a/c	62%	76%
Use of credit		
High Street	25%	32%
Non commercial	15%	8%
Pawnbrokers/loan sharks	5%	3%
No credit at all	55%	57%
Home contents insurance	46%	68%
Savings products		
Long-term savings	8%	15%
Post office schemes	18%	30%
Easy access savings	33%	44%
No savings products	54%	39%
Life insurance products	19%	27%
Endowment mortgages	3%	5%

*   Compiled from *Vulnerable Consumers and Financial Services, Appendix 4—The Consumer Survey* (OFT, 1999).

Those who are on very low or low incomes who do have a bank account also face potential, and one may assume unwanted, exclusion, as they are likely to be the most affected by branch closures. Over the period 1989–1996 the number of bank branches fell by 22%, falling fastest in rural areas. Although there has been an increase in the number of automatic teller machines (atms) and in telephone banking, these are unlikely to be of assistance to those on low incomes. The majority of cash dispensers are installed at bank branches, and of those that are not, very few are situated in poorer areas. The range of services offered by atms is limited, and increasingly banks are charging if customers of other banks use their atms.[15] As regards telephone or internet banking, those most affected by branch closures are those least likely to have access to a telephone or computer. Three times as many households in poor neighbourhoods do not have their own telephone compared with other areas.[16] One survey found only 26% of those on low incomes had access to a telephone, and only 8% of the poorest fifth of households own a computer, compared to

---

of atms, based on a flat rate per transaction, exemplifies the tendency of the poor (who tend to make lower value withdrawals) to pay more, since charges are greater relative to the value of the transaction on lower value withdrawals.

[16]   Social Exclusion Unit *Bringing Britain Together* para 1.27.

57% of the richest fifth.[17] A further survey found that 18% of people overall felt alienated from information technology and a further 40% remained unconvinced or were concerned about it, with the highest figures concentrated amongst those from poor backgrounds.[18]

Vulnerable consumers do not only face problems of exclusion from certain services, but may be disproportionately affected by questionable marketing techniques, although as the recent pensions misselling scandal highlighted all consumers can be misled by dubious sales tactics.[19] Added to these problems is the fact that poorer consumers are less likely to use their legal rights as consumers than those on higher incomes. Knowledge and understanding of the legal position and of where to seek assistance decline as one progresses down the socio-economic groups. In addition to a deficiency of knowledge, lack of confidence may be another explanation why the less affluent do not take advantage of their legal rights. It may be that low expectations of success deter many from complaining. Alternatively, consumers may be unwilling to jeopardise their relations with a business by complaining, for example, if it is their sole source of credit.

3   THE CONSUMER AS CITIZEN

The present work adopts a narrow view of the consumer interest and focuses mainly on citizens entering transactions to obtain products and services from commercial enterprises. Transactions involving land are mentioned only incidentally. In this sense the scope of the book coincides with what is generally regarded as the thrust of consumer protection legislation; such legislation confines itself to transactions involving 'goods' and 'services'. The meaning of 'goods' does not extend to tenancy agreements or to social welfare benefits,[20] although the definition of services is more extensive, encompassing a contract for work, including work of a professional nature (but not under a contract of employment).[1] In another way much regulation relevant to consumer protection has a wider ambit than the present work, since it applies to transactions between

---

[17] OFT *Vulnerable Consumers and Financial Services: The Report* pp 23–24.
[18] Social Exclusion Unit *Bringing Britain Together* para 1.27.
[19] OFT *Vulnerable Consumers and Financial Services: The Report* pp 16–17; on pensions misselling see J Black and R Nobles 'Personal Pensions Misselling: The Causes and Lessons of Regulatory Failure' (1998) 61 MLR 789. For an excellent account of a wide range of dubious selling tactics see A Leff *Swindling and Selling: The Story of Legal and Illegal Congames* (Macmillan, 1976).
[20] For example, Fair Trading Act 1973, s 137(3); Supply of Goods and Services Act 1982, s 12, cf Trade Practices Act 1974 (Aust), ss 4(1), 74(3).
[1]   Unfair Contract Terms Act 1977, s 6(2)–(3).

commercial parties as well as to consumer transactions. In this sense the present book is about what the Germans call the *Endverbraucher*—the ultimate consumer. Some recent legislation is specifically confined to *consumer* transactions. Thus exemption clauses are generally nullified in *consumer* sales but not automatically in commercial transactions. Statutory orders can be made under the Fair Trading Act 1973 if the economic interests of *consumers* are prejudiced. In general terms a 'consumer' is defined in the Fair Trading Act 1973 as one who does not contract in the course of a business carried on by him but who deals with someone who does.[2] The Unfair Contract Terms Act 1977 adds the requirement for consumer deals that the goods must be of the type ordinarily supplied for private use or consumption.[3]

But there is a wider view of the consumer interest in which the term 'consumer' is virtually equated with the term 'citizen'. It is said that the consumer interest is involved when citizens enter exchange relationships with institutions like hospitals, libraries, police forces and various government agencies, as well as with businesses.[4] Indeed, ever since its establishment in 1975 the National Consumer Council has been concerned with the users of public services as well as with users of commercial services, and with their rights to full information, to choice whenever possible, and to treatment with full consideration. It has published a number of reports on the quality of public services and has campaigned actively for greater consumer involvement in setting the standards for service provision. Together with the Service First Unit in the Cabinet Office it conducted research into how users of public services could draw up new service standards and the impact that had on service providers,[5] and advised on the formation of guidelines on consultation practices for government departments and service providers.[6]

The well-known consumer campaigner in the US, Ralph Nader, did much to equate the term consumer with citizen. Originally he began with a narrow focus similar to that adopted in the present work. Quickly he became aware that the cause of consumer protection narrowly defined was inextricably linked with the cause of the consumer as citizen. At the head of Nader publications were the words:

> There can be no daily democracy without daily citizenship. If we do not exercise our civic rights, who will? If we do not perform our civic duties, who

---

2   Fair Trading Act 1973, s 137(2).
3   See further Chapter 3.
4   Mancur Olson *The Logic of Collective Action* (Harvard University Press, 1965) p 166.
5   Service First Unit *Involving Users in the Delivery of Local Public Services* (March 1999).
6   For further information see http://www.ncc.org.uk

can? The fibre of a just society in pursuit of happiness is a thinking active citizenry.

Nader used the idea of citizenship to enhance the notion of consumerism, and by invoking the example of individuals as recipients of public services moved the model of the consumer beyond the concerns of mere consumption to one of active, and rightful, participation of individuals in social and political life. In the last decade or so, however, the argument in the UK has been that rather than recognising individuals as citizens, the introduction of standards stipulating what individuals can expect from public services has turned individuals from citizens to consumers.[7] The mechanisms of public service delivery have been transformed with the introduction of measures such as privatisation, next step agencies, the new public management initiative, citizens' charters, and the contracting out of local authority services. Although accountability of government and other service providers to those who receive those services may at one level appear to have increased, individuals have had very little say in what those standards should be. Rather than being given the opportunity to participate as active citizens in a debate as to what the role of the state should be, individuals have rather been treated as passive recipients, consumers, of those services.

Others might argue that even the concept of the consumer as citizen is limited, because it implicitly accepts the existing order of things. As noted above, much has been written about how advertising creates needs, generates consumption and thus perpetuates modern capitalism—a view given wide currency by Galbraith. Curbing advertising abuse does not affect this fact. Writers like Illich see an all-pervading societal domination over people's lives; in the area of consumption products, rather than non-industrial ways of satisfying needs, dominate. Consumer protection in this view is a mere palliative to such domination, for it perpetuates it, perhaps with slight modification. Illich expresses the point thus:

> Consumers cannot do without cars. They buy different makes. They discover that most cars are unsafe at any speed. So they organise to get safer, better and more durable cars and to get more as well as wider and safer roads. Yet when consumers gain more confidence in cars, the victory only increases society's dependence on high-powered vehicles—public or private—and frustrates even more those who have to, or would prefer to, walk.[8]

An analysis of the role of consumer protection law in promoting consumption and thus upholding capitalism and issues of the nature of

---

[7]   A Barron and C Scott 'The Citizen's Charter Programme' (1992) 55 MLR 526.
[8]   I Illich *Tools for Conviviality* (Calder & Boyars, 1973) p 56.

consumerism are beyond the scope of this book. What is argued, however, is that in the marketplace as it is currently structured consumers are faced with difficulties and disadvantages which can be ameliorated by different forms of law and regulation, whether they are implemented in private or in public law, by the state or by non-state institutions.

4   CONSUMER PROTECTION AND DEVELOPING COUNTRIES

Developing countries have laws which fall within the consumer protection rubric. Some have introduced comprehensive consumer protection legislation covering matters such as weights and measures, food and prices. Such legislation is more likely to succeed where it organically developed from the local legal system, rather than being transplanted from other systems.[9] Where there are laws on the books, however, the administrative infrastructure for their implementation and enforcement is often rudimentary.[10] This does not mean that governments in developing countries are helpless to achieve change of benefit to consumers. One specific example relates to the important concern in the last decade that multinational enterprises (MNEs) have extensively promoted powdered milk for infant feeding in developing countries. Its use increases the risk of infant mortality and malnutrition when mixed with contaminated water and administered by illiterate mothers who do not know how to use it properly. Papua New Guinea was one of the few countries to take legislative action, in the form of the Baby Feed Supplies (Control) Act 1977. The Act and its attendant regulations prohibited advertisements whose intention or likely result was to encourage the bottle feeding of babies and the purchase or use of certain articles associated with it. A survey for the World Health Organisation concluded that the legislation seemed to have positive effects: the number of infants reported as suffering from diarrhoea, gastroenteritis and other signs of malnutrition dropped dramatically, and the proportion of artificially fed infants below 80% of weight for age fell to half what it had been previously.[11]

This example raises the issue of the role of MNEs in developing countries and whether their home governments should impose legal controls over their activities. In particular, MNEs operating in the Third

---

[9]   A Smith 'Consumer Law and Social Justice' (1995) 5 Consumer Policy Review 203.

[10]   Law Reform Commission of Papua New Guinea *Consumer Protection* Working Paper No 17 (1981) pp 9, 11; I Ramsey (ed) *Consumer Law in the Global Economy* (Ashgate/Dartmouth, 1995) especially Chapters 4–7.

[11]   J De Moerloose *Foods for Infants and Young Children: A Survey of Relevant National Legislation* (World Health Organisation) noted in (1981) 7 CLB 813.

World have vigorously promoted certain products (eg high tar cigarettes, drugs) in a manner which would be prohibited in developed countries. The companies argue that consumers in the Third World choose freely to purchase these products and that they are not in breach of local legislation. Critics point out that MNEs create demand by advertising and marketing methods which are sometimes blatantly false and bordering on the corrupt, and that because developing countries lack the resources and experience they do not have the legal controls which are taken for granted in developed countries.[12] A first step would be that products which the law in developed countries has classified as unsafe should not generally be exported to developing countries.[13] Exceptionally, it might be possible for a company to demonstrate that the nature of the risk varies in developing countries and that therefore export should be permitted. Secondly, developed countries might do more at the international level in the way of codes of behaviour to which MNEs would be expected to conform. With voluntary codes problems of content and enforcement loom large, however, while the experience in international organisations such as the World Health Organisation has been that developed countries with important MNEs are not always inclined to altruism. Thirdly, information can be made available to developing countries, for example, about unsafe products, to enable them to take action themselves.

5   CONSUMER GROUPS AND THE CONSUMER INTEREST

Before discussing legal safeguards for the consumer interest it is appropriate to throw some light on the non-legal ways in which consumer protection is advanced. Not everyone agrees that legal measures are necessary or even desirable. The assumption of some is that consumers can exercise a good deal of influence by banding together into pressure groups. Others say that consumer protection is achieved through the operation of the market and that other mechanisms are secondary. These contentions are briefly dealt with in the remaining sections of this introductory chapter. Then in the next chapter attention is directed to the contention that businesses can discipline themselves in the interests of consumers.

[12]   For example, Charles Medawar *Insult or Injury? An Enquiry into the Marketing and Advertising of British Food and Drug Products in the Third World* (Social Audit, 1979).
[13]   Cf Medicines Act 1968, ss 48, 49. See also the EC Directive 92/52/EEC on infant formulae and follow-on formulae intended for export to third countries OJ L 179 01.07.92 p 129 (as amended).

(a)   A theory of consumer groups

Pressure groups are a well-accepted feature of the politics of western society, and among the strongest are those representing commerce and industry. If individual consumers combined in groups they could more effectively pursue their interests like other pressure groups. Other consumers could be sensitised to consumer problems and educated about their rights; resources and support could be given for consumers to enforce their rights; and pressure for change could be exerted on businesses and government. There are limitations on test cases in England, but some might be taken in the courts, for costs could be distributed and the precedent value of decisions given greater weight than if individuals were bringing them. Even if test case litigation were ultimately unsuccessful it could be used to delay objectionable behaviour or to gain favourable publicity.[14]

But are pressure groups representing the consumer interest a likely feature of the political scene? A number of writers take the view that consumer groups will spring up automatically to counter the power of business interests. A writer in the *Canadian Bar Review* put this notion of countervailing power as follows:

> Whenever there is a substantial concentration of power ... there is likely to develop a countervailing force representing an aggregation of individual interests. 'Consumer' groups will have their effect both in direct relations with suppliers and in influencing new government policy to regulate the corporations or other business organisations with respect to which the consumer groups may have conflicting interests.[15]

By contrast, there are those who say that the consumer interest will always be poorly represented in society. Everyone is a consumer, and since the consumer interest is so diffuse and widely shared it should not be surprising that people have difficulty in agreeing what the consumer interest entails.[16] In addition, people lack self-awareness of their role as consumers. Anthony Downs argues that people feel more intense about their role as income-earners because they earn their income in one area but spend it in many.[17] Since those who stand to gain most in an area are those who earn their incomes there, they will be the ones prepared to invest the money and expertise to influence government. Thus a business affected

---

[14]   C Harlow and R Rawlings *Pressure Through Law* (Blackwell, 1992).

[15]   Ivan R Feltham 'The New Regulatory State: Economic and Business Regulation Tomorrow' (1973) 51 CanBar R 207, 209.

[16]   Ralph Winter 'Economic Regulation vs Competition: Ralph Nader and Creeping Capitalism' (1973) 82 Yale LJ 890, 901.

[17]   Anthony Downs *An Economic Theory of Democracy* (Harper & Row, 1957) pp 254–255.

by a particular measure can afford to bring pressure to bear, but consumers with many other interests will have no overriding concern impelling them to act. For this reason, government might fund a special office to represent the consumer interest at national level.

Furthermore, it is said that rational and self-interested individuals will not join a group purporting to represent the consumer interest, even if the collective benefits to be gained are greater than the total individual costs. An exception is if the group is small or if there is coercion or some other incentive to make them act in common. The 'free-rider' problem, as it is called, results because in large groups the contribution any one individual must make is most probably greater than the benefits to be received, and because in groups with many members it is unlikely than an individual contribution will make a difference. Olson writes:

> Virtually no one would be so absurd as to expect that the individuals in an economic system would voluntarily curtail their spending to halt inflation, however much they would as a group gain from doing this. Yet it is typically taken for granted that the same individuals in a political or social context will organise and act to further their collective interests. The rational individual in the economic system does not curtail his spending to prevent inflation (or increase it to prevent depression) because he knows, first, that his own efforts would not have a noticeable effect, and second, that he would get the benefits of any price stability that others achieved in any case. For the same two reasons, the rational individual in the large group in a socio-political context will not be willing to make any sacrifices to achieve the objectives he shares with others.[18]

The truth probably lies somewhere between the proponents of countervailing power and those arguing that consumer bodies will never coalesce and have an influence. Certainly consumer bodies are comparatively small in relation to their potential clientele; they lack resources when compared with pressure groups representing business interests, and the very broadness of the consumer interest explains in part the existence of several competing bodies each claiming to represent it.[19] On the other hand a number of factors mean that the position is not totally without hope. People are not always completely self-interested. The very existence of some consumer groups testifies to the fact that there are individuals who are prepared to band together to further the consumer cause. There may be a number of conflicting consumer interests but representation is not impossible. Consumers have a number of identifiable

[18]   Mancur Olson *The Logic of Collective Action* (Harvard University Press, 1965) p 166.
[19]   Leonard Tivey 'The Politics of the Consumer' (1968) 39 Political Quarterly 181, 192.

interests in common: economic efficiency, diversity of purchasing choice, avoidance of monopoly profits and consumer fraud, optimal purchasing information and good quality products in relation to price. That consumer interests can conflict is hardly a conclusive argument that they cannot be reconciled or adequately represented.

There are incentives impelling representation of the consumer interest. Consumer organisations which do comparative testing, like the Consumers' Association, recruit members because they offer a benefit, in the form of information, which otherwise would be very costly for individuals to obtain. Income from the publication of *Which?* enables the Consumers' Association to carry on many other activities of benefit to customers. It is entirely rational for independent consumer advocates like Ralph Nader, who are financed from private sources and can make money from their publications on consumer protection, to devote their effort to exerting influence on behalf of consumers as a whole. In effect their motivation comes from their career orientation.

Representation of the consumer interest has also been fostered by government. One interpretation is that the consumer movement has had an impact on government in the last decades because the political parties have seen the issue as a vote-winner.[20] Recognising that consumer protection measures do not require a large public expenditure, the parties have competed with one another in new initiatives.[1] Another interpretation is that consumer protection measures have often coincided with the economic policies of various governments which have been keen to further competition, to eliminate restrictive trade practices and to reduce inflation.[2] As a corollary governments need the consumer viewpoint to be presented as a counter to business and trade-union pressure when they make policy in the areas of economic planning.[3] Inherent in both interpretations is that the furtherance of the consumer interest has been largely dependent on political decisions.

(b)   Consumer groups in practice

Private organisations representing the consumer interest fall roughly into two categories: comparative testing groups, like the Consumers'

---

[20]   Previously consumers were regarded as having little influence: eg SE Finer *Anonymous Empire* (Pall Mall, 1958) p 122.

[1]   S Beer *Modern British Politics* (Faber, 1965).

[2]   William Roberts 'The Formation of Consumer Protection Policy in Britain 1945–1973' (Kent, PhD Thesis, 1975) p 15.

[3]   See S Peltzman 'The Economic Theory of Regulation after a Decade of Deregulation' in R Baldwin, C Scott and C Hood *A Reader on Regulation* (OUP, 1998).

Association, and the voluntary consumer groups operating at the local level. Other private organisations claim to represent the consumer interest but they cannot be regarded as an integral part of the consumer movement. Trade unions have in the past campaigned on similar issues to consumers,[4] but they are concerned mainly with the working situations of their members and not with their problems as consumers.[5] The consumer co-operatives, in which consumers are actually members of a retail organisation, are in theory aligned with the consumer movement. The political wing of consumer co-operatives in Britain, the Co-operative Party, has in the past sponsored Labour Party MPs and on several occasions advocated consumer sovereignty as the only true classless way.[6] Co-operatives have not been in the forefront of the consumer movement precisely because they have been preoccupied with business and have failed to resolve the conflict between this and the consumer interest. Business achievements are much easier to demonstrate for those running the co-operatives than advances in a particular philosophy. As Axworthy concludes about the Canadian co-operatives: 'By their nature, producer co-operatives push the producer's interests, not the interests of consumers.'[7]

The Consumers' Association has been primarily concerned with publishing information about products and services on a commercial basis. The information consists mainly of the results of comparative evaluation of products and services and of systematic assessment of consumer experiences. Critics point out that the comparative test surveys of Consumers' Association are often not comprehensive and that there are time lags in providing information about modified or new products after they have been marketed. Limitations of finance and the wide range of products and services on the market are obvious explanations for these drawbacks. Members of the Consumers' Association (around 600,000 subscribers to *Which?*)[8] in Britain have an impact on the market by channelling demand for products and services, and figures from the US show that such reports can have an impact on sales figures.[9]

Consumers' associations have also concerned themselves with representing the consumer interest in public policy making. Thus the

---

[4]   For example food subsidies in the 1970s: see the second edition of this book, p 13.

[5]   Solomon Parkin 'Trade Union and Consumerism' (1973) 7 J of Econ Issues 317; Andrew Hopkins *Crime Law and Business* (Australian Institute of Criminology, 1978) p 92.

[6]   TF Carberry *Consumers in Politics* (Manchester University Press, 1969) p 187. See also Christopher S Axworthy 'Consumer Co-operatives and the Rochdale Principles Today' (1977) 15 Os HLJ 137, 144.

[7]   TF Carberry *Consumers in Politics*.

[8]   Information from the Consumers' Association, January 2000.

[9]   Ursula Wassermann 'Comparative Testing of Consumer Goods' (1973) 7 J Wld Trade L 247, 250.

Consumers' Association in Britain has played an important role in the drafting of consumer legislation and other legislation which has implications for consumers (it has been conducting a campaign on the current Freedom of Information Bill for example). It also has acted as a catalyst for other consumer groups by making financial support available, sponsored test cases on the interpretation of consumer law and promoted the introduction of high street consumer advice centres to widen the access of citizens to advice on consumer matters. Yet the consumers' associations face limitations on their advocacy role because their main focus is publishing information of immediate benefit to their members, their membership is not representative of the population, and because of financial and other resource constraints.

Consumers' groups also operate at the European and international level. The Consumers in Europe Group is an umbrella organisation for over 30 consumer groups in the UK that lobbies on consumer issues at the EU level. At an international level, Consumers International, founded in 1960, lobbies for policies that will respect consumers concerns.[10] Its members comprise more than 200 consumer groups from over 90 countries, including the National Consumer Council and the Consumers' Association in the UK. Its head office is in the UK and it has five regional offices, co-ordinating policies at the regional and international level. Recent campaigns include issues relating to health, the environment, trade and foreign direct investment, calling for an assessment of the social impact of trade liberalisation, and the development of international guidelines to protect consumers who buy goods on the internet.[11]

A further representative of the consumer interest in Britain is the National Consumer Council (NCC). The NCC was established in 1975, and there are separate Councils for England, Scotland, Wales and Northern Ireland.[12] The Council has 18 members, appointed by the government, all with consumer, social or voluntary work backgrounds, and 31 full time staff. It is funded by the government but non-statutory in form. It has no executive powers and does not deal directly with individual consumer problems. Rather its role is to campaign on more general issues and in particular to represent the consumer interest in a partisan fashion at the national level. Its stated objectives are to research consumers' own

[10]   For more information see their website: http://www.consumersinternational.org
[11]   A study on internet shopping by the CI found that 10% of items ordered never arrived; 56% arrived without receipts; 73% of traders failed to give crucial contract terms; 25% gave no address or phone number and 24% were unclear about the total cost of items ordered: IC *Consumers@shopping: An international comparative study of electronic commerce* (1999) available at http://www.consumersinternational.org
[12]   For background to its introduction see Department of Prices and Consumer Protection *National Consumers' Agency* (Cmnd 5726 (1974)).

experiences and concerns, formulate policies to get a fairer deal for consumers and promote new and better practices by suppliers and providers of goods and services, campaign for change in parliament and the media, and support the work of other consumer organisations and representatives. Its members and staff also sit on other national and international policy, regulatory or advisory bodies, for example the Cabinet Office Regulatory Impact Unit, the DTI consumer strategy group, the consumer panel of the Financial Services Authority, the European Commission consumer committees on agriculture and world trade, the Association of British Insurers code of practice monitoring committee, the civil justice council and the public utilities access forum.[13]

The broad remit of the NCC means that its resources are necessarily thinly spread and its impact perhaps reduced. It is also not concerned with informing consumers specifically about problems—the OFT fulfils that role. It may be that it would carry more weight if it were statutory in form. Nevertheless it has taken the initiative in several areas where other consumer groups have not campaigned actively, including the provision of public services, noted above. For example, in the last five years it has produced reports and campaigned on pharmaceutical regulation, financial services regulation, the provision of legal services, the self-regulation systems that operate in health care, telecommunications, energy, water and media policy, freedom of information and commercial confidentiality.[14] It conducts 'consumer concerns' surveys on an annual basis, looking for example at the quality of public services and the NHS.[15]

The other major representatives of the consumer interest in the UK are the voluntary consumer groups. Mainly these operate at the grass-roots level and revolve around assessing local services and products. Financed in part by a small annual grant from the DTI, the National Federation of Consumer Groups encourages and co-ordinates the work of voluntary, independent local consumer groups and represents their views at the national level. It also has an individual membership scheme for those who do not live near enough to a group, and related organisations and companies can join as associates. Most of the federated groups produce their own magazine or newsletter. The Federation has co-ordinated some national surveys by member groups but its effort is largely devoted to serving member groups by collecting their publications, and providing resources, expertise and information for members, for example by assisting

---

[13] NCC *About the NCC* http://www.ncc.org.uk/aboutncc.htm (1999).
[14] NCC *Secrecy in Medicines* (1996); *Financial Services and Markets Bill* (1999); *Self Regulation of Professionals in Health Care* (1999); *Ofcom: A Coherent Approach to Regulating Communications* (1999); *Finding a Basis for Water Charges* (1998); *TV's Last Wave* (1998); *Commercial Confidentiality* (1998).
[15] *Consumer Concerns: the NHS* (1999); *Local Charters: A survey of public services* (1998).

them in conducting local surveys. The legislative committee of the Federation has made representations to the government on various consumer matters and Federation members are appointed, in individual capacities, to various bodies to represent the consumer interest. A similar body, the Australian Federation of Consumer Organisations, was formed in 1974, consisting of 50 bodies with several hundred thousand consumers as members.

A further step in representing the consumer interest has been taken in the United States by consumer advocates. One of the principal advocacy organisations is the Consumers Federation of America (CFA), established in 1968. The CFA focuses on six areas: financial services, utilities, product safety, transportation, health care and food safety. As well as preparing policy studies it develops legislative testimony, regulatory filings and comments and amicus briefs that contain policy related analysis.[16] In Canada, the Public Interest Advocacy Centre is a charitable organisation providing legal advice, representation and specialised research on consumer issues on a non-profit basis. It brings test case litigation and makes representations to legislatures, regulators and law commissions. It also provides advocacy training to individuals and groups to enable them to represent themselves more effectively.[17] A hurdle facing consumer advocates—indeed all consumer groups—is whether they have a mandate to speak for the consumer interest. One view is that, unlike other public interests such as education, citizens know so little about what their welfare requires in the area of consumer protection that consumer advocates can quite properly represent their interests.[18] On the other hand some say this view is patronising and that consumer advocates are unrepresentative.

(c)   Legal requirements for consumer involvement

The law has little to say about the activities of consumer groups: such as what issues they can campaign on. Certainly it has some relevance to their formation and operation as distinct entities. For example, one reason why credit unions have had such a slow growth in Britain is that there has been no suitable legislation giving them a separate legal identity and providing the framework in which they can be registered and supervised.[19] The law can also facilitate (or hinder) the growth of consumer groups by economic measures. The law relating to charities, for example, prevents most

---

[16]   For further details see http://www.consumerfed.org

[17]   For further details see http://www.piac.ca

[18]   Mark V Nadel *The Politics of Consumer Protection* (Bobbs-Merrill, 1971) pp 233–234.

[19]   See further HM Treasury *Credit Unions of the Future.*

consumer groups from having charitable status (because they often campaign for changes in the law they are deemed to be engaging in political activities). They are thus denied the tax advantages which charities enjoy, and those giving money to them cannot do so by way of covenant (binding themselves to pay a certain amount over a period and claiming the amount as a tax deduction).[20] The government funds the NCC, but other bodies such as the Consumers' Association receive no public funding. This contrasts with the position in Germany where organisations like the Consumers' Association receive state subsidies to enable them to continue their work on the comparative testing of products and evaluation of services.

The representative function of organised consumer bodies has nevertheless progressively increased in Britain over the last two to three decades. The government now regularly consults organisations like the Consumers' Association and the NCC before introducing consumer protection measures, and increasingly consults them on the consumer impact of more general policies. It is proposed to set up an Advisory Committee on consumer issues, comprised of consumer, business and enforcement interests.[1] Although there is still no general duty to consult imposed on government bodies, some statutes specifically require consultation to occur before delegated legislation or other administrative rules can be introduced. For example the Deregulation and Contracting Out Act 1994 has a specific statutory consultation process built in. The new procedure for publishing and allowing consultation on draft Bills, used for example with respect to the Freedom of Information Bill and the Food Standards Bill, also increases the opportunities for consultation. Legislation may also require consumer representatives to be appointed to regulatory or advisory bodies, for example the Consumer Protection Advisory Committee, which considers statutory orders to be made under the Fair Trading Act 1973.[2] Legislation also requires consumer panels to be appointed for the utilities and financial services regulators although their status is advisory only; they have no vote or veto in policy issues.[3]

---

[20]   M Chesterman 'Foundations of Charity law in the New Welfare State' (1999) 62 MLR 333.

[1]   DTI *Modern Markets: Confident Consumers*, para 8.10.

[2]   Section 3(5)(c).

[3]   Telecommunications Act 1984, s 54; Gas Act 1986 requires the appointment of the Gas Consumers Council; Water Industry Act 1991, s 28 requires the appointment of a maximum of ten Customer Services Committees, which also investigate to see that companies are responding satisfactorily to complaints; Electricity Act 1989 requires the appointment of a Consumer's Committee for each the area covered by each supplier of electricity; the chair of each committee is in turn a member of the National Consumers' Consultative Committee, chaired by the Director General. The existing bodies for telecommunications and water are to be replaced with independent councils, and a single energy council appointed for gas and electricity. For reforms to the arrangements for gas and electricity see

There are six advisory committees on telecommunications; a Gas Consumers Council, and customer services committees for each area covered by water and electricity suppliers. The Financial Services and Markets Act 2000 requires the appointment of a Consumer Panel to advise the Board, a considerable extension of consumer representation in financial services regulation (ss 8, 10). Consumer representatives also sit on advisory panels such as the Competitiveness Council and the Better Regulation Task Force. Finally, a Ministerial Group has been formed to work on consumer issues cutting across government, considering how to improve effectiveness of enforcement and identifying areas where consumer groups could make a more effective contribution in their policy areas.[4]

The increasing recognition of consumer issues in policy making, manifested in the proliferation of consumer representative bodies or advisory groups, marks a distinct advance. However, consumers are not necessarily a homogenous mass with completely aligned interests. As noted above, low income and other vulnerable consumer groups may face quite different problems and have quite different demands than more affluent consumers. There can be a difficulty in finding a completely representative cross-section of consumer interests to sit on such panels however, especially where appointments are unpaid, and the panels often have limited resources for secretariat services, advice and information. Representatives are also untrained, and although guidance on training of consumer representatives has been produced by government and consumer groups,[5] there is limited funding available for its implementation. There is thus a limit to the extent to which they can provide effective representation of the multiple and possible conflicting views of different groups of consumers. Partly for this reason regulators have also undertaken their own consumer research, for example in the areas of telecommunications and financial services.

Greater activism on the part of consumer groups is not protected by some of the same legal privileges that are conferred on trade unions, although those privileges have themselves been dramatically reduced over the last 20 years. Members of a local consumer group organising a boycott, blacklist or picket against a business notorious for its malpractices could be the subject of an injunction, or be sued for damages for committing torts such as conspiracy, defamation, trespass or private nuisance. Trade unions have a degree of immunity when they act in a similar manner in the furtherance of a trade dispute.[6] The position of consumer and similar

---

the Utilities Bill 2000. Further reform of telecommunications will follow in a White Paper in 2000–2001.
4   DTI *Modern Markets: Confident Consumers*, para 9.3.
5   DTI *Modern Markets: Confident Consumers*, para 8.8.
6   Trade Union and Labour Relations (Consolidation) Act 1992, ss 219–221.

groups is nicely illustrated by the decision in *Hubbard v Pitt*.[7] A local tenants' group disapproved of the activity of an estate agent in changing the social character of a neighbourhood and began a small peaceful picket outside the estate agent's office involving the distribution of leaflets explaining their case. The majority of the Court of Appeal held that the estate agent was entitled to an interlocutory injunction, preventing the group from continuing the picket, on the basis that there was a prima facie case that they were committing the tort of private nuisance by interfering with the enjoyment of the plaintiff's premises. Lord Denning dissented on the grounds that picketing was not a private nuisance in itself if it were directed to obtaining or to communicating information, or peacefully to persuading, so long as it was not associated with obstruction, threats or violence. Despite the decision, consumer groups will not automatically be restrained by an interlocutory injunction from distributing leaflets or displaying placards which a business alleges are defamatory, if this is done elsewhere than outside the business's premises. In *Crest Homes Ltd v Ascott*[8] a consumer was angry because he thought some builders had made his front door very badly, so he took the door, attached it to his car and drove around the streets. It bore the words: 'This door is typical of the poor materials used. Be warned.' The Court of Appeal refused to grant an interim injunction because there was a bona fide defence of justification. However, words such as these might in other circumstances be defamatory and a business might be successful in claiming damages from a consumer who publishes them.

6   COMPETITION, MARKET ECONOMICS AND CONSUMER PROTECTION

Competition has a role to play in protecting consumers. Where it is effective consumers will have a choice of products and services, and information in relation to these products and services which producers provide in seeking consumer patronage. Competition is generally more effective in the case of products and services which are purchased frequently, the quality and performance of which are readily identifiable, and whose characteristics are fairly stable. By contrast, competition is weak in markets which involve substantial information gaps and markets where there are 'fly-by-night' businesses which are not interested in building and maintaining goodwill.

After a brief examination of the role of competition (anti-trust) policy in

---

[7]   [1976] QB 142. The matter never came to trial, but of course the interlocutory injunction had the desired effect.
[8]   (1995) Times, 5 February. See also *Bestobell Paints Ltd v Bigg* [1975] FSR 421, 119 Sol Jo 678.

consumer protection, the remainder of this Part directs attention to a strong school of thought which believes that recent consumer protection legislation is an undesirable departure from *caveat emptor*. It should not be thought, however, that proponents of the market see no role for public control. Even the most rigid sometimes support legislation against marketing fraud or to ensure that businesses impart information to consumers. At the same time critics of the market should not be taken to believe that there is no role for competition in consumer protection.

(a)   Competition policy and consumer protection

In many jurisdictions, including the UK, consumer protection and competition policy are incorporated in the same legislation and administered by the same department or agency. Often this is a matter of convenience and the two could just as well have been set out in different legislation and administered separately. Where the two are combined they might well conflict, for example, if preference is given to the indirect and intangible benefits of competition over the specific protection conferred by consumer protection measures. Mainly it is usually argued that it will be possible to handle the two compatibly, by accepting that legislative policy is that the interests of a consumer of goods or services will best be served when manufacturers compete vigorously without adopting restrictive practices and observe prescribed standards of conduct in their dealings with consumers.[9]

The details of competition policy are beyond the scope of this work.[10] It need simply be noted that whereas in some countries competition law acts generally by prohibiting conduct which it is thought will inhibit competition, in others it operates mainly by means of an ad hoc inquiry and investigation to determine whether action should be taken against particular practices, agreements or takeovers. Anti-trust law in the US reflects the first approach, and in the UK tended toward the other, but broad prohibition provisions are now contained in the Competition Act 1998. The main concerns of competition policy can be conveniently divided into restrictive trading agreements, in which parties accept restrictions on their freedom to compete by fixing prices, dividing the market, establishing uniform terms and conditions and so on; monopolistic and anti-competitive

---

9   See for example, DTI *Modern Markets: Confident Consumers* (Cm 4410). For an examination of the dual mandate of the US Federal Trade Commission see N Averitt and R Lande 'Consumer Sovereignty: A Unified Theory of Antitrust and Consumer Protection Law' (1997) 65 Antritrust LJ 713.

10   See I Maher 'Juridification, Codification and Sanction in UK Competition Law' (2000) 62 MLR 544 and generally R Whish and B Sufrin *Competition Law* (Butterworths, 4th edn, 1999).

practices, where a business uses its market power to engage in monopolistic pricing, exclusive dealing, tie-in sales, full-line forcing and so on with the objective of excluding competitors or inhibiting entry into the market; and mergers and takeovers, which may significantly reduce competition. The Competition Act 1998 prohibits agreements and practices that prevent, restrict or distort competition or are intended to do so, whether written or unwritten or formal or informal.[11] It also prohibits the abuse of a dominant position. Practices that may constitute abuse include, but are not limited to, unfair purchase or selling prices, limiting production, the market or technological developments to the detriment of competition, or attaching unrelated supplementary conditions to contracts.[12] The Office of Fair Trading has extensive powers of investigation, and if it determines that there has been a breach of the Act, a firm can be fined up to 10% of its UK turnover. Firms have a right to respond to allegations contained in any complaint or investigation, and a right of appeal to the Competition Commission. Third parties affected by the anti-competitive conduct may complain to the OFT, may in certain circumstances make representations in the course of an investigation, and also have a right to seek damages in the civil courts.

The consumer case for competition is essentially that it widens choice, leads to prices that are lower than would otherwise obtain, and stimulates industry to remain alert to consumer requirements and in tune with changing needs. Competition policy is said to be especially necessary in the consumer goods market given factors such as its relative concentration, product differentiation and other forms of non-price competition (which make comparisons more difficult), and the absence of objective information about products. Since perfect competition is an unrealistic goal to pursue, it is said that the consumer interest is more likely to be enhanced by a policy of seeking effective competition. Policies appropriate to this have been identified as increasing and preserving competition by the traditional means of competition policy, such as the proscription of price-fixing cartels, coupled with more radical action (as in the case of the privatised utilities), such as the forcible breaking up of dominant firms, assisting new entrants by forcing monopolists to provide access to essential services, improving the quality of competition, monitoring and regulating existing monopolies (for example by regulating the prices they may charge) and increasing the market power of consumers.

The case for competition policy often assumes a taken for granted character as far as the benefits to consumers are concerned. Certainly the

---

[11] 'Chapter I' prohibition.
[12] 'Chapter II' prohibition.

criteria set out in competition law might include taking into account the consumer interest, but this by no means stands alone or is necessarily paramount. There are specific instances where competition policy has led to definite benefits to consumers in the way, for example, of lower prices.[13] Indeed, in a world of less than perfect competition there is a clear distinction in economic terms between competition policies which are aimed at improving allocative efficiency and those which seek to enhance the position of consumers (eg improving price competition). As Sharpe notes,

> There is a distinction between laws which protect or enhance 'competition' in the sense of providing or increasing money gains to *consumers*, and laws which seek to increase economic efficiency, which may provide no direct benefit to consumers at all: any gains from efficiency could be appropriated, for example, by shareholders or employees. Conversely, any attempt to increase money gains to consumers might reduce economic efficiency in that the benefits to consumers might be at the expense of misallocating resources of rival producers or some other group.[14]

Moreover, even where competition policy is aimed directly at benefiting consumers, the result does not automatically follow. For example, a wider choice for consumers might be spurious because of product differentiation, which is also wasteful of resources; more competition might mean a reduction in the number of outlets and thus more difficult access for consumers (closure of bank branches is an example), lower prices might be at the expense of quality; and other legal measures might be more effective in making business responsive to consumers. Conversely, it is often overlooked that consumer protection measures might be good for competition by correcting market failures (see further below). Information deficiencies might be reduced because the law requires businesses to disclose information in relation to their products or services or their activities. The same result might be achieved by the law fixing a standard, for although this restricts choice it provides consumers with information that does not require significant processing effort. Similarly, by uncovering deceptive and misleading conduct in the market-place, consumer protection agencies might reduce the average cost to consumers of doing so compared with the costs of organising themselves as a group and overcoming the 'free-rider' problem.[15]

---

[13] Cf Lee Benham 'The Effect of Advertising on the Price of Eyeglasses' (1972) 15 J Law and Econ 337.

[14] Thomas Sharpe 'Refusal to Supply' (1983) 99 LQR 36, 60.

[15] See further Chapter 13.

(b) The Chicago school

For certain economists, the problems that consumers face, such as lack of information, monopoly suppliers, cartels, are seen as aberrations, exceptions from the normal situation of perfect markets. In such perfect markets, it is argued, consumers face no difficulties. There is thus no need for consumer protection measures except to the extent that they are needed to address failures in the market mechanisms. Indeed such measures can be harmful rather than beneficial. A related school of economists argues further that any regulations imposed will simply serve to benefit large producers and suppliers, for legislators or regulators will simply pass the laws that those groups want in return for their support. Others recognise that imperfect markets are the norm rather than the exception, and further that there are other, non-economic reasons why regulation may be justified. They also argue that the regulation introduced does not necessarily benefit large producers and suppliers, but can benefit other groups or society as a whole. So when is consumer protection justified?

There is a strong school of thought associated with the Chicago school of economists which believes that recent consumer protection legislation is an undesirable departure from the principle of *caveat emptor*. It believes government regulation in the consumer interest is mostly superfluous and that consumers are afforded adequate protection through the operation of the market and the common law system. The argument is by no means new, as illustrated by the following exchange between a solicitor (who was also the chairman of a local board of health) and a member of the Select Committee on the Adulteration of Food, which was considering for the public control of food quality in the 1850s.[16]

> Does your opinion go to this extent, that supposing a man having purchased a pound of coffee, goes into another shop, asking for the same article, and gets 75% of chicory, that is one of the innocent adulterations of which you speak as being the result of competition? Certainly, and for this reason, there is no standard of the value of any article, there is nothing to represent the fact that any article shall be sold for a certain price.
>
> Is there not an understanding between the public and the seller that the seller shall give to you what you ask for? I think not, neither do I think it beneficial that it should be so. The same machinery which fixes the price of the one article fixes the price of the other, and you cannot draw a distinction, nor show any reason why competition should not regulate the price of a mixture of coffee and chicory, just as it does the price of coffee alone or any other article. A man purchases a pound of coffee for 1s; he goes to the next shop and purchases a pound of what purports to be coffee, but which is adulterated with

---

[16] *Report from the Select Committee on the Adulteration of Food etc* (1855) Parl Pap 1854–5, viii, p 23.

75% of chicory, and he pays 1s. For it, do you think there is any injustice in that? I believe it should be left to regulate itself.

Of major importance in the outlook of such economists are five main assumptions: that there are numerous buyers and sellers in the market; there are no barriers to entry to or exit from the market; that buyers and sellers have perfect information about the products on the market; that the products are the same; and that the costs of producing the good are borne by the producer and the costs of consuming the product are borne by the consumer—in economists' terms, there are no externalities. On the basis of these assumptions, it is said, markets are perfectly competitive. There is a further key assumption that is made, that is that individuals are rational actors and will act to further their self interest. In the notion of the rational actor it is assumed that individuals have stable preferences which are not altered by the way that choices or decisions are presented to them; that those preferences are transitive and consistent (if a person prefers A to B and B to C he or she will prefer A to C); that individuals act to further their self-interest; that people's preferences can therefore be read from their actions; that they repeatedly face the same choice situations and in those situations can identify and will take the opportunity to pursue a course of action that will maximise their self-interest; and that there is only one optimal outcome.[17]

So, it is argued, consumers can discipline producers or suppliers through the market. For example, if consumers are dissatisfied with the quality of a product in the light of its price, they will inform other consumers and no longer purchase it themselves. Finding that a product is no longer patronised, a business may reduce its price, modify the design or the quality control of its manufacture, or abandon its production completely. Similarly, competition among businesses is a curb on misleading trade practices for if consumers are misled on one occasion, for example by advertising, they will learn from experience and never again enter transactions with the business. Such businesses will quickly modify their trade practices for otherwise they will lose trade to rivals, at least those who depend heavily on repeated sales of the same products or services to the same consumers, or who find it costly to liquidate at short notice.[18] A third example of faith in the market is in the discussion of standard form contracts. Contrary to accepted belief that these are onerous for consumers, the Chicago school says that if a business offers unattractive terms to consumers, competitors will come forward with better terms. 'Thus the

---

[17]   See eg D North *Institutions, Institutional Change and Economic Performance* (CUP, 1990) p 19; J Hanson and D Kysar 'Taking Behavioralism Seriously' (1999) 112 Harv LR 1420.

[18]   Richard A Posner 'The Federal Trade Commission' (1969) 37 U Chi LR 47, 62.

purchaser who is offered a printed contract on a take-it-or-leave-it basis
does have a real choice: he can refuse to sign, knowing that if better terms
are possible another seller will offer them to him.'[19]

The preference for the market and the common law over state regulation
derives from various arguments. The market and common law methods, it
is said, bring about more efficient results than government regulation.
When the market fails to allocate resources effectively, the common law
comes into play and operates in a manner comparable to a market. It relies
on the actions of private self-interested individuals acting in competition
with each other, and its remedies such as damages are similar to those that
would be generated by market forces. At a general level the legislative
process is said to exhibit a less pervasive concern with efficiency and a
much greater concern with wealth distribution. Unlike the situation in the
courts, where the question of relative cost is always close to the surface,
legislatures take relative deservedness into consideration on a regular
basis. Moreover, in legislatures coalitions of special interest groups can
often secure what are inefficient programmes at the expense of
unrepresented large, generalised interest groups such as consumers which,
because of free-rider problems, have difficulty in influencing legislation.[20]

With reference to consumer products it is assumed that the state cannot
determine the quality of products which will maximise efficiency. Even if
government selects an efficient point for production, this will not
necessarily coincide with the preferences of individuals. Were standards
to be set for consumer products, consumers would take less care in using
them with the result that they would wear out more quickly or that accidents
would rise. Total costs would increase because preventing these outcomes
would not be done by those having the comparative advantage. The
increased costs would be paid in the main by consumers in the form of
higher prices. On the other hand leaving it to the market limits information
costs about what degree of product liability is economical because
consumers are in a better position than government to know the exact
uses they plan for products and what degree of quality is appropriate.[1]
This knowledge is transmitted through the existing market system where
consumers can register their preferences as regards cost and quality.
Producers respond to these in terms of the prices they charge, the quality
of the products they market or the policies they adopt when consumers
return dissatisfied. Moreover, government regulation restricts choice and
consumers are no longer able to bear the risks which they had previously
indicated a willingness to shoulder. By eliminating 'mutually advantageous

[19]   Richard A Posner *Economic Analysis of Law* (Little Brown, 2nd edn, 1977) p 85.
[20]   Richard A Posner *Economic Analysis of Law* pp 404–407.
[1]   Ronald N Kean 'Products Liability: Trends and Implications' (1970) 38 U Chi
       LR 3, 44, 52.

exchanges' economic welfare is diminished. The poor are hardest hit because they are obliged to purchase better quality but more expensive products.

It is also argued that if regulation is introduced, it will be to the advantage of the large suppliers and producers rather than consumers. There are two reasons put forward for this. The first is that although regulation may initially be intended to benefit society as a whole, over time the regulator will end up being 'captured' by the firms it is meant to be regulating.[2] Regulators, it is argued, have a life cycle. At the beginning they are youthful and vigorous, and political attention is on them. They will thus be vigilant in pursuing the goals of the public interest. Gradually, however, political attention is diverted away from the regulator onto new issues, and the regulator comes increasingly to talk only to the regulated firms, and further to rely heavily on them for information. Further, regulators will not want to antagonise regulated firms because many who work in the regulatory office will at some point want to seek jobs with those firms, the so-called 'revolving door' phenomenon. So as the agency matures it gradually becomes 'captured' by the regulated firms, until in old age it produces only policies that are in the interests of those firms.

The second variant on the argument that regulation will benefit large producer interests rather than the consumer is known as the economic or 'public choice' theory of regulation. In this theory, regulation does not even start out with public interest goals. Instead, public choice theory sees politics as a marketplace in which regulation is a good sold by politicians to the highest bidder. Bids come in the form of votes and financial support. Large producers and suppliers are likely to be able to organise more effectively and to offer larger bids than the multitude of individual consumers. So politicians will pass legislation that favours large business interests over the interests of small consumers.[3] A more nuanced version of public choice theory is that no single economic interest will dominate, rather politicians will allocate benefits across groups so as to maximise their support. So as long as some consumers can offer some votes or money pure producer protection will not dominate.[4]

2   MH Bernstein *Regulating Business by Independent Commission* (Princeton University Press, 1955).
3   G Stigler 'The Theory of Economic Regulation' (1971) 2 Bell J Economics and Management Sci 3; R Posner 'Taxation by Regulation' (1971) 2 Bell J Economics and Management Sci 22; R Posner 'Taxation by Regulation' (1974) 5 Bell J Economics and Management Sci 211.
4   S Peltzman 'Toward a More General Theory of Regulation' (1976) 19 Journal of Law and Economics 211; G Becker 'A Theory of Competition among pressure groups for Political Influence' (1983) 98 Quarterly Journal of Economics 371; S Peltzman 'The Economic Theory of Regulation After a Decade of Deregulation' (1989) Brookings Papers in Microeconomics, and in R Baldwin et al *Reader on Regulation* (OUP, 1998).

(c) Criticisms of the theories; rationales for consumer protection

Both the theory of perfect competition and the theories of regulatory capture and public choice have been subjected to strong criticism. Markets, it may be argued, are not perfectly competitive. Rather they are imperfect. In the language of economists, there are market failures; in other words the assumptions on which the theory of perfect markets is based rarely, if ever, exist. The norm is not a perfect market but an imperfect one. Markets may not be comprised of numerous buyers and numerous sellers. The market may be dominated by only one supplier (a monopolist) or by a small number of large suppliers (oligopolists), all of whom provide products of a similar quality at similar prices and on similar terms. It may not be easy for others to enter the market, there may be barriers in the way. Barriers may take the form of high costs (for example it is very costly to lay new cables to transmit data, or lay new pipelines for gas or water) or may be imposed by law (requirements that a person has received several years training before they can offer a service). The consumer may not be faced with a range of identical products from which to choose, but from slightly different products, or products whose characteristics change rapidly (personal computers, mobile phones), making comparisons difficult. Product differentiation may not be a sign of competition, but rather of dominance, especially where differences are spurious and serve only to confuse rather than expand real choice. The costs of production or consumption may not be borne entirely by the producer or consumer—the classic example is that of a paint factory which in the course of producing paint emits noxious chemicals into the river, killing the fish in the trout farm downstream. The costs of the dead fish are not incorporated into the price of the paint, but are rather borne by a third party, in this case the trout farmer.

Further, the consumers may not have perfect information, and indeed may face considerable difficulties in obtaining information that they can understand and rely upon. Consumers need information when they buy a product or a service. More particularly, they need three items of information: information about the price of that product or service and other similar ones, the quality, and the terms on which they are buying. That information also has to have certain properties. It has to be readily available, readily understandable, and easy to verify. In an ideal world, or at least an ideal market place, those conditions would be met. Most of the problems that face consumers in the market place arise from the fact that the world, or market, is not ideal—consumers do not usually have all, or any, of the three items of information required, or if they do, they may not understand the information given (the technical specifications, for example) or may have no means of checking that the information given is correct (for example, the nutritional values listed on food packets). The purchasing decisions that they make are thus made on the basis of imperfect information, and as such are unlikely to be the best ones that they could have made.

Obtaining information is costly for consumers. A rational consumer will search for information until the costs of the search outweigh the benefits to be gained. However, that search may not produce the information necessary, not because the search is poorly executed but because the information is simply not easily available. Suppliers have some incentives to produce information—they want consumers to know about their products and to buy them. But the information that suppliers are likely to provide is information which is easy to understand and to check, which can be provided cost-effectively, and which attracts consumers to their products. In other words, information about high quality, low prices and/or favourable terms. Where the information is not easy to understand or to check, suppliers will rely on their reputation to induce consumers to trust that the product is of a high quality or that the terms are fair. However, suppliers are unlikely to provide information which is unfavourable to their product, and their competitors may not be believed if they do so, or may be barred from doing so by advertising regulations. Suppliers may also not have incentives to put out information that, whilst it may be favourable to the product, is costly to produce. This is because they will not necessarily be able to recover the cost of producing that information, for those who may use it may not end up buying the product from that supplier. In economists' terms, information has the properties of a 'public good': ie no-one can be excluded from enjoyment of the good, and the quality of the good does not deteriorate the more that it is used or enjoyed. So, for example, no mobile phone producer has an incentive to produce information on the exact specifications of mobile phones in general, as opposed to their particular package, because all products on the market share the same characteristics. The effect of giving out further information may be to expand the market as a whole, but it might not necessarily increase the market share of the supplier concerned.

Alternatively, suppliers may simply withhold information, or put out misleading information, or bundle together products, giving information about the primary product (eg the package holiday) but not about the 'add on' product (the compulsory insurance policy that accompanies it). Or they may deliberately create a headline piece of information, a focal point, encouraging consumers to direct their attention to that information, and away from other items: the price of the holiday rather than the price of the insurance.[5] Suppliers may compete on the price of the primary product (cutting the cost of the holiday) but not on the secondary (correspondingly

---

[5]   For analysis see London Economics *Consumer Detriment under Conditions of Imperfect Information*, OFT Research Paper 11 (OFT, 1997) pp 51–54.

raising the cost of the insurance). Alternatively, or in addition, suppliers may give out some information in a form that is deliberately complex and confusing, but give other items of information that are deceptively simple, usually prices, thus encouraging the consumer to focus on that item of information. A good example is the selling practices for photocopiers. In selling photocopiers, the cost of the lease, materials and after sales maintenance are bundled together and expressed as a 'cost per copy'. The cost per copy price can vary considerably, and is the key focal point of competition in the market. However it obscures or directs attention away from the terms of the contract: the length of the contract, volume targets that have to be met and penalties if they are not, price escalation clauses for servicing, exclusive supply conditions for materials, and severe termination penalties.[6] Consumers thus place too much attention on the focal point and fail to collect information on the other attributes of the product.

It is sometimes argued that consumers can overcome the problems of obtaining information directly from suppliers and instead rely on retailers or other third parties to provide that information. However, retailers may not be in the best position to provide all types of information. They will usually provide information on price, which they determine. They may be in a position to provide information on terms, but that may depend on whether they are selling a service that will in fact be supplied by a third party. They are not usually as well placed as manufacturers to give information on the quality of the product, but they may perform a function of verifying the information on quality that the manufacturer supplies, for example by selecting from a range of products and providing comparisons. However, retailers, like producers, do not have incentives to provide information on the generic qualities of products, for that information could be used by others and will not necessarily improve their trade. Moreover, retailers may not in fact be independent from producers. They may receive commission payments or other financial advantages (cheap loans, favourable supply rates) from the producer, linked to the quantities of that producers' product that they sell (financial advisers, mobile phone retailers). Third parties may also be sources of information. But the value of third parties providing information arises most where the product is complex either in its structure, or because making comparisons across products or contract terms is difficult. These are exactly the situations where the consumer finds it difficult to evaluate the product; they are also the situations where for the same reasons they will find it hard to evaluate the third party advisor.[7]

6   *Photocopier Selling Practices* (OFT, 1994).
7   For discussion see London Economics *Consumer Detriment under Conditions of Imperfect Information*, OFT Research Paper 11.

It could also be argued that although consumers might start off with imperfect information, they would soon learn from their own experience or from the experience of others all the information that they need: ie information on price, quality and terms. This may be true with respect to some products, those that are frequently purchased and the experience of which does not depend predominantly on personal taste, for example detergents. But not all products have these characteristics. Many are bought only infrequently (furniture, high value electronic goods, funeral services or the services of plumbers or builders, mortgages, pensions), or consumers may be reluctant to adopt a trial and error approach to experiencing them (medicines, safety equipment, eg child car seats). Or even if the product is bought reasonably frequently the product may change rapidly over time (menus in restaurants, personal computers). It may be that with respect to some products, however, that the consumer is never able to assess their quality, so-called 'credence goods'. The consumer simply has to believe that what she has bought is of good quality or does otherwise have the attributes claimed for it: that she did receive good legal advice; that the medicine prescribed will be effective; that the electrics will not short circuit; that the detergent is indeed biodegradable, and that the 'nutritious' breakfast cereal does contain all the vitamin doses claimed on the packet. Experience of the good therefore does not provide any information that can be fed back into future purchasing decisions.

Information deficits, therefore, may not be easily self-correctable by the market. As a result, prices will not accurately reflect all the information about the product, resulting often in consumers paying more for low quality products. Alternatively, and particularly where consumers are unable to assess quality easily, the lack of information may drive high quality products out of the market. The theory, known as the 'market for lemons', is that where consumers cannot assess quality they will make their purchasing decisions on the basis of price. They may not necessarily opt for the cheapest product on the market, but they are unlikely to opt for the most expensive. As a result, those producing high quality but high cost products will not be able to recover those costs, and will be driven out of the market by those offering lower quality products at lower prices.[8]

In all of these cases, regulation may be justified to correct the market failure. This indeed is the argument of welfare economics, or the public interest theory of regulation, which stipulates that regulation is justified, and will exist, where there are market failures. However, as one economist has noted, '[t]he ingenuity of economists ensures that the list of potential

---

[8]   G Akerlof 'The Market for Lemons: Quality Uncertainty and the Market Mechanism' (1970) 84 Qly Jnl of Economics 488 ('lemons' in the US are cars with defects which prove to be irremediable).

sources for market failure will never be complete'.[9] Further, whilst economists are prepared to accept the existence of market failures, they rarely accept that the model of the rational actor is simply an ideal with no corresponding reality.[10]

Consumers simply do not behave in accordance with the model of the rational actor that economics ascribes to them. Consumers are 'boundedly rational'.[11] That is, even if they are acting to pursue their own self interest, they will not seek the optimal outcome, but only one which is satisfactory— they will satisfice. Moreover, in pursuing their self interest they will be ineffective. This may be because they act on the basis of limited information and on information which may be quickly outdated, particularly if products are changing rapidly, for example, personal computers. Further, individuals only have a limited capacity to process and understand information, a capacity which may vary significantly between individuals depending on educational attainment, social background, linguistic competence etc. The range of alternatives that they consider is restricted, and individuals are affected by the way that information is presented to them—the language of the presentation, the context of the choice, the nature of the display (a feature that the advertising industry relies on for its very existence). Individuals tend to adjust their beliefs and desires according to what they think is attainable—making virtues out of necessities, or indulging in wishful thinking. New information will not be received and processed in a logical, rational manner, but in accordance with the individual's own perceptions, their prejudices, biases and rules of thumb. Individuals tend to prefer outcomes that are certain over those that are probable, and do not treat known probabilities in the way rational theory assumes. People tend to overestimate low probabilities and underestimate those that are high. Finally, the theory of the rational actor cannot cope with incommensurables, or multiple optima—the choice between the cinema ticket and the pizza. The exploitation of these characteristics by producers has been identified as creating a newly identified form of market failure— 'market manipulation'.[12]

[9]   See S Peltzman 'The Economic Theory of Regulation after a Decade of Deregulation' in R Baldwin, C Scott and C Hood *A Reader on Regulation* (OUP, 1998) p 95.
[10] For a good exception see London Economics *Consumer Detriment under Conditions of Imperfect Information*, OFT Research Paper 11.
[11] H Simon, *Administrative Behavior: A Study of Decision-Making Processes in Administrative Organization* (Macmillan, 1957).
[12] See J Hanson and D Kysar 'Taking Behavioralism Seriously' (1999) 112 Harv LR 1420 and generally J Elster *Sour Grapes: Studies in the Subversion of Rationality* (CUP, 1983); id (ed) *Rational Choice* (Blackwell, 1986); id *Solomnic Judgements: Studies in the Limitations of Rationality* (CUP, 1989); D Kahneman and A Tversky 'Prospect Theory: An Analysis of Decision under Risk' (1979) 47 Econometrica 263; ids 'The Framing of Decisions and the Psychology of Choice' (1981) 211 Science 438; ids 'Choices, Values, and Frames' (1984) 39 American Psychologist 341; D Kahneman, P Slovic and A Tversky (eds) *Judgement Under Uncertainty: Heuristics and Biases* (1982).

In failing to recognise bounded rationality, the prescriptions for correcting market failure offered may not be appropriate. For example, the solution for information failures is usually more information. If however the consumer is unlikely to understand the information that is produced, then the lack of information is not corrected. Moreover, regulatory prescriptions can tend to ignore the behavioural responses of those being regulated to the new regulations. So suppliers may take advantage of the need to publish some information by turning that information into a 'focal point', whilst altering those characteristics of the product about which information does not have to be disclosed. For example, if information is required on commissions but not charges, suppliers will lower commissions but raise charges. Or, particularly in the case of credence goods, they may respond to requirements to disclose more information on costs by reducing costs. So a business that provides investment advice may reduce costs by cutting back on training, so that the price of the service appears low, but in fact there has been a deterioration in quality that the consumer cannot detect.

Criticisms may also be levelled at the capture and public choice theories of regulation. The capture theory may be criticised for being too crude in its analysis, one dimensional in its conceptualisation, and for over-generalising. Whilst capture may occur in some situations, it cannot be a universal characterisation of all regulatory systems.[13] The principal criticisms of public choice theory are that it adopts too readily the model of the rational actor, and ignores motivations other than self interest (party loyalties, moral stances, blind adherence to certain views). Further, it cannot account for changes in preferences, or the conflicting interests or loyalties that any one person may hold. Finally it assumes that politics is a perfect market place and that politicians are able to introduce whatever regulation they please, whereas in reality there are numerous institutional constraints on the conduct of politicians and regulators.

Nonetheless, regulation itself, even if directed towards increasing overall social welfare, does impose costs: costs of setting up and staffing the regulator, compliance costs for the firm. Regulation may be badly designed—the problem may have been incorrectly identified; the solution may be inadequate, ineffective or disadvantageous to those it was meant to benefit. Regulation can also have consequences that were unintended and unforeseen.[14] But all these arguments mean is that when deciding whether or not regulation is justified in any one instance, the comparison should not be made between perfect markets and imperfect regulation, or

---

[13]   See eg T Makkai and J Braithwaite 'In and Out of the Revolving Door: Making Sense of Regulatory Capture' (1995) 1 Journal of Public Policy 61.

[14]   P Grabosky 'Counter Productive Regulation' (1995) 23 IJ Sociology of Law 347; C Sunstein 'Paradoxes of the Regulatory State' (1990) 57 U Chi LR 407.

indeed between imperfect markets and perfect regulation, but between imperfect markets and imperfect regulation[15]. The concluding chapter assesses the mixture of policies and instruments which affect consumer markets in England and Wales, and which are considered in more detail over the next 11 chapters.

---

[15]   *The OECD Report on Regulatory Reform, vol 2: Thematic Studies* (OECD, 1997), Chapter 3.

PART I

Business self-regulation

Chapter 2

Business
self-regulation

Questions of regulatory technique have become increasingly important to
the design of consumer law, both for policy makers and for commentators.
If there was ever an assumption that regulatory rules could be made and
implemented by some form of government agency in an unproblematic
fashion, then it no longer exists today. We noted in the first chapter that
considerable scepticism has developed concerning the capacity of
government to regulate effectively and efficiently. This scepticism provides
part of the explanation for the trend towards reliance on various forms of
business self-regulation as an instrument to protect consumers. Though
self-regulation attracts its share of sceptics too (including the author of
the first two editions of this book) considerable work has been devoted to
the development of self-regulatory models to try to avoid the worst
shortcomings of relying on businesses to regulate themselves. These
developments in self-regulatory technique largely centre on providing an
appropriate mix of self-regulation with some form of state oversight or
supervision.

I   DEFINING SELF-REGULATION

Self-regulation is a term which does not admit of any precise or agreed
meaning. At its simplest it might refer to the capacity and tendency of all
individuals and organisations to control their own conduct through the
implicit or explicit development of norms, and mechanisms for monitoring
adherence to them. Any business other than the very smallest is likely to
have procedures for carrying out certain tasks, rules about the ways things
are done and systems of monitoring and bringing deviations from the
rules back into line. The term 'self-regulation' is sometimes used in this

sense in the financial services sector to refer to the controls which a firm has over the conduct of its own staff.[1] Public regulators may use this potential to steer firms towards the development of codes of practice, as has occurred with the utilities sectors (discussed further in Chapter 6). Clearly businesses have a range of resources which they devote to such self-regulation, including expertise, information, authority (through contractual relations with employees and suppliers) and wealth.

The term self-regulation is more widely used to refer to the coming together of a number of businesses into some form of trade association to provide for the *collective* control of the activities of the members of the association.[2] Such a process has the characteristic that it draws on the resources of firms, but through the intermediation of a trade association. Self-regulation in this sense (which is the meaning that will be deployed here) has a number of key advantages when compared with public regulation. Self-regulators are likely to have greater information and expertise concerning the regulated domain. They can use authority derived from the consent of regulatees, and so might expect greater co-operation and compliance. The resourcing of self-regulatory regimes falls on the industry itself rather than on tax-payers. Self-regulation as an instrument of consumer protection seeks to develop and exploit the processes and capacities of businesses, to some extent re-programming them to reflect the public rather than private business objectives.

Self-regulation takes a variety of forms in which a key variable is the extent and nature of state involvement in steering the regime. At one end of the continuum is *voluntary* self-regulation, an entirely spontaneous form of self-government (in the sense that the state neither encourages nor facilitates it) typically involving the formation of a trade association and development of a code of practice by a group of businesses. The motivation lying behind such voluntary self-regulation is unlikely to be entirely altruistic. Such regimes often operate in a manner akin to a cartel, designed to exploit the market through reducing competition between businesses and keeping new entrants out. Consumers may derive some benefit from such regimes where the cartel seeks to develop the reputation of its members, for example through rigorous application of a tough code of practice, as a means of keeping new entrants out of the market. The risks for consumers of such regimes are that the protective aspects simply do not merit the enhanced reputation, that the quality of monitoring and enforcement of the code is inadequate or is diminished once the extent of competition is reduced, or that the additional price paid by consumers for the protective aspect of the regime is not warranted and new entrants are prevented from entering the market to pull prices back down. Put another

---

[1]   J Black 'Constitutionalising Self-Regulation' (1996) 59 MLR 24, 26.
[2]   J Black 'Constitutionalising Self-Regulation' (1996) 59 MLR 24, 26–27.

way voluntary self-regulation may bring some benefits to consumers, but the interests of the business self-regulators are always likely to take precedence. Voluntary self-regulation is only likely to be reliable and desirable where the interests of business and consumers are very closely aligned.

It is concerns of this sort which have led to experimentation with a number of models of self-regulation in which some form of state involvement is deployed to pull the regime in the direction of the consumer interest. The objectives behind such experiments are to continue to exploit the advantages of self-regulation while reducing the main risks. Three conceptually distinct mixed forms have been developed in UK consumer protection.[3] With *sanctioned* self-regulation the voluntary aspect is retained in the decision to establish a code of practice, but a state agency, the Office of Fair Trading, uses statutory powers of approval to set minimum standards for the design and operation of the code. In practice this has been a key mechanism for the development of self-regulation in the UK (and it is discussed more extensively in the next section). *Mandated* self-regulation involves government legislating to require the establishment of self-regulatory codes and provide for monitoring of their effectiveness. This technique is exemplified in the UK both for some professional self-regulation (for example by the Law Society and the General Medical Council) and by the financial services regime established by the Financial Services Act 1986, which is to be replaced by more conventional agency regulation. Relatedly *coerced* self-regulation involves the deployment by government of the threat of legislation as the basis for informal bargaining with industry over the establishment or improvement of self-regulatory regimes. Key examples of this 'bargaining in the shadow of the law' are provided by the self-regulatory regimes in the UK for advertising (discussed below) and insurance (discussed in Chapter 6).

Other variables within self-regulatory regimes include the nature of the participants. While the application of most codes of practice is limited to members of a trade association, some, such as that of the Advertising Standards Authority, purport to apply to all who carry out the regulated business. Some codes are administered solely by members of the trade association. Others have substantial external or lay involvement. Standard-setting may be carried out by the trade association itself, or may be carried out by a separate agency established for that purpose (for example the Committee on Advertising Practice) or by a government agency. Thus the rules may be legislative, contractual or extra-legal, and may be 'general or

---

[3]   The terminology used in this paragraph is based on J Black 'Constitutionalising Self-Regulation' (1996) 59 MLR 24, 26–28. See also NCC *Models of Self-Regulation: An Overview of Models in Business and the Professions* (1999).

specific, vague or precise, simple or complex'.[4] Monitoring and enforcement may be carried out by the self-regulatory body (whether a trade association or a special agency such as the Advertising Standards Authority or the Insurance Ombudsman Bureau) or may be carried out by businesses (for example through contracts) or even by government agencies.

2   APPROVED CODES OF PRACTICE

Codes of ethics and social responsibility have sprouted in recent years as the business community has sought to demonstrate its sense of social responsibility.[5] Controversy concerning the marketing of such products as baby milk and tobacco has led to the development of international codes of marketing practice. At the national level codes of practice can be traced back to the attempts of the guilds to regulate the standards of their members, and even in the days of unbridled capitalism there were always individual capitalists who proclaimed the idea that there were acceptable standards which businesses should meet. Contemporary public debates about the social responsibility of the corporation very much emphasise that the making of profit is only one function of the corporation, and responsibility to employees, consumers, the environment and other groups and values can be reflected in the development and application of codes of practice.[6] To the extent that such measures promote the reputation of corporations they may improve market position and thus be rational even within the narrow frame of profit-maximising behaviour. Certainly companies which have been caught exhibiting signs of corporate irresponsibility have suffered as a result from time to time.[7]

A number of trade associations began to develop codes of practice for consumer dealings in the period after World War II. These activities were variously directed at preventing the development of legislative regulatory regimes and protecting business through enhancing reputation or keeping others out of the market. When the Office of Fair Trading was established in 1973 government recognised the spontaneous development of these codes, and the risk that if completely unregulated they might mislead consumers. The OFT was empowered to approve codes of practice for guidance in safeguarding and promoting the interests of consumers

[4]   J Black 'Constitutionalising Self-Regulation' (1996) 59 MLR 24, 28.
[5]   JAC Hetherington 'Fact and Legal Theory: Shareholders, Managers and Corporate Social Responsibility' (1969) 21 Stan LR 248, 274–92.
[6]   Eg J Parkinson *Corporate Power and Responsibility* (1993); G Wilson 'Business, State and Community: "Responsible Risk Takers", New Labour, and the Governance of Corporate Business' (2000) 27 Journal of Law and Society 151.
[7]   J Forbes *The Consumer Interest:Dimensions and Policy Implications* (Croom Helm, 1987).

(s 124(3)). While this provision was not prominent in the legislative process, it has been among the most central of the OFT's consumer protection functions. The power to approve has been interpreted as a power to examine codes which are submitted for approval and designate minimum standards. Thus the OFT has a key role in shaping the content of self-regulatory codes.

In 1991 the OFT adopted formal guidelines setting out the criteria it would apply in considering future codes of practice, thus, in effect, giving a blueprint for those drafting codes.[8] The guidelines provide a number of broad tests to determine whether a code should be given approval. First, a trade association should normally 'have a significant influence on the sector', with a majority of firms in the sector having membership. But approval may be given where a smaller part of the sector is seeking to develop more progressive values, or where the sector is otherwise fragmented. It is a normal requirement that the trade association has consulted with both consumer groups and regulators (such as trading standards departments). The trade association is required to monitor compliance with the code and publish an annual report. It is said to be preferable that the monitoring be carried out by an independent body, though this is not mandatory. Approved codes should address such matters as 'marketing and advertising of goods; quality of product; terms and conditions of supply…; delivery dates; guarantees and warranties; protection of deposits or prepayments; after-sales service, spare parts, etc', though none of these is actually mandatory within the guidelines. The availability of a suitable low-cost mechanism of alternative redress is a condition for approval of codes. In order to be able to evaluate the effects of codes which it has approved the OFT only gives approval for an initial period of two years so that it can carry out a review and decide whether to give full approval.[9]

To date 49 trade association codes of practice have been approved by the Office of Fair Trading, covering the following sectors (in a number of cases with more than one trade association promulgating separate codes): consumer credit; double glazing; domestic electrical appliances; domestic laundry and cleaning services; residential estate agents; footwear; holiday caravans; introduction agencies; direct marketing; mail order trading; direct selling; motor vehicles; ticket agencies; tour operators and travel agents; photography.[10] The OFT reports that of the codes submitted to it, it 'has

---

8   OFT *Guidelines for the Support of Individual Codes* (1991).
9   OFT *Raising Standards of Consumer Care: Progressing Beyond Codes of Practice* (1998) para 2.8.
10 These are listed in OFT *Raising Standards of Consumer Care: Progressing Beyond Codes of Practice* (1998) Appendix A. A summary of the main provisions of the codes in force in 1995 is provided by B Harvey and D Parry *The Law of Consumer Protection and Fair Trading* (5th edn, 1996) pp 336–347.

chosen to support only a very small minority—those which seemed to offer significant benefits to consumers'.[11]

The Office of Fair Trading has been particularly keen to encourage suitable codes of practice, as the process of issuing statutory orders under Part II of the Fair Trading Act 1973 to control trade practices which are against the economic interest of consumers, rapidly fell into disuse, having only been used four times up to 1976 and not at all since then. The OFT doctrine that businesses are, in any case, more responsive to self-regulation than statutory control, will be tested if the government acts on its plans to develop a new statutory rule-making power for the Office of Fair Trading.[12] In addition to the power of approval of codes, the Director General of Fair Trading can also apply competition law rules which prohibit agreements, decisions and concerted practices which adversely affect UK markets and have as either their object or effect the prevention, restriction or distortion of competition.[13] The exercise of enforcement powers may be used as a lever with trade associations to improve the content of industry codes and associated relationships.

In some respects the codes of practice approved by the OFT are ahead of the law, covering trade practices which are not yet subject to legal regulation. For example some codes require the provision of written estimates, or oblige the clear display of prices where this is not a legal obligation. The Association of British Travel Agents' code was for a long time ahead of the law in providing flexible and immediate remedies where tour operators were unable to fulfil obligations—giving consumers the choice of alternatives or a refund—and these provisions have now been legislated for in the Package Travel Regulations 1992 (discussed further in Chapter 6). Precisely because the codes of practice are in some respects in advance of the law it is anticipated that they will channel its development. It was an early objective for the OFT that, in considering whether a business has fulfilled a consumer contract, the courts will refer to the relevant code of practice as containing the customary terms and the usage of the trade.[14]

Codes of practice are useful in areas which are ill-suited to statutory control. The Office of Fair Trading thought that codes were especially adept in improving the standard of services, which it said could not easily

---

[11] OFT *Raising Standards of Consumer Care: Progressing Beyond Codes of Practice* (1998) para 2.4.

[12] *Modern Markets, Confident Consumers* (Cm 4410 (1999)).

[13] Competition Act 1998, s 2(1). The provision can also be applied in legal proceedings by third parties—competitors and perhaps even consumers who are adversely affected. See I Maher 'Juridification, Codification and Sanction in UK Competition Law' (2000) 63 MLR 544.

[14] MJ Methven 'The Role of the Office of Fair Trading' (1975) City of London LR 10.

be achieved by legislation.[15] Examples of code provision which are probably not the stuff of legislation and perhaps should not give rise to legal liability are the undertakings to deal expeditiously with complaints, those to ensure that people handling complaints are adequately trained and those to offer delivery of an item or a service within a definite number of days. Codes of practice also provide a flexibility which is sometimes difficult to incorporate in legislation. Often matters within codes are not the kind of obligation for which the courts will grant specific performance, and there is no quantifiable loss and therefore little possibility of damages. Codes may also be useful where abuse is confined to one area of the market place and it is not worthwhile to bring to bear the whole legislative machinery to deal with the problem. Codes have proved particularly valuable in sectors where consumers engage in high value but infrequent transactions, with the consequence that they lack both experience and clout that consumers have with transactions they make frequently.[16] Key examples are purchases of secondhand cars and building contracts.

Trade associations have been well disposed to codes approved by the Office of Fair Trading. Codes attract favourable publicity for an industry because of the impression that it is introducing voluntary consumer protection measures. It is no surprise that codes approved by the OFT are concentrated in fields where there have been high levels of consumer dissatisfaction. Table 2.1 shows the numbers of complaints received by local authorities and Citizens Advice Bureaux for 1998, broken down by sector.

Table 2.1 Consumer complaints to local authorities and CABx in year to September 1999

Sector	Number of complaints
House fittings and appliances	309,038
Other household requirements	104,645
Personal goods and services	176,843
Other services	50,710
Transport	168,040
Leisure	88,428
Grand total	897,704

(Source: *Office of Fair Trading Annual Report 1999* pp 80–81.)

NB The statistical method changed during the reporting year. This table provides a consolidation of two sets of half-year data which had somewhat different bases.

---

[15] *Annual Report of the Director General of Fair Trading*, November 1973–December 1974 (1975) p 9.
[16] OFT *Raising Standards of Consumer Care: Progressing Beyond Codes of Practice* (1998) para 1.7.

A key issue with codes is the extent of coverage they have in the sector—what proportion of traders are members? The hope is that once codes are publicised, non-members will find it commercially advantageous to join. Some of the sponsoring trade associations have engaged in recruitment drives since launching their codes of practice. Monitoring has found that in some cases the standards of non-members has also improved after the introduction of the relevant code. This might indicate that the adoption of a code of practice by the greater proportion of a trade actually induces higher standards throughout the trade as a whole. In particular cases other factors may be involved, for example economic forces such as the need to improve trading practices in order to meet weaker consumer demand. The fact remains, however, that codes can never guarantee to apply across the board in the same way as law.

Most of the codes establish conciliation and arbitration procedures funded mainly by the sponsoring trade associations, to assist in the resolution of any consumer complaints against member organisations. A contract term which *requires* the use of arbitration, thus excluding the jurisdiction of the courts, is unfair under the terms of the Arbitration Act 1996 (ss 89–92).[17] It is arguable that even the decision to refer a dispute to arbitration is not binding, and that a consumer dissatisfied by the results of an arbitration could reopen the matter in court proceedings, notwithstanding any provision in the arbitration agreement which excluded appeal to the courts.

Initially a trade association will use its good offices to try to settle a complaint informally if the consumer has already taken up the matter with the business involved. Under the codes, adherents undertake to expedite the settlement of genuine complaints. The aim is to reach a settlement—without any close attention to the consumer's entitlement at law. This approach cuts both ways: on the one hand the consumer may be disadvantaged by a compromise solution. But on the other hand conciliation can deal with matters like dilatoriness, erroneous billing and poor service, which may not amount to legal wrongs. Where a dispute is referred to arbitration an independent arbitrator, a member of the Chartered Institute of Arbitrators, is appointed, under the terms of the Arbitration Act 1996. Arbitrators may be assisted by expert assessors, who are members of the sponsoring trade association, and they may obtain an independent report if necessary. Consumers must pay a fee, but this is

---

[17]   See also the Unfair Terms in Consumer Contracts Regulations 1999, SI 1999/ 2083, Sch 2, para 1(q) where contract terms 'excluding or hindering the consumer's right to take legal action or exercise any other legal remedy, particularly by requiring the consumer to take disputes exclusively to arbitration not covered by legal provisions' are listed in the indicative and illustrative list of terms which may be unfair.

usually the limit of their liability, and the fee is refundable at the discretion of the arbitrator. Arbitration is nearly always carried out on the papers alone, with no hearing. Arbitrators can award sums of money or order a business to take specific action (eg to replace goods).

Responses to a recent OFT consultation document indicated that consumer agencies often advise consumers to pursue claims under the small claims procedure in the county court, rather than through arbitration schemes, because the small claims procedure appeared to them to be more impartial and easier to use. Some trade associations also reported that they steered consumers away from arbitration because the costs of arbitration have to be borne by the association.[18]

As to the more general enforcement of codes of practice, the first line of action lies with the trade association. Some codes recognise the possibility of trade associations imposing 'fines' on their members if they fail to observe their obligations.[19] This is a relatively simple means of disciplining members and inducing them to pay close attention to proper practices. The alternative procedure is to issue a reprimand, which lacks the bite of a fine. The ultimate sanction behind the codes is that sponsoring trade associations can expel members who persistently breach the terms. Expulsion may be a serious threat with a prestigious trade association, or one which confers important benefits on members. Trade associations hope that adherence to a code of practice will eventually become an important benefit to businesses as consumers become familiar with its existence and choose to patronise businesses which indicate adherence to its terms, for example by displaying an appropriate symbol.

These sanctions have drawbacks in that few trade associations seem prepared to invoke them. They adopt a relatively lenient attitude to transgressions, although the Office of Fair Trading requires them to undertake systematic monitoring of members' trade practices, which is necessary if sanctions are to be a real threat. Moreover, once a trade association takes a hard line and expels a member, its sanctions are expended and the business can continue operating in defiance of the code unless membership is a condition of operating.[20] The only consolation to consumers is that a trade association may undertake to pay redress in those circumstances where a business has failed to pay compensation as required when it was a member. One possibility is that the OFT might use its powers under Part III of the Fair Trading Act 1973 to seek assurances that the business will endeavour to comply with the terms of the relevant

18 OFT *Raising Standards of Consumer Care: Progressing Beyond Codes of Practice* (1998) para 2.18. See the discussion of alternative dispute resolution in Chapter 3 below.
19 Such 'fines' were upheld in *Thorne v Motor Trade Association* [1937] AC 797.
20 OFT *Raising Standards of Consumer Care: Progressing Beyond Codes of Practice* (1998) para 2.16.

code.[1] Persistent breach of a code could be made an explicit basis for the Director General of Fair Trading to seek a cease and desist order. Without independent monitoring it is difficult to say whether the codes of practice are being implemented. Trade associations work from the complaints they receive and conclude that things are quite satisfactory.

Other mechanisms of enforcement are linked to the civil and criminal law. Codes of practice may have a number of effects on contracts with consumers. Codes often require their adherents to write particular terms into their contract. Where terms are not written into contracts, a court may nevertheless hold that the terms of the code are incorporated into the contract. Where codes provide that the sponsoring trade association will establish some form of pre-payment insurance regime, it has been held by the Court of Appeal that the consumer may be able to enforce the code directly against the trade association as a form of collateral contract. In *Bowerman v ABTA*[2] a consumer successfully sued the Association of British Travel Agents for a refund of money paid for a holiday to an ABTA member which subsequently became insolvent. Where a trader provides a false or misleading indication that they adhere to a code of practice or are a member of a trade association they may be committing an offence under the Trade Descriptions Act 1968, for which they can be prosecuted by local authority trading standards departments (see further Chapter 8 below). In practice local authorities are likely to advise traders as to how to comply with the law in most cases, but the criminal law may be invoked in cases of persistent intentional conduct which has pronounced effects for consumers.[3] One final mechanism of enforcement is for the OFT to incorporate agreement to comply with a code in an assurance given under Part III of the Fair Trading Act 1973 (discussed further in Chapter 11 below).

An early evaluation of the costs and benefits of codes of practice for consumers concluded that overall there had been beneficial effects for consumers, though these were not measurable.[4] The advantages were said to lie in the enhanced awareness among consumers of their rights, the reinforcement with businesses of legal prohibitions, the provision of better information to consumers, an improvement in the quality of goods and services, and improved mechanisms for redress. The costs to consumers included the effects of the false assurance where a trader did not adhere to the terms of a code, the reduction in choice (for example ruling out the

---

[1]   *Annual Report of the Director General of Fair Trading 1980* (1981) p 73.
[2]   [1995] Trading Law and Trading Law Reports 246.
[3]   B Harvey and D Parry *The Law of Consumer Protection and Fair Trading* (5th edn, 1996) pp 346–347.
[4]   J Pickering and D Cousins 'The Benefits and Costs of Voluntary Codes of Practice' (1982) 6 European Journal of Marketing 31.

chance to take a lower quality service for a lower price), the possibility of higher prices and more generally the risks of possible cartelisation (noted above).

The limitations which the OFT recognises with approved codes of practice have caused it to carry out a major evaluation of possible future directions. In this review the OFT identified problems with publicity, standard setting, enforcement and redress. The objective of the review was to find ways to 'preserve the best features of self-regulation, its flexibility, speed of amendment, acceptability to business, and the voluntary adoption of higher standards from a position of enlightened self-interest...' while ensuring that self-regulatory regimes are properly publicised and have 'truly independent, alternative forms of redress and disciplinary procedures...'.[5] The OFT identified the conditions for success of codes to be 'the availability of a strong sanction; a plausible threat of statutory regulation; a clear wish by the good players in the industry to distinguish themselves from others; and obvious benefits to consumers, sufficient to affect their choice of trader.'[6] These factors were said rarely to be present in a 'sufficiently strong combination'.

In light of its review of the approved codes of practice regime the OFT has proposed a new regime under which more general standards of trading practice will be developed by the British Standards Institution with the involvement of consumers and traders. Compliance with these general standards will entitle businesses to use a 'better trader' logo.[7] Additionally sector-specific standards may be developed to address the particular problems of particular sectors.[8] The processes used by the BSI for setting standards are felt by the OFT to be more transparent and participatory than the current bilateral negotiations held between trade associations and the OFT.[9] Compliance with the new core standards and sector-specific standards would remain voluntary. Businesses wishing to adopt the standards would have the choice of self-certifying compliance or seeking external accreditation from an independent accreditor.[10] A new national body will be established to grant approval and supervise compliance via

---

[5]   OFT *Raising Standards of Consumer Care: Progressing Beyond Codes of Practice* (1998) para 2.24.

[6]   OFT *Raising Standards of Consumer Care: Progressing Beyond Codes of Practice* (1998) Appendix C, para 8.

[7]   OFT *Raising Standards of Consumer Care: Progressing Beyond Codes of Practice* (1998) para 3.38.

[8]   OFT *Raising Standards of Consumer Care: Progressing Beyond Codes of Practice* (1998) para 3.10.

[9]   OFT *Raising Standards of Consumer Care: Progressing Beyond Codes of Practice* (1998) para 3.15.

[10]   OFT *Raising Standards of Consumer Care: Progressing Beyond Codes of Practice* (1998) paras 3.21–3.22.

self-certification or external accreditation. Traders failing to follow the standards could be deregistered by the approval body and the reasons for their expulsion made public.[11]

Linked to these proposals, the OFT is seeking to develop schemes for redress which are independent of trade associations. A key model for development here is ombudsman schemes which have apparently proved more popular with consumers than arbitration and other mechanisms of alternative dispute resolution. The relative popularity of ombudsman schemes may be explained by the fact that they cost the consumer nothing, have investigative as well as adjudicative powers, and have developed reputations for robust independence.[12]

The government is proposing to operationalise the ideas set out by the OFT in legislation empowering the OFT to give a seal of approval to codes which meet core principles:

Outline core principles for code:
Consumers should see:
— truthful adverts
— clear, helpful and adequate pre-contractual information
— clear, fair contracts
— staff who know about and meet the terms of the code as well as their
— legal responsibilities
— an effective complaints handling system run by the business
— if problems cannot be resolved in-house, an effective and low cost redress mechanism
— publicity about the code from the business and the sponsors, including a report on the operation of the code.

Behind the scenes
— the sponsor should have a supervisory body for the code made up of people from the sector and consumers, with some independent members
— the sponsor should tailor the core principles to develop its own code, taking into account the needs and characteristics of the sector such as the size of businesses within it, and keep it up to date
— businesses in the sector should agree to deliver on the principles in the tailored code and report regularly to the sponsor on the operation of the code
— the sponsor should provide an effective and low cost redress mechanism in the event of an unresolved dispute between a member and a consumer

---

[11]   OFT *Raising Standards of Consumer Care: Progressing Beyond Codes of Practice* (1998) para 3.50.
[12]   OFT *Raising Standards of Consumer Care: Progressing Beyond Codes of Practice* (1998) para 3.43. For further discussion of these proposals see OFT *Raising Standards of Consumer Care—Report on a Conference held at New Hall College, Cambridge* (1999).

— the sponsor should put into place an effective system to underpin compliance and to address breaches by members
— the redress and compliance systems should, wherever necessary or possible, include an independent element
— the sponsor should publish a report on compliance with the code and on complaints about its operation.[13]

Non-compliance with codes is to be addressed through new statutory enforcement procedures. In some industries, such as the building trade, government is taking a greater involvement in the drawing up of codes to address particular concerns about 'cowboy builders'.[14]

3   ADVERTISING SELF-REGULATION

Advertising is a central part of the consumer society, providing the capacity of mass producers to mass market their products.[15] For some commentators advertising is chiefly a mechanism for providing information to consumers about the existence or properties or price of a product, so that consumers can better exercise their preferences in the market place.[16] For subscribers to this liberal theory the main tasks of advertising regulation are to ensure the accuracy and honesty of advertisements. These objectives are capable of being pursued by such laws as the Trade Descriptions Act 1968 which makes it an offence to provided false or misleading descriptions of goods (s 1) and to knowingly give a false or misleading description in respect of services (s 14) (these provisions are discussed further in Chapter 8). Civil liability may also flow from misleading advertising, either through misrepresentation or breach of a contract term. In *Smith v Land and House Property Corpn*[17] the plaintiff succeeded in a misrepresentation action against the defendant vendor who had advertised property for sale saying that it had 'a very desirable tenant' when it knew that the tenant was a bad payer. Similarly in *Moorhouse v Wolfe*[18] loans were advertised as being available 'on easy terms', and the interest rate for the particular consumer was about 125% with security. The main reason that the courts do not give consumers a remedy in private law for advertising claims is that they do not regard most of them as binding in law. *Esso Petroleum Ltd v Customs*

---

[13]   DTI *Modern Markets: Confident Consumers* (Cm 4410 (1999)) p 27.
[14]   DTI *Modern Markets: Confident Consumers* p 29.
[15]   S Ewen *Captains of Consciousness* (McCraw-Hill, 1976).
[16]   See the statement by two American regulators: C Peeler and M Rusk 'Commercial Speech and the FTC's Consumer Protection Program' (1991) 59 Antitrust LJ 985.
[17]   (1884) 28 Ch D 7.
[18]   (1882) 46 LT 374; cf *Richardson v Silvester* (1873) LR 9 QB 34.

and Excise Comrs[19] should not be seen as heralding a change of attitude because the decision turned on the very definite nature of the advertising claim, which was quite unlike most claims to which critics of advertising take objection. There Esso offered a World Cup coin with every four gallons of petrol bought. A majority in the House of Lords held that there was an intention to create legal relations by the statement which gave rise to a contract. The minority, however, thought that the statement was not intended to give rise to contractual relations because the offer was so trivial.

Advertising controls must be able to cope with instances of half-truth, ambiguity, undue emphasis and exaggeration as well as blatant dishonesty. They must be capable of examining the total impression created by the advertisement, not just the words and should be able to require substantiation by advertisers of claims made and testimonials used. Only really in the tort of passing off do legal controls come close to meeting these requirements. The elements of the tort are

(1) a misrepresentation,
(2) made by a trader in the course of trade,
(3) to prospective customers of his or ultimate consumers of goods or services supplied by him,
(4) which is calculated to injure the business or goodwill of another trader (in the sense that this is a reasonably foreseeable consequence) and
(5) which causes actual damage to the business or good will of the trader by whom the action is brought.[20]

Actions under this head are brought by competitors but may have the incidental effect of protecting consumers from misleading advertising. In *McDonald's Hamburgers Ltd v Burger King (UK) Ltd*[1] it was held that an advertisement for a Burger King Whopper headed 'Its not just Big, Mac' was likely to mislead consumers into thinking that the advertisement was for a McDonalds product. In *Reckitt & Colman Products Ltd v Borden Inc*[2] it was held that consumers were likely to be misled into thinking that lemon juice sold in a yellow plastic lemon-shaped container was the Jif Lemon brand and accordingly the owners of Jif Lemon were entitled to an injunction to prevent the continued used of plastic lemon-shaped

---

[19] [1976] 1 All ER 117, [1976] 1 WLR 1. See also *Carlill v Carbolic Smokeball Co* [1893] 1 QB 256.
[20] Lord Diplock in *Erven Warnink BV v J Townend & Sons (Hull) Ltd ('Advocaat')* [1979] AC 731.
[1] [1986] FSR 45.
[2] [1990] 1 All ER 873, [1990] 1 WLR 491, HL.

containers by a competitor. Cases such as these are disturbing both because of the extent to which they present consumers as naïve and unable to distinguish products and brands, and because of the potential effect of the decisions on stifling competition. In any event the use of such actions by competitors is strategic and sporadic and could not be expected to have instrumental effects in protecting consumers in any systematic way.

Others subscribing to a substantially liberal view both of consumer behaviour and of the appropriate boundaries of state activity see problems with the economic effects of advertising. Here there are difficulties both from the perspective of forging consensus and developing appropriate controls. The most important economic aspect of advertising is whether it fosters market power by raising marketing costs and creating barriers to entry. Statistical studies over a number of industries disagree on the degree of association between advertising intensity and market concentration.[3] How far there is an association depends on the product and the industry involved. For example, there is much less advertising for industrial goods than for certain consumer goods, irrespective of the market structure, because of the smaller number and greater knowledge of buyers. Other factors besides advertising, such as economies of scale, play an important role in market power. Advertising may create entry barriers but new entrants may actually use it to challenge market dominance. Even if advertising is a substantial barrier to small firms and new entrants, there still may be substantial competition within an industry. Despite these qualifications, it is clear that particular industries with a high degree of market power are characterised by large amounts of advertising, higher profit rates than normal and product stagnation.[4]

Certainly there is a case for provision in competition legislation to limit advertising where it has the requisite anti-competitive effect. There are difficulties with such controls which might push expenditure into other forms of promotion and might penalise the small firm or new entrant.[5] Another idea is to promote or subsidise independent sources of information for consumers which would challenge the claims of advertisers and encourage a change in the character of advertising.

For others of a more critical persuasion advertising is seen as a mechanism for shaping preferences, not through the provision of information, but through exploitation of the desires and weaknesses of

[3]   For example, CJ Sutton 'Advertising, Concentration and Competition' (1974) 84 Econ J 56; WD Reekie 'Advertising and Market Share Mobility' (1974) 21 Scot J of Pol Econ 143; TT Nagle 'Do Advertising Profitability Studies Really Show that Advertising Creates a Barrier to Entry?' (1981) 24 Journal of Law and Economics 333.

[4]   AJ Duggan 'The Great Soap Opera' (1978) 11 Melb ULR 467.

[5]   WD Reekie *Advertising* (Macmillan, 1974) pp 119–124.

consumers.[6] It is argued that the persuasive power of advertising leads to consumer being brainwashed into purchasing what they do not really want. It is also said that advertising creates illusions far removed from reality which render people less able to adjust to real life.[7] A constant criticism has been that advertising generates unacceptable values, for example by reinforcing stereotyped images of women. There are also charges that advertising trivialises serious matters and fosters materialism. Other social effects of advertising include an undue dependence on advertising revenue by the mass media and the possibility that this can expose it to undesirable pressure. For proponents of this latter view problems of inaccuracy in advertisements are just the beginning of their concerns. More pervasive and difficult to control is the attempt by advertisers to shape preferences and to boost consumption through the association of products with particular life styles. This is all the more problematic from a regulatory point of view because of the lack of public consensus on the nature and extent of problems associated with advertising. The result is that some issues related to the social effects of advertising (for example with alcohol and tobacco[8]), judged incapable of statutory regulation, are addressed by codes of practice, whereas others are left untouched by present-day voluntary or legal controls.

Self-regulation is widely thought to provide a better mechanism for controlling these more challenging aspects of advertising technique. There are a number of reasons for this. Firstly, self-regulation is best placed to exploit the expertise of advertisers themselves. Secondly, advertisers are likely to be more co-operative with self-regulators than with a regulatory agency. Thirdly, it is easier to capture the objectives of the regime in the kind of more open-textured rules which can be used in a self-regulatory code, and the code can be said to be binding in both spirit and letter. Fourthly, the costs of the regime fall on the industry rather than on the tax-payer. Any evaluation of the self-regulatory regime established to control print advertising in the UK must ask how successful government has been in fostering the development of appropriate controls through the

---

[6]   JK Galbraith *The Affluent Society* (Andre Deutsch, 4th edn, 1984) p 127ff; J Williamson *Decoding Advertisements* (Marion Boyars, 1978); J Holder 'Regulating Green Advertising in the Motor Car Industry' (1991) 18 Journal of Law and Society 323.

[7]   See the extensive analysis of the cultural studies literature and it application to advertising regulation by I Ramsay, *Advertising, Culture and the Law* (Sweet & Maxwell, 1996) Chapters 2–4.

[8]   Though it should be noted that the UK government is currently in the process of implementing an EC Directive which requires Member States to ban tobacco advertising: Directive 98/43/EC OJ L 213 30.07.98 p 9, Article 3. The validity of the Directive is being challenged before the ECJ: Joined Cases C-376/98 and C-74/99 *Germany v European Parliament and Council*. The Advocate General has proposed that the court should anull the Directive.

threat of more substantial intervention. Such government activity now operates at two levels, with the immediate capacity of the Director General of Fair Trading to seek injunctions against misleading advertisements, and the more general threat of government to legislate should the self-regulatory regime, in combination with the DGFT's injunctive power, prove ineffective in promoting desired public policy outcomes.

4   THE BRITISH CODES OF ADVERTISING AND SALES PROMOTION

The British Codes of Advertising and Sales Promotion are not promulgated by a trade association, and consequently fall outside the approval regime operated by the Office of Fair Trading.[9] The self-regulatory system in Britain, for advertisements other than those on television or radio, began in the early 1960s when the Advertising Association drew up a Code of Advertising Practice and constituted a Code of Advertising Practice (CAP) Committee and a small secretariat to enforce it.[10] The action was taken under the threat of statutory control as a result of the work of the Molony Committee.[11] To give self-regulation a veneer of independence the Advertising Association also established an Advertising Standards Authority (ASA), a company limited by guarantee, to supervise the code and its enforcement. Following earlier decisions concerning the amenability to judicial review of private bodies exercising public functions it has been held that the ASA is subject to judicial review.[12] The ASA model of self-regulation has been widely adopted in other European jurisdictions.[13]

The ASA's responsibilities are to investigate complaints about advertisements, publish case reports giving the results of its investigations and conduct a programme of monitoring to check compliance with the Code. Its chairman is an individual from outside the industry and two-

---

[9]   OFT *Raising Standards of Consumer Care: Progressing Beyond Codes of Practice* (1998) para 2.2.

[10] See Lord Drumalbyn 'Advertising Control: The Evolution of the Self-Regulatory System' (1974) 41 Advertising Quarterly 4; JC Braun 'Voluntary Control within the Profession' in A Wilson (ed) *Advertising and the Community* (1968); P Thompson 'Informal Resolution of Disputes in Advertising—The Role of the Code of Advertising Practice Committee' (1982) Trading Law 233.

[11] R Baggott and L Harrison 'The Politics of Self-Regulation: The Case of Advertising Control' (1986) 14 Review of Politics 143.

[12] *R v Advertising Standards Authority, ex p Insurance Services plc* (1989) 9 Tr LR 169. As with the decisions of other self-regulatory organisations the Divisional Court has applied a light hand to oversight of the ASA, for example holding that even inconsistency in approach as between ASA adjudications affecting the same company would not render the decision flawed: see *R v Advertising Standards Authority, ex p DSG Retail Ltd (t/a Dixons)* [1997] COD 232.

[13] *Advertising Self-Regulation in Europe* (EASA, 1997).

thirds of its members must have no connection with advertising. The advertising members are supposed to sit as individuals and not as representatives of any sectional interest. Co-ordinating the executive actions of the system is the CAP Committee, which works under the general supervision of the ASA. The Committee consists of persons nominated by the various trade and professional associations supporting the Code and is responsible for drafting, monitoring and revision of the content of the Code and the application of the Code to the industry.

The Code of Advertising Practice is drawn up broadly to reflect community standards and is interpreted in this way by the ASA in applying it.[14] The general principles of the Code are that advertisements should be 'legal, decent, honest and truthful', should be 'prepared with a sense of responsibility to consumers and to society' and should 'respect the principles of fair competition generally accepted in business'.[15] The Code prohibits advertising which is likely to cause 'serious or widespread offence' (para 5.1) and has been criticised on the basis that such a narrow basis for regulation prevents the ASA from tackling the more pervasive effects of stereotyping in advertisements for example on the position of ethnic minorities and women.[16]

Special rules apply to certain consumer sectors. Thus for alcoholic drinks advertisements should not encourage excessive drinking (para 46.3) nor show persons under 25 drinking (para 46.5), or be directed at persons under 18 (paras 46.4, 46.6). Advertisements directed at children 'should contain nothing that is likely to result in their physical, mental or moral harm' (para 47.2), nor 'exploit their credulity, loyalty, vulnerability or lack of experience' (para 47.3). There are special rules also for advertisements relating to motoring products, environmental claims, health and beauty products and therapies, slimming products, distance selling, employment and business opportunities, financial services and products, betting and gaming and cigarettes. The Cigarette Code (paras 66 ff) is particularly restrictive on what can be depicted in advertisements for tobacco products, causing many tobacco manufacturers to engage in surreal advertising of various forms so as to avoid risking inadvertent breach of the codes.

The CAP Committee is solely responsible for handling complaints by one advertiser against another—a point which should be underlined because it has been mentioned how self-regulation can be used to stifle competition. A copy panel gives pre-publication guidance on copy and advises on post-publication problems. The Code relies on adverse publicity as its main sanction, for the ASA publishes details of complaints—these

---

[14] Committee of Advertising Practice *The British Codes of Advertising and Sales Promotion* (10th edn, 1999).

[15] *Advertising Code* (10th edn, 1999) paras 2.1–2.3.

[16] I Ramsay *Advertising, Culture and the Law* (1996) pp 123–127.

are often reported in the press—including whether they have been upheld and the names both of the advertiser and the advertising agency who handled the campaign. In a case where an advertiser sought a judicial review of an ASA adjudication the Divisional Court refused an interim injunction to prevent the publication of the case report prior to the outcome of the full judicial review hearing. The court exhibited a marked reluctance to prevent publication, stating that an interim injunction would only be granted where publication would cause irreparable damage.[17]

The ultimate sanction is that the media adherents to the code have undertaken not to publish any advertisements found to be in breach of the Code and not to accept advertisements from agencies which defy the authority of the ASA. Recently the ASA has introduced an intermediate sanction of requiring an advertiser to submit all copy for pre-clearance (a measure normally only required under the Code for certain classes of advertisement) for a specified period. This new measure is both a sanction and a remedy to the problems associated with deliberate breach of the rules by advertisers seeking to shock, and for whom ex post publicity about their breach of the code may be a benefit rather than a sanction. Critics of the ASA regime argue that it should have the power to fine, and that this is the only effective way to deal with wilful non-compliance with the Code's provisions.[18]

Under the threat of legislation both the Code and the procedures for its operation have been changed from time to time. Following criticism in 1974 by the government and the Office of Fair Trading of weaknesses in the self-regulatory system, several changes were made. The size of the CAP-ASA secretariat was increased; an advertising campaign was undertaken to familiarise consumers with the existence of the Code; the independent ASA members now sit on CAP committees; the ASA began publishing names of advertisers against whom complaints were made (although for the first 11 years this was refused on the grounds that it would undermine confidence); and to help emphasise the independence of the ASA, it is no longer financed by the Advertising Association, but by a surcharge on display advertisements. Following developments of complaints procedures affecting public sector bodies, the ASA introduced a system for independent review of its adjudications in March 1999 to provide a quicker and cheaper form of appeal than that provided by judicial review. The grounds for review are either the availability of additional evidence or a substantial flaw in the adjudication (para 68.36).

---

[17] *R v Advertising Standards Authority, ex p Vernons Organisation Ltd* [1992] 1 WLR 1289.
[18] B Middleton and D Rodwell 'Regulating Advertising: Time to Get Tough?' (1998) 8 Consumer Policy Review 88.

The proponents of the Code claim that self-regulation has many advantages over legal control. Legal controls are said not to be adapted to identify advertisements which do not live up to the best professional standards. There is no absolute truth in many areas of advertising, and it is thus said that there is no yardstick by which cases can be compared. The Code is said to maintain standards in areas like good manners and taste which defy legal definition. In the view of its supporters the Code can be applied speedily and flexibly and is enforced in spirit as well as in the letter. Finally the Code can foreshadow developments in the law, as with bargain offers.

The majority of complaints to the ASA are not pursued because inadequate details are received, because there is no case to investigate or because they are judged to be outside the scope of the Code. In 1999 12,141 cases were considered. 7,746 cases were not investigated. 2,015 complaints were upheld, 1,108 not upheld and 737 resolved informally.[19] Complaints on subjective matters like decency account for a small percentage of those dealt with. Mail-order complaints, relating usually to service rather than to copy claims, account for a substantial percentage of the total. The ASA has expressed particular concern that a significant number of complaints upheld have resulted in claims not being satisfactorily substantiated on request. This is especially significant because of strong criticism of the substantiation provision that it does not require that the substantiation be independent or made public.

The ASA regime has long been criticised for its reactive nature. Enforcement actions are triggered only by complaints and cannot be initiated by the ASA without a complaint. A number of attempts have been made to assess the extent to which advertisers comply with the provisions of the Code of Advertising Practice. The ASA itself has developed an ongoing programme of research examining a representative sample of advertisements in regional and national press and magazines. The second *National Advertising Review*, published in 1998, found that 97% of advertisements surveyed complied with the Code. Of the breaches discovered, about three-quarters were said to be technical rather than substantive (ie requiring only a slight alteration to make them acceptable). These technical problems included the failure to include VAT in mail-order advertisements (in breach of para 15.2) and failure to include the advertiser's address outside the response coupon (para 52.5). The substantive breaches largely consisted of breach of the special rules in the health and beauty sector requiring substantiation of claims.

There are a number of points to be made about the Code's operation. Firstly, most investigations arise from complaints by individual consumers

---

[19]   Advertising Standards Authority *Overview of 1999 and Statistics* (2000).

or by other bodies. By themselves complaints are an inadequate way of detecting breaches of the Code. Organizations will only raise a matter when an advertisement touches on their area of interest and individual consumers are unlikely to complain to a great extent, proportionate to the number of breaches, because they do not know about the Code or its provisions or because they are not sufficiently affected to go to the trouble. The ASA has now introduced a monitoring programme supposed to overcome these problems (noted above).

Secondly—and this is a related point—the number of breaches of the Code dealt with annually was relatively small in the early years. Independent surveys of advertisements by consumer groups before the reforms in 1974 detected as many breaches of the Code over a relatively short period as the ASA handled in a year. After publicity campaigns for the Code there has been a substantial increase in complaints, which was particularly ironical because the ASA had always trumpeted the smallness of their number as evidence that the self-regulatory system was working satisfactorily. The ASA was quick to emphasise—and it was certainly true—that the increase was because more consumers were aware of the Code's operation.

Thirdly, the Code operates ex post facto, and an advertisement in breach can continue until the ASA issues a ruling. While it may be impossible to operate a pre-vetting system for the millions of advertisements published annually, this is no reason for not requiring it for particular types of advertisements: those directed at vulnerable sections of the population, those where abuse is known to occur, those for products which are socially dangerous, and those which play on fears of social and physical inadequacy. Moreover there is no provision for advertisers to compensate those who have suffered loss as a result of a contravention of the Code.

The fourth point to note is that in recent years 60–70% of complaints actually investigated have been upheld. Breaches of the Code have been found not to be confined to those marginal or provincial journals which did not adhere to the code. Misleading advertisements have included some by leading manufacturers and service providers, inserted on their behalf by some of the leading advertising agencies.

Finally, there has been concern at the attitude of the ASA to advertisements in breach of the law. The ASA's general view has been that it neither possesses nor seeks the sanctions available in the courts and the Code is designed to complement and not to usurp legal controls. For example, when the Price Marking (Bargain Offers) Order 1979[20] was introduced the provision regarding price comparisons and worth and value claims in the Code was suspended on the basis that this permitted truthful

[20]   SI 1979/364 as amended by SI 1979/633, SI 1979/1124.

price and value claims which had been made unlawful. Where there appeared to be a breach of the law it advised consumers complaining to it to approach their local consumer protection departments. The Director General of Fair Trading concluded, however, that the ASA should review its policy towards breaches of the Order brought to its attention in the light of the general requirements of the Code that all advertisements should be legal, decent, honest and truthful.[1]

5   REGULATION OF BROADCAST ADVERTISING

Television and radio advertising are also subject to self-regulation, but within the statutory framework of the Broadcasting Act 1990 and agency regulation by the Independent Television Commission and the Radio Authority.[2] The ITC (the television regulator) has a Code of Advertising Standards (set out in very similar terms to the Code of Advertising Practice discussed above), a separate Rules on Advertising Breaks and a Code of Programme Sponsorship. The Code of Advertising Standards goes beyond its ASA counterpart in requiring that advertisements are 'clearly distinguishable as such and recognisably separate from the programme' (r 5)). The Breaks Code is concerned both with the length of advertisements and their location within schedules. ITC Guidance notes issued on the application of these codes are binding on broadcasters. The revisions to legislation in the 1990s produced significant liberalisation of the advertising rules for broadcasters. Whereas sponsorship of programmes had been prohibited under the Broadcasting Act 1981,[3] it is now permitted and has become routine, in particular for major dramas broadcast on commercial television.[4]

6   INJUNCTIVE POWERS

The injunctive power of the Office of Fair Trading derives from an EC Directive which originally targeted only misleading advertising likely to adversely affect the economic interests of consumers.[5] The Directive has

---

[1]   Director General of Fair Trading *Review of the Price Marking (Bargain Offers) Orders 1979* (1981) para 2.13.

[2]   See T Gibbons *Regulating the Media* (Sweet & Maxwell, 2nd edn, 1998) p 193ff. *R v British Advertising Clearance Centre, ex p Swiftcall* (16 November, 1995, unreported), Div Ct.

[3]   Section 8(6)–(9).

[4]   T Gibbons *Regulating the Media* (2nd edn, 1998) p 199ff.

[5]   Directive 84/450/EEC; Control of Misleading Advertisements Regulations 1988, SI 1988/915, reg 2(2); *Complaint against X* Case C-373/90 [1992] ECR I-131.

recently been extended to cover also comparative advertising.[6] The thrust of the 2000 Regulations which implement the 1997 Directive is to permit comparative advertising only where it is not misleading, or denigratory and is based on objective comparison (reg 4). The regime for seeking injunctions (which is discussed more fully in Chapter 11 below) is applied to advertisements in breach of these obligations (reg 6).

In negotiating the terms of the EC Directive on misleading advertising the British Government was reluctant to abandon the emphasis in Britain on self-regulation. Accordingly the Directive was drafted in such a way as to permit Member States to continue to place priority on self-regulatory mechanisms, with the use of state action to seek injunctive relief acting as a backstop. This model creates a hierarchy of regimes which might be expected to bolster the self-regulatory regime through the capacity of the ASA to point to the injunctive sanction exercisable by the Office of Fair Trading. While the injunctive power has been rarely used, it may be that it has been used sufficiently to reinforce the self-regulatory regime.

In *Director General of Fair Trading v Tobyward Ltd*[7] the Director of Fair Trading sought an interlocutory injunction to restrain the continuing use of an advertisement for a slimming product in respect of which there was strong prima facie evidence of false claims about permanent weight loss. The defendant continued to place the advertisement after a complaint had been upheld by the ASA, and consequently the ASA had referred the case to the Office of Fair Trading. Hoffman J granted the injunction to restrain the use of the advertisement and other advertisements in similar terms.

7   THE DEVELOPMENT OF ADVERTISING REGULATION NORMS

Independently of the institutional issues of the appropriate mix of self-regulation and agency regulation in the advertising domain, experience in other jurisdictions suggests that there is considerable scope for the development of new principles and techniques to be applied to advertisers to encourage or require them to ensure the accuracy of advertising claims.[8]

Affirmative disclosure has been used by the US Federal Trade Commission on several occasions to ensure that consumers are not misled.

---

[6]   Directive 97/55/EC; Control of Misleading Advertisements (Amendment) Regulations 2000, SI 2000/914.

[7]   [1989] 2 All ER 266.

[8]   A valuable, if dated, account of innovation in the United States is R Pitofsky 'Beyond Nader: Consumer Protection and the Regulation of Advertising' (1977) 90 Harv LR 661.

In one case the court upheld an FTC order that future advertisements about a purported cure for baldness should disclose that up to 95% of all cases of baldness were not curable.[9] Affirmative disclosure can perform the additional function of ensuring that advertisements actually provide information to consumers to allow them to make intelligent choices. Modern advertising is often uninformative on precisely those matters like durability, performance and comparative value which consumers need to know. There are a number of instances in English law where affirmative disclosure is required (and not exclusively in advertising) and these are the subject matter of Chapter 9 of this book. At this stage some of the difficulties of affirmative disclosure should be mentioned: there are finite limits to the amount of information consumers can absorb, consumers are selective in what they take in, some are less able to cope that others and information is more digestible if it is presented in a relatively simple form. Another point to be considered is that affirmative disclosure in advertising is likely to meet strong resistance because it goes against the grain of modern advertising and because in many respects it is directly against producers' interests to emphasise factors like utility and comparative value.

Claim substantiation can have two effects: it can give consumers useful information and it can act as a deterrent to prevent advertisers from making false claims. Neither result seems to occur with the claim substantiation provisions of the Code of Advertising Practice.[10] Information made available is treated as confidential. A new policy of claim substantiation was adopted in the United States in 1971.[11] Under the Federal Trade Commission's interpretation 'a firm's failure to possess and rely upon a reasonable basis for objective claims constitutes an unfair and deceptive act or practice in violation of s 5 of the Federal Trade Commission Act.'[12] Under this doctrine information in support of a claim must generally have been developed *before* a claim is made, so that ex post substantiation of a claim is usually insufficient to avoid liability. A systematic programme was followed whereby manufacturers in various industries were called upon to provide complete documentation for advertising claims. A case where a business could not substantiate its claim was *Firestone Tyre and Rubber Co v FTC*.[13] The company had advertised that its 'Super Sports Wide Oval tyre 'stops 25 per cent quicker'. Quite apart from the fact that it had only

---

9   *Ward Laboratories v FTC* 276 F 2d 952 (1960); cert denied 364 US 827 (1960). See also *J B Williams Co v FTC* 381 F 2d 884 (1967).

10 Advertising Code (10th edn, 1999) paras 3.1–3.4.

11 L Weiner 'The Ad Substantiation Programme' (1981) 30 Am ULR 429.

12 FTC *Policy Statement Regarding Advertising Substatiation* (nd).

13 481 F 2d 246 (1973): cert denied 414 US 1112 (1973). See *also National Commission on Egg Nutrition v FTC* 570 F 2d 157 (1977) cert denied 439 US 821 (1978).

compared its own inferior tyre, the court held that the claim was unsubstantiated because the tests were carried out only on one type of surface. It upheld a cease and desist order that prohibited the company from making comparative claims without first making tests to assure their accuracy.

Information under the Federal Trade Commission claim substantiation programme has been made available for public inspection, but this aspect proved disappointing because in many cases the information was too technical for consumers to understand or out of date. This factor, combined with a perception that the proactive programme was very costly relative to the limited enforcement benefits achieved, resulted in the displacement of the proactive approach by a case-by-case approach.[14] The FTC has adopted a revised programme seeking substantiation for only major themes in advertisements and requesting the response to include a summary in non-technical language. Ideally, consumer groups should obtain the information and publish it in simplified form. There are other difficulties with claim substantiation. Firstly, it may induce advertisers to provide even less information. Secondly, it needs a substantial investment of administrative resources to enforce and access to independent experts (perhaps in other government departments). Thirdly, it is confined to claims which businesses chose to make. Finally, it needs to be backed by strong criminal penalties against unsubstantiated claims and not just by an injunctive power.[15]

Counter-advertising obliges the media to carry, free of charge, advertising prepared by public interest groups which rebuts claims made by commercial interests. Counter-advertising has been used in the United States where public interest groups have taken advantage of the 'fairness' doctrine applying to television and radio broadcasting to get their views broadcast.[16] This doctrine has been applied to cigarette advertising and commercials for large cars on the grounds that such advertisements raise the requisite controversial issue of public importance (health, pollution).[17] However, the courts have said that the fairness doctrine does not invariably require counter-commercials and that the Federal Communications

---

14   FTC *Policy Statement Regarding Advertising Substatiation* (nd).
15   The objection that it 'reverses the onus of proof' is misconceived; so do many other aspects of consumer law (eg licensing). See *Review of the Trade Descriptions Act 1968* (Cmnd 6628 (1976)) pp 55–56.
16   Comment 'And Now a Word Against Our Sponsor: Extending the FCC's Fairness Doctrine to Advertising' (1972) 60 Calif LR 1416; Note 'Application of the Fairness Doctrine to Ordinary Product Advertisements' (1979) 20 Boston LR 425.
17   *Friends of the Earth v FCC* 449 F 2d 1164 (1971); *Banzhaf v FCC* 405 F 2d 1082 (1968); cert denied 396 US 842 (1969).

Commission has discretion not to apply it to a product advertisement (the policy it adopted in 1974).[18]

An initial problem with counter-advertising is the width of the coverage. Is it to be confined to matters of public controversy or will it extend to all commercials? Another issue is whether counter-advertisements must come immediately following an advertisement by a commercial interest. If 'equal time' is not to be given, what percentage of advertising space should be allocated to counter-advertising? One method of counter-advertising might be to conduct discussion programmes in which consumer organisations report on the tests they have conducted on products. It is said that counter-advertising on a broad basis would threaten the viability of the media. But before this occurs, and before counter-advertising becomes really effective, the government would have to subsidise public interest groups heavily, for few have the resources at present to launch a counter-advertising campaign.

Corrective advertising might counteract the residual effects of deceptive advertising and deter businesses from using it in the first place. The first aspect is necessary because even after a deceptive advertisement has ceased it can continue to influence consumers, albeit subconsciously, if it has planted a factual claim in their minds or has generated goodwill which leads to later purchases. The deterrent aspect stems from the damage corrective advertising might do the reputation of a business and to its financial position from a loss of sales. In the United States the FTC orders for corrective advertising give an advertiser an option of ceasing to advertise for a year or devoting 25% of its advertising to corrective advertisements.[19] A notable example was an order directing the Warner-Lambert Co to include the following statement in its advertisements for mouthwash until it had spent an amount equal to its average annual advertising budget over a ten year period: 'Listerine will not help prevent colds or sore throats or lessen their severity.'[20] Research on the impact of the order discovered that even after the corrective advertising campaign 39% continued to use the product to prevent colds and sore throats.[1] Ramsay suggests that a less prescriptive approach might be adopted under which advertisers are required to secure that the message of the

---

[18] *National Citizens Committee for Broadcasting v FCC* 567 F 2d 1095 (1977); cert denied 439 US 926 (1978).

[19] R Cornfield 'A New Approach to an Old Remedy: Corrective Advertising and the Federal Trade Commission' (1976) 61 Iowa LR 693; Note 'Corrective Advertising and the Limits of Virginia Pharmacy' (1979) 32 Stan LR 121.

[20] *Warner-Lambert Co v FTC* 562 F 2d 749 (1977); cert denied 435 US 950 (1978).

[1] W Wilkie, D McNeill and M Mazis 'Marketing's "Scarlet Letter": The Theory and Practice of Corrective Advertising' (1984) 48 Journal of Marketing 11.

corrective advertising reach a certain percentage of the targeted population.[2]

The EC Directive on Misleading Advertising permits the compulsory use of corrective advertising by Member States.[3] But the Trade Descriptions Act 1968 Review Committee in Britain had already recommended against corrective advertising and nothing has been done. It thought that corrective advertising might fail to reach those who were misled.[4] This argument loses much of its force if a corrected version must be run in the same sources and for the same period as the original. Equally specious is the argument that corrective advertising might reach those who were not originally misled, and in so doing cause damage to an advertiser out of all proportion to the original infraction. Two points can be made: at present penalties in law need not be equivalent to the damage occasioned to consumers or the gain accruing to a business. Secondly, the prime aim of corrective advertising is to introduce sufficient power in the law to deter misleading advertising. Advertisers which take preventive action from the outset need have no fear of disproportionate losses. It is interesting to note that the Federal Court of Australia can order corrective advertising under s 80A of the Trade Practices Act 1974 on the application of the regulatory authorities.[5]

The UK position on remedies for deceptive advertising remains remarkably barren with no alternatives for regulators and self-regulators other than prosecution (under the Trade Descriptions Act 1968, discussed in Chapter 8 below), adverse publicity and instructions to media not to carry further advertisements (under the Code of Advertising Practice) and injunctions to prevent continued use of an advertisement (under the 1988 Regulations (as amended)).

Doubts have been expressed about how effective the remedies applied by the FTC have been. In particular, it has been suggested that the legalistic and procedural baggage surrounding public agency actions has discouraged the use of such remedies.[6] Incorporation of the European Convention on Human Rights into English law[7] is likely to make any attempt by state authorities to control advertising more vulnerable to attack as

2   I Ramsay *Consumer Protection: Text and Materials* (Weidenfeld & Nicolson, 1989) p 407.

3   Directive 84/450/EEC, Article 6(a).

4   *Review of the Trade Descriptions Act 1968* (Cmnd 6628 (1976)) pp 58–59.

5   *Annand & Thompson Pty Ltd v TPC* (1979) 25 ALR 91.

6   W Whitford 'Twenty Years of Consumer Protection' (1986) Wisconsin Law School Alumni Bulletin extracted in I Ramsay *Consumer Protection: Text and Materials* (1989) pp 408–9.

7   Human Rights Act 1998.

being in breach of the Convention right of freedom of expression.[8] Given the climate of doubt about the desirability of enhancing the powers of public regulatory bodies (discussed in Chapter 1) it might be most appropriate to consider giving the ASA a wider range of remedial powers, possibly backed by legislation.

8   SELF-REGULATION IN PERSPECTIVE

Self-regulation is a very well-established aspect of the UK consumer protection regime.[9] The choice for policy makers is not self-regulation *or* public regulation, but rather a question of how to harness the self-regulatory capacities of business to deliver public policy objectives through the combination of public and self-regulation. A diverse range of scholars have encouraged policy makers to think about a wide range of different forms of self-regulation which can mixed with state oversight to secure effective control.[10] Where self-regulatory regimes are established the risks of ineffective or self-serving operation can be identified in a number of aspects.

First, rule making may tend to favour the existing members of the industry, through limiting or excluding new entrants. Examples of such rules were found in the rules of the Pharmaceutical Society of Great Britain which sought to limit competition from in-store pharmacies in department stores and were held to be an unreasonable restraint of trade.[11] In another instance the rules of the Association of British Travel Agents restricting its members from dealing with tour operators or travel agents who were not members of the Association were upheld by the Restrictive Practices Court on the grounds that they advanced the public interest in ensuring that there was a bonding scheme in place in the event of the failure of a tour operator.[12] These cases suggest that there is the potential for scrutiny of the anti-competitive potential of self-regulation, both at common law and under

---

[8]   Even prior to the incorporation of the Convention rights into English law the right of freedom of expression had been invoked on a number of occasions. See, eg, *R v Advertising Standards Authority, ex p City Trading Ltd* [1997] COD 202, where the claim based upon breach by the ASA of Article 10 (right to freedom of expression) of the ECHR was rejected on the grounds that prior to the Human Rights Act 1998 there was no duty to have regard to the Convention rights in decision making.

[9]   R Baggott 'Regulatory Reform in Britain: The Changing Face of Self-Regulation' (1989) 67 Public Administration 435.

[10] Compare A Ogus 'Rethinking Self-Regulation' (1995) 15 Oxford Journal of Legal Studies 97–108 with I Ayres and J Braithwaite *Responsive Regulation* (OUP, 1992) Chapter 2.

[11] *Pharmaceutical Society of Great Britain v Dixon* [1970] AC 403.

[12] *Re ABTA's Agreement* [1984] ICR 12.

competition legislation, but realisation of this potential should be kept under systematic review as consumers are not able adequately to protect themselves against such anti-competitive effects.

Rule making within self-regulatory regimes may be carried out in such a way that consumers derive inadequate protection. There are a number of mechanisms through which this risk can be addressed. First, self-regulatory rules may be subjected to approval procedures such as that operated by the Office of Fair Trading. As we have seen this mechanism has allowed the OFT to set out a blueprint which trade associations must follow in order to secure approval. The regime could be bolstered by requiring membership of a trade association and following of a code as a condition of trading, as happens in certain safety-critical consumer sectors such as the installation and servicing of gas appliances.[13] More extensive agency approval of codes would take up more state resources (though arguably rather less then would be the case for the establishment of legislative rules) and risk the creation of a state sanctioned cartel for the industries affected.

A possible way around the problem of cartels and an alternative technique of the control of self-regulatory rules is to promote competition among self-regulatory regimes.[14] Where consumers have good information about the nature and content of competing self-regulatory regimes, then collective market decision making may result in the gradual fine tuning of self-regulatory rules so that they find an equilibrium which is neither over-protective of the industry, nor of consumers. Within this market theory of self-regulation we might expect some consumers to pay more to receive a higher level of protection associated with a trade association applying higher standards. However it is questionable whether in practice a market in self-regulation could operate sufficiently well for it to have the controlling effects advocated for it, and even if it did some might be reluctant to accept the implication that consumers paying higher prices would benefit from better protection, since this challenges the principle of universality in levels of protection.[15] The flow of information to consumers may be assisted by a state agency providing scoring of different self-regulatory regimes against certain criteria, though in many sectors the task of agreeing meaningful criteria would be impossibly complex.[16] An alternative model for harnessing competition is to have trade associations bid to operate a monopolistic self-regulatory regime for a set period. Potential self-

---

[13]   Gas Safety (Installation and Use) Regulations 1998, SI 1998/2451, reg 3(3).

[14]   A Ogus 'Rethinking Self-Regulation' (1995) 15 Oxford Journal of Legal Studies 97–108.

[15]   NCC *Models of Self-Regulation: An Overview of Models in Business and the Professions* (1999) p 27.

[16]   A Ogus 'Rethinking Self-Regulation' (1995) 15 Oxford Journal of Legal Studies 97–108.

regulators could be required to submit details of their proposed rules and monitoring and enforcement procedures, with the successful bidder being subject to monitoring for compliance with the bid by the state franchising authority, in a manner analogous to the arrangement operated for the franchising of railways under the Railways Act 1993.[17]

A third technique to control the making of self-regulatory rules is to promote the participation of representative organisations in the drawing up of rules. This principle can be extended to the regular review of the rules. A fourth is the use by government of the threat of legislation to promote the establishment and development of adequate self-regulatory rules. This technique appears to have secured periodic improvements in both the ASA regime and the regime of self-regulation under the Association of British Insurers' Statements of Insurance Practice.[18] However, the effective use of this technique is dependent on the commitment of government both to monitor and provide the effective threat of statutory intervention in the event of self-regulation being inadequate, and this credible commitment has all too often been lacking in recent British history.

A second raft of problems associated with self-regulation lies in the monitoring and enforcement function. Satisfactory rules may be monitored poorly, or sanctions may be inadequate to promote compliance. Again there is a choice of techniques for addressing these problems. The creation of competition among self-regulatory regimes is one possibility. A second technique is to create residual rights of either state agencies and/or public interest groups to enforce the rules. As we have seen this occurs in the advertising sector, where the ASA can refer intransigent advertisers to the Office of Fair Trading which can seek an injunction against and advertiser. In this case the effectiveness of these back-up powers would be increased if there were more transparent guidance from both the ASA and the OFT on when the reserve power will be invoked.[19] The threat of expulsion from a trade association linked to the right to trade in the particular sector could provide a further more routine sanction. Requiring the participation of industry outsiders in monitoring and enforcement procedures, thus giving them the capacity to blow the whistle on

---

[17] A Ogus 'Rethinking Self-Regulation' (1995) 15 Oxford Journal of Legal Studies 97–108.

[18] R Baggott and L Harrison 'The Politics of Self-Regulation—The Case of Advertising Control' (1986) Policy and Politics 14(2): 143–159; R Lewis 'Insurers' Agreements Not to Enforce Strict Legal Rights: Bargaining With Government and in the Shadow of the Law' (1985) MLR 48: 275.

[19] A point made by Hoffman J in *DGFT v Tobyward Ltd* [1989] 2 All ER 266, the first of only ten cases referred to the OFT in the first ten years of the regime. See NCC *Models of Self-Regulation: An Overview of Models in Business and the Professions* (1999) p 38.

inadequate implementation, would act as a further control on regimes. For example the Code of Banking Practice, followed by banks and building societies, is monitored by the Independent Review Body for the Banking and Mortgage Codes, which includes substantial independent representation (though it has been criticised for devoting inadequate resources to monitoring).[20] Lying behind these techniques is the credible threat to replace self-regulation with statutory regulation.

The National Consumer Council has recently recommended that self-regulatory regimes should more routinely be nested within statutory powers for state agencies to intervene. The NCC sees the potential for the development of the powers of the Office of Fair Trading under Part III of the Fair Trading Act 1973 to allow the OFT to take action against unfair practices which are defined within self-regulatory codes, thus creating a mixed enforcement regime, alongside the mixed standard setting techniques already employed by the OFT. These techniques by themselves need to be linked to the promotion of the kind of cultural approach within which industries see their mandate as aligned with, rather than opposed to, the interests of consumers. Where such alignment is not possible self-regulation is unlikely to be viable and arguments for agency regulation will be stronger.

---

[20]   NCC *Models of Self-Regulation: An Overview of Models in Business and the Professions* (1999) p 25.

Private law

Chapter 3

Private law in perspective

Historically there was no area of 'consumer law' within the private law, and a consumer's legal rights derived primarily from the ordinary law of contract and negligence. Businesses either do not meet the strict standards of performance required by the law of contract or the standards of reasonable care laid down by the law of negligence. Increasingly these common law rights have been modified by statute, specifically of benefit to consumers. There is a common assumption, in particular among lawyers, that private law is the best hope for consumer protection. Writing in 1969, Professor Jolowicz saw consumer protection as prevention on the one hand and financial redress for consumers when things go wrong on the other. He was sceptical about the extent to which law and lawyers could effectively contribute to consumer protection in the first sense.

> The criminal law can, no doubt, do something towards this end, but consumer and producer education seem to me to be more important. Consumer protection in its second sense, however, is something which the law, and in the ultimate result the law alone, can provide.[1]

Educating and informing consumers remains a central instrument both at domestic level and in the European Community.[2]

One aim of this Part of the book is to demonstrate that the private law is often an inadequate tool of consumer protection. We return to the theme at various points in the book, especially in the chapters in this Part, which

---

[1]   JA Jolowicz 'The Protection of the Consumer and the Purchaser of Goods under English Law' (1969) 32 MLR 1, 2.
[2]   DTI *Modern Markets: Confident Consumers* (Cm 4410 (1999)) Chapter 3; S Weatherill 'The Role of the Informed Consumer in European Community Law and Policy' (1994) 2 Consumer Law Journal 49.

deal with specific aspects of private law rights. Private law is not generally instrumental in character—it is not directed at achieving particular social goals such as consumer protection.[3] The relevant legal principles are often unfavourable to consumers, although in some cases legislation has been enacted because of judicial reluctance to bring the law into line with modern social conditions. Historically the law of contract was based on the assumption of equal bargaining power between parties—quite inappropriate where consumers are bound to accept the terms dictated by businesses. Doctrines like privity of contract and negligence continue to impose fetters on the ability of consumers to sue businesses which are responsible, in fact, for their losses.

Specific doctrines of private law and their inadequacies are examined in the following chapters. The burden of the present chapter is to highlight the problem of standard form contracts and the practical difficulties of implementing private law rights. These difficulties cast doubt on the effectiveness of private law to protect consumers, unless substantially modified.

I   STANDARD FORM CONTRACTS AND LEGAL CONTROL

(a)   'Freedom of contract'

Writing in 1943, Friedrich Kessler concluded that while appearing to be non-authoritarian, contract law protected the unequal distribution of power in society and in particular enabled 'powerful industrial and commercial overlords' to 'impose a new feudal order of their own making upon a vast host of vassals'.[4] It is still the case that consumers are bound to contracts, in the main standard form contracts, to which patently they do not agree but which they are obliged to accept if they want the products and services normally taken as an incidence of living in society. The underlying philosophy of the law is that all members of society are basically free to enter contracts and, that being the case, they must take care for their own interests. This approach, forged in the context of dealings between commercial parties, is hardly appropriate when a consumer is involved. In England, the problem is accentuated because while there is a large volume of commercial litigation in the higher courts, where the approach is constantly reinforced, there are few consumer cases—partly because of

---

[3]   A Ogus *Regulation: Legal Form and Economic Theory* (OUP, 1994) p 26.
[4]   'Contracts of Adhesion—Some Thoughts about Freedom of Contract' (1943) 43 Col L Rev 629, 640. The subsequent literature is vast but see, eg, H Collins *The Law of Contract* (Butterworths, 3rd edn, 1998) pp 111–116; J Adams and R Brownsword *Key Issues in Contract* (Butterworths, 1995) pp 55–80.

the jurisdictional limits and partly because of the obstacles to consumer claims considered later in this chapter.

When the occasional consumer contract has reached the higher courts, the temptation has been to treat the matter as if it involved a charterparty. Illustrative is the rule about signature: the consumer who signs a contract will rarely be able to avoid its terms, albeit that they remain unread, and if read, unintelligible.[5] In *United Dominions Trust Ltd v Western*,[6] a consumer signed a personal loan agreement in blank which he thought was a hire purchase agreement and which the dealer then fraudulently filled in as to the amounts. The Court of Appeal rejected the argument that there was no consensus ad idem between the consumer and the finance house to whom the dealer had sent the agreement. Scarman LJ, for example, said that there was no difference between signing 'blind' a completed document the contents of which had not been read, and signing a printed document with blanks which one authorised another person to complete. 'It seems to me that such a man does make the document that he is signing his document; he takes responsibility for it; and he takes the chance of a fraudulent filling in of the blanks.' The actual decision in *Western*'s case, that the consumer had to bear the loss, is no longer good law in the light of the Consumer Credit Act 1974, but the underlying approach of the court is typical and has changed little over the last hundred years.

Another aspect of contract law which is relevant to the discussion is the parol evidence rule, whereby verbal evidence is in general not allowed to derogate from the terms of a written contract. The argument in favour of the rule is convenience, but there would not seem to be any great objection in consumer cases in deciding what was actually said at the time the contract was made. Certainly in most consumer transactions the natural tendency is to rely on what a business's employees say without reading the written terms of any agreement proffered, and there are cases where the former has been given precedence when it was within the employee's ostensible authority to make a promise.[7]

The doctrines of contract law have always been stated as applying equally to all, but in practice it has been businesses who have taken advantage of them. The law in effect protects the bargains of one segment of society and so confirms the exercise of their power. Lord Denning expressed the point this way:

---

[5]   The classic case is *L'Estrange v F Graucob Ltd* [1934] 2 KB 394. *Curtis v Chemical Cleaning and Dyeing Co Ltd* [1951] 1 KB 805 recognises misrepresentation about a clause's effects as an exception.

[6]   [1976] QB 513.

[7]   For example, *Mendelssohn v Normand Ltd* [1970] 1 QB 177. See also *Lease Management Services v Purnell Secretarial Services* [1994] CCLR 127, 13 Tr LR 337.

None of you nowadays will remember the trouble we had—when I was called to the Bar—with exemption clauses. They were printed in small print on the back of tickets and order forms and invoices. They were contained in catalogues or timetables. They were held to be binding on any person who took them without objection. No one ever did object. He never read them or knew what was in them. No matter how unreasonable they were, he was bound. All this was done in the name of 'freedom of contract'. But the freedom was all on the side of the big concern which had the use of the printing press. No freedom for the little man who took the ticket or order form or invoice. The big concern said, 'Take it or leave it.' The little man had no option but to take it. The big concern could and did exempt itself from liability in its own interest without regard to the little man. It got away with it time after time. When the courts said to the big concern, 'you must put it in clear words', the big concern had no hesitation in doing so. It knew well that the little man would never read the exemption clauses or understand them.[8]

The extremities to which the law has been taken are well rehearsed in the standard works on contract. Exclusion clauses excluding liability in contract and negligence are the most common instance dealt with by the English courts. *Thompson v London, Midland and Scottish Rly Co*[9] is perhaps the most remarkable case, where an illiterate woman, injured while descending from a train which had stopped short of the platform, was bound by conditions, referred to on the ticket, which her niece had obtained for her. To the court deciding the cases in 1929, the decision to enforce the conditions, in particular the exclusion clause, was quite natural; to ordinary consumers it would have been blatantly unjust, especially since the actual exclusion clause was contained in a timetable which was only obtainable on an additional payment.

Some judges have seen the rules of English contract law as a means of minimising disputes and providing a clear solution when disputes arise. Others no doubt have been motivated, perhaps in some cases unconsciously, by more fundamental policy aims, such as promoting self-reliance or supporting the operation of the market system. Ideologically, freedom of contract was a counterpart of free enterprise, a point well accepted in the writings of the nineteenth century.[10] Another factor which cannot be ignored is that sometimes the courts have been overly concerned with conceptual analysis and the application of precedent, to the detriment of the social implications of their decisions. English contract law has

8   *George Mitchell (Chesterhall) Ltd v Finney Lock Seeds* [1982] 3 WLR 1036, 1943; on appeal [1983] 2 AC 803. Cf G Gilmore 'Products Liability: A Commentary' (1970) 38 U Chi LR 103, 113.
9   [1930] 1 KB 41; see J Wightman *Contract. A Critical Commentary* (Pluto, 1996) p 60.
10   See PS Atiyah *The Rise and Fall of Freedom of Contract* (Clarendon, 1979).

focused on the formalities—offer/acceptance, consideration, etc—rather than the substance of what the parties agreed. Too much should not be made of this point, however, for in other areas of the law the courts have displayed an ingenuity in developing new doctrine.

Nevertheless, standard form contracts are a necessity in modern business transactions. Bureaucracies want routine and certainty and they need to be able rationally to plan risks (eg the number of consumer claims) if they are to operate efficiently. Moreover, standard form contracts perform other functions within large businesses: they standardise and formalise procedures; allow a corporation to control its agents, preventing them from compromising the corporation by general deals with individual consumers; and act as a means of internal communication, for example indicating the extent of future payments.[11] One study found that finance and insurance companies used exclusion clauses in their consumer agreements as a form of psychological pressure to convince consumers to take the agreement seriously or to settle out of court in a dispute.[12] There can be little objection to standard form contracts in arms-length dealings between businesses of relatively equal bargaining power. There are even advantages for consumers because it is hardly possible to negotiate terms each time they enter contracts, and that is extremely frequent in everyday life. The objection to standard form contracts on the part of consumers is that frequently they are compelled to accept disadvantageous terms. In a way compulsion operates at two levels: in the first sense, about which little can be done, consumers have no option but to enter certain contracts if they are to act as ordinary members of society.[13] Secondly, and this is the real objection, there is compulsion in that the adverse terms are forced upon consumers and may subtract from or set at naught the rights which the law would otherwise give them or which it is reasonable for them to expect.[14]

If it is accepted that standard form contracts are an inevitable feature of modern society, the need is to formulate criteria for identifying objectionable aspects. One line of argument, which derives very much from the classical model of contract, is to ask: what would consumers agree to if they could

[11]   S Macaulay 'Private Legislation and the Duty to Read' (1966) 19 Vand LR 1051, 1059; I Macneil 'Bureaucracy and Contracts of Adhesion' (1984) 22 Os HLJ 5.
[12]   D Yates *Exclusion Clauses in Contacts* (Sweet & Maxwell, 2nd edn, 1982) pp 20, 29.
[13]   Cf M Radin 'Contract Obligation and the Human Will' (1943) 43 Col LR 575, 578–579; Johnson 'Autonomy and Contractual Liability' (1983) 2 Law and Philosophy 271.
[14]   See F Reynolds 'Formulation of Standard Terms and their Incorporation in Contracts' in *Standard Terms in Contracts* (Council of Europe, 1979) pp 18–109.

freely bargain? Perhaps the analogy is to the approach of the commercial courts which think hard before giving effect to a conclusion which is counter to the reasonable expectations of honest business people.[15] For those drafting the Uniform Commercial Code in the United States, the notions of surprise and oppression in bargaining became the benchmarks for identifying unconscionable contracts. In their view one asked: did consumers have access to expert advice, time to reflect on the terms, the experience to suggest alternatives, and so on. The whole notion of bargaining is rather unreal, for consumers are in no position to deliberate every time they enter a contract, even if enterprises were prepared to enter negotiations if they did. More importantly, however much consumers may be able to bargain, the end result will be that large businesses can use their power to force contract terms onto consumers. It is no use saying that consumers can deal with other businesses who would offer more favourable terms because the reality is that in matters of vital concern many enterprises offer identical, or nearly identical, terms.

Another way of dealing with standard form contracts, suggested by Slawson,[16] is generally to enforce only those terms to which consumers have explicitly or impliedly given consent. To give an example, a consumer handed a receipt which he signs without reading has only accepted a 'receipt'; ie what a receipt can reasonably be expected to contain, such as the date and the price. Slawson suggests that a business's behaviour has some role in determining what consumers can reasonably be regarded as having agreed; thus, exclusion clauses in standard form contracts would be disregarded if businesses do not publicise them. Slawson's argument has an appealing simplicity, but it seems rather difficult to apply it to the more complex standard form contracts. It is fairly easy to guess at what contracting parties have consented to or would consent to in relatively simple contracts, but what of the more complicated transactions like insurance, where some of the contingencies are so remote from ordinary experience that consumers will never appreciate them? Moreover, even if consumers expect onerous clauses in particular types of contract, this is no argument for their continuation, because consumers might not appreciate that their deletion is possible.

[15]   Eg *First Energy (UK) Ltd v Hungarian International Bank Ltd* [1993] 2 Lloyd's Rep 194, 196.
[16]   W Slawson 'Standard Form Contracts and Democratic Control of Lawmaking Power' (1971) 84 Harv LR 529. Standard form contracts might be enforced in the absence of private consent if they comply with standards in the public interest.

(b)   The judicial response

The approach in Britain to objectionable features of standard form contracts and to exclusion clauses has been to proceed on a purely ad hoc and rather limited basis, depending on what terms have appeared to cause the greatest hardship and what have attracted the most publicity. Exclusion clauses relating to unsatisfactory products and services have been the main concern, although in limited circumstances the courts deal with onerous terms (eg under the doctrines of undue influence and unconscionability and they have also been empowered to reopen extortionate credit bargains.) In addition, we shall see in Chapter 7, the Consumer Credit Act 1974 provides that consumer credit agreements should be in writing and contain certain terms. The Unfair Contract Terms Act 1977 and the Unfair Terms in Consumer Contracts Regulations 1999 have various provisions designed to tackle the unfair terms in standard form contracts.

Despite the symbolic importance of freedom of contract the English courts, at the instigation of a few judicial mavericks, have conducted forays against exclusion and onerous clauses in standard from contracts. In a number of cases the courts have found that the ordinary formalities of contracting have not been complied with because a consumer has not been able to read the standard clauses before entering a contract,[17] or because a business has misrepresented, albeit innocently, the true nature of a clause.[18] The burden of notification is especially heavy if a clause contains a wide exclusion or an especially onerous provision. Such a clause needs the 'red hand' treatment—it needs to be highlighted, with a red hand or its equivalent drawing the reader's attention to it. In what is now the leading case, the court refused to give contractual effect to a clause which was merely one of a number in four columns of terms printed at the foot of a delivery note.[19]

---

[17]   *Beta Computers (Europe) Ltd v Adobe Systems (Europe) Ltd* [1996] CLC 821. See the Australian consumer case *Dillon v Baltic Shipping Co* (1989) 21 NSWLR 614, [1991] 2 Lloyd's Rep 155.

[18]   For example, *Daly v General Steam Navigation Co Ltd* [1979] 1 Lloyd's Rep 257, on appeal [1980] 3 All ER 696, [1981] 1 WLR 120; *Mendelssohn v Normand Ltd* [1970] 1 QB 177. See also *Tilden Rent-A-Car Co v Clendenning* (1978) 18 OR (2d) 601 (consumer's reasonable expectations). It is fair to say that *Tilden Rent-A-Car* has been distinguished in several Canadian cases, and in *Hunter Engineering Co Inc v Syncrude Canada Ltd* (1989) 57 DLR (4th) 321, Dickson CJC suggested that the lack of knowledge or opportunity of acquiring it of a contractual signatory is to be treated as an aspect of unconscionability (341–342, La Forest J agreeing).

[19]   *Interfoto Picture Library Ltd v Stiletto Visual Programmes Ltd* [1989] QB 433, [1988] 1 All ER 348.

Use of the *contra proferentem* rule has also been possible in some circumstances to construe unfair clauses narrowly; thus is has been held that to exempt itself from negligence, a business must state that quite categorically.[20] Moreover, if a clause is to have any chance of excluding liability for the oral misrepresentations made by a business's employees, that must be mentioned explicitly for otherwise it may be confined to written misrepresentations. An associated approach is for the courts to confine the ambit of entire agreement clauses—clauses which provide that the entire agreement between the parties has been reduced to writing and that any oral statements are to be disregarded.[1] Interpretation has had only a limited effect, however, because businesses properly advised incorporate widely-drawn exclusion clauses in their contracts covering every contingency.

At one time another line of attack on exclusion clauses was through the doctrine of fundamental breach. The doctrine was enunciated in 1956, received a set-back in the House of Lords in 1966 which decided that it was simply a rule of construction, once again assumed the status of a rule of law in the Court of Appeal in 1970, but subsequently was reasserted by the House of Lords to be only a rule of construction.[2] Essentially, the doctrine of fundamental breach provided that a business could not exclude its liability for breaches of fundamental obligations or those which went to the root of a contract.[3]

There is no general principle in English law whereby a consumer can obtain relief because a contract is harsh, or that contracts can be set aside if there is on one side superior bargaining power.[4] Equity intervenes in cases of undue influence—actual undue influence (analogous to duress) and presumed undue influence (presumed in certain established categories, eg parent-child, or presumed because of the nature of the relationship in which one party reposes trust and confidence in another).[5] Presumed undue influence requires manifest disadvantage, a considerable hurdle to

---

[20] Eg *White v John Warwick & Co Ltd* [1953] 2 All ER 1021, [1953] 1 WLR 1285; *EE Caledonia Ltd v Orbit Valve plc* [1995] 1 All ER 174, [1994] 1 WLR 1515 (a case coming out of the Piper Alpha disaster).

[1] *Thomas Witter Ltd v TBP Industries Ltd* [1996] 2 All ER 573.

[2] See *Photo Production Ltd v Securicor Transport Ltd* [1980] AC 827.

[3] Eg *Levison v Patent Steam Carpet Cleaning Co Ltd* [1978] QB 69

[4] *Bridge v Campbell Discount Co Ltd* [1962] AC 600 at 614, 626; *National Westminster Bank plc v Morgan* [1985] AC 686 at 708. See J Cartwright *Unequal Bargaining* (Clarendon, 1991) pp 215–220.

[5] *Barclays Bank plc v O'Brien* [1994] 1 AC 180. There is a considerable case law, eg *Midland Bank plc v Serter* [1995] 1 FLR 1034; *Massey v Midland Bank* [1995] 1 All ER 929; *Royal Bank of Scotland v Etridge (No 2)* [1998] 4 All ER 705. There is also considerable literature: see especially P Birks & NY Chin 'On the Nature of Undue Influence' in J Beatson and D Friedmann (eds) *Good Faith and Fault in Contract Law* (Clarendon, 1995).

the consumer.[6] There are also a number of cases where courts have set aside unconscionable contracts because one party has taken advantage of its economic position and the weakness of the other (illiteracy, poverty, mental instability, etc).[7] Only in unusual circumstances are such doctrines applied to consumer transactions. However, in recent times where undue influence has featured is in situations when a bank has been held to have notice of the undue influence of others. The leading case contemplated a husband exercising undue influence over his wife so that she would give security over her property to support his business' debts to the bank. It establishes that a bank will be responsible in this situation if it is aware of the husband-wife (or similarly close) relationship and fails to ensure that the party giving the security is warned of the risks or receives legal advice.[8]

(c)   Extortionate credit bargains

Following the Report of the Select Committee on Moneylending, which documented many abuses by moneylenders, the courts were given the power to reopen harsh and unconscionable moneylending transactions. It was soon accepted that this provision enabled the courts to reopen transactions merely because excessive charges made them harsh and unconscionable, irrespective of other factors.[9] The Moneylenders Act 1927 established the figure of 48% as the interest which would be regarded prima facie as excessive. As with other aspects of private law, few consumers actually initiated actions under the provision, but in a number of instances it proved useful as a defence to claim by moneylenders for repayment of credit.[10]

The power to reopen extortionate credit bargains contained in the Moneylenders Act is continued in somewhat expanded form in the Consumer Credit Act 1974. The power extends to all credit bargains involving individuals—even those falling outside other provisions of the Act—and need not rest on an examination of the agreement alone. Section 138 defines a credit bargain as extortionate if it requires the debtor or a relation to make payments which are grossly exorbitant or if it otherwise grossly contravenes ordinary principles of fair dealing. The section then

---

6   *Dunbar Bank plc v Nadeem* [1998] 3 All ER 876.
7   *Crédit Lyonnais Bank Nederland NV v Burch* [1996] 5 Bank LR 233; N Bamforth 'Unconscionability as a Vitiating Factor' [1995] LMCLQ 538.
8   *Barclays Bank plc v O'Brien* [1994] 1 AC 180. See also *CIBC Mortgages plc v Pitt* [1994] 1 AC 200. See B Fehlberg *Sexually Transmitted Debt: Surety Experience and English Law* (Clarendon, 1998).
9   *Samuel v Newbold* [1906] AC 461.
10   See Meston *The Law Relating to Money-lenders* (Oyez, 5th edn, 1968) Chapter 12.

directs the courts to have regard to various matters in making this determination—the interest rate prevailing at the time the bargain was made; the age, experience, business capacity and state of health of the debtor; the degree to which at the time of making the credit bargain the debtor was under financial pressure; the degree of risk having regard to the security; the relationship to the debtor and whether the cash price for any item or service involved was colourable; and other relevant considerations.[11]

Unlike the Moneylenders Act there is no figure of 48% as an interest rate which will be prima facie extortionate. A court deciding that a bargain is extortionate may, for the purpose of relieving the debtor or surety from payment of any sum in excess of that fairly due and reasonable, set aside the whole or part of any obligation, require the creditor to repay the whole or part of the sum whether the sum was paid to it or someone else or alter the terms of the agreement.[12] For example, a court may decide that a lesser rate of interest is justified and order that the consumer pay this amount. Consumers can raise the issue that a credit bargain is extortionate on their own initiative, but it arises in the majority of cases where the creditor initiates proceedings and the consumer raises it as a defence to the claim. As soon as a debtor or surety alleges that a credit bargain is extortionate, the onus is then thrown onto the creditor to prove the contrary.

The extortionate bargain provisions have failed. One aspect is the statutory wording. There is some authority that it is to be equated with 'harsh and unconscionable' in its equitable sense.[13] Moreover, the burden cast on creditors to show that a credit transaction is not extortionate is discharged by showing that on its face it is a proper and not extortionate commercial bargain and that they acted in a way that an ordinary commercial lender would be expected to act.[14] Secondly, there seems to be a judicial reticence to interfere with credit transactions pursuant to the legislation.[15] An Office of Fair Trading report examined the 15 cases up to 1991 which decided whether a credit transaction was extortionate.[16] Eleven of these involved secured loans, but in only two of these did the consumer succeed before the county court. In one, a loan of 39% was reduced to 30%, and in the other 42% was reduced to 21%. In one of the four instances of

---

[11]   Section 138(2)–(5).
[12]   Section 139(2).
[13]   *Shahabinia v Giyahchi* (5 July 1989, unreported), per Russell LJ; *Castle Phillips Finance Co Ltd v Khan* [1980] CCLR 1. Cf *Davies v Directloans Ltd* [1986] 1 WLR 823.
[14]   *Coldunell Ltd v Gallon* [1986] QB 1184 at 1202, per Oliver LJ.
[15]   L Bentley and G Howells 'Judicial Treatment of Extortionate Credit Bargains' [1989] Conv 164, 234.
[16]   *Unjust Credit Transactions* (OFT, 1991) Annex A.

unsecured loans, commercial loans of 78, 104 and 156% were all reduced to 30%.[17]

For reasons shortly to be considered, there are many instances where consumers do not complain in the case of extortionate credit bargains. The Office of Fair Trading report contained examples of real interest rates in their figures. Extreme cases included £50 borrowed over 14 weeks, £5 repayable per week—a real interest rate of 4,288%. Moreover, the report listed as exploitative tactics locking consumers into a cycle of debt by re-lending before existing credit is repaid, targeting needy borrowers to whom cheaper forms of credit are not available, making no rebate for early repayment, and not making clear the true cost of credit.[18]

The Office of Fair Trading Report concluded that the concept of extortionate credit bargain should be replaced by that of 'unjust credit transaction', one factor in which would be excessive payments. The notion of 'grossly exorbitant' would go, as also would that of credit transactions contrary to the ordinary principles of fair dealing.'[19] In addition to the existing factors to be considered in deciding whether a credit transaction is unjust, regard would also be had to a creditor's failure to check the borrower's creditworthiness and capacity to repay. Most importantly, the Director General of Fair Trading would have the power, along with trading standard authorities, to initiate proceedings in the public interest for a declaration that a particular type of credit transaction was unjust. This would overcome the problem that insufficient cases have come to court.[20] It is difficult to understand why the recommendation was confined to a power to seek a declaration, without a power also to seek an individual remedy.

In 1998 the Department of Trade and Industry commissioned research on the effectiveness of the extortionate credit bargain provisions of the 1974 Act. This report recommended reforming the 1974 Act: to permit third parties (such as trading standards departments) to initiate proceedings on behalf of borrowers; to enable judges to re-open credit bargains on their own initiative; to provide information and guidance to judges on interest rates and credit terms and conditions. The report further suggests that interest rate ceilings might be introduced, coupled with the provision of some form of social lending to those who would not be able to borrow on a commercial market to which interest rate ceiling applied.[1] The DTI is

17   *Shahabinia v Giyahchi* (5 July 1989, unreported). Cf *A Ketley Ltd v Scott* [1981] ICR 241 (48% unobjectionable).
18   *Unjust Credit Transactions* (OFT, 1991) pp 19–22.
19   *Unjust Credit Transactions* (OFT, 1991) pp 26–29. See also *Transfer of Land— Land Mortgages* Law Com No 204, HC5 (1991) pp 67–68.
20   *Unjust Credit Transactions* (OFT, 1991) p 30.
1   E Kempson and C Whyley *Extortionate Credit Bargains in the UK* (DTI, 2000).

seeking to implement only one of the recommendations—that the court should be able to open extortionate credit bargains at its own initiative.[2] It has been suggested that the DTI is unwilling to embrace the wider implications of the research which it commissioned.[3]

2   UNFAIR CONTRACT TERMS LEGISLATION

Modern legislative attempts to deal with exclusion clauses began with the Hire Purchase Act 1938, which made the implied conditions of merchantability and fitness for purpose non-excludable. The Molony Committee recommended that a similar step be taken for sales transactions, and some 12 years later, following a Law Commission Report, the Supply of Goods (Implied Terms) Act 1973 rendered void terms in consumer sales and hire purchase transactions, purporting to exclude the implied terms as to title, compliance with description, merchantability and fitness for purpose. Steps were subsequently taken to prohibit certain statements rendered void by the Act; these are considered in Chapter 11. After further consumer pressure and another Law Commission Report, the Unfair Contract Terms Act, a Private Member's Bill, was enacted with government support in 1977. Its remit goes wider than exclusion clauses. More recently, to implement an EC Directive on the matter, the Unfair Terms in Consumer Contracts Regulations 1994 were introduced, and gave an additional layer of protection to consumers in the event of certain unfair contracts. These regulations were repealed and replaced by the Unfair Terms in Consumer Contracts Regulations 1999.[4]

(a)   The Unfair Contract Terms Act 1977

The Unfair Contract Terms Act 1977 (UCTA) continues the provisions of the Supply of Goods (Implied Terms) Act 1973 in favour of a person dealing as consumer (s 6).[5] Similarly, in other contracts under which goods are

---

[2]   DTI Discussion paper on the Extortionate Credit Provisions in the Consumer Credit Act 1974 (DTI, 2000).

[3]   T Levene 'Why Loan Sharks Still Make a Killing' (2000) Guardian, 8 April.

[4]   The repeal of the 1994 Regulations was made following the initiation of the proceedings by the European Commission for failure to implement the Unfair Terms in Consumer Contracts Directive adequately. Notably the 1994 Regulations had failed to provide for the application of the administrative enforcement provisions by interest groups, reserving these powers to the Director General of Fair Trading. The 1999 Regulations make good this deficiency (discussed below).

[5]   A party to a contract deals as consumer if he neither makes the contract in the course of a business nor holds himself out as doing so, the other party makes the

supplied (eg contracts of hire, contracts for work and materials) liability cannot be excluded in consumer transactions in respect of terms as to title, correspondence with description, quality and fitness for purpose (s 7(3A)). In addition, contractual terms which exclude or restrict the liability of a party to a contract for a misrepresentation made by him before the contract was made, or any remedy available to another party to the contract by reason of such misrepresentation, are of no effect unless they satisfy the requirement of reasonableness (s 8(1)).[6]

The main innovations of UCTA are with respect to negligence and certain contractual terms. (The 'guarantee' provision, s 5, is discussed in Chapter 5.) Negligence is defined widely to include breach of any obligation arising from the express or implied terms of a contract to take reasonable care or exercise reasonable skill in the performance of a contract and of any common law duty to take reasonable care or exercise reasonable skill (but not any stricter duty) (s 1(1)). The provisions are thus relevant to contracts for work and materials and contracts for the performance of a service. UCTA provides that a business cannot by reference to any contract term, or to a notice given to persons generally or to particular persons, exclude or restrict its liability for death or personal injury resulting from negligence (s 2(1)). Neither can a business so exclude or restrict its liability for negligence in the case of other loss or damage (eg property damage) except in so far as the term or notice satisfies the requirement of reasonableness (s 2(2)). Because invalidity in s 2(2) turns on reasonableness, businesses may continue to exclude or restrict liability for negligence, claiming that the requirement is satisfied. Aggrieved consumers who challenge this exclusion or restriction will be few, for the reasons considered later in this chapter.

Section 3 of UCTA contains what is potentially a wide power for the courts to render invalid terms in contracts where one party deals as consumer, or on the other's written standard terms of business. Whether a contract is on the party's written standard terms is a question of fact and

---

contract in the course of a business, and any goods involved are of a type ordinarily supplied for private use or consumption (s 12(1)). R Kidner 'The Unfair Contract Terms Act 1977—Who Deals as a Consumer?' (1987) 38 NILQ 46. But on a sale by auction or by competitive tender the buyer is not in any circumstances to be regarded as dealing as consumer (s 12(2)). General examinations of the Act include GH Treitel *The Law of Contract* (Sweet & Maxwell, 9th edn, 1995) pp 227–245; D Yates *Exclusion Clauses in Contracts* (Sweet & Maxwell, 2nd edn, 1982) pp 73–109; R Lawson *Exclusion Clauses* (Longman, 4th edn, 1995). For criminal liability for using certain terms invalidated by the Act, see pp 413–415 below.

6   *Walker v Boyle* [1982] 1 All ER 634, [1982] 1 WLR 495 and *South Western General Property Co Ltd v Marton* [1982] 2 EGLR 19 are applications of the section.

degree: the terms need not be employed invariably or without material variation, but they must be regarded by the party which advanced them as those on which it habitually contracts.[7] As against that party a business cannot by reference to any contract term (a) when itself in breach of contract exclude or restrict its liability in respect of the breach, or (b) claim to be entitled to render a contractual performance substantially different from what is reasonably expected, or to render no performance at all, except in so far as in any of these cases the contract term satisfies the requirement of reasonableness. An example covered by (b) might be a clause whereby a tour operator can substitute a different holiday from the one originally booked.[8] Another example would be a public utility with a clause enabling it to terminate a service without good cause.[9]

UCTA 1977 is intended to have wide effect. To the extent that UCTA prevents the exclusion or restriction of any liability, it also prevents making the liability or its enforcement subject to restrictive or onerous conditions, excluding or restricting any right or remedy in respect of liability, or subjecting a person to any prejudice in consequence of pursuing these, and excluding or restricting the rules of evidence or procedure (s 13(1)). Examples of such limitations are restricting liability to a certain sum for each article lost or damages, excluding certain remedies, or requiring that any complaints be made within three days.[10] To the extent that UCTA prevents the exclusion or restriction of any liability the provisions relating to negligence, guarantees and the supply of products also prevent excluding or restricting liability by reference to terms and notices which exclude or restrict the relevant obligation or duty (s 13(1)). Much depends in practice, of course, on whether the courts construe a term positively stating primary obligations as an exclusion or restriction of liability.[11] The House of Lords has said that a court must ask itself whether, but for the existence of the term, there would have been primary obligations. If so then the term is subject to the Act.[12] Indemnity clauses are also prevented if unreasonable, as is evasion by means of a secondary contract or a choice of law clause (ss 4, 10, 27(2)).

---

[7] *Chester Grosvenor Hotel Co Ltd v Alfred McAlpine Management Ltd* (1991) 56 BLR 115.

[8] Cf *Anglo-Continental Holidays Ltd v Typaldos Lines (London) Ltd* [1967] 2 Lloyd's Rep 61.

[9] *Timeload Ltd v British Telecommunications plc* [1995] EMLR 459, CA.

[10] Eg *Stewart Gill Ltd v Horatio Myer & Co Ltd* [1992] QB 600. See E Macdonald, 'Exclusion Clauses: The Ambit of s 13(1) of the Unfair Contract Terms Act 1977' (1992) 12 Leg Stud 277.

[11] Critics have said that the provision goes too far because it might require the deletion of a primary obligation which is an essential characteristic of the transaction and which the parties knowingly and willingly concluded: N Palmer and D Yates 'The Future of the Unfair Contract Terms Act 1977' (1981) 40 CLJ 108, 127.

[12] *Smith v Eric S Bush* [1990] 1 AC 831.

A written agreement to submit present or future differences to arbitration is not treated under the Act as excluding or restricting any liability (s 13(2)). However, consumers could be severely disadvantaged by compulsory arbitration provisions, framed by the business with which they deal. The Consumer Arbitration Agreements Act 1988 struck out such contractual provisions. That Act has now been repealed by the Arbitration Act 1996, which applies the Unfair Terms in Consumer Contracts Regulations— shortly to be considered—to arbitration agreements requiring consumers to refer claims to arbitration, provided the pecuniary value of the claim is below a value set by order.[13] Whereas the 1988 Act was framed in such a way that consumers were unlikely to have to go to arbitration, pursuant to an arbitration clause, unless they specifically consented to it after a dispute arose, now if they refuse to go to arbitration they must be prepared to argue that the arbitration clause, contrary to requirement of good faith, causes a significant imbalance, to their detriment, in the rights and obligations under the contract. It is a most unfortunate change.

As indicated certain exclusions and restrictions of liability under UCTA 1977 are not prevented absolutely but only if a reasonableness requirement cannot be satisfied. In relation to a contract term, the requirement of reasonableness is that the term shall have been a fair and reasonable one to have been included having regard to the circumstances which were, or ought reasonably to have been, known to or in contemplation of the parties when the contract was made (s 11(1)). Reasonableness is assessed without regard to post-formation events.[14] In sales cases, Sch 2 provides certain guidelines for the application of the reasonableness test. For example, the relative bargaining power of the parties, taking into account alternative means by which the consumer's requirements could be met; whether competitors' contracts contain a similar term; the consumer's knowledge of the term and its ambit; and whether the goods were made or adapted to the consumer's special order. Similar factors are taken into account in non-goods cases. Appellate courts will not interfere with a judge's decision on the issue of reasonableness unless satisfied that it proceeded on some erroneous principle or was plainly and obviously wrong.[15]

The obvious limitation is that reasonableness is assessed at the time the contract was made, which is defended on the grounds of certainty and the undesirability of changing the rules of the game. Yet clearly there are

---

[13]   Sections 89–91.

[14]   For a detailed consideration of these factors in a commercial case: *Photoprint Ltd v Foward Trust Ltd* (1993) 12 Tr LR 146. See H Beale 'Inequality of Bargaining Power' (1986) 6 OJLS 123; S Thal 'The Inequality of Bargaining Power Doctrine' (1988) 8 OJLS 17.

[15]   *Edmond Murray Ltd v BSP International Foundations Ltd* (1992) 33 Con LR 1, CA.

claims where unobjectionable contractual terms can be put to unfair use, and where what was reasonable originally transpires to be unreasonable in the context of later circumstances (as where the consumer would be left without any remedy). Reasonableness as confined under s 11(2) cannot cope with these performance-related risks.

One suggestion is that reasonableness ought to turn on whether the consumer is offered a choice of terms, with liability and without liability, varying with price.[16] This would be undesirable since there is a natural tendency for people to underestimate risk and to pay the lower price without taking out their own insurance. From the point of view of social policy it is frequently much better if businesses insure, rather than expecting consumers to do so individually. (An exception might be for motor cars where consumers themselves ought to take out comprehensive insurance.) Moreover, as a practical matter, many businesses would find it impossible to operate a dual pricing system.

In relation to a notice not having contractual effect, the requirement of reasonableness is that it should be fair and reasonable to allow reliance on it, having regard to all the circumstances obtaining when the liability arose or (but for the notice) would have arisen (s 11(3)). Where by reference to a contract term or notice a business seeks to restrict liability to a specified sum of money, and the question arises whether it satisfies the requirement of reasonableness, regard shall be had in particular to the resources which it could expect to be available to it for the purpose of meeting the liability should it arise, and how far it was open to cover itself by insurance (s 11(4)).

Fortunately the courts have been sympathetic, in the main, in interpreting UCTA 1977. It is doubtful if they could have developed the common law to an extent comparable to the Act's provisions, if only because the lack of litigation would not have provided an opportunity to do so. UCTA recognised that in the consumer context freedom of contract is largely illusory. Yet the truth is that the title, Unfair Contract Terms Act 1977, was a misnomer, because given its scope and the specific exemptions to it, many unfair terms caught in other jurisdictions fall outside its ambit.[17] Insurance contracts were excluded, for example, although standard clauses in these have been grossly unfair to consumers.[18]

[16] On reasonableness, see eg *Rasbora Ltd v JCL Marine Ltd* [1977] 1 Lloyd's Rep 645; *R & B Customs Brokers Co Ltd v United Dominions Trust Ltd* [1988] 1 All ER 847, [1988] 1 WLR 321; J Adams and R Brownsword *Key Issues in Contract* (Butterworths, 1995) pp 263–269.

[17] An incisive critique is F Reynolds 'Unfair Contract Terms: A Comment' in Alan C Neal (ed) *Law and the Weaker Party* (Professional Books, 1981) vol 1.

[18] See Law Commission *Insurance Law: Non-disclosure and Breach of Warranty*, (Law Comm no 104 (1980)); Law Reform Commission (Australia) *Insurance Contracts* (Report no 20 (1982)); N Huls 'Critical Insurance Law' in T Wilhelmsson (ed) *Perspectives of Critical Contract Law* (Dartmouth, 1993).

(b)   The Unfair Terms in Consumer Contracts Directive

The EC Directive on Unfair Terms in Consumer Contracts[19] had a long gestation. Unfair contract terms were on the EC's preliminary programme for consumer protection in 1976, and a memorandum and set of articles for a Directive were issued at that time.[20] Preliminary work was carried out but was abandoned. In 1984 the European Commission published a document setting out two paths for action, firstly, the harmonisation of laws, and secondly, stimulating negotiations between consumers and businesses on standard terms. New draft articles were circulated[1] and finally, as indicated, a Directive was agreed in 1993.[2]

The Unfair Terms in Consumer Contracts Regulations 1999 (the UTCC Regulations, replacing the UTCC Regulations 1994) implement in the UK the EC Directive.[3] The Regulations add a layer of regulation to consumer contracts, while leaving the existing law in place. The creation of a dual regime has added confusion to the English law and the DTI has pledged to consolidate the 1977 Act and 1999 Regulations in due course.[4] The Regulations are at once both narrower and broader in scope than the Unfair Contract Terms Act 1977. They are narrower in being confined to consumer contracts; UCTA applies to both consumer and commercial contracts. On the other hand the regulations extend well beyond exclusion clauses: the list of unfair terms specifically mention other clauses as well which occur in a wide range of consumer contracts.[5] Moreover, the regulations do not have the same exclusions written into them as UCTA, and so apply to insurance contracts. There is also the important provision that the written terms of a consumer contract must be in plain, intelligible language.[6] This is not necessarily plain English. If there is any doubt about a written term, the interpretation most favourable to the consumer prevails.

[19]   [1993] OJ L 95/29.
[20]   See [1980] OJ C 291/35.
[1]   Eg [1990] OJ C 243/2.
[2]   See eg H Brandner and P Ulmer 'The Community Directive on Unfair Terms in Consumer Contracts: Some Critical Remarks on the Proposal Submitted by the EC Commission' (1991) 28 CML Rev 647; M Dean 'Unfair Contract Terms: The European Approach' (1993) 56 MLR 581; R Brownsword, G Howells, T Wilhelmsson 'The EC Unfair Contract Terms Directive and Welfarism', in R Brownsword, G Howells, T Wilhelmsson (eds) *Welfarism in Contract Law* (Dartmouth, 1994).
[3]   SI 1999/2083; SI 1994/3159. The remainder of this section is adapted from R Cranston *Principles of Banking Law* (Clarendon, 1997) pp 159–168.
[4]   DTI *Modern Markets: Confident Consumers* (Cm 4410) para 6.15.
[5]   Unfair Terms in Consumer Contracts Regulations 1999, Sch 2.
[6]   Unfair Terms in Consumer Contracts Regulations 1999, reg 7(1). See also *Plain English for Lawyers* (NCC, 1994); OFT 'Plain Intelligible Language' (1997) 4 Unfair Contract Terms Bulletin 12.

(i)   Scope of UTCC

The UTCC Regulations apply to any term in a contract concluded between a seller or a supplier and a consumer. 'Consumer' is defined as a natural person who is acting for purposes which are outside his or her business.[7] Business includes a trade or profession. This is language different from the meaning of the term 'consumer' in other UK legislation, notably UCTA. The point arises of the individual contracting partly for business, partly for other purposes. Since the regulations do not require a consumer to be acting 'wholly' outside the business, it seems arguable that so long as one purpose or more was outside the person's business, he or she could still be a consumer despite there being a business purpose. A more restrictive test, while still recognising that having some business purpose will not disqualify a person from being a consumer, is to read the definition as requiring the consumer to act *primarily* for purposes which are outside his or her business. This would be consistent with other areas of the common law. Focusing on the primary purpose or purposes to determine whether a person is acting outside a business seems also consistent with European Union law. The Directive only strikes at standard terms; despite earlier drafts the Directive, as finally adopted, does not apply to every term in a consumer contract, nor indeed to a consumer contract at all if every term has been individually negotiated. However, the definition of terms which have not been individually negotiated is very broad. Thus the UTCC Regulations apply to any term in a contract concluded between a seller or supplier and a consumer where the term has not been individually negotiated.[8] Notwithstanding that a specific term or certain aspects of it have been individually negotiated, the regulations apply to the rest of the contract if an overall assessment of it indicates that it is a pre-formulated standard contract.[9] Under the regulations the onus of establishing that a term was individually negotiated is on the business.[10]

The distinction between standard and individually negotiated terms derives from German law; the Standard Contract Terms Act 1976 provides that there are no standard contract terms where the conditions of the contract have been negotiated in detail. The approach differs from UCTA, where s 3 applies if a party deals on the other party's written standard terms of business. Under the UTCC Regulations a party could be dealing in that way but not be able to attack a particular term in the contract as unfair because it was individually negotiated. Obviously the key issue is to identify the individually negotiated term. Reflecting the Directive, the regulations provide that a term is always to be regarded as not having

---

[7]   Unfair Terms in Consumer Contracts Regulations 1999, reg 3(1).
[8]   Regulation 5(1).
[9]   Regulation 5(3).
[10]   Regulation 5(4).

been individually negotiated when it has been drafted in advance.[11] Clauses from precedents, manuals or even one previous agreement would be covered. Consequently, even if a consumer negotiates hard over such a term, but at the end of the day fully accepts a pre-formulated term, that is not an individually negotiated term and can be attacked as unfair. Similarly, if a consumer is given a choice of a number of pre-formulated terms, those terms are not individually negotiated. But if there are gaps in a pre-formulated term, which are filled in after negotiation, then the term might be an individually negotiated term. In the Directive, a term is always regarded as not being individually negotiated when it has been drafted in advance 'and the consumer has not been able to influence the substance of the term...'.[12] If the seller or supplier is genuinely open to persuasion, but at the end of the day the consumer agrees to the bank's position, the term is arguably still individually negotiated. It will be necessary to examine the circumstances surrounding the negotiation of the term. The difficulty facing the seller or supplier will be in establishing that it was open to persuasion—and the onus is, as indicated, on it.

A very significant limit on the reach of the UTCC Regulations is that the core provisions of a contract cannot be questioned.[13] In other words, it is only the subsidiary terms of a contract which can be attacked as unfair. This limitation on the scope of the UTCC Regulations reflects the position ultimately agreed for the Directive, that consumers should not be able to re-open a bad bargain. Any control of the essence of the business-consumer relationship, it is said, would be in breach of the fundamental tenets of the free market and consumers would no longer shop around for the best terms. The first point is purely rhetorical, as we have seen in the discussion of standard form contracts. The argument about moral hazard, that consumers would be less careful if the substance of the contract were reviewable, even if only at the margin, would seem counterbalanced by other considerations. However, the Directive accords with the English common law reluctance to examine the value of consideration. The result is, however, that the title of the Directive is a misnomer, like that of the 1977 Act. At most these core terms might fall foul of the requirement in the regulations that all terms in a consumer contract be clearly expressed, or of provisions in the general law such as those against extortionate credit bargains.[14] There is a good argument that a term cannot be a core term unless it is expressly drawn to the consumer's attention.

---

[11]   Unfair Terms in Consumer Contracts Regulations 1999, reg 3(3).
[12]   Regulation 5(3).
[13]   Regulation 6(2).
[14]   Regulation 7(1); Consumer Credit Act 1974, s 137. But provisions for default have been held not to be core terms: *Director General of Fair Trading v First National Bank* [2000] 1 All ER (Comm) 371, CA. See also the county court judgment in *Falco Finance Ltd v Michael Gough* (1999) 17 Tr LR 526.

The unfair terms which are not capable of review under the regulations are those which relate to 'the definition of the main subject matter of the contract' or to 'the adequacy of the price and remuneration'.[15] Inevitably there will be quibbles about what is encompassed by the main subject matter of the contract.[16] Take a basic sale contract. Is the main subject matter of the contract the description of the goods and the price? Or does it extend to the manufacturer's guarantee which comes with the product? In theory it should not be possible for a seller or supplier to inflate the main subject matter of a contract by qualifying its description. But if the seller advertises a 'guaranteed product' there is still the issue of whether the main subject of any contract includes the guarantee.

The 'adequacy of the price and remuneration'—words taken from the Directive—is referred to as the 'quality/price ratio' in its preamble. Both terms 'price' and 'remuneration' arguably differ between themselves. Neither is equivalent to the English concept of consideration which encompasses money and money's worth. On one construction of the Directive and regulations interest might not be a core provision, since there is a specific exemption built into the list of potentially unfair terms relating to variable interest rates.

Excluded from the scope of the regulations is a term incorporated in a consumer contract in order to comply with or which reflects (i) statutory or regulatory provisions of the UK; or (ii) the provisions or principles of international Conventions to which the Member States or the Community are party.[17] 'Statutory provisions' are straightforward and would include terms inserted in consumer credit agreements in line with the Consumer Credit Act 1974 and its attendant regulations. 'Regulatory provisions' are also fairly readily identifiable and would include terms inserted in customer investment agreements as required by the rules of, say, the Financial Services Authority. In both cases the justification, set out in the preamble to the Directive, for excluding such terms from the test for unfairness, is met, namely, that the legislator or regulator in performing its public functions will presumably take the consumer interest into account in formulating such terms.

What of self-regulation, for example the terms required by a Code of Practice—do they reflect regulatory provisions? If there were to be a substantial public input into the code, or if a public body such as the Office of Fair Trading had a veto power over its contents, the question may have some force. Even then it might be said that the substantial public input or veto would have to have consumer protection purposes.

---

[15]   Unfair Terms in Consumer Contracts Regulations 1999, reg 6(2).
[16]   R Brownsword and G Howells 'The Implementation of the EC Directive on Unfair Terms' [1995] JBL 243, 248–249.
[17]   Unfair Terms in Consumer Contracts Regulations 1999, reg 4(2).

In other words, it would not be enough for the Office of Fair Trading to have primarily in mind competition or other reasons. The exclusion of provisions demanded or reflecting international conventions has a narrow ambit. Were the UK to be an adherent of an international Convention, however, implementing legislation would most likely have been passed so that the regulations would not apply by reason of statutory provision.

As indicated, the UTCC Regulations apply to any term in a contract concluded between a seller or supplier and a consumer. The meaning of 'seller' is clear—a seller of goods making a contract in the course of a business. 'Supplier' also includes someone providing goods, not by sale but by other means such as hire. A supplier also includes a person who, acting for purposes related to his or her business, supplies services.[18] The definition does not require that the service be provided to the consumer. Thus a guarantee is covered, albeit that the bank is providing the service (ie finance) not to the consumer guarantor but to the borrower, and that the borrower is not a consumer.[19] Where a consumer borrower is itself providing the security, it is arguable that the security forms part of a financing package—indeed there will be cross referencing—so that it must be read together with the loan contract, and both together involve a service.[20] 'Services' is not defined but clearly a wide range are covered, as indicated by the indicative list of unfair terms in the Annex to the regulations.[1]

(ii)   Unfair terms

English lawyers are not unfamiliar with the task of assessing whether credit bargains require a payment which is grossly exorbitant or grossly contravenes the ordinary principles of fair dealing, and whether a transaction is manifestly disadvantageous or at a considerable undervalue. Testing terms in consumer contracts for their unfairness under the Directive and UTCC regulations is not conceptually very different, albeit that the definition of unfairness is new and invokes the notion of good faith which, familiar to lawyers from civil law systems and the United States, has an alien ring to English ears.[2] To be unfair under the UTCC regulations a term

---

[18]   Unfair Terms in Consumer Contracts Regulations 1999, reg 3(1).

[19]   Cf Case C-45/96 *Bayerische Hypotheken-und Wechselbank AG v Dietzinger* [1998] ECR I-1199.

[20]   DTI *The Unfair Terms in Consumer Contracts Regulations 1994. Guidance Notes* (1995) p 8.

[1]   On the application of the UTCC Regulations to land: S and C Bright 'Unfair Terms in Land Contracts' (1995) 111 LQR 655; T Hartley 'Five Forms of Uncertainty in European Community Law' [1996] CLJ 265, 266–273.

[2]   Eg R Summers 'General Duty of Good Faith—Its Recognition and Conceptualization' (1982) 67 Cornell LR 810; H Lücke 'Good Faith and Contractual Peformance' in P Finn (ed) *Essays on Contract* (Law Book, 1987).

must, contrary to the requirement of good faith, cause the significant imbalance specified in the regulations.[3] The language, lifted from the Directive, indicates that the question is not whether the term (a) *is* in breach of good faith; *and* (b) causes the significant imbalance, but rather whether the term (a) *being* in breach of good faith (b) *causes* the significant imbalance. In other words good faith does not stand alone but must be linked causally to the significant imbalance. Theoretically one can posit a situation where there has been a breach of good faith but some other factor, not it, has caused the significant imbalance; that would be outside the regulations. In practice this type of situation is unlikely, but the causal language points us in the direction of the primary meaning of good faith—taking into account the interests of the consumer.

Having regard to the preamble of the Directive it is clear that good faith in the UTCC Regulations demands a dedication to the interests of consumers on the part of the business. For this reason the concept in particular contexts might not coincide with the standard of reasonableness in UCTA. While a similar result is in many cases likely to be achieved when applying the two concepts, this will not always be the case. The factors which the courts have addressed in applying the reasonableness standard need not necessarily involve an inquiry into whether a business has dealt fairly and taken into account a consumer's interests.

The lack of good faith must cause a significant imbalance in the parties' rights and obligations under the contract to the detriment of the consumer. Thus fairly obviously the nature of imbalance between a business and a consumer customer is not the immediate focus of inquiry although it might be the reason for the imbalance in rights and obligations. This contrasts with an important factor in determining reasonableness under UCTA, whether or not there is inequality of bargaining power. The natural imbalance between a business and consumer need not necessarily lead to an imbalance in contractual rights and obligations; in any particular contract this will be a matter of inquiry.

One difficulty is the meaning to be attached to 'significant' in the description of the imbalance in rights and obligations. One connotation of the term is that the imbalance must be really serious or exceptional. This would accord more with the traditional approach of English law to upholding

---

[3]   Unfair Terms in Consumer Contracts Regulations 1999, reg 5(1). See H Collins 'Good Faith in European Contract Law' (1994) 14 OJLS 229; R Brownsword, G Howells, T Wilhelmsson 'Between Market and Welfare: Some Reflections on Article 3 of the EC Directive on Unfair Terms in Consumer Contracts' in C Willett (ed) *Fairness in Contract* (Blackstone Press, 1996); J Steyn, 'The Role of Good Faith and Fair Dealing in Consumer Law—A Hair-Shirt Philosophy?' [1991] Denning LJ 131; J O'Connor *Good Faith in English Law* (Dartmouth, 1990); G Sepe 'National Models of European Contract Law: A Comparative Approach to the Concept of Unfairness in Directive 93/13' [1997] Consum LJ 115.

bargains but enabling hard cases to be upset in a consumer context outside the specific doctrines of unconscionability, undue influence and duress. Another connotation of 'significant' is important; the term has been inserted in recognition that imbalances permeate consumer contracts, so that there is a need to filter out those which are trivial. But as long as the balance is non-trivial it satisfies the definition of unfairness. There is support for this approach in the exclusion from the UTCC Regulations of the core provisions of a contract. The justification for this exclusion is that consumers should not be able to re-open a bad bargain. To require a serious imbalance in subsidiary terms before unfairness can be invoked would be to extend the protection to bad bargains well beyond the core terms. Moreover, the indicative list has unfair terms which do not all seem to contain a serious imbalance.

Finally, there has been some discussion of the phrase 'to the detriment of the consumer' in the context of the imbalance. One argument is that the words have no operative effect but are simply words of description—the imbalance has to be to the detriment of the consumer, not the business.[4] On the other hand, since the phrase is unnecessary to indicate the direction of the imbalance, they must be given some independent effect. If this is the case how is effect to be given to a requirement that the imbalance be to the detriment of the consumer? The first, and obvious, point is that the words of the regulations do not require that the detriment be significant (as the imbalance must be); we are not looking for a serious detriment comparable to the manifest disadvantage which the applicant in an undue influence action must presently demonstrate.[5] Secondly, it would seem that the test must be objective, rather than being geared to the character of the consumer in any particular case, especially since the regulations are confined to standard form contracts. Thirdly, there must be few terms causing a significant imbalance in rights and obligations which are not simultaneously to the detriment of the consumer.

Determining whether a term is unfair demands an inquiry into the matters so far considered, taking into account 'context'—the nature of the banking or financial service and referring to the circumstances attending the conclusion of the contract, other contractual terms, and other contracts on which it is dependent.[6] Since the regulations are concerned only with

[4]   R Brownsword, G Howells, T Wilhelmsson 'Between Market and Welfare: Some Reflections on Article 3 of the EC Directive on Unfair Terms in Consumer Contracts' in C Willett (ed) *Fairness in Contract* (Blackstone, 1996).

[5]   Page 80 above.

[6]   Unfair Terms in Consumer Contracts Regulations 1999, reg 6(1). See the European Community Database of decisions about the Directive which includes notes on over 700 applications of the Directive in the UK by lower courts and by the Office of Fair Trading: http://europa.eu.int/clab/en/index.htm

standard form contracts, the relevant inquiry into context would seem to be less wide-ranging than were negotiated terms to be potentially unfair as a result of the Directive. Generally speaking, if a standard term in a particular type of contract were to be fair for one consumer, it would be a recipe for uncertainty were it to be unfair for another. Exceptionally a consumer might belong to a particular class of consumers rendering a term unfair when it would otherwise be fair—a standard form contract proffered, say, to a member of a non-English speaking ethnic minority. The assessment of context is to be made at the time of the conclusion of the contract. In this respect the regulations reflect the approach of UCTA.

As mentioned, the Regulations contain a list of indicative and non-exhaustive terms, taken from the Directive, which may be regarded as unfair.[7] It is a grey list, not a black list. Although some of the terms are already caught by UCTA, the list helpfully extends to other matters—forfeiture and penalty clauses, clauses empowering a business to vary or extend the contact (eg increase the price) and clauses which affect the business' performance (eg giving it the right to determine whether it has performed, or to transfer its obligations with a detriment to the consumer). It is likely that the European Court of Justice will be drawn into the development of an authoritative interpretation of some of the key concepts in the Directive (and thus the Regulations) in due course.[8]

(c)   The alternative legal techniques

Legislative control over the imposed terms of standard form contracts can be formulated along a number of lines. First, it can render invalid specific features of contracts which are considered objectionable. As we have seen, this has tended to be the approach in England. The advantage of specific legislative provisions is certainty. In practice there are various drawbacks. While the use of particular clauses may be rendered invalid, additional steps are necessary to prevent businesses continuing to incorporate them in their standard terms. Another of the problems is the time involved in controlling new terms. For example, a decade elapsed before implementation of the Molony Committee's recommendation that the implied terms in sales transactions should be made non-excludable. Another obvious problem is that the clauses prohibited are not the only kinds which are unfair. Conversely, it may be that the clauses prohibited

---

[7]   Unfair Terms in Consumer Contracts Regulations 1999, Sch 2.
[8]   S Weatherill 'Prospects for the Development of European Private Law through Europeanization in the European Court—the Case of the Directive on Unfair Terms in Consumer Contracts' (1995) 3 European Review of Private Law 307.

are not always unfair. The EC Directive on Unfair Terms in Consumer Contracts therefore adopts the approach of presumptive unfairness, with its grey list, but the danger of this is uncertainty. A further problem of specific legislative control is the complexity of the remedial legislation and the inflexibility which this entails. Inasmuch as this is the case it is largely a function of the narrow interpretation of statutes and the attempt by the drafters to minimise this by spelling out in detail what is to be covered.

A second approach to standard form contracts is by requiring contractual terms of meet a broad standard along the lines of the good faith provision in the EC Directive on Unfair Terms in Consumer Contracts. Traditionally, English law has refused to countenance the doctrine of good faith—except in the context of insurance law where both parties must act in utmost good faith to each other—although in practice they can often reach by other routes the conclusion which such a doctrine would demand.[9] Similarly, the Uniform Commercial Code of the United States contains a general provision allowing a court to refuse to enforce an unconscionable clause or contract.[10] It is said that unconscionable means 'grossly unfair', and the Official Comment to the section says that the basic test is whether against the commercial background the clauses are too one-sided: 'The principle is one of the prevention of oppression and unfair surprise ... and not of disturbance of allocation of risks because of superior bargaining power.' The unfair surprise aspect, for example, covers the situation where a business takes advantage of the ignorance or carelessness of consumers. Section 2-302 of the UCC has been put to considerable use, although the facts in cases where relief has been granted are fairly extreme. An exorbitant price in relation to the value of a product has been held to be unconscionable.[11] Apart from substantive terms like price, section 2-302 has been used to invalidate the procedural aspects of consumer contracts such as when consumers have no opportunity to read the small print.[12]

The main justification for a good faith or an unconscionability provision is that only a broad standard can cope with the unforeseen and perhaps

---

9   *Interfoto Picture Library Ltd v Stiletto Visual Programmes* [1989] QB 433, [1988] 1 All ER 348; *Balfour Beatty Civil Engineering Ltd v Docklands Light Railway Ltd* (1996) 78 BLR 42, 67–68. Cf *Walford v Miles* [1992] 2 AC 128.

10   UCC §2-302. See A Leff 'Unconscionability and the Code—The Emperor's New Clause' (1967) 115 U Penn LR 485; J White and R Summers *Uniform Commercial Code* (West, 1988) vol 1, Chapter 4; J Dawson 'Unconscionable Coercion: The German Version' (1976) 89 Harv LR 1041.

11   Eg *FN Roberts Pest Control Co v McDonald* 208 SE 2d 13 (1974); *Kugler v Romain* 279 A 2d 640 (1971); *Sho-Pro of Indiana Inc v Brown* 585 NE 2d 1357 (1992).

12   Eg *Williams v Walker-Thomas Furniture Co* 350 F2d 445 (1965), still a leading case. See also, eg, *Waters v Min Ltd* 587 NE 2d 231 (1992).

marginal features of consumer transactions. The courts, it is said, are the most appropriate body to give substance to such a broad standard because of the wide range of fact situations which will be litigated and its capacity to generalise by analogy. A broad provision, supporters argue, avoids judges having to do justice by stealth because a particular case falls outside the tight compartments available in specific legislation. The objection that a good faith or an unconscionability clause introduces an uncertainty into the law is said to ignore the way courts have historically narrowed wide discretion. Counter-arguments, however, caution against too great a faith being placed in a general standard without the underpinning of specific provisions. Quite apart from the barriers to consumer litigation considered shortly, there is a question whether the courts possess the necessary breadth of vision for such a discretion to be entrusted to them.[13] While this is partly a matter of social values it is also a structural issue, that generalised decision-making is not always appropriate or possible in the context of particular cases. On one interpretation the German and United States courts have been cautious and conservative in exercising their powers under the good faith and unconscionability clauses.

It is possible to meet some of these criticisms by fleshing out a good faith or an unconscionability provision on the basis of legislative and judicial experience in the area of consumer contracts. While entrusting the courts with a general discretion to consider whether a contract or a provision of a contract is not in good faith or unjust, having regard to the public interest and all the circumstances of the case, it is possible to direct them to give attention to factors such as any material inequality in bargaining power, prior negotiations, the practicability of the applicant negotiating an alteration or the rejection of any provisions of the contract, and conditions in the contract which are unreasonably difficult to comply with or not reasonably necessary for the protection of legitimate interests. Other relevant factors include the capacity of parties (or their representatives) to protect their interests given their age or physical or mental condition; the relative economic circumstances, educational background or literacy of the parties; the physical form and intelligibility of contractual language if in writing; the presence of independent legal or other expert advice; the extent of explanations of the legal and practical effect of a contract and whether these were understood; undue influence, unfair pressure or unfair tactics exerted or used; the conduct of the parties in similar contracts or courses of dealing; and the commercial or other

---

[13]   Eg M Trebilcock 'An Economic Approach to the Doctrine of Unconscionability' in B Reiter and J Swan (eds) *Studies in Contract Law* (Butterworths, 1980) pp 389–390, 396–404.

setting, purpose and effect of the contract.[14] Indicative lists of possibly objectionable terms are also possible, as in Sch 2 to the UTCC Regulations.

To be successful any broad standard must focus not simply on the situation at the inception of a transaction but also on its subsequent performance, in other words on substantive as well as procedural fairness. In addition the courts' remedial power must extend beyond refusing to enforce, setting aside or varying the transaction to other aspects such as orders with respect to the disposition, sale or realisation of property, the payment of money, compensation for third parties whose interests might otherwise be prejudiced, the supply/repair of goods and services, the creation and enforcement of a charge on property, and the appointment of a receiver of property.[15]

A third approach to standard form contracts is that a public agency is authorised to take legal action to have offending terms declared void and their use prohibited. It might also be envisaged that the agency will seek voluntary action by businesses by negotiation and by drafting model contracts. Swedish legislation along these lines has operated since 1971. Under the Act Prohibiting Improper Contract Terms, the Consumer Ombudsman examines standard form contracts and standardised terms, and intervenes when he thinks that a clause is improper, ie 'it gives entrepreneurs an advantage or deprives consumers of a right and thereby causes such one-sided relations in the parties' rights and obligations under the contract that a reasonable balance between the parties no longer exists'.[16] The Act deliberately excludes any requirement that impropriety be manifest. Terms can be referred to the Market Court, which can issue an injunction against their future use. Certain clauses are deemed to be improper. Other clauses against which action has been taken include those which enable a business more than three weeks to decide whether to go through with a transaction, and those which give a business the categorical right to cancel a contract and forfeit a deposit for delay in payment. Also subject to review are clauses which allow the contractual price to be raised (except for changes in taxation).

The third approach is now part of UK law as a result of the EC Directive on Unfair Terms in Consumer Contracts. In the long history of the Directive, it was accepted that control of unfair terms should focus not only on individual contracts but on unfair terms as a marketing practice. That required control systems which leading commentators such as Professor

---

[14]   Cf Contracts Review Act 1980 (New South Wales), s 9.
[15]   Contracts Review Act 1980 (New South Wales), ss 7–8, Sch 1.
[16]   See U Bernitz 'Consumer Protection and Standard Contracts' (1973) 17 Scandinavian Studies in Law 11; T Wilhelmsson 'Control of Unfair Terms and Social Values: EC and Nordic Approaches' (1993) 16 JCP 435.

Hondius argued should be two-layered: at the first level the consumer interest should be represented by consumer groups or a public agency, which would engage in negotiations with businesses and trade associations to achieve changes in standard terms, while at the second level there would be a board or court which could issue cease and desist orders against objectionable terms.[17] In the result Article 7 of the Directive obliges Member States to introduce a means of preventing the continued use of unfair terms which 'shall include provisions whereby persons or organisations, having a legitimate interest under national law in protecting consumers, may take action ... before the courts or before competent administrative bodies' in relation to unfair terms.

The need for a public action is underlined by the work of the Director General of Fair Trading, who reports that unfair terms examined conflict with the UTCC Regulations.[18] An acknowledged limitation on the Director General's work is the lack of power to secure redress for consumers who complain. Fortunately the Director General has taken an active approach to reg 7, which requires written terms (including the core terms) to be in plain language. His interpretation is that this requirement is pointless unless consumers are given sufficient time and opportunity to read contract terms, in other words, the regulation is breached unless, before they enter any contract, consumers are able to read and understand all its written terms. Moreover, Article 5 of the Directive excludes the *contra proferentum* rule in relation to public enforcement action, in other words, it enables the Director General to take action against the continued use of terms which, being ambiguous, could be seen as having a potentially fair meaning. In doing this, the Director General has regard to a term's least favourable meaning.

Compared with the legislative history and the words of the Directive, the UTCC Regulations are unduly narrow. The Director General of Fair Trading must consider any complaint that any contract term drawn up for general use is unfair, unless either it is frivolous or vexatious or another 'qualifying body' has notified the Director that it is taking up the complaint.[19] The concept of the 'qualifying body' was introduced by the 1999 Regulations in order to comply with the provisions of the Directive that other administrative agencies and consumer groups should have the capacity previously restricted to the Director to seek undertakings or an injunction against the continued use of the term or a similar term. These

[17] E Hondius *Unfair Terms in Consumer Contracts* (Molengraaff Institute for Private Law, 1983) pp 224–228.
[18] See the Bulletin published from time to time by the Unfair Terms Unit of the Office of Fair Trading. A National Audit Office investigation concluded that OFT activity had resulted in savings of £100m to consumers through action to modify contract terms of one mortgage lender and eight mobile phone companies: *The Office of Fair Trading: Protecting the Consumer from Unfair Trading Practices* (The Stationery Office, 1999) p 53.
[19] Unfair Terms in Consumer Contracts Regulations 1999, reg 10.

qualifying bodies include the utilities regulators (for example the Office of Telecommunications) and the Consumers' Association.[20] The regulations are drafted in such a way as to give the Director a general co-ordinating function, for example by requiring the qualifying bodies to notify her of any complaint which they are taking up.[1] The powers of the Director General (and by analogy also the qualifying bodies) have been interpreted to restrict the power to act to circumstances where a complaint has been received about the use of unfair terms.[2] Fortunately complaints have flooded in from ordinary consumers and trading standards officers. So far many businesses and public bodies have agreed to drop objectionable terms, or undertakings have been given.[3] Objectionable terms dealt with include variation clauses (enabling the price to be increased without giving the consumer the right to withdraw), entire agreement clauses (whereby oral misrepresentations are said not to be binding on the business) and penalty clauses (imposing financial penalties on consumers, eg retention of deposits, but not on the business).[4] It is clear from reading the OFT's regular bulletins that the Director General's approach to the application of the Regulations is to use the grey list in Schedule 2 as a checklist against which to compare terms, though without precluding the possibility that terms of a type not within the list may also be unfair.[5] The Director General has taken one case to the High Court and on appeal.[6]

Mandatory approval of standard form contracts is a fourth technique of consumer protection. It has not been widely used, although a few agreements like package holiday and consumer credit agreements must contain certain clauses presented in a form which, it is assumed, will be comprehensible to consumers.[7] Consumer groups have drawn up a number of model standard form contracts, mainly for publicity purposes, and with the hope that consumers would use them when they wanted work done, but they have been given short shrift by businesses which regard them as unfairly loaded against them. Yet another approach is Israel's Standard Contracts Law 1982, which establishes a Standards Contracts Tribunal to which businesses can apply to have restrictive terms in standard form

---

[20]   Unfair Terms in Consumer Contracts Regulations 1999, Sch 1.
[1]   Regulation 12(2).
[2]   Compare reg 10(1) and reg 12(1).
[3]   For a critique R Colbey 'Unfair Terms and the OFT' (1998) 148 NLJ 46. For details see the OFT Unfair Terms Bulletins.
[4]   OFT Unfair Contract Terms Bulletins, 1996–present.
[5]   OFT 'A Short Guide to Finding Unfair Terms' (1997) 4 Unfair Contract Terms Bulletin 11.
[6]   *Director General of Fair Trading v First National Bank* [2000] 1 All ER (Comm) 371, [2000] 07 LS Gaz R 39, CA (discussed above).
[7]   Package Travel, Package Holidays and Package Tours Regulations 1992, SI 1992/3288, reg 9. Failure to include the terms means the tour operator cannot enforce the contract: reg 9(3). On the consumer credit requirements see p 364 below.

contracts approved.[8] (Consumer groups and the Attorney General can also apply to have unfair standard terms disallowed.) In carrying out its task the Tribunal must consider if, in the light of the surrounding circumstances, the clause is prejudicial to consumers or gives an unfair advantage to suppliers likely to prejudice consumers. Failure to approve them renders the term(s) unenforceable, while approval prevents subsequent invalidation for a period of five years. In those cases where the Supreme Court has become involved, it has adopted a liberal interpretation in recent times. The problem of a clearance system is that it will break down in the event that even a relatively small proportion of the standard form contracts in existence have to be submitted to it.

In the light of limited administrative resources, prior approval of standard form contracts is probably best concentrated in specific areas where the need for consumer protection is greatest. Insurance contracts would be an ideal place to start, although they now fall within the UTCC Regulations. (They were excluded from the effects of s 3 of the Unfair Contracts Terms Act 1977.)[9] Pre-vetting on insurance contracts by public agencies is well accepted elsewhere—albeit that it is often for non-consumer purposes (eg the liquidity and solvency of the insurers)—which is another reason to begin work there.

3   IMPLEMENTATION OF PRIVATE LAW RIGHTS

A general feature of private law is that it is not self-implementing. Consumers must take the initiative to enforce their legal rights. The assumption is that consumers know their rights and are sufficiently motivated to press them. If they are harmed because a business infringes their rights, self-interest will impel them to take action, including court proceedings if a settlement cannot be achieved. Of course, consumers frequently fail to utilise their rights in this way. Consumers may not know of their rights to take advantage of them. For example, consumers frequently attribute responsibility for faulty products to manufacturers whereas the law imposes it on retailers.[10] A common way in which consumers take the initiative when they are dissatisfied is not by enforcing their rights through

---

[8]   Comment 'Administrative Regulation of Adhesion Contracts in Israel' (1966) 66 Col L Rev 1340; K Berg 'The Israeli Standard Contracts Law 1964: Judicial Controls of Standard Form Contracts'(1979) 28 ICLQ 560; S Deutch 'Controlling Standard Contracts—The Israeli Version' (1985) 30 McGill LJ 458.

[9]   See Association of British Insurers, *The Unfair Terms in Consumer Contracts Regulations 1994. Guidance for Insurance Companies* (1995). And see the discussion on insurance contracts in Chapter 6 below.

[10]   See Chapter 5.

the legal system but by refusing to pay amounts which they do not believe are due. For example, they may stop paying credit instalments on the grounds that a product is defective. Such actions can have tragic consequences because the business involved may repossess the product, and/or obtain a default judgment and then an attachment order against the consumer's earnings if the judgment is not met.[11]

One theoretical approach to claims and claiming is a 'naming, blaming and claiming' model where people pass through the different stages, or fail to do so if access is in some way blocked. Another approach is to conceptualise the process as much more complex, for example, where attributions of fault are affected by the process itself.[12] In either case there is a pyramid, as consumers pass from identifying a problem, attributing blame for it to someone, claiming and then, in only a few cases, pursuing legal remedies. Some idea of the pyramid is derived from data collected in the 1994 Office of Fair Trading *Consumer Dissatisfaction* survey:[13]

% where matter taken up with solicitor, CAB, OFT, trading standards, small claims, arbitration or ombudsman	1–2%
% of occasions when consumers with cause to complain took action	32% (goods)
	25% (services)
% with cause of complaint (prompted answers)	48%
total respondents	100%

There is comparable data in another national survey, this one for the National Consumer Council/BBC *Law in Action* programme.[14] In the previous three years, 1,019 persons in the survey had had serious disputes. Of these 8% involved faulty goods and 7% faulty services. Of those with a faulty goods dispute, 9% went for help to a solicitor, and 16% to a CAB.

---

11 In theory consumers may have a right to a set-off, ie a right to withhold payment, but only for the amount of damages they can claim under the general law. See P Wood *English and International Set-Off* (Sweet & Maxwell, 1989) Chapter 4.

12 Eg H Kritzer 'Propensity to Sue in England and the United States of America: Blaming and Claiming in Tort Cases' (1991) 18 J Law & Soc 400; S Lloyd-Bostock & L Mulchahy 'The Social Psychology of Making and Responding to Hospital Complaints: An Account Model of Complaint Processes' (1994) 16 Law & Policy 123.

13 *Consumer Dissatisfaction* (OFT, 1996). The figures in the table are presented as percentages of the same base. Unfortunately full information is not available and the calculations of the data should be treated with care. See also the data on action taken by consumers receiving faulty goods or services in the more recent research by H Genn (with National Centre for Social Research) *Paths to Justice* (Hart Publishing, 1999) p 39.

14 *Seeking Civil Justice* (NCC, 1995).

(The figures for services were 25% and 12% respectively.) Of all those whose dispute was resolved—619 in all—only 1% of those with a faulty goods dispute, and 12% of those with a faulty services dispute, had invoked proceedings before a court or tribunal. (In the case of faulty goods the court/tribunal was the small claims procedure in the county court in all cases, although with faulty services this was the position in only $^2/_3$ of cases.)

Consumers may not pursue their rights for various reasons. First, consumers may not perceive that there is a problem, for example, that the law obliged the business they dealt with to provide a written contract or that a financial service is ill-suited to their retirement needs (which will not be discovered until much later). Moreover, consumers may not realise that their problem is capable of remedy—they may simply accept a particular result in ignorance of the fact that it falls below the legal standard.[15] The Oxford national study on accident victims found that a key factor which helped to explain the higher rates of claiming amongst road accident and industrial accident victims was the availability of information about legal rights immediately after the accident occurred.[16] Again, consumers may accept competing interpretations of the problem, that, say, a defect in a product is temporary until the product is 'broken in', or has manifested itself because the product is not being used properly. Further, consumers may not think a problem is sufficiently serious to do anything about it—a particular item might not have cost very much, they may be more robust

[15]   A study undertaken for the Citizen's Charter Complaints Task Force found that the most common reason for not making a complaint was that it will not do any good: *Complaints Handling in the Public Sector* (HMSO, 1995). See generally A Best and A Andreasen 'Consumer Response to Unsatisfactory Purchases: A Survey of Perceiving Defects, Voicing Complaints, and Obtaining Redress' (1977) 11 Law & Soc Rev 701; A Best *When Consumers Complain* (Columbia UP, 1981); S Sibley 'Who Speaks for the Consumer', Nader's *No Access to Law* and Best's 'When Consumers Complain' [1984] ABA Res J 429; R Oliver 'An Investigation of the Interrelationship Between Consumer (Dis)satisfaction and Complaint Behaviour' (1987) 14 Advances in Consumer Research 218; N Vidmar 'Seeking Justice: An Empirical Map of Consumer Problems and Consumer Responses in Canada' (1988) 26 Os HLJ 757.

[16]   D Harris et al *Compensation and Support for Illness and Injury* (Clarendon, 1984). For example, a study in Manchester evaluated a scheme to improve access to legal services by distributing leaflets giving advice to accident victims and offering a free initial interview with a solicitor. The scheme achieved its objectives of facilitating access for those who would not otherwise have obtained it: H Genn *Meeting Legal Needs? An Evaluation of a Scheme for Personal Injury Victims* (SSRC Centre for Socio-Legal Studies, 1982). With industrial injuries, the energy of local union officials and shop stewards, the availability of literature, and the importance of doctors in alerting patients to their rights have been found to be important in mobilising claims: W Felstiner and R Dingwall *Asbestos Litigation in the United Kingdom: An Interim Report* (American Bar Foundation and Centre for Socio-Legal Studies, Oxford, 1988).

than other individuals and capable of tolerating inconvenience, they may also be philosophical about being 'ripped off' or reluctant to admit it, and they may themselves be able to fix a defect sufficiently. Even if consumers know their rights there are reasons why they should not seek to enforce them. Some of the factors inhibiting consumers from upholding their legal rights are that they think the business involved will ignore them, that they feel helpless in the face of corporate power, or that they simply do not know how to enforce them. As far as legal proceedings are concerned, the courts can appear remote and forbidding to individual consumers. By contrast legal action is less daunting to businesses, particularly if they handle it as a matter of routine.

An important factor in deterring consumers from pursuing their legal rights is the transaction costs, including the opportunity cost of the time and effort.[17] Taking even a conservative figure for the cost of a consumer's time and costing telephone calls, visits and letters, the cost of complaining is likely to be significant. Consumers can quite rationally decide that the opportunity cost of attempting to secure redress is not justified if the amount involved is less than the cost of complaining. It is difficult to say whether consumers are influenced by cost considerations from the pattern of their complaints. Figures in the Office of Fair Trading *Consumer Dissatisfaction* survey show that action was taken in a high percentage of cases which involved new cars, furniture and costly electrical equipment, but the relationship between price and propensity to take action was not statistically significant. On the other hand, the relationship was statistically significant with services—relatively costly services like building work, holidays and double-glazing insulation were associated with more action being taken. (There was an exception with mail order, which had a high percentage of actions considering the relatively low cost.) Other factors may be distorting these results, such as whether consumers think it worthwhile taking any action.[18] Likewise because many consumer problems involve a small amount it is not worth while for consumers to litigate them. Justice Brandeis of the United States Supreme Court noted:

> [A]lthough the aggregate of the loss entailed may be so serious and widespread as to make the matter one of public consequence, no private suit would be brought to stop the unfair conduct, since the loss to each of the individual affected is too small to warrant it.[19]

The exception is that the value of litigation may be greater than the immediate sum at stake if a consumer is taking a test case and receives support from other sources.

[17] A Ogus *Regulation: Legal Form and Economic Theory* (OUP, 1994) p 27.
[18] *Consumer Dissatisfaction* (OFT, 1996) pp 18–22.
[19] *FTC v Klesner* 280 US 19, 18 (1929).

If social and economic factors do not inhibit consumers from complaining, they still face barriers in enforcing their legal rights. An approach to the business involved will often lead to a satisfactory outcome, but in the event that it fails there is a problem for consumers in obtaining assistance from those likely to know the law and how to implement it. Most lawyers have little interest in consumer problems or experience of consumer cases. If they have handled consumer matters, this is at least as likely to be because they have represented a business in its dealings with a particular consumer or with consumers in general (eg in drafting standard form contracts). The reason lawyers do not encourage consumer problems is principally that they are a loss financially, unless damages for personal injuries are involved, although it may also be that they fear a client's close interest in a case will be too great a nuisance. Other possibilities are that lawyers recognise that they could lose work from businesses if they create difficulties on behalf of consumers, or that they identify with businesses and regard complaints as illegitimate.

Of course, lawyers do occasionally handle consumer matters for an established client (a 'loss-leader' service—clearly the wealthier benefit) or for friends, relatives or neighbours. But in this event they are likely to advise that it is not worth while pursuing the matter, to provide information on what the consumer ought to do on their own behalf, to refer the consumer to another source of assistance, or to act as an informal mediator with the business.[20] Few legal aid matters have involved consumer problems, one reason being that lawyers do not put matters forward for legal aid. In 1995, a Green Paper on legal aid noted that the existing legal aid scheme

> tends to channel clients and money to solicitors. It encourages a system of lawyer led services, and delivers what lawyers are best able to supply. This is a particular problem in civil cases where lawyers have tended to concentrate on personal injury and divorce work. By contrast, although lawyers do provide help with other legal problems, they do not do so to anything like the same extent...There is a strong consensus of opinion among lawyers and advice agencies that need for legal services arises in a wide range of problems which affect people on low incomes in an acute form. Particular needs arise in connection with — ...consumer disputes; debt...[1]

---

[20] S Macaulay 'Lawyers and Consumer Protection Laws' (1979) 14 Law and Society Review 115, 124–127.

[1] *Legal Aid—Targeting Need* (Cm 2854 (1995)). See also T Goriely 'The Government's Legal Aid Reforms' in A Zuckerman and R Cranston (eds) *Reform of Civil Procedure* (Clarendon, 1995) p 349. Law centres give low priority to consumer matters: R Campbell 'The Inner Cities: Law Centres and Legal Services' (1992) 19 J Law & Soc 101, 102–103; J Richardson 'Law Centres' Experience of Information Work' in R Smith (ed) *Shaping the Future* (LAG, 1995).

Current changes to the scheme involve more targeting of legal aid moneys to non-lawyer advice centres, which should benefit consumers with problems such as debt.[2]

The major burden of consumer advice and assistance falls on media 'action lines' (eg newspaper advice columnists and television programmes), Citizens Advice Bureaux, other advice agencies, ombudsmen and trading standards (consumer protection) departments.[3] A study of media action lines in the United States concluded that the most disadvantaged complain infrequently and that forces within media organisations tend to push action lines in the direction of passive referral services, which simply transmit complaints to traditional public and private authorities.[4] Adverse publicity by the media can operate as a powerful weapon against recalcitrant businesses, but advertiser boycotts and threats of defamation may curtail aggressive action. There were some 700 Citizens Advice Bureaux in 1998 and over another 1,759 linked outlets. They dealt with over 6.2 million problems, of which nearly a fifth involved consumer and credit problems.[5] Many consumer enquiries to CABx are solved by simply advice, but CAB workers may contact the business and negotiate on behalf of consumers, in most cases successfully. The Federation of Independent Advice Centres comprises some 900 advice centres nation wide, some generalist and others specialist (eg the Mary Ward Legal and Financial Advice Centre). Money advice was pioneered by the Birmingham Settlement in the 1970s, and in addition to the local service it also operates National Debtline, which is a national telephone helpline for consumers with debt problems. Advice is given over the telephone at no cost. There are over 700 money advisers in various Citizens Advice Bureaux and advice centres throughout the country.[6]

---

[2]   *Modernising Justice* (Cm 4155 (1998)) p 30.

[3]   Compare the more general survey of the nature of justiciable problems (ie not just consumer problems) faced by a sample of over 600 people in the UK, the strategies by which they addressed the problems, and the outcomes in H Genn (with National Centre for Social Research) *Paths to Justice* (Hart Publishing, 1999). Particularly interesting was the finding (p 83) that the largest first source of advice was solicitors (24%), with CABx (21%), local councils (9%) and the police (7%) the next most significant sources of advice.

[4]   F Palen 'Media Ombudsmen: A Critical Review' (1979) 13 Law & Soc Rev 799.

[5]   National Association of Citizens Advice Bureaux *Annual Report 1997–1998* (1998) p 18. There are a limited number of telephone helplines, eg National Debtline: see G Bull and J Seargant *Alternative Methods of Delivering Legal Services* (PSI, 1996) p 29. The DTI has announced plans to extend the use of telephone helplines, using call centre technology: *Modern Markets: Confident Consumers* (Cm 4410 (1999)) paras 5.10–5.11. A pilot scheme is scheduled to be evaluated in April 2001.

[6]   *Dealing With Your Debts* (National Debtline/Money Advice Trust, 1997). See also M D'Ingeo 'Money Advice Services' (1994) 144 NLJ 1275; *Funding Money Advice Services* (NCC, 1992); R Mannion *Dealing with Debt* (HMSO, 1992).

High street consumer advice centres were a very positive development in the delivery of advice and assistance to consumers in the 1970s. Services offered included pre-shopping advice about the comparative performance of consumer durables, local price surveys and advice and assistance on consumer complaints. In some cases the centres actually took up complaints and attempted to negotiate a settlement with businesses on behalf of consumers. Centres were usually prepared to advise consumers on bringing legal action where a business remained adamant, and a few went so far as to send a consumer advice worker to court to assist a consumer present a claim.[7] The first consumer advice centre to give pre-purchase advice and help with complaints opened in Berlin in 1928. Developments in Britain derived from the initiative of the Consumers' Association, which financed an experimental consumer advice centre in Kentish Town in North London in 1969. Central government sought the assistance of local authorities in building up a network of local advice centres to give help and information to consumers. From 25 centres in March 1974, the number grew to over 130 by mid-1978. The new Conservative government withdrew central government grants to consumer advice centres in mid-1979 on the basis that they were not cost-effective. All the evidence pointed the other way, estimates being that complainants received compensation or redress equivalent to many times the cost of the service. As a result of the then government's action most consumer advice centres closed. At present local authority trading standards departments do not give the same level of advice as the consumer advice centres did.[8]

If consumers get to the stage of suing in court they still face difficulties in enforcing their rights. Ordinary court documents and procedures are complicated by legal niceties. Procedure at a court hearing is quite foreign to consumers who are not used to the techniques of examination and cross-examination, and to whom hearsay is a natural way of presenting evidence. An attempt to make the courts more accessible, particularly to consumers, is the procedure discussed below for dealing with small claims. The procedure is simplified, court staff assist in the completion of the relevant documents and consumers tend to handle their own case. Should

---

[7]   See R Cranston *Regulating Business* (Macmillan, 1979) pp 20–21, 61–69, 82–98; *The Fourth Right of Citizenship: A Review of Local Advice Services* (NCC, 1977) pp 12–26; G Borrie *Advice Agencies* (NCC, 1982). For elsewhere see M Eisenstein 'The Swedish Public Complaints Board: Its Vital Role in a System of Consumer Protection?' in M Cappelletti and Weisner *Access to Justice*, vol 2.

[8]   D Hutton 'Local Authority Consumer Advice Services in Need of Improvement', *Help and Advice (Institute of Consumer Affairs)* No 30 (February 1998) p 1. In Sweden, for example, municipalities provide local consumer advice centres: *Consumer Policy in OECD Countries* (OECD, 1997) p 14.

a case fall outside the small claims jurisdiction, however, consumers face the possibilities of an ordinary court hearing. If less than £15,000 is involved, under Lord Woolf's 'fast track' introduced in the county court, then there is a more truncated procedure than usual.[9]

A particular obstacle to consumers in legal proceedings is the difficulty of proving their case. Many consumer transactions are more informal than commercial transactions and consumers are unlikely to keep a detailed record or to note carefully the circumstances of a transaction. Take as an example the problems facing consumers in proving misrepresentation. Salespersons will generally not commit a misrepresentation to paper, but a salesperson's oral misrepresentations will normally be made in the absence of independent witnesses because it is not usual for consumers to take third parties with them for consumer transactions. Moreover, an oral misrepresentation which a consumer seeks to prove may be directly contradicted by the written contract which is ultimately signed. What is needed in cases where there are a number of complaints against one business is for consumer protection officials to pretend to be genuine consumers so that clear evidence is obtained of misrepresentation. Similar fact evidence of this nature should be admissible in civil proceedings.

Consumers may face similar problems in defending proceedings, for example, where a business claims that they owe money on a transaction. At one time receipts had to be given if requested for transactions over £2, bearing the requisite stamp duty.[10] Now there is no obligation on a business to issue a receipt, unless it can be argued that it is customary in the type of transaction and thus a common law obligation. Retailers automatically provide a till-slip, but others, such as builders providing a service, must take positive action to do so. Persons who pay by cheque are at an advantage at present because production of a cheque cleared by a consumer's bank is evidence that the payee has received the money.[11] Use of a credit card or debit card also generates good evidence of payment.

The Consumer Credit Act 1974 has improved the position of consumers as regards documentation of payment under regulated consumer credit transaction. A consumer is entitled on payment of 5p to a copy of a consumer credit or consumer hire agreement and to a statement as to what has been paid and what remains to be paid under it.[12] A business which

---

[9]   Civil Procedure Rules (May 1999 as amended) Part 26. See also M Friedrichs 'Fast Track' (1993) 1 San Diego Justice J 443.
[10] Stamp Act 1891, s 103r. Finance Act 1970, s 36(8). Of course a receipt does not close the matter: oral evidence might contradict that it accurately states the transaction which took place, and there is nothing to prevent a creditor accepting a lesser sum in what the receipt says was 'in full settlement': *Ferguson v Davies* [1997] 1 All ER 315 is one of many decisions.
[11] Cheques Act 1957, s 3.
[12] Consumer Credit Act 1974, ss 77–79.

fails to respond to the request cannot enforce the agreement until it does, and it also commits a criminal offence if it has not done so within a month. Similarly, consumers can request a business to issue a written statement acknowledging that the agreement has ceased and that the debt has been fully repaid.[13] The business must either comply with the request or issue a statement in which it disputes that the debt is extinguished. Statements of account and of termination are usually binding on the business.[14]

Many consumer cases turn on expert evidence, for example, about the exact quality of products or services. Experts are expensive to employ, particularly where small claims are involved. What is reasonable payment to an expert for his time will often seem to the consumer to be so great that it is better to abandon a claim. One solution is for small claims judges/ adjudicators to build up an expertise in common sources of consumer complaint. Another possibility is that there should be schemes whereby consumers can obtain cheap, impartial opinions from experts about the true quality of products and services. It should not be too difficult for trade and professional associations to devise such schemes, and there have been some moves in this direction. For example, under the voluntary Code of Practice for Footwear, an independent Footwear Testing Centre has been established to which consumers can forward shoes, mainly through retailers or consumer bodies, for an independent test of quality at a relatively low fee.

4   SMALL CLAIMS

Writing in 1913, Roscoe Pound advocated the establishment of small claims courts.[15] He chided lawyers for their concentration on the substantive principles of law and urged them to recognise the inadequacies and injustices obtaining for ordinary people. It was an injury to society that the will of individuals was subject to the arbitrary will of others because legal protection was too cumbrous and expensive to be available for the less well-off against aggressive opponents, who had the means or inclination to resist. 'It is here that the great mass of urban population, whose experience of the law in the past has been too often experience only of the arbitrary discretions of police officials, might be made to feel that the law is a living force for securing their individual as well as their collective interests.'[16] Pound recognised that it was impossible to have lawyers for

---

[13]   Consumer Credit Act 1974, s 103.
[14]   Consumer Credit Act 1974, s 172.
[15]   R Pound 'The Administration of Justice in the Modern City' (1913) 26 Harv LR 302.
[16]   (1913) 26 Harv LR 315.

every person engaged in small claims litigation and instead advocated that claimants should be assisted by court officials and the judge, who could no longer be an umpire as in traditional legal settings.

Successive reforms have adopted Pound's rationale for small claims courts: to make the service of the courts more easily available to ordinary people; to simplify practice and procedure in such cases; to eliminate delay and reduce costs; and generally to promote public confidence in the administration of justice. Yet for 60 years Pound's call for a small claims procedure went unheeded in England and Wales. The myth was perpetrated that the county courts were 'the poor man's civil courts'. That fallacy was rudely exposed in 1970 with the publication of the document *Justice Out of Reach*.[17] Taking a sample of six county courts in England, the author found that nearly three-quarters of the summons were trade cases involving actions, usually for quite small amounts, against individuals for debt for goods or services. Plaintiffs were frequently the same large firms, and this could only lead to the conclusion that they were in the habit of giving credit without making proper inquiries about creditworthiness.[18] There was not a single case of a consumer suing a business, except perhaps one for which details were not available. There were small numbers of instances, however, where consumers entered a defence, which usually led to an action being withdrawn.[19]

The upshot of *Justice Out of Reach* was the introduction in England and Wales of a small claims procedure within the existing county court structure. The first innovation in 1972 was to introduce pre-trial review by the county court registrar (now district judge), and to simplify documentation with a view to helping unrepresented claimants prepare their cases adequately for the hearing. The pre-trial review was designed to afford an opportunity for identifying the real issues, dealing with the admissibility of evidence, estimating the length of hearing, and fixing a day for the hearing convenient to both parties.[20] Eventually it was abandoned as being unnecessary in most cases and because it required two visits to the court. Now preliminary hearings are exceptional, and in deciding whether to order one district judges must have regard to the desirability of minimising the number of court attendances by the parties.

[17] (HMSO, 1970).
[18] *Justice Out of Reach* p 14.
[19] *Justice Out of Reach* pp 14–15. The results of *Justice Out of Reach* were replicated in a study of one London country court in 1980–1981: individuals were only 10.9% of the plaintiffs, whereas they were the vast majority of the defendants: M Cain 'Where Are The Disputes? A Study of a First Instance Civil Court in the UK' in M Cain and K Kulcsar (eds) *Disputes and the Law* (Akademiai Kindo, 1983) p 122.
[20] G Appleby 'Small Claims in England and Wales' in M Cappelletti and Weisner (eds) *Access to Justice* pp 697–698, 707–709.

The second innovation, introduced in 1973, was the statutory form of arbitration for small claims: matters will normally go to arbitration as soon as a defence to a claim has been received, if not more than a certain amount is involved (the 'small claims limit'), whatever the views of the parties.[1] From April 1999 that limit is £5,000 except for personal injury and housing cases. The £5,000 limit is consistent with the upper limit elsewhere, and should encourage claimants who otherwise may not have sued.[2]

Woolf's report on access to justice has resulted in further major reform of civil procedure in England and Wales (April 1999), with a new orientation towards both efficiency and serving users of legal services more satisfactorily. The managerialist aspect is reflected in rules requiring the courts to manage cases, thus taking greater control over ensuring that the most appropriate procedures are followed. The 'overriding objective of enabling the court to deal with cases justly' is reflected in new principles requiring the courts to ensure parties are on an equal footing, to save expense and deal with cases in ways which are proportionate.[3]

The small claims track today (the term arbitration has been abandoned) is coupled with rules which provide that in claims under the small claims limit no legal costs should be payable except those shown on the claim, an amount for legal advice when the claim is for an injunction or specific performance, costs incurred in enforcing the award, and such further costs which have resulted through the unreasonable conduct of the opposite party.[4] Thus the court cannot order an unsuccessful party to pay a successful party its costs in the ordinary way. The no-costs rule cannot be evaded by artificially inflating a claim. Consumers are not prevented by the rule from taking along a friend or relative to help them present their case, and it is in this way that some advice centres provide assistance to consumers making a claim.

The small claims track and the no-costs rule are designed to simplify procedure and to encourage small claims, in particular consumer claims. Standard court procedures—for example, disclosure and exchange of witness statements—do not apply to the small claims track. When arbitration was introduced it was also anticipated that the strict rules of evidence would be dispensed with and that hearings would be in private so as to ensure as much informality as was consistent with each party

---

[1]   Civil Procedure Rules 1998 (May 1999 as amended) Part 27.
[2]   *Access to Justice. Interim Report on the Civil Justice System in England and Wales by Lord Woolf* (1995) pp 103–105; Semmens and Adams *Evaluation of the Small Claims Program* (Ministry of Attorney General, British Columbia, 1992), p 21.
[3]   CPR 1998, Pt 1.
[4]   CPR 1998, r 27.14.

being given a fair and equal opportunity to present the case.[5] The Touche Ross research for the Civil Justice Review found that under the pre-Woolf small claims procedure the most frequently used source of help was solicitors.[6]

Data for the period prior to the 1999 reforms indicated that the number of small claims cases brought, relative to the number of consumer complaints each year was low.[7] Use of the small claims procedure has been increasing however: in 1974 there were 3,771 judgments by arbitration; in 1980, 13,945, and in 1997, 98,000. While aiming to make court procedures for straightforward for users, the emphasis of the 1999 reforms is on finding the appropriate dispute resolution procedure for the parties. Even if the reforms are effective we should not therefore anticipate an increase in litigation, since alternative dispute resolution (discussed below) may often be more appropriate to consumer claims. A better indicator for the effectiveness of the reforms would be data on satisfaction at the way disputes are resolved.

There is no systematic evidence of who used the old small claims jurisdiction. Regrettably the Touche Ross research for the Civil Justice Review used the categories 'small' and 'larger' litigants, with the former including small business, shops, sole traders and professionals, as well as individuals. However, it seemed that some 38–48% of plaintiffs were private individuals.[8] (On the Touche Ross categorisations, 75% of plaintiffs were 'small' litigants, and 88% of defendants). Bowles in a small sample of 100 cases (drawn from a larger population) in one country court found that private individuals brought just 12% of small claims, although 80% of their cases against a firm, trader or company were defended. Yet individuals comprised a large proportion of defendants.[9] By contrast with the Bowles research, Baldwin found that some 40% of his 109 plaintiffs were individuals.[10] One of the most disturbing features of the small claims

---

5 *Practice Direction* [1973] 1 WLR 1178. An early study showing consumer perceptions of formality was *Simple Justice. A Consumer View of Small Claims Procedures in England and Wales* (National and Welsh Consumer Councils, 1979) p 52.

6 Touche Ross *Civil Justice Review. Study of the Small Claims Procedure* (London: LCD, 1986) Table 18.

7 *Judicial Statistics* (Cm 3980 (1997)) shows that the number of county court trials in 1997 was only 15,500.

8 Touche Ross *Civil Justice Review. Study of the Small Claims Procedure* (London: LCD, 1986) Table 2.

9 See C Whelan 'Small Claims in England and Wales: Redefining Justice' in C Whelan (ed) *Small Claims Courts* (Clarendon, 1990) p 118.

10 J Baldwin *Small Claims in County Courts in England and Wales* (Clarendon, 1997). See also J Baldwin *Monitoring the Rise of the Small Claims Limit: Litigants? Experiences of Different Forms of Adjudication* (Lord Chancellor's Department, Research Series No 1/97, 1997).

procedure is the drop-out rate. It seems that only a minority of cases in which claims are issued and a defence filed are heard. Non-appearance is a major problem, yet non-appearance is a recipe for failure.

Even under the 1999 reforms the small claims track does not go as far as the separate small claims courts in other jurisdictions. One of the advantages of a separate small claims system is that it starts with a completely new image, which can encourage consumers to bring actions to enforce their legal rights. In addition, it is easier to adopt techniques to which objection would be taken if they were used within the framework of the ordinary courts. Thus some small claims courts elsewhere deliberately seek publicity with a view to having a salutary effect on business practices. Some are also directed to proceed in a manner 'fair and equitable to all parties', which is a useful indication to adjudicators to ignore settled law if this is moulded on premises such as freedom of contract which are inappropriate to modern conditions.[11] The danger is that adjudicators might give compromise decisions, and consumers might be induced to settle, when a case demands that full judgment be given in a consumer's favour.[12] Similarly, some small claims courts elsewhere have a wide order-making power—the payment of money, the performance of work, and the rectification of defects.[13] As a halfway house to a separate system each county court could have a separate 'Small Claims Division' clearly labelled and recognised as such, intended to promote the creation of a distinctive new identity for small claims.

Some consumers are probably still deterred and suspicious of a system which has been traditionally associated with debt-collecting.[14] Much has been done to overcome this resistance and to publicise the possibility on consumers making claims. Guides have been prepared on how to make a claim and county court staff are now required to advise claimants about procedure and refer them to agencies like the Citizens Advice Bureaux and advice centres if there are queries about the law. In the Touche Ross research for the Civil Justice Review there was a high percentage of plaintiffs who said they were very likely to use the procedure again, although as the consultants themselves note, this may have reflected the

---

[11] See NY Chin and R Cranston 'Small Claims Tribunals in Australia' in C Whelan (ed) *Small Claims Courts* (Clarendon, 1990).

[12] M Rosenberg and M Schubin 'Trial by Lawyer: Compulsory Arbitration of Small Claims in Pennsylvania' (1961) 74 Harv LR 448, 457; K Economides 'Small Claims and Procedural Justice' (1980) 7 Brit J Law and Society 111, 118.

[13] Thus a manufacturer might be ordered to rectify defects even though not in direct contractual relations with the consumer: *Fairey Australasia Pty Ltd v Joyce* (1981) 2 NSW LR 314.

[14] C Ervine 'The Importance of Small Claims Courts in the Resolution of Consumer Disputes in the United Kingdom' [1995] Consum LJ 24, 27.

inclusion of business as well as private litigants in this sample.[15] In terms of fairness, reactions vary with whether a party was successful, although nearly half of those who lost their cases thought the proceedings were fair. Litigant satisfaction in the Scottish research could not be explained entirely by whether they had won or not. The overwhelming majority of litigants praised the sheriffs for their fairness, irrespective of the outcome of cases.[16] These results accord with the current wisdom that the opportunity to give their grievance a good airing is perceived by litigants as important, if not more important for some, than outcome.[17]

Reform of small claims courts in some jurisdictions has attempted to reduce business claims by limiting the number of suits which can be brought in any period. Suggestions have also been made that a small claims court should have two divisions, one for business and one for individuals, and that the facility of the former should be confined to businessmen not guilty of shady or unlawful practices. However, heavy use of small claims courts by business claimants is not necessarily at the expense of individual litigants. Extensive American research in the 1970s examined 15 small claims courts in a variety of jurisdictions. It found that permitting collection agencies as plaintiffs greatly increased the courts' work-load but there was no relationship between that and individual filing rates per 1,000 population. Indeed the authors argued that when collection cases are filed in the ordinary way outside the small claims jurisdiction, lay people cannot defend without a lawyer and therefore many meritorious defences are overlooked.[18] More recent American research came to the same conclusion. It examined small claims courts in 12 jurisdictions and found that while permitting collection agencies reduced the percentage of cases involving individual plaintiffs, it did not seem to affect individual filings per 1,000 population.[19]

A number of United States jurisdictions and some Australian states have adopted the simplest and most practical solution: businesses have been barred from being claimants in small claims courts. But this approach

15   Touche Ross *Civil Justice Review. Study of the Small Claims Procedure* (London: LCD, 1986) p 24.
16   H Jones, A Platts and J Tombs *Small Claims in the Sheriff Court in Scotland: an Assessment of the Use and Operation of the Procedure* (Scottish Office, 1991) p 110.
17   T Tyler 'What is procedural justice? Criteria used by citizens to assess the fairness of legal procedures' (1988) 22 Law & Soc R 104; W O'Barr et al 'Law expectations of the civil justice system' (1988) 22 Law & Soc R 131.
18   J Ruhnka, S Weller *Small Claims Courts. A National Examination* (National Center for State Courts, 1978) pp 47–50.
19   J Goerdt *Small Claims and Traffic Courts* (National Center for State Courts, 1992) pp 45–46. See also N Vidmar 'The Small Claims Court: A Reconceptualization of Disputes and an Empirical Investigation' (1984) Law & Society R 515; I Ramsay 'Small Claims Courts in Canada' in C Whelan (ed) *Small Claims Courts* (Clarendon, 1990) p 29.

still has the difficulty that businesses can pursue judgments against consumers in other courts, although there may be some attrition of claims because of higher initial costs and closer scrutiny of claims. If a judgment is obtained the costs to an unsuccessful defendant consumer may be greater than if the case were heard in a small claims court. A solution would seem to be to devise some procedure whereby cases in which consumers have not paid for some valid reason are transferred into the small claims court. A solution would seem to be to devise some procedure whereby cases in which consumers have not paid for some valid reason are transferred into the small claims track. The most radical proposal is that businesses should be barred completely from pursuing through any court, small claims court or otherwise, any claim associated with products supplied on credit at the retail level.[20] Professor Ison justifies this reform on three main grounds: (1) by enforcing claims of credit grantors the courts are assisting businesses engaged in disreputable trading practices; (2) it is unfair that the legal system should allow retailers to pursue their claims when consumers have great difficulty in doing the same; and (3) businesses achieve satisfactory payment in the vast majority of cases. To ensure repayment, Ison argues, businesses would have a greater incentive to exclude the poorer risks from the outset and could also use sanctions such as an adverse credit report against non-payers.

Apart from the political problems of excluding business claimants now that the small claims jurisdiction has permitted them for over 25 years, research elsewhere casts some cold water on the theory that their presence deters individual litigants. What is important in encouraging individuals to use the procedure are a range of factors, such as its public image and the assistance individuals can obtain in framing and pursuing a claim. It does seem that there is a greater awareness of the small claims procedure than there was when *Simple Justice* reported widespread ignorance in 1979. In a very small research sample taken in south-west England, it was found that only two people had never heard of it and the majority (26) gave a broadly accurate description of its function.[1]

The small claims track in England and Wales attempts to discourage legal representation through the rule that legal costs cannot normally be recovered from the other party where the amount at stake is less than the limit.[2] It seems doubtful whether the cost sanction in claims for less than this deters those who have the money and think that they will be successful

---

[20]   TG Ison 'Small Claims' (1972) 35 MLR 18, 24–26; TG Ison *Credit Marketing and Consumer Protection* (Croom Helm, 1979) pp 284–289.

[1]   M Blacksell, K Economides, C Watkins *Justice Outside the City, Access to Legal Services in Rural Britain* (Longman, 1991) p 151.

[2]   CPR 1998, r 27.14.

if they are represented. Road traffic accident cases frequently involve representation for one or other parties, funded by an insurance company or under legal expenses insurance.[3] Certainly, larger businesses have every reason to employ legal representation because it is a matter of routine and an ordinary business expense. In Baldwin's research, one in 50 small claims hearings had both parties represented, but in his 1996 research this had risen to one in four. The increase seems confined to road traffic accident cases.[4] In any event, Baldwin found the effect of representation problematic: in the majority of cases the district judges either side-lined legal representatives or preserved their interventionist role. In the Touche Ross research solicitors acted at hearings in 30% of cases for one party (in 12% for the plaintiff and in 27% for the defendant), and in 9% of cases for both parties. Solicitors were more likely the larger the claim and the larger the claimant.[5]

If representation is unnecessary in small claims there seems no reason why it should not be barred completely. The alternative of providing legal representation for consumers engaged in small claims would seem to be too costly. Some North American and Australian jurisdictions bar legal representation in small claims courts. The rationale is that lawyers mean longer, more costly and formal hearings and that they perpetuate inequalities if employed by one party only. Access to justice for individuals might be compromised since those who cannot afford lawyers will be deterred from suing. Denying legal representation really only affects businesses, because at present, consumer claimants are rarely represented.

Research suggests, however, albeit not unequivocally, that a ban on legal representation might be unnecessary so long as other steps are taken to assist the unrepresented litigant. Thus the leading American research found, surprisingly, that a sizeable number of litigants sought legal advice for small claims, even if they were not represented at the hearing. The proportion who consulted a lawyer increased significantly as the amount of claim increased. The poor were as likely to see a lawyer as the better off. The research concluded that the great failing of the system was for the unrepresented defendant, who did as badly when facing an unrepresented as a represented plaintiff.[6] The follow-up study by the National Center for State Courts found that representation at trial by a lawyer was not a statistically significant correlate of success at trial after

3   D Greenslade, 'Small Claims Arbitration and the Solicitor' (1996) 146 NLJ 118, 120.
4   J Baldwin 'Increasing the Small Claims Limit' (1998) 148 NLJ 274.
5   Touche Ross Civil Justice Review. Study of the Small Claims Procedure (London: LCD, 1986) Table 12.
6   J Ruhnka, S Weller Small Claims Courts. A National Examination (National Center for State Courts, 1978) p 194.

controlling for other independent variables. (In courts that allowed lawyers at the hearing 26% of hearings involved a lawyer; both parties had a lawyer in only 2% of cases.) The strongest correlates of whether a plaintiff won (at least in part) were case type and defendant type. As to the former plaintiffs in debt collection cases won more; as to the latter, plaintiffs suing individuals tended to win cases more. While on the bare statistics it appeared that both plaintiffs and defendants enhanced their chance of winning by 11–13% with a lawyer at trial, controlling for these other factors eliminated the advantage and supported the policy prescription of the earlier research.[7]

There can clearly be an inequality of representation in small claims cases where an inarticulate, unrepresented consumer is opposed by an experienced and knowledgeable businessperson. Some redressing of this imbalance was to be afforded by s 11 of the Courts and Legal Services Act 1990, as a result of which lay representatives have rights of audience in many small claims matters.[8] Much depends, however, on the quality, cost and ethical standards of such lay representatives. Lord Woolf recommended that there should be duty representatives from advice agencies at busy courts, and that these should be eligible for public funding.[9] In the absence of representation for the consumer it needs the judge to break away from the adversarial approach normally prevailing in English courts to redress the balance by taking an active inquisitorial role in the proceedings.

From his observations Baldwin found that there were vast differences in judges' interpretation of what it means to be interventionist. He identified four different approaches to the conduct of hearings: 'going for the jugular' (identifying the central issues at an early stage); 'hearing the parties'; 'passive' (talking to each of the parties like a solicitor interviewing clients); and 'mediatory' (encouraging the parties to agree their own solution). However, he also found that there is now widespread acceptance of the desirability of the interventionalist role and that hearings are conducted in a pragmatic, down to earth manner. Significantly he concluded that in terms of providing a forum in which the ordinary lay person can function reasonably effectively, the district judges can be said to score highly. In his 'Access to Justice' inquiry, Lord Woolf emphasised the need for an active judiciary.

---

[7] J Goerdt *Small Claims and Traffic Courts* (National Center for State Courts, 1992) pp 55–56.

[8] The Lay Representatives (Rights of Audience) Order 1992, SI 1992/1966. See F Zemans 'The Non-Lawyer as a Means of Providing Legal Services' in R Evans and M Trebilcock (eds) *Lawyers and the Consumer Interest* (1982) pp 283–284.

[9] See especially *Access to Justice. Interim Report on the Civil Justice System in England and Wales by Lord Woolf* (1995) Chapters 16–17.

'The role of the judge in small claims is not only that of an adjudicator. It is a key safeguard of the rights of both parties. In most cases, the judge is effectively a substitute for a legal representative. His duty is to ascertain the main matters at issue, to elicit the evidence, to reach a view on the facts of the matter and to give a decision. In some cases he may encourage the parties to settle. In doing so he should ensure that both parties have presented the evidence and called the witnesses germane to their case and that he has identified and considered any issue of law which is pertinent to the case in hand. He must also hold the ring and ensure that each party has a fair chance to present his own case and to challenge that of his opponent.'[10]

Since Baldwin's research was completed the new Civil Procedure Rules have been introduced and the judges have been retrained in the management of cases, which is now part of the 'overriding objective' of the civil justice system generally, not just small claims. This reorientation of civil procedure may result in future empirical research finding more uniform and more satisfactory management of cases by judges.

Enforcement is a recurrent problem with small claims: litigants find that having surmounted the many obstacles to obtaining a successful judgment they cannot collect it. In 1996 a National Audit Office survey found that nearly 40% of those who obtained judgment did not recover; and in his report Baldwin found that many small claims claimants had such a bad experience of enforcement that they would think twice about using the procedure gain.[11] In the United States collection rates range from a low of 25–75%.[12] In the Scottish small claims research half of lay advisers said that enforcement problems were commonplace and court staff noted that they were not infrequently asked for advice by successful pursuers on how to begin enforcement proceedings.[13] The Touche Ross report noted that 'it was apparent from the litigant interviews that one of the grounds for dissatisfaction with the system was the inability to secure payment of the award in some cases'.[14] Even in Northern Ireland, where enforcement is through the Enforcement of Judgments Office, enforcement remains a major weakness from the individual litigant's point of view. In particular the enforcement fees are said to be too high, especially since litigants are already at a financial loss.[15] The normative effects of small claims judgments

---

[10]   *Access to Justice. Final Report by the Rt Hon Lord Woolf* (HMSO, 1996) p 108.

[11]   J Baldwin 'Enforcing Small Claims Judgments' (1997) 7 Consumer Policy R 194.

[12]   E Clark 'Recent Research on Small Claims Courts and Tribunals: Implications for Evaluators' (1992) 1 JJA 103, 122.

[13]   H Jones, A Platts and J Tombs *Small Claims in the Sheriff Court in Scotland: an Assessment of the Use and Operation of the Procedure* (Scottish Office, 1991)

[14]   Touche Ross *Civil Justice Review. Study of the Small Claims Procedure* (London: LCD, 1986) p 16.

[15]   General Consumer Council for Northern Ireland *How to Make Small More Beautiful* (Belfast, 1992) pp 43–44, 51.

may be enhanced by new rules introduced in 1999 to the effect that small claims arbitrations are no longer to be in private, creating a potential for newspapers to report the outcomes of actions by consumers against traders, with a concomitant threat to the trader's reputation (CPR 1998, r 39.2).

5   NEW MECHANISMS FOR IMPLEMENTING PRIVATE LAW RIGHTS

Further reform is likely as the Lord Chancellor's Department is consulting on introducing similar rights to appeal as exist in ordinary civil legislation.[16] What is needed if private law rights are to be adequately enforced is to ensure that worthwhile claims are initiated and ultimately get to court if necessary. Consumer education is one way of ensuring that individual consumers are aware of their rights. But institutional reforms are required, because even if consumers know their rights there is no guarantee that they will be acknowledged by businesses. Small claims courts are one such reform. This section looks at two other reforms for ensuring that consumers' private law rights are vindicated through appropriate processes; these are (1) class actions, and (2) alternative dispute resolution mechanisms.

(a)   Class (or multiparty) actions

Class actions enable a number of consumers to have similar complaints determined at one time instead of in separate proceedings. One or two consumers sue on behalf of all the other consumers similarly affected where a business is in breach of the civil law. A successful judgment binds the defendant business as regards all members of the class. The class action thus has an advantage over the test case, which may be ignored with reference to any consumers other than the successful plaintiff. Another advantage over the test case is that the class action limits the ability of a business to avoid an unfavourable precedent by settling with the plaintiff, for settlement of a class action should require court approval. Class actions obviously have advantages in terms of saving time and money over individuals instituting separate proceedings. A number of small claims can be aggregated into an action of some substance, and it becomes easier to cover the legal costs.

Class actions can also attract useful publicity because of the significance and number of people involved. For example, a consumer may sue on behalf of all purchasers of a product or service, alleging that the advertising was false. A deterrent effect on businesses may also result from class actions when they find that their trade practices no longer pass

---

[16]   *June 2000—Access to Justice—Small Claims Appeals: Proposed New Procedures* (LCD, 2000).

unchallenged. A dishonest trader may not be overly sensitive about adverse publicity surrounding litigation against it. But an action that poses a potential liability towards a class possibly numbering hundreds or even thousands is another matter. A threat of this magnitude may well provide the check that will stop the business from carrying out its plans. Class actions can also have an important psychological effect on consumers and can provide an incentive for the formation or continuation of consumer groups.

(i)   A rule for class (multiparty) litigation

At least four principles should underline any rule for class (multiparty) actions. The first is that the rule should be comprehensive, covering all potential class litigation from consumer claims, through public law matters, to the disaster actions. Elsewhere, especially the United States, there is some debate about whether the so-called mass torts (disaster litigation) sit comfortably alongside other class actions. Consequently, it is said by some that there ought to be a set of different, substance based rules for different kinds of class actions. However, one comprehensive rule seems the better approach, although it should give sufficient flexibility to the courts to establish an appropriate structure for the litigation. In some cases solving the generic issue will allow the remainder of the actions to be resolved. In other cases, however, such as pharmaceutical negligence cases, where individual issues of causation are crucial, this approach may not work. Then it may be that a test or lead case provides a superior approach, so long as this is an efficient way of using judicial resources.

The second general principle is that the rule should provide for sufficient discretion for the creative handling of different matters, but not unbridled discretion which can lead to inconsistencies and injustices. The last thing wanted is satellite litigation on whether the rule has been properly applied. At the same time there must be confidence in its predictable application over time, and between different courts. The rule must identify the criteria which ought to be taken into account, although it should eschew the mandatory exercise of discretion. Thirdly, the rule must be informed by the principle of court control. In one sense this is self evident, but the United States' experience serves as a reminder that the courts must be forever vigilant about managing multiparty litigation, even when it appears to be over. For example, the problems with class settlements have already been mentioned: it would appear that some United States courts could have exercised greater control over settlement proposals, which were really in the interests of the lawyer and a limited number of class members rather than the class as a whole. Early and continuous case management and court control are essential to a satisfactory handling of multiparty litigation.

Finally, the rule must allow for an accommodation to the interests of court efficiency on the one hand, and individual justice on the other. The days of giving parties the licence to run litigation as they will, without concern for others, are numbered. Promoting access to justice for the many means limiting the complete autonomy of the few. So too with class litigation: if it is to work at a pragmatic level it is clear that the interests of the group as a whole must sometimes prevail. In other words, the individual justice which the courts normally strive for in our system must be qualified. The justification is that without class litigation, many members of the group would not have obtained access to justice in the first place. Similarly, attempts by defendants to conduct litigation by attrition must be curbed— appealing every interlocutory matter, discovering huge numbers of irrelevant documents and generally seeking to wear down the plaintiffs are examples.

(ii)   Multiparty litigation procedures in England and Wales

It has become the convention to classify class (multiparty) litigation as involving consumer and environmental claims on the one hand and disasters on the other. The consumer claim and environmental claim as concepts are fairly self-evident. Disasters are subdivided into 'sudden disasters', which result when a number of persons are affected by the same accident or catastrophe, and 'creeping disasters', where similar claims for losses are attributable to a single cause such as a defective drug, but incurred at different times and in different circumstances.[17] So far class litigation in Britain has mainly involved disasters. Funding has been available through legal aid to enable lawyers to act for groups affected by either sudden or creeping disasters. Consequently, it is not surprising that the debate has focused on this type of class action, and in particular on its continued and better financing. While disasters are an important aspect of multiparty litigation, they are only part of the story.

The history of class actions in Britain can be traced back to the asbestosis and silicosis cases of the 1960s. The plaintiffs in this litigation had the advantage of trade union support and both sides accepted the result of the test cases brought. The thalidomide affair led to a block fund settlement for victims, and that was followed by the Eraldin drug cases. Then in the 1980s there were a serious of disasters—leading to large class litigation—such as the Piper Alpha oil platform tragedy, several air crashes and more drug related injuries.[18] Though it has been possible to handle

[17]   Eg *Group Actions: Learning from Opren* (NCC, 1989).
[18]   See M Day, P Balen, G McCool *Multi-Party Actions* (LAG, 1995) and C Barker, I Willock, J McManus *Multi-Party Actions in Scotland* (The Scottish Office Central Research Unit, 1994), both of which contain details of the various cases.

such disaster litigation within the context of the old rules,[19] following the Woolf report the LCD has introduced new rules on multiparty litigation, which are informed by a number of basic principles.[20] First the rules confer a general power to make appropriate orders at any stage in the class action and specific provision on a number of matters. There are three basic mechanisms for pursuit of class actions.

The first possibility at present is the representative action. This had its origins in Chancery and is now provided for in the Civil Procedure Rules 1998 (r 19.6). This provides that where numerous persons have the same interest in any proceedings, these may be by one or more of those persons representing the whole group. A judgment or order obtained in representative proceedings is binding on all. (The rule also applies to representative defendants, although this discussion concentrates on the representative plaintiff.) For a long period the rule was stifled by the *Markt* case,[21] which reasoned that if members of a group were seeking damages, each could not have the same interest in the proceedings. On this interpretation of the rule it would not apply to all the consumers who purchased a particular type of car with the same fault, since each consumer would have a separate contract with a different retailer, and would have a separate claim for damages, although the contractual terms in each case might be identical. This narrow approach is probably no longer the law,[1] but the experience here and in comparable jurisdictions is that there are definite limits to the weight the rule can bear.[2]

There are a number of drawbacks to representative actions. The first is that the representative plaintiff is in charge of the proceedings and may conduct, settle or discontinue them in whatever way he or she pleases. The court does not have any particular control over the representative plaintiff or over his or her lawyers. Members of the class might have to be

---

[19]   See *Guide for Use in Group Actions* (Working Party of the Supreme Court Procedure Committee, May 1991); M Mildred 'Group Actions Present and Future' [1994] J Personal Injury Lit 276. A new rule is proposed for such cases: *Access to Justice. Multiparty Situations: Proposed New Procedures. A Consultation paper* (Lord Chancellor's Department, 1997).

[20]   Of particular importance are: *Access to Justice. Final Report by the Rt Hon Lord Woolf* (HMSO, 1996) Chapter 17; Scottish Law Commission *Multi-Party Actions: Report by Working Party* (1993); *Multi-Party Actions: Court Proceedings and Funding*, DP 98 (1994). See also *Group Actions Made Easier. A Report of the Law Society's Civil Litigation Committee* (1995).

[21]   *Markt & Co Ltd v Knight Steamship Co Ltd* [1910] 2 KB 1021.

[1]   *Irish Shipping Ltd v Commercial Union Assurance Co plc* [1991] 2 QB 206.

[2]   *Foskett v McKeown* [1997] 3 All ER 392 involved an order appointing the plaintiff as representative of all purchasers of land in an unsuccessful development. See *Carnie v Esanda Finance Corpn Ltd* (1995) 69 ALJR 206 (High Court of Australia). See D Kell 'Renewed Life for the Representative Action' (1995) 13 Aust Bar R 95; C Dabezies 'The Representative Order—A Form of Class Action?' Legal Action, September 1998, p 28.

listed, although they need not have notice of the proceedings. Perhaps even more importantly, the representative plaintiff has sole responsibility for costs: even though the class as a whole may benefit, they have no obligation to make any contribution.

Secondly, it is possible to issue a claim on behalf of a number of claimants, which can be followed by one statement of claim setting out the parts common to all, with a separate schedule setting out the allegations peculiar to each. Under the Civil Procedure Rules this is referred to as a Group Litigation Order (GLO) (r 19.11). A GLO involves the establishment of a register of claimants for 'the case management of claims which give rise to common or related issues of fact or law (the "GLO issues")'. Clearly for there to be a class action there must be an identifiable group. Lord Woolf recommended against specifying the number in the rule. Rather, the court would only certify a class action if this was the preferable procedure for the fair and efficient resolution of common issues. The number of parties would obviously enter this equation. Subgroups could be constituted. For certification the claims of the parties must raise common issues, although there is a divergence between jurisdictions as to whether these common issues must predominate over issues affecting only individual members. In the British Columbian legislation this is only one of the factors taken into account in determining whether a class proceeding would be the preferable procedure for the fair and efficient resolution of the common issues, along with whether a significant number of the members of the group have a valid interest in individually controlling the prosecution of separate actions; whether the proceeding would involve claims that are or have been the subject of any other proceedings; whether other means of resolving the claims are less practical or less efficient; and whether the administration of the class proceeding would create greater difficulties than those likely to be experienced if relief were sought by other means.

Just as it is important to identify the group by means of certification on the register, it is equally important that individuals can request to be removed from the register and this is provided for in r 19.14. Class action rules in other jurisdictions tend to adopt an 'opt out' approach, so that a person's rights may be determined in a class action without his or her express consent to or participation in the litigation.[3] Members of the group may, however, opt out. If they opt out, a person is not able to benefit from any award of damages, although they may always bring a separate action.

---

[3]   The approach is under rule 23 in the US, and in Ontario, British Columbia and Australia. Lord Woolf says either opt in or opt out may be appropriate, depending on the circumstances: *Access to Justice. Final Report by the Rt Hon Lord Woolf* (HMSO, 1996) p 236. However, the Scottish Law Commission has suggested as a provisional view an opt in approach: Scottish Law Commission *Multi-Party Actions: Report by Working Party* (1993) p 192.

The disadvantage of an opt in provision is obviously that, as a practical matter, many who qualify for class membership through reasons of ignorance, unfamiliarity with the law or timidity, may not take the affirmative step of sending to court a request for class membership. For personal injury claims, however, an opt out scheme may be unfair to defendants unless they know the number of claims and their nature. This problem is overcome, however, by requiring that a register be established and imposing cut-off dates for membership of a class, although those seeking to place their name on the register late would not necessarily be precluded from doing so.[4] This would depend on factors such as their knowledge of the proceedings, the stage the proceedings have reached, the impact on the proceedings of their joining late and whether they are under a disability. In any event, even if not joined up late, their claims could be held as pending until the outcome of any trial on liability or a second group might be formed.

The 'opt out' approach obviously means that a group member has liberty to discontinue or settle his or her case at any time. There is one caveat to this freedom, which is that the court must have power to vet opt out cases where generic issues are to be decided. Otherwise the smooth resolution of the group litigation could be disrupted. There are suggestions from the United States that in some cases persons are opting out from class actions because they are using it as a bargaining tool against the rest of the group. Particularly worrying is the suggestion that opting out is being recommended by lawyers in order to secure themselves higher contingent fees.[5] It seems that as an unintentional result of several court decisions, if a judgment in a class action is favourable, the self-excluded class member can secure a judgment against the defendant without any effort, expense or risk. If the class action is unsuccessful, nothing prevents the opted out member bringing a separate action since he or she is not bound by the class action result.[6] Not only is this unfair on other members of the group, it also disadvantages defendants. They are benefited by group actions which are fair and consolidate similar claims, but not if those opting out can later claim damages. There is also the increased burden on judicial resources. Opting out with the prospect of bringing a subsequent individual suit exposes the defendant to multiple judgments, filed virtually cost free by former group members. In the absence of contingent fees, and given that much class litigation in England will

---

[4]   See CPR 1998, Practice Direction 19B, para 13.

[5]   J Coffee 'The Regulation of Entrepreneurial Litigation: Balancing Fairness and Efficiency in the Large Class Action' (1987) 54 U Chi LR 877, 911.

[6]   M Friedman 'Constrained individualism in group litigation' (1990) 100 Yale LJ 745, 754.

continue to be legally aided, and therefore subject to controls by the Legal Services Commission, it may be that excessive concern about this type of opting out is misplaced.

For example, take a class action where there are many consumer claims, each of which is small. There is little to recommend in a rule making notice to each potential claimant mandatory. The costs of identifying potential claimants, and preparing and sending the notice will make the litigation as a whole uneconomic. In any event, where such claimants receive the notice and choose to opt out, they will receive nothing. Because with small claims it is uneconomic for them to litigate individually, they will almost invariably remain members of the group. In the United States, in small claims group actions, very few of the tens of thousands—in some cases millions—of potential plaintiffs actually notified choose to opt out.[7] Accordingly, courts must have the discretion to dispense with notice enabling parties to opt out having regard to factors such as the cost, the nature of the relief, the size of individual claims, the number of members of a group, the chances that members will wish to opt out and so on.

Once the claims become more substantial, however, individual notice is economically possible. It is difficult to set a figure and the matter must be left to judicial discretion, taking into account the factors previously mentioned. Yet even if the court decides that notice must be given to members of a group, it should have a discretion as to how this is to be done—individual notification, advertising, media broadcast, notification to a sample group, or a combination of means, or different means for different members of the group.

Under Rule 23(d) in the United States, a federal court has the power to appoint the lawyers for the litigation. Thus the courts approve the appointment of a lead lawyer for a class. If a plaintiff's suggested lawyer does not demonstrate the necessary experience or resources to prosecute an action, the courts have refused to appoint him or her as lead counsel.[8] Lead lawyers may be given an authority to conduct the litigation to the exclusion of other lawyers. They generally co-ordinate discovery, employ experts and arrange for support services. They also play a significant role in settlement: indeed they may even propose a settlement to the court without obtaining the approval of every lawyer, although a failure to communicate and consult is a ground for a court to reject a settlement. The federal courts have interpreted Rule 23 to give them a power to appoint a steering or plaintiffs' committee of lawyers. They will have the authority to conduct the litigation. Moreover, courts have awarded compensation

---

[7]   J Macey and G Miller 'The plaintiffs' attorney's case in class actions and derivative litigation' (1991) 58 U Chi LR 1, 28.

[8]   Eg *Cullen v New York State Civil Serv Comm'n* 566 F 2d 846, 847 (2d Cir 1977).

for their additional work, for example by ordering each lawyer not active in the committee to pay the lead lawyers part of his or her fee. In many cases in England, the Legal Services Commission will have identified and appointed a lead lawyer for a class action, since class actions will often be legally aided.

Pre-action disclosure may be especially appropriate to class actions since it could lead to a significant saving in costs if the idea of proceedings is consequently abandoned. The courts have already demonstrated a commendable flexibility to the way disclosure is to be effected in practice in class action proceedings.[9] It may be that disclosure is not appropriate in particular types of cases: thus the British Columbia legislation empowers the court to refuse discovery depending on the stage of the proceedings and the issues to be determined at that particular stage, whether the disclosure is necessary in view of the defences of the party seeking it, the approximate monetary value of individual claims, if any, and whether it would result in oppression or in undue annoyance, burden or expense for the group members sought to be discovered. Restrictions on normal discovery have already been imposed in class actions in this country.[10]

Already mentioned has been the concern in the United States with class action settlements—the risk of collusion between lawyers and between lawyers and class representatives to the detriment of the group as a whole. Clearly the way lawyers are paid is an important incentive for abuse: contingent fees come out of any award the plaintiffs obtain. Lawyers could rationally want settlement, even though there is a good chance of a higher award at trial, since their fees may be proportionately greater in terms of the work done than they would be after trial—quite apart from the fact that if they are unsuccessful at trial they obtain nothing. In weighing the chances of no fee or a higher fee after trial, on the one hand, against the certainty of a guaranteed fee on settlement on the other, plaintiff lawyers on a contingent fee have a strong incentive to settle. While there may be special reasons for a concern about class action settlements in the United States, court scrutiny seems justified in any event when all members of the group are to be bound by the settlement. One difficulty facing the courts will be a lack of information. When the parties have agreed a settlement the courts will have a natural reluctance to interfere, especially since they may have little independent access to information which will enable them to test the settlement.[11]

In the United States there is less financial risk for someone initiating a class action, since each party bears its own costs and lawyers work for

9   *Davies v Eli Lilly & Co* [1987] 1 WLR 1136.
10   *Chrzanowska v Glaxo Laboratories* (1990) Independent, 12 March.
11   See W Schwarzer 'Settlement of Mass Tort Class Actions: Order Out of Chaos?' (1995) 80 Cornell LR 837.

contingency fees. This is not the case in England, where the general rule is that legal costs are paid by the unsuccessful party. Consequently, in many situations no claimant would have the financial incentive to institute a class action, because of the possibility of having to pay the other party's costs as well if unsuccessful. Accordingly, under a class action procedure in England there is merit in the court being able to exercise a discretion that each party bear its own costs. For example, Ontario's Class Proceedings Act provides that the court in exercising its discretion with respect to costs may consider whether the class proceeding 'was a test case, raised a novel point of law or involved a matter of public interest' (s 31(1)). Thus in *Garland v Consumers' Gas Co*[12] the court denied costs to a successful defendant where the case met all of the criteria spelled out in s 1(1), ie it was a test case, raised a novel point of law and involved a matter of public interest. The action was against Consumers Gas for the restitution of some $112 million representing late payment penalties alleged to have been paid. It was dismissed on summary judgment. Moreover, the court should be able to decide that costs need not be borne equally within the group. Thirdly, in some cases it will be fair that the group as a whole bear a proportionate share of the costs. This was the approach in the well known decision involving the drug Opren.[13] However, this approach cannot be adopted as an invariable rule for class litigation. In the Opren litigation the plaintiff's legal advisers hoped that the lead cases could be chosen from those legally aided plaintiffs with nil contribution. When the Court of Appeal held that costs should be borne equally amongst all plaintiffs, the privately funded clients would have discontinued because of the threat which costs posed to them, although a private benefactor agreed to underwrite their costs and the case was soon after settled without trial.

Class actions involving personal injuries such as the pharmaceutical cases, have continued to be funded by legal aid. Legal aid procedures have been tightened, however, as a result of the benzodiazepine litigation, which involved an expenditure of legal aid funds of some £30–35m. Some 93% of plaintiffs were legally aided and initially around 13,000 legal aid certificates were granted, but the litigation later collapsed. In response the Legal Aid Board introduced class action regulations in 1992 to enable it to enter into contracts with solicitors to undertake generic work in personal injury class actions. The idea is for basic issues to be thoroughly investigated before massive expenditure is incurred. The Legal Aid Board is now proposing additional arrangements in relation to the funding aspects of such cases.[14] Another suggestion is for a class action fund, which

[12]   (1995) 22 OR (3d) 451, 767.
[13]   *Davies v Eli Lilly & Co* [1987] 1 WLR 1136.
[14]   Legal Aid Board *Issues Arising for the Legal Aid Board and the Lord Chancellor's Department from Multi-party Actions* (1994).

would be started initially by government, but then subsequently funded by a percentage levy on successful litigations. A precedent is Ontario's 'class proceedings fund', funded by the Law Foundation of Canada. The fund is to provide financial support for plaintiffs to class proceedings in respect of disbursements—not legal costs generally—related to the proceedings, and for payments to defendants in respect of costs awards made in their favour against plaintiffs who have received financial support from the fund. The principal advantages of such a fund are that it would be entitled to assist all class litigations, not just those with incomes low enough to qualify for legal aid.

The effect of a GLO in England and Wales is that any judgments on GLO issues are binding on the parties to all the other claims on the group register, unless the court orders otherwise (CPR 1998, r 19.12).

The third possibility is that in some situations a claimant may launch an action which effectively determines an issue. The individual who obtains an injunction, say, against a product hazard benefits all those who may have been affected by it, even though they have nothing to do with the legal action. However, there will not be a similar beneficial effect from a decision in favour of one person seeking damages, even for those with the same or a very similar claim, unless the defendant will agree that the case will be a test case in relation, say, to liability for all those claimants in the same position. In high profile cases the weight of government or public opinion may force a defendant to treat one case as a test case binding it in relation to others. (A court may strike out as an abuse of process a case which attempts to relitigate a point determined in a lead action, but to avoid disputes it is better for there to be express orders in advance of the trial of the lead actions that all will be bound by the results.) Moreover, with a test case it is also necessary to overcome the problem of funding the case—as a matter of law it is only persons to the litigation who have any responsibility as to costs. In the absence of agreement the legal burden will fall on the named litigants. There are also problems if the test case turns out to be atypical—if it is disposed of on particular grounds or if the judgment is couched in such a way that it leaves undetermined the similar issues in other cases. The court can order that group litigation proceeds as a test claim, and has power to substitute cases where the initial test case is settled (CPR 1998, r 19.15).

(iii)   Class (multiparty) rules elsewhere

The reform of the multiparty litigation rules in England and Wales has followed the earlier lead of some other common law jurisdictions which have introduced new rules in an attempt to handle class (multiparty) litigation more efficiently. This experience is important because of the novelty of the English rules introduced in 2000. The United States has been to the fore and so some discussion of their federal class action rules is inevitable. (Class action rules at state level are not dealt with here.) There has been some discussion elsewhere in Europe about class actions.[15] Jurisdictions in Canada and Australia, with rules of court and procedures closer to those in England, have followed.

Rule 23 of the United States Federal Rules of Civil Procedure authorises class actions. The rule has been used to bring an enormous number of cases, ranging from consumer and environmental claims, through mass accident litigation, to investors' actions and equal opportunities claims. Rule 23(a) establishes four prerequisites to maintaining a class action: that the number of people in the class are too numerous to permit ordinary joinder; that members of the class share common questions of law or fact; that the claims or defences of the representative parties are typical of the claims or defences of the class; and that the representative parties will fairly and adequately protect the interests of the class. Once the demands of section (a) are satisfied, the party requesting class certification must demonstrate compliance with one of the three subdivisions found in section (b). Litigants may maintain suits under sections (b)(1) and (b)(2) where separate actions might result in judgments subjecting the party opposing the class to inconsistent standards of conduct, resulting either from conflicting injunctions or from an inability to satisfy all claimants when money damages are at issue.

Rule 23(b)(3) is mainly available where class litigation involves claims for damages. Here the additional prerequisites to be satisfied are whether it would be convenient and desirable for a class action and whether questions common to the class predominate over the questions affecting individual members. The first issue goes to the manageability of the class action and for a time was used by judges to refuse certificates simply because their courts were overloaded. Whether the group aspects predominate obviously depends on the circumstances. In some actions the breach of contract or tort affecting many may be the same, so that the common issues predominate, even if each member of the class suffers a distinct loss.

The rules demand that the court give 'the best notice practicable under all the circumstances', including individual notice to all class members 'who can be identified through reasonable effort'. This is at the expense of the claimant and is an obvious deterrent to litigation where each individual claim is small. However, a court may require advertisement if it is not possible through 'reasonable effort' to give individual notice.

---

[15]   Eg T Bourgoiginie (ed) *Group Actions and Consumer Protection* (Story Scientia, 1992).

There are several important matters which arise from the experience with rule 23 in the United States over a number of decades. The first is the suitability of the rule for all types of multiparty litigation. The rule was never intended to apply to what are now called mass torts, ie personal injury litigation arising out of the sudden or creeping disasters as described above.[16] One strand of thought uses this as a justification for treating mass torts separately—perhaps by consolidation, test cases and so on. To fit mass torts within rule 23 leads, it is said, to insuperable management difficulties, as well as undermining the individual's rights to a separate trial and individualised compensation. There is also the issue as to whether as a matter of law mass torts can be fitted within the terms of rule 23. On the other hand, there is another strand of opinion which sees rule 23 as the most readily available tool for handling mass torts outside of insolvency. In fact class actions have been certified in mass tort cases such as Agent Orange, the Dalkon Shield and the breast implant cases. Individual action, in this view, is inefficient, wasteful and impractical. Even when consolidated—in other words using other than a class action—there are limits to how many separate claims supported by different evidence can be decided by the one jury. Moreover, mass torts do present common issues which are resolvable under rule 23.[17] Since classes are typically certified under rule 23 for settlement—the so-called settlement class— there is no need to address the issue of judicial authority under the rule.

This issue of the settlement class raises another important issue. At one level since rule 23 does not contain any criteria for approving a settlement, there is a good argument that it should. It has been suggested that, in the absence of such criteria, courts have been presented with cases of settlement which have been in the interests of the lawyers, and possibly some class members, and at the expense of the class as a whole. Recent legislation in the United States has expressed a concern with class action abuse. However, it is confined to a very limited area—multiparty litigation in actions by investors who claim that false statements had been made in the promotion of shares and other securities. In brief the legislation limits lawyers' fees in class actions, prohibits bonus payments by plaintiffs' lawyers to named plaintiffs, lays out procedures to choose a lead plaintiff, requires plaintiff certification of the complaint, and improves settlement

---

[16] See eg W Schwarzer 'Settlement of Mass Tort Class Actions: Order Out of Chaos? (1995) 80 Cornell LR 837.

[17] D Rosenberg, 'Class actions for mass torts: doing individual justice by collective means' (1987) 62 Ind LJ 561.

notices to class members.[18] The primary concern, which motivated the legislation, was of meritless 'strike suits' being promoted by lawyers when a company's stock declined. It was said that these strike suits were discouraging the raising of capital, especially in high-tech, but risky, industries. High on the agenda of complaints was that legal actions were being promoted by lawyers in order to extort settlements—of which lawyers would receive a substantial percentage. Critics of the legislation argued that the judiciary already had the authority to throw such actions out of court. President Clinton, whose veto of the legislation was overridden, said that it could erect so high a barrier to bringing legal actions that even the most aggrieved investors with the most powerful losses might be thrown out of court before they had a chance to prove their case.

There are a number of lessons to be learnt from the United States experience. Firstly, it seems fair to say that rule 23 has facilitated a range of litigation, both in the sense of encouraging certain claims which would never have been brought, but also in handling efficiently litigation of a multiparty character which, because of the issues at stake, would probably have found entry into the federal courts anyhow, by a separate route. Secondly, rule 23 may not provide all the answers, and there is considerable debate over whether mass torts sit easily within its confines. However, there is much to be said for the view that the need for judicial economy demands class action treatment for most mass torts. Thirdly, there is a potential for abuse in multiparty litigation, although the focus of concern in the United States has been on 'strike suits' on behalf of investors, a type of litigation largely unknown elsewhere. This third point underlines the needs for strong court control of class action litigation, in particular of settlements.

Quebec has had class action proceedings for some time, but it seems more relevant to focus on Canadian common law jurisdictions. The Ontario Class Proceedings Act came into effect in January 1993 and already there has been a considerable body of litigation under it. There have been

---

[18]   Private Securities Litigation Reform Act of 1995. There is some empirical evidence: J Aledander 'Do the Merits Matter? A Study of Settlements in Securities Class Actions' (1991) 43 Stan LR 497; R Romano 'The Shareholder Suit: Litigation Without Foundation'(1991) 7 J Law Econ & Organ 55. An earlier study with similar results is T Jones 'An Empirical Examination of the Resolution of Shareholder Derivative and Class Action Lawsuits' (1981) 60 Boston ULR 542 The tentative conclusion to be drawn from such studies is that in the securities area in the United States, class actions and derivatives suits have been in important respects lawyer-driven. In some cases they may have been without legal merit, but have had a nuisance value which has led defendants to settle. Even in cases with legal merit, plaintiff lawyers might have settled for relatively low amounts, so long as they obtained their fees.

consumer cases as well as disaster and investor disputes. There are important divergences in the legislation from the recommendations of the Ontario Law Reform Commission *Report on Class Actions*.[19] For example, the Act requires mandatory certification of a class action without any reference to whether the common predominate over the individual issues. However, the Divisional Court in Ontario has reintroduced this approach back into the Act.[1] British Columbia's Class Proceedings Act 1995 is too recently introduced for any definite conclusions to be drawn. Class actions are now possible in the Federal Court in Australia (as well as at state level). As in Ontario their introduction followed a report of a law commission: the Australian Law Reform Commission argued that class actions would enhance access to justice and gave examples, including consumer matters, where it believed that would occur.[2] The Federal Court Act was amended in 1991, although it does not seem to have been used a great deal. This may reflect the specialised jurisdiction of the Federal Court of Australia.

(b)   Alternative dispute resolution and Ombudsman schemes

The term alternative dispute resolution (ADR) refers to a variety of mechanisms for resolving disputes other than by reference to the courts, including 'arbitration, early neutral evaluation, expert determination, mediation, and conciliation.'[3] Ombudsman schemes and the utility regulators and related consumer councils provide more institutionalised mechanisms for informal resolution of disputes (the latter are discussed in Chapter 5).

ADR is said to have advantages in being simpler, cheaper and quicker than litigation, with less stress to participants and less damage to relationships.[4] But it is not suitable for all disputes, for example where the precedent value of litigation is important. And some forms of ADR are

---

[19]   (Toronto, 1982).

[1]   *Abdool v Anaheim Management Ltd* (1995) 31 CPC (3d) 197.

[2]   *Grouped Proceedings in the Federal Court*, ALRC No 46 (Sydney, 1988). See D Ryan 'The Development of Representative Proceedings in the Federal Court' (1993–94) 11 Aust Bar R 131.

[3]   Lord Chancellor's Department *Alternative Dispute Resolution: A Consultation Paper* (1999).

[4]   Lord Chancellor's Department *Alternative Dispute Resolution: A Consultation Paper* (1999) p 10. See also LCD *ADR Discussion Paper: Summary of Responses* (2000); R Thomas 'Alternative Dispute Resolution—Consumer Disputes' (1988) 7 Civil Justice Quarterly 206.

inappropriate to particular relationships. For example mediation is unlikely to be appropriate where there is a significant imbalance in bargaining power between the parties.[5] These kinds of consideration tend to suggest that arbitration maybe the most appropriate form only for some consumer disputes. A more fundamental critique of the shift towards ADR generally fears that it might provide a form of second class justice in which consumers are disadvantaged.[6] Arbitration schemes are a common part of industry codes of practice, and generally a precondition for approval by the Director General of Fair Trading (discussed in Chapter 2). However Genn's study (completed before the 1999 reform of the Civil Procedure Rules) suggests that the impact of ADR on dispute resolution in the UK has been neglible.[7] Following the 1999 reforms ADR is likely to be resorted to more frequently in consumer disputes, as courts actively channel claimants towards less costly and more effective ways of resolving disputes.

Ombudsmen in the UK were initially confined to the public sector, initially to central and local government, and then expanding to, for example, the health service (in 1974), and prisons (1994).[8] Various forms of the Ombudsman model also now proliferate in the private sector, where both statutory and voluntary schemes have been established covering areas as varied as financial services, lawyers, estate agents and funeral directors.[9] There is no single Ombudsman model, but one generic definition is that an Ombudsman is an independent person or body that can receive complaints, investigate them, and direct or recommend a remedy.[10] Ombudsmen schemes are usually intended to provide a means by which consumers of public and private services can seek redress from a firm, but without having to go to court. The procedures are designed to be more flexible than court procedures, more accessible, and to operate at either a low cost to the applicant, or at no cost at all. Ombudsmen differ from courts in four further

---

[5]   Lord Chancellor's Department *Alternative Dispute Resolution: A Consultation Paper* (1999) p 14.

[6]   M Palmer and S Roberts *Dispute Processes: ADR and the Primary Forms of Decision Making* (Butterworths, 1998) Chapter 2.

[7]   H Genn (with National Centre for Social Research) *Paths to Justice* (Hart Publishing, 1999) 261.

[8]   See further C Harlow and R Rawlings, *Law and Administration* (Butterworths, 2nd edn, 1998) pp 398–401; D Longley and R James, *Administrative Justice: Central Issues in UK and European Administrative Law* (Cavendish Publishing, 1999) pp 47–72.

[9]   R James *Private Ombudsmen and Public Law* (Ashgate, Aldershot, 1997) provides a good study of six private ombudsman schemes. See also A Mowbray 'Ombudsmen—The Private Sector Dimension' in W Finnie et al *Edinburgh Essays in Public Law* (Edinburgh University Press, 1991); D Longley and R James, *Administrative Justice: Central Issues in UK and European Administrative Law* (Cavendish Publishing, 1999) pp 72–94.

[10]   R James *Private Ombudsmen and Public Law* p 3.

important respects. Firstly, the aim of most of the schemes is to produce a conciliated outcome, rather than to declare winners and losers. Secondly, although each Ombusdman varies in the procedures adopted, all follow an inquisitorial model, seeing it as their role to investigate complaints as well as to adjudicate upon them. Most have powers to seek information from those subject to their jurisdiction. Thirdly, decisions are not usually made on the basis of causes of action in private law, but on the basis of what is 'fair and reasonable in all the circumstances', taking into account any codes of practice or industry norms. The schemes thus do not seek to be determinants of legal rights. Finally, schemes vary as to whether or not their decisions are binding on the applicant or the firm being investigated, and on whether their decisions are appealable on point of law to the courts. This latter factor has an effect on the extent to which legal norms intrude into the Ombudsman process, however, even if the Scheme is only subject to judicial review, the operation of that review can have the same effect.[11]

Ombudsmen have been particularly predominant in the area of financial services and have taken a range of forms. There have been separate ombudsmen for banking, insurance, building societies, occupational pensions, and for investment services. Some, like the Banking Ombudsman and the Insurance Ombudsman Bureau (IOB) were voluntary schemes, set up and funded by the industry itself. Others, like the Building Societies Ombudsmen and Pensions Ombudsmen were set up under statute.[12] Yet others, such as the Investment Ombudsman and the Personal Investment Authority Ombudsman Bureau were set up by self regulatory bodies authorised and operating under statute (the Financial Services Act 1986), but funded by the industry.[13] In total, there were nine separate Ombudsmen offices dealing with different aspects of financial services.

All but the Pensions Ombudsman will be combined into a single Financial Services Ombudsman Scheme (FSOS), operating under the Financial Services and Markets Act 2000 (FSMA).[14] The Scheme is anticipated to be the largest in the world, with a budget of approximately £20 million, between 350–400 staff and 15–20 Ombudsmen. The Scheme has a compulsory jurisdiction—certain firms must be subject to the Scheme, and a voluntary

---

[11]   J Black 'Reviewing Regulatory Rules: Responding to Hybridisation' in J Black, P Muchlinski and P Walker (eds) *Commercial Regulation and Judicial Review* (Hart Publishing, 1998).

[12]   Building Societies Act 1986; Social Security Act 1990.

[13]   For details of the nature and scope of the schemes see R James *Private Ombudsmen and Public Law* (Ashgate, Aldershot, 1997); FSA, CP 4 *Consumer Complaints* (December 1997) Appendices 1 and 2.

[14]   Note that at the time of writing the details of the Scheme had not yet been formalised into rules, and so may be subject to some alteration.

jurisdiction—certain firms may seek to be covered by the Scheme, but do not have to be. At least 10,000 firms are expected to be subject to the Scheme's compulsory jurisdiction, which applies to firms authorised under the FSMA who deal with individuals and small businesses. The FSA has discretion to specify which activities of those firms are covered by the Scheme, which it will use to exclude non-financial activities from the scheme's scope, for example estate agency.[15] Initially, it will cover only those financial activities that were covered under one of the previous schemes. In the longer term, however, FSA aims to extend the compulsory jurisdiction to those activities not already covered by existing schemes, for example general insurance broking and advice and independent mortgage broking and advice.[16] The Scheme's voluntary jurisdiction currently covers those activities of unauthorised firms that were covered by existing schemes. Finally, those activities that were not covered by any previous scheme and are not covered by the compulsory jurisdiction will be brought under the voluntary jurisdiction over a period of time (eg consumer credit and the selling of general insurance). Even without those extensions to its jurisdiction, based on the experience of the existing schemes which it is replacing the FSA estimates that the FSOS will receive on average each year 30,000 written complaints requiring conciliation or arbitration, 30,000 written enquiries and 150,000 telephone enquiries.[17]

Following the standard Ombudsman model, awards are to be made on the basis of what is 'fair and reasonable in all the circumstances', taking into account codes of conduct and general standards of good industry practice. The maximum award that can be made under both jurisdictions to compensate for financial loss will be £100,000, although it can be higher if both parties agree. A separate amount may be awarded to compensate for distress and inconvenience, which has no maximum limit.[18] Awards of £100,000 or less will be binding on both parties if the complainant agrees to the decision within the time limit, but if the complainant does not agree then the award will be binding on neither party, leaving the complainant free to pursue the claim in court if they so wish. There will be no further appeal against the Ombudsman's decision within the Scheme, although there will be an independent Complaints Commissioner to whom complaints about the operation of the Scheme procedures (although not the decisions) may be made, and the Ombudsman's decisions will be subject to judicial review.

---

[15]   CP 33, paras 3.40, 3.51.
[16]   CP 33, para 3.40.
[17]   FSA, CP 33 *Consumer Complaints and the new Single Ombudsman Scheme* (November 1999) paras 1.17 and 1.18.
[18]   The initial proposal of a maximum of £1,000 was dropped: CP 4, para 128.

The position of the Financial Services Ombudsman differs from the Pensions Ombudsman in that the decisions of the latter are appealable to the High Court on a point of law. This provision has had a dramatic impact on the operation of the Pensions Ombudsman, and it has been argued that the court's interpretation of the Ombudsman's powers has adversely affected its operations, and effectively negates its role as an alternative to the courts for resolving disputes.[19] The Ombudsman was established in 1993 under the Social Security Act 1990 and his jurisdiction covers public and private sector occupational pension schemes. He has authority to investigate and remedy 'injustice in consequence of maladministration',[20] these terms being undefined in the legislation. His determinations, unusually amongst Ombudsman schemes, are binding on both parties without having to be first accepted by the complainant, and are enforceable in the courts. Where the Pensions Ombudsman makes a determination, he may also order the respondents 'to take, or refrain from taking, such steps as he may specify.'[1] This includes the payment of money awards, which can be high, to the order of several million pounds. The intention of the Act seems thus to create an investigative body which may adjudicate on the basis of a broad standard of maladministration, in turn establishing standards of good administration. However, in successive cases the courts have demonstrated that they are uneasy with the investigative and inquisitorial role of the Ombudsman and have resisted its attempts to establish new standards rather than impose existing ones. They have narrowed the definition of maladministration, stipulating that it refers only to existing causes of action at private law (negligence, breach of trustee's duties), and have restricted the remedies that may be granted to small, relatively inconsequential sums.[2] They have also further resisted the Ombudsman adopting any standard setting role by establishing evidential burdens which make it difficult for the Ombudsman to establish standards of good practice.[3] The result, Nobles argues, is that the 'cumulative effect of judicial decisions has been to nullify the Ombudsman's ability to identify and enforce good standards of administration, and to confine his role to that of an inferior tribunal with powers of investigation'.[4]

[19]   R Nobles 'Enforcing Employee's Pension Rights—The Court's Hostility to the Pensions Ombudsman' (2000) Industrial Law Journal (forthcoming).
[20]   Pension Schemes Act 1993, s 146(1).
[1]   Pension Schemes Act 1993, s 152.
[2]   R Nobles 'Enforcing Employee's Pension Rights—The Court's Hostility to the Pensions Ombudsman' (2000) Industrial Law Journal (due September 2000).
[3]   R Nobles 'Enforcing Employee's Pension Rights—The Court's Hostility to the Pensions Ombudsman' (2000) Industrial Law Journal (due September 2000).
[4]   R Nobles 'Enforcing Employee's Pension Rights—The Court's Hostility to the Pensions Ombudsman' (2000) Industrial Law Journal (due September 2000).

The Legal Services Ombudsman (LSO)[5] differs again from both the Pensions Ombudsman and the Financial Services Ombudsman in that its primary objective is not to resolve a grievance between a consumer and a firm, or even to raise standards or advise on good practice, but rather to monitor the self regulatory complaints mechanisms of the legal profession.[6] He is a regulator of self-regulatory bodies, not a mechanism for investigation and dispute resolution. The LSO's principal function is to investigate the way in which the complaint has been handled by a professional body (the Law Society, the Bar Council and the Council for Licensed Conveyancers). He may investigate the original complaint but is under no obligation to do so.[7] Both the low priority given to dispute resolution and the adequacy of the LSO's regulatory powers have been criticised. Investigations into the original complaint itself occur in only 10–12% of cases.[8]

He has powers only to recommend that the body reconsider the complaint or exercise any of its disciplinary powers, and where he has investigated the original complaint he may recommend that compensation be paid by the professional body or the lawyer against whom the complaint was made.[9] There is no limit on the amount that may be awarded, but the sums have usually been small.[10] The professional body must report on the action it has taken or its reasons for taking no action, but where none has been taken and/or no reasons given, the only power the Ombudsman has is to publicise that fact and the facts of the case. The Scheme was extended in 1999 to empower the LSO to make orders as an alternative to recommending compensation.[11] The LSO has no powers to require the complaints procedures of the professional bodies be altered, only to make recommendations to that effect.[12] In fact he has rarely used these powers,

---

[5] Established under the Courts and Legal Services Act 1990 (as amended by Access to Justice Act 1999, ss 49–50).

[6] R James and M Seneviratne 'The Legal Services Ombudsman: Form versus Function?' (1995) 58 MLR 187; M Seneviratne *The Legal Profession: Regulation and the Consumer* (Sweet & Maxwell, 1999) Chapter 6.

[7] Courts and Legal Services Act 1990, s 22.

[8] R James and M Seneviratne 'The Legal Services Ombudsman: Form versus Function?' (1995) 58 MLR 187 at 193.

[9] Courts and Legal Services Act 1990, s 23.

[10] R James and M Seneviratne 'The Legal Services Ombudsman: Form versus Function?' (1995) 58 MLR 187; D Longley and R James *Administrative Justice: Central Issues in UK and European Administrative Law* (Cavendish Publishing, 1999) p 74.

[11] Courts and Legal Services Act 1990, s 23(2A), as amended.

[12] Courts and Legal Services Act 1990, s 24.

preferring instead to operate informally or to express criticisms in his annual reports.[13]

Given the variety in the structure and scope of Ombudsmen schemes, it is difficult to draw universal conclusions as to their effectiveness. Three main issues of actual or potential concern may nonetheless be identified. Firstly, the independence and accessibility of Ombudsmen schemes. Consumers often doubt the independence of Ombudsman schemes.[14] As noted, many schemes, both statutory and non-statutory, are funded by the industry, and where the scheme is non-statutory, the Ombudsman is usually appointed by the industry. Their procedures are also not particularly transparent, making their independence or otherwise harder to assess. Further, although the schemes are designed to be accessible, individuals first have to go through the firm's internal complaints procedures; given that only between a third to a half of all those who are dissatisfied complain at all,[15] the number who will continue to pursue a complaint through to the Ombudsmen will be even less. Various proposals have been made for the establishment of a regulator of Ombudsmen, building on the current non-statutory British and Irish Ombudsman Association to promote good practice in Ombudsmen schemes.[16] Secondly, there is a certain ambivalence in the Ombudsman's role. The standard on which they make their decisions is on the basis of what is fair and reasonable in all the circumstances, taking into account codes of practice and industry practice. To what extent, however, should they be seeking to raise those standards? James's study found that some Ombudsmen, and certainly many in the firms subject to their jurisdiction, resisted such a regulatory role for Ombudsmen.[17] But to what extent indeed, given that standards are often very generally articulated, if at all, can they fail to be placing their own interpretation on what those standards should be?

Finally, to what extent can and should Ombudsmen procedures be juridified? Ombudsmen are meant to provide an alternative to legal redress. However, to the extent that they are deemed to be public bodies their procedures and decisions will be subject judicial review and to the Human Rights Act 1998 which also imposes additional procedural requirements.

---

[13] R James and M Seneviratne 'The Legal Services Ombudsman: Form versus Function?' (1995) 58 MLR 187 at 199.

[14] NCC 'Ombudsman Services: Consumer's View' (London, 1993); R James *Private Ombudsmen and Public Law* pp 219–222.

[15] *Handled with Care? Consumer Complaints 1991–1997* (Consumers' Association, 1998).

[16] D McKechnie 'The Future of Ombudsmen' (1995) 5(6) Consumer Policy Review 213; D Longley and R James *Administrative Justice: Central Issues in UK and European Administrative Law* (Cavendish Publishing, 1999) pp 90–91.

[17] R James *Private Ombudsmen and Public Law* pp 216–217.

Trying to ensure that Ombudsmen's procedures meet judicial expectations and the requirements of the Human Rights Act whilst retaining flexibility can be a difficult balance to strike, as the debates on the design of the Financial Services Ombudsman illustrate.[18] Further, as noted, the courts, either through judicial review or, as in the case of the Pensions Ombudsman, because an Ombudsman's determination is appealable on a point of law, may overly juridify the Ombudsman's operations, forcing it to operate in a manner more akin to a court, to the detriment of its ability to provide a quick and accessible alternative mechanism for dispute resolution.

---

[18]   Joint Committee on Financial Services and Markets, First Report, *Draft Financial Services and Markets Bill,* para 298; FSA, CP 33 *Consumer Complaints and the new Single Ombudsman Scheme* (November 1999) para 4.7.

Chapter 4

Minimum quality standards for products: retailers' liability

One of the most important issues in consumer protection is the quality of products and services.[1] Every year hundreds of thousands of consumers complain to retailers, manufacturers and consumer protection agencies that the goods they have bought are defective or that the services they have contracted for are sub-standard. A very small proportion of these complaints include consumers who have suffered personal injury as a result of a defective product or sub-standard service, although most complaints are about shoddy, as distinct from unsafe, products and services. This and the following two chapters examine those parts of the private law relating to the quality of goods and services. There are aspects of the public law relevant to the issue—the Food Safety Act 1990 and Food Standards Act 1999 set standards and facilitate regulations for food standards, the Medicines Act 1968 regulates the manufacture and marketing of drugs, under the Consumer Protection Act 1987 and European Communities Act 1972 standards may be set for the safety of consumer goods, while the 1987 Act and the General Product Safety Regulations 1994 set general safety standards for goods. Some of these public law provisions are capable of grounding civil claims for damages. Thus both standard setting and the provision of remedies in respect of poor quality goods and services are the product of a mixture of the public law provisions (discussed in other chapters) and the private law discussed in these chapters.

The previous chapter laid bare the procedural drawbacks to private law. This and the succeeding chapters discuss deficiencies in legal doctrine

---

[1]   A wide-ranging set of analyses is offered by D Dewees (ed) *The Regulation of Quality* (Butterworths, 1983).

which relate to the quality of products and services. The previous editions of this work highlighted the doctrines of privity of contract and negligence as the cause of the greatest deficiencies. There has been substantial reform of the application of both these doctrines to poor quality goods and services since then. Nevertheless, it remains true that even under the reformed privity doctrine manufacturers are not generally liable in contract for the quality of what they produce, since consumers buy from the retailer and not from the manufacturer ('vertical privity'). Consumers must sue the retailer for breach of contract, although it in turn may sue the manufacturer. If substantial loss is involved the situation is hardly satisfactory when the retailer has gone out of business or has few assets. Privity of contract also means that in most circumstances only purchasers can take legal action against a retailer in the absence of negligence ('horizontal privity'). In other words, if a consumer-purchaser has given what turns out to be a defective product to a third party—a member of the family, a friend, etc—that third party consumer has no remedy in contract, unless the contract expressly provides that it shall be enforceable by the third party or the contract benefits an identified third party and there is no indication of intent that the term should not be enforceable.[2]

Consumers can only generally sue manufacturers where they suffer losses consequential upon the defect in a product (for example personal injury or property damage) and have no remedy against a manufacturer for the loss of value in the product itself associated with the defect. Reform of the law introduced by the Consumer Protection Act 1987 means that where there is manufacturing defect (ie the product did not leave the factory in the form intended) then liability is strict and relatively straightforward to establish. Furthermore the liability extends to other persons with responsibility for the product (importers into the EU, other processors of the goods, those who apply their own brand label to the goods (eg supermarkets and suppliers who fail to identify the producer) and thus finding someone to sue is relatively straightforward also. However, in the case of design defects, which have created much more difficulty for claimants (as with the Thalidomide case, discussed in Chapter 5 below), it is likely that the same kind of balancing act as is used in negligence litigation will be applied, even under the strict liability regime. Thus victims of design defects, such as the Thalidomide children, may be no better off in pursuing claims against manufacturers even after the major statutory reform intended to improve the position.

This chapter examines the retailer's position, primarily its liability to compensate consumer-purchasers under the Sale of Goods Act 1979 (as amended in 1994) where it supplies shoddy or sub-standard products. A retailer is also strictly liable under this provision where a consumer-

---

[2]   Contracts (Rights of Third Parties) Act 1999, s 1(1).

purchaser is injured by a defective product. These remedies do not generally extend to third party consumers (unless they can show that the parties intended them to be available or that the third party was identified in the contract and there was no intention that the remedies not be available) and may even prove illusory for consumer-purchasers where a retailer has gone out of business or has few assets. The next chapter focuses on the legal responsibilities of manufacturers under the statutory and common law regimes of liability for harm caused by defective products. Chapter 6 examines liability for services: what is the responsibility of persons like car repairers or medical practitioners regarding the standard of work they perform, or the expected quality of providers of holidays, financial, insurance and utilities services? In English law manufacturers have a minimal responsibility for products which are simply shoddy or sub-standard, although in practice some issue guarantees or offer maintenance by which they undertake to repair products if faults develop. But the legal position is that the main burden for shoddy or sub-standard products falls on retailers.

I   BACKGROUND TO PRODUCT STANDARDS

There is no agreed definition of product quality despite the fact that it is regarded as a major factor in consumer transactions. At one end of the spectrum are the objective criteria of physical/chemical or microbiological standards; at the other is the marketing concept of a consumer's 'subjective assessment' of quality.[3] The former governs the approach of the quality control departments of manufacturing concerns and the latter the approach of the marketing departments. Although the first book on quality control for industry was published in 1931, it was not until after the Second World War that widespread application of its techniques were made. This rise in interest is ascribed to competitive pressure and the requirement of high levels of precision within the manufacturing process itself.[4] However, uniform standards which were established (eg those of the British Standards Institution) met with some opposition on the grounds that they restricted innovation. Despite the rise in quality control, many manufacturers continued to market low-quality goods.

One of the best indicators of quality in consumer markets today is data on consumer complaints. While we need to use the figures with caution, as consumers are less likely to complain about poor quality, low-cost

[3]   R Mason 'Price and Product Quality Assessment' (1974) 8 European Journal of Marketing 29.
[4]   A Willsmore *Modern Product Control* (Pitman, 3rd edn, 1963) p 187; M Dewis et al *Product Liability* (Heinemann, 1980) Part II.

products, nevertheless they provide considerable insight into the extent to which consumers experience difficulties both with the quality of produces and securing appropriate remedies. The Office of Fair Trading collects statistics about the number of complaints to trading standards departments, consumer advice centres and Citizens Advice Bureaux. For the 12 months up to the end of September 1998, the OFT recorded the following complaints totals:

Table 4.1

Furniture (not upholstered or nursery), pictures etc	22,523
Upholstered furniture	34,615
Carpets and other floor coverings	16,037
Radio, TV and other electrical goods	70,062
Major appliances	43,642
Clothing	46,861
Footwear	18,977
Prams, push-chairs and other nursery furniture	10,048
New motor cars	9,822
Second-hand motor cars	90,456
Sports goods, etc	11,430

(Source: *Office of Fair Trading Annual Report 1998* Appendix E.4.)

Looking at these figures it is necessary to remember that these are only those complaints which make it as far as consumer agencies. Furthermore many other areas of complaint for which data is collected by the OFT include goods and services. They suggest that the total number of complaints made about goods is much higher, because most complainants are unlikely to take the matter further than the retailer. To fill in the gaps in the complaints data the OFT has for a number of years collected information about consumer dissatisfaction (now referred to a 'consumer detriment'). This research uses a sample of the UK adult population as the basis for estimating the frequency of consumer problems with traders and now also to attempt to establish the costs imposed on consumers by these problems (many of which will amount to breach of contract). The most recent research suggests that annually consumers experience nearly 86 million problems with goods and services. Within this figure, it is suggested that there are nearly three and half million problems with personal clothing, shoes and jewellery, two million problems a year with household appliances and nearly two million problems a year associated with TVs, videos, hi-fi, radios and Walkmans.[5] Typical problems were that the item was incomplete, faulty or defective (16.2%), the item was damaged (5.2%), the quality of the item was below standard (14.9%) and the product did not perform as

[5]   *Consumer Detriment* (OFT, 2000) Table 5.1.

specified (15.3%).[6] Each of these main sources of complaints ab
could provide the basis for a claim for breach of contract. In near
instances of problems consumers were either dissatisfied
dissatisfied with the outcome,[7] suggesting that there is a major task to be
achieved in improving the ways in which traders respond to problems
(whether by legal or extra-legal means). The OFT estimates that the cost to
consumers of problems with goods and services is £8.3 billion each year
or 1.5% of annual consumer expenditure.[8]

The present state of private law, combined with the procedural
difficulties of using it, are inadequate to ensure satisfactory product quality.
Perhaps this is not surprising because private law operates only to a
limited extent as a means of social control. Its usual remedy of damages is
to compensate an injured party, not to punish or correct the other side. A
business responsible for defective products or sub-standard services can
still be in a profitable position after paying compensatory damages and
the calculation of other amounts such as opportunity costs. The amount
of damages awarded to a successful consumer is unrelated to the purpose
of deterrence and will only have that effect if it is less expensive for the
business to alter its behaviour than to give relief to that consumer and
others likely to take similar action in the future and succeed. As Leff notes:
'One cannot think of a more expensive and frustrating course than to seek
to regulate goods or "contract" quality through repeated law-suits against
inventive "wrongdoers".'[9]

How, then, can manufacturers be encouraged to improve design and to
step up inspection of products as they come off the production line? How
can they be induced to assess carefully the potential market, to test
thoroughly prototypes, and to introduce a check-up system to find out
consumer reactions and feed them back into the design and production
process? Voluntary measures are one way, although they suffer drawbacks.
The British Standards Institution, for example, which is financed by
subscriptions from industry, government grant and the sale of standards,
concerns itself with drafting standards of size, quality and performance in
a number of industrial and commercial fields. Draft standards are adopted
by consensus in committees comprising manufacturers, distributors,
technical experts and sometimes consumer representatives. Interest in
consumer products has always been incidental to the main work of the
BSI. Even the 5,000-odd standards it identifies for consumer products are
not of crucial importance to consumers in terms of the OFT data mentioned.

[6] *Consumer Detriment* (OFT, 2000) Table 5.2.
[7] *Consumer Detriment* (OFT, 2000) Table 7.1.
[8] *Consumer Detriment* (OFT, 2000) para 2.1.
[9] A Leff 'Unconscionability and the Crowd—Consumers and the Common Law
Tradition' (1970) 31 U Pitt LR 349, 356.

A second mechanism of control is through the market. It is argued that vigorous competition should encourage producers to target markets more effectively and to compete on quality. Membership of the European Community and the development of free movement of goods within the EU are said to assist in that development. However, in practice, many sectors are dominated by a small number of producers, in many cases using advertising both to persuade consumers of their reputation and to inhibit the entry of others into the market place.

Ultimately public regulation is necessary to improve product quality in addition to voluntary efforts and reform of the private law. The Director General of Fair Trading can obtain assurances, undertakings and orders against businesses which are consistently responsible for sub-standard products and poor services.[10] This power offers the greatest chance for action to be taken to improve the quality of products and services. The Swedish Market Court has used a similar power against manufacturers. Another technique to improve product quality is to require mandatory guarantees for consumer products during which time consumers can have defects repaired without cost.[11] This has been used in New South Wales for motor cars where legislation deems that a mandatory warranty exists in every consumer transaction for the sale of a motor vehicle.[12] Dealers—not manufacturers—are obliged to repair any defect whether it existed at the time of sale or not, so as to place the vehicle in a reasonable condition having regard to its age. For new cars the warranty is 12 months or 20,000 kilometres; for used cars it is on a sliding scale depending on the price, although it can be excluded completely by disclosure before sale. The dealer is still liable when a car is sold on hire purchase, and with new cars subsequent owners can take advantage of the warranty. The warranty does not apply to defects in specific accessories (eg tyres) or to those attributable to an accident or consumer misuse (s 28).

Consideration might also be given to enforcing minimum quality standards. A number have been enacted for safety reasons under s 11 of the Consumer Protection Act 1987 and s 2 of the European Communities Act 1972 (discussed in Chapter 10 below). Something along these lines operated during the Second World War, and the post-war period until 1952 under the Utility Schemes, which covered a wide range of consumer products.[13] The supply of material to manufacturers was made dependent on the production of goods which conformed to certain broad descriptions

---

[10] See p 440 below.
[11] Various reform initiatives applying to manufacturers' guarantees are discussed below, pp 174–180.
[12] Motor Dealers Act 1974, s 27.
[13] *Final Report of the Committee on Consumer Protection* (Cmnd 1781 (1962)) pp 76–89.

and specifications. Admittedly there would be difficulties in introducing product standards today with the huge range of products currently on the market and the great variety of tastes. For these reasons clothing, for example, would generally be a poor candidate for product standards.

Multi-level standards might overcome the objection that they lead to uniformity and the lowest common denominator. There has in fact been considerable development of voluntary quality assurance schemes, but these often focus on the manufacturing process rather than on the quality of the product produced.[14]

2   PRODUCT QUALITY

In many cases consumers will obtain satisfaction from a retailer when they complain about a faulty product they have purchased. Some retailers give an automatic refund or exchange. This often extends to where consumers find that the size is wrong or the colour is not what they thought, or where they have simply changed their mind—situations where there is no legal right to redress in the absence of misrepresentation. Consumers may still have to demonstrate proof of purchase, which is most easily done by producing the receipt or till-slip. A credit card statement will provide proof that a purchase was made from the retailer, though it may not establish what item was the subject matter of the transaction. In situations where retailers are not as obliging as this, the law provides two actions for the purchaser of the faulty product against the retailer: an action for misrepresentation if the product was misdescribed, and an action for breach of the implied conditions incorporated in sale of goods contracts by the Sale of Goods Act 1979 to the effect that goods should correspond with their description and with any sample shown (for example with floor coverings), and should be of satisfactory quality and fit for any purpose specified by the purchaser. The 1979 Act provides a range of important remedies for consumer for breach of these implied conditions.

The EC Directive on Consumer Guarantees, adopted in 1999,[15] requires the UK government to make significant amendments to the sale of goods regime as it affects consumers. The chief ostensible justification for the Directive is that the disparate sale of goods laws of the Member States discourage consumers from engaging in cross-border shopping (for fear that they may be less well protected in other Member States than in t⌐ own).[16] Accordingly the Directive aims to approximate the s⌐¹

---

[14]   See H Collins and C Scott 'United Kingdom' in G Brügg⌐
        von Qualitätsmanagementvereinbarungen und EG-Binn
[15]   OJ L 171, 07.07.99 p 0012–0016.
[16]   See in particular recitals 3, 4, and 5 of the Directive.

the Member States as they affect consumers (Article 1). While the scope of the Directive may be thought of as somewhat more fundamental to the English law of contract than the earlier Unfair Terms in Consumer Contracts Directive (discussed in the previous chapter), in contrast with the earlier Directive it does not require the adoption of any new principles. Rather it provides for significant modification of the application of existing principles, both in respect of substantive requirements and remedies for breach. At the time of writing it is not clear exactly how the DTI proposes to implement the new requirements, and it seems unlikely that UK implementation will be in place much before the deadline of 1 January 2002. Accordingly discussion of the requirements of the Directive is incorporated in the text discussing the Sale of Goods Act 1979 which follows. If the government follows the newly enunciated doctrine of legislative consolidation (which it is seeking to apply in bringing together the separate regimes of the Unfair Contract Terms Act 1977 and the Unfair Terms Regulations 1999) then we would expect the DTI to proceed by means of legislative amendment to the Sale of Goods Act 1979. This would require the measure to be in Queen's speech in November 2000 on the basis that the government would allow sufficient parliamentary time for a Bill. If, as seems likely, ministers feel that other measures should take priority, then the DTI will have to proceed by statutory instrument and reproduce the highly unsatisfactory results which have followed from the creation of parallel regimes both in respect of unfair terms, discussed in the previous chapter, and general product safety (discussed in Chapter 10 below).

(a)   Misrepresentations about quality

Retailers can incur civil liability, as well as criminal liability under the Trade Descriptions Act 1968, when they misrepresent the quality of products and services either orally or in writing. For example, if they describe a product as being in excellent condition and it is not, a consumer may be able to rescind the contract or claim damages. It need not matter that the business did not know the statement was untrue. An oral statement might constitute an actionable misrepresentation when it distorts a written representation. A clear case is *Curtis v Chemical Cleaning and Dyeing Co Ltd*,[17] where a shop assistant accepted a dress from a consumer for cleaning but innocently misrepresented that the exemption clause on the receipt only covered things like beads and sequins, whereas it covered all damage. The Court of Appeal held that the consumer could claim damages when the dress was returned stained because the assistant's statements

[1951] 1 KB 805.

had created a false impression in the consumer's mind. The case also illustrates the point that retailers are in general vicariously liable for misrepresentations by their employees in the course of their employment. Criminal liability for employees under the Trade Descriptions Act 1968 is much more limited. The following discussion focuses on representations about the quality of products, but the principles are general and consumers may have a remedy for misrepresentation about other matters like the price or the identity of the seller (eg a misrepresentation by a doorstep seller that she is from an education authority). Generally speaking the law only gives relief for misrepresentations of existing fact. A statement of opinion might be regarded as a statement of fact if, say, the facts on which it is based are peculiarly within the knowledge of the person making it. An action does not generally arise from misrepresentations about the law or about what a person promises to do (eg repair a car) unless the promise is contractual or unless the person has no intention of carrying out the promise.

Not all misrepresentations give rise to civil liability. The parol evidence rule makes it difficult for consumers to sue on an oral misrepresentation when it adds to or is inconsistent with the terms of written contract. In an Australian case the court held that a consumer could not rely on an oral misrepresentation by a sales person that a car was in very good mechanical condition when the transaction was completed on the basis of an express 30-day or 1,000-mile warranty.[18] In practice the courts are increasingly using the device of collateral contract to avoid the parol evidence rule and to regard a statement additional to or inconsistent with written terms as giving rise to a separate contract, consideration for which is entering the main contract. The courts have always allowed some latitude to sales 'puffs' or commendations, which will not give rise to an action for misrepresentation. Puffs, or commendations, are the laudatory statements businesses use in marketing products, the vacuous claims of modern advertising like 'whiter than white', which everyone is expected to take with a grain of salt. If this is the case, however, it is difficult to see why puffs are so widely used. There are no modern English cases in the consumer field deciding that a statement was a puff. In *Andrews v Hopkinson*[19] the court had no doubt that a statement by a dealer that a car was 'a good little bus; I would stake my life on it' was not a puff. Some United States cases take a robust view of consumers' ability to see through advertising claims.[20]

---

[18] *Lough v Moran Motors Pty Ltd* [1962] Qd R 466.
[19] 1957] 1 QB 229; cf *Esso Petroleum Co Ltd v Mardon* [1976] QB 801; *Marks v Hunt Bros (Sydney) Pty Ltd* (1958) 58 SRNSW 380; *JJ Savage & Sons Pty Ltd v Blakeney* (1970) 119 CLR 435.
[20] *Carpenter v Alberto Culver & Co* 184 NW 2d 547 (1970).

Misrepresentation may give rise to a claim for damages or rescission. Damages are payable if the misrepresentation is fraudulent, negligent or contractual.[1] The law says that a misrepresentation is a term of the contract if in the circumstances it can be said that this is what the parties intended. In practice the courts give substance to this rather unsatisfactory test by examining various factors such as the nature of the representation and the knowledge available to the parties. There is little difficulty in establishing that the representation is contractual if it is incorporated in a written contract.[2] Generally speaking representations by businesses in transactions with consumers are likely to be contractual because of the disparity in knowledge between the parties. The consumer in *Dick Bentley Productions Ltd v Harold Smith (Motors) Ltd*[3] obtained damages for breach of contract when a car dealer innocently misrepresented that the car he bought had travelled a limited mileage. In the reverse situation, where a consumer was selling a car in part-exchange to a dealer and innocently misrepresented what model it was, this was not a term of the contract because the dealer was in a position to know whether or not the statement was true.[4]

The difference between a mere representation and a representation which is a term of the contract is less important than it was prior to the Misrepresentation Act 1967, because the Act imposes a statutory liability for damages where a person 'has entered into a contract after a misrepresentation was made to him by another party thereto and as a result thereof has suffered loss…unless he [the representor] proves that he had reasonable grounds to believe and did believe up to that time the contract was made that the facts represented were true' (s 2(1)). It is a difficult matter for a person to show reasonable grounds.[5] The court also has discretionary power to award damages in lieu of rescission in circumstances where a person has entered into a contract after a misrepresentation has been made to him and he would be entitled to rescind the contract (s 2(2)).[6] This discretionary remedy is available irrespective of whether the rescission is still available in the particular case, provided that the agreement was capable of being rescinded at some earlier stage.[7]

---

[1]   H Collins *Law of Contract* (Butterworths, 3rd edn, 1997) pp 181–184.
[2]   *Liverpool and County Discount Co Ltd v AB Motor Co (Kilburn) Ltd* [1963] 1 WLR 611; *Academy of Health and Fitness Pty Ltd v Power* [1973] VR 254.
[3]   [1965] 1 WLR 623.
[4]   *Oscar Chess Ltd v Williams* [1957] 1 WLR 370.
[5]   *Howard Marine and Dredging Co Ltd v A Ogden & Sons Excavations Ltd* [1978] QB 574.
[6]   See *William Sindall plc v Cambridgeshire County Council* [1994] 3 All ER 932 for a consideration of the factors relevant to the exercise of the discretion.
[7]   *Thomas Witter Ltd v TBP Industries Ltd* [1996] 2 All ER 573.

Previously the consumer's only remedy for innocent misrepresentation was rescission. The 1967 Act provided an early form of statutory control over exemption and limitation clauses in respect of such remedies.[8]

Rescission for misrepresentation arises at law with fraudulent misrepresentation and in equity for innocent misrepresentation. Breach of a representation in a contract entitles a consumer to claim damages and might also give rise to a right to 'rescind' it. With serious breaches a right to treat the contract as having been repudiated is automatic for it arises by virtue of the breach rather than the misrepresentation.[9] The right to rescind a contract for misrepresentation can be lost on general equitable principles where a consumer has expressly affirmed the contract, where *restitutio in integrum* is impossible (eg the consumer has substantially modified the product or it has been seriously damaged through his fault), where an innocent third party would be prejudiced, or where a reasonable time has elapsed. The purchaser in *Leaf v International Galleries*[10] purported to rescind on the basis that a painting was not a Constable, but the Court of Appeal regarded the five-year period since the sale as being too long. The justification was that the purchaser had ample opportunity to examine the painting in the first few years after he had bought it. Weighed against this, however, is the fact that the painting could have been returned quite easily in the same state as when it was sold. *Long v Lloyd*[11] is an unsatisfactory case. There a lorry was described as being in exceptional condition but almost immediately the purchaser found that it was defective. A few days after the sale he complained to the dealer who agreed to pay half the cost of repairs. The purchaser then sent the lorry on a long journey during which it broke down. Six days after the sale, being thoroughly dissatisfied, the purchaser purported to rescind the contract for misrepresentation. The Court of Appeal held that the purchaser had lost his right to rescind, presumably because he had affirmed the contract by making the agreement about the repairs or because the lapse of six days was too long. Pearce LJ gives as a major reason for the decision that the purchaser could have had the lorry examined by an expert before or immediately after he bought it.[12] The Law Reform Committee concluded that the bar on rescission as applied in *Long v Lloyd* was too rigid.[13]

The rules about misrepresentation are unduly complicated and inadequate. In part this derives from the drafting of the Misrepresentation

---

8   Section 3 as amended by s 8 of the Unfair Contract Terms Act 1977, discussed more fully in Chapter 3 above.
9   For example *Porter v General Guarantee Corpn Ltd* [1982] RTR 384.
10 [1950] 2 KB 86.
11 [1958] 1 WLR 753.
12 [1958] 1 WLR 753, 760.
13 Law Reform Committee *Tenth Report (Innocent Misrepresentation)* (Cmnd 1782) p 4.

Act 1967 which had the opportunity (but did not take it) of codifying the law on the subject. Another factor is that in misrepresentation cases the courts tend first to decide whether to give a remedy; they then have to force the misrepresentation into the appropriate legal category. The rules about misrepresentation are also limited in scope and do not apply to much misleading advertising or to statements used in sales techniques like 'bait and switch'. The basis for the calculation of damages for negligent misrepresentation under the 1967 Act (s 2(1)) was left unclear though it has now been held that the same principles should be applied as for the tort of deceit, with the potential for considerably more generous awards than for common law negligence, permitting all consequential loss to be recovered (rather than limiting recoverable loss to what is foreseeable).[14] Discretionary awards in lieu of rescission under s 2(2) in cases of innocent misrepresentation are likely to be based on the contractual measure of damages, as the order is intended to compensate the plaintiff in lieu of rescission, rather than for the global effects of the misrepresentation.[15] At the present time the best advice to consumers when there has been misrepresentation is probably to complain to a trading standards department which may investigate the case for breach of the Trade Descriptions Act 1968. Then the business may be more willing to give redress because of the threat of criminal proceedings. If the case comes to court and the prosecution is successful consumers can claim compensation under the procedure set out in s 130 of the Powers of Criminal Courts (Sentencing) Act 2000.

There is a strong case for legislative reform of the law regarding misrepresentation. A business should be strictly liable for misrepresentations (including silence) if consumers are adversely affected. The New South Wales Law Reform Commission has suggested legislation along these lines.[16] Any representation would give rise to a civil action if the natural tendency was to induce a consumer to buy a product and if the consumer bought in reliance on it. The provision would apply to all misrepresentations including those in advertisements. Notice would be taken of to whom the representation was directed. Thus gullible sections of the population, like children, would be protected even if ordinary people would see through the misrepresentation. The Ontario Law Reform Commission goes one step further and would apply such provisions to sales puffs and mere language of commendation in recognition of the importance of modern advertising techniques in influencing consumers'

---

[14] *Royscott Trust Ltd v Rogerson* [1991] 2 QB 297.
[15] *William Sindall plc v Cambridgeshire County Council* [1994] 3 All ER 932; *Witter Ltd v TBP Industries Ltd* [1996] 2 All ER 573.
[16] *Working Paper on the Sale of Goods* (1975) pp 34–45.

buying decisions.[17] As the New South Wales Commission points out, there is a clear moral basis for these reforms, which is recognised in the old cases like *Redgrave v Hurd*[18] where Jessel MR said that persons should not be allowed to profit from misstatements which they now admit are false or which are shown to be inaccurate or untrue.

(b)   Implied conditions in the Sale of Goods Act 1979 and the prospects for reform

Prior to the Industrial Revolution most products were relatively simple in nature to evaluate, and purchases were mainly within fairly closed, stable groups.[19] Where trade with strangers was engaged in it was assumed that this was 'an arm's length proposition, with wits matched against skills'. Courts in the nineteenth century began developing implied terms in sales transactions in response to the commercial—not the consumer—problems thrown up by industrialisation. As Karl Llewellyn noted:

> Overseas trade in seaports introduces cargo-lot dealing and dealing in goods at a distance, before they can be seen. Markets widen with improved transportation—internal waterways, railroads. This means reliance on distant sellers. Middlemen's dealings mean, sometimes, the postponement of inspection; always they mean some ignorance in the seller of the history of the goods. Industrialisation grows out of and produces standardisation, grading and sizing of lumber, grading and branding of flour or hardware, a certain predictability and reliability of goods. Contracts made by description, or by sample, which is a form of description, or by specification, which is an elaborate form of description, become the order of the day. Contracts come increasingly to precede production. Sellers begin to build for good will, in wide markets, to feel their standing behind goods to be no hardship, no outrage, not threat to their solvency from a thousand lurking claims, but the mark of business respectability and the road to future profit. The law of seller's obligation *must* change, to suit.[20]

As eventually settled, the courts decided that there was no general implied term as to the quality of goods.[1] But where a sale was by description

[17]   *Report on Consumer Warranties and Guarantees in the Sale of Goods* (1972) p 29; *Report on Sale of Goods* (Ministry of the Attorney General, 1979) p 140.
[18]   (1881) 20 Ch D 1, 13.
[19]   See WN Hamilton 'The Ancient Maxim Caveat Emptor' (1931) 40 Yale LJ 1133, 1138; PS Atiyah *The Rise and Fall of Freedom of Contract* (Clarendon, 1979) p 545.
[20]   Karl N Llewellyn *Cases and Materials on the Law of Sales* (Callaghan & Co) p 204.
[1]   *Barr v Gibson* (1838) 150 ER 1196, 1200.

and the buyers had no opportunity to inspect the goods—the typical commercial situation with goods on the high seas—there was an implied term that they should conform to their description and be of merchantable quality.[2] Buyers were not protected in circumstances when it was possible to inspect the goods at the time of sale—the typical consumer transaction. An exception was if they said something to make known to the seller the purpose for which the goods were wanted in order to demonstrate reliance on the latter's skill and judgment, whereupon the courts implied a warranty that the goods were reasonably fit for the purpose.[3] Clearly the doctrine of implied terms was for the benefit to commercial interests; *caveat emptor* was still the prevailing philosophy in sales to consumers.

The implied conditions in ss 13 and 14 of the Sales of Goods Act 1893 were a codification, but in some respects an important extension of the rules developed in the earlier part of the century. The draftsman of the Act, Chalmers, justified the legislation on the grounds that it was easier and cheaper to amend than the common law and that certainty was of great importance in commercial matters. He went on to note: 'Sale is a consensual contract, and the Act does not seek to prevent the parties from making any bargain they please.'[4] This philosophy led to unequal contracts between businesses and consumers because the former were able to use exclusion clauses to avoid the liability for defective products imposed on them by ss 13 and 14. This was finally prevented by legislation in 1973.[5] Following this legislative reform, which made attempts to exclude the implied terms void as against consumers, the Office of Fair Trading carried out research which indicated that many businesses were continuing to purport to exclude this liability. Using powers under the Fair Trading Act 1973, the Office of Fair Trading made it a criminal offence to purport to exclude the implied terms.[6] Businesses responded by including in any notice or term which might be construed as excluding the implied terms a statement 'This does not affect your statutory rights.' Thus it is common to see beneath signs in shops which state that there will be no refunds on returned underwear, earrings or sale items, and adjacent to manufacturers' quality guarantees on chocolate bars the statement 'This does not affect your statutory rights.' Enforcement authorities have apparently accepted

[2]   *Gardiner v Gray* (1815) 171 ER 46; *Jones v Just* (1868) LR 3 QB 197.
[3]   *Gray v Cox* (1825) 107 ER 999; *Randall v Newson* (1877) 2 QBD 102.
[4]   *Chalmers Sale of Goods* (Butterworths, 18th edn, 1981) Introduction to 1st edn, p viii.
[5]   Supply of Goods (Implied Terms) Act 1973, s 4 (now Unfair Contract Terms Act 1977, s 6).
[6]   Consumer Transactions (Restrictions on Statements) Order 1976, SI 1976/1813 as amended by SI 1978/127. The Regulations are discussed in more detail in Chapter 11 below.

that this statement complies with the 1976 regulations, even though it is patently obvious that most consumers are unaware of its true meaning—that if the goods are defective they have a statutory right to a refund or damages.

Nevertheless, the Sale of Goods Act 1893 afforded greater protection to consumers than the common law, for they were no longer obliged to inspect goods for defects, and sellers were liable even if they did so long as inspection would not have revealed the defects. The protection of the implied terms was extended to hire purchase transactions in the Hire Purchase Act 1938 and other contracts for the transfer of property in goods and hire contracts in 1982.[7] However there are still some situations where are there are no implied terms because there is no contract. Consumers must then resort to non-legal remedies. An example is faulty goods supplied by way of gift.[8] In the absence of negligence, consumers will have no recourse against a retailer where they are injured while taking a defective product off a supermarket shelf because there is no contract until they reach the check-out.[9]

(c)   The current law

The three principal implied terms protecting consumers against poor quality goods are those requiring correspondence with description (s 13), that goods be of satisfactory quality (s 14(2)) and that goods be fit for a particular (specified) purpose (s 14(3)). Atiyah describes these provisions as creating a gradation in the standards required for products.[10] Correspondence with description is the lowest standard—a product might be what it claims to be but also be highly defective. The requirement of satisfactory quality is the default requirement applying to all goods. The highest standard—fitness for a particular purpose—can be applied by the consumer specifying to the seller the purpose for which the goods are required. This standard may be more demanding than fitness for normal purposes. Under the Unfair Contract Terms Act 1977 it is not possible for a business to exclude any of these implied conditions in consumer sales. We may note also that

[7]   Hire Purchase Act 1938, s 8 (now Supply of Goods (Implied Terms) Act 1973, ss 9, 10; Consumer Credit Act 1974, Sch 4, s 35); Supply of Goods and Services Act 1982, ss 4, 9, 10.

[8]   *Esso Petroleum Ltd v Customs and Excise Comrs* [1976] 1 WLR 1; cf *Chappell & Co Ltd v Nestlé Co Ltd* [1960] AC 87; *Buckley v Lever Bros* [1953] 4 DLR 16.

[9]   *Pharmaceutical Society of Great Britain v Boots Cash Chemists (Southern) Ltd* [1953] 1 QB 401.

[10]   JN Adams *Atiyah's The Sale of Goods* (Pitman, 9th edn, 1995) p 112.

the lowest of these standards (correspondence with description) is implied into all sale of goods contracts whereas the other two are only implied where the vendor sells in the course of business.[11] Thus the Act offers only limited protection to consumers purchasing in private sales (for example from the classified advertisements of a newspaper, at a car boot sale or in response to a private internet advertisement).

3   CORRESPONDENCE WITH DESCRIPTION

Section 13(1) provides that a product must correspond with its description where it is sold by description.[12] Most sales are sales by description. Clearly where a product is a 'future good' (eg not yet made) and/or where the consumer does not see it before it is sold (as with mail order and including e-commerce), there must be a sale by description. Legislation confirms that there can be a sale by description even where a product is selected by a consumer from those on display (s 13(3)). Thus a product selected by a consumer from the shelves of a supermarket must comply with the description on its label as to brand and contents. It seems that only where consumers buy a product as a specific thing on their own assessment of its value that there will not be a sale by description.[13] This seems to leave to the court considerable discretion to decide whether a sale has been by description—with the consequence that non-correspondence will entitle the buyer to reject the goods.[14] It is likely that in consumer cases that discretion will generally be exercised in favour of the buyer.

In some cases the courts have taken a wider view of the implied condition in s 13 and regarded it as having relevance to the quality of a product. *Beale v Taylor*[15] is an example, where a private motorist advertised his car

[11]   There has been a significant amount of litigation, in a variety of legislative contexts, concerning the meaning of the term 'in the course of business'. It is unlikely to raise many problems in the area of consumer sales. The Court of Appeal has removed the requirement that to be acting 'in the course of business' there should be a regularity in dealing in goods of the type concerned: *Stevenson v Rogers* [1999] 1 All ER 613; J de Lacy 'Selling in the Course of a Business Under the Sale of Goods Act 1979' (1999) 62 MLR 776.

[12]   The equivalent provisions dealing with other contracts for the transfer of property in goods and contracts for hire of goods are ss 3 and 8 of the Supply of Goods and Services Act 1982 respectively.

[13]   *Harlingdon & Leinster Ltd v Christopher Hill Fine Art Ltd* [1991] 1 QB 564.

[14]   JN Adams *Atiyah's The Sale of Goods* (Pitman, 9th edn, 1995) p 120.

[15]   [1967] 1 WLR 1193; See also *Hall v Queensland Truck Centre Pty Ltd* (1970) Qd R 231 (truck described as CBEW type in fact CADY type). See also discussion of cases under the Trade Descriptions Act 1968 in Chapter 8 below.

for sale as a 'Herald Convertible, white, 1961, twin carbs.' The buyer saw the car and drove in it with the seller, but unbeknown to either, the car was an amalgam of two parts, the front half being an earlier model. The Court of Appeal held that the buyer was entitled to succeed. In *Alton House Garages (Bromley) Ltd v Monk*[16] an advertisement for a secondhand Rolls-Royce car indicated that the 'full history' was available. The service record of this type of car enhances its value and the buyer checked when he took delivery of the car that it was there. Later he found that it was the service record of another car. He successfully claimed that the contract was a sale by description and that by not supplying the record the car did not correspond with its description. However, the House of Lords has warned that the implied condition in s 13 really concerns descriptions which allow the product to be identified; in other words, which characterise it as belonging to a particular class.[17] In that particular case the House of Lords held that an animal foodstuff still corresponded with its description despite contamination. Clear examples where a description relates to identity are a consumer who gets a secondhand car when he contracts for a new one, or a Ford when he contracts for a BMW.[18] The House of Lords has deprecated earlier cases which give buyers a remedy, however trivial the breach of description, and has said that the right approach is to ask whether a particular item in a description constitutes a substantial ingredient in the identity of the thing being sold.[19] Nevertheless, it would still seem that extensive contamination or substantial defects may affect identity and give consumers a remedy because of the implied condition.[20] In other words a product of very bad quality may not come within the contractual description but be of a different kind from what the consumer agrees to buy.

In most cases where a product is defective consumers will rely on the satisfactory quality and fitness for purpose provisions of the Sale of Goods Act 1979. These are the main instruments whereby the law ensures a minimum quality for both new and second hand products. Subject to some qualifications the section implies conditions that a product will be satisfactory and also fit for the purpose for which it is supplied. Under the Unfair Contract Terms Act 1977, sellers cannot exclude liability under it in

---

[16]   (1981) unreported.
[17]   *Ashington Piggeries Ltd v Christopher Hill Ltd* [1972] AC 441. This approach diminishes the rights of consumers: See B Coote 'Correspondence with Description in the Law of Sale of Goods' (1976) 50 Australian Law Journal 17.
[18]   *Andrews Bros (Bournemouth) Ltd v Singer & Co Ltd* [1934] 1 KB 17; *Clarke v McMahon* [1939] SASR 64, 67.
[19]   *Reardon Smith Line Ltd v Hansen-Tangen* [1976] 1 WLR 989, 998.
[20]   *Osborn v Hart* (1871) 23 LT 851 (undrinkable wine described as superior old port); *Wilson v Rickett Cockerell & Co Ltd* [1954] 1 QB 598, 608 (coalite containing explosive).

consumer sales. With both conditions the retailer is strictly liable and whether it exercised reasonable care is irrelevant.[1] Liability extends to the container in which a product is supplied as well as to the product itself.[2] The onus of establishing that a product is not satisfactory or fit for the purpose is on the consumer.

4   SATISFACTORY QUALITY

The satisfactory quality and fitness for purpose provisions are confined to sales in the course of a business—unlike the implied condition that a product must correspond with its description. 'Business' includes profession and the activities of any government department, or local or public authority (s 61(1)). Sales in the course of a business include those which are ancillary to the main trade of a seller, those by a seller who has not previously dealt with a particular line and those where the seller carries on the business on a modest part-time basis.[3] The major arguments for confining liability to business sales are that in private sales there is a substantial parity of bargaining power between the parties and that the courts should not be overburdened with disputes between private individuals which commonly involve items of comparatively low value. One would have thought, however, that in many cases private sellers will acquire considerable knowledge of something they own and later sell to put them at an advantage over buyers. At the same time there seems little reason to impose on private sellers liability for consequential losses, which can be very high in cases of personal injury.

The main quality condition of the Sale of Goods Act 1893 was an implied condition that goods were of 'merchantable quality'. Amendments to the Act in 1973[4] supplied a definition of the term which was subsequently incorporated into the Sale of Goods Act 1979. It was a contentious issue both with judges and commentators whether the introduction of a statutory definition of merchantable quality should sweep away the old case law. Overall the courts appear to have gained continuing assistance from case law pre-dating the introduction of the statutory definition, and the controversial issue continued with the displacement of the merchantable quality concept by the implied condition of 'satisfactory quality' with its

---

[1]   *Frost v Aylesbury Dairy Co Ltd* [1905] 1 KB 608.
[2]   *Wilson v Rickett Cockrell &Co Ltd* [1954] 1 QB 598; cf *Aswan Engineering Establishment Co v Lupdine Ltd* [1987] 1 WLR 1.
[3]   *Stevenson v Beverley Bentinck Ltd* [1976] 1 WLR 483; *Blakemore v Bellamy* (1982) 126 Sol Jo 852; *Stevenson v Rogers* [1999] 1 All ER 613.
[4]   Supply of Goods (Implied Terms) Act 1973.

new definition.[5] We may conclude that the courts are likely to continue to find old cases helpful, both for reasons of culture and because it aids them in exercising discretion under the Act.

The implied condition that goods are of satisfactory quality in s 14(2) of the 1979 Act, and the equivalent provisions in other contracts where property in goods passes and contracts of hire, was introduced by an amendment under the Sale and Supply of Goods Act 1994 following the Report of the Law Commission *Sale and Supply of Goods*.[6] The terminology of the 1893 Act, involving 'merchantable quality', which was carried over into the 1979 Act was no longer felt to be appropriate to many contemporary transactions where the buyer was seeking to use the goods rather than to sell them on. While arguably no more precise than the terminology which it replaced,[7] the concept of 'satisfactory quality' appears to be closer in nature to what most consumers would expect of goods which they purchase. Under the (amended) s 14(2) 'goods are of satisfactory quality if they meet the standard that a reasonable person would regard as satisfactory, taking account of any description of the goods, the price (if relevant) and all the other relevant circumstances' (s 14(2A)).[8] The reference to price is relatively unimportant unless a substantial difference is involved.[9] Thus 'sale goods' must live up to the normal standard although the consumer must expect slight damage or a degree of shop-soiling if the description 'seconds' is used.

The amendment to the 1979 Act brought considerable change to the list of matters to be considered in determining whether the quality condition had been complied with or not. Aspects of the quality of goods are listed and include fitness for all the purposes for which goods of that kind are commonly supplied, appearance and finish, freedom from minor defects, safety and durability (s 14(2B)).[10] Explicit inclusion of durability and safety were new additions in 1994, although the courts had previously recognised these as elements of merchantable quality. The inclusion of durability was a long overdue reform, but remains a vague requirement. The Law

---

5   JN Adams *Atiyah's The Sale of Goods* (Pitman, 9th edn, 1995) p 140ff.
6   Law Com no 160 (Cm 137). The equivalent provision for contracts for the transfer of property in goods and contracts for the hire of goods are ss 4(2) and 9(2) of the Supply of Goods and Services Act 1982 (as amended) respectively.
7   JN Adams *Atiyah's The Sale of Goods* (Pitman, 9th edn, 1995) p 140.
8   The equivalent provision for contracts for the transfer of property in goods and contracts for the hire of goods are ss 4(2A) and 9(2A) of the Supply of Goods and Services Act 1982 (as amended) respectively.
9   *BS Brown & Son Ltd v Craiks Ltd* [1970] 1 WLR 752.
10   The Supply of Goods and Services Act 1982 provides no equivalent definition for contracts for the transfer of property in goods and contracts for the hire of goods. It appears likely, however, that the courts would derive assistance from the definition in s 14(2B) of the Sale of Goods Act 1979 (as amended).

Commission rejected any attempt to precisely specify the period for which goods should last to satisfy a requirement of durability, indicating that goods should last a reasonable time, and that this would not be the same period for all goods.[11] However the EC Directive on Consumer Guarantees[12] requires Member States to make available to consumers the remedies under the Directive (discussed below) for a period of two years as from the delivery of the goods (Article 5(1)). In effect this creates a specification of durability with a *minimum* period of two years.

Some critics suggest that the durability requirement should be extended, as it is in some other common law countries, to oblige manufacturers to maintain sufficient spare parts and/or repair facilities for a minimum period of time.[13] The Law Commission did not feel able to support such proposals for the UK, as it felt that the primary obligation should remain with the retailer, and that small retailers should not be burdened by excessive requirements.[14]

The requirement of 'freedom from minor defects' appears to reverse case law which had suggested that whether goods could be expected to be free from minor defects depended on the price paid. Many of the cases involve cars.[15] Thus in *Bernstein v Pamson Motors (Golders Green) Ltd*[16] it was said that while a Rolls-Royce car buyer might not put up with scratches on the bodywork the buyer of a more modest car might have to. The courts were effectively legitimating sloppy manufacturing processes by sanctioning minor defects, even in new cars, by reference to the expectations of buyers. In contrast the Law Commission thought it unsatisfactory that in *Millars of Falkirk Ltd v Turpie*[17] a consumer was left without a remedy for a leak in the power-assisted steering system of a new car. They thought it unacceptable in such a case that 'the buyer should have to put up even with minor defects without a remedy...'[18] The

---

[11]   *Sale and Supply of Goods* (Law Com no 160 (1987)) para 3.49.

[12]   Directive 1999/44/EC, OJ L 171 07.07.99 pp 0012–0016.

[13]   See the New Zealand Consumer Guarantees Act 1993, s 12 (but subject to an exception s 42 where the consumer is notified prior to purchase that the manufacturer does not undertake to supply repair facilities and spares); Consumer Protection Act 1996 (Saskatchewan), ss 48, 50(2) (both noted and reproduced in CJ Miller, BW Harvey and DL Parry *Consumer and Trading Law: Text, Cases and Materials* (OUP, 2nd edn, 1998). Cf California Civil Code (1987), ss 1793.2, a classic example of a 'lemon law'.

[14]   *Sale and Supply of Goods* (Law Com no 160 (1987)) para 3.66.

[15]   *Leaves v Wadham Stringer (Cliftons) Ltd* [1980] RTR 308; *Millars of Falkirk Ltd v Turpie* 1976 SLT (Notes) 66; *Spencer v Claud Rye (Vehicles) Ltd* unreported, cited in M Whincup 'Reasonable Fitness of Cars' (1975) 39 MLR 660, 661–162; cf *Jackson v Chrysler Acceptances Ltd* [1978] RTR 474.

[16]   [1987] 2 All ER 220. cf *Rogers v Parish (Scarborough) Ltd* [1987] 2 All ER 232.

[17]   1976 SLT (Notes) 66.

[18]   *Sale and Supply of Goods* (Law Com no 160 (1987)) para 3.43.

line taken by the courts can partly be explained by the fact that a finding that the implied condition had been breached would give the buyer the right to reject the goods (unless the right had been lost through acceptance or for other reasons) and that the remedy appeared disproportionate to the loss suffered where defects were minor. The Law Commission addressed this problem in its 1987 report and as a result the legislation removes the right to reject in commercial contracts where defects are minor, though retains the right for consumers (s 15A). Additionally the 1994 Act gives buyers the right of partial rejection (s 35A), addressing circumstances where one, separable, part of the goods is defective, but the remainder satisfactory.

The satisfactory quality condition does not apply to defects specifically drawn to the consumer's attention before the sale (s 14(2C)(a)). The word 'specifically' requires that the precise defect be identified: general statements by retailers that there may be defects are inadequate. Further it does not apply if a consumer examines a product before the sale, as regards defects which that examination ought to reveal (s 14(2C)(b)). Signed statements on sale documents that a consumer has examined the product cannot substitute for a genuine examination and will also be void as an exemption clause. The proviso protects the consumer who does not examine a product before purchase, although she may yet be denied recovery for any loss incurred on the grounds of not treating the product properly or of not mitigating losses.

5   FITNESS FOR A SPECIFIED PURPOSE

An alternative to a claim that a product is not of satisfactory quality is s 14(3) of the Sale of Goods Act 1979, which provides:

> Where the seller sells goods in the course of a business and the buyer, expressly or by implication, makes known—
> (a)   to the seller, or
> (b)   where the purchase price or part of it is payable by instalments and the goods were previously sold by a credit-broker to the seller, to that credit-broker,
> any particular purpose for which the goods are being bought, there is an implied condition that the goods supplied under the contract are reasonably fit for that purpose, whether or not that is a purpose for which such goods are commonly supplied, except where the circumstances show that the buyer does not rely, or that it is unreasonable for him to rely, on the skill or judgment of the seller or credit broker.

The courts accept that there is no need for a consumer specifically to state the purpose of a product when it is obvious and they are prepared to infer a reliance on the retailer's skill and judgment in selecting stock unless there is evidence to the contrary.[19] The section can also be used to ensure a higher than normal standard in a product as long as the consumer informs the retailer about this.[20] If a consumer buys a small car and on enquiry is told that it will pull a caravan although normally this would not be expected, she has a remedy if the retailer's assurances prove unfounded.[1] There will be a breach of the implied term if a consumer is assured that a particular cloth is suitable for making dresses although normally it would only be used for industrial purposes, like making bags.[2] A consumer with a peculiarly sensitive skin will have a remedy if she develops dermatitis as a result of wearing clothing, if she has been assured by the retailer that it is suitable for all skins.[3] As long as there is partial reliance by a consumer on the retailer's skill and judgment there will be a breach of the implied term even if the consumer has relied to a greater extent on his own judgment. Simply because a consumer selects products in a self-service store or inspects a product before buying does not exclude the section.[4] But if a consumer provides a retailer with a complete specification for a product and places no reliance on its judgment, the retailer is only responsible for sub-standard workmanship and not for the lack of suitability of the product for the purpose needed.

The EC Directive on Consumer Guarantees[5] uses the general concepts of conformity and non-conformity with the contract to encapsulate the substantive obligations of the seller (Article 4). Aspects of conformity include correspondence with descriptions and samples (Article 4(2)(a)), fitness for particular purposes made known by the buyer to the seller (Article 4(2)(b)), 'fitness for the purposes for which goods of the same type are normally used' (Article 4(2)(c)), and showing 'the quality and performance which are normal in goods of the same type and which the consumer can reasonably expect...' (Article 4(2)(d)). It would appear that the implied terms of the Sale of Goods Act 1979 (as amended) already comply with these definitions of conformity and this would suggest that no amendment to these aspects of the current regime is required. It is possible, however, that in their detailed application the concept of non-conformity might be held to have a different meaning than that currently

---

Grant v Australian Knitting Mills Ltd [1936] AC 85; *Godley v Perry* [1960] 1 WLR 9; cf *Henry Kendall & Sons v William Lillco & Sons Ltd* [1969] 2 AC 31, at 84, 106–107, 124–125.
20   See *Wormell v RHM Agriculture (East) Ltd* [1986] 1 All ER 769.
1   Cf *Baldry v Marshall* [1925] 1 KB 260.
2   Cf *BS Brown & Sons v Craiks* [1970] 1 WLR 752.
3   *Griffiths v Peter Conway Ltd* [1939] 1 All ER 685. See also *Ashington Piggeries Ltd v Christopher Hill Ltd* [1972] AC 441.
4   For example, *Priest v Last* [1903] 2 KB 148.
5   OJ L 171 07.07.99 pp 0012–0016.

given to breach of an implied condition by the English courts. A major change effected by the Directive is that the European Court of Justice will become the final arbiter of the interpretation of the Act, by means of the preliminary reference procedure and there is considerable scope for testing of the UK provisions by this means.

6   REMEDIES

The law provides two remedies for consumers who receive faulty products in breach of the implied terms of quality of ss 13–14 of the Sale of Goods Act 1979 (as amended): the right to reject them and the right to money damages. The EC Directive on Consumer Guarantees,[6] noted above, requires significant changes to the range and nature of remedies available under the 1979 Act. We noted above that many retailers have policies under which they accept the return of goods and provide refunds without the consumer having to allege or prove breach of express or implied contract terms. Where available the application of such policies will dispose of most complaints which the consumer may have regarding the quality of a product. Many retailers, particularly smaller ones, do not operate such policies. Some consumer complaints (for example for damage to other goods or personal injury consequential upon the defects in the product) would not come within these voluntary policies. Furthermore most voluntary policies of this kind operate for a limited period only, typically 14 or 28 days. Many retailers will want to resolve disputes quickly and straightforwardly and are likely to provide immediate remedies for defects drawn to their attention falling outside their voluntary policies. These remedies might include credit notes, allowances on future purchases, repair and replacement in addition to refunds. Acceptance of these remedies may provide the most practical means of resolving disputes, though acceptance of a credit note or allowances on future purchases causes the consumer to lose the statutory right to reject the goods. Accepting a repair or a replacement might foreclose the consumer's possibility of rejecting, but in any event he can still claim damages for a continuing or new defect. It is important to understand the legal remedies available to understand the ways in which retailers exercise discretion over complaints and the approach of the courts in that very small number of cases which reach litigation.

---

[6]   OJ L 171 07.07.99 pp 0012–0016. The Directive requires the UK government to implement the necessary changes by 1 January 2002.

(a)   Rejection

The immediate response of many consumers when they find a product is defective is to attempt to reject the product and to recover any money paid to the retailer. The implied terms of quality in ss 13–14 of the Sale of Goods Act 1979 are conditions, breach of which may entitle consumers to reject.

Consumers lose the right to reject a faulty product once they 'accept' it. This is the effect of s 11(4) of the Sale of Goods Act 1979:

> Subject to section 35A below where a contract of sale is not severable and the buyer has accepted the goods or part of them, the breach of a condition to be fulfilled by the seller can only be treated as a breach of warranty, and not as a ground for rejecting the goods and treating the contract as repudiated, unless there is an express or implied term of the contract to that effect.

Section 61(1) provides that the remedy for breach of warranty is damages.

Acceptance is defined in ss 34–35 of the Act; their effect can be summarised as follows:

(a)   consumers are deemed to accept a product where they intimate to the retailer that they have accepted ('express acceptance');

(b)   consumers are not deemed to accept if they have previously examined a product delivered to them until they have had a reasonable opportunity to do so: s 34(1);

(c)   where consumers have examined a product, or have had a reasonable opportunity to do so, they are deemed to accept if (1) they do any act in relation to the product which is inconsistent with the retailer's ownership; (2) after a lapse of a reasonable time[7] they retain the product without intimating to the retailer that they have rejected it: s 35(1).

Express acceptance will be unusual in the consumer context. It mainly occurs in commercial dealings when a buyer tests a product and indicates satisfaction that it meets any requirements. It seems that a consumer who signs a receipt merely acknowledging delivery will not be accepting a product. Previously retailers could include written in contracts terms excluding the right to reject or limiting the period in which rejection had to occur. Such clauses were not common in consumer transactions and in any event are now rendered void in consumer sales.[8]

Implied acceptance is more difficult: what is an examination or a reasonable opportunity to conduct one? what is an act inconsistent with the retailer's ownership? and what is the lapse of a reasonable period? If

---

[7]   By s 59 what constitutes a reasonable time is a question of fact.

[8]   Unfair Contract Terms Act 1977, s 13; Unfair Terms in Consumer Contracts Regulations 1999, SI 1999/2083, Sch 2, para 1(q).

consumers fail to complain to a retailer about an obvious defect when they buy a product or when it is delivered, they will lose the right to reject. *Milner v Tucker*[9] is an old case but a useful illustration. A chandelier was incomplete when it was delivered to the consumer but nothing was done for six months. The court held that if the consumer had wanted to reject, he 'should have given the plaintiff notice immediately; and have returned it as soon as he could'.[10]

A typical situation these days is where a product has a latent defect which does not manifest itself until sometime after the consumer starts using it. The consumer complains and the retailer promises a repair. After attempts at repair prove abortive the consumer finally purports to reject. Now on one interpretation of the relevant sections it could be argued that the consumer loses the right to reject in these circumstances. Use of a product could be said to be inconsistent with the retailer's ownership and might also mean that a reasonable period has elapsed.[11] The same points could be made if a consumer agrees to a product being repaired. In each case the underlying policy argument against allowing rejection would seem to be that substantial use or having repairs done would prevent the consumer returning the product in the same condition as when it was bought.

On the other hand there are strong arguments for allowing consumers to retain the right to reject in the circumstances outlined. Many defects in modern consumer durables are latent and not apparent until after considerable use.[12] Consumers cannot be expected to employ experts to examine every product they buy, even if it is prudent to do so for some items like secondhand cars when organisations like the Automobile Association operate advisory services.[13] Moreover, consumers should not be prejudiced into postponing rejection just because they are misled by a retailer's assertion that a product can be repaired.[14] For these reasons it is desirable that the courts interpret the concept of acceptance in the Act as narrowly as possible. Consumers who use a product before a latent defect develops should be regarded as subjecting it to reasonable examination, which is not inconsistent with the seller's ownership, as long

---

9   (1823) 171 ER 1082.
10   At 1083.
11   Cf *Armaghdown Motors Ltd v Gray Motors Ltd* [1963] NZLR 5 (registration of car in own name inconsistent with seller's ownership).
12   See Brett J's judgment in *Heilbut v Hickson* (1872) LR 7 CP 438.
13   *Long v Lloyd* [1958] 1 WLR 753 and *Leaf v International Galleries* [1950] 2 KB 86 can be distinguished on these grounds; they involve products where expert examination was practical.
14   *Shofield v Emerson-Brantingham Implements Co* (1918) 43 DLR 509; *Freeman v Consolidated Motors Ltd* (1968) 69 DLR (2d) 581.

as the time period involved is not excessive. It should be irrelevant that a product cannot be returned in the same state as when the consumer purchased it. Overall, the losses businesses consequently incur can be regarded as counterbalanced by those consumers suffer in terms of lost time, opportunity costs and mental anguish.

The problem of acceptance with consumer products has never been properly considered by the English courts, although several decisions touch on it. A liberal approach has been adopted on the parallel issue of affirmation in several hire purchase cases.[15] But the courts have not uniformly applied similar reasoning in sale of goods cases involving consumers. In *Bernstein v Pamson Motors (Golders Green) Ltd*[16] it was held that the consumer-purchaser of a new car had accepted the goods by virtue of having had possession of them for a reasonable time, when the car had been in his possession for three weeks, during which period he had driven 140 miles. The defect in the car was a serious one, a piece of sealant coming loose and cutting off the oil supply to the camshaft, causing the car to stop with potentially dangerous consequences while being driven on a motorway. There was no doubt that the seller was in breach of the implied condition in s 14(2). As a consequence of it being held that he had accepted the car he was entitled only to damages: the value of lost petrol, the cost of repair, compensation for a 'totally spoiled day' and for five days he was without the car before he turned down the offer of a replacement vehicle. This decision appears particularly hard on the consumer. In other cases much longer periods have elapsed between sale and rejection. Thus in *Rogers v Parish (Scarborough) Ltd*[17] the buyer had had the car for many months and it had been replaced, but the Court of Appeal did not allow the defendants to argue that the goods had been accepted. The buyer was entitled to reject.

Where the courts interpret the Sale of Goods Act 1979 narrowly, to limit the circumstances in which consumers can reject for breach of the implied terms regarding quality, consumers will be confined to an action in damages. This may be fine in commercial transactions to prevent buyers seizing on a technical breach to avoid taking goods on a falling market, but the situation is entirely different in consumer transactions.

A possible explanation for the restrictive approach of the courts is that the remedy of rejection may be viewed as disproportionate to the loss

---

[15]   *Farnsworth Finance Facilities Ltd v Attryde* [1970] 1 WLR 1053 (rejection of new motorcycle permitted after four months with various attempts at repair); see also *Jackson v Chrysler Acceptances Ltd* [1978] RTR 474.
[16]   [1987] 2 All ER 220.
[17]   [1987] 2 All ER 232

suffered where defects are minor or easily remediable or where defects only affect a relatively small part of a product. The legislature has addressed this problem in two ways. First the Sale and Supply of Goods Act 1994 created the right of partial rejection, where a defect only affects some of the goods and the buyer accepts the remainder (s 35A). This might occur where one discrete part of a product is defective, as with speakers on a hi-fi system, or where one item of a batch is defective (a situation more likely in commercial contracts). The second aspect of the 1994 reforms was the removal of the right of buyers in non-consumer sales to reject the goods where the breach is so slight that rejection would be unreasonable (s 15A). Thus consumer-purchasers retain the right to reject for any breach of the implied condition, whereas non-consumer-purchasers can only reject where the breach is serious. While it might appear that this provision does not affect consumers, it is supportive of the general policy of the 1994 reforms in making it clear that minor defects may breach the implied condition of satisfactory quality, since in non-consumer cases courts can find that minor defects are in breach without the automatic consequence of a right to reject. Put another way, consumers retain the right to reject for minor defects. Consumers typically have to live with minor defects, such as scratches or other minor damage, whereas the effects of minor defects for business purchasers are much less serious. In previous editions of this work arguments were made for reform to broaden the circumstances under which serious breach of the implied conditions should give rise to the right to reject, by narrowing the interpretation of acceptance under the 1979 Act. Such arguments will be overtaken by the substitution for rejection and damages as the main remedies for breach of repair or replacement in the EC Directive on Consumer Guarantees (discussed below).

(b) Damages

Consumers may claim damages for breach of the implied terms of satisfactory quality and fitness for purpose in s 14 of the Sale of Goods Act 1979 (as amended). Alternatively, if the retailer sues for the price, consumers may set up a breach of the implied terms in diminution or extinction of the claim. Three situations can be identified where consumers will seek damages rather than rejection of the product. Firstly, it may be more advantageous to have a defect remedied than to receive back the purchase price, as where supplies of a product are short and it is relatively difficult to obtain. A second situation is where consumers have suffered personal injury because of a defect and need to sue for consequential damages to cover the losses involved. Consumers can obtain substantial amounts in these circumstances, out of all proportion to the cost of the product involved, which becomes largely irrelevant. In *Grant v Australian*

Knitting Mills[18] the plaintiff was awarded £2,450 for dermatitis contracted from underwear, and in *Godley v Perry*[19] a six-year-old boy obtained £2,500 for the loss of his eye caused by a faulty catapult. Thirdly, there are those situations where consumers have no choice but to sue for damages because they have lost the right to reject, as discussed above, by accepting a product within the terms of the Act.

Under English law it is the consumer's responsibility to establish her damages. The measure of damages according to the first branch of the rule in *Hadley v Baxendale*[20] is the loss flowing directly and naturally from the breach of the implied terms. In the case of breach of warranty of quality, s 53(3) establishes a prima facie rule that the loss is the difference between the value that the product would have had without the defect and it actual value at the time of delivery. The prima facie rule would seem also to apply to products which do not conform to their description or which are not fit for their purpose. The value of a consumer product without a defect will generally be the contract price, so the prima facie rule means that damages are equivalent to the difference between the contract price and the value of the product with its defects. Frequently latent defects are not discoverable until some time after delivery and in these circumstances the prima facie rule is displaced and the difference in value is the contract price minus the value when the defect becomes manifest.[1] Delay on the part of the consumer in bringing a claim, however, may cause damages to be assessed at the time of delivery.[2]

If a defect renders a product completely useless the consumer should recover the full contract price under these rules. Some consumer products can be sold despite their defects, if only for scrap value, and this is good evidence for calculating the value difference.[3] Many damaged products cannot be disposed of once they have defects, and in these circumstances a court has to do the best it can in determining their value. In practice the difference in value can often be calculated from the cost of repair.[4] The cost of repair is of no assistance, however, in those cases where it costs more to repair a product than to purchase a new one. In applying these rules the Canadian courts favour consumers, by adopting the full purchase price as the prima facie measure of damages, and placing the onus on the retailer to demonstrate that a defective product retains some value.[5]

---

[18]　[1936] AC 85.
[19]　[1960] 1 WLR 9.
[20]　(1854) 9 Exch 341.
[1]　*Ashworth v Wells* (1898) 78 LT 136.
[2]　*Robert Holt & Sons Ltd v Lay* (1972) 7 Recent Law (NZ) 226.
[3]　*Vella v Eagers Retail* [1973] 1 QL 236 (Unroadworthy car = contract price – worth for spare parts).
[4]　But see *Ruxley Electronics and Construction Ltd v Forsyth* [1996] AC 344.
[5]　*Ford Motor Co of Canada v Haley* (1967) 62 DLR (2d) 329.

consumer can also claim damages for consequential loss resulting from a defective product, as long as the loss is not too 'remote'. This is the second part of the rule in *Hadley v Baxendale*, and the House of Lords has interpreted it to mean that there must be a 'serious possibility' or that it must be not unlikely that the consequential loss will occur.[6] Mention has been made of claims for losses incurred by personal injury, and damages in these cases are assessed on the same basis as similar cases in tort. Indeed, the circumstances may be such that the consumer can bring an action under Part I of the Consumer Protection Act 1987 or in negligence. Since strict liability of producers for harm caused by defective products was introduced by the 1987 Act, there is arguably not much difference in the basis of liability in contract (against the retailer) and in tort (against the producer). In many cases the producer may have deeper pockets and a bigger reputation to protect. An action under the 1987 Act will be particularly attractive where consumers injured by a defective product are not in a contractual relationship with the retailer. This issue is discussed at greater length in Chapter 5.

Another example of consequential loss is where a defect in a product causes property damage, as where the brakes of a car fail and it is involved in a collision. The transport costs of returning a defective product can also be claimed under this head. A number of interesting practical questions have never been considered by the courts. Launderette charges are no doubt recoverable if a washing machine develops a defect, and a consumer can claim an amount for bus and taxi fare or car hire when a car is off the road because of a fault.[7] A court in the United States has gone as far as awarding loss of wages incurred by a consumer in taking time off to try to negotiate a settlement with a retailer about a defective product.[8] It seems unlikely that an English court would reach a similar conclusion.

Consumers must mitigate their losses and may not recover damages in full if they fail to do so. Mitigation may involve the consumer in accepting an offer by a retailer if it is without prejudice to any rights she may have. The normal rule is that consumer should not use a defective product if they suspect that further damage will result, but there may be circumstances where a consumer who acts reasonably in seeking to mitigate may recover additional loss thereby incurred. Mitigation is especially relevant to consequential losses; for example, the consumer who suffers personal injury must seek medical assistance. Similarly, the consumer who buys a defective car must use her second car if one is available, employ public

---

6   *Koufos v C Czarnikow Ltd* [1969] 1 AC 350.
7   Cf *Bernstein v Pamson Motors (Golders Green) Ltd* [1987] 2 All ER 220.
8   *Zoss v Royal Chevrolet Inc* 11 UCC Rep Serv 527 (1972).

transport if that is convenient, and if neither of these is feasible and she hires a substitute car she must do so at competitive rates.[9]

(c)   Reform of remedies

The only remedies for breach of the implied conditions in the Sale of Goods Act 1979 are rejection and damages. The Law Commission considered creating a statutory right in consumer transactions for the seller to cure defects (by repair or replacement) where breaches were relatively slight.[10] However ultimately the Law Commission rejected this option on the grounds first that it was 'too adverse to consumers' interests' and second that the proposed new remedy would be too complex in practice.[11] The Law Commission suggested that the numbers of consumers unreasonably (but legally) seeking to reject goods was relatively small. Their worry was that '[a]ny legal ground upon which rejection might arguably be resisted, however weak such ground might be on the facts, gives the seller a potential weapon with which to undermine the position of the ordinary consumer...There should be no ambiguity or misunderstanding about the rights of the consumer buyer'.[12]

Notwithstanding the reservations of the Law Commission, the EC Directive on Consumer Guarantees requires Member States to provide that the chief remedy for non-conformity of the goods with the contract shall be a right for the consumer to have the goods brought into conformity by replacement or repair (Article 3(3)). Only where the repair or replacement remedies are not available or where the seller has not carried out the remedial work within a reasonable time or without significant inconvenience to the consumer, is the consumer to be entitled to have a reduction in the price or rescission of the contract (ie rejection) (Article 3(5)). The new repair or replacement remedy is not available where it is impossible or disproportionate. In those circumstances the consumer will only be entitled to a reduction in the price or damages. The rescission remedy is not to be available where the lack of conformity is minor.

Assessing the terms of the Directive, on the one hand it is progressive in the emphasis it places on the new remedy of repair or replacement which, in many cases, is as much as the consumer wants and is less costly

---

9   Cf *Dimond v Lovell* [2000] 2 All ER 897, [2000] 2 WLR 1121, HL.
10   *Working Paper No 85* (1983) paras 4.43–4.47.
11   *Sale and Supply of Goods* (Law Com no 160 (1987)) para 4.14.
12   *Sale and Supply of Goods* (Law Com no 160 (1987)) para 4.14. Compare the Saskatchewan Consumer Protection Act 1996, ss 57, 59 which put into practice a cure remedy similar to that discussed by the Law Commission.

to the business than rejection.[13] Additionally it will remove the significance of the concept of acceptance, since the main remedies under the Directive are not barred where goods are accepted, but continue to be available for two years (Article 5). On the other hand implementation of the Directive will mark a significant step backwards for consumer rights if it reduces the availability of the rejection remedy, removing its availability in cases where defects are minor. While it may be unreasonable for a consumer to reject goods when defects are minor, the certainty associated with the unqualified right to reject defective goods creates a relatively strong bargaining position for consumers and, in cases where there is a total loss of confidence in a retailer or a lack of appropriate response it permits the consumer to terminate the relationship completely.

It is open to the UK to implement the Directive in such a way as to maintain the more stringent rights currently available to consumers (eg a right to reject for minor defects) (Article 8). However, there may be some reluctance to do so because of the provision of the Directive that the remedies under it shall be available for two years from the date of delivery. A possible solution would be to remove the right to reject for minor defects on acceptance (reflecting the current law) while complying with the Directive by providing that rejection is available for non-minor defects for two years. It is open to the UK to give consumers additional protection to that anticipated by the Directive by maintaining rejection as the chief remedy, and placing the repair/replace remedy in a lower position in the hierarchy—being available in every case where a consumer does not want to exercise the right to reject.

---

[13]   For a general assessment and comparison with current English law see C Twigg-Felsner and R Bradgate 'The EC Directive on Certain Aspects of the Sale of Consumer Goods and Associated Guarantees: All Talk and No Do?' (2000) 2 Web JCLI.

Chapter 5

Minimum quality standards for products: manufacturers' liability

For many products the chief reasons for consumers choosing them are linked to the reputation and marketing of the manufacturer. Though the retailer is often merely a conduit in this more remote manufacturer-consumer relationship it bears the chief legal responsibility for the quality of the product (discussed above, Chapter 4): the responsibility of manufacturers for quality has traditionally been rather limited. But pressures during the twentieth century have considerably narrowed the immunity from liability, and this trend seems set to continue. The difficulty faced by consumers in the age of mass production and globalisation is that they are unlikely to have any direct relationship, contractual or otherwise, with those who produce the goods they consume. The privity of contract doctrine has historically both prevented third parties to retail contracts having the burden of that contract placed upon them (thus protecting manufacturers from liability) while at the same time excluding the consumer from the benefit of the contract under which the manufacturer supplied the product to a distributor or retailer. This problem is compounded for consumers adversely affected by defective products which they did not purchase, as they are not even in a relationship of privity with the retailer.[1]

The privity of contract doctrine has been evaded in a number of ways, through a finding of a collateral contract between manufacturer and customer (in limited circumstances) on the basis of statements made by the manufacturer (either generally, or in the form of a manufacturers' guarantee), and through the imposition of common law negligence and

---

[1] *Donoghue v Stevenson* [1932] AC 562.

statutory strict liability in tort for property damage, personal injuries and death caused by defective products. The last years of the twentieth century saw clamour for reform of the privity of contract doctrine, and legislation enacted in 1999 will considerably reduce the impact of the doctrine. In this chapter we consider the somewhat limited liability of manufacturers in contract and the more extensive liability in tort. In practice we note that the guarantees voluntarily made to consumers (but possibly enforceable directly as contracts) provide the most significant basis for claims by consumers against producers. The provision of remedies for defective products under such manufacturers' guarantees is rather hidden from the mainstream of legal practice, because, though many thousands of claims are met or settled each year (leading us to the hypothesis that they are more significant than product liability claims in tort) they are rarely, if ever, the subject matter of reported litigation.

I   CONTRACTUAL LIABILITY FOR MANUFACTURERS' STATEMENTS AND GUARANTEES

There have been several cases where the courts have held that an express representation by a manufacturer to a consumer as to the quality of its products gives rise to a collateral contract.[2] The leading case of *Carlill v Carbolic Smokeball Co*[3] recognised that a statement in a manufacturer's advertisement could give rise to a collateral contract with a consumer who bought the product from a retailer.[4] The precedent is there; whether the courts will apply it to modern advertising depends on whether they are sufficiently attuned to its techniques and subtleties. The difficulty is that the courts do not regard most statements in advertisements as being intended to create legal relations. It seems that there must be an unambiguous promise, as with *Carlill*, where the manufacturer offered to pay £100 to anybody who bought and used the smokeball in the prescribed manner and subsequently caught influenza.[5] The doctrine applies not only to statements about quality, but also to other forms of promise linked to the purchase of products (and for that matter services).[6] Recently the

---

[2]   But different considerations may apply in contracts between businesses. See *Lexmead (Basingstoke) Ltd v Lewis* [1982] AC 225.

[3]   [1893] 1 QB 256.

[4]   See also *Wood v Letrik* (1932) Times, 13 January (£500 guarantee); *Goldthorpe v Logan* [1943] 2 DLR 519 (results guaranteed); *Murray v Sperry Rand Corp* (1979) 23 OR (2d) 456.

[5]   A full historical account of the background to the case and its doctrinal significance can be found in AWB Simpson *Leading Cases in the Common Law* (OUP, 1995) Chapter 10.

[6]   *Bowerman v ABTA* (1995) 14 TR LR 246.

lower courts have applied the doctrine in numerous cases arising out a bungled promotion made by the major electrical retailer Hoover.[7] The company promised free flights to consumers who purchased Hoover products to a value exceeding £100, but dramatically underestimated the demand for the offer. This case provides an important lesson to manufacturers about the potential pitfalls of special offers of this kind.

In other jurisdictions it is possible to enforce statements made about the quality of products directly against a manufacturer, in the absence either of a direct contractual relationship or of some specific promise as to a remedy should the product not comply with the statement. The courts in the United States had no difficulty in applying the doctrine of breach of express warranty where assertions in manufacturers' advertisements about product quality proved untrue.[8] The same result is achieved in Australia by legislation, which provides that a consumer can sue a manufacturer for loss or damage by reason of the failure of a product to comply with an undertaking, assertion or statement in relation to its quality, performance or characteristics, the natural tendency of which is to induce persons to acquire it.[9]

In certain limited circumstances the Contracts (Rights of Third Parties) Act 1999 provides a right for consumers to enforce a term of a contract between manufacturer and retailer. The right will arise where the contract expressly provides for enforcement by such a third party (which is not likely to be very common in cases involving consumers) or where the contract benefits an identified third party and there is no indication that the term should not be enforceable (s 1(1)). The clearest case where the Act might benefit consumers is where goods are made to order by a manufacturer and sold through a retailer, as often happens with furniture such as sofas and beds. The sale of other products which are delivered, though not made, to order (for example cars) might also meet the second test for the operation of the Act. In each case the quality provisions in the contract of sale to the retailer might be enforceable by a consumer. This might be of particular importance where a retailer has become insolvent or otherwise disappeared such that a consumer is unable to secure a remedy.[10]

---

[7]   See, eg, *Freeman v Hoover Ltd* (1995) 5 Consumer Policy Review 218; R Lawson 'Sales Promotion Schemes: The Participants' Rights' (1994) 13 Trading Law 41.

[8]   *Baxter v Ford Motor Co* 12 P 2d 409 (1932); *Greenman v Yuba Power Products Inc* 377 P 2d 897 (1963).

[9]   Trade Practices Act 1974, s 74G. The limitation 'in relation to the quality, performance or characteristics' of a product excludes, for example, a manufacturer's promise in relation to servicing. For New Zealand see S Todd 'Consumer Law Reform in New Zealand: The Consumer Guarantees Act 1993' (1994) 2 Consumer Law Journal 100.

[10] See, eg, the circumstances of the litigation in *Lexmead (Basingstoke) Ltd v Lewis* [1982] AC 225 (especially the Court of Appeal decision).

Quite distinct from the application of the 1999 Act a credit lender who has a pre-existing arrangement with a supplier of goods or services for the giving of credit to consumers (for example by means of a credit card or for purchase of a car or furniture) is jointly and severally liable with the supplier for breach of contract and misrepresentation by the supplier, in respect of contracts for values over £100. This provision of the Consumer Credit Act 1974 (s 75) is discussed more fully in Chapter 7 below.

In many cases manufacturers offer consumers explicit guarantees in relation to the quality of their products, with undertakings that repairs will be made (often with one or both of free parts and labour) within a certain period from the date of purchase. The consumer typically has to complete a registration form which, arguably, has the effect of creating direct contractual relations between consumer and producer. If manufacturers' guarantees were litigated today the courts would have available a range of approaches, ranging between the formal analysis which searches for all the elements of a valid contract, much as occurred in *Carlill*, and the more modern approach which examines all the circumstances of the case to determine whether what passed between the parties amounted to an enforceable arrangement.[11] A more problematic situation arises where the goods have been sold or given to another consumer. In these circumstances it might be extremely difficult for the new owner to establish either a collateral contract with a manufacturer or a right to enforce the manufacturer-retailer contract under the terms of the 1999 Act.

Whatever the strict legal position, research carried out for earlier editions of this work suggested that most manufacturers seek to honour the guarantees they make. One producer said:

> We deal with any complaint irrespective of its source at the highest possible level, as the ability to bring about customer satisfaction is the best way we can protect the brand image and ensure future sales of products.

Among a sample of 26 manufacturers, mostly operating nationally, the quantity of complaints relative to the output of products ranged from the 'infinitesimal' to 2–3%. Major areas of complaint were servicing, failure of components (in domestic electrical appliances) and spoilage in the case of perishable products. Minor areas included early wear on parts and a poor supply of spare parts. None of the manufacturers mentioned complaints about personal injury or death. That most manufacturers are generous

---

[11]   *Butler Machine Tool Co Ltd v Ex-Cell-O Corpn (England) Ltd* [1979] 1 All ER 965. Note also that the EC Directive 1999/44/EC of the European Parliament and of the Council of 25 May 1999 on certain aspects of the sale of consumer goods and associated guarantees (OJ L 171 07.07.99 p 12) will require the UK government to make manufacturers' guarantees enforceable (Article 6, noted below).

with genuine consumer complaints, at least those involving claims about shoddy goods, is a good argument for bringing the law into line with the practice and making manufacturers jointly liable with retailers.

Guarantees issued by manufacturers typically offer such remedies as replacement of unsatisfactory products (eg food) and rectification of manufacturing defects which become manifest within a specified period like six months or a year (eg cars, domestic electrical equipment). Guarantees perform a promotional function for manufacturers, as well as acting as a system of quality control whereby information can be obtained about the performance of a product, and valuable marketing information collected about consumers.[12] The advantage of a generous guarantee to consumers is that it gives them a remedy without the formality of establishing a legal claim. It can also mean that a product will be repaired by the manufacturer, who has the resources and expertise which the retailer lacks, although the latter is legally responsible. Retailers often try to avoid their legal responsibility by pointing to a manufacturer's guarantee. Relying on the guarantee, then, may be the most practical means for consumers of settling a dispute. A possible disadvantage is that where manufacturers decide against giving redress, consumers may not be able to exercise the right to reject as against the retailer because of the delay and may be confined to an action for money damages.[13]

At one time the term 'guarantee' was clearly an abuse of language, because many manufacturers used a 'guarantee' to exclude their liability for negligence in a situation where a consumer suffered personal injury from a defective product. The Law Commission recommended that consumers should have legal protection because they could not be expected before accepting a guarantee to evaluate precisely the risk involved.[14] Section 5 of the Unfair Contract Terms Act 1977 provides that liability for loss or damage cannot be excluded or restricted by reference to any contract term or notice contained in or operating by reference to a guarantee of a product, ordinarily of a type supplied for private use or consumption, where the loss or damage arises from the product proving defective while in consumer use and resulting from the negligence of a person covered in its manufacture or distribution. 'In consumer use' is defined widely to cover situations where a person is using a product, or has it in his possession for use, otherwise than exclusively for the purpose of a business. Anything in writing is a guarantee if it contains or purports to contain some promise or assurance that defects will be made good by complete or partial replacement, by repair, by monetary compensation or

---

[12] G Priest 'A Theory of the Consumer Product Warranty' (1981) 90 Yale LJ 1297.
[13] See pp 164–167 above.
[14] *Exemption Clauses* (Law Com no 69 (1975)) p 40ff.

otherwise.[15] The upshot is that manufacturers' guarantees now give consumers additional remedies without subtracting from any of their legal rights.

Nevertheless guarantees may not be as extensive as consumers expect. Consumers may still be liable for labour and transport charges where a product is repaired under guarantee. A guarantee may not extend to defective accessories and it may not apply at all if repairs have been attempted by the consumer. Then there are guarantees which, in addition to limitations like these, contain an additional clause which renders them virtually useless: 'In implementing this guarantee the Company and/or the Retailer may charge at their discretion for any service rendered.'[16] On one occasion Lord Denning spoke scathingly about guarantees of this nature which, in his view, could hardly be called 'guarantees' when the additional benefits they conferred were so restrictive.[17] There is widespread agreement that if consumers are lured into buying a product in part because of the promise of a guarantee, then it is highly undesirable that the terms of the guarantee (usually not known to the consumer until after the completion of the transaction) fall significantly below the level of the consumer's expectation, both for reasons of fairness and economic efficiency.

Various attempts have been made to regulate the content of guarantees, going beyond the policy of the Unfair Contract Terms Act 1977, that guarantees should not reduce existing legal rights. The objective of these initiatives has been to create a minimum standard to which any document calling itself a guarantee must conform. Thus the Office of Fair Trading has deployed soft law, in the form of a guide designed to improve on a voluntary basis the clarity, scope and presentation of guarantees. The minimum standards in the OFT guide were that guarantees must include a commitment to undertake repair or replacement of all or specified defective parts for a stated period free of charge (including labour and carriage) and to extend the period where the product is out of action for a significant time. The guide also listed the kind of undesirable restrictions which were to be avoided.[18] The OFT has also been responsible for statutory control, introduced under Part II of the Fair Trading Act 1973, which makes it an offence for a manufacturer to give an indication on a product which appears to have the effect of excluding the inalienable rights of consumers (by virtue of the Sale of Goods Act 1979, ss 12–15 and the Unfair Contract

---

[15] See D Cusine 'Manufacturers' Guarantees and the Unfair Contract Terms Act' [1980] Juridical Review 185.
[16] 'Guarantees' (1976) *Which?* April, p 79.
[17] *Adams v Richardson and Starling Ltd* [1969] 1 WLR 1645, 1648–1649.
[18] *Guarantees: A Guide for Manufacturers* (OFT, 1979),

Terms Act 1977, s 6) to goods corresponding to description, and of satisfactory quality, and fitness for purpose.[19]

A number of statutory reform initiatives have been floated in recent years. A Private Members Bill in 1992 sought to implement the recommendations of a National Consumer Council report which had proposed that the use of the term 'guarantee' be restricted to promises given free of charge. The basic approach was based on disclosure, with standardised labels—'total guarantees', 'retailers' total guarantees' and 'limited guarantees'—to be mandatory, each involving a minimum standard of promise.[20] The Bill was not acceptable to the government of the day and was not adopted into law.[1] A more limited legislative proposal was put out for consultation by the government at that time, which would have made the terms of manufacturers' guarantees civilly enforceable against retailers, manufacturers (if in the UK) or importers.[2] Ultimately this proposal was not pursued by the government.

The UK government is now required to implement the terms of an EC Directive on Consumer Guarantees (discussed more fully above, Chapter 4). The provisions of the Directive do not go as far as a minimum standards approach. Rather they seek to ensure that consumers are not misled by guarantees by requiring that guarantees state that the statutory rights of the consumer against the retailer are not affected by the guarantee, and by requiring that such guarantees are themselves legally enforceable by the consumer.[3] Although the Directive provides that guarantees are to be 'set out in plain intelligible language the contents of the guarantee and the essential particulars necessary for making claims under the guarantee, notably the duration and territorial scope of the guarantee as well as the name and address of the guarantor' (Article 6(2)), the substantive standards of the guarantee are to be set by the offeror rather than by legislative policy. Thus the EC Directive will do nothing to address a major reason for lack of consumer confidence in guarantees, the fact that the rights they offer the consumer are often very limited. UK implementation will require that it be made clear for the first time that guarantees are legally enforceable. The DTI is expected to publish a consultation document on the implementation of the Directive in 2000. Under its new doctrine of legislative

---

[19]   Consumer Transactions Restrictions on Statements Order 1976, SI 1976/1813, article 5. See Chapter 4.

[20]   NCC *Competing in Quality* (1989).

[1]   C Willett 'The Unacceptable Face of the Consumer Guarantees Bill' (1991) 54 MLR 552.

[2]   DTI *Consultation Document on Consumer Guarantees* (1992).

[3]   Directive 1999/44/EC of the European Parliament and of the Council of 25 May 1999 on certain aspects of the sale of consumer goods and associated guarantees (OJ L 171 07.07.99 pp 0012–0016) Article 6.

consolidation (which has led the DTI to propose a consolidation of the Unfair Contract Terms Act 1977 and the Unfair Terms in Consumer Contracts Regulations 1999) then we might expect implementation to be by means of amendment to the Sale of Goods Act 1979. However the DTI may not have sufficient time for the passage of a Bill through Parliament.

In recent years the manufacturer's warranty has been supplemented by the new consumer product of the extended warranty. This is a promise of servicing and sometimes replacement for goods for a period beyond the manufacturers' warranty, which is offered by many retailers. In many instances this is a form of insurance against breakdown (the contract being with a third party), in others it is simply a commitment by a retailer to provide a repair service. These extended warranties have been controversial for a number of reasons.[4] Firstly, they have been the subject of pressurised sales techniques by some retailers. Secondly, they are sometimes rather costly relative to the value of the product. Thirdly, they may amount to the purchase of a right to durability which is already a contractual right under the Sale of Goods Act 1979 (s 14(2)).

2   TORTIOUS LIABILITY FOR PROPERTY DAMAGE, PERSONAL INJURIES AND DEATH

(a)   Background to the current regime

Non-contractual liability for defective products is substantially restricted to personal injuries, death and property damage (ie damage to property other than the product). Neither common law negligence nor the statutory regime of strict liability introduced by Part I of the Consumer Protection Act 1987 will provide remedies in respect of the quality of the goods themselves (which is classed as pure economic loss at common law[5]) nor for other pure economic loss.[6] The reasons for such limitations are that tort law is not generally concerned with the value expected to be secured under a contract. Accordingly tort law does not recognise any harm where, because of a defect, a product is worth less than the purchase price. Such a loss belongs to the realm of contract law. Whereas pure economic loss through products being defective is extremely common, instances of personal injury, death and damage to other property appear to be

---

[4]   C Twigg-Flesner and H Bohling 'Insurance Regulation: When a Warranty is not a Guarantee' (1999) 9 Consumer Policy Review 193; Institute of Trading Standards Administration *Guarantees or Warranties* (1999).

[5]   *Murphy v Brentwood District Council* [1991] 1 AC 398.

[6]   See the discussion of liability for pure economic loss in negligence in Chapter 6 below.

comparatively rare. One indicator which supports this claim is the incidence of litigation. In the twelve years since strict liability was introduced for personal injury, death and property damage caused by defective products there has been virtually no reported litigation under the 1987 Act. This statistic might be explained by reference to the Act having created a regime which is so certain in its effects that no litigation has been required. If this hypothesis is correct then it would suggest that the claims which do arise are simply being settled. However, data collected by the European Commission in the context of its Green Paper reviewing the effectiveness of the Product Liability Directive[7] suggests that neither producers nor their insurers are in fact meeting lots of claims.[8] One possibility is that in combination the strict liability regime, together with the proactive regulatory initiatives of government General and others (discussed further in Chapter 10) and the commercial incentives on producers are keeping products at least sufficiently safe that consumers are rarely harmed by them. Another possibility is that although consumers are injured by products the injuries are relatively minor for consumers, and thus not worth litigating, and that even where injuries are more serious much of the costs is covered by state health care schemes.[9] Whatever the explanation for the paucity of litigation, the European experience is strikingly at odds with that of the United States, where soaring rates of litigation for product liability have created perceptions of a crisis, particular because of the difficulty manufacturers face in securing liability insurance.[10]

Though it may be true that consumers are rarely harmed by defective products, the quantity of harm caused when defective products do reach the market can be substantial. The statutory regime of strict liability introduced in 1987 was in part a response to the widespread harm caused by the marketing in the 1960s of a defective pharmaceutical product known in the UK as Thalidomide. Developed in Germany by the company Chemie Gruenethal, Thalidomide was manufactured in several countries under license and promoted widely as a safe tranquilliser without side effects. Its marketing and use by pregnant women resulted in 8,000–10,000 children

---

[7]   European Commission *Green Paper on Liability for Defective Products* COM (1999) 396 Final. The responses to the Green Paper are published on the Internal Market Directorate General website. See, eg, the response of the Confederation of British Industry which was unable to supply data but suggested that the litigation rates are low and that the few cases that do arise are generally settled out of court.

[8]   This evidence may be compared with evidence collated by the *Royal Commission on Civil Liability and Compensation for Personal Injury* (Cmnd 7054) pp 256–257, which suggested that between 30,000 and 40,000 injuries a year were caused by defective products, including drugs.

[9]   For evidence as to why consumers do or do not litigate see H Genn *Paths to Justice* (Hart, 1999).

[10]   WK Viscusi *Reforming Products Liability* (Harvard University Press, 1991).

being born seriously deformed.[11] Quite apart from its other implications, the Thalidomide tragedy demonstrated the complete inadequacy in the law of most countries either to prevent the marketing of an unsafe drug or to compensate those injured when it was marketed.[12]

The main difficulty facing the Thalidomide children in Britain in seeking compensation for their injuries was in grounding a good cause of action against the company marketing the drug, the Distillers Company (Biochemicals) Ltd. First there was the absence of clear authority on whether the common law provided a remedy for those suffering from a pre-natal injury caused by another's fault. The English Law Commission said that a court would have decided the question favourably, but the matter was not clear.[13] The rights of children to sue for harm caused to them prior to their birth was subsequently clarified by legislative reform.[14] More important was the necessity to establish negligence—that the company had fallen below the standard of care in marketing the drug and/or as to the withdrawing of it once evidence of its effects became apparent.[15] As to the manufacture of Thalidomide, the German company had subjected the drug to only a small number of unsystematic clinical tests, most of which were conducted by doctors in a regular commercial relationship with the firm who lacked special training for the purpose. No proper evaluation of synergistic effects was made and certainly there was no testing for teratogenic effects. Early reports of adverse side-effects were suppressed by Gruenethal, who lied when doctors enquired whether such side-effects had been previously encountered; they had also tried to suppress unfavourable reports and promoted favourable publicity, in some cases by dishonest means.[16]

What of the British distributors, Distillers? In their advertisements they claimed that the drug could be safely administered. A particular claim was that the drug could be given with complete safety to pregnant women and nursing mothers. Distillers carried out no scientific tests themselves before marketing the drug to establish the validity of this claim. The key question in any civil action, therefore, was whether Distillers were negligent in not doing so. Their argument was that tests for teratogenic effects were not

---

[11]   Sunday Times Insight Team *Suffer the Children* (1979).
[12]   H Teff and C Munro *Thalidomide—The Legal Aftermath* (1976).
[13]   *Injuries to Unborn Children* (Law Com no 60 (1974)) pp 2–3.
[14]   Congenital Disabilities (Civil Liability) Act 1976, s 1(1). There may also be a common law duty not to cause pre-natal injury: *McKay v Essex Area Health Authority* [1982] QB 1166; *B v Islington Area Health Authority* [1991] 1 All ER 825.
[15]   H Teff 'Products Liability in the Pharmaceutical Industry at Common Law' (1973) 20 McGill LJ 102, 120.
[16]   H Sjöström and R Nilsson *Thalidomide and the Power of the Drug Companies* (1972) Chapters 3–5.

customary at that time, although critics argued that they did not even follow the best testing procedures of the time. Almost all the legal authorities, including lawyers for the children, thought it unlikely that negligence would be established on this point, although there was greater hope for the time between when Distillers where first notified of suspected teratogenic effects by the Australian obstetrician, Dr William McBride, and before the drug was actually withdrawn from the market some months later.

The belief that the case was too weak for trial on the first point was based primarily on the assumption that at the time Thalidomide was marketed it was not accepted practice to test drugs for teratogenic effects. Scientific opinion then prevailing did not conceive that drugs would damage the developing foetus, especially if they caused little harm to the mother. This assumption about the standards has been challenged, however, and the *Sunday Times* has alleged that in accepting it the lawyers for the children failed to mount as effective a case as possible in the circumstances. Certainly the issue was less clear cut elsewhere.[17]

The English High Court approved a settlement in a test case in 1969 for some of the children.[18] That settlement was quite inadequate in the eyes of many, and at one stage when Distillers made an offer for the remaining children conditional on all parents accepting it, the Court of Appeal upheld the refusal of a number of parents to agree. The court held that, as best next friends of their children, the dissident parents were entitled to have regard to the interests of their children irrespective of the interests of the Thalidomide children as a whole.[19] Meanwhile public opinion from various quarters pressed Distillers to make a more favourable settlement: parliamentary opinion expressed disfavour at the company's proposals; shareholders of the company, including local authorities and institutional investors such as insurance companies, pledged their support for generous treatment, other large enterprises expressed their displeasure at the tardy progress, including a major chain store which threatened to boycott Distillers' other products. Finally a settlement was reached which extended to those who had earlier compromised their claims.[20]

Procedural difficulties also faced the Thalidomide children. An overriding factor was the time delay: over a decade had passed before compensation was finalised. The absence of class actions as compared

---

[17] Cf *Distillers Co (Biochemicals) Ltd v Thompson* [1971] AC 458, 465–466.
[18] *S v Distillers Co (Biochemicals) Ltd* [1969] 3 All ER 1412, [1970] 1 WLR 114.
[19] *In Re Taylor's Application* [1972] 2 QB 369. A constraint on Distillers was their insurance. J Franks 'The Thalidomide Claim: Laws, Fantasy and Reform' (1973) 117 SJ 643.
[20] *Allen v Distillers Co (Biochemicals) Ltd* (1973) Times, 3 July. See also *Allen v Distillers Co (Biochemicals) Ltd* [1974] QB 384.

with the United States meant that the children had to issue separate proceedings alleging the individual circumstances of their injury. A degree of consolidation of these actions was achieved in Britain where the legal aid authorities encouraged all claims to be processed by the same firm of solicitors. A further hitch was the limitation period, which required the institution of proceedings of this nature within three years of the cause of action arising. A large number of children were outside the limitation period and it was necessary to obtain special leave under the extended time provisions of the Limitation Act 1963. The general point is that substantial periods can elapse before drugs are discovered to be dangerous and legal proceedings contemplated. A homely illustration is that the serious danger to human kidneys, caused by ingesting phenacetin in aspirin, is cumulative and only becomes apparent after a number of years. The difficulty is now overcome: the limitation period in the case of personal injury runs from when the prospective plaintiff first knows that an injury is significant and that it is the defendant which caused it.[1]

The weaknesses of the substantive and procedural law in compensating the Thalidomide children have been outlined. But this is not the end of the law's failings, for in Britain the law actually stepped in to hinder the children from benefiting from extra-legal tactics to further their claims. In effect it prevented the use of one weapon the children had to pressure Distillers to increase the settlement offer—the force of public opinion—by granting an injunction to prevent publication of a critical article by the *Sunday Times*.[2] Six years later the European Court of Human Rights held this injunction to violate Article 10 of the European Convention on Human Rights regarding freedom of expression.[3]

(b)   Reform

By contrast to the situation in many countries, the United States suffered comparatively little from Thalidomide. Because its safety was never satisfactorily demonstrated, the Food and Drug Administration there never gave marketing approval for the drug. The legal provision used was introduced following a Thalidomide-type tragedy in the United States in 1937, where a liquid form of new sulpha drug caused nearly a hundred deaths. The Thalidomide tragedy led to the introduction in the UK of controls similar to those in the United States, whereby drugs are not

---

[1]   Limitation Act 1980, ss 11, 11A, 14.
[2]   *A-G v Times Newspapers Ltd* [1974] AC 273, cf *Schering Chemicals Ltd v Falkman Ltd* [1982] QB 1.
[3]   *Sunday Times v United Kingdom* (1979) 2 EHRR 245.

approved for marketing unless they are regarded as safe (see Chapter 12, below). Certain dangerous substances, notably tobacco and alcohol, were excluded from the new UK regime, and government has relied heavily on voluntary measures to reduce the risks to health from these commodities. The statutory regime for issuing regulations controlling particular products (introduced by the Consumer Protection Act 1961, now contained in s 11 of the Consumer Protection Act 1987) imposed strict liability in civil law for harm caused by breach of the regulatory requirements, under a statutory action for breach of statutory duty.[4] But the scope for deployment of this measure is limited by the need to show that the harm was caused by non-compliance with the specific regulations. In practice there is little evidence of litigation grounded on this provision being brought.

In addition to new regulatory developments, the Thalidomide tragedy stimulated pressure for reform of the civil liability rules governing defective products.[5] Though a UK Royal Commission and the English Law Commission had earlier recommended major reforms,[6] it took the adoption of an EC Directive to force a change in the English law.[7] The Law Commission had advanced a number of arguments in favour of reform.[8] Firstly there was a moral argument: losses associated with a defective product should be borne by the manufacturer who creates the risk by putting it into circulation for commercial gain. Secondly, there was the consideration of equity: the easiest way of spreading the loss fairly is to place it on the manufacturer who can recover the cost of insuring against the risk in the price charged for the product. Thirdly, there were matters of efficiency: it is desirable to impose liability on manufacturers because they are in the best position to exercise control over the quality and safety of products, and they can most conveniently insure against the risk, rather than leave it to individual consumers to arrange their own first-party insurance.[9] Finally, there is the political argument: it is desirable to bring the law into line with consumers' expectations, who are led to believe by advertising and promotional material that manufacturers are liable.

These factors in favour of stricter liability were felt by policy makers and legislators to outweigh the disadvantages of the change. Any tendency

---

[4] Consumer Protection Act 1987, s 41.

[5] See the excellent history and analysis in J Stapleton *Product Liability* (1994) Chapter 3.

[6] *Royal Commission on Civil Liability and Compensation for Personal Injury* (Cmnd 7054 (1978)); *Liability for Defective Products* (Law Com no 82 (1977)). See also European Convention on products liability in regard to personal injury and death, European Treaty Series No 91, 1977.

[7] EEC Directive 85/374.

[8] *Liability for Defective Products* (Law Com no 82 (1977)) pp 6–7.

[9] G Calabresi and K Bass 'Right Approach, Wrong Implications: A Critique of McKean on Products Liability' (1970) 38 U Chi LR 74.

of this liability to discourage innovation is more than counterbalanced by the need to compensate adequately those injured by defective products. Despite stricter liability, it seems that companies will be impelled to develop new products for their continued existence, possibly with a greater emphasis on safety to avoid legal actions. It is unlikely to lead to an increase in the currently small number of spurious claims, because consumers still have to establish that the defect caused the harm within a strict liability regime. Further, there is little reason to think that the change to stricter liability will make consumers more careless because their claims will no longer be defeated, or at best reduced, on the basis of contributory negligence. It is unrealistic to think that at present consumers know the law, appreciate the risks they face from defective products or take steps to avoid them. Most consumers undervalue the likelihood of their own involvement in accidents.

It is unlikely that consumers acquire much information about product-related risks from personal experience, since they are unlikely to experience multiple incidents of product-related accidents. Though increasingly common the sharing of information among consumers, via the media or the internet, is still fairly marginal compared to the scale of consumption generally, and is most likely to occur only after a defect has become manifest. Of course manufacturers may have little incentive to provide the information. But even if consumers knew the risks, there is no reason to think that they could take preventive action to avoid every possible accident. The conclusion is obvious: negligence has no deterrent effect on consumers and the introduction of strict liability is unlikely to affect their behaviour.

The most serious objection to strict liability is the cost. Unfortunately an evaluation of studies carried out on the impact of strict liability rules in the United States suggests that there is no reliable basis for understanding the effects of the regime.[10] It would appear, however, that US producers face a heavier burden of claims than is true of UK producers. In any case it seems clear that factors in the United States creating pressures for a large number of high value product claims are not present elsewhere. In particular the UK does not yet have a developed contingency fee system (discussed above, Chapter 3) of the kind which encourages American lawyers to seek personal injury litigation in return for a percentage of any amount awarded. It has, for example, been estimated that in the mid-1970s there were only two UK product liability claims filed for every 700 such claims in the US.[11] The high cost of medical care in the United States is a

---

[10]   J Stapleton *Product Liability* (1994) p 69.
[11]   J Stapleton *Product Liability* (1994) p 79 citing P Atiyah 'Tort Law and Alternatives: Some Anglo-American Comparisons' (1987) 198 Duke LJ 1002, 1013.

large component of personal injury awards there, whereas UK awards are lower, in part because so much health care is publicly funded through the National Health Service.[12]

(c)   Strict liability and negligence today

Notwithstanding the existence of many detailed and well-articulated arguments in favour of strict liability for harm caused by defective products, when the principle was adopted in the UK it was chiefly for reasons of harmonisation of laws in the European Community (as an aid to the completion of the internal market) rather than for purposes of consumer protection.[13] The EC Directive on Product Liability was intended to create a more level playing field for producers, such that they would face equivalent legal risks, regardless of which member state was chosen for the marketing of their products. Equally consumers were to be encouraged to shop in any member state, confident that they would benefit from equivalent legal protection to that which they had at home. It has been argued that a central effect and intent of the product liability directive was to pre-empt the kind of more radical reform which might result in the replacement of tort liability generally with the kind of accident compensation scheme which operates in New Zealand.[14]

Part I of the Consumer Protection Act 1987, which implements the EC Directive, has at its heart the principle that producers shall be liable for defects in their products which cause harm to consumers. The concept of producer is rather widely drawn, so as to catch not only the actual manufacturer, but also others involved in processing, businesses which apply their own-brand label to products (for example supermarket chains), and importers of products into the EU (s 2(2)). Additionally suppliers of products who fail to identify the producer can be held liable as if they were the producer (s 2(3)). So, for example, a pharmacist issuing generic drugs who is unable or unwilling to identify the producer can liable under the Act. Where more than one producer is involved, for example with a product made up of a number of components, the Act provides both for joint and several liability (s 2(5)) and for a defence for components manufacturers where the defect is the result of the design of a subsequent producer (s 4(1)(f)). The objective lying behind these scope provisions is to ensure

---

[12]   *Liability for Defective Products* (Law Com no 82 (1977)) pp 14–15. J Stapleton *Product Liability* (1994) p 70 suggests that the claim that US awards are higher than in the UK may be overstated, on the basis of comparative research on asbestos litigation.

[13]   S Weatherill *EC Consumer Law and Policy* (1997) p 92.

[14]   J Stapleton *Product Liability* (1994) p 52ff.

that an injured consumer always has someone available to sue, even where the actual manufacturer is unidentified, or unreachable (because outside the EU). Nevertheless the scope of liability is somewhat narrower than that provided for in the American Third Restatement of the Law of Torts, which extends liability to anyone selling or distributing defective products in the course of business.[15] The explanatory notes to this provision are explicit in their recognition that products liability in American law is a *sui generis* blend of contract and tort principles.

The extent of the protected class under the 1987 Act is somewhat slippery. In general businesses are not intended to receive protection from the Act. Thus damage to property not intended for private use (either by the producer or by the owner) is excluded from the provisions of the Act (s 5(2)). However all personal injury is recoverable under the Act, where attributable to a defective product. Harm caused by primary agricultural products and game was excluded from the 1987 Act (s 2(4)), following the terms of an option offered by the Directive (Article 15(1)(a)). However the Directive has been amended to require Member States by December 2000 to remove any exemption for primary agricultural products and game.[16] It does not matter whether the defective product is being used for private or commercial purposes at the time the harm is caused. An injured factory worker is as able to claim damage from a defective chemical or piece of equipment as a consumer injured by a defective item of household equipment.

The statutory definitions of the potential defendants and claimants may be contrasted with the common law position, where both defendants and claimants in negligence actions are defined by reference to foreseeability (a producer could foresee that a failure to take care would cause harm to the ultimate consumer[17]). The duty in negligence extends beyond producers of finished products to encompass manufacturers of component parts.[18] Additionally others who ought to foresee that failure to take reasonable care might harm consumers owe a duty, and this class of persons extends considerably beyond the scope of the statutory regime to include retailers, repairers and those who hire out products, and also those responsible for the testing and certification of products.[19] Thus negligence liability continues to have relevance, even though the statutory regime is likely to be preferred where it is available. In negligence the range of liability is limited by reference to a requirement of proximity between

---

[15]   American Law Institute, *Restatement of the Law Third, Torts: Product Liability* (1998) Chapter 1, § 1.
[16]   Directive 99/34/EC OJ L 141 4.06.99 pp 20–21. Implementation is to be achieved via the Consumer Protection Act 1987 (Product Liability) (Modification) Order 2000, in draft at the time of writing.
[17]   *Donoghue v Stevenson* [1932] AC 562, 599.
[18]   *Lexmead (Basingstoke) Ltd v Lewis* [1982] AC 225.
[19]   *Miller: Product Liability and Safety Encyclopedia* para **III [11]**.

defendant and claimant, conceived of in product liability claims in terms that there was 'no reasonable possibility'[20] or 'no reasonable prospect'[1] of intermediate examination of the product between the time it left the producer and reached the ultimate consumer. In *Donoghue v Stevenson* itself the requirement of proximity was satisfied because the ginger beer bottle in which there was alleged to be the remains of a decomposing snail was opaque, with the effect that neither the retailer nor the friend who purchased the drink could examine the contents. Under both statute and common law the range of protection extends beyond the consumer to others injured by defective products (with the qualification in negligence that they must be foreseeable as likely to suffer harm[2]).

With the exception of the basic principle of the 1987 Act, under which liability is not to depend on the consumer proving that the presence of the defect was attributable to the producer's fault, it is widely assumed that the key elements of liability—the concept of defectiveness, principles of causation, and scope of harm for which recovery is permitted—are virtually identical under the legislation as under common law negligence. Consequently the common law which pre-dates the 1987 Act continues to be a valuable aid to understanding the contemporary liability regime, though the statutory regime should strictly speaking be considered to operate alongside the common law, rather than to mesh with it.

A product is defective under the 1987 Act where 'the safety of the product is not such as persons generally are entitled to expect' (s 3(1)).[3] This test is resonant of the implied term of satisfactory quality under the Sale of Goods Act 1979 (s 14(2)), and similarly requires an evaluation based on a balancing of factors. Indeed, it may be thought that the use of such a balancing test to determine whether or not a product is defective is akin to the test of negligence at common law, such that liability is no more strict under the Act than at common law.[4] Factors to be taken into account in applying this standard include the way in which and purposes for which it is marketed, the presence of instructions and warnings, 'what might reasonably be expected to be done with the product' and 'the time when the product was supplied by its producer to another' (s 3(2)). Thus where an accident would have been averted had the user heeded the warnings there will be no liability.[5] This list of factors is non-exhaustive.

[20]   *Donoghue v Stevenson* [1932] AC 562, 599.
[1]   *Murphy v Brentwood District Council* [1991] 1 AC 398.
[2]   *Stennett v Hancock and Peters* [1939] 2 All ER 578.
[3]   See A Stoppa 'The Concept of Defectiveness in the Consumer Protection Act 1987: A Critical Analysis' (1992) 12 Legal Studies 210.
[4]   A Stoppa 'The Concept of Defectiveness in the Consumer Protection Act 1987: A Critical Analysis' (1992) 12 Legal Studies 210 at 215; P Cane *Atiyah's Accidents, Compensation and the Law* (6th edn, 1999) pp 85–86.
[5]   *Relph v Yamaha Motor Co Ltd* (24 July 1996, unreported), QBD.

There is no explicit reference in the Act to the kind of cost-benefit analysis often said to be present in common law reasoning as to whether a producer has breached the standard of care, under which a balance is struck between the costs of taking additional precautions (such as safety devices and warnings) as against the risk and gravity of likely harm.[6] It is clear that the Act does not require absolute safety but it is an open question whether the failure to make possible safety improvements (usually considered as an aspect of negligent conduct at common law) is an aspect of the definition of what is defective. The statutory test, noted above, is one of consumer expectations. Other factors not referred to in the Act which might be relevant to consumer expectations include whether the danger is obvious or hidden, and whether the product complies with statutory safety regulations.[7]

In practice we may think of defects as falling into two main classes: design defects and manufacturing defects. With manufacturing defects it is possible that only one or a small number of products are affected, and it may be difficult to prove the existence of the defect at the time that the product left the producer's control. The actual fact of there being a defect is less likely to be a problem. *Donoghue v Stevenson* itself provides an example of this kind of case where the claim is that due to a manufacturing defect the product was not supplied as intended. In that case the container was sealed, and the defect could only practically be explained by reference to something which happened in the factory. In other cases the involvement of more than one producer may make it difficult to establish the nature and/or responsibility for the defect. In *Evans v Triplex Safety Glass Co Ltd*[8] a consumer had bought a car fitted with a Triplex toughened windscreen. About a year after purchase, when the car was being used, the screen suddenly broke for no apparent reason and the occupants were injured. The court held that the consumer had not discharged the onus of establishing that the glass broke because of negligence on the part of the component manufacturer. The disintegration was possibly due to the strain imposed on the windscreen in its fitting rather than faulty manufacture. In this case the consumer's difficulty, having to prove that one or other of the car manufacturer and the glass manufacturer caused the defect, has been substantially removed by the 1987 Act providing that each is a producer and that they shall be jointly and severally liable (s 5), thus

---

[6]   This balancing approach is often referred to at the 'Learned Hand test' after the American judge who rendered the approach explicit in *United States v Carroll Towing Co* 159 F 2d 169 (2d Cir 1947). See further C Veljanovski *The Economics of Law—An Introductory Approach* (London: Institute of Economic Affairs, 1989) pp 66–67.

[7]   *Miller: Product Liability and Safety Encyclopedia*, para **III [255]**.

[8]   [1936] 1 All ER 283.

entitling the consumer to pursue either or both. Since liability is strict there is no need to prove negligence.

Design defects are characterised by the product having the features intended by the producer, with either some basic flaw in the design, or inadequate warnings or instructions in respect of risks associated with the use of the product. Adequate warnings can make a product safe, within the definition of the legislation, whereas it would not be safe in the absence of such a warning. Such design defects create the potential for much wider liability, as potentially all users of the product will be affected. The difficulties for consumers are likely to lie in establishing that a particular design (with or without warnings) is defective, rather than in proving the condition of the product.[9] In *Vacwell Engineering Co Ltd v BDH Chemicals Ltd*[10] a warning to the effect that a chemical called boron triboromide caused harmful vapour was inadequate as it failed to refer to the risks of explosion should the chemical make contact with vapour. Accordingly the defendant chemical company was held liable for death, personal injury and property damage caused by an explosion. The adequacy of warnings may depend on their location and prominence. Some risks are sufficiently great as to require the placing of prominent warnings on the product, as well as in instruction manuals. An example is the risk presented by the tendency of the blades of rotary lawn mowers to continue spinning after power has been disconnected. The practice is to place prominent warnings on the product itself, using materials which cannot easily be dislodged by use.

In its Third Restatement of the Law of Torts, the American Law Institute abandoned the attempt to make a single provision in respect of manufacturing defects, design defects, and failure to provide adequate warnings or instructions has been abandoned. The experience of litigation in the United States suggested that the strict liability rule in respect of design defects was both too onerous and unprincipled. Thus § 2 of the Restatement provides:

A product is defective when, at the time of sale or distribution, it contains a manufacturing defect, is defective in design, or is defective because of inadequate instructions or warnings. A product:

(a)   contains a manufacturing defect when the product departs from its intended design even though all possible care was exercised in the preparation and marketing of the product;

(b)   is defective in design when the foreseeable risks of harm posed by the product could have been reduced or avoided by the adoption of a reasonable

---

9   *Miller: Product Liability and Safety Encyclopedia*, para **III [18]**.
10   [1971] 1 QB 88; see also *Fisher v Harrods Ltd* [1966] 1 Lloyds Rep 500.

alternative design by the seller or others distributor, or a predecessor in the commercial chain of distribution, and the omission of the alternative design renders the product not reasonably safe;

(c)   is defective because of inadequate instructions or warnings when the foreseeable risks of harm posed by the product could have been reduced or avoided by the provision of reasonable instructions or warnings by the seller or other distributor, or a predecessor in the commercial chain of distribution, and the omission of the instructions or warnings renders the product not reasonably safe.[11]

Thus, whereas liability for manufacturing defects is said to be strict, liability for design defects and defective instructions is premised upon concepts of reasonableness and foreseeability more familiar within the reasoning of negligence. The explanation put forward for the difference in approach is that consumer expectations and indeed quality control considerations suggest that products should always comply with their specification, and liability should follow for harm caused where they do not so comply. By contrast a 'reasonably designed product still carries with it elements of risk that must be protected against by the user or consumer since some risks cannot be designed out of the product at reasonable cost'. Thus in the case of design defects it is appropriate to engage in a balancing exercise between considerations of cost and safer design rather than to impose strict liability. In this respect it is likely that the application of Part I of the Consumer Protection Act 1987 will be similar to that envisaged by the Third Restatement.[12]

Often the fact that a product is defective and that a consumer has been harmed will be sufficient to create the inference, sometimes on the basis of circumstantial evidence, that the defect caused the harm. Difficulties are likely to arise where the presence of a defect is not the only possible cause of the harm, as where the consumer has some pre-existing condition rendering them more susceptible to harm of the type suffered, or where the consumer's own use of the product may have caused the harm.

Recovery of damages for personal injuries, death or damage to property other than the product itself is relatively unproblematic. The common law and the 1987 Act each provide for recovery for these types of damage (s 5). Some limitations are placed by the 1987 Act. No claims for damage to property under £275 in value are permitted (s 5(4)), nor are claims in respect of damage to property which are not generally intended for private use, or not actually intended by the claimant to be for their private use (s 5(3)). The product liability Directive permits Member States to place a ceiling on

[11]   American Law Institute *Restatement of the Law Third, Torts: Product Liability* (1998).

[12]   C Stolker and D Levine 'The Reasonable Alternative Design Test: Back to Negligence' [1997] Consumer Law Journal 41.

recoverable loss, but the UK government did not take advantage of this option (Article 16(1)). Damage to the product itself is not generally recoverable either at common law nor under the Act. In negligence such loss is classified as purely economic, comparable to the reduction in the value of a building owing to negligent construction, inspection or survey.[13] At common law considerable difficulty has been presented by cases where a defect has not yet caused harm, the question being whether the cost of repair to prevent the harm is recoverable. The question has been pursued most directly in cases involving defective buildings, rather than defective products, but in *D & F Estates Ltd v Church Comrs for England*[14] the analogy to products liability was directly made to support the reasoning of the House of Lords. Lord Oliver said:

> …in no other context has it previously been suggested that a cause of action in tort arises in English law for the defective manufacture of an article which causes no injury other than injury to the defective article itself. If I buy a secondhand car to which there has been fitted a pneumatic tyre which, as a result of carelessness in manufacture, is dangerously defective and which bursts, causing injury to me or to the car, no doubt the negligent manufacturer is liable in tort on the ordinary application of *Donoghue v Stevenson*. But if the tyre bursts without causing any injury other than to itself or if I discover the defect before a burst occurs, I know of no principle on which I can claim to recover from the manufacturer in tort the cost of making good the defect which, in practice could only be the cost of supplying and fitting a new tyre. That would be, in effect, to attach to goods a non-contractual warranty of fitness which would follow the goods into whosoever hands they came. Such a concept…is, in my opinion, contrary to principle.[15]

Where the conduct of consumers is held to contribute to their own harm it is possible for the court to reduce the level of damages to reflect this, both in respect of negligence[16] and liability under the 1987 Act (s 6(4)). The doctrine under which a court may reduce the damages for contributory negligence is not without its critics, who argue that the fault of a consumer is not, as the doctrine assumes, the mirror image of the fault of the producer.[17]

Tort law has long provided a number of defences to liability in negligence arising from the marketing of defective products. Central among these common law defences is the 'state of the art' defence—the defence that

[13]   *Murphy v Brentwood District Council* [1990] 2 All ER 908.
[14]   [1988] 2 All ER 992.
[15]   At 1010; see also *Murphy v Brentwood District Council* [1990] 2 All ER 908. See further the discussion of pure economic loss in Chapter 6 below.
[16]   Law Reform (Contributory Negligence) Act 1945.
[17]   P Cane *Atiyah's Accidents, Compensation and the Law* (6th edn, 1999) p 46.

the product was safe at the time of production having regard to the state of scientific knowledge at the time. This defence is available where the relevant knowledge that a product was unsafe only became known after the product had been put into circulation, and typically only after the harm had been caused to the consumer. This form of defence was the subject of protracted argument in the EC legislative process concerning the product liability directive, but was within the final version adopted by the Council of Ministers, albeit with permission to derogate from its provision (Article 7(e)). The UK government had been among the strongest proponents of making the defence available and elected not to use the derogation provision. The government's support for and implementation of the defence in the Consumer Protection Act 1987 was premised upon the belief that not to offer the defence would stifle innovation.[18] It may be noted that the UK is a major producer of pharmaceutical products, and the pharmaceutical industry is among the major beneficiaries of the defence.

The state of the art defence has no bearing on manufacturing defects, but provides a defence where there is a design defect and

> the state of scientific and technical knowledge at the relevant time was not such that a producer of products of the same description as the product in question might be expected to have discovered the defect if it has existed in his products while they were under his control. (Consumer Protection Act 1987, s 4(1)(e)).

Critics of this provision argue that it effectively reintroduces a negligence test, and thereby dilutes the strict liability of the 1987 Act. It was pointed out by a government minister that this defence might have been available in the Thalidomide case, provided that the producer could demonstrate that they had carried out the research and trials normal within the industry at that time.[19] The wording of the 1987 Act was the subject matter of infringement proceedings by the European Commission, which felt that the legislative wording just quoted was more favourable to manufacturers than the wording of the Directive which it purported to implement. In particular the 1987 Act appears to provide a subjective test of knowledge of the manufacturer, whereas the wording of the Directive was more objective and absolute. In formal terms the Commission lost the case. The European Court of Justice held that the Commission had failed to demonstrate that the 1987 Act would not achieve the effect intended by the Directive. Because there had been no cases brought under the 1987 Act the Commission was not able to adduce any evidence that the English courts would interpret the provision in a manner inconsistent with the Directive.[20] However, the Commission's action was successful to the extent

[18]   HC Deb Vol 991, cols 1110–1111, 4 November 1980 (Mrs Oppenheim).
[19]   HL Deb Vol 414, col 1455, 12 November 1980 (Lord McKay of Clashfern).

that it produced strong dicta to the effect that the 1987 Act must be interpreted in a manner consistent with the Directive, such that it may now be thought that it is the wording of the Directive which more adequately reflects the state of English law.[1]

A number of other defences are available to producers under the 1987 Act, each addressing particular contingencies. First, evidence that the defect was a product of compliance with other EC legislation provides a defence (s 4(1)(a)). The effect of this provision is to give precedence to vertical EC safety legislation (ie rules addressing particular products or sectors, discussed further in Chapter 10 below), such that a product complying with such rules is by definition not defective. It seems unlikely that a court would hold a product complying with EC safety rules was defective under the Act. A defence is also available to the producer who can show that it did not supply the product to another (s 4(1)(b)). This defence would be available to a producer from whom products had been stolen, where this had resulted in their reaching the market, or where products injured employees in a factory prior to being supplied. Production outside the course of business is effectively exempted from the Act by means of a defence for non-commercial business, such as university laboratories or hospitals undertaking research (s 4(1)(c)). A fourth defence is that the defect did not exist in the product at the time it left the producer's control (s 4(1)(d)). Finally, a producer has a defence where it can show that the defect was attributable to the design of a subsequent product or compliance with the instructions of the producer of the subsequent product (s 4(1)(f)). This defence would be available to a producer of component parts, where the defect was caused by the way that those components had been incorporated in another product.

3 CONCLUSION

Taken together reforms to the privity rules and the introduction of strict liability for producers of defective products might be expected to have created something of a revolution in the liability of manufacturers. But this does not yet appear to have happened. There is little evidence of litigation proceeding against manufacturers, and sellers continue to provide a better target for claims for those consumers able to pursue them. The introduction of strict liability for defective products was largely a result of issues which

[20] *Commission v United Kingdom* Case C-300/95 [1997] ECR I-2469.

[1] Article 7(e) of the Directive provides for a defence 'that the state of scientific and technical knowledge at the time when he put the product into circulation was not such as to enable the existence of the defect to be discovered'.

arose from the poor regulation of pharmaceutical products. Not only has much been done to diminish the weaknesses of pharmaceutical regulation, but also the legislation which introduced strict liability provided for the availability of a state of the art defence which is likely to defeat claims by consumers in cases where the regulatory system fails (and would likely have defeated the Thalidomide victims). More generally, it may well be that the failure of consumers to pursue claims, and the incentives of the market for producers to meet claims, both under warranties and independently of them, are sufficient to keep legal doctrine and lawyers very much at the boundaries of the consumer-producer relationship, at least within the EU. Put another way the relationship has yet to be radically juridified, notwithstanding the considerable doctrinal development.

Chapter 6

Minimum quality
standards for services

The nature of relations between consumers and those who provide services
to them is markedly different from relations in respect of contracts for the
sale of goods. Whereas goods are often, even typically, manufactured in
some remote factory, with the consumer never having direct contact with
the manufacturer, services are more typically provided in face to face
transactions without the intervention of the equivalent of distributors and
wholesalers (though it is increasingly likely that a franchisee will provide
the service in some sectors such as fast food and printing). Consequently
relationships are generally less complex and the identification of those
responsible when things go wrong more straightforward.[1] On the other
hand many important contracts for services engage consumer and supplier
in long-term relationships, the epitome of the relational contract,[2] within
which the supplier may exercise considerable continuing power. Typical
examples are financial services contracts and contracts of insurance,
though in the latter cases the development of competition has tended to
reduce the average length of these relationships, as consumers are more
willing and able to switch insurers than was the case 20 years ago. The
same is true of another long-term contractual relationship: banking.
Contracts for services may also include the provision of goods (either
contracts of hire or contracts for work and materials in the old parlance)
and this adds some complexity. Typical examples of such contracts include
home improvements and car repairs. Furthermore the identification of
appropriate standards and judgment as to whether those standards have
been met is often likely to be more problematic for services. Additionally

---

[1] J Chait 'Continuing the Common Law Response to the New Industrial State: The
     Extension of Enterprise Liability to Consumer Services' (1974) UCLA LR 401,
     405.
[2] I McNeil *The New Social Contract* (Yale University Press, 1980).

privity of contract may be a problem in respect of services, not because there is some remote producer falling outside the contract, but rather because the consumer ultimately intended to benefit from the contract is not a party to it. Consequently the provision of professional services has provided a key territory for the development of principles concerning the boundaries of contract and tort law. In this chapter we consider the general principles of contract and tort applying to the provision of services and then proceed to consider the development and application of more particular rules which apply to particular service sectors: holidays, insurance, financial services and public services.

1   GENERAL PRINCIPLES

(a)   Contract or tort?

Most services are provided to consumers under contract. A major exception to this concerns service providers who have a statutory duty to provide the service in question, some of whom do not receive payment at point of use from the consumer. Regional electricity companies provide an example of such a statutory duty to supply, and it has been held that consequently there is no contract, even though payment is made at point of use.[3] The provision of health care under the National Health Service is another example of a statutory service provider, but in this case most services are free at the point of use (exceptions are the provision of dental services and prescriptions where payment is made by most consumers). In the case of the NHS also there is no contract, whether or not payment is made.[4] In other cases there may be a contract under which services are provided, but the contract is not made directly with the consumer or intended beneficiary under the contract. Thus in most cases where a barrister is hired in respect of particular advice or litigation the client makes the contract with the solicitor not the barrister. Where a consumer contracts with a solicitor for the making of a will, the intended beneficiaries of the will not be part of the contractual relationship. Where a survey is carried out prior to a mortgage lender granting a mortgage, the contract is usually between the lender and the surveyor, even though the survey benefits the consumer

[3]   *Norweb plc v Dixon* [1995] 3 All ER 952. Indeed a Northern Ireland court was so persuaded of the public character of a privatised electricity supplier it was prepared to permit a judicial review action: *Re Sherlock and Morris* (29 November 1996, unreported, QBD(NI)), noted by A McHarg (1997) 8 Utilities Law Review 123.
[4]   I Harden *The Contracting State* (1992) Chapter 5; S Whittaker 'Unfair Contract Terms, Public Services and the Construction of a European Conception of Contract' (2000) 116 LQR 95.

and is often at the consumer's expense. In each of these cases where the consumer is not part of a relevant contract (or where there is no relevant contract) it will be difficult to apply contractual principles to the determination of disputes. Consequently these kinds of circumstances have been central to the development of the principles of negligence in respect of poorly delivered services.

In circumstances where there is a contract to which the consumer is a not a party the force of the privity of contract rules has been somewhat diminished by the Contracts (Rights of Third Parties) Act 1999. The 1999 Act, which implements a Law Commission report,[5] provides that a third party to a contract 'may in his own right enforce a term of the contract if— (a) the contract expressly provides that he may, or (b)...the term purports to confer a benefit on him' (s 1(1)). The latter condition is not met where as a matter of construction the parties did not intend the third party to have an enforceable benefit (s 1(2)). The definition of possible third parties is widely drawn to include not only persons expressly identified in the contract by name, but also members of a particular class or answering a particular description (s 1(3)). These provisions may have a marked impact on consumer services, since there are many cases where consumers are third parties to contracts under which they benefit. The circumstances of *Smith v Eric S Bush*,[6] where a surveyor was hired by a mortgage lender to survey a property which a consumer was buying provides such an example, though in that case the presence of a clause excluding liability in negligence to the consumer provided pretty clear evidence that the parties did not intend to confer an enforceable benefit, and the 1999 Act expressly provides that s 2(2) of the Unfair Contract Terms Act 1977 cannot be invoked by a third party to challenge the terms of a contract in which the rights of that third party are excluded or limited (s 7(2)). A key example where the 1999 Act is likely to be effective is in the purchase of holidays, where one member of a party contracts for a group or family holiday, but typically all the parties are expressly named in the contract. It would be good practice to re-write such contracts to expressly confer an enforceable benefit on those third parties, rather than to leave it to a matter of construction as to whether the parties intended to create an enforceable benefit. Prior to the 1999 Act the courts had to find ingenious ways around the privity of contract rule, as in *Jackson v Horizon Holidays Ltd*.[7]

5   *Privity of Contract: Contracts for the Benefit of Third Parties* (Law Com no 242 (1996)).
6   [1990] 1 AC 831.
7   [1975] 3 All ER 92. Though the Package Travel, Package Holidays and Package Travel Regulations 1992, SI 1992/3288 (as amended) already provided that beneficiaries and transferees of contracts should receive the benefit of the regulations (regs 2(1), 10); see below pp 218–220.

(b)　Contractual standards and liability

A key source for the setting of standards in contracts for services is the express terms provided for in the contract. A potential difficulty is that even though there may be a clear breach of such terms it is difficult to find that the consumer suffered damage in conventional terms. The value to a consumer of a contract for a service may be considerably more than the contract price, and the consequence of defective performance inadequately reflected in conventional ideas about the award of damages.[8] This was reflected in the decision in *Jarvis v Swan Tours Ltd*[9] where a holidaymaker was awarded damages for disappointment, upset and frustration when he found—contrary to the statements in the brochure about his Swiss skiing trip—that there was no welcoming party, that the bar was not open on several evenings, that there were no full-length skis or house-party arrangements, that a suitable yodler failed to appear and that he did not receive the delicious Swiss cakes promised for afternoon tea. The lower courts now routinely award damages for disappointment to holidaymakers.[10]

Notwithstanding the importance of express terms, particularly in respect of the description of the services and any goods provided under the contract, much of the standard-setting for contracts for services occurs through the terms which are implied by law into such contracts. These implied terms (both in respect of goods and services) were developed in the common law and codified by the Supply of Goods and Services Act 1982. The provisions relating to goods provided under contracts for work and materials and contracts of hire are generally similar to those of ss 12–15 of the Sale of Goods Act 1979, and were similarly amended by the Sale and Supply of Goods Act 1994 (see Chapter 4). Reasons in favour of implying terms analagous to those in the Sale of Goods Act are firstly, a supplier of work and materials usually has recourse against its supplier; secondly, it usually charges customers more for the materials than they cost so there is no serious injustice in imposing the same liability as if it were the seller; thirdly, it is only logical that it should be under at least as high, if not higher degree of obligation with regard to the materials it supplies than a seller, who may be a mere middleman.

Whereas the liability for defective goods in contracts of hire and contracts for work and materials is strict (in similar fashion to the liability under contracts for the sale of goods), the main terms implied into such contracts and into contracts for services *simpliciter* involve a more

---

[8]　D Harris, A Ogus and J Phillips 'Contract Remedies and the Consumer Surplus' (1979) 95 LQR 581.
[9]　[1973] QB 233.
[10]　See D Oughton and J Lowry *Textbook on Consumer Law* (1997) pp 249–252.

subjective element which has elements which are similar in character to the standard of care in negligence. Thus:

> In a contract for the supply of a service where the supplier is acting in the course of a business, there is an implied term that the supplier will carry out the service with reasonable care and skill. (Supply of Goods and Services Act 1982, s 13).

This provision applies to all contracts for services (whether they involve transfer or hire of goods), though not contracts of service (ie employment contracts) or apprenticeship.[11] The obligation to exercise reasonable skill and care is the central implied term in respect of services. This is the common law standard, incorporated into legislation. At common law the duty requires that a business must use the skill appropriate to a reasonably competent member of the relevant trade. For example a lower standard is required of a jeweller piercing ears than of a medical practitioner.[12] In holding itself out as qualified to do certain work, however, a business warrants that it possesses those skills and so may be held to a higher standard.

Expert carpet-layers were held to be in breach of the standard when they left hall carpet in such a condition that it constituted a danger to anyone using the premises they knew to be occupied, even if such occupiers exercised reasonable care.[13] Motor repairers must provide good workmanship and are liable for defective work by sub-contractors, even if the consumer has consented to the work being done by a particular sub-contractor, unless the consumer does not place any reliance on the main contractor but chooses a sub-contractor himself.[14] The implied term that a newly-constructed house must be finished in a workmanlike manner requires, for example, that fittings like water taps and baths be properly installed and that walls be plastered.[15]

---

[11] But notice that the Secretary of State has exercised powers to exclude certain sectors from the provisions of the Act by statutory instrument: Supply of Goods and Services Act 1982, s 12(4); Supply of Services (Exclusion of Implied Terms) Order 1982, SI 1982/177; Supply of Services (Exclusion of Implied Terms) Order 1983, SI 1983/902; Supply of Services (Exclusion of Implied Terms) Order 1995, SI 1995/1. These orders provide limited exemption to the services provided by advocates, company and building society directors and arbitrators.

[12] *Phillips v William Whitley Ltd* [1938] 1 All ER 566.

[13] *Kimber v William Willett Ltd* [1947] 1 All ER 361.

[14] *Stewart v Reavell's Garage* [1952] 1 All ER 1191.

[15] *Perry v Sharon Development Co Ltd* [1937] 4 All ER 390; cf *McKone v Johnson* [1966] 2 NSWR 471. It must also be fit for habitation. Cf *Batty v Metropolitan Property Realisations Ltd* [1978] QB 554. Section 1 of the Defective Premises Act 1972 confirms these common law obligations: a person taking on work for or in connection with the provision of a dwelling (erection or renovation) owes a duty to the person ordering the work and to subsequent persons who acquire a

Firms which are entrusted with goods are liable for loss sustained if they have not exercised reasonable skill and care. In *Morris* v *CW Martin & Sons Ltd*[16] the consumer sent a stole to be cleaned, but when in possession of the defendants it was stolen by an employee although there was no reason to suspect his loyalty. The Court of Appeal held that the defendants, as bailees for reward, had failed in their duty to exercise reasonable care and were responsible for the actions of the employee to whom they had delegated the job. It has been held that in the event of goods disappearing while in the care of a bailee then the burden of proof is on the bailee to show that she was not negligent in caring for them.[17] If consumers park their car in an unattended car park adjacent, say, to a hotel or to shops, that would not ordinarily give rise to a contract or to a bailment. Consequently car park owners may avoid responsibility for theft when strangers take the car.[18] Comprehensive car insurance offers protection to consumers in these cases, although they may lose their 'no claims' bonus. Legislative provision enables airlines, for example, to limit their responsibility when consumers' luggage goes astray.[19]

The reasonableness standard is similar to that used in negligence (discussed below), and essentially requires the consumer to show not that a service was defective, but rather that the provider was at fault in the way they provided it. The reasons for the different type of standard for services when compared with goods are historical.[20] Previous editions of this work have made a strong case for abandoning the reasonableness test and replacing it with strict liability for defective services. The case for reform is similar to that for abolition of negligence principles and their replacement with strict liability for non-intentional harm. The central argument is that it is very difficult for consumers to know whether professional services or repairs to goods have been carried out to a standard of reasonable skill and care or not. There is also the difficulty of proving breach of the standard. It is argued that an individual who has suffered

---

legal or equitable interest in the dwelling to see that work is done in a workmanlike or professional manner with proper materials and so that the dwelling will be fit for habitation when completed. The duty is non-excludable (s 6(3)).

[16]   [1966] 1 QB 716. See also *Houghland v RR Low (Luxury) Coaches Ltd* [1962] 1 QB 694.

[17]   *Levinson v Patent Steam Carpet Cleaning Co Ltd* [1978] QB 69.

[18]   *Ashby v Tollhurst* [1937] 2 KB 242; cf *Mendlessohn v Normand Ltd* [1970] 1 QB 177 (consumer had to leave keys); *Sydney Corpn v West* (1965) 114 CLR 481; N Palmer *Bailment* (Sweet & Maxwell, 2nd edn, 1991).

[19]   *Fothergill v Monarch Airlines* [1981] AC 251; *Collins v British Airways Board* [1982] 1 All ER 302.

[20]   We will note later that under the Trade Descriptions Act 1968 the criminal law similarly imposes strict liability for false and misleading statements about goods, whereas the test of liability in respect of services involves mens rea elements.

loss should be compensated on the basis of strict liability, with the costs being redistributed among other customers and insurers. The Australian Trade Practices Act 1974 provides that in consumer contracts for services, there shall be an implied warranty that that both services and goods provided shall be suitable for any particular purpose made known by the consumer to the supplier (s 74(2)).[1] A draft EC Directive put forward by the European Commission, but never adopted, offered a different approach, providing that suppliers of services should be liable for physical injury and property damage caused by them in provision of a service unless they could prove the absence of fault.[2]

The second main term applying to such contracts is that, in the absence of any express provision, the supplier will carry out the service within a reasonable time—a question of fact (s 14). In *Charnock v Liverpool Corpn*[3] the plaintiff took his car to the defendants' garage for repair after it had been involved in a collision. The repair, which should have taken five weeks at a maximum took eight weeks because the garage prioritised other work; the plaintiff successfully claimed for three weeks replacement car hire.

The third main implied term creates an obligation on the purchaser of the service, in the absence of any express provision as to the contract price, to pay a reasonable charge (s 15). There is no equivalent provision in respect of contracts for the sale of goods, because it is much less common for such contracts to be agreed with no provision either as to what the price shall be or how it shall be calculated. However in contracts for the provision of services it is quite common for the price to be left open, dependant on what work is actually carried out. Thus a contract for the repair of a car will often involve a diagnosis of what is wrong, together with appropriate corrective action, and neither the amount of labour nor nature of the parts required can be determined in advance. While such cases often give rise to dispute the service provider is in a strong position as in many cases (eg repair of a car) it holds a contractual lien over the goods (in this case the car) until payment is made.[4] With house repairs (for example by an emergency plumber or locksmith) a consumer may pay an exorbitant charge because they fear a county court summons.[5] Once the consumer has paid she is in a much less favourable bargaining position.

---

[1]   See also *Greaves & Co (Contractors) Ltd v Baynham, Meikle & Partners* [1975] 3 All ER 99.

[2]   Proposal for a Council Directive on the Liability of Suppliers of Services Com (90) 482 Final, November 1990. This proposal fell victim to the subsidiarity debate within the EC and was never adopted into law. COM (94)260, discussed in S Weatherill *EC Consumer Law and Policy* (1997) pp 100–102.

[3]   [1968] 3 All ER 473.

[4]   *Green v All Motors Ltd* [1917] 1 KB 625; *Albermarle Supply Cos Ltd v Hind & Co* [1928] 1 KB 307.

[5]   *Services and the Law: A Consumer View* (NCC, 1981) p 17.

Only in respect of consumer credit is there provision for regulation of the price charged for a service (Consumer Credit Act 1974, ss 137–139, discussed in Chapter 3 above). The provision of a quotation is one way of minimising difficulties, for the consumer knows what she has to pay and the business knows the consumer understands the price and has consented to it. The business cannot bind the consumer to pay for additional work not provided for in the quotation.[6] If it finds that additional repairs are necessary it must approach the consumer to vary the original contract. While it is generally accepted that 'quotations' are a definite promise to do work at a fixed price, and 'estimates' are estimates of the total cost which may or may not be exceeded when the charge comes to be calculated, whether either is binding is dependent on the intention of the parties. In *Croshaw v Pritchard and Renwick*[7] an owner of premises wanting alterations done contacted builders and invited them to tender for the work. They wrote a letter headed 'estimate' in which they gave £1,230 as the cost of the alterations. The owner wrote telling them to go ahead with the work but some time later they contacted him to say that a mistake had been made and they must withdraw. The owner sued successfully for the difference between the estimate and what he paid other builders to do the work. The court rejected the argument that the word 'estimate' avoided a final and binding agreement and held that the letter was intended to give rise to such.

(c)   Tort standards and liability

The most straightforward issues concerning tortious liability for services are those where the harm caused is in the form of personal injury, death or property damage. A key area of litigation is medical negligence claims arising is the provision of health care by the National Health Service. At the end of March 1999 the NHS had potential liabilities in negligence of £2.4 billion outstanding.[8] Here the general principles of negligence apply. Medical staff owe a duty of care to those they treat. That standard is set at the level of reasonably skilled medical practitioner of the type who offers the service.[9] The scope of liability is for all the damage caused by the negligent act. While the scope of the duty is well established, the standard of care and issues of causation have, in practice given rise to a considerable quantity of litigation. The determination of whether the relevant

---

6   *Forman & Co Pty Ltd v The Liddlesdale* [1900] AC 190.
7   (1889) 16 TLR 45.
8   National Audit Office *NHS (England) Summarised Accounts 1998–99* HC 356 1999/2000 (The Stationery Office, 2000), though it appears that the *actual* cost to the NHS of meeting claims was £84m in 1998: P Fenn, S Diacon, A Gray, R Hodges and N Richman 'Current Cost of Medical Negligence in NHS Hospitals: Analysis and Claims Database' (2000) 320 BMJ 1567.
9   *Bolam v Friern Hospital Management Committee* [1957] 2 All ER 118.

professional standard has been met requires the calling of evidence from other professionals. In *Bolitho v City and Hackney Health Authority*[10] the House of Lords held that the evidence provided must be reasonable and responsible, indicating that courts should investigate and 'be satisfied that the exponents of the body of opinion relied can be demonstrate that such opinion has a logical basis'. Similar principles would apply in respect of other professionals such as solicitors.[11] Some of the difficulties associated with the rise in medical negligence litigation, and in particular distrust between the parties, are addressed in the Clinical Negligence Protocol, linked to the Woolf reforms to civil procedure. The protocol seeks to develop a 'less adversarial expert culture', and to place greater reliance on dispute resolution outside the courts.[12] Further difficulties associated with medical negligence litigation, concerned with the nature of informed consent and causation, fall outside the scope of this work.[13]

Somewhat more complex issues arise in cases where the type of damage caused is not personal injury, death or property damage. Two main classes of damage fall outside this core territory of negligence actions. First, psychiatric illness and second pure economic loss. The boundaries of liability for psychiatric illness have been tested in a number of important House of Lords decisions in the 1980s and 1990s, but substantially fall outside the scope of this chapter.[14] More germane to the development of consumer law has been an important sequence of litigation concerned with defining the boundaries of tortious liability for negligently inflicted pure economic loss. Pure economic loss is a loss suffered to economic welfare which occurs other than as the product of personal injury, death or damage to property. It is a somewhat obscure concept, which includes loss of profit and the reduction in value of an item of property. Thus, where a surveyor values a house at £100,000 but, because of a defect in the property which the surveyor ought to have detected, the property is only worth £80,000 this is classified as pure economic loss, because there is no damage to property as a result of the negligence, but only a reduction in its value to the owner. The value of property is, of course, the very thing the consumers contract for when they enter into contracts for the sale of goods or property, and pure economic loss is recoverable in contract as the loss of expectation under the contract. But in negligence the courts have long been hostile to the recovery of pure economic loss.

10   [1998] AC 232, HL.
11   *Edward Wong Finance Co Ltd v Johnson, Stokes & Master* [1984] AC 296.
12   Clinical Negligence Protocol, paras 4.2, 5.3.
13   See *Clerk and Lindsell on Torts* (17th edn, 1995) paras 8.25–8.68.
14   *McLoughlin v O'Brian* [1983] 1 AC 410; *Alcock v Chief Constable of South Yorkshire* [1991] 4 All ER 907; *White v Chief Constable of South Yorkshire Police* [1999] 1 All ER 1, HL. See the discussion in M Brazier and J Murphy *Street on Torts* (10th edn, 1999) pp 203–210.

The landmark case on pure economic loss in negligence was *Hedley Byrne & Co Ltd v Heller*.[15] In this case the House of Lords held that under limited conditions a professional person making a statement might owe a duty of care to persons to whom the statement was made, where the professional knew that the recipient would rely on it, and that person had relied on it to their detriment. At the time the case was decided it appeared to provide a rather narrow exception to the principle of non-recovery for pure economic loss, in circumstances where there was a close relationship between a professional adviser and the recipient of the advice which was very similar in character to a contract. Subsequently that case was used as the basis for litigation which sought to expand the scope of the exception, reaching a high water mark in the late 1970s and early 1980s with the House of Lords apparently accepting that pure economic loss might be recoverable in a wider range of circumstances.[16] The House of Lords rapidly pulled back from that position and by 1990 had sought to re-establish the narrow range of liability laid down in *Hedley Byrne & Co Ltd v Heller Industries plc*. In *Caparo v Dickman*[17] their Lordships held that pure economic loss was only recoverable where it was foreseeable the claimant would suffer a loss if they relied on the statement, where there was a close relationship of proximity between the claimant and the defendant (the claimant being directly in the contemplation of the defendant—a narrower definition of proximity than that deployed in personal injury litigation) and where it is just and reasonable to impose liability.[18] More generally their Lordships advocated a narrower approach to establishing the existence of a duty of care.[19] Thus the law would now appear to restrict liability to circumstances where a statement was made to a particular individual with the intention that they should rely on it.

Notwithstanding the apparently narrow range of liability set down in *Caparo Industries Ltd v Dickman* the House of Lords has shown a consumer-orientation in at least two major decisions where somewhat laxer tests were applied. In *Smith v Eric S Bush*[20] a consumer suffered a loss of value in a property which they bought as a result of a negligent

---

[15]　[1964] AC 465.
[16]　*Anns v Merton London Borough Council* [1978] AC 728; *Junior Books Ltd v Veitchi Co Ltd* [1983] 1 AC 520.
[17]　[1990] 2 AC 605. See also *Murphy v Brentwood District Council* [1991] 1 AC 398 which directly overturns the earlier House of Lords decision in *Anns v Merton London Borough Council*.
[18]　[1990] 2 AC 605 at 617–618 (per Lord Bridge of Harwich). Subsequently the Court of Appeal offered a somewhat more detailed list of factors to consider which are pertinent to determining the question whether the claimant has sufficient proximity to the defendant: *James McNaughton Paper Group Ltd v Hicks Anderson & Co* [1991] 2 QB 113, 125–27.
[19]　See M Brazier and J Murphy *Street on Torts* (10th edn, 1999) pp 172–182.
[20]　[1990] 1 AC 831.

survey carried out in a contract with their mortgage lender. Their Lordships held that in this case, even though there was a clear clause in the contract between the consumer and the mortgage lender excluding any liability to the consumer in respect of the survey (and thus the consumer's case might have been expected to fail on the ground that the surveyor did not assume responsibility for the contents of the survey), nevertheless the surveyor owed a duty of care. Lord Griffiths expressly pointed out that the decision was made 'in respect of a dwelling house of modest value'[1] which was material to the decision because the surveyor would have known that it was highly likely that the consumer would rely on the survey rather than go the expense of having their own survey carried out. In *White v Jones*[2] their Lordships held that the intended beneficiaries of a will which had not been executed owing to the negligence of a solicitor were entitled to recover their economic loss against the solicitor, even though there was no evidence of reliance by the claimants. It is not clear whether the lower courts demonstrate a similar consumer orientation and the exact boundaries of extra-contractual liability for negligence causing pure economic loss are consequently somewhat unclear.

2   QUALITY STANDARDS IN PARTICULAR SERVICE SECTORS

Examination of particular service sectors against the background of the general common law and statutory rules finds significant areas of concern not capable of being readily addressed by general rules. Consumers of investment services face severe difficulties in acquiring sufficient information to be able to rely on advice they receive. The common law rules on insurance contracts have developed in such a way that legal assumptions about risk have acted very much against the interests of consumers. The development of a mass market for holidays has created a dependence of consumers on tour operators to arrange products comprising a number of different types of services (such as hotels and flights) with potential problems of fragmented liability.[3] The privatisation of the utilities sectors and more general application of consumer principles to public services has revealed problems of responsiveness to consumer needs, often linked to substantial elements of private or public monopoly. In each of these areas, explored below, distinctive legal responses to the particular problems can be identified.

---

[1]   [1990] 1 AC 831, 859.
[2]   [1995] 2 AC 207, HL.
[3]   See MMC *Foreign Package Holidays* (Cm 3813 (1997)).

3   THE PROVISION OF INVESTMENT SERVICES

Common law clearly applies to the provision of investment services. In the case of a contract to give advice, it is an implied term that the adviser will exercise reasonable care and skill in giving advice.[4] The standard is that which is to be expected of a professional person of ordinary competence and experience.[5] It is also possible that a third party could claim that an advisor exercised undue influence over them, although such a situation is likely to be established only rarely and where the third party is commercially and financially unsophisticated.[6] A duty of care will arise in tort, following the leading case of *Henderson v Merritt Syndicates Ltd*,[7] when a person has voluntarily assumed responsibility for another.[8] Such a responsibility is assumed, inter alia, where a person gives advice or makes a representation in circumstances in which a reasonable person would know that trust was being placed on him and that his skill and judgment were being relied upon. If the third party in fact places reliance on the exercise of reasonable skill and care by that person, then a duty of care arises. If the breach of that duty causes economic loss that was reasonably foreseeable, then the third party will have an action in negligence. The duty of care in tort can run concurrently with that in contract.[9]

The court may find that a fiduciary relationship arises between the parties if there one has placed trust and reliance on the other, and is in a position of vulnerability vis à vis that other . The person owing the fiduciary duty is also under a duty to exercise reasonable skill and care, not to have a conflict of interest with the beneficiary, not to make secret profits, and not to have a conflict between their duty to one beneficiary and their duty to another. Finally, advisers and others providing investment services under contract are subject to common law and statutory duties not to make misrepresentations as to material facts.[10]

The common law has however played only a residual role in ensuring the standard in accordance to which investment services have to be provided. The benchmarks for those standards are set by rules made

---

[4]   Supply of Goods and Services Act 1982, s 13.
[5]   *Bolam v Friern Hospital Management Committee* [1957] 1 WLR 582.
[6]   *Lloyds Bank Ltd v Bundy* [1975] 3 All ER 757; *Barclays Bank plc v O'Brien* [1993] 4 All ER 417; *Bank of Credit and Commerce International v Aboody* [1990] 1 QB 923.
[7]   [1995] 2 AC 145.
[8]   An extension of the duty relating to negligent misstatement as established in *Hedley Byrne & Co Ltd v Heller* [1964] AC 465 and further *Spring v Guardian Assurance plc* [1995] 2 AC 296 (discussed above).
[9]   *Henderson v Merritt Syndicates Ltd* [1995] 2 AC 145.
[10] See further pp 148–153.

under statute by the financial services regulators, at present by the Financial Services Authority under the Financial Services and Markets Act 2000. The regulatory requirements for those providing investment services to disclose information are discussed in Chapter 9. However, as is noted, there are a number of factors which mean that disclosure is only ever going to be of limited use in protecting the consumer. Investment products are complex, consumers will have different abilities to understand the information that they are given, moreover the products are long term in nature and their value depends on the subsequent performance of the product. In addition to the problems of poor quality or biased advice, the consumer is thus also prey to poor quality investment decisions being made by the product provider, and to opportunistic behaviour—rather than investing the money, the provider may use it to cover its own costs to an inordinate degree, or otherwise appropriate the money through fraud. No amount of information at the point of sale can overcome these problems.[11] Regulation that focuses on disclosure is thus only ever going to be partially effective.

There are a number of different ways in which regulation attempts to ensure the quality of the investment service being provided in addition to requirements to disclose information. These are through the initial licensing of investment advisors and others providing investment services, regulation of the structure of the market for investment advice, the setting of standards of advice, and the provision of systems of complaint, compensation and redress.[12] The licensing system is intended to ensure that only those of a certain minimum competence are able to advise on and sell investment products. Before a person can provide investment services they have to satisfy the Financial Services Authority (FSA) that they are 'fit and proper',[13] and they have to comply with the rules on training and competence that the FSA has set out.[14] The rules also stipulate the structure of the market for investment advice, in an attempt to reduce biased and partial advice to consumers. The rule on 'polarisation' requires that investment advisors either sell only the products of one company (tied agents) or that they sell the products of all companies (independent

---

[11]   See further J Black *Rules and Regulators* (Clarendon Press, 1997) pp 141–144; D Llewellyn *The Economic Rationale for Financial Regulation* (FSA Occasional Paper Series 1 (1999)); A Page and R Ferguson *Investor Protection* (Butterworths, 1992) Chapter 5; *The Protection of the Small Investor* (JUSTICE, 1992).

[12]   For a general discussion see M Clarke *Citizens' Financial Futures: The Regulation of Retail Investment Products in Britain* (Ashgate, 1999).

[13]   FSMA 2000, s 41, Sch 6; FSA CP 20, *The Qualifying Conditions for Authorisation* (1999).

[14]   The rules are formulated by the Financial Services Authority, acting under the Financial Services and Markets Act 2000, s 138: FSA, CP 34 *Training and Competence Sourcebook* (1999).

financial advisors (IFAs)). As a result, advice is provided by three different types of advisor: those who are employed directly by a product provider, that is a life assurance or pensions company, those who are self-employed or run their own businesses but who have an agreement with a product provider to sell only their products, so called 'tied agents' (for example most large banks and building societies have an agreement with a life assurance company to sell the latter's policies through their branches), and IFAs, who are independent from any particular product provider.

All advisors are under a central duty to provide a certain standard of advice. They are required to advise on and recommend only investment products that are *suitable* for the consumer. The duty is coupled with a requirement that the advisor 'know the customer'. In other words that advisors obtain from the customer sufficient information about the customer's financial circumstances, including their attitude to risk, to enable the advisor to give suitable advice. The suitability and know your customer rules are central planks in the investor protection regime, and have been likened to the 'fitness for purpose' standards that apply in the sale of goods.[15] However, exactly what duty they impose on advisors has been a matter of some uncertainty and controversy.[16] With respect to the 'know your customer' obligations, the rules differ between tied agents and IFAs in the extent to which they set out the different types of information that should be sought,[17] but the overall intention of the rules is that advisors gain enough personal and financial information from the investor to be able to form a complete picture of the investor's financial requirements, their attitude to risk, and their ability to make regular payments into an investment where relevant. With respect to the suitability rule, the

---

[15]   Joint Committee on Financial Services and Markets, First Report, para 39 (in response to a call from the National Consumers' Council and the FSA Consumer Panel for a separate 'fitness for purpose' requirement in the rules).

[16]   See further J Black and R Nobles 'Personal Pensions Misselling: The Causes and Lessons of Regulatory Failure' (1998) 61 MLR 789; M Sah and G Cameron 'Controlling the Quality of Financial Advice: The Use of Regulatory Form to Satisfy Fiduciary Obligations' [1997] JBL 143.

[17]   This differentiation is a legacy of the initial structure of financial services regulation. The Financial Services Act 1986 delegated regulatory powers to the Securities Investments Board, including the power to recognise self-regulatory organisations (SROs). Initially seven SROs were recognised, which through a process of mergers reduced to three by 1997. IFAs used to be regulated by one self-regulatory organisation, FIMBRA, and life assurance companies, their salesmen and tied agents by another, LAUTRO. The two organisations had separate rule books, and although most of the firms they regulated moved to the Personal Invesment Authority (PIA), formed in 1994, the PIA did not create a single rulebook but continued to use those of FIMBRA and LAUTRO. Under the FSMA 2000 the SROs no longer exist, and the rules are currently being amalgamated into a single Handbook by the FSA, due to be finalised at the end of 2000–2001.

regulators' view is that the duty embodies two principles: that the investment that is recommended must not be one which on any view the investor would be better off without, and that an advisor should not recommend a product when another would plainly be more appropriate.[18] If the advisor did not sell that product, the advisor would have to forego a sale.

In addition to the know your customer and suitability rules, advisors are under an obligation to give 'best advice'. The requirement operates differently with respect to tied agents and direct salesmen on the one hand and IFAs on the other. Tied agents and direct salesmen must inform themselves on the products available from their product provider, and recommend only that which is most appropriate for the investor. IFAs must inform themselves about all products on the market on a continuing basis, and recommend only that which is most appropriate for the investor from that entire range (IFAs can specialise in providing certain types of advice, eg on pensions only, but they have to make that specialisation clear to the investor at the outset). The 'best advice' requirement is bolstered by the 'better than best' requirement: that advisors only recommend an investment product if they are not aware of another that would better meet the investor's needs. The implications for direct salesmen and tied agents is that if there is another product sold by another product provider which would be more appropriate, again the advisor is meant to forego the sale.

The rules on polarisation and on the standards of advice have been the subject of continuing controversy. The debate on polarisation concerns the effect they have had on the market for advice The polarisation rules had the unintended and unexpected consequence of reducing the availability of independent advice,[19] and have been repeatedly scrutinised by the Office of Fair Trading for their anti-competitive effects.[20] The central issue with respect to the standards of advice is non-compliance, and the effectiveness, or rather ineffectiveness, of those standards in preventing misselling. The biggest single instance of misselling that has occurred is that of personal pensions. Between 1988 (when the regulation began) and 1994, over half a million people were missold personal pensions, and over 700,000 cases have still to be reviewed.[1] Under a process of redress

---

[18]   SIB, Discussion Paper 2, *Retail Regulation Review* (1991).

[19]   See further J Black *Rules and Regulators* (Clarendon Press, 1997); J Black and R Nobles 'Personal Pensions Misselling: The Causes and Lessons of Regulatory Failure' (1998) 61 MLR 789.

[20]   The most recent report is *The rules on the polarisation of investment advice, A Report by the Director General of Fair Trading* (OFT, August 1999).

[1]   Melanie Johnson, economic secretary to the Treasury, written answer, Hansard, 10 January 2000, col 106W. See further J Black and R Nobles 'Personal Pensions Misselling: The Causes and Lessons of Regulatory Failure' (1998) 61 MLR 789.

instituted by the regulators, companies have had to compensate investors to a total estimated cost to the industry (including administration expenses) of over £10 billion.[2] The personal pensions scandal is the biggest instance of misselling, but by no means unique. In 1992–94 thousands of investors were missold products called home income plans,[3] and in 1999 concern focused on the misselling of endowment mortgages (mortgages accompanied by life insurance policies, the value of which was meant to repay the mortgage and provide the investor with some additional money).

Firms are required to pay investors compensation if they missell products or otherwise breach the rules,[4] and in addition consumers have a right to bring a civil action in the courts[5] (although no-one has yet done so, preferring to rely on the regulatory structures rather than the courts). If the firm is still in business, then the consumer has to first of all complain to the firm that sold them the product, and if the firm does not agree to pay compensation, then the consumer can take the matter to the Financial Services Ombudsman. The Ombudsman will investigate the matter and make an award that is binding on the firm, though not on the consumer.[6] If the firm has become insolvent, then the consumer can apply to the Investors' Compensation Scheme for compensation. All regulated firms have to contribute to the scheme, which determines whether the firm breached the rules and the amount of compensation that should be awarded.[7] Both the Ombudsman and the compensation schemes require the consumer to take action: they therefore depend on the consumer being aware that they have been missold a product. Because of the difficulties that are inherent in assessing product quality, it may be that a consumer is

2   PIA Consumer Panel (1998).

3   Under a home income plan, a person who had paid off the mortgage on their house (therefore usually an elderly person) would re-mortgage it, and with the money gained spend some and invest the rest. The value of the investment was meant to repay the interest on the mortgage, and then when the person died, the sale of the house would enable the capital amount to be repaid. The investor was however exposed to the risk that interest rates would go up at the same time that the return on their investment fell, meaning they would be unable to cover the interest payments (and usually as the person was retired, they had insufficient income to cover those payments otherwise than from the investment). This is exactly what happened, and many were left owing thousands of pounds in interest payments which they could not make, with the consequence that they were threatened with repossession.

4   FSMA 2000, s 382, Investors Compensation Directive 97/9/EC OJ L 084.

5   FSMA 2000, s 71.

6   Under the pre-FSMA structure each SRO had its own Ombudsman or arbitration system; these have now been consolidated into one structure, the Financial Services Ombudsman, whose powers are set out in FSMA 2000, ss 225–233; FSA, CP 33 *Consumer Complaints and The New Single Ombudsman Scheme* (1999).

7   FSMA 2000, s 234; FSA, CP 5, *Consumer Compensation* (1999) and CP 24, *Consumer Compensation: A Further Consultation* (1999).

not aware that they have been the subject of misselling. Arguably there is thus a case for regulators being proactive in requiring firms to give compensation, and this is exactly what happened in the case of personal pensions. Regulators took the initiative and required firms to review each sale to see whether or not it complied with the rules and to write to those to whom they had sold personal pensions informing them that they might be entitled to compensation. If the sale did not comply, then the firm had to pay compensation or make alternative pension arrangements for that person equivalent to those they should have had had misselling not occurred. In fact early on in the process firms conceded that sales had not complied with the rules and focused instead on identifying how much compensation should be paid. Over two million sales have had to be reviewed with redress to be given to an anticipated one million consumers. The review and redress process, initiated in 1994–95, is not expected to be completed until 2002.

The examples of misselling, particularly pensions misselling, illustrate all too graphically the failures of regulation in ensuring that certain standards are maintained in the provision of investment services. The rules have failed to prevent misselling, but what of 'misbuying'? The rules clearly impose an obligation on advisers and salesmen to act on the consumer's behalf, but what of the consumer's responsibility to ensure that the product he or she is buying is that which is most appropriate? We have already pointed to the difficulties that consumers face in the market for investment services, but given those difficulties, where does the balance of responsibility lie between the consumer and the seller to ensure that the consumer's needs are met? The goal of investor protection, according to the system's original architect Professor Gower, was to ensure that 'reasonable people were not made fools of'.[8] The phrase is easy to state but difficult to give content to. To what extent should the principle of *caveat emptor*, let the buyer beware, apply to consumers entering the investment markets? Should the consumer be entitled to rely entirely on the expertise of the investment adviser and on their obligations to act in the consumer's interest, or should they treat all recommendations with complete scepticism, trusting no one? The Financial Services and Markets Act provides that the FSA is to have regard to the principle that consumers should take responsibility for their own investment decisions, but both the National Consumers' Council and the FSA Consumer Panel argued that the principle of *caveat emptor* negates the principle of investor protection and should be deleted entirely from the Act.[9]

---

[8]   LCB Gower *Review of Investor Protection: Discussion Document* (HMSO, 1982); *Review of Investor Protection, Report, Part I* (Cmnd 9125 (1984)).

[9]   Joint Committee on Financial Services and Markets, First Report, paras 32–37.

4   INSURANCE

As consumers have become wealthier their potential losses from theft, accident and illness have grown in scale, a massive consumer insurance industry has sprung up. The essential characteristics of insurance relations are that risks are pooled by those who face them via the intermediation of an insurer, typically within a long-term contractual relationship. The policy holders know they face a risk of theft or accident, but do not know whether such thefts or accidents will actually occur to them. Insurers equally do not know who the victims will be, but can use actuarial methods to calculate what percentage of the pool of policy holders will put in claims and for what amounts. Thus insurers pool the risk. Life insurance is somewhat different from insurance against theft, accident and illness, because insurers and policy holders alike know that the policy holder will die in due course. Whereas most insurance is designed to provide an indemnity should the risk turn out, life insurance provides for payment when a certain contingency is met (and not on an indemnity basis). Many life insurance policies provide a mechanism of saving (and are properly treated as part of the financial services industry) for known events, rather than a mechanism for pooling risk.

Among the wide range of insurance products on the market consumers are likely to have contracts of insurance in respect of: home contents; buildings (for owner-occupiers); car accidents;[10] holiday delays or cancellation; loss of employment; and extended care for consumer products (discussed in Chapter 5). Each of these insurance products raises similar legal issues. The chief quality issues in consumer insurance relate to the speed and effectiveness with which claims are processed. A central issue is the validity of claims where consumers have failed to disclose fully information, or have failed to carry out obligations such as ensuring prescribed security measures are in place. The nature of insurance as dealing with risk has led to the development of special common law rules governing insurance contracts. These rules, which are protective of the interests of insurers, operate harshly against consumers and, to date, proposals to reform the law have not been implemented. Although government exercises regulatory powers over the establishment of insurance providers (under the Insurance Companies Act 1982 which implements a number of EC Directives) government has elected not to introduce statutory control of contract terms in the industry. Instead government has placed reliance on industry self-regulation to mitigate the harshest aspects of the common law regime. Additionally the industry has

---

[10]   Third party liability insurance is compulsory for drivers under the Road Traffic Act 1988, ss 143, 145.

established an ombudsman scheme, the Insurance Ombudsman Bureau, to handle consumer complaints in respect of insurance contracts.

The difficulty faced by insurers is that they are highly dependent on the information provided to them by those who take out insurance with them. This information is central to the determination of the level of risk, and thus the determination of the premium (or price) for the service. Information relevant to the risk depends on the particular matter being insured. However, the claims history of the applicant is always relevant, as is any criminal record, since each affects the 'moral hazard' being taken on by the insurer. For insurance in respect of cars and home contents postcodes are used in a standard way to calculate risks, as these differ in different parts of the UK. Typically premiums in respect of inner city postcodes are higher, and those in respect of rural postcodes are lower, and insurers may refuse to take on consumers in particular high risk areas altogether, a practice known as 'red-lining'.

Three distinctive doctrines govern the provision of information by consumers in insurance contracts. First, the old doctrine of *uberrimae fides* or utmost good faith, creates a duty on policy holders to provide all information which would be material to the reasonable insurer, whether or not the insurer requests that information. Breach of the duty entitles the insurer to avoid the contract. This doctrine operates in contrast with the general contractual principles under which there no general duty of disclosure (though under misrepresentation doctrines information which is disclosed must be accurate). Thus in *Woolcott v Sun Alliance and London Insurance Ltd*[11] an insurer was held under a contract of buildings insurance to be entitled to avoid its obligations to an policy holder who had failed to disclose his history of criminal convictions (including for robbery) even though he had not been asked any questions about such matters in the proposal form. The court accepted evidence that a serious criminal conviction affected the moral hazard faced by the insurer, and in this case there was a serious material non-disclosure. It was immaterial whether the matter which the policy holder failed to disclose was implicated in the loss which he suffered.[12] The doctrine has the potential to operate harshly against consumers. It is unreasonable to expect consumers to know all the information which an insurer considers material to the risk. Given most insurance contracts include the submission of a proposal form (exceptions include temporary cover and some holiday insurance) it would be possible to make it standard practice (as indeed it is for many forms of insurance) for insurers to specifically ask about all matters which are

---

[11] [1978] 1 All ER 1253.
[12] The leading case on the disclosure doctrine is *Pan Atlantic Insurance Co Ltd v Pine Top Insurance Co Ltd* [1994] 3 All ER 581, HL.

material. Surely this would provide insurers with sufficient protection. In response to a Law Commission report which recommended retention of a residual duty of positive disclosure the National Consumer Council has argued for a separate regime for consumer insurance contracts under which consumers would owe no duty to insurers other than to provide accurate answers to questions posed in the proposal form. A similar more limited duty would exist in respect of renewals, where again insurers would have to ask questions about matters on which they wanted information disclosed.[13]

A second doctrine specific to insurance contracts concerns warranties made by policy holders, which take effect as if they were conditions, entitling the insurer to repudiate the contract in the event that information which is provided is inaccurate. Warranties in insurance contracts can relate not only to past conduct, but also to present and future behaviour. Thus a policy holder may warrant that an insured vehicle will be kept habitually at a particular location when not in use and breach of this continuing warranty entitled the insurer to avoid the contract.[14] Equally a policy holder might warrant that a vehicle will be kept roadworthy, or that a bicycle or a house will be kept properly secured. Breach of such warranties entitle an insurer to repudiate the contract even where the breach is immaterial to the risk. 'Basis of the contract clauses' convert any statement into a warranty. However, the introduction of the Unfair Terms in Consumer Contracts Regulations 1994[15] has led at least one commentator to question the validity of basis of the contract clauses because of their obscurity.[16] It cannot be long before the Office of Fair Trading takes regulatory action on the basis of a complaint.

The courts have traditionally applied a high standard of disclosure in respect of information requested on proposal forms.[17] However a recent Court of Appeal decision, *Economides v Commercial Union Assurance Co plc*[18] suggests that the appellate courts may be open to a more

---

[13]   NCC *Insurance Law—Non-Disclosure and Breach of Warranty* (1981).
[14]   *Dawsons Ltd v Bonnin* [1922] 2 AC 413.
[15]   Now replaced by SI 1999/2083.
[16]   JE Adams 'Basis of the Contract Clauses and the Consumer' [2000] JBL 203.
[17]   In *Kumar v Life Insurance Corpn of India* [1974] 1 Lloyd's Rep 147 the policy holder, when asked about any history of surgical operations in a life insurance proposal form, declared that she had had no surgical operations. She signed the proposal form making her answers the 'basis of the contract' between herself and the insurer. There was persuasive evidence provided to the effect that she believed that the delivery of a child by caesarean section a few months before she took out the life insurance was not a surgical operation, although medical evidence was pretty clear to the effect that it was properly considered to be an operation. The policy holder died about two years later owing to an ectopic pregnancy, in which the fertilised egg grows in the fallopian tubes. The death was said to be completely unrelated to the earlier caesarean section operation. The insurer was held to be entitled to avoid payment on the policy on grounds of breach of warranty.
[18]   [1997] 3 All ER 636.

consumerist orientation. In that case a student had failed to adequately increase the declared value of his house contents for insurance purposes when his parents came to live with him. Rather he declared a more modest increase (a figure suggested by his father, a retired senior police officer). The sum insured was £16,000 at the time a theft of goods worth £31,000 occurred from his flat and the insurer sought to repudiate the policy. It was held that the policy holder's duty was only to make an honest disclosure of the matters requested by the insurer and he had done so. He had no reason to disbelieve that valuation suggested to him by his more experienced father.

The Law Commission recommended that contractual statements made by policy holders should only be treated as warranties when they are material to the risk and that breach of warranty should not entitle insurers to repudiate the contract where the loss was of a different type from that which the broken warranty was intended to safeguard. The Law Commission additionally recommended that 'basis of the contract' clauses should be ineffective in converting statements about past or present fact into warranties, but should only be effective in relation to future conduct. The government did not find these proposals attractive. Rather the insurance industry was encouraged to develop a self-regulatory code, *The Statements of Insurance Practice*, under which the harshness of the rules would be mitigated in practice by the way there were operated by insurers. One commentator described this as 'bargaining in the shadow of the law'—ie self-regulating in order to avoid legislation.[19] Under the statements any declaration signed by policy holders should be restricted to completion according the policy holder's knowledge and belief and no attempt should be made to convert statements of past or present fact into warranties. In respect of claims insurers are not to repudiate policies:

(i) on grounds of non-disclosure of material fact which a policy holder could not reasonably be expected to have disclosed;
(ii) on grounds of misrepresentation unless it is a deliberate or negligent misrepresentation of a material fact;
(iii) on grounds of a breach of warranty or condition where the circumstances or the loss are unconnected with the breach unless fraud is involved.[20]

Whilst the principles of the statements might be satisfactory, they create wide discretion to insurers in applying them. The *Commercial Union*

---

[19] R Lewis 'Insurers' Agreements not to Enforce Strict Legal Rights: Bargaining with Government and in the Shadow of the Law' (1985) 48 MLR 275.
[20] ABI *Statement of Non-Life Insurance Practice* (2nd edn, 1996). A new self-regulatory body, the General Insurance Standards Council, was established in July 2000, though its *General Insurance Code for Private Customers* relates chiefly to marketing issues and thus does not overlap with the ABI Code.

case, discussed above, provides some evidence that the courts are beginning to internalise the self-regulatory code and adapt the common law to meet it. However the common law remains in need of reform. Though insurance contracts were excluded from the provisions of the Unfair Contract Terms Act 1977[1] they are regulated by the Unfair Terms in Consumer Contracts Regulations 1999 (see Chapter 3), so where express terms (as opposed to common law rules) operate unfairly they may be regulated by action of the Director General of Fair Trading, although the terms of the Directive on which the Regulations are based exclude the regulation of terms which 'clearly define or circumscribe the insured risk'.[2]

5   HOLIDAYS

The provision of holiday services has been the subject of a range of common law decisions, and extensive statutory and self-regulatory activity. The importance of holidays derives from the fact that they are a relatively expensive purchase for consumers with high expectations that they will be very good. As the mass market in holidays developed after the Second World War, inevitably so did consumers experience growing problems, in particular associated with misdescription of services provided. The intentional provision of misleading descriptions relating to services is an offence under s 14 of the Trade Descriptions Act 1968 (discussed in detail in Chapter 11) but has also given rise to a considerable amount of contractual litigation. Included within the ambit of the criminal law is the practice of airlines of overbooking seats[3] and this is also subject to EC rules requiring airlines to provide minimum compensation and set procedures for dealing with overbooking situations in respect of scheduled flights.[4]

As noted above the high consumer expectations in relations to holidays have been reflected in case law suggesting that consumers can be compensated for disappointment where the supplier breaches express terms of the contract. In *Jackson v Horizon Holidays Ltd*[5] one member of a family who had contracted for a family holiday was able to claim compensation on behalf of the whole group for disappointment. The common law contractual liability for misrepresentation is supplemented by the provisions of the Package Travel, Package Holidays and Package

---

[1]   SI 1999/2083.
[2]   Directive 93/13/EEC, recital 19.
[3]   See Chapter 8 below.
[4]   Regulation 295/91/EC, OJ L 36/5 8.2.91 recital 19. The Commission has proposed revisions to the Regulation to provide better compensation and also new self-regulatory initiatives: European Commission Communication on the Protection of Air Passengers in the European Union COM(2000)365 final (June 2000).
[5]   [1975] 3 All ER 92. See also *Jarvis v Swans Tours Ltd* [1973] 1 All ER 71.

Tours Regulations 1992[6] which create civil liability in respect of misleading descriptive matter relating to the package, the price of the package and any other misleading information supplied as part of the contract (reg 4). This provision applies both to travel agents and tour operators.

As regards the statutory implied term that service providers should act with reasonable skill and care, when applied to holidays this meant that a tour operator, though it was obliged to ensure that hotel facilities met relevant national standards, this did not mean that the glass in a patio door had to comply with the higher standards which would have applied had the hotel been located in the UK.[7] It is very common for tour operators to use sub-contractors for some parts of a holiday package. The Privy Council has held that where a tour operator by its brochure undertakes to provide all the services then, although it may be free to sub-contract some of those services, it is not absolved from the duty to exercise reasonable skill and care, and will be liable if a sub-contractor fails to comply with that duty.[8]

The Privy Council may have been encouraged in their expansive view of the liability of tour operators by the legislative policy lying behind the Package Travel, Package Holidays and Package Tours Regulations 1992.[9] The Regulations implement an EC Directive[10] and provide that tour operators shall be contractually liable for breach of all obligations related to a package holiday,[11] irrespective of whether the obligations are to be performed by the operator or by some other supplier (such as an airline or hotelier). This liability is relatively strict, though subject to exceptions where the breach was not attributable to the tour operator or their supplier (reg 15(2)). Terms are implied into every contract for a package holiday that where a significant proportion of the services contracted for are not provided, then the organiser will make suitable alternative arrangements, compensating the consumer for any difference in value, or if this is not possible or acceptable to the consumer, will arrange to transport them back to their point of departure and compensate the consumer 'where appropriate' (reg 14). The 1992 Regulations also use the technique of compulsory disclosure (discussed in detail in Chapter 9 below).

In practice the experience of consumers is often shaped by the provisions of the self-regulatory code administered by the Association of

---

6   SI 1992/3288. See also SI 1998/1208 which modified the application of the 1992 Regulations in relatively minor respects.

7   *Wilson v Best Travel* [1993] 1 All ER 353.

8   *Wong Mee Wan v Kwan Kin Travel Services Ltd* [1995] 4 All ER 745, PC.

9   SI 1992/3288.

10   Council Directive 90/314/EEC.

11   Defined as any pre-arranged combination consisting of at least two of accommodation, transport and ancillary services offered for sale at an inclusive price (reg 2(1)).

British Travel Agents (ABTA). The ABTA code has very wide coverage in the UK holiday industry, as it formerly incorporated a stabilizing provision to the effect that ABTA tour operators could only sell their holiday through ABTA travel agents, and ABTA travel agents could only sell holidays of ABTA tour operators.[12] This restrictive practice was tolerated on the grounds that it ensured that nearly all holidays sold in the UK were subject to the protection ABTA's bonding scheme under which members of the Association paid into a fund from which customers were compensated in the event of the failure of a member (discussed in more detail in Chapter 11).[13] The 1992 Regulations oblige tour operators to make appropriate insurance or bonding arrangements in respect of customers' money (regs 16–18) with the consequence that the public interest defence for the restrictive nature of ABTA's agreement with its members was no longer justified, and the stabilising aspect of the Code was removed in 1993.[14] It has been held that the ABTA notice displayed in travel agents' windows can have the effect of creating a collateral contract between the consumer and ABTA, so that compensation provisions under the code become a contractual obligation.[15]

6   PUBLIC AND PRIVATISED SERVICES

The provision of public services by public and privatised service providers is often characterised by an element of monopoly, meaning that a central self-help remedy for consumers seeking services from other providers, may be absent when things go wrong. Notwithstanding this feature, and the considerable importance of these services in consumers' lives, the provision of public services was for a long time treated as falling outside the concerns of consumer law, being more akin to issues explored in administrative law. Earlier editions of this book, for example, make no reference to the liability of public service providers to consumers. Even administrative law treatments of the issues tended to exclude grievance handling.[16] This omission was explicable in part by reference to the fact that public services were typically governed by particular statutes or

---

[12]   D Oughton and J Lowry *Textbook on Consumer Law* (1997) p 238.

[13]   See *Re ABTA Ltd's Agreements* [1984] ICR 12. More recent intervention under competition law powers has sought to prohibit the practices of compulsory insurance and tour operator financial discounts: Foreign Package Holidays (Tour Operators and Travel Agents) Order 1998, SI 1998/1945; *R v Secretary of State for Trade and Industry, ex p Thomson Holidays Ltd* (2000) Times, 12 January, CA.

[14]   D Oughton and J Lowry *Textbook on Consumer Law* (1997) p 239.

[15]   *Bowerman v ABTA Ltd* [1995] NLJR 1815.

[16]   A McHarg 'Separation of Functions and Regulatory Agencies: Dispute Resolution in the Privatised Utilities' in M Harris and M Partington *Administrative Justice in the 21st Century* (1999) p 215. But see C Harlow and R Rawlings *Law and Administration* (2nd edn, 1997) pp 385–388.

administrative rules, and ordinary rules of contract were held not to apply. The limited remedies available for poorly delivered services had to be sought through applications to tribunals, complaints to statutory consumer committees, complaints to MPs or local councillors (with the possibility of the complaint being referred on for investigation to the appropriate ombudsperson) or possibly by way of judicial review of administrative action.

The landscape of public service provision has changed markedly in the last 20 years with significant effects on the liability regimes for poorly delivered services. Most dramatically the privatisation of most utility services (telecommunications, gas, electricity, water and rail),[17] accompanied by re-regulation and liberalisation,[18] has exposed utilities service providers both to new administrative mechanisms for resolving consumer complaints, and to the possibility of contractual liability for failure to honour obligations such as timely installation or repair of telephone lines and electricity services. Less dramatically new expectations have been applied to publicly provided services which have remained in the public sector, with the application of new doctrines as to the way services are managed and their relations with their customers. The consumer aspect of these transformations was consolidated by the Conservative administration of John Major in 1991 under the rubric of the Citizen's Charter programme,[19] subsequently adopted by the Labour government elected in 1997 and re-badged Service First.[20] Furthermore the European Community has taken an interest in the development of norms of minimum service quality across the so-called 'services of general interest',[1] as well as legislating for general principles which will apply to public and private services alike.[2]

(a) Privatised services[3]

During the era of public ownership of utility services such as telecommunications, electricity, water and gas, these were provided to customers under the statutory duties imposed on the public corporations

---

[17] C Graham and T Prosser *Privatising Public Enterprises* (OUP, 1991).
[18] T Prosser *Law and the Regulators* (OUP, 1997).
[19] A Barron and C Scott 'The Citizen's Charter Programme' (1992) 55 MLR 526.
[20] C Scott 'Regulation Inside Government: Re-Badging the Citizen's Charter' [1999] Public Law 595.
[1] European Commission Communication *Services of General Interest in Europe* COM (96) 443 Final, 11 September 1996
[2] S Whittaker 'Unfair Contract Terms, Public Services and the Construction of a European Conception of Contract' (2000) 116 LQR 95.
[3] See generally C Graham *Regulating Public Utilities* (Hart, 2000) Chapter 5.

which operated the services. Typically this legislation obliged the public corporation to meet all reasonable demand for service. The customer had no contract, and no legal rights against the service provider *qua* consumer, but only the more general relationship which exists between citizens and the state. Consequently faults with telephone lines, delays in repairing electricity wires, delayed or poor quality train services could only give rise to complaints via administrative or political channels, and did not generally attract any form of legal redress. Dissatisfaction with the operation of these public corporations surfaced in the 1970s with concerns both about their efficiency, and the considerable drain which the public corporation placed on scarce government funds.[4] Though a variety of reform proposals were mooted, the policy course chosen by the Conservative administration of Margaret Thatcher in the 1980s was to privatise all of the utilities services, in most cases through converting the public corporations into public limited companies and selling shares to the public. The consumer revolution in utilities services was, initially at least, an incidental by-product of that privatisation process. Customers were encouraged to buy shares, and concerns with the efficiency of utility companies heralded the creation of new regulatory offices charged both with regulating price and quality of service and the introduction of competition.[5]

(i)   Contractualisation

A first consequence of the privatisation process is that most utilities services are now provided under contract. As a consequence the normal incidents of any contract for services will generally apply, including the implied terms from the Supply of Goods and Services Act 1982 (as amended and noted above). Contractualisation also opens the way to judicial and administrative regulation of express terms in contracts. Thus it has been held that the provisions of the Unfair Contract Terms Act 1977, when coupled with the licence obligations owed by British Telecom to meet all reasonable demand, may make a contract term permitting BT to disconnect a customer at with one month's notice unfair.[6] Additionally the Unfair Terms Unit of the Office of Fair Trading has been very active in requiring mobile phone companies to re-write contracts which were unfair because the obligations of the customer were not balanced by the obligations of the companies.[7]

---

[4]   C Foster *Privatisation, Public Ownership and the Regulation of Natural Monopoly* (Blackwell, 1992).

[5]   C Scott 'Privatization, Control and Accountability' in J McCahery, S Picciotto and C Scott (eds) *Corporate Control and Accountability* (1993).

[6]   *Timeload Ltd v British Telecommunications plc* [1995] EMLR 459.

[7]   Office of Fair Trading Unfair Terms Unit *Unfair Terms Bulletins*.

Whilst contract law might provide a fall-back position in respect of disputes between consumers and utility companies, in practice most complaints are addressed within internal complaints procedures which are a statutory obligation on the companies concerned.[8] Regulators and other complaints handlers will generally refer the consumer back to their supplier in the event that their complaint has not exhausted the internal complaints procedures.

(ii)   Self-regulation

Linked to the contractualisation process, the utilities regulators have promoted the development of codes of practice by utility companies, with guaranteed service standards and compensation where such standards are not met. Utility companies typically offer compensation to customers for missed appointments and for delays in installation or repair of services. For example BT offers to compensate customers at a rate of one month's networks rental charge per day in the event of delays in installation or repair of lines, or pay compensation for the actual loss where this can be shown to be greater.[9] Rail companies offer compensation for delays and cancellation to services in the Passenger's Charter documents, which are referred to in the National Conditions of Carriage which apply to all rail operators. It is arguable that the terms of these codes are incorporated into the contracts suppliers have with their customers, and therefore take effect as express contractual terms.

(iii)   Grievance-handling

Relatively minor, but frustrating complaints about aspect of utilities services will in many cases not justify a consumer in litigating where satisfaction cannot be secured through an initial complaint to the company concerned (under the procedures discussed above). At privatisation various alternative mechanisms for handling of disputes were established. Each of the utilities regulators has a statutory duty to consider complaints[10] and has established mechanisms for handling such complaints. Additionally some of the industries have consumer representative committees. Thus complaints about water services are handled by regional Customer Service

---

8   Telecommunications Act 1984, s 27E; Gas Act 1986, s 33E; Electricity Act 1989, s 42B; Water Industry Act 1991, s 86A. This duty was introduced by the Competition and Service (Utilities) Act 1992, and the procedures are subject to the approval of the Directors General.
9   British Telecom *Code of Practice for Consumers* (nd) Part 5.
10 Telecommunications Act 1984, s 49; Gas Act 1986, s 31; Electricity Act 1989, s 45; Water Industry Act 1991, s 30.

Committees, and complaints about gas by the Gas Consumers' Council.
Only complaints which cannot be resolved through the informal brokerage
role of these bodies, either because the complainant is not satisfied, or
because it appears desirable that formal regulatory powers are applied to
the problem, are referred to the regulatory office. In each sector there
appears to be an implicit distinction drawn between customer complaints
(which are regarded as inappropriate for regulatory action) and more
substantial disputes on which regulators are prepared to invoke licence
conditions and formal powers. The consequence is that most consumer
complaints are treated as falling outside the concerns of the regulators
(even where, as in telecommunications, there is not separate representative
committee to act as first port of call) and even where the source of complaint
is a breach of licence, this is unlikely to be detected or acted upon.[11]

The statutory powers exercised by the regulators over customer
complaints include both the referral of such complaints to arbitration and
the determination of disputes dealing with such matters as terms and
conditions of supply to customers,[12] deposits[13] and meter accuracy[14] by
orders. Power for the Directors General to determine billing disputes have
not yet been brought into force.[15] The regulators owe a common law duty
in exercising these powers to treat all the parties fairly, for example by
revealing full information to them about the way the dispute is being
handled.[16]

Evidence concerning the use of these procedures is mixed. When OFTEL
received the new powers to resolve disputes or refer them to arbitration in
1992 it decided not to use them.[17] OFTEL's public statements concerning
consumer complaints do not refer to these statutory powers and suggest
that it can only act as an honest broker in negotiating settlements between
consumers and phone companies. Some change in this position has
resulted from the implementation of an EC Directive which is likely to

[11]   Cf A McHarg 'Separation of Functions and Regulatory Agencies: Dispute Resolution in the Privatised Utilities' in M Harris and M Partington *Administrative Justice in the 21st Century* (1999) pp 232–242.
[12]   Telecommunications Act 1984, s 27F; Gas Act 1986, s 14A; Electricity Act 1989, s 23; Water Industry Act 1991, s 30A.
[13]   Telecommunications Act 1984, s 27I.
[14]   Gas Act 1986, Sch 5, paras 1–4; Electricity Act 1989, Sch 7, para 1(7); Water Industry Act 1991, ss 38, 95.
[15]   Telecommunications Act 1984, s 27G; Gas Act 1986, s 15; Electricity Act 1989, s 44; Water Industry Act 1991, s 150A.
[16]   *R v Director General of Gas Supply, ex p Smith* (31 July 1989, unreported), DC.
[17]   C Hall, C Scott and C Hood *Telecommunications Regulation: Culture, Chaos and Interdependence Inside the Regulatory Process* (2000) pp 188–192. An official investigation found that OFTEL's complaint handling function was not carried out efficiently, noting unacceptable delays and the poor quality of staff training and decision letters: National Audit Office *The Office of Telecommunications: Licence Compliance and Consumer Protection* HC 529, 1992–93.

cause OFTEL to use powers to refer disputes to arbitration in future.[18] The advantage of using both the arbitration and determination powers, even if only occasionally, it that it is likely to strengthen the hand both of the regulator and of the consumer in negotiating informal settlements.[19] More generally it appears that the regulators have favoured seeking informal solutions to problems. Occasionally a matter of consumer complaint raises issues of very wide application, and this may cause a regulator to propose a licence modification to address the matter and/or make a reference to the Competition Commission to investigate the issue complained of.[20] New powers for the regulators to take action against anti-competitive agreements and abuse of dominant position came into force in April 2000,[1] though it remains to be seen how actively these powers will be used, and whether they are deployed to address consumer issues.

Institutional changes are likely to follow from the election of the Labour government in 1997, with a mandate to increase the consumer orientation of the utilities sectors. A review of the utilities sectors completed by the DTI in 1998 resulted in proposals that consumer protection should be made a primary duty of the utilities regulators and that independent consumer councils should be established in those sectors where they did not already exist.[2] Proposals to implement some aspects of this proposed reform are contained in a Utilities Bill before Parliament in 2000, while others have been deferred for later implementation. The importance of the new consumer councils is linked to a perception that the regulators who routinely bargain with utility companies may permit wider strategic issues to blunt their effectiveness as complaints handlers.[3]

---

[18]   OFTEL *Proposed New Dispute Resolution Procedures for Fixed Telecommunications* (1999).

[19]   C Hall, C Scott and C Hood *Telecommunications Regulation: Culture, Chaos and Interdependence Inside the Regulatory Process* (2000) Chapter 10.

[20]   An example is provided by the complaints of excessive charges for calls to mobile phones, which resulted in OFTEL proposing a licence modification to cap these charges, and a subsequent reference to the Monopolies and Mergers Commission (the predecessor to the Competition Commission established by the Competition Act 1998). See MMC *Cellnet and Vodafone* (The Stationery Office, 1998). The MMC agreed that a licence modification was appropriate to deal with the problem and consequently OFTEL introduced its proposed price cap on the previously unregulated area of charges to mobiles.

[1]   Competition Act 1998 (see Chapter 1 above).

[2]   DTI *A Fair Deal for Consumers: Modernising the Framework for Utility Regulation* (Cm 3898 (1998)).

[3]   N Lewis and P Birkinshaw *When Citizens Complain* (1993) p 219; A McHarg 'Separation of Functions and Regulatory Agencies: Dispute Resolution in the Privatised Utilities' in M Harris and M Partington *Administrative Justice in the 21st Century* (1999) pp 217, 222–223; C Hall, C Scott and C Hood *Telecommunications Regulation: Culture, Chaos and Interdependence Inside the Regulatory Process* (2000) pp 188–192.

(iv)   Regulation, service quality and price controls

Perhaps the most central aspects for consumers of the regimes established for the privatised utilities services were the regulatory controls established over the price and quality of service, and incorporated in the licences (or equivalent authorisations) issued to service providers. Price controls have been used to ensure reductions in the price of services in the telecommunications, gas and electricity sectors. (With water, the government permitted undertakings to increase prices in order to pay for new investment to improve the quality of drinking water to meet the terms of EC legislation.)

The early privatising statutes did not include powers for the regulators to control service quality. However the introduction of the Citizen's Charter in 1991 caused government to harmonise the provisions of the earlier statutes (relating to telecommunications and gas) with those of the later enactments (electricity and water) and gives powers to all the regulators to determine appropriate levels of service.[4] OFGAS has elected not to use these statutory powers, relying instead on enforcement of licence conditions.[5] While OFTEL has generally eschewed the use of these powers, it has recently indicated that problems of service quality associated with the provision of local access telephone service by new providers using BT's infrastructure will cause it to develop statutory standards.[6]

(b)   Public services and Service First

The Citizen's Charter programme heralded the introduction of a number of consumer-oriented principles across the public sector, including improved provision of information to customers, the development of independent grievance-handling mechanisms, and the specification of service standards. A central aspect of this programme has been the development of Charter documents for each public service setting out details of the standards of service to be provided, together with information on remedies and grievance handling mechanisms when things go wrong. In some cases (typically where payment is made at point of use) these documents promise monetary

---

[4]   Telecommunications Act 1984, s 27A; Gas Act 1986, s 33A; Electricity Act 1989, s 39; Water Industry Act 1991, ss 38, 95.

[5]   A McHarg 'Separation of Functions and Regulatory Agencies: Dispute Resolution in the Privatised Utilities' in M Harris and M Partington *Administrative Justice in the 21st Century* (1999) p 216, n 25.

[6]   OFTEL Press Release 90/99 'Oftel Demands Improvement to Quality of Service for Calls and Access Product' (December 1999).

compensation, creating a relationship somewhat akin to contract. In other instances the provision of a satisfactory remedy is at the discretion of the service provider, with the possibility of a complaint to an ombudsperson (the Parliamentary Ombudsman in the case of central government and many non-departmental public bodies). Official figures indicate that there are about 40 national charter documents,[7] covering services such as the payment of taxes, provision of social security payments, the National Health Service, housing, the courts, schools, higher education, etc. To take an example, the Benefits Agency Charter provides for minimum opening hours for all offices, responses to letters within ten working days, responses to complaints within seven working days, and published standards for answering telephones.[8] However it does not provide for any remedy for breach of these standards. Only the usual remedies for maladminstration exist—internal review of a complaint and possibly a complaint to the Ombudsman via an MP. By contrast the London Underground Passengers' Charter, where payment is made at point of use, provided for a refund on the ticket price (by voucher) in the event of a delay of more than 15 minutes.[9] Overall the chief changes introduced by the introduction of charter documents has been to increase the transparency of the service quality issue, rather than to create widespread enforceable remedies where things go wrong. There is little data to suggest how effective these changes have been in improving public services.

7   CONCLUSIONS

Considerable advances have been made in the law relating to the quality of services through the codification of general obligations in respect of both goods and services by legislation, the creation of special legislative standards together with regulatory arrangements for dispute resolution, and the development of voluntary codes (with the encouragement of the Office of Fair Trading or other government agencies). The provisions of the Unfair Terms in Consumer Contracts Regulations 1999 have filled some of the gaps left by the Unfair Contract Terms Act 1977 in respect of the use of unfair terms, and the Office of Fair Trading has applied its new powers to police contracts for compliance with the Regulations with considerable vigour. These developments notwithstanding, consumer research suggests

---

[7]   Cabinet Office *Service First: The New Charter Programme* (1998) para 4.5.

[8]   Benefits Agency Customer Charter (October 1999 edition).

[9]   London Underground Customer Charter (1999).

considerable continuing dissatisfaction with service providers as disparate as car repairers, banks, holiday companies and utilities service providers.

A possible development is to create a general duty on businesses to trade fairly (enforceable by the Office of Fair Trading) with voluntary codes providing evidence of the detailed standards of fairness for each sector (discussed in further detail in Chapter 11). An alternative approach is to create more detailed statutory regimes (as exist for holidays and utility services). During the heyday of the deregulatory era in the 1980s it would have been unthinkable to imagine marked development of sectoral statutory regimes for services, but the combination of EC membership (which has required the implementation of new consumer protection measures in the UK, governing such services as holidays, telecommunications and postal services) together with the political expediency for government to be seen to be protecting consumers have changed that, and further legislative development in response to particular concerns now seems possible. The successful development of new norms has often been accompanied by new institutional arrangements for oversight, either regulatory or self-regulatory

Chapter 7

Consumer credit

I THE DEVELOPMENT OF CONSUMER CREDIT[1]

Credit is one of the essential features of modern capitalism for it enables businesses to sell goods and services to consumers which their current income or wealth would not otherwise enable them to buy. As Galbraith puts it: 'The process of persuading people to incur debt, and the arrangements for them to do so, are as much a part of modern production as the making of the goods and the nurturing of wants.'[2] Trade credit, in which consumers were presented with a periodical bill to be paid in full, had developed in the seventeenth and eighteenth centuries, and pawnbroking had been regulated by legislation as early as 1603 because of the abuses practised against the many ordinary consumers who obtained credit in this way.[3] Banks provided credit by way of overdraft, but until relatively recently bank accounts were held mainly by the middle, professional and upper classes. Building societies made specialist credit available for house purchase, and became increasingly important as the trend moved from renting to buying property. It is not surprising that important developments in consumer credit coincided with the production of mass-produced consumer durables, for credit enabled businesses more readily to market their goods and at the same time gave them a tidy profit. At first sewing machines, pianos and furniture were the subject of these new forms of credit, and then later in the twentieth century they were

---

[1]   Credit is also dealt with elsewhere in this book: pp 81–84 above, pp 362–367 below.

[2]   JK Galbraith *The Affluent Society* (Andre Deutsch, 4th edn, 1984) p 148.

[3]   There is an historical study of consumer credit in *Report of the Committee on Consumer Credit* (Cmnd 4596 (1971)) vol 1, Chapter 2 [hereafter called Crowther Committee].

extended to cars, radios, televisions, videos etc, so that now consumers can obtain most products and most services through credit.

Initially these new forms of credit were provided by manufacturers and retailers, but from the 1920s separate finance houses had been established which specialised in advancing credit to enable consumers to finance the purchase of products from retailers which did not give credit themselves, either as a matter of policy or because their financial assets were insufficient or directed to other purposes. Finance houses obtained finance from banks and the deposits of investors and institutions. One judge described the development in 1929:

> There were, of course, many cases in which a person or firm had a motor car which they wished to sell and in which a customer was found who desired to purchase but had not the money to pay for it in a lump sum; and on the other hand the owner did not want the bother of a hire-purchase agreement. That this was a common situation was shown by the fact that there had sprung up all over the country a system of calling in the assistance of business firms which existed largely, if not solely, for the purpose of giving assistance to both classes of persons by carrying out negotiations of the following nature. The company or firm not infrequently called itself a finance company. They bought the car and then proceeded to let it out on a hire-purchase agreement to the person who was desirous of acquiring it.[4]

Finance houses, now often owned by banks, have never captured the whole market for point of sale credit and retailers continue to play a vital role. For them credit boosts demand (retailers in this context includes mail order companies, many of which provide goods on credit). Manufacturers never came to provide credit to the same extent as in some other countries. These sources of credit to consumers must be considered along with others. Government policy favouring house ownership boosted the building societies but also encouraged banks and others to advance this type of credit. Banks have penetrated to all classes and building societies have extended their services beyond home loans (some converting into banks). Bank overdrafts, credit cards and personal loans are often secured by second mortgages on homes. Since financial liberalisation in the 1980s, banks have fiercely competed to provide credit to consumers. Independent

---

4   *Automobile and General Finance Corpn Ltd v Morris* (1929) Times, 19 June, per Acton J; (1929) 73 Sol Jo 451, quoted in E Campbell-Salmon *Hire Purchase and Credit Sales* (Pitman, 1962) pp 10–11. See also A Drury *Finance Houses: Their Development and Role in the Modern Financial Sector* (Waterlow, 1982).

credit card companies are also active. Credit continues to be provided to the poorer sections of society by pawnbrokers and money-lenders.[5]

From the consumer's viewpoint buying on credit has its advantages. It may simply be convenient either at the point of sale or in enabling payment to be made for something over a period.[6] With major purchases consumers can obtain the present enjoyment of products, services and property without the need for immediate payment; there is a good argument that the use of credit in this way is a desirable form of forced saving for some people. Any doubt about the integral role that consumer credit has in the economy is belied by the enormous amounts currently outstanding (see Table 7.1).[7] In particular there was a very significant rate of increase in consumer credit in the 1980s—faster than the growth in the economy—reflecting both supply (financial liberalisation and competition) and demand (consumer buoyancy and increased incomes for the better off).[8] There was also a great surge in credit card ownership in that period, from 16.6 million in 1980 to 29.8 million in 1990. In the mid-1990s promotional credit came into its own for retailers, whereby the offer deferred payment on zero-interest loans.

The effects of credit for consumers are not uniformly advantageous. Some think that it dampens desirable investment either directly because consumers no longer save, or indirectly because it ingrains the consumption ethic.[9] There is also a relatively high level of fraud associated with some forms of credit, such as credit cards, and the loss sometimes falls on consumers.[10] Of more immediate interest, credit also causes untold hardship for many consumers who are induced to over-commit themselves by the blandishments of sales or promotional techniques or the pressures

---

[5]   K Rowlingson *Moneylenders and their Customers* (PSI, 1994). (There are some 1,200 licensed moneylenders, 27,000 agents lending and collecting door to door each week, and three million customers. Moneylenders are reluctant to lend to the very poor, but lend to those who find it difficulty getting credit elsewhere, eg those in low paid casual employment.) On unlicensed moneylending: E Oxford 'I Was a Teenage Loan Shark' (1994) Independent, 19 September, Supp, pp 2–4. J Macleod 'Pawnbroking: A Regulatory Issue' [1995] JBL 155, 174 ('leaving shops' are unregulated, although functionally equivalent to pawnbrokers: they buy the goods on the understanding they will be resold to borrowers when they repay).

[6]   See eg *Overindebtedness. A Report by the Director General of Fair Trading* (1989) pp 16–24.

[7]   *Financial Statistics* No 458, February 1998 (Office for National Statistics, 1998) Table 3.2B.

[8]   NCC *Credit and Debt* (HMSO, 1990) Chapters 1–2.

[9]   See generally N Runcie *The Economics of Instalment Credit* (University of London Press, 1979); JK Galbraith *The Affluent Society* (Andre Deutsch, 4th edn, 1984) Chapter 3.

[10]   M Levi and J Handley *The Prevention of Plastic and Cheque Card Fraud Revisited* Home Office Research Study No 82 (Home Office, 1998).

of their social milieu, and who find that they default on their repayments when unexpected events like sickness or unemployment occur.[11] For the poor credit has been a necessity for survival, given limited welfare benefits and employment, if it has been available, which is casual rather than long-term. Credit leads to debt which leads to more credit.[12] It is these casualties of the credit system who feature prominently in the courts and about whom a large part of this chapter is concerned.

Table 7.1: Consumer credit and other personal sector borrowing, £m outstanding at end of period

	1993	1994	1995	1996
Total consumer credit	53,295*	58,051*	68,205*	77,494*
Banks	41,768	44,821	49,845	55,609
Building societies	770	1,104	1,237	1,476
Other specialist lenders	6,725	8,189	13,282	16,572
Retailers	2,562	2,644	2,509	2,586
Insurance companies	1,471	1,293	1,332	1,251
Loans secured on dwellings	357,305	375,864	390,385	409,446
Other borrowing from banks	36,465	35,768	36,667	34,798

* of which credit cards involved 10,658 (1993), 11,914 (1994), 13,836 (1995), 16,161 (1996).

(a) Forms of consumer credit

After the 1890s hire purchase was adopted as the preferred method of instalment credit in Britain for purchasing products. In law, hire purchase involves the consumer in hiring an item, either from a retailer or from a finance house to whom the retailer has sold it, with an option to purchase it at the end of a period if all the instalments are paid. Apparently hire purchase had developed in the early nineteenth century in France and in

---

[11] Eg G Parker *Getting and Spending. Credit and Debt in Britain* (Aldershot: Avebury, 1990). The former Director General of Fair Trading criticised credit providers for lack of caution in granting credit: G Borrie 'The Credit Society: Its Benefits and Burdens' [1986] JBL 181, 188–191.

[12] J Ford *Consuming Credit. Debt and Poverty in the UK* (Child Poverty Action Group, 1991).

the United States, where furniture was leased for periodic payments to the wealthy, who after a period could buy it if they wished. There was no inherent reason why hire purchase should have become the norm in England—conditional sale, in which consumers agree to buy an item, but do not acquire property in it until all payments are made, has been widely used in the United States and Canada—and indeed until the late nineteenth century the differences between hire purchase and conditional sale were hardly important. The reason for the change in popularity of hire purchase in England was that alternative forms of instalment selling became less desirable The technicalities of the Bills of Sale Acts meant that the chattel mortgage never really took root, in which the consumer buys an item but gives security over it for the credit extended. More importantly, as the result of the Factors Act 1889, consumers purchasing a product on conditional sale could, in certain circumstances, pass good title to an innocent third party and thus defeat the rights of the seller.[13] Hire purchase on the other hand secured the seller's rights against third parties on the basis, established by the House of Lords in *Helby v Matthews*,[14] that the consumer under hire purchase was simply hiring an item and not committed to buying it. The seller, as owner, could seize the goods under the *nemo dat* principle from third parties into whose hands they had fallen. That conceptualisation of the transaction was artificial, for it ignored the fact that almost all consumers entered hire purchase with the intention of acquiring ownership.

Gradually hire purchase was subject to greater control both by Parliament and the courts as abuses by particular businesses became apparent. The first major step was the Hire Purchase Act 1938, which introduced documentary formalities for hire purchase contracts and imposed restrictions on businesses' remedies, for example, a court order was needed for an item to be repossessed after a third of the purchase price had been paid. Some 20 years later the courts accepted the artificiality of hire purchase and began attacking the unequal terms in hire purchase agreements with traditional contractual doctrines like the rule against penalty clauses.[15] A persuasive argument is that the larger credit providers accepted these restrictions without great objection because they legitimised credit-buying in the eyes of the public and also made trade difficult for the smaller finance companies, 'which were giving hire purchase a bad name, and were cutting into the profits of the larger companies'.[16]

---

[13]   *Lee v Butler* [1893] 2 QB 318.
[14]   [1895] AC 471.
[15]   For example *Bridge v Campbell Discount Co Ltd* [1962] AC 600.
[16]   JJ McManus 'The Consumer Credit Act' (1975) 2 Brit J of Law & Soc 66, 68.

By the 1960s hire purchase had fallen out of favour with some of the larger finance providers. Hire purchase was subject to legal restrictions, including terms controls (eg minimum deposits were required) imposed as a matter of economic policy to dampen consumer demand. It was not thought as essential to have a security interest in items being sold on credit because their resale value when repossessed was sometimes quite low (although not for items like cars), and because it was possible with the increase in personal wealth and the establishment of credit reference agencies to be assured initially about the credit worthiness of the great bulk of consumers. Moreover, consumers began needing finance for what the law categorised as services, like the installation of central heating and home improvements, for which hire purchase (which deals with goods) was not really appropriate.[17] The outcome of these various factors was that a number of finance providers began leasing products to consumers or, more importantly, began providing personal loans to consumers to be used for the purchase of products and services from retailers with whom they had arrangements. Legally, the consumer uses a personal loan to buy the product or service from an independent retailer in a transaction quite distinct from that in which the loan is obtained from the finance house.

One of the benefits which the loan and sale arrangement gave to finance providers was that, unlike in hire purchase transactions, they had no responsibility for the quality of the merchandise supplied. The Consumer Credit Act 1974 overturns this result by making credit providers liable for the quality of the products and services obtained with its credit pursuant to, or in contemplation of, arrangements with its retailers.[18] Consumers, of course, have little inkling of the difference when they approach a retailer to obtain something on credit and are asked to complete a personal loan agreement, rather than a hire purchase agreement, which is then forwarded to the finance house for approval.

Retailers still provide directly to consumers a large amount of credit for the purchase of products and services. Hire purchase may be used but credit sale, in which property passes to the consumer immediately, is the more common method used by large department stores. Large retailers have their own charge (store) cards and typically take other credit cards. Some stores and mail order companies use revolving credit, in which a consumer periodically repays and in return receives revolving credit greater than that amount.[19] The cost to consumers of this type of account may be the 'service' charge imposed, for example, on the monthly balance.

---

[17]   See also RM Goode 'Introductory Survey' in RM Goode (ed) *Consumer Credit* (Sijthoff, 1978) p 19.
[18]   Section 75. See below.
[19]   R Berthoud and E Kempson *Credit and Debt* (PSI, 1992) Chapter 5.

Many other forms of credit are available to consumers.[20] Banks, of course, provide credit to consumers to purchase goods and services, although the facility is usually only available to those with accounts. Bank overdrafts, a form of revolving credit, are more likely to be available to the better off. Check trading has a long history in Britain, mainly for those in the lower socio-economic groups. Credit is given in the form of trading checks and vouchers which can be used in retail outlets which have arrangements with the check trading company. Retailers are reimbursed by the check companies when trading checks are used there; they must pay a commission by the trading company of the business. The check company collects from consumers by instalment.[1]

Credit cards have been a fast growing category of credit since they were introduced in the 1950s. Credit cards are used for the purchase of a wide range of goods and services, including transactions in the higher price ranges such as holidays and travel.[2] Many consumers use credit cards not so much to obtain credit but for convenience. Terms between credit cards vary.[3] Bank credit cards generally offer a system of revolving credit, whereby consumers are issued monthly accounts, part of which must be paid within so many days with interest being charged on the balance. 'Travel and entertainment' or 'charge cards' charge an amount per annum for use of the card and usually demand immediate settlement of a monthly account, otherwise charging so much interest per month. 'In house' cards are issued to customers by or on behalf of department stores, garages, hotels, and so on; they may involve extended credit. The different methods of operation are of direct legal significance: bank credit cards are generally regulated consumer credit agreements within the Consumer Credit Act 1974, but charge cards are exempt agreements if, for one, they demand repayment immediately of a monthly account in one instalment. Issuers of the latter are not jointly liable with the retailer when a consumer receives a defective product or substandard service.[4]

The Credit Cards (Price Discrimination) Order 1990[5] was the result of criticism that credit cards disadvantaged those paying cash, because of the 'no discrimination' policy—that those paying by credit card should

[20] R Berthoud and E Kempson *Credit and Debt* (PSI, 1992) Chapter 6.

[1] See Monopolies and Mergers Commission *Trading Check Franchise and Financial Services* HC 62, 1981.

[2] K Rowlingson and E Kempson *Paying With Plastic* (PSI, 1994) p 11.

[3] Monopolies and Mergers Commission *Credit Card Services* (HMSO, 1989) Chapters 2–3.

[4] Sections 16(5)(a), 25, 75. See G Stephenson *Credit Debit and Cheque Cards* (Central Law Publishing, 1993) pp 126, 143.

[5] SI 1990/2159, made under Fair Trading Act 1973. See *R v Monopolies and Mergers Commission, ex p Visa International Service Association* (1991) 10 Tr LR 97.

pay the same price as those paying by cash—which credit card companies imposed on retailers. Critics also said that credit cards had a direct effect in pushing up prices because retailers have to recoup the 'commission' which they pay to credit card companies. In response the credit card companies said that differential pricing would confuse consumers and that in any event the use of credit cards increased the turnover of stores and thus had a dampening effect on prices. Moreover, there was not the same need for security arrangements as with cash. Consumers also benefited because they were assured that a retailer who accepted credit cards had been vetted by the credit card company for the quality of its merchandise and/ or service (partly the effect of s 75 of the Consumer Credit Act 1974). Unlike Britain and countries like Belgium and Sweden, not all EC members have abandoned the non-discrimination rule. The European Commission has raised the competitive disadvantage to consumers of any rule which prevents consumers having to pay extra for payment by credit (or debit) cards. However, it is well to note that the European consumer organisation, BEUC, takes a neutral view on the issue, since its national constituent members are divided on whether a charge would benefit consumers.

Under the Order agreements are now unlawful which prevent retailers from surcharging credit card users or from offering discounts to cardholders who pay by cash, cheque or similar means. However, little advantage seems to have been taken of this provision, probably because retailers fear it would alienate credit card users. Retailers imposing differential prices on credit card users must give adequate notice to consumers of any difference since otherwise they may commit a misleading price offence under s 20 of the Consumer Protection Act 1987.[6]

The Consumer Credit Act 1974 contains provisions which apply specifically to credit cards and similar forms of credit. The mass mailing of unsolicited credit cards, which was used in the early years to attract custom, is forbidden.[7] A consumer is not liable if a credit card is lost and used fraudulently before it is signed (or a receipt for it signed) or before it is first used. A consumer may have to pay up to a maximum of £50 if a credit card is lost and used fraudulently after that point, unless the company is notified of the loss before the card is used, whereupon there is no liability.[8] Limiting liability in this way is justified because the credit card companies can spread the risk among many consumers and are also in the best position to take preventive steps against fraud through card design or the way they

---

[6] Pages 306–307 below.
[7] Section 51. See *Elliott v Director General of Fair Trading* [1980] 1 WLR 977, [1980] ICR 629.
[8] Section 84. Oral notification must be followed by written confirmation (s 84(5)). On fraudulent use by the consumer see *R v Lambie* [1982] AC 449.

can be used. That the consumer can be liable for up to £50 provides an incentive to ensure that the card is kept safely.

Credit advanced to enable consumers to purchase housing is secured by mortgage over the property.[9] The bank or building society can repossess the property and sell it, should the consumer be in default. Interest payable on home mortgages can be fixed, but Britain has always had large numbers of flexible rate mortgages where the interest rate fluctuates in accordance with the level of interest rates in the economy as a whole. Consumers are said to have an equity in their homes, although negative equity was a feature of Britain in the late 1980s and early 1990s, when with the collapse of property prices the amount consumers owed exceeded the market value of their homes. 'Equity release' involves the bank or building society making advances to the consumer—to fund home improvements or other spending–on the basis of the existing mortgage, a second mortgage or a remortgaging of the property.

(b) The law of consumer credit

The relevant legal principles relating to credit for consumers are drawn widely from common law principles, the Consumer Credit Act 1974, other statutory law from the Bills of Sale Acts to the Insolvency Act 1986, and procedural law. The Consumer Credit Act 1974 is derived from the work of the Crowther Committee which was established in 1968 to review existing and alternative arrangements for consumer credit. The main thrust of the Committee's exhaustive analysis was directed to improving consumers' rights and to rationalising the law into a new coherent framework. As far as consumers were concerned, the Committee proceeded on the basis that credit contributes to the well being of consumers as a whole and that only a small number of people, who, as it put it, for some reason or another are incapable of managing their own affairs or who are unable to cope with sudden sickness or unemployment, have repayment difficulties. Since the problem of default as the Committee saw it was not inherent in credit transactions, the Committee concluded that the best policy was to interfere as little as possible.[10]

Rationalisation, according to the Committee, should proceed along various lines: credit transactions should be regulated according to their substance, not their form; consumer transactions should be given separate

---

[9] Mortgage law is not dealt with at length here. Note that the Law Commission has proposed that land mortgages should no longer come within the Consumer Credit Act but should be regulated under a proposed Land Mortgages Act: Law Commission *Transfer of Land. Land Mortgages* (Law Com no 204 (1991)).

[10] *Crowther Committee* pp 152–153.

treatment from commercial transactions; and credit when provided in loan form should be assimilated with that provided in a hire purchase or similar instalment sale contract.[11] Two pieces of legislation were recommended: a Lending and Security Act to rationalise the treatment of security interests and conflict between secured parties, primarily along the lines of Article 9 of the American Uniform Commercial Code,[12] and a Consumer Sale and Loan Act which would licence those in the consumer credit market and extend protection currently applying to hire purchase to all forms of consumer credit agreement. The Lending and Security Act has never been implemented on the grounds of its complexity and unnecessary cost,[13] but the proposals for a Consumer Sale and Loan Act became, in effect, the Consumer Credit Act 1974.[14]

The Consumer Credit Act 1974 was hailed as a great advance in consumer protection, and certainly the licensing scheme for all engaged in consumer credit (considered in Chapter 12) seems to have improved standards. But given the philosophy behind the Act it is not surprising that some of its provisions relating to consumers' rights and obligations are less protective than the law elsewhere. Certainly the larger finance houses had nothing to fear from the Act because it did not impose undue restrictions and in the main confirmed their existing practices. A director of one member firm of the Finance Houses Association, in welcoming the Act, commented:

> There are two aspects of competition to which attention should be drawn. The impact of government controls over banks and finance houses in the past twenty years has consistently led to the promotion and growth of smaller fringe companies who have contrived to 'escape the net' and in many cases to remain unaffected by the controls imposed on the larger and more reputable companies—to the extent that this will no longer be possible (as a result of the licensing system) the Bill is to be welcomed.[15]

When, some 20 years after its enactment, the Director General of Fair Trading consulted on the scope and operation of the Consumer Credit Act 1974, he found no respondent, from the credit industry or otherwise, who seriously called into question the basic framework of regulation under

---

[11]   *Crowther Committee* pp 184ff.
[12]   *Crowther Committee* p 183.
[13]   Similar reasons were given for rejecting proposals along the same lines by Professor Aubrey Diamond *A Review of Security Interests in Property* (HMSO, 1989).
[14]   *Reform of the Law on Consumer Credit* (Cmnd 5427 (1973)) (hereafter White Paper).
[15]   G Tipping 'Reform of the Law on Consumer Credit' *Credit* vol 14 (1973) p 83. See generally, JJ McManus 'The Emergence and Non-Emergence of Legislation' (1978) 5 British J Law & Soc 185.

the Act, the need for its protective provisions, and the broad success of the Act in achieving its goal.[16] The credit industry has no doubt incorporated the legislative provisions into its standard practices and operation procedures. Familiarity, and institutional inertia, can lend powerful support to consumer protection, once the battle for its adoption has been won.

The Consumer Credit Act 1974 is rather complex, partly because existing forms of credit like hire purchase, conditional sale and personal loan agreements continue in existence, and partly because a great deal of the law is contained in regulations made under the Act.[17] It is necessary to appreciate the coverage of the Act to understand the substantive provisions. Most of the protections in the Act are confined to consumer credit agreements, which are in effect agreements in which creditors provide individuals with credit not exceeding £25,000 (increased over time from the original £5,000 limit).[18] Credit includes a cash loan and any other form of financial accommodation such as allowing a consumer time to pay.[19] Interest and certain ancillary charges are excluded when calculating the £25,000 limit in fixed sum credit agreements, while in running account credit agreements (like bank overdrafts, some store accounts and some credit cards) the £25,000 figure is the credit limit, or probable credit limit, when the agreement was entered.[20] In particular circumstances there can be nice questions about whether the £25,000 figure is exceeded. In *Huntpast v Leadbeater* the Court of Appeal held that although £18,500 had been advanced (as a personal loan on a mortgage of the consumer's home), £2,960 had been bridging loan interest and deducted from the advance,

[16]   *Consumer Credit Deregulation* (OFT, 1994) p 6.
[17]   Standard works include RM Goode *Consumer Credit Legislation* (Butterworths, looseleaf); AG Guest and E Lomnicka *Encyclopedia of Consumer Credit Law* (Sweet & Maxwell, looseleaf); G Harding *Consumer Credit and Consumer Hire Law* (Sweet & Maxwell, 1995).
[18]   Section 8(1)–(2). The £25,000 figure replaced at £15,000 limit as from 1 May 1998: Consumer Credit (Increase of Monetary Limits) (Amendment) Order 1998, SI 1998/996. Credit for unincorporated businesses is covered (see definition of individuals in s 189(1)). At one time it was proposed to remove them from the scope of the Act, except licensing: OFT *Consultation Document on the Treatment of usiness Consumers under the Consumer Credit Act 1974* (1993); *Deregulation of United Kingdom Consumer Credit Legislation* (DTI, 1995) p 6. The proposal was surprising in the light of the abuses reported in *Photocopier Selling Practices* (OFT, 1994).
[19]   Section 9(1). *Dimond v Lovell* [2000] 2 All ER 897, [2000] 2 WLR 1121, HL.
[20]   Sections 9(4), 10(2), 10(3)(b)(iii); Consumer Credit (Total Charge for Credit) Regulations 1980, SI 1980/51. The ancillary charges excluded include (a) default charges, (b) certain charges payable even if the transaction were for cash, (c) charges for incidental services or benefits, (d) certain maintenance charges, (e) certain bank charges, (f) certain insurance premiums: reg 5.

together with £3,925 payable to credit brokers, with the result that the agreement was within the financial limits then obtaining of £15,000.[1]

Hire purchase agreements are regarded as credit agreements and credit is regarded as being provided to the extent of the total price of an item, less the aggregate of any deposit and credit charges.[2] Because of their functional similarity to credit agreements, many provisions in the Act apply to consumer hire agreements, which are defined as bailments capable of subsisting for more than three months which do not require the hirer to make payments exceeding £25,000.[3] However, this catches many short-term hire agreements, as where tools are hired out for a few days at a time on the understanding that the customer will pay for the number of days used, because they are capable of lasting for more than three months. It is proposed to exempt such hire agreements, where there is a flat fee for a hire period of up to a week with no penalty for early or late return of the equipment hired.[4]

As will be seen later in the chapter, a further definition to be appreciated in considering the application of the Consumer Credit Act 1974 is of the *debtor-creditor-supplier* agreement.[5] A debtor-creditor-supplier agreement can involve two parties, the consumer and the creditor-supplier, as with hire purchase where the finance house is the creditor and supplier. The other type of debtor-creditor-supplier agreement is the tripartite agreement. This is a restricted use credit agreement where the agreement is made by a creditor under existing or contemplated arrangements with a supplier, or where a creditor advances unrestricted-use credit in the knowledge that it will be used with a supplier with whom it has pre-existing arrangements. A simple example is where a finance house provides a personal loan for a consumer to purchase a motor car from a retailer who has an arrangement whereby it introduces consumers to the finance house for credit. Under the Act, a *debtor-creditor* agreement is a residual category: it is a regulated consumer credit agreement other than a debtor-creditor-supplier agreement. Basically, it is an agreement for the lending of money with no supplier involved such as with a personal loan.[6]

Most provisions of the Act—the advertising and extortionate credit bargain provisions are exceptions—apply only to regulated consumer

---

[1]   [1993] CCLR 15. However, deductions for a fire insurance premium and legal costs were not excluded in calculating the £15,000 figure.

[2]   Section 9(3).

[3]   Section 15(1). See N Palmer and D Yates 'The Application of the Consumer Credit Act 1974 to Consumer Hire Agreements' (1979) 38 Cambridge LJ 180.

[4]   DTI *Clarification and Simplification of United Kingdom Consumer Credit Law. A Consultation Paper* (1998) pp 13–14. Section 15 will be amended by order under the Deregulation and Contracting Act 1994.

[5]   Section 12.

[6]   Section 13.

credit agreements and regulated consumer hire agreements, meaning those which are not exempt. Exempt consumer credit agreements include ordinary mortgages by banks and building societies; fixed sum debtor-creditor-supplier agreements where the number of payments does not exceed four within a maximum period of 12 months, and debtor-creditor-supplier agreements where the rate of total charge for credit does not exceed the sum of 1% and highest of any of certain bank base rates.[7] Moreover, some provisions in the Act do not apply to non-commercial agreements (which may include a business engaging in a private or uncommon transaction, eg a loan to an employee[8]) and to small agreements, where the credit or hire charge does not exceed £50, not being hire purchase or conditional sale agreements or secured transactions.[9] Bank overdrafts are excluded from the provisions of Part V of the Act, which stipulates the content of consumer credit agreements and what information consumers must be given.[10]

2   OBTAINING CREDIT[11]

(a)   A right to credit

Like other businesses credit providers have wide freedom to grant or deny their facilities to whom they choose. But there are limitations. Creditors are now forbidden to discriminate on the grounds of sex, race or disability.[12] In *Quinn v Williams Furniture Ltd*[13] for example, the Court of Appeal held that a retailer was in breach of the former provision in insisting on a married woman having her husband guarantee a hire purchase agreement, when it would not have imposed a similar requirement on a married man whose circumstances were in all material respects similar. In addition the Director General of Fair Trading in exercising its licensing powers must have regard to whether a creditor has practised discrimination on the grounds of sex, colour, race or ethnic origins.[14] In the United States, the

---

[7] Consumer Credit Act 1974, s 16; Consumer Credit (Exempt Agreements) Order 1989, SI 1989/869 as amended by SI 1998/1944.

[8] See *Hare v Schurek* [1993] CCLR 47.

[9] Sections 17, 189.

[10] Section 74(1)(b).

[11] Credit advertising and truth in lending are considered elsewhere in the book: pp 373–374; pp 362–367.

[12] Sex Discrimination Act 1975, s 29; Race Relations Act 1976, s 20; Disability Discrimination Act 1995, s 19.

[13] [1981] ICR 328.

[14] Consumer Credit Act 1974, s 25(2)(c).

Equal Credit Opportunity Act and legislation at the state level deal specifically with a number of objectionable practices which may not fall within the sweep of the UK legislation.[15] Nonetheless, there is empirical evidence that discrimination continues: one Chicago study demonstrates that white men were systematically offered better prices on new cars than blacks and women.[16]

If there is some protection against creditors discriminating on sexual or racial grounds, what of other types of discrimination? Reference has been made to the problems which the less affluent have in obtaining credit. There have been instances of direct discrimination against the poor where they were denied credit even though they were creditworthy. For example, some creditors have refused to grant credit to all those living on a particular street or council housing estate, whatever the merits of an individual applicant, because in the past they had a disproportionate number of defaulters from the area.[17]

Larger creditors now use credit scoring, designed to predict the probability of a person repaying any credit advanced. Scoring is based on the personal characteristics of the debtor, either matching them statistically to the profile of others who have repaid (applicant scoring) or examining the borrower's own behaviour with existing indebtedness (behavioural scoring). Scoring is associated with targeting, with financial institutions able to market a range of financial products (including credit) to those with favourable scores.

In principle credit scoring is a rational method of making credit decisions. No one shall be denied credit simply because they live in a particular street or on a particular estate. However, those on low incomes (or state benefits) and without property—which can be used as security or is taken as evidence of financial stability—are still unlikely to obtain high scores. They will have limited access to mainstream credit providers or will be excluded altogether. Ford writes:

> Those with limited incomes, low-status jobs or no jobs are disadvantaged. This group includes many women and members of ethnic minority groups, because of broader social and economic processes that allocate them to low-paid and/or part-time jobs, or high levels of unemployment. In addition, non-economic factors play a part in structuring access to credit. Knowledge of financial

[15] Eg A Geary 'Equal Credit Opportunity' (1976) 31 Bus L 1641; E Griffith 'The Quest for Fair Credit Reporting and Equal Credit Opportunity in Consumer Transactions' (1994) 25 U Mem LR 37; A Farley 'The Spousal Defense—A Ploy to Escape Payment or Simple Application of the Equal Opportunity Act?' (1996) 49 Vand LR 1287.
[16] I Ayres 'Fair Driving: Gender and Race Discrimination in Retail Car Negotiations' (1991) 104 Harv LR 817.
[17] See the examples in *Consumers and Credit* (NCC, 1980) pp 90, 274–276.

processes and financial institutions is unequal, and the rational assumptions about 'shopping around', even amongst limited alternatives, may be relinquished in favour of familiarity and certainty of acceptance.[18]

There is a Guide produced by the trade associations, and endorsed by the Director General of Fair Trading, which aims at clarifying best practice in credit scoring and avoiding the threat of legislation.[19] More consideration needs to be given to the factors it takes into account and the weight given to them. However, the Guide obliges credit providers to inform consumers why they have been denied credit and to provide an appeal mechanism when credit is refused. Unfortunately the Data Protection Act 1998, which implements an EC Directive, does not contain a legal obligation on credit providers to explain to consumers that decisions have been based on credit scoring.[20]

The law can do a little to overcome the lack of income of poorer consumers. However, it has a role in institution building, as we see later in the chapter in the discussion on credit unions. It can help curb the undesirable practices of those lending to the consumers with impaired credit ratings (called non-status lending). For example, in 1997 the Director General of Fair Trading threatened to withdraw the licences of several companies providing non-status loans and reissued guidelines for lenders and brokers in the non-status lending market identifying practices considered to be deceitful, oppressive or otherwise unfair or improper, even if not unlawful.[1] In the United States the Equal Credit Opportunity Act protects against discriminatory practices used in relation to the poor. The Act makes it unlawful to discriminate against a consumer because of age or because all or part of the applicant's income derives from any welfare programme.[2] However, it does not constitute discrimination for a creditor to make inquiry about the applicant's age or whether his income derives from any public assistance programme 'if such inquiry is for the purpose of determining the amount and probable continuance of income levels, credit history or other persistent element of creditworthiness as provided in regulations.'[3] Perhaps more importantly, the Community

---

[18] J Ford *Consuming Credit. Debt and Poverty in the UK* (Child Poverty Action Group, 1991) pp 35, 37. See also S Fleming 'Cash at the Price of a Lifetime' (1996) New Statesman, 16 August, p 22; B Wildavsky 'Keeping Score' (1996) National Law Journal, 10 February 10, p 527 (on US criticism).

[19] *Guide to Credit Scoring 1993* (Credit Industry Working Party on Credit Scoring, 1993).

[20] Section 13(2), (6), (7). See Directive 95/46/EC [1995] OJ 281/31.

[1] *Guidelines for Non-Status Lenders and Brokers* (December 1998) (covering, for example, high default interest rates for late payers and exorbitant redemption penalties).

[2] 15 USC §1691(a)(2).

[3] 15 USC §1691(b)(2).

Investment Act of 1977 was designed to counter the practice of red-lining, which involves denying or restricting credit for the purchase or improvement of homes in particular areas (notably, poorer neighbourhoods).[4] The Act does not establish specific standards for bank performance, but the banking regulators use it as a lever to have financial institutions meet informal standards of matching the credit needs of a community where an institution is based.[5] Moreover, community groups have mobilised around the opportunities provided by the Act when local banks have been acquired or sought to restructure: the banks have been obliged to enter agreements, involving changes in the terms and standards for loans (eg lower interest rates for certain home and business loans) or the provision of basic banking services in a community.[6]

(b)   Creditworthiness and credit reference agencies

Credit reference agencies are businesses which provide information about the financial standing of consumers. With the growth of modern credit scoring, they are not as important as they once were to the decision to grant credit. Some agencies are profit-making bodies, but others are trade protection associations operated as a service to members. The largest credit reference agencies have files covering millions of consumers. Credit reference agencies draw on a number of sources of information: public records like county court judgments, the reports of bankruptcy proceedings and the electoral register, and trade members who supply items for the files such as information about bad debts and repossessions. Credit reference agencies record the enquiries which they receive about a consumer, and if the record shows a number of enquiries over a period with no derogatory information reported, the consumer is likely to be regarded as very creditworthy. Reports in which local enquiries are made from neighbours and traders are relatively rare in the case of individual consumers, although more common with business concerns. The Younger Committee on Privacy concluded that checking creditworthiness prevented reckless or dishonest people from obtaining credit, kept down overheads and prices by reducing

---

4   12 USC §2901.
5   J Norton and S Whitley *Banking Law Manual* (Matthew Bender, looseleaf), §7.04[2].
6   C Bradford and G Cincotta 'The Legacy, the Promise and the Unfinished Agenda' in G Squires *From Redlining to Reinvestment* (Temple UP, 1991) pp 241, 147; C Marasill 'Beyond the Boundaries of the Community Reinvestment Act and the Fair Lending Laws: Developing a Market-Based Framework for Generating Low- and Moderate-Income Lending' (1996) 96 Colum LR 710, 711.

bad debts and stimulated trade by facilitating the ready granting of credit in appropriate cases.[7]

Despite the value of credit reference agencies in determining the creditworthiness of consumers, there have been concerns. Privacy is one: most consumers will not object if a credit provider contacted a credit reference agency when they intended to buy on credit, although they would no doubt condemn the leakage of this information to others.[8] Accuracy is another. In 1993 the Data Protection Registrar reported:

> Of those complaints assessed, 2,628 (63%) were about problems associated with credit reference activities. Many relate to concerns about the extraction of third party information. Particular concerns expressed by complainants included the extraction of information about the financial history of every member of the credit applicant's family ... However, individuals are also questioning the information held by credit reference agencies in other ways. For example, in relation to the length of time for which specific items of data are held and as to whether the data held for the purposes of credit reference are adequate.[9]

Subsequently, the Data Protection Tribunal has approved enforcement notices against the four main credit reference agencies, which in broad terms prevent them from passing to credit providers third party information, unless there is some relationship of family or residence between the applicant and the third parties. Third party information may be further limited where, for example, there is no financial relationship between the individuals concerned.[10]

Situations such as that identified by the Data Protection Registrar are personally damaging to consumers and also lead to inefficiency in the provision of credit. The Consumer Credit Act 1974 and Data Protection Act 1998 go some way to ensuring that information in the files of credit reference agencies is accurate. Accuracy is one of the principles which those collecting personal data must comply with under the Data Protection Act 1998. More directly, consumers can contact a credit reference agency, request a copy of the information held about them, and have the data corrected if it is inaccurate.[11] A major advance under the data protection

---

[7]   *Report of the Committee on Privacy* (Cmnd 502 (1971)) p 78.

[8]   Confidentiality was emphasised by those interviewed for I Crow, G Howells and M Moroney 'Credit and Debt: Choices for Poorer Consumers' in G Howells, I Crow, M Moroney (eds) *Aspects of Credit and Debt* (Sweet & Maxwell, 1993) p 49.

[9]   *Ninth Report of the Data Protection Registrar 1993* (HMSO, 1993) Chapter 5.

[10]   *CNN Case, Infolink Case, Equifax Europe Case, CDMS Case* in S Charlton et al (eds) *Encyclopedia of Data Protection* (Sweet & Maxwell, looseleaf).

[11]   Consumer Credit Act 1974, ss 158–160; Data Protection Act 1998, ss 7–8, 12. As a matter of practice a request will be made under the former, since the charge is lower (£2).

legislation has been a provision enabling consumers to sue for compensation for damage or distress suffered because of information which continues to be inaccurate.[12] Whenever consumers negotiate with a creditor or with a retailer with a view to purchasing on credit, they can demand to know the name and address of any credit reference agency from which information about their financial standing has been sought.[13] This information must be provided whether or not credit was refused, but there is no need for the creditor or retailer to reveal what the credit reference agency said or whether it affected any decision about the application for credit. Once consumers know the name of the credit reference agency, however, they can then obtain a copy of the information on file.

The Consumer Credit Act 1974 and Data Protection Act 1998 tackle the major problem with the information collected by credit reference agencies—that it may be inaccurate. But there are other undesirable practices which can occur: for example, information could be collected by credit reference agencies on matters like the personal behaviour of consumers, which is irrelevant to their creditworthiness. Status information of this sort is unusual but the Data Protection Act 1998 goes some way to restricting the type of information that can be stored in that it must be relevant and not excessive in relation to the purposes for which it is processed.[14] Stale information must also be weeded out of the files of credit reference agencies.[15]

(c)   The right to copies and to cancel

Consumers entering regulated agreements come under the Consumer Credit Act 1974, they are entitled to receive at least one, and in many cases, two copies of an agreement with the aim of informing them of their rights and obligations and of making it more difficult for any retailer to engage in fraud. In the common situation where the consumer signs an agreement and it does not become an executed agreement immediately (eg the consumer's creditworthiness must first be checked or a finance house must decide on the proposal submitted through the retailer), the consumer must be supplied with a copy of the unexecuted agreement.[16] Moreover, when the agreement becomes executed (ie the creditor approves the credit)

---

[12]   Section 11. Even if it were possible, an action in defamation might be defeated by the defence of qualified privilege.
[13]   Consumer Credit Act 1974, s 157. See also Consumer Credit (Conduct of Business) (Credit References) Regulations 1977, SI 1977/330; Consumer Credit (Credit Reference Agency) Regulations 2000, SI 2000/290.
[14]   Data Protection Act 1998, Sch 1, Principle 3.
[15]   Data Protection Act 1998, Sch 1, Principle 4.
[16]   Consumer Credit Act 1974, s 62(1).

the consumer must be supplied with a copy of the executed agreement, and any other document referred to in it, within seven days of its being made, unless the agreement is actually sent to the consumer for signature and thereupon becomes an executed agreement.[17] In the special case where an unexecuted agreement is personally presented to the consumer and it becomes executed when he signs it, the consumer must receive a copy of the executed agreement there and then and must also be sent a notice of his right to cancel within seven days.[18]

Failure to supply the copies makes the agreement non-enforceable without a court order, so that in theory consumers can keep possession of an item without having to pay for it, but may be liable for conversion if they part with it to a third party.[19] As a matter of practice the courts will be lenient in granting orders to creditors to enforce agreements, despite a failure to send copies within the time limits required, so long as the consumer is not, in their view, in a different position than if he or she had received a copy, and he or she is given a copy of the executed agreement before legal proceedings are commenced.[20] In other words, the non-enforceability provision is not necessarily a sanction: criminal penalties are needed to achieve this result.

The cancellation ('cooling off') provisions apply to regulated agreements in which the antecedent negotiations included oral representations made in the presence of the consumer unless the unexecuted agreement was signed by the consumer at related business premises.[1] Credit agreements secured on land, or for the purchase of land, are excluded because of what are said to be the difficulties in cancelling these types of agreement. There is no need for the end representations to have been intended to induce, or in fact to have induced, the agreement.[2] The cancellation provisions apply mainly to doorstep transactions, although there are other situations which can be envisaged as being covered; for example, an agreement signed at a trade display or a fair or the consumer's place of work. Unscrupulous businesses operating door to door can avoid the effects of the cancellation period quite simply by conning the consumer at home and then bundling him off to business premises to sign the agreement. The limitation of the cancellation provisions to mainly doorstep transactions also ignores the point that pressure can be applied to consumers at business premises. As a matter of

---

[17]   Section 63(2).
[18]   Sections 63(1), 64(1)(b).
[19]   Section 65.
[20]   See s 127; *Nissan Finance UK v Lockhart* [1993] CCLR 39, CA.
[1]   Section 67.
[2]   *Moorgate Services Ltd v Kabir* [1995] CCLR 74, CA.

policy, it is desirable to allow consumers some time for reflection with major credit agreements because of their onerous and complex nature. There should be no prejudice to businesses in making this the law; they need simply to hold off delivering goods or providing services or advancing credit until the cooling-off period has elapsed.

A cooling-off period is of little value if consumers are not fully informed of their right to cancel within the time set for its exercise. The Consumer Credit Act 1974 fails to achieve this. With cancellable agreements there must be included in every copy of the unexecuted and executed agreement mentioned above a notice of the consumer's right to cancel, how and when that right is exercisable, and the name and address of the person to whom it may be given. A separate notice of cancellation is required in the special case where the agreement becomes executed when the consumer signs it.[3] There seems to be no reason why the Act should not provide for a separate notice of cancellation to be sent in all cases to notify consumers of their rights, for it is clear that consumers cannot be expected to, and in fact rarely, read complicated agreements like those covered by the Act, and thus tend to remain ignorant of the right to cancel. The Crowther Committee recommended that consumers should be provided with a notice of cancellation which could simply be signed and posted within the period created.[4]

The actual period in which cancellation can take place normally begins when the consumer signs the unexecuted agreement and finishes on the end of the fifth day following the day on which the consumer receives a copy of the executed agreement or the requisite notice about cancellation.[5] In total, then, the consumer has some 12 days to cancel compared with seven days in the case of non-credit transactions, which are subject to a cooling-off period under regulations implementing EC Directives.[6] Consumers sending a notice of cancellation by post are deemed to exercise their right at the time of posting, even if it is never received, and notice of cancellation can be served not only on the creditor or owner, but also on a person it has specified, any agents, a credit broker or supplier who was a negotiator in antecedent negotiations, and any person who in the course of a business acted on behalf of the consumer in any negotiations for the agreement.[7]

The effect of cancellation is to render void the agreement, a separate sale transaction (in the event of a debtor-creditor-supplier agreement for

---

[3]   Section 64. With credit card agreements the rules are more lax.
[4]   *Crowther Committee* p 189.
[5]   Section 68(a).
[6]   Page 427ff below.
[7]   Section 69.

restricted use credit) and other 'linked transactions' (exceptions include a contract of insurance). The consumer is released from further liability for payment and is entitled to recover payments made.[8] The consumer must be ready to return any goods received except if goods have been incorporated into land or other goods, whereupon liability arises for the cash price, but with perishable goods, or those consumed by use which have been consumed, the consumer is under no obligation either to return or to pay the cash price.[9] Specific provision is made for cancellation where part-exchange goods are involved, and consumers are entitled to recover a sum equivalent to the part-exchange agreed (otherwise a reasonable allowance) if the goods are not returned within ten days of cancellation.[10]

3   CREDIT AGREEMENTS

Credit agreements are typically standard form contracts and are therefore subject to some control under the general law and the unfair contracts terms legislation considered in Chapter 3. For example, the Director General of Fair Trading has sought to act against the use of dual interest rate schemes by non-status lenders.[11] Under this structure, if a debtor falls into default the second, and much higher, rates come into effect. If creditors wish to recoup the administrative costs involved in default, says the Office of Fair Trading, they should do so by reasonable direct charges to debtors.[12] Unless carefully expressed, a dual interest rate could also be in breach of the common law rule against penalties, as not being a genuine pre-estimate of the loss the creditor suffers on default. The Court of Appeal has held that the provision in a simple rate loan agreement for contractual

---

[8]   Section 70. For 'linked transactions', s 19; Consumer Credit (Linked Transactions) (Exemptions) Regulations 1983, SI 1983/1560, reg 2(2).

[9]   Sections 69(2)–(3), 72. The provision regarding perishables has the underlying policy intention of not inhibiting consumers from exercising the right to cancel, for example in relation to a freezer where food was also supplied, where if they cancelled they might still have to pay for the perishables.

[10]   Section 73.

[11]   OFT Press Release No 27/97; see also the county court judgment in *Falco Finance Ltd v Michael Gough* (1999) 17 Tr LR 526

[12]   The OFT takes the view that a dual interest rate terms is in substance a term making provision for payment of compensation upon breach of an obligation, and is thus not a core provision: see Unfair Terms in Consumer Contracts Regulations 1999, SI 1999/2083, reg 4(2). On core terms see *Director General of Fair Trading v First National Bank* [2000] 1 All ER (Comm) 371, [2000] 2 WLR 1353, CA (appeal to House of Lords pending, June 2000). See also the reference in Sch 2—potentially unfair terms—to a term requiring any consumer who fails to fulfil his obligations to pay a disproportionately high sum in compensation: see *Non-status Lending* (OFT, 1997) pp 17–18.

interest to accrue on any judgment obtained by the lender was unfair under the Regulations.[13]

In addition to these private law controls, credit agreements may attract regulatory protection. In Britain this is now because they fall under the Consumer Credit Act 1974. For example, in relation to the problem just mentioned of very high default interest rates, s 93 of that Act prohibits any increase in interest on default under a regulated consumer credit agreement. The following sections outline some of these specific controls in consumer credit agreements arising from the Consumer Credit Act 1974.

(a)   The contents and form of an agreement

The Hire Purchase Acts traditionally empowered the executive to control the form and content of the contractual documents. The Consumer Credit Act 1974 continues the provision so that basic information can be provided to consumers as to the terms of the regulated agreements upon which they are embarking. Non-commercial agreements (eg between friends) and certain small debtor-credit-supplier agreements for restricted use credit are not covered.[14] Contractual documents will furnish consumers with essential information on matters such as the rights and duties conferred or imposed by the agreement; the amount and rate of the credit and the protections and remedies available (eg the right to cancel). Regulations can also be promulgated regarding the manner in these matters are set out in the documents.[15] Under the Consumer Credit Act 1974 non-compliance with the provisions about the form and content of regulated agreements makes a credit transaction unenforceable without a court order.[16] A court in making an enforcement order must have regard to the prejudice caused and the degree of culpability for non-compliance.[17] Where essential information is omitted by reason of fraud on the part of a dealer—for example, the dealer has the consumer sign the proposal form in blank—a court clearly could not enforce the agreement as later completed.[18] Even where non-compliance with the requirements of the Act is a product of widespread misunderstanding or ignorance of provisions of the Act the courts have not been sympathetic to lenders. *Dimond v Lovell* was a case

---

[13]   *Director General of Fair Trading v First National Bank* [2000] 1 All ER (Comm) 371, [2000] 2 WLR 1353, CA (appeal to House of Lords pending, June 2000).

[14]   Sections 60, 74.

[15]   Section 60.

[16]   Consumer Credit Act 1974, ss 61(1)(a), 65.

[17]   Section 127(1). See *Nissan Finance UK v Lockhart* [1993] CCLR 39; *Rank Xerox v Hepple* [1994] CCLR 1; N Cawley and G Goldberg 'Protecting Borrowers' [1997] LM & CLQ 406.

[18]   Section 172(3).

which was appealed to the House of Lords to test the validity under the Act of car hire agreements made to customers of insurance companies whose cars were put out of action by road accidents, with payment deferred until an insurer paid on an insurance policy.[19] The case arose by way of an insurer defending a claim for car hire by a consumer on the basis that the agreement between the consumer and the hirer did not comply with the provisions of the 1974 Act, was unenforceable, and consequently did not create any liability for the insurer. Lying behind the insurer's action was a concern in the insurance industry that the rate of hire on these deferred payment hire agreement was considerably greater than for an ordinary hire agreement. Put another way, consumers were failing to mitigate their losses. Their Lordships held the agreement to be unenforceable. It was said by the Vice Chancellor in the course of proceedings that 40,000 similar cases turned on the outcome. The future implications of the decision are less clear since it might be open for a car hire company to comply with the terms of the Act or frame the agreement in such a way as to secure exemption.

Parliament rejected the course of actually mandating a statutory form for credit contracts, with a standard set of terms laid out in uniform manner, on the basis that this would inhibit the evolution of new forms of credit and be an unnecessary burden on businesses.[20] The result is that agreements contain not only the statutory information but other material besides, and in language which ordinary consumers might not understand. The argument for standard forms is that existing documentation is concerned less with consumer understanding than industry advantage, and that the industry should welcome shorter, clearer contracts to 'save time, paper and anxiety about compliance with the legislation'.[1] Certainly, there seems no reason that the task of facilitating changes in a standard form should be as exacting as some suggest. Wherever the balance lies in the argument for standard forms, there is a clear case for requiring greater simplification of the language in which credit documents are drafted, for with many only the most sophisticated consumers can readily comprehend them. The Australian Consumer Credit Code, which came into force in 1996, requires that all consumer agreements and notices must be clearly expressed, and that they may be considered unjust and liable to be re-opened if unintelligible.[2]

Contractual documents are not necessarily the most appropriate means of conveying information to consumers. Consumers will not engage in

---

[19]   [2000] 2 All ER 897, [2000] 2 WLR 1121, HL. The implications of the decision are discussed in a series of articles by I McLaren 'Consumer Credit Hire' (2000) 150 NLJ 748, 765, 837.

[20]   *Crowther Committee* p 267.

[1]   Justice White *Fair Dealing with Consumers* (Govt Printer, 1975) p 36.

[2]   Sections 70(2)(g), 162(1). See C Shum 'The New Consumer Credit Law in Australia' [1997] JBL 254.

comparative shopping if it is only then that they first become aware of credit terms and charges. By the time they get the documents they will in most cases be committed to a transaction. Moreover, consumers commonly sign credit documents without knowing what they contain, so that they may be in complete ignorance of the terms until the possibility of withdrawal or cancellation has passed. The Consumer Credit Act 1974 tries to get around this to some extent, and contains a regulatory power to oblige disclosure to consumers of specified information before a regulated agreement is consummated.[3] However, no regulations have ever been made under this section. Later in the book we see that if there is pre-contractual disclosure, this must comply with the regulations governing advertising, which are designed to give consumers a fair and reasonable indication of the credit terms available.[4] Requirements that creditors and credit brokers must on request provide consumers with a quotation and detailed information regarding credit terms were repealed and not replaced in 1997.[5]

Since 1985, regulations have been in operation regarding the content and form of regulated credit agreements.[6] These provide that the agreement must be recorded in a document which records all its terms, is signed by both the business and consumer, and is readily legible. (However, there are no requirements governing the size of lettering as there were under the Hire-Purchase Acts.) Some terms must always be contained in the signature document, but other terms may be included either in the signature document or in another document referred to in it. In broad terms, the agreement must contain a heading (eg 'Credit Agreement regulated by the Consumer Credit Act 1974'), the name and address of both the business and consumer, a clear description of any security, details of any default charges, and certain financial information (eg the cash price of the product, services or land, any deposit, the amount of credit, the charge payable for the credit, the timing and amount of repayments and the annual percentage rates (APR)).

---

[3] Consumer Credit Act 1974, s 55. The section has yet to be implemented.

[4] Pages 362–367 below.

[5] Consumer Credit (Quotations) Regulations 1989, SI 1989/1126 repealed by Consumer Credit (Quotations) (Revocation) Regulations 1997, SI 1997/211. Though a deregulatory measure it was achieved by use of the powers under the Consumer Credit Act 1974. New, but more limited requirements as to quotations were introduced in 2000, requiring the issuing of warnings where credit might be secured on real property: the Consumer Credit (Content of Quotations) and Consumer Credit (Advertisements) (Amendment) Regulations 1999, SI 1999/2725.

[6] Notably Consumer Credit (Agreements) Regulations 1983, SI 1983/1553, as amended; Consumer Credit (Cancellation Notices and Copies of Documents) Regulations 1983, SI 1983/1557 as amended.

Most importantly, there must be a statement of the protections and remedies provided to the consumer, notably the right to cancel (if that applies) and to a rebate on early settlement. Here the regulations are prescriptive, for the agreement must reproduce specified words which must be of a certain prominence. An example are the words explaining 'YOUR RIGHT TO CANCEL', which must appear in a box. There must also be a signature box for all regulated agreements, for the customer's signature and its date. The box can be of any size and location, but the wording must be as specified (eg 'This is a Credit Agreement regulated by the Consumer Credit Act 1974. Sign it only if you want to be legally bound by its terms.')

(b)   Control over credit

Over the years it has been said that consumers can be induced by marketing into transactions on credit when they cannot really undertake the repayment responsibilities. Their budgets are so tightly committed that the least interruption by illness or unemployment will produce default. The Crowther Committee set out what has become the conventional wisdom:

> It would appear that responsibility for the majority of court cases rests with a small number of credit-granting bodies which habitually grant credit without making any enquiries about creditworthiness of the debtor. Sometimes the same creditor is issuing judgment summonses against a debtor while through its agents it is persuading that debtor to accept extra credit.[7]

The Committee concluded that the best policy was not to restrict the granting of credit, but to ensure that creditors were most careful in assessing creditworthiness and to assist those who defaulted.[8] It recommended that the body administering licensing under the Consumer Credit Act 1974 should be empowered to receive information on default rates and overdue accounts from creditors and to take appropriate action (it was not clear what this would entail) if it appeared that creditors were extending credit unwisely and that they were still able to operate successfully despite high rates of bad debt.[9]

In the late 1980s and early 1990s the then Director General of Fair Trading expressed concern at the over-extension of credit to many consumers and indicated that he would take account of it in exercising his licensing powers under the Act. The credit industry has responded, and the Code of Practice for the major representative body for the finance and leasing industry in the UK obliges its members to 'take reasonable steps

[7]   *Crowther Committee* p 140.
[8]   *Crowther Committee* p 145.
[9]   *Crowther Committee* p 150.

to satisfy themselves as to customer's ability to repay' and to 'continuously monitor their credit granting practices and their assessment techniques to ensure that they are prudent and realistic in the prevailing economic circumstances'.[10] Can the too-ready extension of credit by businesses be inhibited in other ways? It might be made unlawful to pressure consumers into credit transactions, but such a provision would probably only catch the most blatant cases. Restrictions could be imposed on the remedies which creditors are able to enforce in the event of default to induce them to be more careful in extending credit. Retailers' commission on business which they introduce to creditors could be controlled if it encouraged retailers to push credit onto consumers who were in no real position to repay it. (Another mischief with retailers' commission is if consumers think that they are obtaining an objective evaluation about the comparative advantages of a particular type of credit when in reality a retailer's advice is determined by which credit institution provides the highest commission. Disclosure is an answer to this.)

Controlling the effective cost of credit (requiring minimum deposits, limiting the repayment period, etc) may be another way of encouraging consumers not to undertake transactions when there may be a risk of getting into difficulties. Terms control was first introduced in Britain during the Second World War, but with the purpose of supporting price control by preventing excessive prices being hidden in credit charges. After that terms control was utilised as an instrument of macroeconomic policy but was abandoned in 1982.[11] Changes in terms control were made depending on how the government wished to regulate consumer expenditure. Its advantages as an economic regulator were that it took effect immediately and that it is one of the few instruments that acts solely on consumer expenditure and not on business investment, in contrast, say, to changes in interest rates. However, terms control is discriminatory, applying only to point of sale credit. Moreover, the fact that a consumer can pay a large deposit is not guarantee in itself that he can repay the instalments, and thus terms control is no substitute for a creditor properly assessing credit-worthiness. Terms control can also be evaded in practice, for example by inflating the trade-in price of an item given in part-exchange.

(c)   Rate regulation and extortionate bargains

Rate regulation has a long history deriving from the suspicion with which moneylending has always been regarded. In England the common law

[10]   Finance and Leasing Association *Code of Practice* (1996) paras 5.3, 5.5.
[11]   FR Oliver and N Runcie 'The Economic Regulation of Instalment Credit in the United Kingdom' in AL Diamond (ed) *Instalment Credit* (Stevens, 1970).

held that it was unlawful if a Christian took any kind of usury; and thus if a person were found to have committed usury, after his death all his chattels were forfeited by the king and his lands escheated to the lord of the fee.[12] Methods were found of evading the prohibition; raising loans on mortgage was one way, for the profit made by the creditor was not regarded as reducing his debt. Eventually the statute 37 Hen VIII, c 9, while making usury unlawful, recognised the realities and fixed a legal rate of interest for commercial and real transactions at 10%, subsequently reduced to 5% by 12 Anne, c 16. Writers like Adam Smith, Bentham and JS Mill in the eighteenth and nineteenth centuries declared that the rate of interest was fixed by market forces and to restrict it was harmful. A Select Committee of the House of Commons agreed in 1818: restrictions on usury were being evaded, it concluded, but by methods which impeded commercial transactions and only caused litigation. Finally, the laws against usury were repealed in 1854. The consequence was that abuses multiplied, as demonstrated in the report of the Select Committee of the House of Commons which considered the matter in 1898. As a result of the report the Moneylenders Act 1900 required moneylenders to register and provided that the courts could re-open transactions where the interest was excessive. The Moneylenders Act 1927 substituted licensing for registration and introduced the figure of 48% as prima facie excessive.

Rate regulation has sometimes been suggested in modern times as a means to encourage creditors to lend more prudently, because no longer would they have the same latitude to cover the cost of default by high credit charges, and to prevent the exploitation of more vulnerable consumers by excessive credit charges. Implicit in both arguments is that existing measures, like information disclosure and the power of the courts to open extortionate credit bargains, are inadequate in protecting consumers. Consumers themselves have mixed views about credit charges, although often they have little choice in the credit they can use and thus the rates they pay. In general, most people seem to think that the cost of credit they use is more or less as they plan and that its cost is reasonable.[13] People tend to use particular forms of credit for reasons of habit, convenience, ignorance and indifference to alternatives. Those without bank accounts, poorer and older people, had a narrower choice of credit—for example, credit cards, bank loans and overdrafts are generally ruled out. Charges

---

[12] *Hawkins Pleas of the Crown* Book 1, Chapter 82. Much of the material in this paragraph is derived from H Bellot *The Legal Principles and Practice of Bargains with Moneylenders* (Stevens & Haynes, 1906) Chapters 1–3. See also PS Atiyah *The Rise and Fall of Freedom of Contract* (Clarendon, 1979) pp 66–67, 550–552, 571.

[13] *Consumers and Credit* (NCC, 1980) pp 47–49.

for the credit sources open to them are usually high when they take out second mortgages or borrow from moneylenders and others.[14] The Director General of Fair Trading has described some of this lending as socially harmful, since the costs substantially exceed levels which would be generated by fully competitive markets or are so exploitative that no sensible person, independently advised, would find them acceptable.[15] The Director General gave as examples of common types of exploitation locking debtors into a cycle of debt by reloaning before an existing debt was repaid, targeting needy borrowers to whom cheaper forms of credit were not available, discharging loan balances with a new loan, making no rebate for early repayment and not making clear the true cost of the loan since the borrower would normally look only at the size of the weekly payments.

A form of rate regulation existed under the Moneylenders Acts, for on a loan covered by the Acts, it was noted above, a true interest charge of greater than 48% per annum was regarded as prima facie excessive and the transaction harsh and unconscionable, enabling the courts to reduce it if the money-lender could not establish the contrary.[16] This approach was replaced by the power in the Consumer Credit Act 1974 to re-open extortionate credit bargains if the payments required are grossly exorbitant or if the terms otherwise grossly contravene principles of fair dealing.[17] All credit agreements when the debtor is an individual are subject to these provisions, whatever the sum involved. However, the wide discretion given to the courts in considering bargains for their extortionate character, and the fact that so much can depend on the individual circumstances of a credit transaction, mean that little control of credit charges has resulted from the enactment of this provision. Moreover, in the words of the Director General of Fair Trading, the courts have adopted 'a restrictive interpretation of the provisions'. Interest rates of 42.5% and 48% have been permitted as the normal going rates,[18] although in two cases where consumers had secured loans a county court reduced rates of 39% to 30% and 42% to

---

[14] Eg R Berthoud *Credit, Debt and Poverty* (HMSO, 1989) p 17.
[15] *Unjust Credit Transactions* (OFT, 1991) p 3, Annex B of the report. See also R Berthoud and E Kempson *Credit and Debt. The PSI Report* (PSI, 1992) p 99.
[16] Eg *Reading Trust Ltd v Spero* [1930] 1 KB 492.
[17] Sections 137–140. Section 138(3), (4) lists factors to be considered in assessing transactions such as the individual circumstances of the debtor, whether he or she was under financial pressure and the risk to the creditor.
[18] *Woodstead Finance Ltd v Petrou* [1986] CCLR 107, CA; *A Ketley Ltd v Scott* [1980] CCLR 37; J Ford *Consuming Credit. Debt and Poverty in the UK* (Child Poverty Action Group, 1991) p 5.

21% respectively.[19] The courts have tended to concentrate on interest rates and neglected the phrase 'otherwise grossly contravenes ordinary principles of fair dealing', which could be applied to many of the unacceptable practices described in the Director General's report. Another disadvantage is that the existing provision only becomes operative when court proceedings are taken by debtors or creditors. Almost invariably this means that it will be used as a shield when consumers are sued and not as a sword to challenge a wide range of interest rates, for consumers who enter extortionate credit agreements are among those least likely to be in a position to invoke the provisions of private law.[20]

Instead of recommending a return to prescriptively excessive, or threshold, rates the Director General proposed that the notion of an 'unjust credit transaction' would replace that of an extortionate credit bargain. Excessive payments would be a factor in finding injustice. The reference to ordinary principles of fair dealing would be replaced by a test of deception, oppression, impropriety and unfairness. There would be a responsibility on a creditor to check the borrower's creditworthiness and capacity to repay: failure to do so would be a factor in finding injustice. The Director General would be able to take the initiative to apply for a declaration that a credit transaction was unjust. A recent study commissioned by the DTI recommended that interest rate ceilings be introduced, coupled with the provision of some form of social lending to those who would not be able to borrow on a commercial market to which interest rate ceiling applied.[1] There is no evidence that the DTI is likely to implement this recommendation.[2]

Yet more specific control of credit charges operates in other jurisdictions. Rate regulation in France and Germany is in terms of the market rate: it is unlawful to charge more than a certain amount above that rate.[3] A threshold operates in other jurisdictions as well. For example in Canada it is a criminal offence to enter an agreement or arrangement to receive interest at a criminal rate or to receive a payment or partial payment of interest at a criminal rate.

[19] *Derogate v Jaris* (1987) unreported, Sevenoaks County Court; *Prestonwell Ltd v Capon* (1988) unreported, Corby County Court, both cited in *Unjust Credit Transactions* (OFT, 1991) p 34. See also *Shahabinia v Giyahchi* (5 July 1989, unreported), when a strong Court of Appeal reduced rates of 78%, 104% and 156% to 30%: these were unsecured loans for business purposes.
[20] *Unjust Credit Transactions* (OFT, 1991). See also L Bentley and G Howells 'Judicial Treatment of Extortionate Credit Bargains' [1989] Convy 164. Parallel provisions can be invoked in a person's bankruptcy: Insolvency Act 1986, s 244.
[1] E Kempson and C Whyley *Extortionate Credit Bargains in the UK* (DTI, 2000).
[2] DTI Discussion paper on the Extortionate Credit Provisions in the Consumer Credit Act 1974 (DTI, 2000).
[3] G Howells 'Controlling Unjust Credit Transactions' in G Howells et al (eds) *Aspects of Credit and Debt* (Sweet & Maxwell, 1993) pp 102–105.

A criminal rate of interest means an effective annual rate of interest that exceeds 60% on the credit advanced.[4] The United States has a heritage of state governments fixing rate ceilings, usually at market level, designed to prevent loan sharking. Under the Uniform Consumer Credit Code, which has been adopted in some of the states, there is a ceiling rate.[5]

Rate regulation is generally regarded as undesirable by those who accept the conventional wisdom that it is better to leave matters to the market.[6] The first argument against rate regulation is that it causes distortion, as businesses inflate the cash price of items and services to enable them to charge the same price as would be payable without a regime of control. Whether such distortion would occur on a wide scale depends on a number of factors, such as the proportion of transactions of a particular type involving credit. If this was relatively small, inflated cash prices in credit transactions would be obvious and it would simply be a matter of allocating adequate enforcement resources to prevent it. Secondly, it is said that there would be a large administrative burden to imposing rate regulation because different credit institutions charge widely differing amounts and credit charges vary according to consumers' individual circumstances. The argument is hardly as strong as the critics make out because the larger credit institutions tend to charge a uniform rate to consumers once they decide that they are creditworthy. The real point is that credit involving home collections involves a high administrative cost, which leads to very high interest rates. Those dependent on this type of credit are in a segmented market characterised by a lack of competition on the interest rates charged.

Finally, it is said that if rate regulation were introduced certain forms of credit would disappear, to the disadvantage of consumers. Whether this is undesirable depends on the value of the type of credit, who is affected, and whether alternative institutional arrangements are possible. For example, opponents of rate regulation argue that low income consumers have an inelastic demand for credit which will force them into the arms of loan sharks if rates are fixed. One answer to this is that credit unions and government-supported loan schemes (such as the social fund in Britain) could be developed to provide a better service to low-income consumers than at present. The greater competition in the credit market which would result would have a beneficial effect on credit rates, perhaps as well for consumers other than those who would be the immediate beneficiaries. Perhaps the most practicable means of reform is to foster these institutional changes, which could be supplemented by other measures. For example,

[4]   Criminal Code, §305.1
[5]   UCCC §2-201, 3-508.
[6]   D Cayne and M Trebilcock 'Market Considerations in the Formation of Consumer Protection Policy' (1973) 23 U Toronto LJ 396, 411–418.

there could be a ceiling establishing a prescriptively unjust level of credit charges to prevent loan sharks, with enforcement agencies being empowered to issue court challenges on behalf of consumers.

(d)   Creditors' liability for retailers' breach

There has been a long held concern that finance providers have not exercised sufficient care in the choice of retailers through whom they have provided credit to consumers. Fraudulent, and in some cases criminal, secondhand car dealers survived, it was said, because finance houses were so eager to acquire their business that they failed to investigate their records or references.[7] A limited step was taken in the Hire Purchase Act 1964 to make finance providers liable for the misrepresentations of retailers, but the provision was confined to hire purchase and associated transactions.[8] Because of the legal nature of hire purchase, where a financier is the hirer, it has long been the case that financiers have been liable for the title to products taken on hire purchase, and for their correspondence with description, satisfactory quality and fitness for purpose. From the early 1960s, however, credit was increasingly provided through personal loans so that financiers had no direct legal responsibility for these matters. Some contractors canvassed for the installation of central heating and home improvements door to door, and induced consumers to sign documents by high pressure tactics, including the application for a loan from a financier. The work was often inadequate, in some cases not even begun—yet some financial institutions took the view that they were not legally liable and since they were ignorant of the contractors' malpractices had no moral responsibility either.

The upshot of practices like these was a recommendation by the Crowther Committee that a creditor providing credit for consumers for specific deals with a retailer with whom it had connections should be responsible for misrepresentation by that retailer and for defects in the goods.[9] Over the objections of some finance houses, credit card companies and others, the recommendation was embodied in the Consumer Credit Act 1974. A justification for the move was that it would induce creditors to exercise their economic power over retailers to discourage malpractices. The assumption was that retailers which make misrepresentations or supplied defective products or services could only continue in business if they were able to provide credit.

7   R Harris et al *Hire Purchase in a Free Society* (Institute of Economic Affairs, 3rd edn, 1961) pp 130–131.
8   Section 10(1); then Hire Purchase Act 1965, s 16(1).
9   *Crowther Committee* pp 279–283.

The means by which the law achieves joint and several liability on the part of creditors and retailers is not straightforward. Tripartite debtor-creditor-supplier agreements are dealt with by s 75(1) of the Consumer Credit Act 1974. It provides that if a debtor under certain debtor-creditor-supplier agreements has, in relation to a transaction financed by the agreement, a claim against a supplier in respect of a misrepresentation or breach of contract, he or she 'shall have a like claim against the creditor, who, with the supplier, shall accordingly be jointly and severally liable to the debtor.'[10] Debtor-creditor-supplier agreements are those where the agreement is a restricted-use credit agreement and the loan is made by a creditor under pre-existing arrangements or in contemplation of future arrangements between the creditor and the dealer, or is an unrestricted-use credit agreement made by the creditor under pre-existing arrangements between itself and the supplier in the knowledge that the credit is to be used to finance a transaction between the debtor and the supplier. The section does not apply to non-commercial agreements. Consumers in situations like this who, say, receive a defective product have a 'like claim' against the financier or credit card company as they have against the supplier. A 'like claim' means that the consumer is not confined to suing for the credit advanced but can include a claim for consequential losses, which in the case of personal injury can be considerable.[11] There is joint and several liability, although the creditor has an indemnity against the supplier. A claim must relate to a single item to which the supplier has attached a cash price, more than £100 but less than £30,000.[12] The average credit card purchase is for less than £100, and so falls outside the protection of the section. However, it applies notwithstanding that the debtor, in entering into the transaction, exceeded any credit limit or otherwise contravened any term of the agreement.[13]

Section 75(1) applies to a financier which advances a loan to a consumer to acquire a produce or service from a supplier with which it has existing arrangements or with which it contemplates future arrangements. It also applies to a credit card company as regards retailers with whom, as a result of a credit card company-retailer agreement, consumers are entitled to use the facility. An area of uncertainty occurs where there is no direct link in the form of a contract between the card-issuer and the retailer. These days most retailers have a single payment handling agreement with one card issuer which deals with all card payments made to the retailer, whether or

---

[10] On the meaning of 'like claim' see Goode *Consumer Credit Law and Practice* (Butterworths, looseleaf) para **IIB [5.145]**; *United Dominions Trust Ltd v Taylor* 1980 SLT 28 (Sh Ct).
[11] Cf Director General of Fair Trading *Connected Lender Liability* (OFT, 1995) p 6.
[12] Section 75(3).
[13] Section 75(4).

not by means of that issuer's card.[14] Card issuers contend that s 75 does not apply—this type of four party situation was not contemplated in 1974—but nonetheless honour claims.[15] However, they do not honour claims when the card is used abroad. There is significant force in the argument that the place where the card is used is irrelevant for the purposes of s 75.[16] Non-credit card transactions, with a foreign element, such as a loan from a British bank to purchase a time-share abroad, can generate claims against the bank under s 75.[17]

Where the retailer itself is the creditor or hirer, liability is direct as regards title to products and their correspondence with description, satisfactory quality and fitness for purpose.[18] Similarly in hire purchase transactions the finance house has a direct responsibility in an almost identical manner by virtue of the Supply of Goods (Implied Terms) Act 1973.[19] A slight difference in the provisions, taking into account the nature of the transaction, is that to benefit from the implied condition of fitness for purchase it is sufficient for the consumer to make that purpose known to the retailer.[20] Retailers in hire purchase transactions may be liable for a misrepresentation on a collateral contract, the consideration for which is the consumer entering the main contract with the finance house.[1]

What of a financier's responsibility for the retailer's misrepresentation? Misrepresentations in relation to the supply transaction trigger the application of s 75, but not if these relate solely to the credit transaction. However, s 56(2) of the Consumer Credit Act 1974 means that the negotiations with a debtor conducted by a retailer may be deemed to be conducted by the retailer in its capacity as agent of the financier as well as in its own capacity.[2] Consequently, any misrepresentation by a retailer in relation to the credit agreement, including a misrepresentation in an advertisement, is attributable to the financier and is actionable by the

---

[14] A Campbell 'Credit Cards and Section 75' [1996] 12 JIBL 527, 531.
[15] But the banks appear willing only to honour claims up to the value of the transaction, not for the entire liability (including consequential losses) which a consumer may have suffered: *Butterworths Trading and Consumer Law* (looseleaf) para 4[161].
[16] Director General of Fair Trading *Connected Lender Liability* (OFT, 1995); P Dobson 'Purchases Abroad and Credit at Home' (1997) 141 Sol Jo 40, 41.
[17] *Jarrett v Barclays Bank plc* [1999] QB 1.
[18] Sale of Goods Act 1979, ss 12–14; Supply of Goods and Services Act 1982, ss 7–9.
[19] Sections 8–10.
[20] Section 10(3)(b).
[1] *Andrews v Hopkinson* [1957] 1 QB 229.
[2] The ambit of s 56(2) is complicated, but a major gap does not extend to leasing agreements: P Dobson 'Agency in the Equipment Leasing Business' (1994) 138 Sol J 992.

consumer. For example, in several cases a consumer has had to be indemnified by a second financier where the dealer taking a motor vehicle in part-exchange for another vehicle on hire-purchase/conditional sale, did not, as promised, pay out the financier of the first vehicle.[3] By virtue of s 56, financiers may also be liable for retailer fraud such as where a retailer misappropriates a deposit.

Can finance houses avoid this liability for the behaviour of retailers? In the United States—and to some extent in Britain[4]—retailers would provide credit themselves by getting consumers to give a promissory note or bill of exchange payable by instalments, but then discounting these to a finance house. In law the finance house as holder in due course of the promissory note or bill of exchange could avoid responsibility for any misrepresentation or breach of contract on the part of the retailer.[5] In Britain the Consumer Credit Act 1974, s 123 now prevents creditors and owners from taking a negotiable instrument like a bill of exchange or a promissory note from a consumer in relation to a regulated agreement. If a negotiable instrument is taken in contravention of the section, the agreement is only enforceable by court order, and the person who takes it is not to be regarded as a holder in due course and capable of enforcing the instrument.[6] The section does not apply to cheques, but these can only be negotiated to a banker.[7]

In Britain block discounting has been used to some extent, whereby retailers have written credit agreements themselves but then sold them to finance houses at a discount on the value of the contract rights on the face of the agreements.[8] The finance houses have usually retained the retailer as the agent for collection and have not bothered to call for formal assignment of the agreements. Even were an assignment to be effected, finance houses could not by block discounting avoid their liability for retailers' actions under s 75 because a creditor is defined in the Consumer Credit Act 1974 to include those to whom rights and duties under an agreement have passed by assignment or operation of law.[9]

---

[3]   *United Dominions Trust v Whitfield* [1987] CCLR 60; *Forthright Finance Ltd v Ingate* [1997] 4 All ER 99; cf *Powell v Lloyds Dowmaker Ltd* [1996] CCLR 50.
[4]   *United Dominions Trust Ltd v Kirkwood* [1966] 2 QB 431, 448–89.
[5]   V Countryman 'The Holder in Due Course and Other Anachronisms in Consumer Credit' (1973) 52 Tex LR 1.
[6]   Sections 124, 125.
[7]   Section 123(2). See also s 125(2).
[8]   RM Goode *Hire-Purchase Law and Practice* (Butterworths, 2nd edn, 1970) pp 657–661.
[9]   Section 189(1).

4   DETERMINATION OF A CONSUMER CREDIT AGREEMENT

Most consumer credit agreements terminate with the consumer repaying the credit in the manner anticipated by the agreement. Occasionally consumers wish to pay out the creditor what is owing before the agreement is due to expire—they have won the lottery, a wealthy aunt has died, they have received redundancy money, or some other reason. The Consumer Credit Act 1974 gives consumers the right to do this, and provides that they should receive a rebate for early payment on the charges outstanding.[10] The rebate is not a simple reduction in the total credit charge related to the time the agreement has to run because this would not compensate the creditor for the cost of setting up the transaction. The Crowther Committee therefore recommended that a mathematical calculation, known as the 'rule of 78', be made mandatory to calculate the rebate. However, the 'rule of 78' becomes increasingly inaccurate as the interest rate and the term of a transaction increase, and constitutes an implicit penalty on consumers when they wish to repay credit before time.[11] The rebate payable for regulated loans is controlled by regulations, but the Director General has called for these to be reviewed.[12] For unregulated secured loans, the Office of Fair Trading said in 1997 that use of the 'rule of 78' should be discontinued at the earliest opportunity and should not be applied rigidly to existing loan agreements without some form of cap.[13] Alternative methods of calculating the settlement figure, such as the actual reducing balance or actuarial methods should be used, so that the charges for early redemption are no more than the actual costs incurred.

Although most consumer credit agreements terminate as contemplated—or in some cases before then—we shall concentrate in this section on situations where consumers experience serious difficulties in meeting their repayments.[14] For convenience these situations are called default situations. Concentrating on default is clearly justified because the courts are primarily concerned with this type of problem case; as the Crowther Committee remarked, if all debtors repaid on time the law would be quite simple.

---

[10]   Sections 94–95. The provisions are also relevant where an asset is sold or traded in by way of part exchange.

[11]   Eg J Hunt 'The Rule of 78: Hidden Penalty for Prepayment in Consumer Credit Transactions' (1975) 55 BULR 331.

[12]   Consumer Credit (Rebate on Early Settlement) Regulations 1983, SI 1983/1562. See OFT *Non-Status Lending. Guidelines for Lenders and Brokers* (London, 1997) p 19.

[13]   See OFT *Non-Status Lending. Guidelines for Lenders and Brokers* (London, 1997) p 19.

[14]   The discussion is concerned with default for non-payment; default may also occur through the bankruptcy or death of the consumer.

(a)   The nature of default

The incidence of default among consumers is relatively small. One National Consumer Council survey found that only 3% (nine people) of the credit-buying sample had had a problem over some aspect of the credit arrangement after purchase. Of these apparently only 1% (four people) had found difficulty in making payments.[15] The nineteenth century view that defaulters are the authors of their own misfortune still finds expression in authoritative sources. The Crowther Committee recognised that consumers often experienced difficulties with credit because of matters beyond their control, like sickness and unemployment, but it still saw their irresponsibility as an important cause.

> There are many, particularly in the low-income group, who are not reckless so much as improvident. They lack the ability to budget or to manage their income. They have little or no sense of values and are not motivated by rational considerations in selecting their purchases. Such people will, for example, spend a slice of their income not on articles they really need but on other less important items; and they will spend regardless of whether they are getting value for money.[16]

Here we have the conventional stereotypes of defaulters: there are cases of genuine misfortune, but equally strong numbers of feckless defaulters who enter credit transactions irresponsibly, and professional defaulters who from the outset never have any intention of repaying. The reality of repayment difficulties from the point of view of those involved is somewhat different from the common stereotypes. In interviews with judgment debtors at one county court, researchers from Queen Mary College found that 70% of debtors said they were unable to pay, 17% refused to pay and the remainder gave other reasons which concentrated mainly on the debt not being their responsibility or that default was caused by payment misunderstandings. The reasons given parallel those of similar studies previously and elsewhere:[17] unemployment (42), followed by a

---

[15] *Consumers and Credit* (NCC, 1980) p 202. See also *Consumers and Debt* (NCC, 1983).

[16] *Crowther Committee* p 232.

[17] R Cotterrell et al 'The Recovery of Judgment Debts in the County Court' in I Ramsay (ed) *Debtors and Creditors* (Professional Books, 1986) p 90; J Phipps *Individual Judgment Debtors in One London County Court* (Centre for Commercial Law Studies, 1991) pp 20–21. Some debtors gave more than one reason. See also D Caplovitz *Consumers in Trouble* (Free Press, 1974); M Trebilcock and A Schulman 'The Pathology of Credit Breakdown' (1976) 22 McGill LJ 415; Jane Phipps and previous editions of this book mention other UK surveys.

spouse's unemployment (19), sickness (15), marital problems (14), income reduction (11) and misunderstandings (10). Most of the debtors who gave inadequacy of income mentioned their over-commitment, with other debts, although some mentioned unexpected expenses or unexpectedly high bills. Of the 17% of debtors who said they were refusing to pay the debt, 80% focused on creditor fault of some kind (faulty goods, services, failure to respond to complaint), while the remainder refused for reasons including that it was not their debt (they were guarantors) or the item was stolen. It is difficult not to feel sympathy for some of those who knew they were over-committing themselves; for example, for those who did it as an escape from a low standard of living. In another study of credit card users there was not much evidence of their being used recklessly by those who could not afford them. Job losses and changes in family circumstances were important factors in credit card default.[18] Such surveys tend to uncover that a disproportionate number of consumers from the lower socio-economic groups have repayment difficulties. Some consumers seem caught in a circle of poverty—consumers who are least able to afford it are seduced into credit transactions which further undermine their economic position.

If the primary reasons for default are unemployment and inability to pay and not irresponsibility or fraud, there seems no need for creditors to use harsh collection methods. As Caplovitz notes:

> Perhaps the most impressive finding is that substantial numbers of debtors resume payments regardless of the reason for their default and the type of credit threat. We have repeatedly made this observation in order to question the basic premise of the credit industry—that harsh collection devices are needed to control the credit system.[19]

A creditor, if it is sensible, will accept that in the great majority of cases the best approach is to treat consumers leniently if they are in temporary difficulties, for there is the assurance that ultimately they will be paid without having to incur the cost of collection procedures. Indeed consumers in difficulty find that their creditor behaves in a sympathetic manner when contacted. A real problem, however, is that consumers in difficulty frequently feel inhibited from approaching the creditor to explain their plight before action is taken against them.

Initially creditors use extra-judicial methods to induce defaulters to pay. Typically creditors rely on sending letters to consumers which become increasingly threatening if default continues. There are isolated instances of creditors using harassment where letters fail to prompt payment, but it

---

[18]   R Rowlinson and E Kempson *Paying With Plastic* (PSI, 1994).
[19]   D Caplovitz *Consumers in Trouble* (Free Press, 1974) p 270.

seems that these are less frequent than formerly. There are different types of harassment used; for example, frequent calls at the home of the debtor leaving threatening cards, informing neighbours of the debtor about his or her indebtedness under the guise of seeking information, and writing to an employer under the guise of avoiding the need for the debtor to absent himself from work to attend court. One debt collection firm indicated its robust approach by the legend which appeared at the foot of their stationery: 'It's no use dying to avoid us—we pursue debtors to the gates of Hell if necessary in order to recover our clients' money!'[20] Consumers defaulting because of misfortune are peculiarly vulnerable. Harsh methods are sometimes adopted, although economically the time and effort cannot be justified, because the creditor believes that it is dealing with a fraudulent debtor or that otherwise it would gain the reputation of being too lenient and thus attract a number of bad accounts.[1] Another factor is that a creditor may sell bad debts to a collection firm without recourse instead of simply employing it as an agent, so that there is every incentive for the latter to collect the debt.

The private law contains remedies for trespass, assault and harassment, which may be used against certain types of collection harassment. To say falsely that a person refuses to pay his debts, is deliberately delaying payment of them, or is unable to pay them may be defamatory.[2] Needless to say, the typical defaulter is not a person who will utilise his private law rights. Criminal law offers some protection, although a major problem is lack of enforcement. Section 40(1) of the Administration of Justice Act 1970 makes it an offence if, with the object of coercing another to pay a debt, a person (a) falsely represents that criminal proceedings will lie for failure to pay; (b) falsely represents that he has official authorisation to enforce payment; (c) wrongly uses a document which appears to be official; and (d) unreasonably harasses '… with demands for payment which, in respect of their frequency or the manner or occasion of making any such demand, or of any threat or publicity by which any demand is accompanied, are calculated to subject him or members of his family or household to alarm, distress or humiliation'.[3] The offence under s 40(1)(d) is not restricted to cases where the creditor intends to cause alarm, distress or humiliation, but extends to conduct which though unintended is likely to have these

---

[20] *Mephistopheles Debt Collection Service (A Firm) v Lotay* [1994] 1 WLR 1064.

[1] P Rock *Making People Pay* (Routledge, 1973) pp 53–54.

[2] *Stubbs Ltd v Russell* [1913] AC 386; *Stubbs v Mazure* [1920] AC 66. There may also be an action for invasion of privacy in jurisdictions which recognise this as a cause of action.

[3] Section 40(1), (3). The County Courts Act 1984, s 136 prohibits the false representation of official documents. See J Noonan et al 'Federal Trade commission Developments in Consumer Financial Services' (1991) 46 BusL 1093, 1104–6.

consequences.[4] Legislation elsewhere is somewhat wider and prohibits other practices, such as conducting inquiries at a person's place of employment, with a view that he will then pay because of the fear of being dismissed if the matter becomes public knowledge. The biggest restraint on undesirable collection methods in Britain is that businesses collecting debts must obtain a licence under the Consumer Credit Act 1974, and to do so they must be able to demonstrate that they do not engage in undesirable trade practices.[5] The Director General of Fair Trading refuses a licence to any debt collector who persists in using such methods as the threat or use of physical violence; the parking of vans outside debtors' houses with the name and business of the debt collector prominently displayed; visiting people at their place of employment, and using letters couched in terms suggesting it is a legal summons (sometimes referred to as a 'blue frightener').[6]

Most consumers in repayment difficulties consult with their family, friends or even their creditor, but at the very least for reasons of cost there is an understandable disinclination to be involved with the legal profession. Only a number of consumers with debt problems consult bodies like the Citizens Advice Bureaux, legal advice centres and charitable organisations which engage in debt counselling, mainly if they have a 'link' with those agencies (eg through a relative) or by previous use.[7] Most important are the money advice services, which expanded considerably in the 1980s.[8] In some cases they provide direct services to the public; in others they are a back-up to general advice services. Many are associated with the independent voluntary sector, such as the Citizens Advice Bureaux, others with local authorities, in particular their trading standards departments. Money advice services can often negotiate short-term accommodation with creditors on behalf of debtors and then they may be able to achieve something on a long-term basis. In negotiating with creditors, money advice centres are attempting to get the best deal they can for consumers. In a few cases they may serve as a conduit through which regular payments can be made, reducing indebtedness. Legal advice to consumers may be defensive, or it may also be to advise on legal procedures like an administration order.

One line of criticism of money advice centres is that they may be functioning as a benign form of collection agency appended to the courts.

---

4   *Norweb plc v Dixon* [1995] 1 WLR 636.
5   Sections 145(1), (7), 147(1).
6   Eg G Borrie 'Legal and Administrative Regulation in the United Kingdom of Competition and Consumer Policies' (1982) 5 UNSW LJ 80, 89.
7   J Phipps *Individual Judgment Debtors in One London County Court* (Centre for Commercial Law Studies, 1991) p 96.
8   T Hinton and R Berthoud *Money Advice Services* (PSI, 1988).

Debt is being seen as a repayment problem, rather than one of legal rights.[9]
The criticism may have added force. Warnings have been issued in the
past against business enterprises using titles like 'credit counsellor', who
claim to assist consumers with their financial problems. The activities of
similar firms in the United States were so notorious that they were banned
in more than 20 states. The worst excesses in Britain are now curbed
because debt counsellors must be licensed under the Consumer Credit
Act 1974.[10] The case law illustrates the pitfalls of consumers entering
refinancing agreements through the offices of credit counsellors. In *Snook
v London and West Riding Investments Ltd*[11] the consumer was paying off
a car on hire purchase—he had paid nearly the full amount cash down—
with Totley Investments (TI), when he saw an advertisement by Auto
Finance (AF) which offered to assist consumers by refinancing hire
purchase debts enabling them to pay off an amount over a longer period.
The consumer approached AF who prepared documents which he signed,
clearly without appreciating their full import. One was a letter saying that
he had sold his rights in the car to AF, and the other was a new hire
purchase agreement with the London and West Riding Investments Ltd
(L&W) L&W accepted the hire purchase agreement, paid £300 to AF,
which paid out TI and gave £125 to the consumer, keeping £15 itself.
When the consumer fell behind with his repayments through unemployment
the car was repossessed by AF (acting as agents for L&W), who refused
the consumer's offer to pay off the arrears. The car was sold for £575; AF
paid L&W £280 and kept the balance of £295. In other words, the consumer
found himself without a car on which he had paid some £800 for falling
behind in two instalments worth under £30. The majority of the Court of
Appeal upheld the result—Lord Denning saw the injustice and dissented—
because the consumer by his conduct had allowed AF to represent that it
was the owner, and thus title passed to L&W. The transaction between
the consumer and AF could not be said to be a sham, said Diplock and
Russell LJJ, because L&W were not aware of it. The upshot of the decision
is that the law preferred an ignorant finance house to an ignorant consumer,
although the former was undoubtedly in a better position to uncover the
realities of the transaction and to bear any loss.

[9]   J Davies 'Delegalisation of Debt Recovery Proceedings: A Socio-Legal Study of
      Money Advice Centres and Administration Orders' in I Ramsay (ed) *Debtors and
      Creditors* (Professional Books, 1986) p 135; I Ramsay 'Credit, Class and
      Normalisation of Debt Default' in G Howells et al (eds) *Aspects of Credit and
      Debt* (Sweet & Maxwell, 1993) p 73.
[10]   Sections 145(1)(b), (c), (5), (6), 147(1).
[11]   [1967] 2 QB 786. See also *Eastern Distributors Ltd v Goldring* [1957] 2 QB 600.

(b)   The creditors' remedies

Where a consumer is in default with repayments under a regulated agreement, a creditor will have at least one of a number of remedies. Before it can become entitled, by reason of the breach, to terminate the agreement, to demand earlier payment of any sum, to recover possession, to treat any right conferred on the consumer by the agreement as terminated, restricted or deferred, or to enforce any security, it must serve a default notice on the consumer specifying the nature of the alleged breach, if it is capable of remedy and the remedial action required or, if none is possible, the payment required as compensation.[12] If the consumer can remedy the breach within seven days it is treated as not having occurred.[13] If the amount given in a default notice is an overstatement, the notice is invalid, since consumers need to know precisely what to do to put matters right.[14] The Act is intended to be protective of consumers, who are at a disadvantage when contracting with financial organisations, especially as the contract is likely to be in standard form and relatively complex.[15]

The idea of the default notice is that consumers should be given an opportunity to make the payments owing or to apply to a court for an extension of time. In addition, preparation of a default notice has the advantage that it might lead the creditor to discover a mistake in its claim. Once a period of seven days expires from service of the notice, the creditor can then proceed to enforce its remedies. Default notices by themselves assume that a consumer in default can spot an inaccuracy, and so have the notice cancelled, or can correct the default within a relatively short period, or if not will seek a court order. The typical defaulter, previously described, is hardly likely to be in a position to do either and in general the only effect of a default notice will be to postpone the creditor's remedies for seven days.

A creditor or owner under a credit or hire agreement is entitled to claim the instalments as they become due. Should a consumer be in default under a regulated consumer credit agreement, legislation provides that the creditor cannot charge a higher rate of interest (default interest) than in the agreement.[16] In any event the Office of Fair Trading takes the view that terms providing for default interest can never be a core term of a

---

[12]   Sections 87–88. In proceedings for the possession of an item s 134(1) must also be complied with.
[13]   Section 89.
[14]   *Woodchester Lease Management Services Ltd v Swain & Co* [1999] 1 WLR 263.
[15]   *Woodchester Lease Management Services Ltd v Swain & Co* [1999] 1 WLR 263.
[16]   Section 93.

contract and thus are subject to review under the Unfair Terms in Consumer Contracts Regulations 1994, even if not invalid at common law as a penalty clause. An acceleration clause may provide that a consumer in default becomes liable for the full outstanding balance. Acceleration clauses are said to be justified because otherwise creditors would have to bring a series of actions as each instalment becomes due, or wait for the agreement to run its course when the chances of recovery will be increasingly remote.[17] The injustice of acceleration clauses to consumers is obvious because the agreement may provide that they can be invoked in the event of a single default—incidentally defeating the whole purpose of purchasing on credit. The validity of an acceleration clause has been upheld, as being a genuine pre-estimate of the creditor's loss and non-penal in effect, under which the consumer had to pay the outstanding balance, but only a proportion of the charges in accordance with the rule of 78.[18] Their existence is recognised in the Consumer Credit Act 1974.[19] But acceleration clauses will not be given unlimited effect by the courts and should be construed strictly because of their nature. Indeed an acceleration clause is unenforceable as a penalty if, under it, in addition to the principal, the consumer has to pay the whole of the charges, without any rebate, although credit is no longer outstanding. Another possible attack on an acceleration clause is that its operation contravenes the extortionate bargain provisions of the Consumer Credit Act 1974 because it requires payments which are grossly exorbitant or because it grossly contravenes the ordinary principles of fair dealing.[20] Whether the extortionate bargain power can be brought to bear against acceleration clauses depends very much on how widely the courts interpret it.

Repossession is perhaps the strongest weapon a creditor can have because of its immediacy. The Finance Houses Association informed the Crowther Committee that its members repossessed about one in forty of the cars being purchased on hire purchase.[1] Repossession is less useful when utilised against some household domestic appliances because their resale value hardly justifies the effort. Nevertheless, the threat of repossession can still be used as a tactic by creditors against consumers in default. One suggestion is that the law should deny creditors the right to repossess, except for expensive items like cars, in order to prevent empty threats of repossession which cause consumers unnecessary distress.

---

[17]   R Goode and J Ziegel *Hire Purchase and Conditional Sale* (British Institute of International and Comparative Law, 1965) p 110.

[18]   *Wadham Stringer Finance Ltd v Meaney* [1980] 3 All ER 789, [1981] 1 WLR 39.

[19]   Section 76. See also ss 86, 87.

[20]   Sections 137–140.

[1]   *Crowther Committee* p 287.

Legally a consumer does not became the owner of an item being acquired on hire purchase until all the instalments are paid and the option to purchase is exercised. Businesses thus have the right at common law to repossess an item on hire purchase if a consumer is in breach of the agreement.[2] The courts held that relief against forfeiture was not possible in the case of hire purchase—a result which would have gone part of the way to mitigating the harshness for consumers.[3] Public concern about how some businesses used their rights to 'snatch back' items led to reform in the Hire Purchase Act 1938.[4] In introducing this part of the legislation—a Private Members Bill—the MP responsible, Ellen Wilkinson, referred to the 'snatch back' as the 'cancer' afflicting hire purchase. She gave an example of how the 'snatch back' operated.

> For instance, a poor woman got furniture for which she was to pay a total of £27 1s 6d. With some difficulty, she paid £25 16s 9d, and then she got behind in her payments and was prosecuted, the court ordering £6 8s 9d for costs. While she was out charing, a van called, took away all the goods and what was considered to be £5 worth of other goods for the court costs.[5]

The protection is now embodied in the Consumer Credit Act 1974 and provides that a creditor in a regulated hire purchase or conditional sale agreement must obtain a court order to repossess an item when more than one-third of the total purchase price has been paid.[6] The Act provides that the protection ceases if the consumer terminates the agreement.[7]

Under the Hire Purchase Acts, the Court of Appeal in *Mercantile Credit Co Ltd v Cross*[8] held that a consumer who gives up possession of an item voluntarily to a creditor loses the protection of the one-third rule. The decision turned on the wording of the hire purchase legislation—an owner could not enforce a right to recover possession of protected goods, and merely passively to accept was not to enforce. The Consumer Credit Act 1974 is much wider and prohibits the creditor from recovering possession without a court order. But it has been argued that creditors can now take advantage of s 173(3) of the Act, which provides that an act which can only be done by court order can also be done with the person's consent given at the time.[9] It is submitted that the courts should be reluctant to use

---

[2] For example *Cramer v Giles* (1883) Cab & El 151.
[3] Contrast the position of those purchasing land on mortgage where relief against forfeiture was possible.
[4] Section 12.
[5] 330 HC Official Report (5th series) col 731, 10 December..
[6] Section 90. See also s 91.
[7] Section 90(5).
[8] [1965] 2 QB 205.
[9] R Goode *Consumer Credit Law and Practice* (Butterworths, looseleaf) para **IIB [5.343]**.

minimum payment clauses as a penalty and not as a genuine pre-estimate of the losses experienced because they mean a consumer will be liable for a substantial percentage of the total purchase price, however little use has been derived from the product. *Bridge v Campbell Discount Co Ltd* [1] is the leading case in hire purchase law, where the House of Lords held that a hire purchase company could not enforce a minimum payment clause obliging the consumer, who had already returned the car, to make payments equal to two-thirds of the purchase price. It seems that it will be difficult to frame a minimum payment clause which the courts will not regard as a penalty clause.[2] A minimum payment clause would also be regarded as a penalty if it did not differentiate between what is payable for trivial default and repudiatory breach. Minimum payment clauses may also be invalid because they constitute a grossly exorbitant payment or grossly violate the ordinary principles of fair dealing in breach of s 138 of the Consumer Credit Act 1974.

What can a creditor claim if a minimum payment clause is invalid? It is fair to say that the law is anomalous. Except in the specific cases mentioned, resort must be had to the agreement and to common law principles. Depending on its nature, the agreement may contain provisions such as an acceleration clause, a provision for the creditor to terminate the agreement in specified events, a power for the creditor to remedy beaches itself and charge the consumer with the cost, and a power for the creditor to terminate and sell the items covered by the agreement or security. So in the case of a credit sale or loan, the creditor will be entitled to sue for the price or the outstanding balance, respectively, both of which will become payable immediately if an acceleration clause can be invoked. Such clauses may be attacked under the unfair terms legislation discussed in Chapter 3.

With hire purchase and conditional sale, as well as repossessing the item the losses for which a creditor can claim lie along a graduated scale:

(a) if the creditor terminates the agreement: the instalments then in arrear only;

(b) if the consumer terminates a regulated hire purchase or conditional sale agreement: the amounts specified in s 99 of the Consumer Credit Act 1974;

(c) if the consumer repudiates: the creditor's loss of profit (with some minor reductions).

---

[1]   [1962] AC 600.
[2]   At common law the rule against penalties seems not to apply when a consumer voluntarily terminates pursuant to contract. The situation is anomalous, and Lords Denning and Devlin in *Bridge*'s case said that the courts should have the power to strike down penalty clauses no matter how an agreement is terminated.

(a) arises if the consumer fails to pay an instalment and the financier exercises its rights to terminate the agreement. In practice this will not usually occur because consumers are likely to do acts which constitute either termination or repudiation, and finance houses will protect their position by invoking an acceleration clause in an agreement. As a matter of public policy there is strong justification for legislation to limit finance houses from claiming arrears in instalments in these circumstances, which is to restrain financiers from ending agreements simply because a consumer is in temporary difficulties but intends to complete.

Sections 99 and 100 of the Consumer Credit Act 1974, which apply generally and not simply to default situations, give consumers the right to terminate a regulated hire purchase or conditional sale agreement by returning the item to the creditor. Unless the agreement provides for a smaller amount they must make up their payments to one-half the total purchase price (if they have not already paid that amount).[3] However, if the court is satisfied that the creditor's losses are a lower amount, it may order payment of that amount instead. Consumers using this right to terminate are liable for an additional payment if they have breached an obligation to take reasonable care of the item.[4] The right to terminate must be exercised before the final payment falls due; consequently, it seems to be defeated if a creditor invokes an acceleration clause.[5] Otherwise the '50% rule' represents the maximum recoverable even in the case where the consumer has been in default, even default sufficient to constitute repudiatory breach. The right to terminate under the '50% rule' only applies to regulated hire purchase and conditional sale agreements, presumably because in other credit agreements the law regards consumers as having committed themselves to buy. Needless to say the difference perpetuates the artificial—and to consumers incomprehensible—distinction between hire purchase and other forms of sale on credit.

Where creditors get back possession of an item, they may try to claim damages for the cost of repair on the basis that the consumer has breached an obligation to take reasonable care of it. Consumers should resist attempts by finance houses to charge them for the cost of bringing the item up to the standard necessary for resale. The Court of Appeal has said that the consumer's obligation in a hire purchase agreement to keep an item in good order and repair only imposes a duty:

---

3   If there is an installation charge, one-half of the total price refers to the aggregate of the installation charge and one-half of the remainder of the total price: s 100(2).
4   Section 100(4).
5   *Wadham Stringer Finance Ltd v Meany* [1980] 3 All ER 789, [1981] 1 WLR 39.

to keep the car in the condition in which it might reasonably be expected to be if he had looked after it properly. He need not put it in a better condition than it was when he hired it. He need only keep it in the condition in which a reasonably minded hirer would keep it. Thus he would repair it if there was an accident, and he would do the immediate repairs in the course of running the car, but no more.[6]

The Consumer Credit Act 1974 considerably limits the remedies of businesses under regulated consumer hire agreements from the position obtaining at common law. Under s 101 of the Consumer Credit Act 1974 the hirer under a regulated hire agreement is entitled to terminate after 18 months. Also s 132 of the Consumer Credit Act 1974 provides that in a regulated consumer hire agreement, if the business recovers possession of an item, a court can give relief to the consumer by ordering that he need not pay any more under the agreement, or that the business must actually repay an amount. In making an order the court must have regard to the amount of enjoyment of the item by the consumer.

(c)   The consumer's position

This section discusses some aspects of the consumer's position when faced with repayment difficulties. It is worth saying at the outset that in the main their rights and the procedures mentioned suffer from the basic deficiency of private law as an instrument of consumer protection—they require the initiative of consumers to invoke them. Consumers in default are often reluctant to do anything for understandable reasons:

> Social attitudes that attribute debt to personal mismanagement merely reinforce the views defaulters hold and they do not, therefore, constitute a point of challenge. The consequences were seen in the accounts of borrowers who delayed action, sought to keep the information private, and who experienced acute anxiety and distress, as well as in the absence of the development of any critique of the housing or credit system.[7]

Consumers in difficulty with a regulated hire purchase or conditional sale agreement, who have no chance of making repayments in the foreseeable future and who are quite clear that they would rather be free of

---

[6]   *Brady v St Margaret's Trust Ltd* [1963] 2 QB 494, 500, per Lord Denning ME with whom Danckwerts and Davies LJJ agreed. See P Shuchman 'Condition and Value of Repossessed Automobiles' (1979) 21 W & MLR 15, whose United States study shows that most repossessed cars range from fair or average to good, with poor condition cares almost offset by the number in good condition.

[7]   J Ford *The Indebted Society* (Routledge, 1988) p 181.

future involvement, might consider terminating the agreement pursuant to s 99 of the Consumer Credit Act 1974. Unfortunately, a decision might have to be made quickly, for a finance house might invoke an acceleration clause if valid which, as we have seen, seems to exclude the possibility of using the termination provision. Whether exercise of the right to terminate is a wise move depends on the circumstances. Consumers who terminate early on in an agreement are at an obvious disadvantage unless it provides for the payment of an amount lower than the 50% figure. Otherwise they must be prepared to go to court for an order that the creditor's losses are less than this amount. Creditors are likely to claim substantial losses if a consumer terminates an agreement early, because they will have recouped little of their profit, even taking into account the resale value of the item. And there is the problem mentioned previously that the values creditors obtain when reselling items are relatively low. On the other hand, consumers terminating an agreement after some time may not be at a great disadvantage in paying the 50% figure: they may already have paid it, especially if the item is one subject to fairly rapid depreciation.

Many default situations will result in a court making a time order under s 129 of the Consumer Credit Act 1974, which gives a consumer additional time to pay instalments and/or reduces their individual (but not total) amount. The court is given wide discretion as to the nature of a time order, but one factor to be considered is the consumer's means. A time order should normally be for a stipulated period on account of temporary financial difficulty.[8] The power to make a time order in the case of consumer hire purchase or conditional sale agreements extends to future instalments, and where a possession order is sought to the whole of the indebtedness, but in other agreements it only applies to payments in arrear unless an acceleration clause has come into operation whereby all remaining instalments are due immediately.[9] In addition to a time order, s 135 of the Act empowers a court to make a suspension order; for example, it might suspend a creditor's power to repossess an item on condition that the consumer keeps up the payments required, A time order can be made on application of a consumer who has received a default notice, as well as when a creditor brings an action in court against the consumer.[10] Because consumers are unlikely to seek a time or suspension order themselves an institutional change would be to confer on advance agencies the right to seek these on account of debtors, where a creditor fails to negotiate a suitable compromise. Another possible reform would be to spell out more expressly in the legislation that relief can be given against the consequences of default where, by reason of any circumstances which

[8]   *Southern and District Finance plc v Barnes* [1995] CCLR 62.
[9]   Section 130(2).
[10]   Section 129(1).

were not reasonably foreseeable at the time of entering into the consumer credit transaction, like illness or unemployment, a consumer is temporarily unable to discharge his obligations.

An orderly payment of debts has the dual advantage of reducing consumer anxiety and at the same time guaranteeing payment to creditors. Short of bankruptcy, one possible measure is for the consumer to enter an individual voluntary arrangement. Under the Insolvency Act 1986, this results in a moratorium on claims.[11] The consumer can then seek a voluntary arrangement with creditors, and if a majority agree with a proposal the minority are bound and cannot pursue their claims to the full. Individual voluntary arrangements are effected under the supervision of an insolvency practitioner.

Another possibility for the orderly repayment of a number of creditors where they might prove resistant in negotiation is to obtain an administration order in the county court, whereby all debts are consolidated and the debtor makes regular payments to the court which distributes them to the creditors.[12] Administration orders ought to be used more extensively following changes introduced by the Courts and Legal Services Act 1990.[13] Previously jurisdiction was limited to a total indebtedness of about £5,000 and to situations where at least one judgment debt was outstanding. Under the 1990 Act there are no such prerequisites. Nor will orders require an application by a debtor but the court may take the initiative itself. An administration order has the advantage of staying most proceedings by creditors to whom it applies, and courts are apparently fairly benevolent in suspending orders when consumers are in temporary difficulties. A composition provision may be attached to an administration order, whereby creditors have to accept only part of their debts. Court-administered debt consolidation like the administration order and the consolidated attachment of earnings[14] is to be preferred to the private enterprise system of debt pooling which operates in some parts of North America. Debt pooling has given rise to various abuses and legislation has been enacted in a number of jurisdictions to control it.[15]

Bankruptcy is the obvious course for defaulters in the more serious cases because it offers the prospect of a fresh start when the order is finally discharged. Present bankruptcy law, however, has a number of

---

[11]   Insolvency Act 1986, ss 252–263. See eg G Howells *Consumer Debt* (Sweet & Maxwell, 1993) pp 97–104.
[12]   CPR 1998, Sch 2; CCR Ord 39.
[13]   See *Civil Justice Review. Report of the Review Body on Civil Justice* (Cm 394 (1988)) p 119; *Credit and Debt* (NCC 1990) p 95.
[14]   Attachment of Earnings Act 1971, s 17. See p 280 below.
[15]   Law Reform Commissions of British Columbia *Debtor-Creditor Relationships, Debt Collection and Collection Agents* Project No 2 (1971) LRC 4, p 31.

disadvantages from the point of view of consumers. There is the obvious effect on a consumer's reputation, coupled with the limitation on his ability to obtain credit because of the legal obligation to inform potential creditors of his bankrupt status.[16] Hardship also arises because a bankrupt has to contribute to his creditors from after-acquired property.[17] Delay in obtaining a formal discharge can also disadvantage consumers. One alternative would be a moratorium on debt recovery actions for consumers, as long as they use new procedures for an orderly repayment of creditors. The procedures would be available outside bankruptcy, and would include arrangements where payment in full was not expected. The procedures would not involve meetings of creditors, but instead creditors would be informed by post and they would signify approval in the same way. The reform would be coupled with a scheme to promote debt counselling.[18]

(d) Enforcement of the judgment debt[19]

A creditor who obtains a money judgment against a consumer in the event of a default—for arrears in instalments, for the full amount outstanding (less a rebate) if an acceleration clause is valid, for the losses incurred if the consumer has repudiated a hire purchase agreement, etc—can seek to enforce it in a number of ways if, as is likely, the consumer cannot satisfy it. A county court judgment may be followed by a warrant of execution whereby personal property of the consumer can be seized (with the exception of the family's clothing and bedding, and the debtor's tools of trade below a certain amount) and sold at a public auction to satisfy the judgment.[20] Execution in this way is not always satisfactory from the point of view of creditors: there may be problems of obtaining access to the property or the warrant may not be satisfied because the property is the subject of hire purchase or leasing agreements—and hence not available

---

[16] Insolvency Act 1986, s 360. J Ford and M Wilson 'Personal Debt and Insolvency' in H Rajak (ed) *Insolvency Law Theory and Practice* (Sweet & Maxwell, 1993) p 104.

[17] Section 307.

[18] M Ryan *The Last Resort: A Study of Consumer Bankrupts* (Avebury, 1995). See also *Insolvency Law and Practice* (Cmnd 8558 (1982)) pp 72–87; *Insolvency: The Regular Payment of Debts* Report No 6 (Australian Law Reform Commission, 1977); Ontario Law Reform Commission, *Report on the Enforcement of Judgment Debts and Related Matters* (Toronto: Ministry of the Attorney General, 1981) vol 1.

[19] For position when creditors seek to enforce mortgages: N Madge 'Mortgage Possession Proceedings' (1997) 147 NLJ 459.

[20] County Courts Act 1984, ss 89, 97.

for execution—or not worth the cost of removal and sale.[1] Consumers can be driven to borrow at high interest rates to stave off execution—in the sense the immediate creditor may be satisfied, but from the point of view of the consumer the situation has hardly improved. Other grave drawbacks to execution for consumers are the limited categories of items which are exempt and the low resale that items fetch when sold.[2] In fact very few of the total warrants issued are enforced by sale and the procedure operates by threat.[3] Difficulties from the point of view of creditors are also associated with other methods of satisfying a judgment such as a charging order on the consumer's home—the Court of Appeal has warned courts against issuing a charging order when a debtor is likely to be insolvent and the order would give an advantage to the creditor applying for it[4]—or initiating bankruptcy, whereupon other creditors will be able to put in rival claims.

A popular form of enforcing judgment now is an attachment of earnings order, a procedure which was introduced in 1971 following the report of the Payne Committee.[5] Attachment of earnings was the quid pro quo for abolition of imprisonment, which had existed for centuries as the ultimate method of enforcing debts. Imprisonment for debt still exists in case of wilful non-payment.[6] Imprisonment for debt is, of course, largely futile in getting consumers to pay because most default arises not from recalcitrance but from misfortune, and because imprisonment cuts off debtors from the capacity to repay. An attachment order directs the debtor's employer to deduct certain amounts from the debtor's earnings and periodically to pay these to the court which distributes them to creditors. The court fixes a rate of earnings so that they will not fall below a certain minimum—the protected earnings rate—usually fixed at the basic benefits level.

A creditor can be awarded costs on applying for an attachment order, which can constitute a substantial additional burden for the consumer. Much concern has been expressed that an attachment order can jeopardise a consumer's employment because the employer might object to the burdens of collection; if this occurred it would defeat the very purpose of the attachment order, because debtors would no longer be in regular employment to pay the order. The Attachment of Earnings Act 1971 tries to avoid this by allowing employers to deduct an amount from the earnings

[1]   J Phipps 'Warrants of Execution in the Recovery of Consumer Debts in the County Court. A Lost Opportunity for Change?' (1990) 9 Civ JQ 234.

[2]   Courts and Legal Services Act 1990, s 15. See *Bailiffs and Sheriffs* (NCC, 1992).

[3]   R Cotterrell et al 'The Recovery of Judgment Debts in the County Court' in I Ramsay (ed) *Debtors and Creditors* (Professional Books, 1986) p 85.

[4]   *Rainbow v Moorgate Properties Ltd* [1975] 2 All ER 821, [1975] 1 WLR 788. Cf *Roberts Petroleum Ltd v Bernard Kenny Ltd* [1983] 2 AC 192. See Charging Orders Act 1979, s 1(5).

[5]   Attachment of Earnings Act 1971.

[6]   R Epstein 'Imprisonment for Debt' (1998) 117 Prison Service Journal 17.

attached for administration.[7] In addition, an employer who dismisses an employee because of an attachment order will probably be liable to pay compensation for unfair dismissal. Nevertheless, one study found that although district judges were not necessarily aware whether anyone had lost their job as a result of an order, they were aware of the possibility. For this reason they operated a system of 'suspended' attachment of earnings orders, which were not enforced if the debtor paid the creditor regularly.[8] Another study found that only a minority of applications for attachment orders succeed, with the majority being rejected as inappropriate or failing to progress because of creditor inactivity.[9]

A Canadian study suggested that attachment orders may undermine the incentive to work because consumers can obtain as much in welfare payments, which are not subject to attachment, as when they are working.[10] On this basis the courts should not impose attachment of earnings orders as freely as they can at present. Attachment of earnings orders should be a last resort for debtors who will not pay voluntarily after receiving suitable counselling and an adequate period of time to pay. As long as the law continues to allow creditors to use its processes to enforce debts, however, attachment of earnings orders seem a more satisfactory method of enforcing judgments against debtors than imprisonment or a rigorous execution against their real or personal property.[11] Of course it requires that debtors have sufficient income to be able to pay without their debt position getting worse overall.

(e)   Reform of the law

A number of disturbing features associated with creditors' remedies have been discussed; for example, even though a creditor may obtain a low value for an item which it has repossessed compared with its retail value, it still has the right to sue for its losses ('deficiency'). One of the reforms in the Consumer Credit Act 1974 is that a creditor cannot enforce any security taken in relation to a regulated agreement (eg over the consumer's other property) so as to benefit to an extent greater than would be the case

---

[7]   Section 7(4).

[8]   Touche Ross *Civil Justice Review. Study of Debt Enforcement Procedures* (Lord Chancellor's Dept, 1986) p 19.

[9]   M Wilson and J Ford 'Recovering Debt: The Effectiveness of Attachment of Earnings?' (1992) 11 Civil JQ 363.

[10]   M Trebilcock and A Schulman 'The Pathology of Credit Breakdown' (1976) 22 McGill LJ 415 at 458.

[11]   W Whitford 'A Critique of the Consumer Credit Collection System' [1979] Wisc LR 047, 1143. For a cogent view to the contrary, see TG Ison *Credit Marketing and Consumer Protection* (Croom Helm, 1979) pp 271–284.

under the agreement itself.[12] Reform in other jurisdictions has taken the course of closing off to creditors one of their two remedies: repossession (proceeding against the security), or the personal action in damages. Several jurisdictions oblige creditors to elect between the two remedies when consumers default ('seize or sue' provisions).[13] Saskatchewan goes further and limits the right of creditors to proceeding against the security; creditors cannot sue for any part of the purchase price.[14] From the point of view of creditors this is probably the least satisfactory course because they say that, except for cars, boats, etc, the resale value of most items sold on credit is very low. The virtue of the Saskatchewan approach is that creditors have every incentive to obtain the best price possible on selling an item which has been repossessed. The alternative of abolishing security in consumer credit transactions seems to have growing support, because it would curb the abuses associated with repossession and the problem of items being resold at a substantial undervalue. Certainly, it would confirm a trend in modern forms of credit, such as retailers' credit sales and credit cards, towards giving credit without security. Even some finance houses have abandoned the idea of security by moving away from hire purchase to personal loans without taking a bill of sale. Mr Justice White, then Chairman of the South Australian Credit Tribunal, suggested:

> Industry reliance upon security ... does not appear to be based so much on present favourable levels of consumer dishonesty and collection efficiency as on lending habits acquired from another age ... and on industry's preference for the well-trodden path of volume (secured) sales to that of making proper inquiries as to creditworthiness. Why go to the trouble and expense of proper inquiries when they might prejudice a possible sale?[15]

A fundamental question is whether creditors should be entitled to any remedies at law. Why should the state lend its support to enforcement of consumer debt? Why should the law become the collection arm of business? The great bulk of consumers—some 95%—repay the credit advanced to them without difficulty, and consumers who strike problems are mainly those on lower incomes who experience illness or unemployment. It is inaccurate to say that consumers freely contract credit agreements, and therefore the state should help creditors enforce them, because many consumers are pressed into credit agreements at both a personal and societal level. There will be a small number of consumers who will practise

---

12   Section 113.
13   J Ziegel and B Geva *Commercial and Consumer Transactions* (Edmond-Montgomery, 1981) pp 1128–29.
14   Limitation of Civil Rights Act, RSS, s 18(1).
15   *Davies v Kobi Finance Co Pty Ltd* (unreported) p 43.

fraud, but they can be dealt with by the criminal law. If creditors were denied the law's assistance, the incentive to consumers to repay credit would not derive from the threat of legal processes at present, but from the fear of an adverse credit rating. To be balanced against this of course is that a greater invasion of privacy might be entailed.

Abolition of creditors' rights to enforce consumer credit transactions might lead to extra-judicial methods of collection, but the criminal law and licensing could do much to curb this. Another consequence of abolishing creditors' legal remedies might be an increase in the cost of credit to cover bad debts.[16] Just how severe this would be is the subject of some doubt, but it does not deter adherents to market economic theory from concluding that an important number of consumers, especially the poor, would be excluded from the credit market. One study which has some bearing on the matter was conducted in Wisconsin after the law there placed curbs on self-help repossession and required notice to be given to debtors and an opportunity for a judicial hearing. It concluded that there had not been a substantial decline in motorcar loans after the change, although there was a marginal impact in restricting credit availability because retailers required larger down-payments.[17] Were the law's assistance to be denied to creditors, alternative institutions, like credit unions, could be encouraged to assist those consumers adversely affected by restrictions on availability.

5   INSTITUTIONAL CHANGES IN CONSUMER CREDIT

Reforms have already been suggested in a number of areas of consumer credit law further to protect consumers. Credit counselling has been mentioned as a development to assist consumers who get into difficulty. Should creditors still be entitled to enforce credit agreements at law, moratorium periods are necessary, longer than those provided by the present provisions for a default notice, to give consumers time to get out of difficulties. Consumer education is a solution suggested by a number of writers, and although its benefits in familiarising consumers with the nature of credit and credit transactions should not be downgraded, it is a little facile to think it will have much effect on the level of default so long as such strong pressures bear on consumers to purchase on credit. If the desirability of credit is accepted then it seems that institutional reforms are one way of ensuring that consumers can obtain credit on reasonable terms with a reasonable prospect of repaying it.

[16]   See W Whitford 'A Critique of the Consumer Credit Collection System' [1979] Wisc LR 1047, 1081–1086.
[17]   W Whitford and H Laufer 'The Impact of Denying Self-Help Repossession of Automobiles: A Study of the Wisconsin Consumer Act' [1975] Wisc LR 607.

Credit unions are a development which has attracted favourable comment in consumer circles. Credit unions began in Europe in the nineteenth century as mutual aid organisations, spread to North America in the early twentieth century, and have taken root in many developing countries since then. The idea of a credit union is the common pooling of financial resources by those having a common bond—occupational, religious, professional, etc— which can then be used to provide loans to its members. Credit unions in their literature draw on the Rochdale principles, drafted by the first consumer co-operative in Rochdale in 1844, and emphasise values such as democratic control in which each member has one vote in the annual meeting of the organisation.

The rate of interest charged by the credit unions is uniform for all borrowers and relatively low. Loans seldom extend over more than three or four years, because otherwise capital is tied up by only a few members. Credit unions usually vet the purpose for which a loan is needed. Loans normally only cover the purchase of consumer durables and are not large enough for house purchase, for example. Borrowers obtain protection insurance so that the loan can be repaid in the event of death or disability of the borrower. The shares of a borrower in the credit union also act as a form of security. In its formative years a credit union usually relies heavily on the voluntary effort of members in running the organisation, but this can have the advantage that annual dividends and interest refunds to borrowers are possible.

Credit unions are strongest the United States, where they are big business: state and national organisations supply services to local credit unions, stabilise the funds of member groups and generally promote credit unions by advertising, and so on. American credit unions use share drafts, which resemble bank cheques. Occupational credit unions are the largest category, associations come next (religious, professional, etc) and residential last. The early credit unions in the United States were directed to productive purposes—mainly loans for small businesses and farmers. The early driving forces behind the credit unions there saw them not as anti-capitalist but as a basically conservative force to make employees more content and efficient and thus less likely to adhere to radical principles.[18] Similarly, American credit unions' leaders in the 1950s promoted credit unions in developing countries because they conceived them as 'bulwarks against Communism'. In the 1960s, those involved in the War on Poverty thought that credit unions might be the answer to the problems which the American poor experienced with credit, as well as providing an example of community action. Generally the movement was a

[18]   J Carroll Moody and C Fite *The Credit Union Movement: Origins and Developments 1850–1970* (University of Nebraska, 1971) pp 354–355.

failure: the default rate was high, poor consumers without employment were hardly in a position to contribute to credit unions' funds and, most importantly, the Republicans cut off federal funding in 1970.[19]

Credit unions in Britain have had a very slow growth.[20] Many have owed their origin to immigrants, who brought the idea with them. By 1997 there were 645 credit unions registered, with a membership of under 200,000 and assets of just over £100 million. However, at current rates of growth most community credit unions would take 50 years to develop an asset base of half a million pounds, sufficient to appoint a part-time paid manager.[1] One factor inhibiting the growth of credit unions in Britain has been the existence of alternative sources of credit like hire purchase and doorstep credit. Some mainstream banks, however, have supported community credit unions, including plans for the creation of a national credit union development fund.

Another explanation has been the lack of a modern legislative framework. The Credit Unions Act 1979, currently under review, creates a legislative framework for the operation and supervision of credit unions.[2] A society which meets the requirements of the Credit Unions Act 1979 may be registered as a credit union under the Industrial and Provident Societies Act 1965 (s 1(1), (2)). Admission to membership of the society must be restricted to those having a common bond (ss 1(2), (5)). The rules must provide that the qualifications for admission to membership is following a particular occupation, residing in a particular locality, being employed in a particular locality or by a particular employer, being a member of a bona fide organisation or otherwise associated, or such other qualification as the registrar approves (s 1(4)). Only registered credit unions can use that description (s 3). Savings must be in £1 shares, and no member can hold generally more than £2,000 in shares (ss 5, 7). Credit unions must have a minimum of 21 members and generally not more than 5,000 members (s 6(1)–(2)). Loans may be made 'for a provident or productive purpose' but cannot be more than £2,000 in excess of a member's total paid-up shareholding, must be repaid with a maximum of five years (if secured) or two years (if unsecured), and generally cannot involve interest in excess of 1% per month on the amount outstanding (s 11). The Chief Registrar can prescribe the manner in which credit union funds may be invested,

19 J Carroll Moody and C Fite *The Credit Union Movement: Origins and Developments 1850–1970* (University of Nebraska, 1971) pp 355–356, 399.
20 Registrar of Friendly Societies *Annual Report 1996–1997* (SO, 1997).
1 E Mayo *A Commitment to People and Place* (New Economics Foundation, 1997). See also G Griffiths and G Howells 'Slumbering Giant or White Elephant— Do Credit Unions have a Role in the United Kingdom Credit Markets' (1991) 42 NILQ 199.
2 Cf Federal Credit Union Act, 12 USC s 1751ff.

and credit unions must establish a general reserve (ss 13, 14). With approval, credit unions can make insurance arrangements to protect members against loss (s 16). The Chief Registrar is empowered to appoint inspectors to investigate the affairs of a credit union, to suspend certain of its operations and to cancel or suspend its registration (ss 18–20).

Views are divided about the manner in which this legislation needs amending.[3] For example, one line of argument is that change is desirable to enable credit unions to advance larger loans and to allow wider common bonds. Particular scope for expansion is thought to lie in occupational credit unions, along North American lines, since trade unions and professional associations have the organising capacity and their members, being in employment, the resources. By contrast another line of argument is that any weakening of the common bond required would undermine the co-operative principles at the base of credit unions. Credit unions would become just one source of credit and the self-help co-operative principles would fall by the wayside. Also to be taken into account is the possible attempt by banks and other financial institutions to curb the privileges of credit unions should they become larger, professionally managed and competitive bodies.

[3]   G Griffiths and G Howells 'Credit Unions in the United Kingdom and Possible Legislative Reforms to the Credit Unions Act 1979' in G Howells et al (ed) *Aspects of Credit and Debt* (Sweet & Maxwell, 1993).

Public control

Chapter 8

Broad statutory standards

The simplest form of public regulation is where legislation announces a standard of behaviour in broad terms and imposes penalties on any deviation from it. In some cases the standard may be taken from the private law, so that it is simply the remedial law that is changed. Broad statutory standards usually operate so that official action is deferred until wrongdoing occurs. The individual has the choice of complying with the standard or of violating it and incurring a penalty.[1] The assumption is that the majority of those being regulated will choose to comply with the standard. So many laws are enacted that if the majority did not obey, law enforcement agencies could not cope. Public compliance with broad statutory standards is assisted if they correspond with societal values and if they are precise and well known so that individuals can bring their behaviour into line without much official guidance. The major difference between broad statutory standards and other forms of public regulation is that they have a ready flexibility to cope with the constant flow of innovations in marketing. Further, they usually need fewer resources for enforcement. The drain on enforcement resources increases, however, if specific exemptions from the standard can be made, or if breaches are difficult to detect or to prove.

Broad statutory standards, backed by criminal sanctions, can be an unsophisticated instrument of regulation and are not always a satisfactory method of controlling undesirable features such as business acts prejudicial to consumers.[2] Firstly, their edge is blunted because they compete with each other for enforcement. A method of counteracting this tendency is to entrust the enforcement of a particular type of standard to a specialised

---

[1] HLA Hart *Punishment and Responsibility* (Clarendon, 1968) p 23.
[2] See R Baldwin and M Cave *Understanding Regulation* (OUP, 1999) Chapter 8.

agency, the success of which is then identified with its vigorous application. Thus consumer laws ought to be enforced by separate consumer protection departments and not by the police. Secondly, if there is some uncertainty as to the application of a broad standard, there is a temptation for enforcement authorities to refrain from taking any action because of the possibility of not being successful. Uncertainty can be mitigated, however, by supplementary provisions, whether in the legislation itself, statute-backed guidance and codes of practice. Thirdly, broad criminal standards are not interpreted liberally because, as a matter of course, courts construe criminal statutes narrowly. While this may be justified where individual liberty is at stake, it is different with matters like consumer offences and imprisonment is hardly ever involved. Fourthly, the details of how the standards are enforced are filled in by enforcement agencies or by industry self-regulation, which can be undesirable on grounds of lack of transparency and accountability. Finally, criminal procedure is inappropriate when applied to intricate consumer offences.[3] Existing criminal procedure evolved for discovering truth in straightforward crimes like murder or theft, where evidence is relatively simple and is capable of being assessed by ordinary citizens comprising a jury or a bench of lay magistrates. By contrast, some consumer offences are relatively complex and in some cases can only be understood by experts. Detailed regulatory control greatly reduces the difficulty in such cases because it narrows the issues and may result in expert witnesses having a larger role in appraising the evidence for the court.

The burden of enforcing broad statutory standards in consumer matters is somewhat eased because the great bulk are strict liability offences. Penalties can be incurred for their unintentional or inadvertent breach.[4] The crucial question is whether the elements of the prohibited act (the *actus reus*) have been committed, and it is irrelevant whether there is *mens rea*. In law there is a presumption that offences require *mens rea* in the absence of a clear legislative indication to the contrary.[5] Quite early, however, it was accepted that consumer protection offences are generally among those regulatory offences where the presumption is displaced.[6] With some consumer protection statutes the courts have been assisted in this interpretation by the need for there to be intention or recklessness in

---

[3]   H Mannheim *Criminal Justice and Social Reconstruction* (Routledge & Kegan Paul, 1946) pp 166–167.

[4]   See C Howard *Strict Responsibility* (Sweet & Maxwell, 1963); L Leigh *Strict and Vicarious Liability* (Sweet & Maxwell, 1982); G Howells 'An Evaluation of the Role of Defences in Consumer Protection Statutes' (1988) 6 Trading L 244; P Cartwright 'Defendants in Consumer Protection Statutes: a Search for Consistency' (1996) 59 MLR 225.

[5]   Eg *Sweet v Parsley* [1970] AC 132.

[6]   Eg *Roberts v Egerton* (1874) LR 9 QB 494.

certain, but not all, aspects of an offence or group of offences; by the fact that imprisonment is not a necessary penalty; and perhaps most importantly, by the insertion of specific defences which would have little role in the absence of strict liability.[7]

The major policy reason for making consumer offences strict liability offences is the overriding need to protect the public from social harm.[8] When an offence occurs consumers are concerned that they have been harmed, and whether the business involved has a guilty mind is irrelevant to them. The assumption is that businesses are never completely innocent, for they can reorder their affairs to avoid breaches of statutory standards even if, as a practical matter, this is uncompetitive.[9] Indeed, as a matter of law, as we shall see below, the statutory defences in consumer legislation enable a business to avoid liability where, to put it in general terms, it is not at fault. Moreover, consumer enforcement agencies introduce notions of fault into their decisions to prosecute, such as whether the offender is regarded as dishonest or unscrupulous, or has failed to respond to previous warnings or advice.[10] For these reasons strict liability in consumer protection matters does not involve punishing the 'morally blameless'. Strict liability also makes for convenience in law enforcement. It would be virtually impossible to penalise undesirable business behaviour if it were necessary to establish *mens rea* in each case. A survey of consumer protection departments and environmental health departments found that the overwhelming view was that strict liability was crucial to the process of investigation and prosecution.[11]

An argument of some commentators against strict liability is that offences are shielded from the process of being regarded as criminal. In other words, because the requirement of *mens rea* is dispensed with offences are not regarded as morally reprehensible, and hence their effectiveness is weakened.[12] The fact is, however, that there are other more important reasons why the impact of the law in areas like consumer protection is diluted. The high status of business people—an outcome, in part, of their association with production—is one reason that those who

---

[7]   Eg *Tesco Supermarkets Ltd v Nattrass* [1972] AC 153; *Wings Ltd v Ellis* [1985] AC 272.

[8]   G Borrie *The Development of Consumer Law and Policy* (Stevens, 1984) p 48.

[9]   C Wells 'Restatement or Reform' [1986] Crim LR 314, 319.

[10] See G Richardson 'Strict Liability for Regulatory Crime' [1987] Crim LR 295, 297–303.

[11] M Smith and A Pearson 'The Value of Strict Liability' [1969] Crim LR 5.

[12] See H Packer *The Limits of the Criminal Sanction* (Stanford University Press, 1969) p 359; S Kadish 'Some Observations on the Use of Criminal Sanctions in Enforcing Economic Regulations' (1963) 30 U Chi LR 423, 436–437; D Tench *Towards A Middle System of Law* (Consumers' Association, 1981); A Ashworth *Principles of Criminal Law* (Clarendon, 2nd edn, 1995) p 1.

commit offences are not condemned by the community. A further argument against strict liability is that it makes it difficult for courts to distinguish between the unscrupulous and the less serious offender, and that there is a tendency to impose uniformly low penalties which are not a burden to the former. In practice enforcement bodies can use the general reputation of a business as an element in exercising discretion to prosecute, and courts might also be able to identify unscrupulous businesses after conviction from the antecedents made known for sentencing.

An important correlation of broad statutory standards is that a fairly wide discretion will repose in the relevant enforcement agency. Some discretion is always present with law enforcement, partly because of the vagueness of language and the need to apply legal categories to specific circumstances, but generally speaking an enforcement body will possess less discretion if standards are detailed and specific. Discretion involves flexibility, and it may be that the legislature chooses a general standard in preference to other forms of regulation which can be adapted according to changing social conditions. In other words it feels incapable of dealing with the details of regulation and deliberately entrusts the task to an enforcement body which, it assumes, will have the advantages of flexibility and accumulated expertise. Of course, broad and vague standards may also result from a failure of legislative draftmanship or because a statute incorporates competing and inconsistent values. When an agency has wide discretion to prosecute, there is an obligation on it to be open about the criteria it uses to enforce the law.

This chapter deals with three types of broad statutory standards in the consumer protection area: those relating to misdescriptions, quality and quantity. It then turns to the complexities of corporate criminal liability as they affect prosecutions for the breach of such standards. There is no doubt some trend away from broad statutory standards in the consumer protection area, as illustrated by the way price misdescriptions are now handled.[13] However, they continue to be an important part of the consumer protection armour, deserving attention.

I   TRADE DESCRIPTIONS

Consumers' buying decisions can be influenced by the manner in which products and services are described. If this is inaccurate, consumers can easily be misled and suffer financial loss. Legislation prohibiting false or

---

[13]   See C Scott 'Criminalising the Trader to Protect the Consumer' in I Loveland *Frontiers of Criminality* (Sweet & Maxwell, 1995).

misleading descriptions goes part of the way to protecting consumers in such circumstances. In Britain the Trade Descriptions Act 1968 is the most important legislation in the area. There is comparable legislation in other jurisdicitons. The predecessor of the Trade Descriptions Act 1968, the Merchandise Marks Act 1887, had its origins in attempts by certain businesses to protect themselves from what they regarded as the threat of unfair competition.[14] As originally conceived, the legislation was directed against businesses which falsely portrayed their products by copying the marks and names of others. Later, it penalised businesses which incorrectly indicated that imported items were manufactured in the UK. The basic prohibition against the application of false, and later misleading, written descriptions was somewhat unclear, had a limited scope and was rarely enforced.[15]

The Trade Descriptions Act 1968, originally entitled the Protection of Consumers (Trade Descriptions) Bill, was an outcome of the report of the Molony Committee on Consumer Protection.[16] Unlike its predecessor, the Trade Descriptions Act 1968 is clearly a consumer protection measure. The Trade Descriptions Act 1968 extended the ambit of the previous law by clearly including oral misdescriptions and false statements about prices and services, by clarifying the law relating to advertisements, and by imposing an obligation on consumer protection departments to enforce the legislation. Misleading pricing offences now fall within Part III of the Consumer Protection Act 1987, and the Property Misdescriptions Act 1991 deals, as the name suggests, with property misdescriptions.

Descriptions dealt with by legislation such as the Trade Descriptions Act 1968 fall conveniently under four main headings: descriptions of products, services, prices and property. From the point of view of enforcement this order seems to reflect the relative importance of the different aspects. In 1996 false descriptions of products accounted for 1,134 prosecutions; services for 220 prosecutions, prices for 147 prosecutions and property for 22 prosecutions. Some of the matters involved in these cases are set out in Table 8.1.[17]

14   Eg *Report from the Select Committee on Merchandise Marks* (1897) c 346, xi, 29, p iii.
15   J Martin and G Smith *The Consumer Interest* (Pall Mall, 1968) pp 161–162; cf *Slatcher v George Mence Smith Ltd* [1951] 2 KB 631, 639.
16   *Final Report of the Committee on Consumer Protection* (Cmnd 1781 (1962)).
17   OFT *Annual Report of the Director General of Fair Trading 1997* (HMSO, 1998) pp 79–82.

Table 8.1. Prosecutions for misdescriptions of products, services and prices (1999)

	Misdescribed products	Misdescribed services	Misleading prices
Second-hand cars	307	12	3
Leisure goods and services	39	6	1
Clothing and clothing fabrics	83	—	6
Home maintenance, repairs, improvements	14	47	—
Food and drink	48	1	10
Others	144	88	39
Total	635	154	59

(Source: *Office of Fair Trading Annual Report 1999*, pp 89–93.)

(a)   Misdescribed products

Section 1(1) of the Trade Descriptions Act 1968 prohibits persons in the course of trade or business from applying a false trade description to products and from supplying (or offering to supply) any falsely described products. The requirement that an offender be in the course of trade or business excludes transactions without some degree of regularity to them.[18] However, the section encompasses ancillary business dealings, as where a car hire firms sells its cars after using them.[19] Actions by professionals can be in the course of a trade or business.[20] The Act deploys a 'specific, yet also comprehensive, legal definition'[1] of what is a trade description, defined as 'an indication, direct or indirect, and by whatever means given', of the matters mentioned in s 2(1):

(a) quantity, size or gauge;
(b) method of manufacture, production, processing or reconditioning;
(c) composition;
(d) fitness for purpose, strength, performance, behaviour or accuracy;
(e) any physical characteristics not included in the preceding paragraphs;
(f) testing by any person and results thereof;

[18] *Davies v Sumner* [1984] 3 All ER 831, [1984] 1 WLR 1301.
[19] *Havering London Borough Council v Stevenson* [1970] 3 All ER 609, [1970] 1 WLR 1375.
[20] *Roberts v Leonard* (1995) 14 Tr LR 536, 159 JP 711.
[1] A Ogus *Regulation: Legal Form and Economic Theory* (OUP, 1994) p 145.

(g) approval by any person or conformity with type approved by any person;
(h) place or date of manufacture, production, processing or reconditioning;
(i) person by whom manufactured, produced, processed or reconditioned;
(j) other history, including previous ownership or use.

Omitted from the list are matters such as the identity and standing of businesses and the contents and authorship of books, films and records. In addition the results and the fact of testing might not be covered if standing alone and not in combination. It can also be said that the section needs widening, for it leaves untouched businesses which create false impressions that consumers are paying trade prices by describing themselves as 'discount stores' or the like. Under the German Law on Unfair Competition 1909 it has been held that a business must not portray itself to a consumer as a wholesaler if its consumer prices are higher than those charged to other businesses, even if the larger part of its sales are to the latter.

The ambit of a false trade description of a product is defined in ss 3–4. Trade descriptions, to be caught by the statute, must be false to a material degree (s 3(1)), but the prohibition extends to trade descriptions which, although not false, are misleading (s 3(2)). Anything which, although not a trade description, is likely to be taken as such is covered (s 3(3)), along with situations where a purchaser uses a trade description in ordering and products are supplied pursuant to the order (s 4(3)). A false trade description can be annexed to a product, made orally, or contained in an advertisement (ss 4–5). An offer to supply a product extends to where a business exposes for supply (to cover invitations to treat) or has it in its possession for supply (s 6). Use of the term 'supply' covers hire purchase, hiring and giving away as part of a promotion, as well as ordinary sales.

A wide range of situations have been handled under s 1.[2] Table 8.1 shows, however, that the rather mundane misdescriptions of secondhand cars feature prominently in prosecutions. The prevalence of these in the offences that come to official attention is attributed to the malpractices of secondhand car dealers and to the willingness of consumers to complain (perhaps because, apart from a house, cars are likely to be the most expensive items they ever purchase). Prosecutions have been successfully directed against the sales techniques of secondhand car dealers, in particular the language employed in effecting sales. For example the phrase

[2] See R Bragg *Trade Descriptions* (Clarendon, 1991).

'beautiful' when applied to a car has been held to refer to both the appearance and running of a vehicle and to constitute a false trade description if the car is unroadworthy.[3]

A large number of detected offences has been in relation to the purported mileage of vehicles. 'Clocking'—the deliberate interference with an odometer so that it registers fewer miles than the vehicle has actually travelled—is a widespread and profitable offence, not infrequently perpetrated by rings involved in other organised crime.[4] An incorrect odometer is capable of being a false trade description in that it is an indication of the history or use of a vehicle (s 2(1)(j)), even though the seller does not know about the falsity.[5] Even dealers who turn the odometer reading back to zero fall within the section.[6] However, secondhand car dealers can protect themselves by disclaimers, which are discussed below. Jurisdictions such as the United States have felt the need for specific prohibitions against tampering with odometers.[7] Because of his conclusion that the practice of 'clocking' cars has reached the level of widespread fraud in the UK, the Director General of Fair Trading has recommended various measures: that the vehicle registration document be redesigned and expanded to list the names and addresses of as many previous keepers as possible to make it easier to check the history of the car; that urgent consideration be given to the introduction of legislation to require the installation of tamper-proof odometers in all new cars sold; and that legislation be introduced requiring the provision of a written statement to accompany used cars, including a statement of whether or not the mileage reading has been verified.[8] A survey of dealers in 1994 found that only 48% said that they always attempted to verify the mileage reading, although this is required under industry codes and membership standards.[9] There are a number of commercial organisations operating data bases, which provide information about the history of vehicles.

In considering whether there is a trade description, whether it is false, and whether it is false to a material degree, the courts use the test: what is the impression likely to be made on the minds of ordinary consumers to

---

[3]   *Robertson v Dicicco* [1972] RTR 431, [1972] Crim LR 592.
[4]   *The Purchase of Used Cars* (OFT, 1996) pp 14–16. One estimate is profits of £100m a year for unscrupulous sellers.
[5]   *Tarleton Engineering Co Ltd v Nattrass* [1973] 3 All ER 699, [1973] 1 WLR 1261; *Smithland Motors Ltd v Peck* [1991] Crim LR 386.
[6]   *R v Southwood* [1987] 3 All ER 556, [1987] 1 WLR 1361.
[7]   49 USC §32703 (added 1994). The law provides for both civil and criminal penalties (the latter for wilful violations), civil actions by the Attorney General to enjoin breach and treble damage suits (up to $1,500).
[8]   *Consumer Difficulties in the Used Car Sector* (OFT, 1980). See also P Turner *Caution! Used Cars* (Penguin, 1994).
[9]   *The Purchase of Used Cars* (OFT, 1996) pp 18–19.

whom it is directed?[10] From this follows a number of subsidiary conclusions. Firstly, even if experts or more experienced consumers can readily interpret, or are likely to discount, a description that does not make it any the less false or misleading.[11] Secondly, the issue is not whether a false description actually affected the consumer whose complaint gives rise to a prosecution, it is whether it is likely to affect ordinary consumers. The fact that the particular consumer was not deceived is immaterial, although it may be a mitigating factor in fixing the penalty.[12] Conversely, evidence that a consumer or that consumers have been misled is not conclusive. Thirdly, a statement of opinion might constitute a direct or indirect indication of the matters constituting a trade description, and in any event is likely to be taken as such.[13] Fourthly some, but not a great deal of, latitude is allowed for 'puff', which consumers discount as meaningless, although there is a case that a statement should be regarded as false to a material case if it has no factual basis.[14] Finally, it is also irrelevant that a particular transaction is on the whole fair to the consumer involved.[15] In determining the effect of a description on ordinary consumers the judges use hunch, and their knowledge and experience of the world (such as it is). Unlike business executives, they do not have access to empirical research about the actual impact on consumer behaviour of descriptions applied to particular products.

In relation to these matters, is it necessary for a significant section of the public to be misled? To put it differently, when assessing the impression likely to be made on the minds of ordinary consumers, are ordinary consumers reasonable consumers or do they encompass, as some decisions elsewhere suggest, 'the ignorant, the unthinking and the credulous, who, in making purchases, do not stop to analyse but are governed by appearances and general impressions'?[16] On the first

---

10 For example *Kensington and Chelsea Borough Council v Riley* [1973] RTR 122, [1973] Crim LR 133; *Horner v Kingsley Clothing Ltd* [1989] Crim LR 911; *West Yorkshire Metropolitan County Council v MFI Furniture Centre Ltd* [1983] 3 All ER 234. See, generally, C Swanson 'Predicting Changes in Consumer Attitudes' in S Britt (ed) *Consumer Behaviour and the Behavioural Sciences* (Wiley, 1966) pp 563–564.

11 *Dixons Ltd v Barnett* [1988] BTLC 311; *FTC v Standard Education Society* 302 US 112, 116 (1937).

12 *Chidwick v Beer* [1974] RTR 415; *Southwark London Borough Council v Time Computer Systems Ltd* (1997) Independent, 14 July.

13 *Holloway v Cross* [1981] 1 All ER 1012, [1981] RTR 146.

14 *Cadbury Ltd v Halliday* [1975] 2 All ER 226, [1975] 1 WLR 649; *Riley McKay Pty Ltd v Bannerman* (1977) 15 ALR 561, 570–571.

15 *Furniss v Scholes* [1974] RTR 133, [1974] Crim LR 199.

16 *Florence Mfg Co v JC Dowd & Co* 178 F. 73, 75 (1910). See also the Australian case *Parkdale Custom Built Furniture Pty Ltd v Puxu Pty Ltd* (1982) 56 ALJR 715.

approach, the falsity of a trade description is assessed in terms of its effect on reasonable consumers and the offence is not for the benefit of persons who fail to take reasonable care of their own interests. This approach is inconsistent with legislative purpose to protect all consumers including the inexperienced, the ignorant and the uneducated. Certainly this is the approach in the United States where a statement is treated as false, even if it is obviously so to the trained and experienced.[17] Of course the class to be protected may vary according to the facts of the case. For example, with relatively expensive items one may, in the ordinary course, expect consumers to exercise somewhat more vigilance than with less expensive items or those with less aesthetic importance. Those considering the purchase of equipment through a specialist magazine will be expected to be more sophisticated than the ordinary consumer.[18]

Despite the wide wording of the prohibition contained in s 1(1)(a) of the Trade Descriptions Act 1968, the English courts have held that to fall within it a false trade description must be connected with the supply of a product. In *Wickens Motors (Gloucester) Ltd v Hall*,[19] 40 days after a consumer purchased a secondhand car he returned to the defendant car dealers to complain. An employee told him: 'There is nothing wrong with the car', whereas it was unroadworthy then and at the time of sale. The Divisional Court held that no offence had been committed because any false trade description applied had not been associated with the sale of the car. The justification for this conclusion was that a broad application had never previously been suggested during 80 years of the Merchandise Marks Acts—strange reasoning when the Act was hardly ever enforced and when it is the nature of appellate litigation to raise points never previously suggested. On the other hand the courts have said that there is no need for a person who applies a false trade description to be a contracting party to the transaction.[20] Moreover, where a business undertakes to supply a product in the future complying with specifications of the consumer an offence is committed if the product fails to meet them.[1]

Under the civil law the sale of many products is regarded as being by description even if consumers select a product themselves.[2] In addition,

---

[17] *FTC v Standard Education Society* 302 US 779 (1937). See also *American Home Products Corp v TTC* 695 F 2d 681 (1982).
[18] *Southwark London Borough Council v Time Computer Systems Ltd* (1997) Independent, 14 July. See generally *British Airways Board v Taylor* [1976] 1 All ER 65 at 68–69, 72.
[19] [1972] 3 All ER 759, [1972] 1 WLR 1418. See also *Robins & Day Ltd v Kent County Council and Trading Standards Department* [1996] BTCL 3.
[20] *Fletcher v Sledmore* [1973] RTR 371, [1973] Crim LR 195.
[1] *Shropshire County Council v Simon Dudley Ltd* (1997) 16 Tr LR 69.
[2] Sale of Goods Act 1979, s 13(3).

where the purpose of a product is obvious, consumers benefit from the condition of fitness implied by law, although they do not specify the purpose for which they require it.[3] Are implied trade descriptions similarly covered by the criminal law? For example, can the mere appearance of a product be held to constitute a trade description about its fitness for purpose under s 2(1)(d)? If these questions are answered in the affirmative, the effect would be to impose criminal liability for products that are below the standard normally expected and the obligations about quality implied in the sale of products by the Sale of Goods Act would be transformed into criminal obligations. Many consumers would support such a move because when they receive shoddy products their remedies in civil law sometimes prove illusory and the criminal law might be a good way of deterring businesses from selling such products.[4] Further, the criminal law applies if consumers ask the right questions and a trade description is used. Why should there be a distinction between a shoddy product sold without being described and the same product sold when falsely described? Commentators point out that the two situations are different because false descriptions may induce consumers to buy when otherwise they would not do so. They also regard the introduction of implied descriptions into the criminal law as undesirable because of the uncertainty it would engender. For example, the purpose of articles is not always self-evident—it is not always clear whether they are bought for design or performance.[5] But the policy question still remains: would not the criminal law be the best means of ensuring that shoddy products are not marketed?

It is clear that there is no need for an express trade description before the Trade Descriptions Act 1968 can be invoked (s 3(3)). It is also clear that an omission may render a description misleading.[6] In addition a trade description is regarded as being applied if used in any manner likely to be taken as referring to a product (s 4(1)(c)). But can the analysis be taken one step further, that the mere appearance of a product might sometimes

---

[3]   Sale of Goods Act 1979, s 14(3).

[4]   In *Shropshire County Council v Simon Dudley Ltd* (1997) 16 Tr LR 69 Phillips LJ said (at p 82): 'If the 1968 Act takes effect in the way that I have postulated, it follows that the offences under the Act will be committed on many occasions where a breach occurs of a contract for the sale of goods ... I do not think that this is a satisfactory state of affairs, but it may be justified by the need to attempt to ensure fair trading in a very wide variety of circumstances... Trading Standards Officers must exercise discretion when deciding whether or not a particular case warrants the intervention of the criminal law.'

[5]   See OFT *Review of the Trade Descriptions Act 1968* (Cmnd 6628 (1976)) pp 44–46.

[6]   For example *Royal Banking Powder Co v FTC* 281 F 744 (1922); *Simeon Management Corpn v FTC* 579 F 2d 1137 (1978).

be such that a trade description can be implied?[7] *R v Ford Co Ltd*[8] has now established that as a general rule there is no scope for implied trade descriptions. That case involved a consumer purchasing a Ford motor car which he thought was new and which was so described in an invoice. The car had been damaged while it was in a compound awaiting retail delivery, but repairs had been effected. The documentation between Ford and the retailer did not contain the word 'new' but the Court of Appeal (Criminal Division) held that the order form was such that it gave an indirect indication that the trade description 'new' was being applied. In considering the matter the court rejected the proposition that whenever there is an implied term of a contract of sale relating to a matter covered by the Act, there is a corresponding application of a trade description.

> This seems to us to go much too far; it would be very startling if, for instance, the effect of the 1968 Act were to make a criminal of every seller of goods by description who delivers goods in breach of the condition of merchantable quality which is implied by s 14(2) of the Sale of Goods Act 1893.[9]

Businesses can circumvent the consequences of their false trade descriptions by the use of disclaimers.[10] Their legal efficacy derives from the fact that whether or not there is a false trade description applied to a product depends on the whole description, and that includes the presence of any disclaimer. Analytically, an effective disclaimer prevents a false trade description arising in the first place. If a disclaimer is not effective in this way it might still constitute a defence under s 24.[11] The policy justification for disclaimers is to enable retailers to negate a description, already applied to a product by a supplier, the truth of which they doubt but which cannot easily be altered. A similar situation arises when a description originally true becomes false but is difficult to change (as in a mail order catalogue). There is the danger that disclaimers can undermine the protection afforded by the legislation. The courts have said that disclaimers must be as bold, precise and compelling as the description. For example, the use of a general disclaimer in one part of a shop cannot negate descriptions on particular products. Another example is that disclaimers of odometer readings generally cannot be effected by casual remarks during negotiations, by small print clauses in contractual

---

[7]   As suggested in *Cottee v Douglas Seaton (Used Cars) Ltd* [1972] 3 All ER 750, [1972] 1 WLR 1408.
[8]   [1974] 3 All ER 489, [1974] 1 WLR 1220. Cf *Janbo Trading v Dudley Metropolitan Borough Council* (1993) 12 Tr LR 190.
[9]   [1974] 3 All ER 489 at 491–492, [1974] 1 WLR 1220 at 1224.
[10] For example *R v Bull* [1997] RTR 123, [1996] Crim LR 438.
[11] Eg *Southend Borough Council v White* (1991) 11 Tr LR 65.

documents, or by a notice inside a dealer's office. Moreover, the words of a disclaimer must be unambiguous and render a description meaningless; if not, the disclaimer itself might constitute a false trade description.

What of unscrupulous businesses applying false descriptions, and then using disclaimers to avoid liability in the hope that the disclaimer will not entirely neutralise the impact of the description? An example is a secondhand car dealer who turns back odometers but uses prominent disclaimers. The courts have held that they will not permit disclaimers in situations where the charge is of applying a false trade description and the circumstances indicate that this was done intentionally.[12] Another problem which disclaimers raise is that businesses might cease to make checks but might us disclaimers to repudiate liability. For example, the failure of used car dealers to investigate the real mileage travelled has been referred to: many dealers simply display disclaimers to avoid liability. The extent to which this can be done generally is limited, however, because traders would generally be reluctant to create apprehension among prospective customers about the quality of their merchandise by widespread use of disclaimers.

Businesses have responded to the growing interest and concern among consumers by marketing claims about the environmental impact of their products. Most such claims are on products and to a lesser extent in advertisements. Consumers need to have confidence in the accuracy of such claims so they can exercise their buying power in particular ways. A survey by the National Consumer Council found that many such claims were unverifiable, or were vague, specious or misleading. Most were accompanied by a bewildering range of logos and symbols. Consumers expressed scepticism about the truth of claims, confusion or ignorance, and these reactions were almost as pronounced among those claiming to be 'green shoppers'.[13]

Environmental claims about the impact of a product, or the way it is processed, manufactured or distributed, are not specifically mentioned in s 2 of the Trade Descriptions Act 1968. Even if they were, they might be too subjective or vague to constitute a trade description (eg 'ozone friendly', 'environmental friendly', 'environmentally responsible'). The approach in the United States and Australia has been to issue detailed

---

[12]   *R v Southwood* [1987] 3 All ER 556, [1987] 1 WLR 1361. There is also the possibility of offences of obtaining property by deception (Theft Act 1968, s 15), and under the Consumer Transactions (Restrictions on Statements) Order 1976, SI 1976/1813 as amended. See P Blish-Cheesman 'Mileage Disclaimers, Effective and Legal' (1982) 9 MR 121; E Newsome 'Trade Descriptions Misconceptions?' [1985] Crim LR 123; R Bragg *Trade Descriptions* (Clarendon, 1991) Chapter 3.

[13]   *Green Claims* (NCC, 1996).

guidelines regulating environmental claims under general prohibitions on misleading conduct. Britain is moving along the same lines, with a Green Claims Code of Practice, introduced by the government in 1998 and endorsed by consumer and professional bodies and by major retailers and manufacturers.[14] At the time of writing the government is reviewing legislative support for the code. Also relevant to green claims are the European Union's ecolabelling scheme and system of energy labelling for domestic appliances.[15]

(b)   Misdescribed services

False statements about services or facilities made knowingly or recklessly in the course of any trade or business are prohibited by s 14 of the Trade Descriptions Act 1968. Section 14(1) provides as follows:

14(1) It shall be an offence for any person in the course of any trade or business:
(a)   to make a statement which he knows to be false; or
(b)   recklessly to make a statement which is false;
as to any of the following matters, that is to say:
(i)   the provision in the course of any trade or business of any services, accommodation or facilities;
(ii)   the nature of any services, accommodation or facilities provided in the course of any trade or business;
(iii)   the time at which, manner in which or persons by whom any services, accommodation or facilities are so provided;
(iv)   the examination, approval or evaluation by any person of any services, accommodation or facilities so provided; or
(v)   the location or amenities of any accommodation so provided.

Unlike other consumer protection provisions, including those relating to the misdescription or mispricing of goods, the offence is not one of strict liability. Liability under s 14(1)(a) has been described as 'semi-strict'. The defendant must know of the falsity of the statement but need not know that the statement has been made.[16] This has implications for continuing statements in publications, brochures and the like: defendants will be liable if they knew that a statement in a publication was false, even if they thought they had taken steps to prevent its continued distribution. Knowledge of an employee can be attributed to the company.[17]

---

[14]   Department of Environment, Transport and the Regions *Green Claims Code* (1998).
[15]   Page 353 below.
[16]   *Wings Ltd v Ellis* [1985] AC 272, [1984] 3 All ER 577.
[17]   Page 327 below.

Recklessness gives rise to liability under s 14(1)(b). Recklessness has a broad meaning and covers situations where businesses simply ignore the truth or falsity of their statements. There is no need to establish dishonesty or that a business has deliberately closed its eyes to the truth.[18] Whereas sub-s (1)(b) does not require knowledge of the making of the statement, that seems to be a prerequisite in sub-s (1)(a).

The departure from strict liability was originally justified because of the novelty of the section. The only present justification must be that this acts as a safeguard because the description of services is likely to be more subjective than of products, and because an indefinite range of matters can be caught by the section. The former argument is now without any basis after 30 years of operation of the legislation. The other argument must be juxtaposed with the illogicality of treating the description of products and services differently when their supply is often closely linked. As long ago as 1968, the Review Committee on the Trade Descriptions Act 1968 concluded that liability for the misdescription of products and of services should be assimilated on the same strict liability basis.[19] No distinction between products and services is made for pricing offences under the Consumer Protection Act 1987. Strict liability obtains in relation to misdescribed services in other jurisdictions. The DTI has accepted the logic of these arguments and is proposing to create a strict liability offence of falsely describing services.[1]

Although s 14 applies to anything likely to be taken for a statement as to any of the matters specified in the section, it is somewhat narrowed by use of the term 'false' (despite the side-heading to the section) and the omission of specific reference to statements which are simply misleading. 'Services' means doing something for another, and includes professional services. 'Accommodation' is taken to mean short-term lettings and arguably applies to time shares. The term 'facilities' is wide enough to cover ancillary aspects of consumer transactions, such as insurance, credit, guarantees or the offer of products on approval or with free carriage.[2] The location of services and facilities would seem to fall outside the Act, as well as statements about the need for them. False statements about the price of services or facilities are not covered by the section unless the price relates to the 'provision' or 'nature' of these or the 'manner' in which

---

[18]   Section 14(2)(b); *MFI Warehouses Ltd v Nattrass* [1973] 1 All ER 762, [1973] 1 WLR 307; *Yugotours Ltd v Wadsley* [1988] BTLC 300.

[19]   OFT *Review of the Trade Descriptions Act 1968* (Cmnd 6628 (1976)) p 20. See also *Kirwin v Anderson* (1991) 156 JP 301.

[1]   DTI *Modern Markets: Confident Consumers* (Cm 4410 (1999)) para 3.19; DTI *Amendments to the Trade Descriptions Act 1968* (2000).

[2]   For example *Bambury v Hounslow London Borough Council* [1971] RTR 1; *Ashley v Sutton London Borough Council* (1994) 159 JP 631.

they are provided.[3] The courts have confined s 14 to statements of fact of which it can be said at the time they are made that they are either true or false. Statements about the future—assurances, promises or predictions—are not caught unless they imply a statement of present fact; for example, about the intention of a business or about its capacity to realise its intentions.[4] The approach is in keeping with the law of misrepresentation where the plaintiff must prove that there is a false representation of fact as distinct from the failure to fulfil a promise. However, in interpreting the section in this way the courts have robbed it of a protection it was originally thought to have.

A well-known case is *Beckett v Cohen*[5] where a builder undertook to complete a garage in ten days and to build it 'as the existing [garage]' but did not finish it within the period nor construct it similar to the one already standing. The Divisional Court held that no offence was committed because the undertaking was a promise, unrelated to existing fact. Lord Widgery CJ said of s 14 that Parliament never contemplated for a moment that the Act should be used to make a criminal offence out of what was really a breach of warranty. The decision would have been different, however, if the defendant had never intended to complete the work as contracted or was clearly unable to do so. It has been suggested that legislation should overturn judicial interpretation of s 14, to make it an offence to supply services or facilities which do not correspond with the description by reference to which they are supplied.[6] A defence would be necessary for persons who, discovering they are unable to supply the service or facility as described, take steps to inform intending recipients.

Many of the cases about future services have concerned statements in the advertisements of travel agents or tour operators which prove to be untrue when consumers take their holidays. Trading standards departments have received thousands of complaints from consumers aggrieved about poor value for money, inferior hotels, inadequate food or poor facilities. The Code of the Association of British Travel Agents purports to regulate some of these matters. The relevant law is considered in Chapter 6, but it is worthwhile noting at this point that under the package travel regulations organisers and retailers must not supply misleading information in any descriptive material concerning a package holiday: if they do so they are liable to compensate consumers for any loss incurred as a result of relying on that information.[7] Convictions have been obtained under s 14 where

---

[3]   As we will see, the Consumer Protection Act 1987 applies to services.
[4]   *R v Avro plc* (1993) 12 Tr LR 83.
[5]   [1973] 1 All ER 120, [1972] 1 WLR 1593.
[6]   OFT *Review of the Trade Descriptions Act 1968* (Cmnd 6628 (1976)) p 34.
[7]   Package Travel, Package Holidays and Package Tours Regulations 1992, SI 1992/3288, reg 4.

advertisements have been interpreted as describing an existing state of affairs. In one, a business issued a brochure purportedly describing a hotel which was not completed, while in another a trip continued to be advertised although it had been cancelled.[8] Contrast *R v Sunair Holidays Ltd*[9] where convictions were quashed because a statement in a brochure as to a swimming pool could be interpreted as a simple promise, unrelated to existing fact, and it was not disputed that the other statements related to the future.

British Airways Board v Taylor[10] is the leading case on statements about the future; it concerned airline overbooking. Many airlines operate a policy of overbooking to counteract 'no-shows', that is, passengers who make reservations on flights but do not appear. No-shows are usually far higher on the main business air routes because some business people who intend to travel on a certain day book every flight in the timetable and then take whichever is most convenient. Airlines could discourage no-shows by suing for breach of contract, but accept them as part of commercial life. The practice inevitably results in the occasional off-loading ('bumping') of passengers who have booked but these are few when compared with the number of no-shows, especially high on some routes.[11]

The decision in the case of *Taylor* ultimately turned on the point that the British Airways Board was not liable for the criminal acts of BOAC, which was the airline involved. But the House of Lords accepted that a breach of the Trade Descriptions Act 1968, s 14 had occurred, since BOAC had written to the consumer confirming his flight without qualification. The confirmation involved BOAC in knowingly making a false statement about its intention as to the provision or timing of a service, since it implied that there was a seat reserved for the consumer when there was always the intention of 'bumping' if more passengers arrived than there were seats available. Three Lords expressly approved MacKenna J's judgment in *R v Sunair Holidays Ltd*.[12]

In the course of the argument in *Taylor*'s case, the policy of overbooking flights was mentioned. The House of Lords refused to countenance whether the policy was commercially sound, fair to passengers, or operated conscientiously. Such questions, it held, were primarily within the control

---

[8]   *R v Clarksons Holidays Ltd* (1972) 57 Cr App Rep 38, [1972] Crim LR 653 is a leading case.

[9]   [1973] 2 All ER 1233, [1973] 1 WLR 1105; cf *Sunair Holidays Ltd v Dodd* [1970] 2 All ER 410, [1970] 1 WLR 1037.

[10] [1976] 1 All ER 65, [1976] 1 WLR 13.

[11] The practice is now regulated by Council Regulation (EEC) No 295/91 of 4 February 1991 establishing common rules for a denied-boarding compensation system in scheduled air transport, OJ L 036 08.02.1991 p 5. See pp 218, above and 425 below.

[12] [1973] 2 All ER 1233, [1973] 1 WLR 1105.

of administrative authorities. One approach is to ensure that it was made clear to consumers that they might be 'bumped'. Another is a scheme under which the airlines must recompense passengers who find themselves off-loaded—payment varying on the length of the flight, and on how long passengers have to wait for another seat. Prohibiting over-booking in the absence of effective measures against no-shows would be uneconomical because airlines would operate at less than their potential capacity. Fares would increase, contrary to the interests of most passengers. On the other hand it is difficult to control no-shows except by imposing reconfirmation requirements, or by obliging prospective customers to place a deposit which would be forfeited if they failed to appear.

Another House of Lords decision involving travel, *Wings Ltd v Ellis*[13] establishes the important point that a statement may be made for the purposes of s 14 not only when it is initially made but as long as it has real effect. The upshot is that a statement which is broadcast, or which is contained in a publication, may give rise to multiple prosecutions. It is a continuing statement until it is somehow exhausted. Prior to that the only limit on multiple prosecutions is that the courts may stay them as oppressive or impose nominal penalties.

(c)   Mispricing

Legislation prohibiting false statements of price is quite distinct from price control. The present concern is not with selling at an unduly high price, but with false representations about price. The initial law in this area, s 11 of the Trade Descriptions Act 1968, was limited when compared with that in other countries. Subsequently it was supplemented by the Price Marking (Bargain Offers) Order 1979, but the consensus seemed to be that this was too convoluted.[14] It was a salutary lesson in the value of broad standards, backed by more detailed controls. The Price Marking (Bargain Offers) Order was an example of regulation so complex that neither regulators nor regulated found it truly comprehensible, so that on the one side there was a failure to enforce, and on the other a failure to take seriously.[15] Moreover, no attempt to cover the field exhaustively ever succeeds, and in this case there were gaps where businesses took advantage, complying with the letter of the law but making a mockery of its spirit.

The upshot was the introduction of a general offence of giving a misleading price indication, s 20(1) of the Consumer Protection Act 1987:

---

[13]   [1985] AC 272, [1984] 3 All ER 577.
[14]   SI 1979/364 as amended.
[15]   A Ogus *Regulation: Legal Form and Economic Theory* (OUP, 1994) pp 145–146.

… a person shall be guilty of an offence if, in the course of any business of his, he gives (by any means whatever) to any consumers an indication which is misleading as to the price at which any goods, services, accommodation or facilities are available (whether generally or from particular persons).

This general provision is backed by a Code of Practice. Misleading is extensively defined in s 21 of the Act—if a business indicates that a price is less than in fact it is; that the applicability of a price does not depend on certain facts and circumstances on which in fact it does depend; that a stated price covers matters in respect of which an additional charge will be made; that, when there is no such expectation, it is expected that a price will be increased, reduced or maintained; and that the facts or circumstances by reference to which consumers might reasonably be expected to judge the validity of any relevant comparison are not what in fact they are. It is not necessary that a misleading price indication be given to any particular consumer or that any particular person be misled.[16]

The Code of Practice, issued under s 25 of the Act, identifies desirable pricing practices.[17] Non-compliance with the Code may be relied on as evidence in determining whether there has been a breach of s 20(1). In other words, the legal question is whether there has been a breach of the general mispricing section, and breach of the Code itself is not necessarily an offence. In practice a breach of the Code will tend to constitute a s 20(1) offence,[18] although there is a case for making many of the provisions in the Code directly enforceable regulations.[19] The Code has not been kept up to date, although the Local Authorities Co-ordinating Body on Trading Standards (LACOTS) issued a circular in 1995 to cover 'factory outlet centres', a recent development where a number of outlets offer discounted prices on items which may be seconds, samples or simply overstocks. DTI plans to update the Code, announced in 1999, have apparently been put on hold.

As well as the general mispricing offence there are regulations on specific points of pricing practice made under s 26 of the Act. These have a limited scope. One set deals with businesses which charge more when, say, a credit card is used as payment: if that is the case, the consumer must be advised before making payment that this method is not covered by any indicated price, as well as the difference payable.[20] Another set of

---

[16] *MFI Furniture Centre Ltd v Hibbert* (1996) 160 JP 178.
[17] Consumer Protection (Code of Practice for Traders on Price Indications) Approval Order 1988, SI 1988/2078.
[18] Cf *R v Parris* (1988) 89 Cr App Rep 68.
[19] As recommended by the majority of the *Monitoring Committee on Misleading Price Indications: Report to Ministers*, nd.
[20] Price Indications (Method of Payment) Regulations 1991, SI 1991/199. Motor fuel is excluded.

regulations oblige bureaux de change to give comprehensive and clear indications of what exchange rates operate.[1] A third set of regulations obliges ticket touts and others reselling tickets for entertainment to give price and other information.[2] Compulsory marking of prices, and unit pricing, are considered in the following chapter. Price indications about credit terms must comply with the Consumer Credit Act 1974. Both regulators and government have also deployed self-regulatory approaches to problems in particular sectors. The telecommunications regulator, OFTEL, has on a number of occasions attempted to regulate the display of prices charged by hotels for phone calls made from guests' rooms. Finding that its powers were deficient it has attempted to secure the incorporation of obligations to display prices in codes of practice used by the hotel trade.[3] More recently the DTI has taken up the issue as part of plans for a new harmonised grading scheme for hotels which will include obligations to display charging information for bedroom telephones.

Misleading price claims, which are potentially within s 20(1), can take many forms. *Overcharging* is one, as where an item on display bears one price, but another, usually higher, price is indicated when its barcode is scanned at the check-out counter.[4] Unless the shop operates a policy of charging the ticket price, an offence is committed since a misleading indication of the actual price—the price 'required to be paid', s 20(6)—is being given. Even if the shop has such a policy, an offence is committed if, despite the policy, items are not available at the ticket price because cashiers and customers do not notice the discrepancies and have them corrected.[5] Obliging shops in these circumstances to make the item available free of charge would be an additional sanction against wrongdoing. As far as dishonest overcharging is concerned, this could found a prosecution for obtaining property by deception.[6]

Price comparisons are a common marketing technique. Under EC law restrictions on price comparisons which are not misleading (eg because they are 'eye-catching') are not permitted, since the operation of the internal market would be impeded.[7] Section 21(3) defines 'comparison' to include 'any comparison of price, or method of calculating the price, of the goods

---

[1]   Price Indications (Bureaux de Change) Regulations 1992, SI 1992/316.
[2]   Price Indications (Resale of Tickets) Regulations 1994, SI 1994/3248.
[3]   C Hall, C Scott and C Hood *Telecommunications Regulation: Culture, Chaos and Interdependence Inside the Regulatory Process* (Routledge, 2000) pp 161–169.
[4]   Dishonest overcharging may constitute a criminal offence under the Theft Act 1968.
[5]   *Toys'R'Us v Gloucestershire County Council* (1994) 158 JP 338. See also Code of Practice, para 2.1.
[6]   *R v Silverman* (1987) 86 Cr App Rep 213; *R v Jones* (1993) Times, 15 February.
[7]   *Schutzverband gegen unwesen in der Wirtschafts v Yves Rocher GmbH* Case C-126/91 [1993] ECR 1-2361.

in question with any price or value or any method of calculation which is stated in the indication or implied by it as a present, past or future attribution of price or calculation'. The Code devotes a great deal of attention to price comparisons. Businesses are told to make clear whether or not a price comparison is being made (para 1.1.1). Any price comparison should always state the higher price, as well as the price which it is intended to be charged (para 1.1.2). It should be clear what sort of price the higher price is, for example whose 'regular', 'usual' or 'normal' price is being referred to (para 1.1.3).

Generally speaking, in any comparison with a business' own previous price, the Code requires that:

(a) the previous price should be the *last* price at which the product was available to consumers in the previous six months;
(b) the product should have been available to consumers at that price for at least 28 consecutive days in the previous six months;
(c) the product must not have been offered at a different price between that 28-day period and the day when the reduced price is first offered; and
(d) the previous price should have applied for that period at the place where the reduced price is now being offered (para 1.2.2).[8]

Otherwise, businesses must explain precisely and prominently the circumstances of the higher price used in the comparison—for example 'these goods were on sale here at the higher price from 1 February to 26 May' or 'these goods were on sale at the higher price in 10 of our 95 stores only' (para 1.2.3). As these permissible comparisons demonstrate, there is an almost impossible burden cast on enforcement officers. Resources are not available to monitor continually a wide range of prices over a long period, and it should not be surprising that prosecutions do not generally occur unless consumers complain. Putting the burden on businesses to justify such price indications will go some way towards lessening the enforcement burden. By way of comparison with the general law of trade descriptions the Code deprecates general disclaimers, for example, that the higher prices indicated have not necessarily applied for 28 consecutive days (para 1.2.3).

The Code covers other comparisons as well, such as 'perfect' comparisons (eg 'seconds £20, when perfect £30') and comparisons for special groups of people (eg lower prices for new customers). Comparisons with another business' prices are also referred to: a business must only make the comparison if it knows that the price quoted is accurate and up to

---

[8]   There are special rules for food and drink, and for catalogue and mail order (paras 1.2.5–1.2.6).

date, the name of the other business and its location is given, and the products involved are the same or substantially the same (para 1.4.6). In *MGN Ltd v Ritters*[9] a national newspaper ran an advertisement offering a £50 watch for £4.99. The Divisional Court dismissed the newspaper's appeal, since under s 20(1) of the Consumer Protection Act 1987, it was necessary in all but exceptional cases to show that there were indeed articles of the description under offer already available for sale on the open market, so that the necessary price comparison could be made.

Comparisons with 'recommended retail prices' and 'manufacturers' recommended prices' have featured in a considerable number of prosecutions. These offences are easy to prove and trading standards departments have justified prosecution because of their prevalence and the way they mislead customers. Should recommended prices be allowed at all? Among arguments in favour of recommended prices is that they are necessary to guarantee the margins of distributors and to avoid excessive price-cutting and other unethical practices.[10] Administrative convenience for retailers in pricing their goods—calculating, negotiating and marking prices—is another factor mentioned, although this is not as compelling a reason where competition means widespread divergence from recommended prices or where retailers handle a small range of products. Recommended prices are also said to assist consumers: they can see whether they are obtaining a bargain and competition between manufacturers is promoted. On the other hand recommended prices may reduce price competition by inducing retailers to charge that price. On this basis power to prohibit them was contained in the Price Commission Act 1977. Moreover recommended prices, when they are well above the actual selling price, can mislead those consumers who regard them as the normal selling price.[11] The discrepancy occurs in areas of trade where competition is vigorous but also where manufacturers deliberately set recommended prices at a high level to enable retailers to show large price cuts, and where several levels of recommended prices exist so that retailers can select those which they will discount. Another reason recommended prices can be misleading is that, unless consumers know the particular recommended price, they cannot assess whether the reduction has been made by the retailer. Thus it falls to enforcement bodies, who have this information, continually to check the products which are subject to recommended price claims.

In 1978 the Director General of Fair Trading recommended that all bargain offer claims which indicate that the seller's price is less than a recommended,

---

[9]   (1997) 16 Tr LR 427.
[10]   Monopolies Commission *Recommended Resale Prices* (HMSO, 1969) p 3.
[11]   See OFT *Bargain Offer Claims* (HMSO, 1975) p 189. See also Price Commission *Recommended Retail Prices* Report No 25 (1977) p 17.

suggested or maximum retail price should be prohibited because they are unhelpful or even positively misleading. The Price Marking (Bargain Offers) Order (as amended) prohibited recommended prices for certain scheduled items, namely, beds, electrically-powered and similar domestic appliances, consumer electronic goods, carpets and furniture.[12] The sectoral approach to banning recommended prices was criticised as leading to confusion and anomalies, and to traders establishing their own list prices as a basis for price comparison advertising, regardless of whether they ever intended to charge those prices. The Director General of Fair Trading reiterated his call for a complete ban on the use of recommended prices, but if the sectoral approach was continued suggested that additional sectors be included, and that any recommended retail prices should be stated in cash terms or that the difference be calculable, and that retailers be prohibited from establishing their own recommended prices.[13]

The Code of Practice contains a permissive regime for recommended prices. It forbids the use of initials or abbreviations, except 'RRP' to describe a recommended retail price, and the abbreviation 'man rec price' to describe a manufacturer's recommended price (para 1.6.2). However it permits the use of such recommended prices, subject to some qualifications. Firstly, it must be a price recommended by a manufacturer or supplier: thus a retailer cannot recommend a price to itself. Secondly, the business must have dealt with the manufacturer or supplier on normal commercial terms. This qualification is designed to prevent powerful retailers pressuring manufacturers or suppliers to 'recommend' a higher price than would otherwise be the case. Finally, the price must not be significantly higher than retail prices at which the product is generally sold at the time of the comparison—another condition designed to put a brake on unrealistic recommended prices.

General 'sale' notices are misleading if the great majority of items are being sold at normal prices, or if the sale items are specially made for the sale. Provided the sale items themselves are properly marked to comply with the Code provisions on price comparisons previously mentioned, sale notices are generally permitted (para 1.9.2). If a business has bought in items especially for a sale, and this is made clear, one price only may be quoted (para 1.9.1). General notices such as 'up to 50% off' must not be used unless the reduction applies to at least 10% by quantity of items on sale. However, sales which are still going on months after they began are too common a feature of the retailing landscape. One largely unexplored possibility is action under the Control of Misleading Advertisements

---

[12] SI 1979/364, article 5; Schedule (as amended).
[13] Director General of Fair Trading *Review of the Price Marking (Bargain Offers) Orders (1979)* (OFT, 1981) paras 5.9.3–5.10.

Regulations 1988.[14] Some European countries have very tight control over sales; for example in Germany they can only be held at certain times of the year.[15]

'Worth' and *'value' claims* can be either vacuous or incapable of substantiation. They are deprecated in the Code—retailers are told not to compare their prices with an amount described only as 'worth' or 'value', and not to use these claims in a way likely to be seen by consumers as a price comparison. *MGN Ltd v Northamptonshire County Council*[16] establishes that there will generally be a breach of s 20(1) in the case of a 'worth' or 'value' claim if a product is not on offer to the general public at the time the advertisement is published at the price which it is said to be worth or valued. In other words, retailers will generally have to establish that there are indeed articles of the description for sale on the open market, so the necessary price comparisons can be made.

False indications of the actual price to consumers include items advertised as being at a price and then a higher price being charged. Under previous legislation the courts held that the maxim *de minimis* had no relevance to mispricing of this nature, however small the discrepancy.[17] Their approach can be justified because although an individual consumer may suffer little, unfair profits accrue to businesses. There is no reason for this approach not to apply to s 20(1) of the Consumer Protection Act 1987. The Code of Practice also deals with other examples of the actual price to consumers being different than what is advertised, as where there are non-optional extras, where the quantities available are limited, or where there are minimum call-out charges. Under the Prices Act 1974 the government has statutory power to require businesses to mark prices and several orders have been made, but we shall see in the next chapter that there has been less obligatory price marking compared with other European countries.

Many ordinary consumers do not know that they can oblige a business to adhere to the *price quoted* in a contract. Even if they do they are at a disadvantage with an intransigent business if they have paid a deposit or they want that particular item, since they are virtually forced to pay the higher price unless they are prepared to incur legal costs.[18] Section 29(2)

---

[14] Page 60 above.

[15] See RG Lawson *Advertising and Labelling Laws in the Common Market* (Jordans, 2nd edn, 1981) Chapter 10, paras 1–4.

[16] (1997) 161 JP 735.

[17] Eg *Doble v David Greig Ltd* [1972] 2 All ER 195, [1972] 1 WLR 703; *Nattrass v Marks & Spencer Ltd* (1981) 89 ITSA MR 211 noted by Peter Clark '"De Minimis": How Not to Deal With It' (1981) 145 JP 753.

[18] *Simmons v Emmett* (1982) 90 MR 97 is a good example: a deposit had been paid on flowers for a wedding: when they arrived on the wedding day a higher price was requested. What customer in this type of situation, when the florist refuses to

of the 1987 Act makes it an offence to give a price indication which, although correct at the time, subsequently becomes misleading if consumers could reasonably be expected still to be relying on it, and the business does not take reasonable steps preventing them from doing so. In fact continuing offers may be brought under s 20(1) as well. In *Warwickshire County Court v Johnson*[19] the House of Lords had to consider an offer that the retailer would beat any price in town by £20 for an identical product. It was a continuing offer, true at the time it was displayed, but rendered untrue when the branch manager refused to honour it. The House of Lords had no difficulty in concluding that the statement was misleading, since to hold otherwise 'would be seriously to restrict the efficacy of this part of the consumer protection legislation'.[20]

An incidental aspect of the subject is that prices quoted should generally be inclusive of VAT. Where most business is with trade customers, then VAT can be quoted separately, so long as it is clearly indicated. Quotations for building work, and fees for future professional services when no precise amount is quoted, can be given as 'plus VAT at x%'.

While an advance on previous legislation, s 20(1) of the Consumer Protection Act 1987 contains some real defects. Firstly, it is confined to misleading indications given to consumers. Therefore it is not an offence for a wholesaler to give a misleading price indication to a retailer, nor to give a misleading indication as to the price of products which by their nature could not have been intended for private use or consumption.[1] There is no such limitation in relation to misdescriptions of products: there is no basis for the distinction. Secondly, it has been held that the phrase 'in the course of any business of his' in s 20(1) excludes the prosecution of employees.[2] While supportable on policy grounds, this conclusion enables employers more readily to invoke the statutory defences, considered below, since an offence can be attributed to the fault of an employee. Thirdly, as we have seen, the Code giving substance to s 20(1) is ripe for review.

(d) Property

Although s 14 of the Trade Descriptions Act 1968 covers services, accommodation and facilities, 'accommodation' does not extend to

---

hand the flowers over unless the higher price is paid, will go out and obtain flowers elsewhere and sue the first florist later for return of the deposit?
[19] [1993] 1 All ER 299.
[20] At p 302.
[1] *MFI Furniture Centres Ltd v Hibbert* (1995) 160 JP 178.
[2] *Warwickshire County Council v Johnson* [1993] 1 All ER 299.

dispositions of substantial interests in property; rather it applies to short-term leases like those associated with holiday lettings.[3] However, descriptions of houses and property may fall within other heads of the Act, such as s 1. In *Breed v Cluett*,[4] 20 days after the exchange of contracts for the sale of a bungalow the builder wrongly stated it was covered by the National House Building Council long-term guarantee. The Divisional Court held, firstly, that statements covered by s 14 are not confined to those inducing the entering into of a contract. 'There may well be statements made after a contract is completed—a contract for repairs to my motorcar, a contract for repair to my roof, stating the effect of what has been done by way of repair which may constitute an offence if made recklessly—even though the contract has been completed and the payment has been made.'[5] Secondly, the court accepted that the builder's statement could be about the provision of services, viz performance of an obligation during the ten-year guarantee period.

However, the Trade Descriptions Act 1968 does not apply to descriptions of the size, position or other characteristics of houses or land. Yet there have been many complaints over the years about the poetic licence, in some cases the dishonesty, of the descriptions used by estate agents and property developers. The licensing of estate agents offers some protection for consumers.[6] Moreover, consumers are normally prevented from major blunders by the expert advice of surveyors or solicitors. However, there is no reason why consumers should incur an unnecessary waste of time and expense in viewing property and perhaps arranging for surveyors when this would never have been done if it had not been misdescribed.

This is some of the background to the Property Misdescriptions Act 1991. Section 1(1) of the 1991 Act creates the offences of making a false or misleading statement about a prescribed matter. The list of prescribed matters is extensive. Matters include the proximity to any services or amenities; accommodation; measurement or sizes; fixtures and fittings;

---

[3] It is arguable that it extends to houses on long leases or for sale; the word is used in these senses by estate agents. See G Stephenson, 'Estate Agents and Trade Descriptions' [1980] Conveyancer 249, 254–255.

[4] [1970] 2 QB 459.

[5] [1970] 2 QB 459 at 462.

[6] See p 448 below. In the United States, there is extensive regulation of land sales, in particular of permissible descriptions: 15 USC §§1701–1720. See also J Oliver 'Beyond Consumer Protection: The Application of the Interstate Land Sales Full Disclosure Act to Condominium Sales' (1985) 37 U Fla LR 945; RM Friedman 'Regulation of Interstate Land Sales: Is Full Disclosure Sufficient?' (1980) 20 Urban L Ann 137.

and history, including the ownership of land.[7] The offences can be committed by estate agents and property developers, but not by anyone providing conveyancing services. It is uncertain whether foreign land is covered. Falsity must be to a material degree but omissions are covered, because a statement can be misleading 'if (though not false) what a reasonable person may be expected to infer from it, or from any omission from it, is false' (s 1(5)(a), (b)). A statement can be made by pictures, although whether a statement can be disclaimed by pictures would depend on whether it is effectively negated.

The Act has had a welcome impact on the accuracy of particulars for houses and land. Flowery language and grandiose claims have been curbed. Moreover, estate agents are now providing additional information such as floor plans. There is some criticism among estate agents but, to avoid being caught under the Act, many of their property descriptions have become so cautious as to be unhelpful. However, misdescriptions of property also give rise to civil liability, and there have been some important cases, so it is somewhat disingenuous to blame the Act alone for any change in estate agency practices.[8] Estate agents and property developers may have a defence under the Act if they have relied on information provided by the seller.[9]

Whether all statements about house and property prices should be controlled is a matter on which some commentators have expressed doubt. A particular aspect is 'gazumping', whereby those selling property agree to sell at a price 'subject to contract' but later withdraw or threaten to do so in expectation of a higher price.[10] The prospective purchaser who has been gazumped is then put in the position of having to pay the higher price or losing the house. Arguments against bringing gazumping within the trade descriptions net are that the problem only arises when houses are in short supply, and that it is unfair to invoke the criminal law against sellers, while leaving buyers free not to continue in order to pay less. The solution may lie in the civil law, where 'lock-out' agreements are enforceable, under which sellers bind themselves for a fee to sell to a particular buyer at a specified price and not to deal with anyone else.[11] Lock out agreements, however, cannot compel the seller to sell. Another

---

[7] Property Misdescriptions (Specified Matters) Order 1992, SI 1992/2834. See R Rowell and J Hancock *Regulating the Sale of Property* (Central Law Publishing, 1993).

[8] Eg *McCullagh v Lane Fox & Partners Ltd* [1996] 1 EGLR 35, (1997) 61 Conv 229

[9] Section 2. See *Enfield London Borough Council v Castle Estate Agents Ltd* (1996) 73 P & CR 343.

[10] M Thompson 'The Fight Against Gazumping' [1997] Amicus Curiae 28.

[11] *Pitt v PHH Asset Management* [1994] 1 WLR 327.

possibility is to oblige sellers to pay buyers' conveyancing and survey costs if they sell elsewhere. Speeding up the conveyancing process would also help, by reducing the time during which other buyers can enter the fray.

(e) Other misstatements

Misstatements other than those mentioned can cause consumer loss, but are not always covered by the legislation outlined. False statements by persons about their qualifications have given rise to difficulty in the past, but in some cases the courts have been able to bring these under the Trade Descriptions Act.[12] Misstatements about availability are particularly worrisome. Non-availability of an advertised product or service can cause consumers loss in time and money if they go to the trouble of visiting the retailer but discover that it is unavailable. Businesses can benefit unjustifiably. The problem is acute with the 'specials' retailers advertise. Once consumers enter a retailer's premises because its advertisements suggest that it has the best 'specials', they may complete a transaction, even if some of the 'specials' are not available, because of the inconvenience of going elsewhere. In its most extreme form non-availability constitutes the practice of 'bait and switch'. 'Bait and switch' is where a seller seeks to attract customers by advertising a product or service, which it does not intend to sell, at an extremely low price. When a consumer responds to the advertisement, the seller discourages him or her from purchasing the 'bait' and instead tries to 'switch' him or her to a higher priced, more profitable, item. In the United States studies have demonstrated that 'bait and switch' advertising is used by ghetto merchants to the detriment of consumers. A closely related practice with services is 'lo-balling', a term developed to cover situations where companies advertise repairs at low prices as an enticement to obtain possession of products so that the owner can be charged for additional, unnecessary repairs.

There is some protection against these practices as a result of a recent amendment of the EC Directive on Misleading Advertising.[13] Under the new regulations comparisons referring to 'special offers' must indicate in a clear and unequivocal way the date when the offers end or, where appropriate, that the special offer is subject to the availability of the product or service (reg 5). If the special offer has not yet begun, the date of the

12 *Edward A Savory & Associates Ltd v Noel Dawson* (26 February 1976, unreported).
13 Directive 97/55/EC [1997] OJ No L 290; the Control of Misleading Advertisements (Comparative Advertisements) (Amendment) Regulations 2000, SI 2000/914.

start of the period must be given. However, there is no legal underpinning that a product or service will be available, despite the advertising.

Can it be argued that the availability of goods is a facility and hence any false statement is actionable under s 14 of the Trade Descriptions Act 1968? In *Westminster County Council v Ray Alan (Manshops) Ltd*[14] the Divisional Court held that there was no infringement of s 14 of the Trade Descriptions Act 1968 when a retailer advertised a 'Closing Down Sale', although in fact it continued to trade. The prosecution had unsuccessfully argued before the magistrates that the advertisement constituted a recklessly false statement within s 14(1)(ii) as to the nature of facilities provided in the course of a trade or business. On appeal Ormrod LJ held that the word 'facilities' in s 14 should be construed *ejusdem generis* with the preceding words 'services'; and 'accommodation'. Although 'facilities' had a very wide meaning, and was increasingly popular in commercial circles, it had to be construed strictly in a penal statute such as the Trade Descriptions Act 1968. Woolf J agreed, but he conceded that if 'facilities' had appeared by itself it could cover shopping facilities. With regard to use of the *ejusdem generis* rule, it can hardly be said that 'services' and 'accommodation' are of the same kind or nature to qualify the meaning of 'facilities'.[15] Moreover, weighed against the penal nature of s 14 is the desirability, in Woolf J's words, 'for there to be some protection for the public which prevented persons advertising something as a closing down sale if it is not such a sale'.

Other countries have specific legislation for non-availability of advertised sale items. For example, under s 56(1) of the Australian Trade Practices Act 1974[16] a corporation commits an offence if it advertises goods or services for supply at a special price but does not intend to offer them for supply at that price for a period that is, and in quantities that are, reasonable having regard to the nature of the market and advertisement.

---

[14]   [1982] 1 All ER 771.

[15]   Ormrod LJ said that 'services' implies activities ('Hotels or business of all kinds provide services, meaning that they do something for the customer'), so that facilities means making things available in a more passive sense (p 774). But why not conclude that facilities implies activities as well, in this case shopping facilities? Cf *Brooks v Club Continental Ltd* (13 October 1981, unreported), noted in G Stephenson 'False and Misleading Price Comparisons' (1982) 45 MLR 710, 712.

[16]   See *Reardon v Morley Ford Pty Ltd* (1980) 49 FLR 401. The Federal Trade Commission in the United States has a regulation making it an unfair or deceptive practice to advertise food for retail if the relevant stores do not have the advertised products in stock and readily available during the effective period of the advertisement (unless the advertisement states clearly that supplies are limited or available in only limited stores): 16 CFR §424.1. The FTC has also issued guidelines describing unlawful 'bait and switch' practices: 16 CFR §238. See *Peterman v US Department of Agriculture* 770 F 2d 888 (1985). See also *Tashof v FTC* 437 F 2d 707 (1970).

To avoid the difficulties of the prosecution having to prove intention, the section also creates an offence if a corporation, having advertised goods or services for supply at a special price, fails to offer such goods or services for supply at that price for a period that is, and in quantities that are, reasonable, having regard to the nature of the market and the nature of the advertisement (s 56(2)). The qualifications in this offence ensure that a genuine selling campaign is not placed at risk. Moreover, the section provides for a corporation facing genuine difficulties in giving it a defence if it establishes that if offered to supply or procure the goods or services advertised within a reasonable time or that it offered to supply or procure equivalent goods or services within a reasonable time (s 56(3)).

2 THE QUALITY OF FOOD

Quality is primarily a matter for private law. Products, for example, must be of satisfactory quality and fit for the purpose, but if they are not it is the consumer who must institute legal action against the business involved. Chapter 10 examines a number of products, potentially dangerous to humans, for which detailed safety standards have been set. A limited number of provisions also exist which incorporate quality standards into the criminal law. Reference can be made, for example, to s 75 of the Road Traffic Act 1988, which makes it illegal to sell, supply, offer to sell or to supply, or to expose for sale, unroadworthy vehicles. The most important of these broad criminal provisions, and the concern of this section, are those directed at sub-standard food and drink.

Legislation in 1860 laid the foundation for the general framework of control for food quality.[17] Until then the quality of food depended on a combination of the common law and specific enactment. The former was concerned with those serious cases where food was potentially injurious to health. It was an offence knowingly to sell someone food injurious to health or to mix noxious ingredients with a food.[18] If someone died as a result of eating unwholesome food the seller could be indicted for manslaughter if he had sold the food knowingly or negligently.[19] In addition, a common law nuisance arose whenever diseased or unwholesome

---

[17] See generally E Stieb *Drug Adulteration Detection and Control in Nineteenth-Century Britain* (University of Wisconsin Press, 1963); I Paulus *The Search for Pure Food* (Martin Robertson, 1974); PS Atiyah *The Rise and Fall of Freedom of Contract* (Clarendon, 1979) pp 546–547; FB Smith *The People's Health 1830–1910* (Croom Helm, 1979) pp 203–215. See also F Engels *The Condition of the Working-Class in England* (Progress Publishers, 1973) pp 98–100.

[18] *R v Dixon* (1814) 105 ER 516.

[19] *R v Kempson* (1893) 28 L Jo 477.

food was exposed for sale.[20] Specific enactments were designed mainly to prevent the adulteration of products on which excise duty was payable. The preambles to legislation on tea, coffee and beer in the eighteenth and early nineteenth centuries recited that adulteration threatened public health, ruined fair trade and diminished the revenue.[1] The latter consideration was apparently paramount. Thus, when a duty was imposed on chicory comparable to that on coffee, the Board of Revenue no longer interfered with the mixture of these substances since its previous concern had been simply to prevent the evasion of excise duty on the latter.[2] Earlier legislation was motivated by a more general concern with public health: bread was regulated from 1266 by the Assize of Bread and Ale,[3] and support was given to guilds in their attempts to suppress food adulteration.

Writers like Hassall described in the nineteenth century how milk was watered, alum added to flour and lead acetate used to sweeten beer. The aim was to lower the price of foods by mixing in other, cheaper substances to improve the appearance of adulterated articles.[4] In some cases the adulterants were of an innocuous character but others were actually injurious to health as well as being a fraud on the public. In the 'Bradford Incident' in 1858, 200 people were poisoned eating adulterated lozenges, 17 fatally. Finally Parliament was impelled to act. Not without some opposition,[5] the view was abandoned that the forces of competition and the knowledge of the consumer were sufficient to guarantee the sale of unadulterated foodstuffs of adequate quality.[6]

Instead of forbidding the use of particular substances or processes, or of directing that food be treated in specified ways,[7] the 1860 legislation contained a broad and simple provision making it unlawful for a person knowingly to sell food which contained injurious substances or which was adulterated or impure. Offenders were subject to a fine and—a sanction not included in later legislation—a court could publicise that a trader had been convicted of a particular offence, perhaps by a newspaper advertisement. In practice, the Act proved a failure because Parliament did

---

[20]   *Shillito v Thompson* (1875) 1 QBD 12.
[1]   Tea: 11 Geo 1, c 30 (1724); 4 Geo 2, c 14 (1731); 17 Geo 3, c 29 (1766–67). Coffee: 5 Geo 1, c 11 (1718); 11 Geo 1, c 30 (1724); 43 Geo 3, c 129 (1803); cf 3 Geo 4, c 53 (1822). Beer: 56 Geo 3, c 58 (1816); 7 & 8 Geo 4, c 52 (1827).
[2]   *Report of the Commissioners of Inland Revenue* 1870, c 82, xx, 193, p 37.
[3]   51 Hen 3, st 6 (Assise Panis et cervisiae).
[4]   For example, AH Hassall *Adulterations Detected, or, Plain Instructions for the Discovery of Frauds in Food and Medicine* (Longmans, 1857).
[5]   For example J Toulmin-Smith *Local Self-Government and Centralization* (Chapman, 1851) p 335.
[6]   For example *Report from the Select Committee on Adulteration of Food etc* 1856, 379, viii, 1, p iv; Parl Deb HC vol 209, 6 March 1872, 1507.
[7]   As in the Licensing Act 1872, 35 & 36 Vict, c 94, s 19, Schedule 1.

not create the machinery for its enforcement,[8] but it represented a major blow to the principle of laissez-faire and established the important principle 'that it was within the proper role of the State to protect the consumer against injury to his pocket and his health'.[9]

The law was strengthened in the Sale of Food and Drugs Act 1875 which prohibited the admixture with food and drugs of ingredients injurious to health, and which made it an offence to abstract an ingredient so as to injuriously affect quality.[10] Most importantly, the Act made it unlawful to sell to the prejudice of a purchaser any article not of the nature, substance and quality demanded.[11] Taken in conjunction with the Public Health Act 1875, which contained provision to deal with the sale of unsound food, the aim was to safeguard the public against hazards to health and to protect it economically. In those early years the latter aim went no further than attempting to guarantee that consumers received what they ordered; but later its scope was enlarged to encompass protection from false descriptions and labelling.

The substance of this early legislation has been re-enacted in subsequent statutes and elsewhere. Safety, and ensuring that consumers obtain what would reasonably be expected, remain the basic aims of the law.[12] Current legislation, the Food Safety Act 1990, creates a number of broad offences in relation to the sale of food. It is an offence to sell food (a) which is injurious to health because of its preparation or processing; (b) which is unfit for human consumption; (c) which is so contaminated that it is not reasonable to expect it to be used for human consumption; or (d) which is not of the nature, substance or quality demanded.[13] There is also a broad trade descriptions type offence of falsely describing or presenting food.[14]

These broad provisions remain basic in controlling the quality of food despite regulations, discussed in a later chapter, which control food additives, compositional standards of food, food hygiene and so on. The 'nature, substance or quality' section quickly became the most important of the provisions in the administration of the legislation, and today many

[8]   E Ballard 'The Work of the Metropolitan Medical Officers of Health' *National Association for the Promotion of Social Science, Papers and Discussions on Public Health* (Faithful, 1862) p 123.
[9]   J Burnett *Plenty and Want. A Social History of Diet in England from 1815 to the Present Day* (Nelson, 1966) p 82. See also Parl Deb, HC, vol 156, 29 February 1860, 2025–2026.
[10]   Sections 3, 4, 9.
[11]   Section 6.
[12]   See EJ Bigwood and A Gerard *Fundamental Principles and Objectives of a Comparative Food Law* (S Karger, 1968) Volume 2, pp 58–59.
[13]   Food Safety Act 1990, ss 8, 14.
[14]   Section 15.

prosecutions are still brought under it.[15] As an illustration, Table 8.2 lists the number of prosecutions reported in the Annual Report of the Director General of Fair Trading, 1997.

Table 8.2. Prosecutions under the Food Safety Act 1990

Unfit food	69
Not of nature, substance or quality demanded	106
False or misleading description	58
Labelling regulations and other	20

The prominence of the 'nature, substance or quality' section is partly because it is an offence of strict liability.[16] Additionally, it is unnecessary to prove that a consumer has sustained actual injury in a 'nature, substance or quality' prosecution. Courts assume that a consumer who receives an article inferior to that expected or contracted for is automatically prejudiced within the meaning of the section.[17] Even if it can be shown that a consumer is not prejudiced economically, because a better quality product would cost more, there might still be prejudice within the meaning of the section. However there will be no prejudice if a consumer is notified at the time of sale that an article is not of the accepted or usual standard.[18] In *Smedleys Ltd v Breed*[19] the House of Lords accepted (Viscount Dilhorne dubitante) that the presence of a caterpillar rendered a tin of peas not of the substance demanded by the consumer, although it was quite harmless through sterilisation in the manufacturing process. Lord Diplock said that the section

> is not concerned with health or hygiene but with breaches of contracts for the sale of food or drugs ... so if the purchaser gets what he contracted to buy there is no contravention of this section, though if the food is injurious to health there may be an offence under some other section even though there is no breach of the contract of sale ... [I]n determining what was 'the food or drug demanded by the purchaser', the words by which the goods that he purchased were described must be understood in their popular sense.[20]

---

[15] For example, WJ Bell *The Sale of Food and Drugs Acts* (Shaw, 1886) p 12. See now *Butterworths Law of Food and Drugs* (looseleaf) para **B(116)**.

[16] *Betts v Armstead* (1888) 20 QBD 771.

[17] *Hoyle v Hitchman* (1879) 4 QBD 233. See also *Pearks, Gunston and Tee Ltd v Ward* [1902] 2 KB 1.

[18] For example *Williams v Friend* [1912] 2 KB 471.

[19] [1974] AC 839.

[20] [1974] AC 839 at 857.

Over the last century there has been a remarkable reduction in prosecutions for deliberately altering food (eg adding cheaper substances to a genuine article) or for compositional deficiency. Whereas packaging and preparation of foods by individual merchants gave every opportunity for such practices, precisely the opposite is the case with large-scale food manufacturers marketing prepacked products throughout the country under their brand names. Today an important concern of enforcement bodies in prosecuting food offences is the presence in food of foreign bodies and mould. Many such prosecutions arise from complaints from dissatisfied consumers rather than from the detection activities of enforcement bodies. This follows because prepacked foods cannot be thoroughly examined until after they have been opened. Insects and pieces of metal are common foreign bodies and result mainly from the mass production of food. Insects enter inadequately screened factories and metals find their way into food from insufficiently maintained machines. Poor stock rotation, especially in small shops, and inadequate storage conditions explain the incidence of many cases of mould.

The wide ambit of the broad prohibitions in food legislation means that prosecutions are relatively straightforward once the presence of a foreign body or of mould has been established. One qualification is that sometimes the presence of a sterile and harmless foreign body will not constitute an offence.[1] It is impossible to devise a test for when this happens because the judges react to the particular facts before them. On one side of the line is the extra bottle top floating in a bottle of milk; on the other, the presence of a small sliver of glass or an object like a beetle.[2] Another minor problem in enforcement is the overlap between food which is not of the nature, substance or quality demanded, and food which is unfit for human consumption or contaminated. Now Statutory Code of Practice No 1, made under s 40 of the 1990 Act, recommends that all prosecutions for contamination, whether by micro-organisms and their toxins, chemicals, mould or foreign matter, and cases involving the microbiological quality of food, should not be brought under the nature, substance and quality provision. The 'unfit for human consumption' offence occurs where food has decomposed or is putrid, and the contamination offence covers foreign bodies, mould, pesticides residues, heavy metals, mite and similar infestation, radioactive contamination and unauthorised additives.[3]

---

[1]   *Edwards v Llaethdy Meirion Ltd* [1957] Crim LR 402, 107 L Jo 138.
[2]   *Edwards v Llaethdy Meirion Ltd* [1957] Crim LR 402, 107 L Jo 138; *Greater Manchester Council v Lockwood Foods Ltd* [1979] Crim LR 593.
[3]   *Butterworths Law of Food and Drugs* (looseleaf) para **B(63)**. See eg *Kwik Save Group plc v Blaenau Gwent Borough Council* (1995) unreported CO/2246/95; *R v F & M Dobson Ltd* (1995) 16 Cr App Rep (S) 957, 14 Tr LR 467.

The major sanction supporting food legislation is the fine. Fines operate *ex post facto*, however, and their level may also be such as not to deter some businesses, which simply treat them as a minor business expense. Enforcement authorities need power to act quickly where food is in breach of the legislation and already on the market. The Food and Drugs Administration in the United States exercises a recall power which is not confined to unfit food only. Although there is no legal power as such, recalls are possible because the FDA has the threat that if businesses fail to comply a court can be requested to issue an injunction or to order a seizure. The recall procedure is not limited to situations where a hazard to health had been found in a product. Chapter 11 will explain the 'cease and desist' order under the Fair Trading Act 1973 which can be obtained against businesses in persistent breach of consumer law, including food legislation. In the case of the latter the Office of Fair Trading has obtained assurances from a number of food businesses.

Section 9 of the Food Safety Act 1990 contains inspection and seizure provisions. The food must be intended for human consumption and appear on inspection to be injurious to health, unfit, or contaminated, or appear other than on inspection to be likely to cause food poisoning or any disease communicable to human beings. The enforcement authorities can either issue a prohibition notice, or seize the food to have it destroyed by order of a magistrate. If the magistrate refuses to condemn it, the enforcement authority must compensate the owner for any depreciation in its value which can be shown to result. Code of Practice No 4 has been issued under s 40 of the Act on the Inspection, Detention and Seizure of Suspect Food.

3   QUANTITY

The broad prohibition against incorrect quantity in force in many countries is illustrated by s 28(1) of the Weights and Measures Act 1985.

> [A]ny person who, in selling or purporting to sell any goods by weight or other measurement or by number, delivers or causes to be delivered to the buyer— (a) a lesser quantity than that purported to be sold or (b) a lesser quantity than corresponds with the price charged, shall be guilty of an offence.

The legislation also contains a prohibition on misrepresenting or misleading consumers about quantity. These provisions are supplemented by others to enable consumers properly to evaluate quantity. A wide range of items must be sold by weight; for many items it is incumbent on sellers to inform consumers about the weight at the time of sale; and a number of commodities must be marketed in prescribed quantities.

A uniform system of weights and measures is obviously essential to commerce and industry. Legislation established the imperial standards in the early nineteenth century, although attempts can be traced back to Magna Carta.[4] All transactions in trade must be conducted by reference to the imperial or metric units required in the legislation. Control of weighing and measuring equipment began some time earlier in 1795–97, when statutes were passed to suppress the use of defective weights and of false and unequal balances. The principles of this earlier legislation remain in the Weights and Measures Act 1985 ensuring that weighing and measuring equipment conforms to the standardised units, is kept in accurate condition and is constructed so as not to facilitate fraud. Weighing and measuring equipment, as prescribed, must be verified as fit for use. Enforcement authorities regularly inspect business premises to ensure that the equipment remains in good working condition. In order to ensure their suitability for use in trade, the government approves patterns of weighing and measuring appliances, both as to the material of which they are constructed and the principles on which they are designed.

Legislation to ensure that the quantities actually sold were what they purported to be originated much more recently. It was long rejected on the grounds that it would constitute an unacceptable intrusion into commerce by the state.[5] Bread and coal were commodities specifically regulated. Both products had to be sold in specified quantities and traders could be punished for short measure.[6] The Weights and Measures Act 1878 imposed a penalty on the fraudulent use of weighing and measuring equipment, but this was ineffectual because of the difficulty of proving fraud and because of the advent of prepackaging.[7] Attention was frequently drawn to the anomaly of controlling weighing and measuring equipment, but of not prohibiting the giving of short weight or measure.[8] Particular concern was expressed that the poor suffered in the absence of such a prohibition.

Finally in 1914 a parliamentary committee accepted the need for a strict liability offence of giving incorrect quantity. While pointing out that the

---

[4] P Kelly *Metrology; or An Exposition of Weights and Measures* (Lackington, 1816) pp 33–82; HJ Chaney *Our Weights and Measures* (Eyre & Spottiswoode, 1897) pp 50–55.

[5] *Weights and Measures, Letter from the Comptroller-General of the Exchequer to the Secretary of State for the Home Department*, dated 9 February 1859, 188, xxv, 291, p 2.

[6] *O'Keefe's Law of Weights and Measures* (looseleaf) paras **O(78)**, **O(92)** (*O'Keefe* is the standard work on the current law). See also CW Parsley *Observations on ... The Measures Weights and Money used in this Country* (Egertons Military Library, 1834) p 81.

[7] GA Owen *The Law Relating to Weights and Measures* (Griffin, 2nd edn, 1947) p 71.

[8] *Report by the Board of Trade in the Proceedings and Business under the Weights and Measures Act 1878* (1882) c 331, xxvii, 715, p 2.

state should interfere with relations between buyers and sellers in only exceptional circumstances, the committee justified legislation because consumers, especially the poor, were vulnerable to business malpractice.[9] After some delay, the Sale of Food (Weights and Measures) Act 1926 penalised short weight and measure in the sale of food and compelled traders to sell a number of foods by quantity. The latter provision was gradually expanded and it now extends it to a wide range of consumer commodities. Enforcement of the short weight prohibition, although it receives little publicity, is of continued importance to ordinary people.

4   CORPORATE CRIMINAL LIABILITY AND THE STATUTORY OFFENCES

This section is concerned primarily with consumer offences committed by companies. Who is to be punished in these circumstances; the employee whose immediate mistake gave rise to the offence, the senior executives whose promotional practices inevitably led to such mistakes being committed, or the company itself? Imposing sanctions on the company confiscates any illegal profits accruing from the offence. Further, prosecuting the company may lead its top management to police observance of legal requirements by those in the organisation. Sometimes there is no alternative to proceeding against a company if a prosecution is to be instituted. Decision-making is diffuse in a large organisation and it may be impossible to locate an individual responsible for a particular occurrence. The same happens if an offence is the accretion of decisions by many individuals.

There are equally cogent reasons for proceeding against the senior executives of a company whose promotional practices are responsible for an offence.[10] If only the company is prosecuted the effect on these individuals is indirect. Assuming that the stigma of a conviction attaches to the company, it is highly unlikely to filter through to the relevant company executives. Similarly, when a company is fined this will rarely affect the senior executives financially. On the other hand there is little value to be gained in prosecuting junior employees unless they have committed consumer offences for their own benefit. They are the captives of promotional practices adopted by their employers and it is quite unfair to lay the blame at their feet.

9   *Report from the Select Committee on Short Weight* (1914) Cd 359, x, 337, p iii–iv. See also Food Council *Short Weight and Measure in the Sale of Foodstuffs* (1926), Cmd 2591, x, 733.
10   See WB Fisse 'Criminal Law and Consumer Protection' in AJ Duggan and LW Darvall (eds) *Consumer Protection Law and Theory* (Law Book, 1980).

In the light of these considerations, what does the law say about offences committed by companies? The subject is best considered under different headings.[11]

(a)   Liability of individual officers

(i)   Top management

Top management may be guilty of aiding and abetting an offence by others, such as the corporation or its employees, but that requires knowledge and an ability to control the actions of the principal offender. Consumer legislation generally provides that if a company is liable for an offence, its top management can also be prosecuted if it is directly responsible or should have taken steps to prevent its occurrence. For example, s 20 of the Trade Descriptions Act 1968 provides that top management such as directors, managers or company secretaries (or those acting in such capacities) can be prosecuted along with their company if the offence has been committed with their consent and connivance, or is attributable to any neglect on their part. Neglect involves failure to perform a duty about which a person knows or ought to know. Consent requires knowledge, but mere suspicion, coupled with acquiescence, may be sufficient for connivance.

A decision of the United States Supreme Court, *United States v Park*[12] is a useful illustration of these points, although the case may not be directly applicable in other jurisdictions. The president and chief executive officer of a large national food chain (Park) was held liable for unsanitary storage conditions in one of the company's warehouses. The enforcement authority had inspected the warehouse, found conditions in violation of the Food, Drug and Cosmetic Act, and notified Park by letter. On receipt of the letter, Park had conferred with his vice-president of legal matters, who informed him that the divisional vice-president would take corrective action. Park argued that he could not have taken more constructive action. The United States Supreme Court disagreed and ruled that under the Act Park had responsibility and authority either to prevent violations in the first instance or promptly to take steps to seek out and correct them once they were discovered. Liability was not predicated on Park's position, title, or on his closeness to the violation, said the court, but because all officers who have power and authority, regardless of how extended and indirect,

---

[11]   Cf J Gobert 'Corporate Criminality: Four Models of Fault' (1994) 14 Leg Stud 393.

[12]   421 US 658 (1975). Cf the approach in *Williams v Natural Life Health Food Ltd* [1997] 1 BCLC 131.

to secure compliance with the law have an affirmative duty to do so. Objective impossibility of preventing a violation, however, would have been a defence. The decision in *Park*'s case is to be welcomed as an indication that company executives should bear a responsibility for violations of the law arising from the way their organisations operate.

(ii)   Employees

If employees are responsible for all the elements of an offence, they can be prosecuted directly.[13] They may also be prosecuted under general provisions such as s 23 of the Trade Descriptions Act 1968, which make it possible to prosecute a person whose act or default has given rise to an offence.[14] As a matter of practice consumer protection departments will rarely prosecute employees. In some special cases, as where the legislation applies to the commission of an offence 'in the course of any business *of his*', the courts might conclude that on such wording proceedings cannot be brought against employees.[15]

(b)   Corporate liability

Since a company is incapable of performing acts itself, a basis must be found for imputing to it acts performed by individuals. English law has approached this problem in two ways.[16]

(i)   Personal liability of company

The law regards certain individuals working for a company as being so closely identified with it that their acts can be treated as its acts. This is sometimes known as the direct, *alter ego* or attribution theory. Those in respect of whose actions liability may be ascribed occupy the top management positions in the organisation. They may be those strictly allowed by the articles of association of a company to exercise its powers or those defined in statutory provisions like s 20 of the Trade Descriptions Act 1968.[17] They are the 'directing minds' of the company, characterised by Denning LJ in a well-known passage:

---

[13]   For example *Hotchin v Hindmarsh* [1891] 2 QB 181; *Melias Ltd v Preston* [1957] 2 QB 380.

[14]   Eg *Olgeirsson v Kitching* [1986] 1 WLR 304.

[15]   *R v Warwickshire County Council, ex p Johnson* [1993] AC 583.

[16]   The leading account is now C Wells *Corporations and Criminal Responsibility* (Clarendon, 1993) especially Chapter 4. See also C Clarkson 'Kicking Corporate Bodies and Damning their Souls' (1996) 59 MLR 557.

[17]   *Tesco Supermarkets Ltd v Nattrass* [1972] AC 153.

A company may in many ways be likened to a human body. It has a brain and nerve centre which controls what it does. It also has hands which hold the tools and act in accordance with directions from the centre. Some of the people in the company are mere servants and agents who are nothing more than hands to do the work and cannot be said to represent the mind or will. Others are directors and managers who represent the directing mind and will of the company, and control what it does. The state of mind of those managers is the state of mind of the company and is treated by the law as such.[18]

(ii)   Vicarious liability of company

A company can be criminally liable for the acts of its employees:

(a)   in the exceptional cases where top management delegates their full discretion to those at lower levels who can act independently of instructions from them.[19] It has been held that the delegation of duties to a branch manager or sales manager, however, does not fall within this head.[20]

(b)   where the courts regard a statute as being intended to create vicarious criminal liability. There is no reason why this should not be the case with consumer statutes. A company will therefore be liable for the acts of even junior employees, even if it is quite unaware of those acts, when they are committed in the course of their employment.[1] The justification for such extensive liability is that substantial authority is delegated to the lower echelons of modern business organisations. Lower officials can endanger the public and profit a business by unlawful acts to the same extent as top management. Vicarious liability also encourages the top management of businesses to supervise closely the activities of their lower officials.

In the last decade, vicarious liability has become more attractive to the English courts as a basis of corporate liability, although it is true to say that there has never been any thoroughgoing analysis of what underlies the criminal regulation of corporate behaviour. A limitation on vicarious liability has been that the courts have been reluctant to infer a parliamentary

---

[18]   *HL Bolten (Engineering) Co Ltd v TJ Graham & Sons Ltd* [1957] 1 QB 159, 172.
[19]   *Mousell Bros Ltd v London and North-Western Rly Co* [1917] 2 KB 836; *James & Son Ltd v Smee* [1955] 1 QB 78.
[20]   *Tesco Supermarkets Ltd v Nattrass* [1972] AC 153.
[1]   *Re Supply of Ready Mixed Concrete (No 2)* [1995] 1 AC 456; *Meridian Global Funds Management Asia Ltd v Securities Commission* [1995] 2 AC 500; *R v British Steel plc* [1995] 1 WLR 1356. See R Wickins and C Ong 'Confusion Worse Confounded: The End of the Directing Mind Theory?' [1997] JBL 524.

intention to impose it in cases where consumer offences require *mens rea*. This has been said to follow from the difficulty of attributing the mental state of one person to another.[2] However, this would seem not to be a major problem with consumer legislation now, given the more expansive view of vicarious liability being taken by the courts.[3] To put the matter beyond doubt, statute could provide that where it is necessary to establish the intention of a corporation it is sufficient to show that one of its employees or agents who engaged in the conduct had that intention.

(c)   Statutory defences: the company

To mitigate the harshness of strict liability, legislation provides certain defences in consumer legislation.[4] The most important defence, exemplified in s 24(1) of the Trade Descriptions Act 1968, is if a person can show: (a) that the contravention was due to a mistake, to reliance on information supplied, or to the act or default of another person, an accident or some other cause beyond its control; and (b) that it has taken reasonable precautions and exercised all due diligence to avoid the commission of such contravention. Defences of this nature vary in detail.[5] Where the allegation is that someone else is to blame most legislation requires the defendant to give the prosecution beforehand information identifying or assisting to identify that other person.

The leading case on defences is *Tesco Supermarkets Ltd v Nattrass*.[6] There a national supermarket was prosecuted for mispricing and successfully raised the defence, under s 24(1) of the Trade Descriptions Act 1968, that it was the fault of its branch manager. The House of Lords held that a branch manager could be 'another person' under the section. He was not at sufficiently high a level to be regarded as a directing mind of the company (instead he was one of the directed), and neither was he a delegate of the directing minds because they always retained control through their chain of command. It had already been accepted that the company had taken reasonable precautions and exercised due diligence instructing its branch managers and other staff on how to avoid mispricing,

---

2   Eg *Coupe v Guyett* [1973] 2 All ER 1058, [1973] 1 WLR 699.
3   See P Cartwright 'Trade Descriptions, Corporations and Mens Rea' [1997] JBL 465. Cf the wider US approach: Foerschler 'Corporate Criminal Intent: Towards a Better Understanding of Corporate Misconduct' (1990) 78 California LR 1287.
4   The defences can be invoked by individuals as well as companies but in practice are used by the latter. See A Ogus *Regulation: Legal Form and Economic Theory* (OUP, 1994) pp 84–86.
5   See P Cartwright 'Defendants in Consumer Protection Statutes: A Search for Consistency' (1996) 59 MLR 225.
6   [1972] AC 153.

by its method of selecting branch managers, by providing adequate staff and conditions, and by its system of area inspectors.

The underlying rationale of the decision in *Tesco*'s case is to avoid making companies criminally liable when they are regarded as not being to blame for a criminal offence. The justification for this approach in Lord Reid's words is: 'But if he has done all he can how can he do more?' But this argument misses several points. Firstly, it is the business that makes any profit when an employee commits an offence.[7] In general terms, the result of a prosecution is simply to deprive the business of this wrongly acquired profit, although in particular cases the business may be fined an amount greater than the profit made or the publicity surrounding the prosecution may cause financial loss in excess of the profit. Secondly, the employees identified by a company as being responsible for an offence are open to prosecution. Yet it is socially undesirable for employees to be punished for such offence which they commit not for their benefit but in the course of their employment. Why should they be blamed? They are locked into a system where they have to carry out a company's production and marketing scheme; in the case of junior employees, for low wages in what may be an uncreative environment. Consumer protection departments may not prosecute them as a matter of practice, but should companies be able to escape liability in such circumstances and transfer it to them?

The most telling point, however, is that some firms are able to operate without committing consumer offences. Comparable businesses have completely different conviction records, and these seem to vary with a company's production and marketing policies and the way it treats its employees. Businesses with low conviction rates eschew procedures and schemes which give rise to offences and create an atmosphere, in terms of the way they treat their staff and the conditions under which they employ them, where the risk of infringement is minimised. What more can a business do, asks Lord Reid? Some businesses can emulate their competitors by introducing better checking procedures, changing certain modes of operation, and improving the position of their staff so that they have an incentive to avoid mistakes. But obviously certain businesses will not do this until the cost of doing so, in terms of the penalties involved, is a sufficient deterrent. Vicarious liability for offences committed by employees in the course of their employment would seem to be the only solution.

Another criticism of the approach in *Tesco*'s case is that it is all too easy for a company to appear to have taken reasonable precautions and to have exercised due diligence. *Tesco* contains warnings against ready acceptance of paper schemes for preventing offences and perfunctory efforts to implement them. Despite these warnings, courts have sometimes

---

[7]   RWL Howells 'A Blow Against Enterprise Liability' (1971) 34 MLR 676, 679.

adopted a lenient view of what has to be done to prevent offences. In *Newcastle-upon-Tyne City Council v Safeway plc*[8] the defendant supermarket detailed its system to avoid mispricing errors—listing price amendments in daily product advice notes, employing a price checker in each store, removing immediately all old material when prices were changed, spot checks, sequencing changes to prevent mispricing (eg removing point of sale material only after price amendments were completed) and so on. However, the required supervision had not taken place in all respects, and the supermarket's own system showed a pricing error rate of 67 errors out of 408 offers in a 13-week period. Nonetheless, the Divisional Court upheld the magistrates' decision that the due diligence defence had been made out. By contrast, in *Balding v Lew-Ways Ltd*[9] the court held that it was not sufficient to show that the toys supplied were submitted to analysts and complied with British Standard BS 5665: the issue was whether due diligence had been exercised, and this required an inquiry of the analysts as to whether the toys complied with the Toys (Safety) Regulations.

A plausible argument for the apparent inconsistencies in the case law, illustrated by these two decisions, is that a breach of safety provisions attracts a more searching judicial approach. By contrast, the courts treat other offences, such as mispricing, where economic interests are threatened, more leniently, and are thus more readily persuaded that due diligence has been exercised.[10] While the difference between economic and safety interests is not always clear-cut, it frequently has a useful explanatory role. The policy argument supporting a narrow interpretation of the due diligence offence in all cases, such as mispricing, is to act as an incentive to business to improve quality control and thus consumer protection. Of course this is most obviously evident in the need for robust checks to ensure compliance with safety regulations.[11]

Guidelines on the due diligence defence in the Food Safety Act 1990 have been issued jointly by the Institution of Environmental Health Officers, the Food and Drink Federation, the Local Authorities Co-ordinating Body on Trading Standards (LACOTS), the National Consumer

---

[8]   (27 June 1994, unreported). See also *Berkshire County Council v Olympic Holidays Ltd* (1994) 158 JP 337. Cf *Denard v Burton Retail Ltd* (1998) 162 JP 545, 162 JP 566.

[9]   (1995) 159 JP 541. See also *Turtington v United Co-operative Ltd* [1993] Crim LR 36; *Padgett Bros (A to Z) Ltd v Coventry City Council v* (1998) 162 JP 673.

[10] D Parry 'Judicial Approaches to Due Diligence' [1995] Crim LR 695. The courts thus approach strictly the special defence in s 10(4) of the Consumer Protection Act 1987—whether a retailer has reasonable grounds for believing that a product fails to comply with safety requirements.

[11] See especially S Weatherill 'Unsafe Goods: Protecting the Consumer and Protecting the Diligent Trader' [1990] JBL 36, 41.

Council, the National Farmers Union and the Retail Consortium.[12] In addition to guidelines given for particular sectors of the food industry, there are some general points set out, which are applicable to all the due diligence defences. Thus it is said that some positive action will always be required. ('Sitting back and doing nothing can never enable a person to make out the defence.') Taking reasonable precautions involves the setting up of a system of control having regard to the nature of the risks involved, say the guidelines, whilst due diligence involves securing the proper operations of that system. Since the legislation speaks of taking *all* reasonable precautions and exercising *all* due diligence, the guidelines conclude, consistently with the case-law, that where there was a reasonable precaution that could have been taken, but was not, the defence would not succeed. The case-law makes clear, however, that since all *reasonable* precautions need be taken, this does not mean that every conceivable precaution need be taken.[13] The guidelines continue that what is reasonable depends on the particular circumstances. Thus operating an inherently high risk process will require greater precautions than operating one which is by its nature safe. Similarly, what is reasonable for a large-scale business may not be so for a much smaller business. The guidelines caution that a control system must cover all aspects of the operations of the business. They conclude with the obvious point that the operation of the system must be kept under review and be amended as necessary.

(d) Statutory defences: suppliers

In addition to blaming employees, companies may be able to use defences such as s 24(1) of the Trade Descriptions Act 1968 to push liability onto their suppliers. Retailers who do nothing would seem to have a heavy job in establishing a s 124 defence following the decision in *Sherratt v Gerald's The American Jewellers Ltd.*[14] That case involved a watch engraved 'water proof', a claim which the consumer demonstrated to be untrue when he dipped the watch in a bowl of water. The retailer attempted to invoke the s 24 defence when prosecuted under s 1 of the Trade Descriptions Act 1968 on the basis that the watch had been obtained from a responsible company and that no previous complaints had been received. The

---

[12] *Food Safety Act 1990. Guidelines on the Statutory Defence of Due Diligence* February 1991. Note also the LACOTS (Local Authorities Co-ordinating Body on Food and Trading Standards) advice in relation to the Package Travel, Package Holidays and Package Tours Regulations: see R Lawson 'Due Diligence Defence' (1996) 140 Sol J 690, 691.

[13] Eg see *Ealing London Borough Council v Taylor* [1995] Crim LR 166.

[14] (1970) 68 LGR 256, 114 Sol Jo 147.

Divisional Court rejected the argument: no precautions had been taken, although the retailer could have done quite easily what the consumer did. Irrespective of a s 24 type defence, however, retailers cannot be liable if it is the supplier which has actually committed the offence. Suppliers may be liable for not properly warning retailers.[15] Moreover, where the commission of an offence by a retailer was due to the act or default of a supplier, the prosecution may be brought directly against the supplier.[16]

There is now clear case-law that retailers must test samples of products from their suppliers for compliance with safety requirements. The samples must be statistically controlled and the tests on the samples properly conducted.[17] Reliance on certificates, indicating compliance with safety standards, will not in itself constitute the exercise of due diligence.[18] The steps that secondhand car dealers must take to satisfy the statutory defences to push blame onto their suppliers have tightened considerably over the years, which reflects the courts' attitude to the continuing need for secondhand car dealers to be prosecuted for trade description offences. For example, secondhand car dealers must generally contact the previous owner and use disclaimers if they are to show reasonable precautions and due diligence in relation to odometer readings.[19]

(e) Statutory defences: manufacturing processes

Defences comparable to s 24 of the Trade Descriptions Act 1968 may be applicable where an offence can be attributed to a fault in the manufacturing process and the manufacturer has taken reasonable precautions and exercised due diligence. *Bibby-Cheshire v Golden Wonder Ltd*[20] involved a prosecution for short-weight crisps, but the court was satisfied that the manufacturer had a defence when it demonstrated that if the machines were functioning normally the error was equivalent to 0.0006% of weekly output, that it was economically impossible to weigh manually the 20 million bags produced weekly, that the filling machine was the most modern available and was adequately maintained, and that various check weighing procedures were in operation.

---

[15] *Coventry City Council v Ackerman Group plc* [1995] Crim LR 140.
[16] *Balding v Lew-Ways Ltd* (1995) 159 JP 541; *Padgett Bros (A to Z) Ltd v Coventry City Council* (1998) 162 JP 673.
[17] See especially *Rotherham Metropolitan Borough Council v Raysun* (1989) 153 JP 37; *Sutton London Borough Council v David Halsall plc* (1995) 159 JP 431.
[18] *Whirlpool (UK) and Magnet Ltd v Gloucestershire County Council* (1995) 159 JP 123.
[19] Eg *Wandsworth London Borough Council v Bentley* [1980] RTR 429. Cf *Ealing London Borough Council v Taylor* [1995] Crim LR 166.
[20] [1972] 3 All ER 738, [1972] 1 WLR 1487.

5   CONCLUSION

The broad statutory standards considered in this chapter are those most frequently used by consumer protection departments in ensuring acceptable standards of business behaviour.[1] By no means are the existing provisions entirely satisfactory and a number of suggestions have been made for reform. For example, the law is inadequate with regard to false statements about services and there is a need for a broad provision making it unlawful to represent that services are of a particular standard, or to mislead consumers as to the nature, characteristics and suitability for purpose or quality of any service. Moreover, there is an urgent need to overturn the *Tesco* decision, which emasculated the liability of corporations for breaches of consumer protection law. Something along the lines of s 84(2) of the Australian Trade Practices Act 1974 provides a model: it deems conduct engaged in on behalf of a company by an employee to be also engaged in by the company if committed 'at the direction or with the consent or agreement (whether express or implied) of a director, agent or servant of the body corporate'. On this basis the branch manager in Tesco would not have been 'another person' for the purposes of the s 24(1) defence.

Enforcement is crucial with broad statutory standards because it is only by constantly bringing prosecutions in the courts that the enforcement authorities can bring home to businesses the need to ensure compliance with consumer law. Moreover, judicial decisions are often necessary to establish the parameters of an enactment incorporating broad standards. *Regulating Business*[2] criticised the operation of some consumer enforcement authorities which too readily adopted an advisory and educative role on the basis that they could ensure compliance with the law simply by informing businesses of its provisions, at the expense of giving businesses sharp reminders through prosecution about the need to present violations. There is now a considerable literature about the nature of the advisory and educative ('compliance') strategy of regulatory agencies and about whether it is either effective or desirable.[3] As to effectiveness,

[1]   Note also the occasional prosecutions under the Theft Act 1968.

[2]   Ross Cranston *Regulating Business* (Macmillan, 1979). More recently the Audit Commission was critical of the wide variations it found in levels of formal enforcement of consumer protection measures: Measure for Measure: The Best Value Agenda for Trading Standards Services (The Stationery Office, 1999) pp 41ff. The government is planning to respond to the problem by setting national standards: OFT Press Release 24/00 (22 June 2000).

[3]   See especially F Pearce and S Tombs 'Ideology, Hegemony, and Empiricism' (1990) 30 Brit J Criminol 423; K Hawkins 'Compliance Strategy, Prosecution Policy and Aunt Sally—A Comment on Pearce and Tombs' (1990) 30 Brit J Criminol 444. See also J Rowan-Robinson, P Watchman and C Barker *Crime and Regulation* (T & T Clark Ltd, 1990); C Wells *Corporations and Criminal Responsibility* (Clarendon, 1993); K Hawkins (ed) *The Uses of Discretion* (Clarendon, 1992); I Ayres and J Braithwaite *Responsive Regulation* (OUP, 1992).

there is just not the evidence to say whether a compliance strategy produces the same degree of lawful behaviour as a more adversarial strategy. As to desirability, there is the need on the one hand to retain business good will, and on the other to ensure that the 'crimes of the powerful' are not being condoned.[4] Notwithstanding the scepticism about the use of a compliance approach, it appears to be the new orthodoxy within government.[5]

At the next level, the 'secondary enforcers'—in the main the magistrates' courts—often seem to overlook the nature and seriousness of consumer offences.[6] Too often businesses can breach statutory standards in the consumer protection area without incurring a great cost in monetary penalties or in stigmatisation. The ambivalence of the magistrates' courts to consumer offences is also evident in the decisions of the superior courts. For example, in giving an expansive interpretation of the mispricing offence in s 20 of the Consumer Protection Act 1987, Lord Roskill said that '[t]o hold otherwise would be seriously to restrict the efficacy of this part of the consumer protection legislation'.[7] By contrast Lord Scarman said in one leading case that the Trade Descriptions Act 1968 'is not a truly criminal statute. Its purpose is not the enforcement of the criminal law but the maintenance of trading standards. Trading standards, not criminal behaviour, are its concern'.[8] In a sense Lord Scarman was simply reflecting a popular view that strict liability, regulatory offences are not 'real crimes' such as those requiring *mens rea*. When dishonesty is clearly involved, however, and the behaviour is akin to traditional offences such as theft and deception, magistrates' courts and Crown Courts have imposed heavier penalties, including prison sentences.[9]

Making breaches of criminal law automatically give rise to civil liability is one way of strengthening the broad statutory standards. In 1856 a select committee recommended that 'a cheap and easy remedy, by summary charge before a magistrate', should be afforded 'to consumers who received

---

4   E Bardach and R Kagan *Going By the Book: The Problem of Regulatory Unreasonableness* (Temple University Press, 1982).

5   DTI *Modern Markets: Confident Consumers* (1999) Chapter 7; Better Regulation Task Force *Enforcement Concordat* (Cabinet Office, 1998).

6   See H Croall 'Mistakes, Accidents and Someone Else's Fault: The Trading Offender in Court' (1988) J Law & Soc 293.

7   *Warwickshire County Council v Johnson* [1993] 1 All ER 299, 302.

8   *Wings Ltd v Ellis* [1985] AC 272.

9   In 1996, 61 defendants received prison sentences in s 1 prosecutions under the Trade Descriptions Act 1968, and 10 defendants in s 14 prosecutions: OFT *Annual Report of the Director General of Fair Trading 1997* (HMSO, 1998) p 78. In 1998, a Crown Court judge sentenced two secondhand car dealers to six years' imprisonment for clocking 38 cars: (1998) Times, 9 January. But that seems to have been a prosecution for conspiracy to defraud. See also *R v Nash* [1990] RTR 343; D Roberts 'Sentencing Under the Trade Descriptions Act' [1991] Trad L 36.

adulterated or falsely described food'.[10] The suggestion was taken up not
in the food and drugs legislation but in the Merchandise Marks Act 1887.
Section 17 of that Act provided that a person applying a trade description
to a product was deemed to warrant that it was true, so that a false trade
description constituted a breach of both the criminal and civil law. The
section was deliberately omitted from the Trade Descriptions Act 1968,
which contains a specific provision that a contract for the supply of a
product is not void or unenforceable by reason only of a contravention of
the Act.[11] In fact the general rule is that contracts are not automatically
void even if there is a breach of criminal law.[12] Unlike with industrial safety
legislation, the courts have rejected an attempt to ground a civil action on
breach of a criminal statute in the consumer protection area.[13] In *Square v
Model Farm Dairies (Bournemouth) Ltd*[14] the Court of Appeal justified
the result because purchasers could already in most cases bring an action
under the Sale of Goods Act, but to give other consumers a civil action on
the basis of a criminal offence would undermine the doctrine of privity of
contract.[15] Consequently, what would be needed is a specific provision in
consumer legislation to the effect that breach automatically gives the
consumer an action in civil law and that any term of an agreement is void
in so far as it has the effect of excluding or restricting such liability. Wide
use of such a provision in consumer legislation would have the advantage
that consumers would readily obtain compensation in the event of a
business committing a criminal offence. More importantly, it would act as
some deterrent to wrongdoing if enforcement authorities instituted mass
restitution suits on behalf of consumers adversely affected, as discussed
in Chapter 3.

[10] *Report from the Select Committee on Adulteration of Food* 1856, Parl Pap 376, viii, 1, p vii.
[11] Section 35. See J Landis 'Statutes and the Sources of Law' *Harvard Legal Essays* (Harvard University Press, 1934) p 220.
[12] Eg *Hughes v Asset Managers* [1994] CLC 556.
[13] The general principles are discussed in the recent House of Lords decisions: *X v Bedfordshire County Council* [1995] 2 AC 633, [1995] 3 All ER 353; *Stovin v Wise* [1996] AC 923, [1996] 3 All ER 801.
[14] [1939] 2 KB 365. See also *Buckley v La Reserve* [1959] Crim LR 451.
[15] Section 130 of the Powers of Criminal Courts (Sentencing) Act 2000 entitles consumers to compensation in the event of conviction. See p 152 above. Cf Trade Practices Act 1974 (Aust), s 82, which enables a person to recover the loss or damage suffered by conduct of another person in contravention of the consumer protection provisions of the Act.

Chapter 9

The provision of information

The Consumer Protection Charter of the Council of Europe espouses the principle of making information available to the consumer 'to enable him to make a rational choice between competing products and services'.[1] Actually forcing businesses to divulge information about their products, practices and processes, under threat of criminal sanction, is now a popular technique of modern consumer legislation,[2] and the promotion of the 'informed consumer' is a key plank of contemporary government orthodoxy.[3] The assumption is that once information is disclosed, consumers will use it to protect themselves. Government's enthusiasm for disclosure regulation is based partly on the fact that it is relatively inexpensive and has a lighter touch when compared with other forms of regulatory control.[4] Compliance can be readily checked where it is simply a matter of determining whether advertisements, contracts in standardised form, or the like contain the requisite information.

The economic justification for disclosure regulation is that it facilitates competition, one of the necessary conditions for which is that consumers possess a high degree of knowledge about products and services in the

---

[1] Resolution 543 in Eur Consultative Assembly, 25th Session, Texts Adopted (1973) p 2 C(i).

[2] See generally W Whitford 'The Functions of Disclosure Regulation in Consumer Transactions' [1973] Wisc LR 400; G Gatwood, R Hobbs, F Miller 'Consumer Disclosure in the 1990s' (1993) 9 Georgia SULR 777; G Hadfield, R Howse and M Trebilcock 'Information-Based Principles for Rethinking Consumer Protection Policy'(1998) 21 Journal of Consumer Policy 131; I Ramsay *Rationales for Intervention in the Consumer Market Place* (OFT, 1984).

[3] DTI *Modern Market: Confident Consumers* (Cm 4410 (1999)) Chapter 3.

[4] A Ogus *Regulation: Legal Form and Economic Theory* (OUP, 1994) p 125.

market.[5] This is recognised explicitly in the Fair Packaging and Labelling Act of the United States, which says by way of preamble: 'Informed consumers are essential to the fair and efficient functioning of a free market economy.'[6] At present there is widespread consumer ignorance because of the vast array of complex products, which are frequently concealed by pre-packing, and of services which are inherently difficult to fathom. In more theoretical terms, disclosure regulation can redress the market failure which arises from the provision of sub-optimal information and the welfare loss which consumers consequently suffer.[7] Moreover an advantage of information disclosure over other types of regulation is if consumers are in a better position than regulators to make decisions about behaving in certain ways.[8] For example, it may be relatively easy for consumers to avoid the hazards associated with a product or service, if properly informed, but quite costly for regulators to take preventive action.[9] Much depends, however, on whether the information is easily understandable and likely to be taken on board by consumers.

Businesses may be deterred from providing information voluntarily because of the cost, but also because of self-interest, since consumer ignorance furthers oligopoly power by impeding the market.[10] Disclosure regulation forces businesses to place greater emphasis on price and quality factors and less on promotion, although the two are not mutually exclusive. This furthers competition and limits the ability of businesses to acquire monopoly power. An illustration is that information about the comparative advantages of products and services made available through *Which?* or *Consumer Reports* makes consumers less vulnerable to promotional advertising. Even a relatively small change in consumer behaviour brought about by such information can have a magnified impact on business behaviour because it may not take much to render particular products or

---

[5]   S Grossman 'The Informational Role of Warranties and Private Disclosure about Product Quality' (1981) 24 J Law & Econ 461.

[6]   15 USC §1451.

[7]   A Ogus *Regulation: Legal Form and Economic Theory* (OUP, 1994) pp 121–123.

[8]   A Ogus *Regulation: Legal Form and Economic Theory* (OUP, 1994) pp 121–124; S Breyer *Regulation and Its Reform* (Harvard University Press, 1982) p 163.

[9]   P Burrows 'Consumer Safety Under Products Liability and Duty to Disclose' (1992) 12 International Review of Law and Economics 457.

[10] S Rhoades 'Reducing Consumer Ignorance: An Approach and its Effects' (1975) 20 Antitrust Bulletin 309, 310. See also H Beales et al 'The Efficient Regulation of Consumer Information' (1981) 24 J Law & Econ 491, 501–513. By the same token disclosure regulation can have monopoly effects, eg by advantaging larger firms: R Higgins and F McChesney 'Truth and its Consequences: The Federal Trade Commission's Act Substantiation Program' (1986) 6 Int Rev Law & Econ 149, 155.

services unprofitable. By enabling consumers to spend their income more rationally, information of this sort leads to a more optimal allocation of society's resources.

Disclosure regulation as the major tool of consumer protection law is espoused particularly by those with political philosophies seeking to minimise the intervention of the state in the economy. The non-interventionists say that regulatory control can never replace *caveat emptor* or substitute for informed decisions by individual consumers. Their view is that regulatory control is necessary in only isolated instances, involving safety and health, or for consumers who are particularly susceptible to exploitation because of their dependence or vulnerability. Instead, the non-interventionists argue that the combination of informed consumers and competition among businesses best serve the cause of consumer protection. In their view ordinary consumers command little sympathy if they lay out appreciable sums of money without first informing themselves. With less expensive items, the argument runs, consumers can easily acquire information from experience. It is conceded that this is less practicable with hazardous or expensive purchases, and for this reason non-interventionists grant government a limited role in compelling businesses to make sufficient information available to consumers for rational choice. This does not mean that those with different political philosophies never advocate disclosure regulation, or that it is inconsistent with their politics, only that they do not see it as the main tool of consumer protection. They are more inclined to advocate other more direct forms of regulation, for they see a number of drawbacks associated with disclosure regulation, some of what are considered later in this chapter. Indeed disclosure regulation is sometimes justified on the basis that consumers have a right to information, in particular about health and safety risks. The analogy is with freedom of information in the public sphere.

Disclosure regulation goes one step further than laws controlling trade descriptions, which are simply concerned with the accuracy of information which businesses elect to make available. Disclosure regulation actually mandates the provision of certain types of information. Potentially its ambit is very wide, covering the quality of products and services, their price, including the cost of credit, and the actual terms of consumer transactions. Traditionally legislation obliging businesses to disclose information was confined almost entirely to product labelling. More recently legislation has concerned itself with information about prices and the cost of credit. Indicative of the narrowness of disclosure regulation, despite the political and economic arguments in support, is the history of ss 8–10 of the Trade Descriptions Act 1968. These sections clothe the executive with wide power to compel the marking or accompanying of their products with, or the insertion in advertisements of, information of value to consumers. Yet to date hardly any orders have been made along these lines.[11] At least two reasons are advanced to excuse the dearth of such orders. It is said that there is an absence of reliable, objective standards to express such information and to measure its use. Then there is the legal opinion that the sections are drafted narrowly, and that within these terms information must be about 'goods' and not about business-consumer transactions.[12] These reasons do not bear close examination as an excuse for inaction, for organisations like the British Standards Institution have drafted numerous objective standards concerning products, which could form the basis of such orders.

I   CHANNELS OF INFORMATION DISCLOSURE

A possible means of analysing laws requiring business to disclose information is to proceed in terms of the way information must be presented under them. The following categories suggest themselves.

(a)   Product labelling

Product labelling has been an important method of protecting consumers for some time. As well as ensuring market transparency, product labelling sometimes has the more direct role of ensuring physical protection by warning consumers about product hazards. Product labelling promotes rational choice by permitting consumers to assess and compare the suitability of items for their individual requirements. The European Court of Justice has pointed out that information supplied at the point of sale, or as part of an advertising campaign, is no substitute for product labelling, not least because the ultimate consumer may not necessarily be the purchaser.[13] It also assists after consumers have purchased an article if there are instructions on matters like care or use. Criteria for introducing product labelling include whether its absence creates difficulties for consumers, whether its presence is important for initial choice or subsequent use, whether important facts about a product or service are identifiable by observation and whether the requisite information is describable within the limits of a label. In the main governments have confined compulsory product labelling to cases involving consumers' health or safety or involving a statement of relatively simple matters of

---

[11] Trade Descriptions (Sealskin Goods) (Information Order) 1980, SI 1980/1150 seems to be the only order extant.

[12] OFT *Review of the Trade Descriptions Act 1968* (Cmnd 6628 (1976)) p 86.

[13] *Criminal Proceedings against Goerres* Case C-385/96 [1998] ECR I-4431.

fact as distinct from value judgments.[14] CE labelling indicates a manufacturer's claim that its products comply with EC Directives on matters such as electrical equipment, gas appliances and implantable medical devices. However, it is not a sign of official quality approval, which is not widely understood (see further the discussion in Chapter 10).[15]

(b)   Advertisements

Corrective advertising has already been considered (in Chapter 2 above). Another possibility is to require advertisements to contain particular information, which is something that the Swedish Market Court can do.[16] An example in Britain is that the government can require tests on the fuel consumption of cars and require the results to be published in various ways.[17] As an integral part of the European Union's strategy to reduce CO_2 emissions the European Commission has adopted a proposed Directive which sets out requirements on Member States to provide consumers with information on the fuel-economy of new cars.[18] Package holiday brochures must clearly and accurately indicate the price and information about matters like destination, means of transport, type of accommodation (plus its location, degree of comfort, main features), included meals and itinerary.[19] A further step involves the state in actually issuing advertisements about the quality of products and services offered by private businesses (eg best buys, safe products). On the whole governments eschew the course of evaluating products and services because objections would be raised that they were favouring one business over another. Germany, for example, avoids this difficulty by subsidising an independent comparative testing organisation similar to the Consumers' Association.[20]

---

[14]   OECD *Labelling and Comparative Testing* (1972) p 5.
[15]   D Taylor 'CE—A Sense of European Direction' (1998) Business Standards, May, p 10.
[16]   Marketing Act 1975, s 3.
[17]   Energy Act 1976, s 15. See Passenger Car Fuel Consumption Order 1983, SI 1983/1486 as amended. On the accuracy of fuel saving claims: *Trade Practices Commission v Vaponordic (Aust) Pty Ltd* (1975) 6 ALR 248; *R v Consumers Distributing Co Ltd* (1980) 57 CCC (2d) 317, 54 CPR (2d) 50.
[18]   Com (98) 489 final.
[19]   Similar information must be in the contract (Package Travel, Package Holidays and Package Tours Regulations 1992, SI 1992/3288, reg 9, Sch 2) and the brochure and contract requirements are supplemented by the requirement to supply other information in good time before the holiday is to start.
[20]   N Reich and H-W Micklitz *Consumer Legislation in the Federal Republic of Germany* (Van Nostrand Reinhold, 1981) pp 60–62.

(c)   Terms of sale

Consumers' ability to compare prices is impaired by the large number of items available, their range of sizes and the variations in the way they are promoted. In a classic study, college-educated women in the United States were instructed to select the most economic package for each of 20 products. The women erred on 43% of their selections, although the results differed between products according in part to the nature of the packaging.[1] Standardised quantities are an illustration of how regulating the terms of sale can inform consumers and overcome some of the confusion in purchase decisions. The requirement is an alternative to unit pricing, and like that practice depends for its effectiveness on whether consumers use the information.

The idea of standardised quantities for products is to reduce the proliferation of sizes at present on the market. Thus the law might compel manufacturers to sell a prepacked product in quantities of 125, 250, 500g and 1000 grammes (1kg), and multiples of whole and half kilogrammes. The aim is to enable consumers to choose more rationally because of the simpler relationships involved. Standardised quantities facilitate comparisons between different sizes and between the same size for different brands. At present as little as a few grams separate pack sizes and different sizes proliferate. Another advantage is that standardised quantities make it more difficult for manufacturers to disguise price increases by a marginal reduction in the quantity of the product.

An EC Directive requires this change from the confusing array of existing sizes to standardised ones for foods and other consumer products such as cosmetics, detergents and aerosols.[2] In Britain full implementation of this Directive is still pending,[3] but various foods (eg biscuits, tea and coffee, breakfast cereals, dried fruits, pasta) and a limited number of other products must be sold in standardised quantities.[4] Prescribed quantities by no means remove consumer confusion if the units chosen are not

---

[1]   M Friedman 'Consumer Confusion in the Selection of Supermarket Products' (1966) 50 Journal of Applied Psychology 529.

[2]   Council Directive relating to the ranges of nominal quantities and nominal capacities permitted for certain prepackaged products, 80/232/EEC [1980] OJ L 51 25.02.80, as amended.

[3]   The government has announced a review and simplification of UK weights and measures legislation which may address the issue: DTI *Modern Markets: Confident Consumers* (1999) para 6.11.

[4]   Weights and Measures (Miscellaneous Foods) Order 1988, SI 1988/2040, as amended by SI 1990/1550; Weights and Measures (Intoxicating Liquor) Order 1988, SI 1988/2039, as amended by SI 1990/1550; Weights and Measures (Knitting Yarns) Order 1988, SI 1988/895.

easily identified. Consumer groups have also said that too many standardised quantities are allowable for some products. This defeats the object of standardised quantities because consumers cannot distinguish standard sizes which are too closely bunched. Unit pricing overcomes this to an extent. Manufacturers have successfully opposed the extension of standardised quantities. A major objection is that standardised quantities will discourage standardised containers, because the same weight of different brands of a product can occupy a different volume because of a variation in density. It is also said that standardised quantities place too great an emphasis on price to the detriment of quality. Both objections cannot bear close scrutiny; even if the first is true it can be solved by varying fills of different brands, and the second is in direct contravention of the consumer's right to know comparative prices.

2   TYPES OF INFORMATION DISCLOSURE

Another means of exposition is to focus on the particular concerns of disclosure regulation laws.[5] Information about credit rates and price and about investment products and services are dealt with separately; here, we shall consider the following categories.

(a)   Safety

Safety is a major consideration of many laws obliging the provision of information. The labelling of drugs is a good example and is dealt with in Chapter 12.[6] Under s 11(1) of the Consumer Protection Act 1987, the government may make safety regulations for the purpose of securing that appropriate information is provided in relation to other products. In particular, safety regulations may require that a mark, warning, instruction or other information be put on or accompany products. For example, certain fireworks must be marked with the words 'This device must not be sold to, or used by, a member of the general public', and packets of sparklers must be marked: 'Warning: not to be given to children under 5 years of age.'[7] Fireworks are inherently dangerous and cause many injuries, especially to children.[8] In the European Community there are provisions for the

---

[5]   Cf B Katz *Public Policy Towards Consumer Product Information* (PhD Thesis, University of Penn 1973) Chapters 5–7.
[6]   Labelling of durable goods is covered in Chapter 10 on product standards.
[7]   Fireworks (Safety) Regulations 1997, SI 1997/2294, reg 7.
[8]   See *Controls on the Availability of Fireworks: A Discussion Paper* (DTI, 1996).

compulsory labelling of dangerous products—products which are explosive, oxidising, flammable, toxic, harmful to health, corrosive, carcinogenic and so on. Labels of these products must contain information, through danger symbols, and the nature of the risk and safe uses (both expressed by standard phrases).[9] Domestic cleansers are a product which could be covered.[10] Compulsory labelling is justified for these products because of their widespread use, diversity and potential danger. A significant number of accidental poisonings from household cleaning products are reported among young children.

The United States was first in the field of safety labelling for cigarettes. The Federal Cigarette Labeling and Advertising Act 1965 made it unlawful to market cigarettes without a prominent statement on the packet that smoking was dangerous to health.[11] Other countries followed suit; cigarette packets had to be labelled and warnings have also to accompany advertisements.[12] In 1972 a Private Member's Bill in Britain to similar effect failed to obtain a second reading. Voluntary agreements were subsequently reached between the government and the tobacco manufacturing industry that warnings must appear on cigarette packets and in poster and press advertisements and would be such that they were easily seen by consumers. Self-regulation continues with press and poster advertisements. These must carry the health warnings which are required to appear by rotation on cigarette packets (discussed shortly). The area of press and poster advertisements for cigarettes used for the health warning must be 20%.[13]

As a result of a European Directive the warnings on cigarette packets have been put on a legal basis.[14] In fact the regulations under s 11 of the Consumer Protection Act 1987 require that cigarette packets contain health warnings more demanding than those in the Directive.[15] The Directive

---

[9]   See *Miller: Product Liability and Safety Encyclopaedia* (Butterworths, looseleaf), Division V.

[10] See also Commission Recommendation 89/542/EEC of 13 September 1989 in *Miller: Product Liability and Safety Encyclopaedia* at **V [1106]**.

[11] 15 USC §1333. M Redish 'Tobacco Advertising and the First Amendment' (1996) 81 Iowa LR 589; Note 'An exercise in administrative creativity: The FDA's assertion of jurisdiction over tobacco' (1996) 45 Cath UL Rev 991.

[12] For example, NSW: Cigarettes (Labelling) Act 1972.

[13] Voluntary Agreement on Tobacco Advertising and Promotion, December 1994. This agreement will be superseded by EC Directive 98/43 on the approximation of laws, regulations and administrative provisions relating to the advertising of tobacco products OJ L 213 30.07.98 p 9. For the government's attempts to implement the Directive see *R v Secretary of State for Health, ex p Imperial Tobacco Ltd* [2000] 1 All ER 572, [2000] 1 CMLR 307.

[14] Tobacco Products Labelling (Safety) Regulations 1991, SI 1991/1530. See also Tobacco Products Labelling (Safety) Amendment Regulations 1993, SI 1993/1947.

[15] Council Directive [on] the labelling of tobacco products, 89/622/EEC OJ 1989 L359, as amended by Council Directive 92/41/EEC.

requires the warning 'Tobacco seriously damages health' on their most visible surface, covering at least 4% of the surface on which it is printed; the regulations require stark health warnings on both the front and back of the packet, taking up 6% of the surface on which they are printed. The warnings in the regulations are 'Smoking Kills', 'Smoking Causes Cancer', 'Smoking Causes Heart Disease', 'Smoking Causes Fatal Diseases', 'Smoking When Pregnant Harms Your Baby', and 'Protect Children: Don't Make Them Breathe Your Smoke'. These must be regularly rotated on the assumption that that way they are more likely to be noticed.

The European Court of Justice rejected a claim by the tobacco industry that the UK regulations, being stricter than the Directive, constituted an obstacle to free trade within the European Community. The Directive stipulated only minimum sizes for the warning, and even if the regulations resulted in unfavourable treatment for domestic products they were justified because of the health risks.[16] A Private Member's Bill in 1995 proposed, along Canadian and Australian lines, that the warnings cover at least 25% of the surface on which they were printed, with prominent borders. It was lent some support by market research that warnings which cover a comparatively small area are easy to ignore and that consumers tend to equate the size of the warning with the magnitude of the risk.[17]

The warnings by themselves do not seem to have greatly affected the consumption of cigarettes—a reminder that simply obliging businesses to provide information to the public is frequently ineffective as a means of consumer protection. One of the few relevant studies found that anti-smoking publicity, taking the form of health scares, reduced consumption by between 3–7% during the year of the scare and the subsequent year.[18] Perhaps this is not surprising: warnings will not overcome the prevalent attitude maintained by advertising, particularly persuasive to the young, that smoking is an acceptable social activity. There are difficulties in trying to give up the habit voluntarily because of the social pressures and because nicotine is addictive. In other words, many smokers will not act on the information readily available to them about the dangers of smoking. The anti-smoking lobby has campaigned for more drastic laws, such as a total ban on all forms of advertising; prominent mention of tar levels on cigarette packets; a significant increase in taxation to make excessive consumption of cigarettes prohibitive; and ultimately a ban on sales.

---

[16]   *R v Secretary of State for Health, ex p Gallaher Ltd* Case C-11/92 [1993] ECR I-3545.

[17]   *Health Warnings on Cigarette and Tobacco Packs. Report on Research to Inform European Standardisation* (Health Education Authority, 1990).

[18]   S Witt and C Pass 'The Effects of Health Warnings and Advertising on the Demand for Cigarettes' (1981) 28 Scottish J of Pol Econ 86–91.

(b)   Quality

Grading is a direct means of indicating quality if there is an agreement on how to set the grades, and providing consumers appreciate the difference between products of different grades. For example, under the Common Agricultural Policy, about 30 fruits and vegetables, together with eggs and wine, are subject to grading regulations in the European Union.[19] The grading is primarily to encourage growers to improve quality and to assist marketing, but it also benefits consumers by informing them about the quality of their purchases. Under the grading regulations for fresh fruit and vegetables, products offered for sale at both wholesale and retail outlets must clearly show the origin; the quality class (Extra, I, II and III); and the variety. It is sufficient for retailers to sell products direct from a container with the requisite information attached if the details are clearly visible to consumers. Otherwise there must be a display card or the information must be on the packet if there is prepacking. The EC grading is not concerned directly with eating quality but with size and condition. Within a class a particular fruit or vegetable must be of a minimum size and within batch the particular fruit or vegetable must not vary in size by more than a specified tolerance. There are difficulties in enforcing the regulations with the multifarious retail outlets for fruit and vegetables.

Grade labelling is more difficult with complex consumer durables than with natural products like fresh fruit and vegetables. Performance characteristics are one way of conveying information about the quality of consumer durables; for example an Appliance Labelling Rule,[1] promulgated by the Federal Trade Commission, requires the disclosure of energy consumption or efficiency information (eg water rate use) in relation to some eleven product categories of household appliance (eg refrigerators, dishwashers, washing machines, lamps). The information must be disclosed in catalogues and at the point of sale in the form of yellow and black Energy Guide labels, and is designed to enable consumers to compare the energy use of competing appliances. The eco-labelling scheme, considered below, is a form of grade labelling.

A common method of disclosing quality information, however, is through compositional labelling. Traditionally, compositional labelling was confined to processed food, but in recent years has been extended to products like textiles. Footwear must be labelled with its main components.[2] Textiles are

---

[19]   The relevant EC Regulations are voluminous: see *Butterworths Law of Food and Drugs* (looseleaf) Division R.

[1]   16 CFR §305.

[2]   Footwear (Indication of Composition) Labelling Regulations 1995, SI 1995/ 2489 implementing European Parliament and Council Directive 94/11/EC, [1994] OJ No L100.

said to be a suitable area for compulsory labelling because consumers face difficulties in distinguishing and in appreciating the characteristics of the many synthetic and natural fibres. European Union countries, the United States, Canada and Australia compel fibre content labelling for textiles.[3] A broad statement of the EC Directive is that the names of fibres must be specified on a garment or in advertisements, together with the percentage of the different fibres used. Further, the limited number of generic names mentioned in the Directive must be used to describe fibres, and restrictions are placed on the use of words such as 'pure' when referring to fibre content.

One aspect of quality labelling in some countries has been to encourage voluntary action on the part of businesses. Quality marks convey a guarantee of a certain quality without normally providing details of use, composition or performance.[4] The marks usually take the form of a symbol, which indicates compliance with a standard fixed by a body like the British Standards Institution. Its 'Kitemark' symbol tells consumers that a product complies with a BSI standard, and that the manufacturer's production process is regularly inspected, its quality control methods checked and a specified number of sample items ready for retail sale tested. Although compliance with some BSI standards is required by legislation, most are issued for voluntary adoption. About 90% of BSI standards now reflect internationally agreed standards. Surveys indicate that there is considerable public ignorance of such quality marks and that consumers, especially those in the lower socio-economic groups, are quite unsure about the properties to which the marks refer.

(c)   Quantity

One of the first pieces of information the law obliged businesses to provide to consumers was a statement of the quantity of products being sold. Quantity marking facilitates inter-produce comparisons by consumers. Legislation obliges manufacturers to mark many prepacked goods with a statement of their weight or other appropriate quantity.[5] If goods are not prepacked, weight may still have to be made known to consumers; one

---

[3]   Directives [on] Textiles No 71/307/EEC, [1971] OJ No L 185; No 83/623/EEC, [1983] OJ No L 353, (implemented in UK by Textile Products (Indications of Fibre Content) Regulations 1986, SI 1986/26, as amended by SI 1988/1350, SI 1994/450, SI 1998/1169).

[4]   See N Reich and H-W Micklitz *Consumer Legislation in the EC Countries* (Van Nostrand Reinhold, 1980) pp 35–36.

[5]   Weights and Measures Act 1985, s 48; Weights and Measures (Packaged Goods) Regulations 1986, SI 1986/2049.

course is to require weighing or counting in the presence of purchasers.[6] A less satisfactory alternative is to allow retailers to have a self-indicating type of scale available for use by consumers with a notice drawing attention to the facility.[7] Observation suggests that few consumers use the facility. The United States Fair Packaging and Labeling Act makes necessary a statement of the net quantity of a serving if representations are made concerning the number of servings.[8]

For marketing executives, the package is often more important than the product it contains. This attitude has led to a situation where packaging often misleads consumers about the nature—in particular the amount—of an enclosed product. Modern packaging is frequently a waste of economic resources and a cause of environmental pollution. It results in consumers spending substantial amounts on what may be discarded as soon as a product is opened. Containers may be necessary for reasons of hygiene and freshness, and to store the product, but promotional considerations frequently dictate an unnecessary extravagance in design. Bulk-buying might achieve considerable savings because the packaging content of products is equivalent to a not insignificant part of the retail price. There is some incentive to reduce excessive packaging as a result of the European Community inspired obligation on producers to recover and recycle packaging waste.[9]

Legislation directed at deceptive practices, such as the Trade Descriptions Act 1968, is only a partial answer to misleading packaging. As a result of s 22(3)(b) of the Weights and Measures Act 1985 regulations may be made obliging containers to be filled to specified levels (eg in percentage terms). South Australian legislation actually lays down percentage levels for the amount of slack—25% in normal cases and 35% where there is an inner container.[10] New Zealand's law attempts to suppress spurious advertising about sizes (eg 'economy size') by making it specifically unlawful to suggest that there is a price advantage associated with a particular size when this is not the case.[11]

6   Weights and Measures Act 1985, s 45(1)(a).
7   See Weights and Measures Act 1985, s 45(3).
8   15 USC § 1453(a)(4).
9   Producer Responsibility Obligations (Packaging Waste) Regulations 1997, SI 1997/648; the Packaging (Esential Requirements) Regulations 1998, SI 1998/1165
10   Packages Act 1969–72 (SA), ss 26, 37. See also 15 USC §1454(c)(4) (regulations may prevent the non-functional slack fill of products (ie filling substantially less than capacity for reasons other than the protection of contents or the requirements of manufacture)).
11   Consumer Information Act 1969, s 10(5).

(d) Origin

Marking of goods with their country of origin is criticised as an unreliable indication of the quality and properties of products, and a hindrance to free trade among countries and thus to consumer welfare. One of its justifications is that it permits consumers to discriminate against imported goods on patriotic, political or personal grounds and that it may inform them about quality. Origin marking can take various forms. It can be limited to ensuring that foreign products are not falsely passed off as to their country of origin.[12] Alternatively, it might require that products be marked with or accompanied by an indication of origin, which might also have to be included in certain advertisements.[13] Generally speaking, there is no obligation in United Kingdom and European law that products bear marks of origin, although there is nothing to prevent voluntary marking.[14] The free trade argument weighs heavily in the European Union approach.

(e) Use

Use marking is mainly voluntary; where compulsory it is largely concerned with safety (eg 'Keep out of reach of children' for poisons and drugs). An exception is that food to be delivered as such to the ultimate consumer must be marked or labelled with instructions for use if it would be difficult to make appropriate use of it in the absence of such instructions.[15] However, care instructions are an aspect of use marking of growing importance. Consumer advocates justify care instructions for textiles because fibre content alone is insufficient to inform consumers exactly what cleaning processes may be used. Without care labelling, appreciable numbers of garments can be rendered useless, causing consumer dissatisfaction and wasting economic resources. In many countries care labelling depends on the voluntary efforts of trade associations. The International Organisation for Standardisation, based in Geneva, has developed a code of graphic symbols for the making of textile articles with information on their care in use.[16]

---

[12]   Eg Trade Descriptions Act 1968, s 16. On misleading trade marks see eg *Re Swiss Miss Trade Mark* [1997] RPC 219.

[13]   For example, Trade Descriptions Act 1972; Trade Descriptions (Place of Production) (Marking) Order 1988, SI 1988/1771, repealed and revoked respectively.

[14]   *Trade Descriptions Act 1968—Origin Marking Guidance Notes* (DTI, 1996).

[15]   Food Labelling Regulations 1996, SI 1996/1499, reg 5(g).

[16]   *Textiles—Care Labelling Code Using symbols* ISO 3758, 1991.

The objection to compulsory care labelling has been mainly that the variety of factors determining how textiles respond to treatment is too great—and includes behaviour solely within the province of consumers—for manufacturers to be threatened with criminal sanctions. The Federal Trade Commission in the United States makes care labelling compulsory for textile wearing apparel under a rule that not to label constitutes an unfair or deceptive act or practice.[17] The rationale of the rule is that technological advance in the apparel and cleaning industries and the host of textiles on the market, each with different characteristics, made it impossible for consumers to inform themselves or to determine care information by the traditional means of trial and error.

(f)   Contractual terms and parties

Chapter 7 contained a discussion of how regulated agreements under the Consumer Credit Act 1974 must contain information about important contractual terms. The Federal Trade Commission in the United States can go one step further than such a provision. It can order particular businesses to disclose orally, in dealing with consumers, information already required to be set down in written form. In *Tashof v Federal Trade Commission*[18] a Federal Trade Commission order was upheld obliging a business located in an area inhabited by low-income consumers, who employed 'bait and switch' (see Chapter 8) with respect to sales, adequately to disclose its charges, both orally and in writing. Oral disclosure was required because customers were relatively unsophisticated and would not benefit from written disclosure alone. Critics argue that requiring oral disclosure of important terms of sale faces insuperable barriers of enforcement. Perhaps a more pertinent point to make is that other forms of regulation (like banning particular modes of sale) are a more efficient method of protecting consumers.

Consumers need an effective means of identifying those behind a business to further their complaints, to sue, or to enforce any judgment. If a business is incorporated it might be possible to trace the controllers of the company through the companies' registry. The Registration of Business Names Act 1916 provided a central registry of business names for those carrying on a business under a name different from their real name or for a company carrying on a business under a name which was different from its corporate name. That Act has been repealed. Instead of a central registry,

---

[17]   Care Labelling of Textile Wearing Apparel and Certain Piece Goods, 16 CFR 423.
[18]   437 F 2d 707, 714 (1970). See also *Encyclopaedia Britannica Inc v Federal Trade Commission* 605 F 2d 964 (1979).

the Business Names Act 1985 introduced a system of disclosure by businesses themselves of their proprietors' names. Disclosure is required in business documents, at business premises and immediately on request in writing to a person with whom anything is done or discussed in the course of a business.[19] Disclosure is not required in advertisements. Breach of the disclosure requirements constitutes a criminal offence. Moreover, a court must dismiss any action brought by a person who is in breach of the provisions, arising out of a contract made in the course of the business, if the breach was in existence at the time the contract was made, and if the defendant shows that he has been unable to pursue a claim arising out of that contract or has suffered financial loss by reason of the breach.[20] A court can permit the proceedings to continue if satisfied that it is just and equitable. The deterrent effect of this provision is undermined considerably by the difficulties of establishing an inability to pursue a claim or financial loss.

At one time in Britain the courts could publicise the fact that a business had been convicted of a consumer protection offence. The nature and outcome of, and the businesses involved in, small claims adjudications are prominently published in local newspapers in some Australian jurisdictions. In addition, some Australian consumer affairs departments publish annual lists of businesses whose methods are open to question or who have given rise to consumer complaints which have not been resolved satisfactorily. In this country the Office of Fair Trading has deliberately publicised the names of businesses against whom it has obtained undertakings for breaches of the civil and criminal law under Part III of the Fair Trading Act 1973. These are some examples of how the law requires that information about business behaviour must be publicised. Such action is not to be disparaged because it can have a powerful deterrent effect on those businesses which are mindful of their responsibilities. The deterrent effect is lessened, however, to the extent that larger firms are prepared to counteract a bad reputation by conducting an advertising campaign, and that smaller firms simply change their name and carry on in the same way.

Generally speaking, there has been a reluctance to countenance measures which would lead to greater dissemination of information about the reputation of individual businesses and business people, such as the publication of blacklists. The culture may be changing. In 1997 the National House Builders Council announced that it would place the names of 'cowboy' builders on a public blacklist. The Council is a voluntary body, which provides a warranty for new houses built by its members, guaranteeing that poor work will be corrected. Previously, the Council did not disclose publicly the names of those it had expelled because of

---

[19]   Section 4(1)–(2).
[20]   Section 5(1).

complaints. Along the same 'name and shame' lines, the Department of Trade and Industry established a 'hot line' in early 1998, enabling the public to pass on information about undischarged bankrupts and directors acting in breach of a disqualification under the Company Directors Disqualification Act 1986. The statistics reveal that undischarged bankrupts and disqualified directors are often associated with companies dealing adversely with consumers.

(g) Post-contractual rights

An underrated aspect of disclosure regulation is providing consumers with information about their legal rights if something goes wrong with a consumer transaction. With cancellable agreements under the Consumer Credit Act 1974, consumers must be notified about their rights to cancel an agreement, but probably few read this and even fewer readily comprehend it.[1] The Consumer Transactions (Restrictions on Statements) Order 1976 requires signs in shops, advertisements, containers and documents issued with products such as manufacturers' guarantees, not to be worded so as purportedly to deprive consumers of their rights when goods are sold without title, do not correspond with their description, or are unsatisfactory or not fit for the purpose.[2] In *Hughes v Hall*[3] secondhand car dealers included the phrase 'sold as seen and inspected' in their documentation. The magistrates dismissed informations for breach of the Order on the grounds that the phrase was too vague and would not enable the dealers to avoid their civil liability. The Divisional Court allowed the prosecutor's appeal. Prima facie, and subject to what else might be expressly said in the contract, the phrase would negate a sale by description and therefore be in breach of the Order.

These are limited steps: concise and understandable information attached to products, set out in written documents or displayed at retail premises should benefit many consumers. Another approach is for the government to promote the establishment of consumer advice centres in major shopping areas, and interactive computer programmes for libraries and the internet, where consumers can obtain advice about their post-contractual legal rights.

---

[1] Consumer Credit Act 1974, s 64(1). Similar provisions for notification of cooling off periods are found in the Timeshare Act 1992; the Consumer Protection (Cancellation of Contracts Concluded away from Business Premises) Regulations 1987, SI 1987/2117; the draft Consumer Protection (Contracts Concluded By Means of Distance Communication) Regulations 2000.

[2] SI 1976/1813 as amended by SI 1978/127.

[3] [1981] RTR 430, 125 Sol Jo 255. Cf *Cavendish-Woodhouse Ltd v Manley* (1984) 148 JP 299.

(h)   Environmental impact

Environmental consciousness has grown enormously in the last decade
and so too has consumer demand for environmental labelling. Eco-labelling
schemes now operate in many countries: the German Blue Angel scheme,
the Nordic Swan, Canadian Environmental Choice and the Japanese Eco
Mark.[4] An EC eco-labelling scheme was introduced in 1992.[5] Its objectives
have been to promote the production and use of products which have a
reduced environmental impact during their life cycle and to provide
consumers with better information on the environmental impact of
products. Eco-labelling is currently available for 12 product groups, such
as light bulbs, washing machines, laundry detergents and T-shirts.
Manufacturers, including those outside the European Union, may apply
for an eco-label and the product must meet certain criteria in order to
qualify. A life-cycle assessment of a product is made, taking particularly
environmental costs into account. Applications are assessed and awards
made by competent bodies within individual Member States. In Britain
there is a specially constituted body, the UK Ecolabelling Board.[6] Successful
manufacturers contract with the competent body for use of the label.

The EC eco-labelling scheme has had a number of flaws and has been
slow to develop. It is voluntary in nature and a major problem has been the
low level of business interest in the scheme. Partly this has been due to
delay in the European Commission in adopting criteria for award of an eco-
label and partly to a lack of enthusiasm among some Member States.
There is also some debate about the misuse of an award for anti-competitive
purposes and about the nature of the assessment criteria. For example, it
has been said that the criteria ought to take into account whether the
product in question is actually needed and is not merely a waste of natural
resources.[7] 'Fitness for use' as required by the Regulation does not extend
so far. Further, the Regulation is not an exclusive scheme, and neither is
the scheme underpinned in Britain by a broad standard prohibiting false
environmental claims. Perhaps most importantly, a recent European survey
is said to have found that some 60% of refrigerators were incorrectly
labelled, thus throwing considerable doubt over the value of eco-labelling.[8]

The EC eco-labelling scheme is currently under review. The Commission
Proposal for revising the Regulation includes the establishment, through

[4]   *Eco-Labelling: Actual Effects of Selected Programmes* (OECD, 1997).
[5]   Regulation (EEC) No 880/92, [1992] OJ L 99.
[6]   United Kingdom Ecolabelling Regulations 1992, SI 1992/2383.
[7]   O McIntyre 'Environmental Labelling—Clear Conscience for the Consumer or a
Missed Opportunity?' [1994] JBL 270, 278.
[8]   (1998) Observer, 20 September, p 16.

an association of competent bodies, of a single European Ecolabelling Organisation which will be responsible for setting the criteria for product groups selected by the Commission and for promoting the scheme. Other aspects include the simplification of procedures for setting criteria; the extension of the right to apply for an eco-label to retailers applying for own brand products; the introduction of a graded eco-label and the imposition of a ceiling on fees chargeable for applying for the eco-label. The Commission Proposal also includes a provision to phrase out national schemes over time, for products where an EC label is available.[9]

3   FOOD LABELLING

A broad prohibition in food legislation seeks to prevent food labelling and advertising which falsely describes a food or which is likely to mislead consumers as to the true character of a food.[10] In addition to the broad prohibition on misleading labelling, the law requires manufacturers to disclose specific information on all food labels. When this aspect of food labelling was first introduced in Britain in 1944 it was simply assumed that it would protect consumers to the same extent as compositional standards.[11] Developments in the technology, processing and marketing of food have strengthened the importance of food labelling. Consumers are now more dependent on food labelling because an increasing proportion of foods is sold prepacked, which partially or wholly prevents visual assessment, and because there is an increasing diversity of foods, the result of factors such as modern processing techniques. Social changes, however, have undermined the extent to which consumers acquire their knowledge from previous generations. An additional factor is that consumers are more aware of risk, associated with particular foods, and thus more demanding that information be available on labels so these can be minimised.[12] The importance of technology is highlighted by the development of genetically modified foods.

In the nineteenth century it was thought sufficient to inform the consumer when an article of food was a mixture and not a pure product. The assumption was that consumers were sufficiently protected as long as they were not misled. They were benefiting by purchasing a mixed and therefore a cheaper article, and they would not be safeguarded further by

---

[9]   [1997] OJ C114/9.
[10] Food Safety Act 1990, s 15. See R Lawson 'Food Claims' (1993) 143 NLJ 520, 557.
[11] *The Labelling and Advertising of Foods* (1942—), Cmd 6482, xi, 113.
[12] A Turner 'Prepacked Food Labelling: Past, Present and Future' (1995) British Food J, v 97, No 5, p 23.

knowing the actual ingredients.[13] A similar attitude was adopted to the labelling of drugs. A select committee which considered the matter in 1914 concluded that labelling would not protect the public since, to the majority of purchasers, a statement of composition or contents would afford no information because of its technical language. Indeed, said the committee, the simplest substances might acquire distinction from being described in complicated chemical terms.[14]

Under s 4 of the Sale of Food (Weights and Measures) Act 1926, a number of prepacked foods had to be labelled with an indication of quantity. Restrictions on the use of preservatives under the Public Health (Preservatives etc in Food) Regulations 1925 were accompanied by a requirement that certain foods containing permitted preservatives had to be labelled to that effect, not so much to benefit ordinary consumers, who were protected by the general limitations on their use, but to benefit children, invalids and other particularly vulnerable persons who, in the absence of any declaration, would if necessary be unable to avoid their use.[15] Wartime conditions provided the impetus for wide-ranging mandatory food labelling. Under the Labelling of Food Order (No 2) 1944, prepacked articles of food had to bear a label indicating the name and address of the business, the common name of the food, its quantity and a list of ingredients in descending order of amounts (although the fact that the ingredients were listed in descending order of amounts did not have to be stated).

The basic requirements have been substantially re-enacted in subsequent regulations where modification has tended to extend labelling requirements. Quantity markings are now governed by the Weights and Measures Acts 1985 and Regulations.[16] The Food Labelling Regulations 1996, implementing various Directives of the European Community,[17] apply to most food which is ready for delivery to the ultimate consumer or to a catering establishment. Food has to be marked or labelled with the name of the food, a list of ingredients, an indication of appropriate durability, any special storage conditions or conditions of use, the name and address of

---

[13] For example, Sale of Food and Drugs Act 1875, ss 7, 8. See also *Report from the Select Committee on Adulteration of Food Act* (1872), 1874, C 262, vi. 243, p v.
[14] *Report from the Select Committee on Patent Medicines* (1914) Parl Paper 414, xi 1.
[15] Ministry of Health *Final Report of the Departmental Committee on the Use of Preservatives and Colouring Matters in Food* (HMSO, 1924) p 45.
[16] Weights and Measures (Packaged Goods) Regulations 1986, SI 1986/2049, as amended, reg 10.
[17] Food Labelling Regulations 1996, SI 1996/1499 (as amended) implementing a number of European Community Council Directives, primarily Council Directive 979/112/EEC (OJ L33 08.02.79). See also the Natural Mineral Waters Regulations 1985, 1985/71.

the manufacturer or packer,[18] and in certain cases particulars of the place of origin of the food (if failure to give such particulars might mislead a purchaser to a material degree as to the true origin of the food) and instructions for use (if it would be difficult to make appropriate use of the food in the absence of such instructions) (reg 5).

Generally speaking, ingredients must be listed in descending order by weight determined as at the time of their use in the preparation of the food (reg 13(1)). But consumers are not always aware that ingredients are listed in this manner and it has been suggested that an explanation should be added to this effect. Now as a result of the so-called QUID directive of the European Community, percentage declarations of ingredients are necessary if a food is characterised by the presence of a particular ingredient or the labelling of the food places special emphasis on this: minimum and maximum percentages are necessary respectively (reg 19(1)–(2)). Simple ingredient labelling will not always enlighten consumers as to the composition of foods. By using two substances with similar functions in a food instead of one, it may appear that a particular type of ingredient is present in lesser amounts than is really the case. In addition, it may be that there is no need for an exhaustive list of ingredients used in manufacturing processes, and that an additive used in an ingredient, but not serving any purpose in the finished product, is exempt.[19]

The regulations attempt to ensure that ordinary consumers should be able to understand the nature of the ingredients listed. The name used for any ingredient must be a name which, if the ingredient in question were itself being sold as a food, could be used as the name of the food (reg 14(1)). In some situations, generic names are permitted. In the case of flavourings it is sufficient simply to use the word 'flavouring' without naming the particular flavouring.[20] Objection has been taken to this because consumers may, as a matter of choice, wish to avoid ingesting particular types of flavourings, which are presently permitted, although there is no evidence of their danger to humans. By contrast, with additives serving a wide range of functions, the function and the additive's specific name (or serial number) must be set out.[1] Where the additive is a sweetener, or there is added sugar and a sweetener, this must be indicated ('with sweetener(s)' or 'with sugar(s) and sweetener(s)').[2]

---

[18] To enable the consumer to contact the person responsible: *Provincia Autonoma di Trento v Deya di Depretto Gino Snc* Case C-83/96 [1998] All ER (EC) 252.

[19] *Pfanni Werke Otto Eckart KG v Landeshauptstadt München und Landesanwaltschaft Bayern* Case C-144/93 [1994] ECR I-4605.

[20] Regulation 14(5).

[1] Regulation 14(9). The functions include as an acid, antioxidant, bulking agent, emulsifier, firming enhancer, gelling agent, preservative, stabiliser, sweetener, and thickener.

[2] Regulation 34(1)–(2).

Broad standards for food are ineffective in dealing with the sale of stale food or food which might have deteriorated. Food needs to be mouldy or 'bad' (in ordinary parlance) rather than simply stale before it is caught by the unfit food provisions. Open-date marking of food is an important solution to the problem. It recognises the consumer's right to know the freshness of food being purchased as well as providing an incentive for retailers to institute a workable system of stock rotation and to ensure that food is in as fresh a condition as is technically possible. Poor stock rotation by retailers can render a manufacturer's date marking inaccurate as an indication of freshness. Yet date marking raises the possibility of consumer pressure on retailers and can thus actually encourage more efficiency in handling stock. A possibility is the selective consumer purchase of foods with later dates, with the consequent wastage of other foods which are still fresh. Proper stock control can reduce this.

As a result of the Food Labelling Regulations 1996[3] an indication of minimum durability is required for many prepacked foods by the words 'best before' followed by the date up to and including which the food can reasonably be expected to retain its optimum condition. In the case of food which is highly perishable, and in consequence likely, after a short time, to pose an immediate danger to health, minimum durability of the food must be indicated by a 'use by' date.[4] There is the argument against 'best before' dates that they lead to unnecessary wastage because of the implication that to eat a food any time later than the 'best before' date is dangerous. Another problem is that consumers store foods differently and 'best before' dates may have to be set to take account of the worst possible storage conditions. It is not an offence to sell food beyond the 'best before' date, although an offence occurs if food is sold beyond a use by date.[5] Date marking is not the complete answer for food freshness for there are other matters such as stock control, temperature control and further food labelling (eg setting out storage conditions).[6]

Special provisions govern the labelling and advertising of certain foods, and the way particular claims about food are made. For example, there are additional labelling requirements for food sold from vending machines and for alcoholic drinks. Certain words and descriptions cannot be used in the labelling and advertising of a food, except in accordance with appropriate conditions.[7] Nutritional labelling is not obligatory, but

---

[3]   SI 1996/1499.
[4]   Regulations 20–21.
[5]   Regulation 41(1)(d).
[6]   Food Safety (Temperature Control) Regulations 1995, SI 1995/2200.
[7]   Food Labelling Regulations 1996, SI 1996/1499, reg 42(1). See also Bread and Flour Regulations 1998, SI 1998/141.

nutritional claims are prohibited on labels or in advertisements unless the food is capable of fulfilling the claim and the particular nutritional characteristics are identified.[8] (Energy, protein, vitamin, mineral and cholesterol claims are similarly restricted.) Claims that a food is capable of preventing, treating or curing a human disease must not be made. Between nutritional and medicinal claims, however, are a range of unregulated health claims. The evidence is that consumers do not distinguish between nutrition and health claims and that they are confused by longer and more complex health claims.[9] The European Commission is considering what approach should be followed at community level to the regulation of claims, including not only compositional claims such as 'light' and 'low-fat', but also health and similar types of claims which are increasingly being made on so-called 'functional foods'.[10]

There has been considerable hostility from consumer and environmental groups to genetically modified foods. Commercial pressures, and the potential benefit from the use of modern biotechnology (eg resistance to herbicides) have meant that such foods have been permitted onto the market. However, to allay consumer fears, there are European Community Regulations establishing common labelling rules for foods containing genetically modified soya and maize and additives.[11] However, products with genetically modified ingredients which are deemed 'chemically identical' or 'substantially equivalent' to conventional foods do not require labelling. This is a considerable gap, and one estimate is that 80% of genetically altered foods are not covered by the regulation. Moreover, the regulation does not prescribe what the labelling should say, with the possibility that warning labels could become promotional claims (eg 'produced with the benefit of modern biotechnology'). In 1998 the European Commission adopted further requirements for the compulsory labelling of products containing genetically modified soya or maize.[12]

---

[8]   Food Labelling Regulations 1996, reg 40, Sch 6.
[9]   *Messages on Food* (NCC, 1997).
[10]   *The General Principles of Food Law in the European Union. Commission Green Paper* COM (97) 176 final, 30 April 1997, p 33.
[11]   Labelling Genetically Modified Foods, Commission Regulation EC/1813/97, [1997] OJ No L 257; Commission Regulation EC/50/2000 [2000] OJ No L 6 p 15.
[12]   Council Regulation EC/1139/98, OJ L 190 p 86, implemented by the Food Labelling (Amendment) Regulations 1999, SI 1999/747, breach of which is a criminal offence. The absence of a standard test for the presence of GMOs in foodstuffs may make the regulations difficult to enforce: 'GM food labelling rules undermined by lack of reliable tests' (1999) 290 ENDS 49. See also the Genetically Modified and Novel Foods (Labelling) (England) Regulations 2000, SI 2000/768.

4   PRICE INFORMATION

Price information is crucial to consumers. It is essential for comparative shopping, in which an increasing proportion of consumers seem for some time to have engaged.[13] Unless prices are displayed, the opportunity cost of comparative shopping increases since more time and effort must be expended. Price information also avoids the situation of consumers entering transactions, despite misgivings, because once they have made personal contact with a business they may feel embarrassed at not going further. Consumers entering a restaurant where the prices are only set out on their menus are an example.

Despite the importance of price information to the economic interests of consumers, compulsory price marking is a relatively recent development. For some time French and German laws have required businesses, including those providing services like credit providers, restaurateurs and car repairers, to display their prices at their place of business.[14] Developments in Britain, however, were must less advanced, although many businesses displayed prices voluntarily. The change in policy was a result of two factors. Firstly, in the 1970s, the government saw price marking as an aspect for both its anti-inflation policy and its consumer protection policy (especially concerned with poorer consumers). Secondly, an EC Directive from 1979 required prices to be marked on foodstuffs and in 1988 this was extended to non-food products.[15] The EC Directives do not apply to services.

Section 4(1) of the Prices Act 1974 provides that:

(1)   The Secretary of State may by order make provision for securing:

(a)   that prices are indicated on or in relation to goods which a person indicates are or may be for sale by retail, whether or not the goods are in existence when he does so;

(b)   that charges are indicated for services which a person indicates are or may be provided, except services which he indicates are or may be provided only for the purposes of businesses carried on by other persons;

(c)   that prices of such goods or changes for such services are not indicated in a manner which the Secretary of State considers inappropriate and that no part of a penny except one half-penny is specified in the amount of an indicated price or charge.

---

[13]   A Gabor 'Consumer Oriented Pricing' in D Thorpe *Research in Retailing and Distribution* (Saxon, 1974) p 50.

[14]   Eg N Reich and H-W Micklitz *Consumer Legislation in the Federal Republic of Germany* (Van Nostrand Reinhold, 1981) pp 35–37; J Calais-Auloy et al *Consumer Legislation in France* (Van Nostrand Reinhold, 1981) pp 83–84.

[15]   Council Directive 79/581/EEC, [1979] OJ L158; as amended by Council Directive 88/315/EEC [1988] OJ L 142, and Council Directive 88/314/EEC [1988] OJ L 142.

Section 4(2) goes on to provide that the regulations can specify how the prices are to be indicated, which includes requiring unit pricing. In addition, the government under the Act can oblige retailers to display information about the range of prices within which particular goods are being commonly sold by retail, in the country as a whole or in particular areas. This provision is limited to food and to necessities which are important to poorer families and are normally the subject of recurrent expenditure by them.[16]

The Price Marking Order 1999[17] requires that the selling price of products being sold at retail must be indicated in writing. Article 7 of the Order, in keeping with the EC Directives, requires that the indication of price be unambiguous and easily identifiable and clearly legible by prospective purchasers.[18] Prices must be inclusive of VAT and any other tax related to the products, although where products are mainly sold to business buyers it is possible to indicate the exclusive price plus the amount of tax (expressed as a sum or percentage). Consequently, consumers who gain access to 'wholesale' stores should beware because the pricing may not be what they are used to. When products are sold at retail with other products or services which have to be paid for along with the former, the price must indicate whether it is inclusive or exclusive of the ancillary products or services. If the latter, the price of the ancillary products or services must also be indicated. There are special rules for displaying petrol prices.

Advertisements are not covered by the Price Marking Order, although if they state the selling price of products they must do so in the manner specified in the Order (which including unit pricing). While certain advertising is not conducive to carrying price indications, in some cases it would be appropriate. Some of the advertising codes require the price to be included: for example, the British Code of Advertising Practice says that advertisements for distance selling must include the charge for delivery.[19]

The Price Marking Order does not cover services. However, there are a limited number of provisions making compulsory price displays for services, or for the combination of products and services where the service element is more than ancillary. Thus premises such as public houses, restaurants

---

[16] Section 5.

[17] SI 1999/3042.

[18] *Allen v Redbridge London Borough Council* [1994] 1 All ER 728, [1994] 1 WLR 139 held that the pricing of products could still satisfy this requirement if they were locked away in a cabinet and consumers needed to ask staff to get them out to see the price. On the Council Directive provisions that pricing has to be in a language easily understood by purchasers: Case C-369/89 *PIAGEME v BVBA Peeters* [1991] ECR I-2971; Case C-85/94 *Groupement des Producteurs, Importateurs et Agents General d'Eaux Minerales Estrangeres, VZW (Piageme) v Peerers NV* [1995] ECR I-2955.

[19] *British Code of Advertising and Sales Promotion* (1999) para 52.3.

and hotels must display in a clear and legible manner the price of food and drinks intended to be consumed on the premises.[20] Another Order requires the display of maximum and minimum prices charged per night for accommodation in hotels and other establishments with not less than four bedrooms or eight beds.[1] Since 1992 it has been compulsory for bureaux de change, which give indications of exchange rates, to do so comprehensively and clearly.[2]

The Price Marking Order 1999 introduces more extensive provision for unit pricing of goods. Unit pricing, which requires goods to be marked with their price per unit quantity, is a means of assisting consumers to compare values. Competing products are often not made up in equal or simply related quantities, and any comparison involves a complex calculation which the average consumer is unable or unwilling to make. It is said that there are drawbacks associated with widespread unit pricing. First, it is said that there are the costs and administrative problems, especially for small businesses, in determining the unit price of products and then ensuring the display of that information. A fluctuation in price necessitates an alteration in the marking, which may discourage 'reduced' offers. But unit pricing might have compensating advantages—tighter inventory control, better space management, fewer price-marking errors, and showing their own-brand labels to advantage. The second drawback of unit pricing is said to be that, unsupported by other information, it is misleading in that it bears little relationship to product quality. Yet unit pricing informs consumers how much they are paying, even if other factors such as quality may determine their final decisions

Unit pricing existed during the Second World War in Britain for a limited number of products.[3] Then with the blossoming of consumer protection in the 1970s it was again invoked for certain basic commodities.[4] However, unit pricing was more firmly grounded in other European countries and in some parts of the United States.[5] Under European Community influence, unit pricing now has an established place in Britain. The Price Marking Order 1999 makes general provision for unit pricing, subject to limited exceptions where the unit price is identical to its selling price goods which

---

[20] Price Marking (Food and Drink on Premises) Order 1979, SI 1979/361.

[1] Tourism (Sleeping Accommodation Price Display) Order 1977, SI 1977/1877 made under the Development of Tourism Act 1969.

[2] Price Indications (Bureaux de Change) (No 2) Regulations 1992, SI 1992/737.

[3] Eg Meat (Maximum Retail) Prices Order 1942, SI 1942/1460, r 4; the Preserves Order 1944, SI 1944/841, Pt 1.

[4] Eg Price Marking (Meat and Fish) Order 1974, SI 1974/1368, Sch, para 4; Price Marking (Prepacked Milk in Vending Machines) Order 1976, SI 1976/796.

[5] See OECD *Package Standardization Unit Pricing and Deceptive Packaging* (1975); N Reich and H-W Micklitz *Consumer Legislation in the EC Countries* (Van Nostrand Reinhold, 1980) p 25.

are pre-packaged in a constant quantity and sold in a small shop, by an itinerant trader or from a vending machine (article 5(3) and see also Sch 2). A small shop is one whose relevant floor area does not exceed 280 square metres (article 1(2)).

Unit price orders require the marking to be clear, legible and easily recognised by consumers. Under the 1999 Order the unit price indication is treated in the same manner as the selling price (ie '(a) unambiguous, easily identifiable and clearly legible; (b) placed in proximity to the products to which it relates; and (c) so placed as to be available to consumers without the need for them to seek assistance from the trader or someone else on his behalf in order to ascertain it' (article 7(1)). The unit of measurement used in unit pricing is crucial, for the higher the unit the more the price differences between products will be accentuated. The mandated units in the 1999 Order range between 10g/ml for such items as herbs, spices and food colourings, through to units as large as 50Kg for coal, though most of the mandated units are 100g/ml (Sch 1).

A final aspect of price disclosure is comparative price information. Assuming that it is not practical for business to provide this directly themselves, an independent or government body has to do so. Consumer journals such as *Which?*, and newspaper articles, contain comparative price information, but this dates quickly and is often limited to relatively expensive items. At one time central government subsidised local consumer groups and consumer advice centres to undertake local price comparison surveys with a view to increasing consumers' purchasing power and stimulating retail competition.[6] Some 300 weekly surveys operated under this scheme covering commonly purchased items in a variety of shops. Monthly and quarterly surveys of non-food products such as fuel and petrol were also common. The information was disseminated by display on notice boards in consumer advice centres, on leaflets distributed by consumer advice centres, Citizens Advice Bureaux and public libraries, and in a few areas through newspaper advertisements. One study concluded that the savings for a consumer in using a price comparison survey was typically in the range of 2½–5%, but suggested that the usage rates might not justify the public expenditure.[7]

(a)   Credit disclosure

One approach would be to ban credit advertisements on the basis that they can never convey enough relevant information about credit

---

[6]   Price Commission Act 1977, s 18; repealed Competition Act 1980.
[7]   D Reeson 'The Economics of Local Price Information Services' (1978) 2 J Cons Studies & Home Econ 35.

transactions and can only be misleading. Law-makers have rejected this approach on the grounds that advertising is an inescapable feature of society and can perform a valuable service in making members of the public aware of credit facilities of which they might otherwise be ignorant.[8] Under the Consumer Credit Act 1974 there is a general prohibition on the credit advertisements covered conveying a false or misleading impression to consumers.[9] More importantly, credit advertisements and advertisements regarding the bailment of goods must disclose detailed information to give a fair and reasonably comprehensive indication of the nature of the credit or hire facilities offered and of their true cost.[10] Advertisements are defined to include display cards and catalogues.[11] It probably includes modern forms of advertising through fax and on the internet. Failure to comply with the credit advertising requirements is a criminal offence,[12] and it may be that a consumer can also obtain a compensation order against a defendant convicted in criminal proceedings for any loss suffered due to the omission of the requisite information.[13]

The main aim of credit disclosure is to redress part of the inequality of bargaining power between consumers and those offering credit by making it easier for consumers to discover the advantages and disadvantages of the alternative credit available. Credit disclosure ('truth in lending') permits the consumer to obtain an accurate description of the total credit charge, to allow easy comparison of different lenders' credit terms, and to help consumers decide whether a purchase should be financed by credit or by other means. An ancillary aim is to sharpen competition between credit institutions—assuming consumers engage in comparative shopping— which may improve the terms on which credit is offered.

The application of this credit disclosure part of the Consumer Credit Act is quite wide and applies to advertisements by anyone carrying on a consumer credit business or a consumer hire business or a business which involves providing credit to individuals secured on land (eg building societies and others financing house purchases on mortgage), whether or not the particular agreements are otherwise regulated by the Act. Exceptions include advertisements which indicate that the credit is only available to corporations, or that the credit must exceed £15,000 and that

---

8   *Crowther Committee* p 259.
9   Consumer Credit Act 1974, s 46. But a statement like the following would seem not to be covered: 'We have to show 23 percent but really it is only about 12 percent flat.'
10   The regulations discussed below are made under s 44. Cf US: Truth in Lending Act, 15 USC §§1601–1665; see also Truth in Lending Regulations (Regulation Z) 12 CFR s 226.
11   Section 189(1).
12   Section 167(2).
13   Powers of Criminal Courts (Sentencing) Act 2000, s 130.

no security is required, or that the security is to consist of property other than land.[14] Advertisements by credit brokers are also covered.[15]

The Consumer Credit (Advertisements) Regulations 1989[16] confine advertisements for credit and bailment to three types, 'simple', 'intermediate' and 'full'. 'Simple' credit advertisements must give no more than the name, logo, address, telephone number and occupation of the business but nothing else indicating a willingness to provide credit. The idea of the simple credit advertisement is to enable credit providers to keep their name before the public. Certain information is obligatory in an 'intermediate' advertisement—the name and address (or telephone number); the security, deposit and insurance required; if the security is the debtor's home, a health warning ('Your home is at risk if you do not keep up repayments on a mortgage or other loan secured on it'); the case price of any goods, services, land, etc specified; the APR;[17] and an indication that written quotations or a full document may be obtained on request. Optional information in 'intermediate' credit advertisements includes a logo, restrictions of credit to particular groups, the extent to which cash and credit consumers are treated differently, and the maximum and minimum credit available.

'Full' credit advertisements must contain all the compulsory information of intermediate advertisements (with slight modifications), information on any restrictions to a particular group, frequency, number and amount of advance payments and of repayments, the extent to which cash and credit consumers are treated differently, and a statement of the total amount payable by the debtor when repayments are at specified intervals or in specified amounts. Substantial compliance with these requirements is not enough, since the regulations provide that 'at least' this information should be in the advertisement.[18] With fixed-sum credit additional information is required in 'full' advertisements—the cash price, the total amount payable,

---

[14] Section 43. Additional exceptions are contained in the Consumer Credit (Exempt Advertisements) Order 1985, SI 1985/621; Consumer Credit (Advertisements) Regulations 1989, SI 1989/1125, reg 1.

[15] Section 151.

[16] SI 1989/1125 as amended by the Consumer Credit (Total Charge for Credit, Agreements and Advertisements) (Amendment) Regulations 1999, SI 1999/3177; the Consumer Credit (Content of Quotations) and Consumer Credit (Advertisements) (Amendment) Regulations 1999, SI 1999/2725 and the Consumer Credit (Advertisements and Content of Quotations) (Amendment) Regulations 2000, SI 2000/1797. The regulations are complex and what follows is a broad outline.

[17] The annual percentage rate of charge (APR) seeks to inform consumers about the effective cost of credit. There have been difficulties in correctly calculating this eg with fixed rate mortgages in their early years: *National Westminster Bank v Devon County Council* (1993) 158 JP 156; *Clarification and Simplification of United Kingdom Consumer Credit Law* (DTI, 1998) pp 3–4.

[18] *Carrington Carr Ltd v Leicestershire County Council* [1993] Crim LR 938.

and either the number of repayments or the period over which they are to be made. Comparative advertising suggesting better terms is permitted in 'full' credit advertisements (but not otherwise), but must be set out and the business making them identified.[19] The requirements for hire advertisements—simple, intermediate and full—are along similar lines.

Obligatory information, and optional information in the case of 'intermediate' credit advertisements, must be presented clearly and easily legible and together as a whole (reg 2(b)). An exception to the latter requirement is that credit advertisements on the premises of a dealer can be split so that certain information (eg the cash price) is displayed on or near products or when consumers enquire, with an indication that other detailed information relating to their supply or credit is displayed or available elsewhere on the premises (reg 6). When a statement of the rate of interest other than the APR is included, the APR must be afforded greater prominence, as by underlining or using bolder print (reg 8). Representative information by way of typical example may be disclosed in certain credit and hire advertisements where an item of information in relation to one transaction differs from that which applies in relation to another transaction of the same class (eg credit terms vary with the subject matter of the transaction or the status of the consumer) (reg 3).

Without the obligation to disclose credit charges and terms businesses could state the cost of an item on credit, or the cost of a loan without specific reference to interest, to other charges and to significant features of any agreement. Advertisements for credit could be in terms of instalments at so much per month or of a global sum to be repaid over a specified period or at the end of a period. Interest, if stated, could be in terms of a confusion of rates—flat rates, reducible rates, compound rates, add-on rates, effective annual rates and nominal rates (ie they might be reduced by bargaining). Flat rate interest (I) is calculated by dividing a hundred times the credit charges (C) by the credit originally extended (P; with purchases this is the case price less the deposit) and the duration of the agreement in years (T). Thus the formula $I = 100C/PT$. As an indication of the cost of credit in instalment transactions, flat rate interest is quite misleading if consumers repay the original credit extended over the period of the agreement and not in a lump sum at its termination. The true rate of interest in such cases is much greater than the flat rate, because in effect consumers are paying interest on money which they have already repaid.

Problems arise where an advertiser of products or services purports to have no credit charge or a modest credit charge but will not sell for cash. With no cash price there is no base to calculate the cost of credit and the advertiser could be charging a substantial amount for it. The Consumer

---

[19]   SI 1989/1125, reg 7(b).

Credit Act 1974 makes it an offence to advertise products or services for sale on credit if they are not available at the same time for cash.[20] Since the section fails to specify the level of the cash price, there is still the possibility of the real cost of credit being hidden by an inflated cash price. United States' law overcomes the problem by making it a violation if a creditor represents as part of the 'cash price' any amount charged in excess of the amount at which a cash sale would be effected.[1] In other words, it makes equivalent the 'cash price' in a credit transaction and the price at which products and services are sold for cash. Yet even here there is the possibility that the price at which cash sales are effected may be inflated and consumers may not realise this because they do not engage in comparative shopping or because it is uncommon to pay cash in such a transaction.

What is the effect of credit disclosure on consumers' knowledge and behaviour? Studies in the United States indicate that after the introduction of credit disclosure, customers were more aware of the general level of interest rates being charged, especially those in higher socio-economic groups. Consumers actually committed to credit transactions were also more knowledgeable about what they were being charged. This says very little, however, because there was still an abysmal ignorance of credit charges, particularly among poorer consumers. In one survey after credit disclosure legislation began operating, only 10% of borrowers could estimate what interest they were paying with a 10% margin of error, and nearly half missed the amount by 50% or more.[2] Very few consumers compare sources of credit before committing themselves to particular transactions, and in this regard credit disclosure had virtually no impact. A survey in California, for example, found that not even a fifth of those noting information about credit charges indicated that it had any effect on past or anticipated behaviour.[3] These surveys are not conclusive, however, particularly since they were conducted soon after credit disclosure was introduced. The effect of credit disclosure is likely to be indirect as consumers gradually become aware that certain sources of credit are cheaper (just as they gradually became aware that some prices at discount houses were lower).[4]

---

[20]   Section 45.

[1]   R Speidel et al *Commercial and Consumer Law* (West, 1974) p 489.

[2]   L Mandell 'Consumer Perception of Incurred Interest Rates' (1971) 26 J of Fin 1143.

[3]   W Brandt and G Day 'Information Disclosure and Consumer Behaviour: An Empirical Evaluation of Truth in Lending' (1973) 7 U of Mich JL Reform 297.

[4]   Another American survey indicates an increased awareness of dollar amounts of credit charges rather than annual percentage charges. T Durkin 'A High-Rate Market for Consumer Loans' in *National Commission on Consumer Finance Technical Studies* (CCH, 1975) vol 2.

To be effective, credit disclosure must be associated with a concerted campaign of educating consumers about credit. There is an overriding need for teaching school children to appreciate the nature of credit transactions and the associated costs and pitfalls. Further, the scope of credit disclosure may need to be widened. Consumers have too little appreciation of the extent to which credit transactions limit their ability to adapt to new needs or unforeseen problems like sickness or unemployment. One suggestion is that charts should be developed which would show how much of a budget under different conditions can safely be committed to credit transactions.

Does credit disclosure achieve the subsidiary aim of furthering competition between credit institutions? A detailed, albeit rather dated, survey of the impact of credit disclosure on the major credit companies in the United States discovered that few companies had lost customers. Only 6% of those companies making consumer finance loans and only 5% of the ones purchasing sales finance contracts found it necessary to reduce their annual percentage rate of charge.[5] One of the reasons that most were not seriously injured was that they were able to move into the more profitable areas of consumer credit.[6] However, the total number of finance companies in the United States fell, and it seems that some were forced out of business perhaps as a result of increased competition arising from the obligation to disclose cost of credit.

(b)   Disclosure in the provision of investment products

Requirements on the provision of information also form a key part of the regulation of the provision of investment services and the sale of investment products. These products include pensions, life insurance, collective investment schemes such as unit trusts. The FSA also regulates some aspects of the sale of mortgages, and has been given reserve powers to extend that regulation in line with that on other investement products. Investment products are highly complex, and they are usually long-term in nature. These characteristics pose considerable problems for consumers: not only is it difficult to understand the products, making it hard to decide which one to buy, the consumer has to wait at least five years, often considerably longer, before the product matures and they can assess

---

[5]   W Starkweather *Effects of Federal Truth in Lending Legislation on Sales Finance and Consumer Finance Companies* (DBA Thesis, Kent State University 1973) pp 100, 121.

[6]   J Epstein 'Consumer Research' (1979) 3 J Cons Studies & Home Econ 269, 272–274, collects some empirical evidence.

whether they made the right choice. Investment products are what economists term 'credence goods': the consumer cannot assess the quality of the product through experience, only through faith. Further, the quality of the product is determined by the performance of the investment after it has been bought. Principal-agent problems necessarily arise as the consumer (the principal) has to rely on the skill and expertise of the agent, the person managing the investment, and has to hope that that person does not divert the investor's money to their own use, either through excessive charges or through fraud.

It is thus very difficult, if not impossible, for the consumer to assess the quality of the product at the point of sale. As a result, when buying an investment product consumers rely heavily on the advice they receive from financial advisors. However, the advisor may not give full information (eg he may not disclose how much commission he will receive for recommending a particular investment), and the information and advice that he does give may be biased. The asymmetries of information that exist between the advisor and the consumer mean that the consumer has no way of assessing the quality of the information given and thus the quality of the advice received. Regulation in this area thus focuses principally on two things: the provision of investment advice, and the marketing and sale of investment products. The rules regulating these activities are made by the Financial Services Authority (FSA), acting under the Financial Services and Markets Act 2000 (FSMA).[7] The rules cover the advertising of investment products, the duties of investment advisors, the information to be given about the advisor and the product at the point of sale, and provide cancellation rights to consumers.[8]

Advertisements for investment products can only be issued by a person who is authorised to provide investment services under the Act, or if they have been approved by such a person.[9] All advertisements have to be clear and not misleading, clearly identifiable as an advert rather than as a news item or editorial for example, and whilst they must state that the person offering the product is regulated by FSA, they must not imply that the regulator has in any way endorsed the product. The person issuing the advert must have reasonable grounds for believing that the statements

---

[7] The Act replaces the Financial Services Act 1986, under which these activities were previously regulated by the Securities and Investments Board (SIB) and a number of self-regulatory organisations. Immediately prior to the FSMA 2000, the self-regulatory body responsible for regulating the provision of financial services to consumers was the Personal Investment Authority (PIA). These bodies have been replaced by the FSA.

[8] The rules are currently contained in the rule books of PIA and the FSA, which are to be combined in the FSA Handbook, due to be finalised at the end of 2000–2001.

[9] FSMA, s 21. The rules on advertisements are to be set out in the FSA Handbook.

made in the advert are true when the advert is issued and will remain so for the duration of the period of the publication of the advert. Adverts for specific investment products (that is for a specific life assurance product rather than brand-name adverts, for example for the Prudential generally) in addition have to show clearly the nature of the investment being advertised, of the investor's financial commitment and of the risks involved, any figures on past performance must state the source from which they are derived and a warning that past performance is no guarantee of future performance, and must make it clear that the value of investments will fluctuate. Those advertisements which make or invite offers to enter into investment contracts (eg by having a tear-off slip that the person fills in and returns) must in addition contain information that is normally contained in the Key Features document (below) and tell the customer to seek advice if they are unsure as to the suitability of the product for them. Such advertisments have at the moment to be printed, but it is likely that this will change to accommodate internet-based investment business as it develops.

At the point of sale, the regulatory rules require two types of information to be given: information about the person advising the customer and selling investments, and information about the product. Those who advise and sell investment products are required either to advise on and sell the products of only one company (tied agents) or the products of all companies (independent financial advisors (IFAs)). Before the advisor starts to tell the consumer about different investments, he or she has to say whether or not he or she is a tied agent or an IFA, and explain what this means (status disclosure). The information that the investor has to be given about the product is also set out by the rules of the FSA.[10] Before a product is sold, the advisor has to give the customer a 'Key Features' document. The Key Features document sets out the nature of the product, the customer's financial commitment, the risk factors associated with the product, what the customer will receive if they cash in the investment within the first five years (the surrender value), the amount of commission that the advisor will receive, projections of future investment returns (based on standardised figures set by the regulators), and the effect that the charges and expenses for administering the product will have on the overall return. The information given has to be made specific to the client's circumstances and to the product being recommended, and has to contain an example of how it will operate. The format of the Key Features document is specified by the regulator, but the standard and form of presentation

---

[10]   The rules vary with the product being sold, but cover most forms of life policy, personal pension and unit trust. Rules governing the sale of mortgages have not been made at the time of writing.

has to be similar to that used for the firm's other brochures or business documents, in an attempt to prevent firms presenting it as simply an 'official' piece of information which has no real significance. The investor must also be informed of any cancellation rights.

The investor must also be given a 'reason why' letter, either at the time the recommendation is made or soon after it. The 'reason why' letter sets out the basis on which the advisor thinks a particular product is suitable for the investor, or if the customer has either not sought the advisor's advice or has decided to buy a product in contradiction to the advisor's recommendation, that this is the case. If the product is one to which cancellation rights apply, then the letter can be sent after the transaction has been entered into but before the post-sale notice of the right to cancel has been sent. In addition, after a product has been sold, the investor is sent another copy of the tables of surrender values, deductions for charges and commision, what return the investor will receive from their investment and the effect of charges etc on that return, details of the commission or remuneration paid to the advisor and details of the advisor's status. Additional information is sent if the investor has bought a with-profits life policy, giving further details of the nature of the policy.[11]

Cancellation rights apply to most types of unit trust, personal pension and life policy taken out by non-business investors as a result of taking investment advice. The reason for giving a right to cancel is to try to ensure that the investor has not agreed to buy the product simply as a result of the hard-sell sales tactics of the advisor. Notice of the right to cancel has to have been given prior to the sale of the product in a manner which is clear, timely, prominent and comprehensive, and has to give information of the duration of the cancellation period and the steps that the investor has to take in order to cancel. Similar information has to be given between 8–15 days after the sale. If the cancellation notices are not given, then the investor can cancel the investment at any time. Further, if the right to cancel does not normally arise but the investor might reasonably have concluded that it did, then cancellation rights arise.

Considerable regulatory attention has been spent on the issue of what information should be disclosed about financial advisors and investment products, and when in the sales process that information should be given.[12] As noted above, investment products are highly complex and technical,

---

[11]   Under a with-profits life policy, the investor pays regular premiums to the life assurance company, and receives a return on that investment annually, plus a bonus when the policy matures; the level of bonus is determined by the life company.

[12]   For a discussion of the policy issues and debates surrounding the development of retail regulation see J Black *Rules and Regulators* (1997) Chapter 4.

and in addition consumers' understanding of such products is very low.[13] In order that consumers can understand the information being given it has to be expressed in a simplified form, which may mean sacrificing technical accuracy in favour of comprehensibility. Further, consumers can only absorb a limited amount of information, and so the issue regulators have to decide is what information is the most important, and whether disclosing only some information is misleading.[14] The danger is that consumers will focus only on the information that they can understand, such as the amount of commission the advisor is receiving, or the projected investment return, and use that as the basis of comparisons at the expense of other aspects of the product which are at least as, if not more, important (such as the effect of charges and expenses on the overall investment return).

In order to try to address these problems, in formulating its rules on what information should be included in the Key Features document and how that information should be displayed, FSA undertook market research to find out how much of the information consumers could in fact understand.[15] Although it modified the rules as a result of the research, there is little evidence that consumer understanding has improved. In a survey conducted in 1998, 80% of consumers viewed the financial services markets as 'baffling'[16] In order to address this concern, one of the new statutory objectives of the FSA is to raise public awareness of financial services and products. In fulfilment of this objective, the FSA is proposing to publish fact sheets on different types of products, and league tables of the costs and charges of different product providers and of their relative performance over time.[17] It is hoped that this will help consumers compare different products, and so reduce both misselling of products by the advisor, and the 'misbuying' of products by consumers. Whether that will improve consumer awareness overall remains to be seen: such information is after all already available from a number of sources, including broadsheet newspapers, specialist investment magazines such as *Money Management*, and a range of internet sites.

In any event, there is little evidence that the disclosure rules have had any impact on consumers' investment decision. The evidence is instead

[13]   See for example *Review of Retail Regulation: Consumer Research by Taylor Nelson Financial* SIB Disclosures Research Report, January 1992; *Savings and Investments, Consumer Issues: An Occasional Paper to the OFT by J Mitchell and H Weisner* (OFT, June 1992)

[14]   See further J Black *Rules and Regulators* (1997).

[15]   SIB *Life Assurance Disclosure—Reports on Market Research Conducted in 1993.*

[16]   Reported in Treasury Select Committee Third Report *Financial Services Regulation* HC 73-I 1998–9, para 32

[17]   Gordon Brown, Budget Speech, HC 9 March 1999, col 179; FSA, CP 15 *Promoting Public Understanding of Financial Services* (1998).

that consumers base their investment decisions on the reputation of the advisor rather than on the information disclosed about the product.[18] The limited awareness and understanding that consumers have of financial products, and indeed that it is perhaps possible or rational for them to have,[19] means that disclosure of information, whilst important, can only play a limited role in ensuring that the consumer actually ends up with an investment product that is best for them. Further, no amount of information disclosure at the point of sale can address the principal-agent problems to which investment services necessarily give rise. Disclosure rules thus have to be bolstered by additional requirements as to the quality of the investment advice to be provided and duties imposed on those who have control over the investor's money (discussed further in Chapter 5).

5   DISCLOSURE REGULATION IN PERSPECTIVE

The evidence suggests that many consumers are not greatly assisted by laws which require businesses to disclose information. The major problem with disclosure regulation is not in securing business compliance, but rather that consumers are unaware of the information disclosed, do not appreciate its significance or simply do not employ the information provided in the market-place. Those who theoretically are likely to benefit most from the information, poorer consumers, may face different market conditions from others, which information disclosure is unable to equalise.[20] The evidence from the United States is that credit disclosure, at least initially, had only a minor impact on consumer behaviour. Surveys of knowledge about detailed food labelling have revealed that consumers are often misinformed about food composition and that although they might study the lists of ingredients when first purchasing a product, they do not really understand them (particularly the technical terms), nor do they know that the ingredients are listed in order of amounts.

A number of factors bear on the effectiveness of disclosure regulation. First, consumers may not have a strong desire for information. This derives partly from habit and partly from a deficiency in consumer education; it is no surprise that it is the middle class who reads consumer publications like *Which?* and *Consumer Reports*. Consumers may also overlook crucial

[18]   London Economics *Independent Financial Advisors and the Impact of Commission Disclosure* (October 1992) pp 36–37 and Annex E.
[19]   See further London Economics *Consumer Detriment under Conditions of Imperfect Information*, OFT Research Paper 11 (1997) pp 78–85.
[20]   I McNeil et al 'Market Discrimination Against the Poor and the Impact of Consumer Disclosure Laws: the Used Car Industry' (1979) 13 Law & Soc Rev 695.

information. For this reason the food compositional standards might be better than food labelling although the latter has the advantages of simplicity, of avoiding the difficulty of definition and of not inhibiting the development of new products. Another factor is that consumers may not regard as important much of the information presently the subject of disclosure law. They may respond differently to an obligation on businesses to inform consumers about crucial characteristics of consumer products like performance and durability.

Next, certain types of disclosure are more effective than others. The United States Supreme Court has indicated a preference for oral disclosure in television advertising, since many people listen to rather than watch television commercials.[1] Information on food labels or in contractual documents may be excessive or incomprehensible to ordinary consumers.[2] Non-technical information can have a greater impact. Examples are the display of prices on supermarket shelves or the dissemination of specific information about businesses (eg public blacklists) or short one-word or one-phrase claims or symbols on the front of food packs.[3] There is a dilemma in communicating technical information to a non-technical audience. Information must be capable of being understood by consumers, but at the same time it must be accurate—and that can mean use of technical expressions. Information associated with one product or service has to compete with the whole range of other information. Consumers may be under tight time restrictions.[4]

> With all the promotional material, media stimuli, and junk mail available to consumers, it is extremely difficult for a government-mandated disclosure even to be heard, let alone achieve its desired objective.[5]

Even simply understood information may not have an impact on consumers, depending on its manner of presentation. When bold and simple warnings are set out (eg 'Your home is at risk if you do not keep up repayments on a mortgage or other loan secured on it'[6]) they may have an

---

[1]   *Morales v Trans World Airlines Inc* 504 US 374, 396 (1992).
[2]   W Magat and W Viscusi *Informational Approaches to Regulation* (MIT Press, 1992).
[3]   *Messages on Foods* (NCC, 1997) pp 19–22.
[4]   J Caswell and D Padberg 'Toward a More Comprehensive Theory of Food Labels' (1992) 74 Amer J Agri Econ 460.
[5]   D Clanton 'Predicting Business Reaction to Consumer Regulation' (1993) 15 Law and Policy 253, 253.
[6]   As required by the Consumer Credit (Advertisements) Regulation 1989, SI 1989/ 125.

impact.[7] Yet even consumers may not be psychologically disposed to take them into account because they have already committed themselves to go ahead with a transaction. Even if the barrier is overcome there remains the complexity of choosing despite adequate and clear information. As Leff noted: 'Anyone who has tried to use Consumer Reports has experienced the frustration of deciding between a superb Frammis with a shock hazard and a not-so-fine Wudgis without.'[8]

Another factor in the relative effectiveness of disclosure regulation is that different types of consumer react differently. Professional social groups, and the more educated, have a greater understanding of APR and the warning about loss of a home as required in consumer credit advertisements.[9] Research shows that label information does not reach certain segments of the population.[10] Even if it does, some consumers may have no choice but to enter certain transactions whatever their state of knowledge. Thus many poor consumers have no realistic alternative to paying high interest rates for credit because they are regarded as bad credit risks by established finance house. Of course other factors are involved in the poor seeking credit.[11] Even if they know of cheaper prices they may prefer to do business with familiar, if more expensive, institutions. A related point is that the impact of information disclosed can be counteracted by other aspects of a consumer transaction. Advertising is a force strongly influencing choice and may offset detailed, objective information available to consumers.[12] Pressures existing at the point of sale—such as ploys of salespersons—can override the knowledge which consumers have obtained. In other words, the problem is sometimes misleading or fraudulent marketing practices and not ignorance on the part of consumers.

Finally, consumers may make a rational choice in disregarding available information. It is quite common for consumers to ignore price information because other factors—quality, the desire to possess a product and so

---

[7]   See W Viscusi 'Predicting the Effects of Food Cancer Risk Warnings on Consumers' (1988) 43 Food, Drug & Cosmetic LJ 283.

[8]   A Leff 'Injury, Ignorance and Spite—The Dynamics of Coersive Collection' (1970) 80 Yale LJ 1, 33.

[9]   Consumers' Appreciation of 'Annual Percentage Rates' (AFT Research Paper 4, 1994).

[10]   P Ippolito and A Mathios 'Information, Advertising and Health Choices' (1990) 21 Rand J Econ 459; D Putler and E Frazao 'Assessing the Effects of Diet/Health Awareness on the Consumption and Composition of Fat Intake' in J Caswell (ed) Economics of Food Safety (Elsevier Science, 1991).

[11]   See p 232 above.

[12]   Good For You? An Overview of Nutritional Information and Advice for Consumers (NCC, 1994).

on—make price a minor consideration.[13] When seeking credit, poor consumers may be more concerned with the size of a deposit and of the monthly repayments than with the interest rate charged. Opportunity costs (the time and effort) associated with using information may not be worth while, especially if small amounts of money are at stake. Thus a rather old survey of consumers obtaining credit for new cars concluded that lack of knowledge was by no means the principal deterrent to their seeking the lowest-cost loan for which they were qualified.[14] There were a variety of other reasons: inconvenience, legitimate impossibility, belief that the low-cost lender was tougher in other respects (larger deposit, more references, etc), too much trouble to join a credit union, and so on.

Because disclosure regulation has these drawbacks, other forms of regulatory control may be the preferred course for legislative action. Even so, disclosure regulation can perform a useful role in consumer protection. In some cases it is the only practicable approach, given the limits on legislative technique and a shortage of enforcement resources.[15] Its continued and more extensive use, together with rising levels of consumer education, will render it more worthwhile with time. For these reasons it is misguided to adopt the attitude that because consumers at present will not use information there is no need for it. Another point which has not yet been mentioned is that disclosure regulation is an invaluable aid for those charged with implementing consumer law, for discrepancies between the substance of business claims and their performance are immediately apparent or subject to investigation. Disclosure regulation can also be justified on other than utilitarian grounds: there is the consumer's basic right in a democratic society to be informed about products and services on the market so that they can have control over their daily decisions.

---

[13]   See J Caswell and E Mojduska 'Using Informational Labelling to Influence the Market for Quality in Food Products' (1997) 23 Amer J Agr Econ 344; F McChesney 'Consumer Ignorance and Consumer Protection Law: Empirical Evidence from the FTC Funeral Rule' (1990) 7 JL & Politics, 42.

[14]   J White and F Munger 'Consumer Sensitivity to Interest Rates: An Empirical Study of New-Car Buyers and Auto Loans' (1971) 69 Mich L Rev 1207, 1227.

[15]   Eg C Chen 'Consumer Protection Through the Regulation of Product Information' (1992) 47 Food & Drug LJ 185, 203.

Chapter 10

Product standards: regulating for consumer health and safety

I INTRODUCTION

The increased complexity of consumer products, typically manufactured at locations far from their point of final consumption, has generated new risks to health and safety for consumers. One response to this problem of increased risks is to suggest that it is not for the state and the law to intervene directly, and that the most appropriate way to proceed is to require producers and retailers to draw the attention of consumers to any risks associated with product and leave consumers to use the information how they choose. Consumers have differing degrees of risk aversion. Some will pay more for a safer product. Others will deliberately increase the risks, for example by removing safety guards from power tools, using ladders propped up on boxes or removing grass from the blades of motor mowers with bare hands.[1] There is considerable evidence that these contrasting behaviours are a product not simply of differing degrees of risk aversion, but also of the fact that individuals are notoriously bad judges of risk. Polls conducted after the Paddington rail crash of September 1999, in which 31 people were killed, revealed a significant proportion of the population who believed, contrary to the evidence, that it was safer to travel by car than by train.[2] If even a small proportion of people were to act on that mistaken belief it would lead to significant increase in deaths, as more consumers took to the roads for journeys they would otherwise have made by train. This is one of the reasons law and public policy have a role to play in developing consumer safety standards.

---

[1] W Oi 'The Economics of Product Safety' (1973) 4 Bell Journal of Economics 3, 22; P Asch *Consumer Safety Regulations* (OUP, 1988) Chapter 4.
[2] S Jenkins 'Risking Our Sanity' (1999) Times, 20 October.

We have already noted (Chapter 5) the response of private law to change, and notably the landmark case *Donoghue v Stevenson* (1932) in which the House of Lords held that a producer of consumer products owes a duty of care to the ultimate consumer to ensure that the product does not leave the factory in such a state that harm is reasonably foreseeable. This negligence doctrine requires the courts to determine the appropriate standard for the manufacture of consumer products in any particular case. As we have seen this negligence doctrine has been largely superseded by statutory rules of strict liability in tort.

Subsequent to this judicial decision a variety of factors have led governments to question the adequacy of private law (both contract and tort) for the development and maintenance of high standards for consumer health and safety. Firstly, there is the development of official data on accidents and their causes. The collection of such data since 1976 by the Home Accident Surveillance Scheme (HASS) ought to provide the basis for more rational policy making, though, as noted below, there are some doubts about whether this is the case. HASS, and the related Leisure Accident Surveillance Scheme (LASS), uses data collected from the accident and emergency units of 18 UK hospitals to build up a detailed picture of the causes of accidents. This sample data is then scaled up to provide estimates on the numbers of accidents with information about the circumstances of the accident (in the garden, doing DIY, linked to toys, etc) in the UK as a whole. This data is fed into the design processes of manufacturers, the research strategy of the DTI and the policy processes of government in an effort to reduce the numbers of accidents. What is striking about the figures is the diversity of the ways in which accidents happen. For the major accident categories covered by the schemes, there were reported to be 3,699 deaths (1995 figures) (roughly equivalent to the number of deaths caused by road accidents in the UK each year) and 2,493,000 injuries (1996 figures).[3] Of these accidents, 23,000 injuries were linked to the use of toys, 464,000 were garden accidents, 112,000 involved people doing DIY activities, and 100,00 were linked to the packaging of goods.

The largest category of accidents (over a million injuries and nearly 2,000 deaths a year) was falls, which do not necessarily involve consumer products. While this data is important it is limited in the information it conveys about unsafe products. Even for the large number of accidents which do involve products the dataset is not sufficiently sophisticated to give any idea whether some defect in the design or manufacture of the product *caused* the accident. While the level of home accidents has remained relatively stable over the last ten years, the collection of

---

[3]   HASS, 21st Annual Report, 1997 Data (1998) p 19.

reasonably reliable data on food poisoning has shown a five-fold increase in incidents, to over 90,000 cases a year since 1982.[4] Again with this data it is not possible to identify the *cause* of the harm. There is a suspicion that many cases of food poisoning are attributable to poor hygiene in retail outlets and the home, rather than defects in manufacturing. The EU also maintains a European Home and Leisure Accident Surveillance Scheme (EHLASS) to which all 15 Member States contribute data.

Secondly, government and citizens alike have formed higher expectations of what the state can do for them. During the period of food shortages in the Second World War government extended the medieval regime[5] for regulation of the composition of food substitutes in order to maintain nutritional diets for the general population. More generally food safety regulation has been the subject matter of evolutionary development as a response to food scares of various types.[6] At the time of writing the risks both to consumers and to the continuing development of a European market in foodstuffs have caused the European Commission, newly installed in October 1999, to make the development of food safety regulation an early priority.[7] The massive development of the pharmaceutical industry caused governments to take on the task of granting prior approval before new drugs could be marketed. To secure approval under the Medicines Act 1968 the producer must engage in clinical trials (though controversially these trials do not always involve trials on children, who are likely to react differently to drugs) (see pp 469–477 below). Concerns about various other ultra-hazardous products caused governments to take powers to set down specific standards which such products should meet. The European Community institutions have been important actors in these developments, as trade in unsafe products presents a particular risk to the European internal market. Most recently the criminal law has been deployed to create general requirements that consumer products should be reasonably safe.

This chapter examines the regimes directed at enhancing consumer health and safety together. Though food regulation has had a distinct and longer history from the regulation of other consumer products, and retains a distinctive legislative basis, there is some evidence of convergence of the regimes, notably under the main general legislation governing product

---

4   *The Food Standards Bill* House of Commons Research Paper 99/65 pp 21–28. The increase in reported cases needs to be treated with some caution. Food poisoning has long been an illness which doctors have a duty to report to public health authorities, but doctors may be more likely to attribute illnesses to food poisoning under circumstances where food poisoning has a higher profile.

5   Compositional standards can be traced back at least as far as the Statute of Bread and Ale (1266) which was aimed at reducing the adulteration of bread and ale with cheaper but less nutritious ingredients. See pp 318–323.

6   I Paulus *The Search for Pure Food* (Martin Robertson, 1974).

7   EC White Paper on Food Safety, 12.1.2000. COM (1999) 719 final.

safety, the General Product Safety Regulations 1994, which apply to all
consumer products (including foodstuffs and medicines). In any case the
issues of regulatory technique and conceptual structures for food control
and general product safety regulation are sufficiently similar to merit a
combined treatment. Three main themes pervade the examination of the
issues in this chapter. Firstly, the responsibility for setting and enforcing
product standards is highly fragmented, with national and supranational
governmental and non-governmental involvement in standard setting and
national and local involvement in enforcement. Secondly, the effect of the
diffuse arrangements is to create a 'hierarchy of norms' under which
specific product standards (whatever their provenance) generally take
precedence over more recently developed general norms. Thus, in contrast
with the broad statutory standards discussed in Chapter 8, the function of
general rules in the product standards domain is to fill in the gaps which
are inevitably left in the regimes of more specific standards. Thirdly, and
relatedly, the development of more general norms, together with enhanced
self-regulatory capacities both for standard-setting and enforcement, has
been a response to worries that the more interventionist detailed sectoral
regulation has been ineffective.

2   SETTING STANDARDS

The task of setting standards of safety, whether undertaken by courts,
government, industry groups or enforcement officers, necessarily requires
some kind of balancing between the costs of design, modification or
withdrawal of products for safety relative to the benefits of permitting
products to be marketed and likely benefits of any enhancement to safety.[8]
This requirement is most obvious in the case of products which necessarily
have features which create risks of harm to consumers. Examples include
steam irons (which to be effective necessarily have the capacity to inflict
burns) and cars (which necessarily have the potential to cause injury and
death both to their occupants and to others). Any explicit or implicit
standard for such products must balance the benefits of permitting the
products to be freely available at affordable prices against the costs
associated with improving design (for example by incorporating automatic

---

[8]   This balancing act was famously set out by Learned Hand in *United States v
Carroll Trading Co* 159 F 2d 169, 173 (2d Cir 1947). See C Veljanovski *The
Economics of Law* (Institute of Economic Affairs, 1991) pp 65–67. Interpreting
a statutory duty to provide safe working conditions 'so far as is reasonably
practicable' Lord Oaksey said: 'What is "reasonably practicable" depends on a
consideration whether the time, trouble and expense of the precautions suggested
are disproportionate to the risk involved' *Marshall v Gotham Co Ltd* [1954] 1
All ER 937 at 939.

cut-out devices in steam irons, or seat belts and airbags in cars) or requiring the incorporation of warning signs or devices or requiring that a product be withdrawn from the market. Put another way safety standards implicitly require some conception of what is an acceptable level of risk for a consumer product.[9] Whilst the calculation of the risk of harm associated with a product (risk assessment) is a technical exercise (as is the effect on risk of safety enhancement measures) the determination of what level of risk is acceptable (risk-management) is one of non-technical or political judgment, over which views are likely to differ, even among consumers.[10]

The DTI has recently indicated that the 'precautionary principle' (under which potential risks are assessed in advance and efforts made to reduce or eliminate them, rather than waiting for hazards to be created) may have an important role to play in its policies on consumer safety.[11] One body of evidence presented to the Phillips investigation into the government response to the discovery of Bovine Spongiform Encephalopathy (BSE or 'mad cow disease') suggests that the precautionary principle was not followed, with disastrous results.[12] On the other hand, recent controls over the commercial exploitation of techniques of genetic modification suggest the application of the precautionary principle at play.[13] There is a suspicion that the governmental approach to particular risk issues is, in some cases, determined by the weight of lobbying. Thus, the weak approach to the BSE crisis may be explained by the existence of a powerful agricultural lobby and a weak consumer lobby. But apparently irrational legislative responses may also occur which favour consumers at the expense of industry, as with the issue of regulations in 1984 to prohibit the supply of scented erasers in the UK, following a media campaign led by the television programme *That's Life*. Scented erasers were thought to present a choking risk to young children who might eat them, mistaking them for food. Evidence from hospital data showed many other objects where much greater risk was tolerated without the issue of regulations— for example marbles.[14] Pressure from consumers and the media may

[9]   A Ogus *Regulation: Legal Form and Economic Theory* (1994) pp 190–205.
[10]   I Ramsay *Consumer Protection: Text and Materials* (1989) p 472.
[11]   DTI *Modern Markets, Confident Consumers* (Cm 4410 (1999)). For an analysis and discussion of the wider analysis of risk regulation see R Baldwin, C Scott and C Hood 'Introduction' in Baldwin, Scott and Hood *Reader on Regulation* (1998) pp 15–17.
[12]   See also the National Audit Office report *Ministry of Agriculture, Fisheries and Food and the Intervention Board: BSE—the Cost of a Crisis* HC 853 Session 1997–1998.
[13]   J Black 'Regulation as Facilitation: Negotiating the Genetic Revolution' (1998) 61 MLR 621, 628–629
[14]   Scented Erasers Order 1984, SI 1984/83, now superseded by the Food (Imitations) Safety Regulations 1989, SI 1989/1291. The case is extensively documented in I Ramsay *Consumer Protection: Text and Materials* (1989) pp 478–489.

independently cause producers to change their approach to particular products.

The allocation of the right to set standards is extremely important for a variety of reasons. These reasons include not only the political issues noted above, but also considerations of expertise and effectiveness. Under private law regimes decisions about acceptable risk are implicitly made by the courts (see the discussion in Chapter 5 above). The vertical regimes of detailed product safety rules which have developed in the UK and the EC have allocated the decision-making power to ministers, acting alone in the case of the UK, or acting collectively through the Council of Ministers in the EC. In each case a dense web of expert advisory committees has grown up, amid concerns that industry interests are over-represented.[15] These arrangements have the strength that they recognise the political nature of decisions about safety and, in theory, provide a more democratic mechanism to resolve safety issues. However in at least one consumer product sphere, that relating to food, a series of food scares in the 1980s and 1990s led to a loss of confidence in the capacity of ministers (advised by experts) to make safety decisions which properly served the public interest (both in terms of protecting consumers and maintaining confidence in consumer markets). The BSE affair, discussed above, was a key example. The decision of the government to establish an independent Food Standards Agency has been a partial response to these concerns.[16] The Agency, established by the Food Standards Act 1999, provides a central advisory function on food policy to the government, it being advised by various advisory committees, and has a lead role in monitoring the UK food market over safety and standards issues, including monitoring of enforcement.[17] The Republic of Ireland had already established a similar agency.[18] The European Community is also planning the establishment of an independent food agency in response to various crises of confidence both in relation to particular foodstuffs, and in the independence and authority of the policy process. A proposed European Food Authority will play a lead role in risk assessment and risk communication in respect of foodstuffs in the EU, but the legislative and policy role of risk management will remain the

[15] W Sauter and E Vos 'Harmonisation under Community Law: The Comitology Issue' in P Craig and C Harlow (eds) *Lawmaking in the European Union* (1998) pp 182–184; F Snyder (ed) 'A Regulatory Framwork for Foodstuffs in the Internal Market', EUI Working Paper LAW 94/4 (1994).
[16] See P James *Food Standards Agency: An Interim Proposal* (1997); *The Food Standards Agency: A Force for Change* (Cm 3830 (1998)).
[17] Food Standards Act 1999, ss 5–9, 12–14.
[18] P Wall 'The Food Safety Authority of Ireland' (1999) 9 Consumer Policy Review 188.

responsibility of the Commission, Council of Ministers and European Parliament.[19]

It has been argued that the American approach—under which detailed accident data is collected by an independent agency, the Consumer Product Safety Commission—has led to a more rational safety policy than the *ad hoc* development of regulations in the UK.[20] Though considered by the UK government, a similar institutional development for general product safety was rejected.[1] Both UK and EU plans to create independent food authorities reflect a reluctance to cede real authority to unelected regulators, their roles being restricted to advisory roles in relation to policy.[2] Thus under these proposals the objective is to attempt to show the advisory function on food to be credible and independent, while the policy and legislative functions remain in the political sphere.

Contemporary product safety regimes (both within the UK and other jurisdictions) often generate a hierarchy of norms, within which the presence of detailed statutory standards take precedence, but if there are no such statutory standards then private or industry standards govern the products. Only where there are no detailed standards of any kind can enforcement officers and courts fall back on general safety standards which, because they are necessarily open-textured, give wide discretion in their interpretation. In practice the detailed content of general safety standards is often filled in by private standards set by standardisation institutions or industry groups. It is argued that the presence of the capacity of government to set statutory standards encourages industry to develop effective self-regulation, obviating the need for the statutory approach. Clearly for such an incentive mechanism to work government has both to monitor industry self-regulation carefully and act in such a way that the threat of new regulation is credible.[3]

Since the mid-1980s government has adopted the rhetoric of deregulation, and placed considerable pressure on departments such as the DTI, to reduce the extent of the regulatory burdens it places on

[19] European Commission Press Release 'Commission adopts White Paper on Food Safety and sets out "Farm to Table" Legislative Action Programme' 12 January 2000; European Commission *White Paper on Food Safety* COM(1999)719 Final, January 2000.

[20] The CSPC was not without its problems, however. Excessive procedural requirements were blamed for slowing rule making down, so that it took many years to promulgate new safety standards: R Hirshorn 'The Administration of the Hazardous Products Act' in D Dewees (ed) *The Regulation of Quality* (1983).

[1] DTI *Consumer Safety: A Consultative Document* (Cmnd 6398) pp 28–29.

[2] On the EC White Paper on Food Safety see the *Financial Times* leader 'The Politics of Food Safety' (2000) 12 January.

[3] I Ayres and J Braithwaite *Responsive Regulation* (OUP, 1992) Chapter 2.

business, by requiring a form of cost-benefit analysis to be applied to proposed regulations (now referred to as regulatory impact assessment), and an evaluation to be conducted of existing regulations with a view to slimming them down or scrapping them.[4] The effects of the deregulation initiative on consumer safety regulation appear to be fairly marginal. A rare example of a complete revocation (without replacement) of safety regulations is provided by the Stands for Carry-Cots (Safety) Regulations 1966.[5] But even in this case, the DTI was explicitly not fully liberalising the product concerned, but rather seeking to place reliance on the statutory general safety requirement, in combination with voluntary standards.[6] Recently the government-appointed Better Regulation Task Force has set down a formal guide to regulating, which highlights the virtues of doing nothing, or promoting self-regulation over the more intrusive requirements of new regulation. Unless handled very carefully such deregulatory initiatives run the risk of reducing the credible threat of government intervention, and thus reducing the incentive on business to self-regulate to keep more formal intervention at bay.[7] However, in practice much of safety regulation in the UK (both vertical and horizontal) today originates with EC legislation, with the consequence that the scope for any EC Member State government to reduce the protections offered to consumers is tightly circumscribed.[8]

3   DETAILED LEGAL STANDARDS

The development of detailed statutory standards was at the forefront of regulatory developments in consumer safety after the Second World War. The Consumer Safety Act 1961 empowered ministers to lay down regulations in respect of the manufacture of particular products. The power to make regulations was subsequently amended by the Consumer Safety Act 1978 and the Consumer Safety (Amendment) Act 1986. The regulations made under these provisions are often referred to as 'vertical regulation' since they typically only apply to one sector or one type of product, rather than being of general application. Whilst the UK government has been active in developing regulations under the 1961 Act and subsequent

---

[4]   A detailed administrative history of the UK deregulation programme is found in J Froud et al *Controlling the Regulators* (Macmillan, 1998).

[5]   SI 1966/1610 revoked by SI 1996/2756.

[6]   DTI *Consumer Safety: Report by the Secretary of State for Trade and Industry for the Period 1 April 1993–31 March 1998* (1998) para 28.

[7]   These issues of institutional design for regulation are discussed in greater detail in Chapter 13.

[8]   See DTI *Consumer Safety: Report by the Secretary of State for Trade and Industry for the Period 1 April 1993–31 March 1998* (1998) paras 22–25.

legislation—regulations are currently issued under s 11 of the Consumer Protection Act 1987, and many regulations made under earlier legislation continue in force as if made under the 1987 Act—in practice much of the detailed legal regulation of consumer products in the UK derives from EC legislation which, in the form of regulations, is directly effective, and in the form of Directives is typically implemented in the UK under regulations issued by ministers either under s 11 of the 1987 Act or using the powers of s 2 of the European Communities Act 1972. From the perspective of the UK, the source of the legislative obligations is not particularly important, though at the margins EC-derived legislation may require the application of rather different principles of interpretation to purely domestic legislative rules.

The main powers to promulgate safety regulations are widely drawn and give broad discretion to ministers. The Consumer Protection Act 1987 provides that the powers may be used to make regulations under the negative resolution procedure (s 11(6)), for the purpose of securing that goods are safe, that unsafe goods do not reach the market or particular parts of it (for example children), and that appropriate information is provided with goods (s 11(1)). Safety is defined as creating 'no risk or no risk apart from one reduced to a minimum' that death or personal injury will be caused by the goods or a variety of functions associated with the goods (s 19(1)). In addition to addressing matters of composition, design, construction, finishing and packing, such regulations may require that goods receive approval before being marketed, and provide for the charging of fees for such approval regimes (s 11(2)(a)–(e)). Thus prior approval requirements could be applied to any class of goods where safety concerns warranted such a regime. Additionally regulations may provide for inspection regimes and for the prohibition of particular goods (s 11(2)(g)). The main procedural requirements associated with the making of regulations are a duty on the minister to consult 'such organisations as appear to him to be representative of interests substantially affected by the proposal'…and 'such other persons as he considers appropriate' (s 11(5)). A producer succeeded in a judicial review action against the Department of Health where the minister had put forward regulations prohibiting the production of oral tobacco product, because the producer was the only producer of those products in the UK and not been consulted sufficiently.[9] However, this modest procedural requirement can be overridden where regulations are needed urgently, though such regulations cannot have effect for a period exceeding 12 months (s 11(5)). The power

---

[9]   *R v Secretary of State for Health, ex p United States Tobacco International Inc* [1992] QB 353. The Secretary of State responded by consulting afresh and producing new regulations to the same effect: Tobacco for Oral Use (Safety) Regulations 1992, SI 1992/2134.

to make regulations without consultation was used to introduce the Fireworks (Safety) Regulations 1996.[10]

A very wide range of safety regulations have been made under the s 11 powers and their predecessors under the 1961 and 1978 Acts.[11] Detailed statutory standards may impose negative or positive requirements in relation to the product, and although these requirements are typically applied at the production stage, they may also apply at the marketing stage. Marketing stage controls are most prominent in the food safety regime, notably in respect of food hygiene practices, which are the subject matter of stringent regulation,[12] and also the storage of food. Examples of different types of control applying at each stage are shown in Table 10.1.

Table 10.1 Examples of safety requirements under regulations

Regulatory requirements	Stage at which requirement applied	
	Production	Marketing
Negative	Prohibition on use of certain substances in cosmetic products (Cosmetic Products (Safety) Regulations 1996 (SI 1996/2925) (as amended)	Prohibition on supply of cigarette lighter fuel refill canisters containing butane to persons under age of 18 (Cigarette Lighter Refill (Safety) Regulations 1999, SI 1999/1844)
Positive	Fitting of safety guards to heating appliances (Heating Appliances (Fireguards) (Safety) Regulations 1991, SI 1991/2693)	Labelling of secondhand furniture not complying with safety regulations in transitional period (1988–1993) (Furniture and Furnishings (Fire)(Safety) Regulations 1988, SI 1988/1324)

---

[10]   SI 1996/3200.
[11]   They are detailed in Division IV of *Miller: Product Liability and Safety Encyclopedia*.
[12]   Food Safety (General Food Hygiene) Regulations 1995, SI 1995/1736.

A further distinction which may be drawn in promulgating and evaluating regulations is between performance and design standards. Performance standards indicate what tests a product should be able to meet to comply with the standard, for example the amount of weight that a product should be able to withstand. Design standards specify detailed design issues—for example pushchairs must be fitted with five point harnesses. While performance standards have the merit of leaving producers considerable discretion in design, and seem to be closely linked to the instrumental objectives of the standards promulgated, design standards are more straightforward to enforce. Performance standards have become predominant in the UK in recent years,[13] though in most cases these are expressed in BSI standards rather than in statutory regulations (discussed below).

A particular issue addressed by regulations is that of the marketing of novel products. In the case of foodstuffs the government has an advisory committee on novel foodstuffs and processes (ACNFP). There are specific statutory powers to issue regulations to address particular procedures such as food irradiation. Food irradiation is the process of applying large doses of ionising radiation to food, inducing chemical changes, which may delay ripening and sprouting (in fruit and vegetables), kill certain bacteria, such as listeria, salmonella and campolybacter, or kill insects in certain foods, such as spices. In the face of disagreement about the scientific evidence concerning the safety of irradiated foodstuffs, some countries have legalised the process, and others not. Though a major issue at the time of the passage of the Food Safety Act 1990, controls on irradiation were not provided for in that Act, but fell to be controlled by regulations made under s 16(1)(c) of the Act, possibly subject to some form of licensing (Sch 1, para 4(b)).[14] For genetically modified organisms, the system of control requires the approval of the Health and Safety Executive and specific approval from the Secretary of State for field trials before plants can be grown. Field trials are assessed by ACNFP, which receives advice from a number of advisory committees. Marketing consent is only provided by the Secretary of State once there has been a full risk assessment.[15] A more general approach has been taken by the EC, which has established a regime for notification to public authorities in respect of the marketing of

---

[13]   A Ogus *Regulation: Legal Form and Economic Theory* (OUP, 1994) pp 165–171.

[14]   C Scott 'Continuity and Change in British Food Law' (1990) 53 MLR 785, 797–800

[15]   Genetically Modified Organisms (Deliberate Release) Regulations 1992, SI 1992/3280.

novel substances (ie not previously marketed in the EC). The notification must include a detailed, independent risk assessment. [16]

In respect of foodstuffs, the development of statutory standards extends beyond safety matters to cover composition and related marketing standards for foodstuffs.[17] A key area of specific safety regulation is in respect of food additives, and the approach is rather different from that employed in respect of consumer products generally. The use of food additives is tightly controlled, whilst regard is had to the useful functions such additives have: inhibiting spoilage and reducing the danger of microbial disease and enabling food to be transported long distances and stored for extended periods. The main food additives are preservatives (which limit food spoilage by inhibiting microbe growth or combating specific reactions), antioxidants (which retard oxidisation of fats), colorants (designed to make food more appealing to consumers), emulsifiers (to delay separation of the ingredients of prepared food, such as to prevent less dense liquids floating to the top, solids settling, gas being lost), thickeners, sweeteners (the emphasis on weight control has led to the replacement of sugar) and other flavouring agents. The regulatory approach in the early part of the twentieth century was to ban additives which were demonstrably harmful, but that strategy was superseded by the contemporary technique under which additives may only be used where they are specifically permitted, a case having been made to the expert Food Additives and Contaminants Committee. The Food Safety (General Food Hygiene) Regulations 1995[18] similarly impose general (or horizontal) requirements across the food industry requiring all businesses dealing with food to take responsibility for food hygiene and to implement a system of hazard analysis. This formalised system of Hazard Analysis at Critical Control Points (HACCP) provides a mechanism for producers and retailers to identify and address risks in their processes. Sectoral hygiene regulations exist for certain sectors where particular risks have been identified and catered for, such as dairy products,[19] red meat premises[20] and white meat premises.[1]

Compositional standards operate vertically, in respect of particular product sectors and are directed at consumer health (ie promoting good

---

[16] Council Directive 67/548/EEC (as amended) implemented in the UK in the Notification of New Substances Regulations 1993, SI 1993/3050 (amended by SI 1994/3247).
[17] Food Safety Act 1990, ss 16–19.
[18] SI 1995/1763. The regulations implement EC Directive 93/43.
[19] Dairy Products (Hygiene) Regulations 1995, SI 1995/1086.
[20] Fresh Meat (Hygiene and Inspection) Regulations 1995, SI 1995/539.
[1] Poultry Meat, Farmed Game Bird Meat and Rabbit Meat (Hygiene and Inspection) Regulations 1995, SI 1995/540.

nutrition) and protection of economic interests. Such standards may relate to the identify of a foodstuff, to the method of preparation or to its minimum quality. An example of an identity-based standards is used for butter, and a preparation-based standard for ice-cream.[2] More common are quality standards, for example prescribing the minimum quantity of fruit in jam or fruit juice, or of meat in mince.[3] Such compositional standards reduce risks of deception and may promote healthier eating than would otherwise occur in an unregulated market. The EC has been in involved in implementing international standards for the marketing of fresh produce such as peaches and asparagus.[4] A long-standing dispute over the compositional requirements for foodstuffs marketed as chocolate has resulted in a failure to regulate at EC level, with the suggestion that this results in consumers being misled as the quality of products marketed as chocolate in some Member States. A compromise reached by the Council of Ministers will permit the marketing of chocolate containing up to 5% of non-cocoa vegetable fats, provided it is clearly labelled as 'family milk chocolate' to distinguish it from products which do not contain non-cocoa vegetable fats.[5]

Detailed vertical standards were the preferred mode of safety rule for consumer safety in both the UK and EC from the initiation of the regimes after the Second World War until the mid-1980s. More recently considerable doubt has emerged about the appropriateness of detailed vertical regulation for product safety. At a practical level the capacity of government, whether national or EC, to set detailed standards for all those products and sectors which are deemed to require regulatory intervention has been questioned because of the experience of slow legislative processes and the difficulties of keeping up with technological change. At a more theoretical level the reflex reaction that perceptions of risk associated with particular products or sectors should be met automatically with statutory intervention has been questioned on two grounds, firstly that increasing 'materialisation' tends to degrade the general claims to legitimacy of legal systems, and secondly that highly detailed legal rules may strain to breaking point the capacity of law to govern behaviour.[6] On

---

2   Commission Regulation 880/98 (butter); Ice Cream (Heat Treatment, etc) Regulations 1959, SI 1959/734.

3   Eg Jam and Similar Products Regulations 1981, SI 1981/1063 (as amended); Fruit Juices and Fruit Nectars Regulations 1977, SI 1977/927 (as amended).

4   Eg Marketing Standard for Asparagus, Regulation 2377/1999, OJ L 287 10.11.99; Marketing Standard for Peaches and Nectarines, Regulation 2335/1999, OJ L 281 4.11.99.

5   Agence Europe 26/05/2000.

6   G Teubner 'Juridification: Concepts, Aspects, Limits, Solutions' in G Teubner (ed) *Juridification of Social Spheres* (1987) reproduced in R Baldwin, C Scott and C Hood *Reader on Regulation* (OUP, 1998).

this last point it is argued that the legal system cannot properly comprehend the production systems which it seeks to regulate, and thus statutory regulation is unlikely to modify behaviour to maximise safety, unless accompanied by other forms of activity, such as fostering of self-regulatory institutions.

The response to these concerns, that 'interventionist' consumer law may not be effective has been the development of a post-interventionist style of law.[7] This new style of law takes at least four forms. Firstly, highly detailed vertical measures of regulation from the EC have, since the 1980s, been gradually displaced by so-called 'new approach' or 'framework' directives. These legislative instruments set out minimum requirements while leaving the filling in of much of the detail to voluntary standards or 'soft law'.[8] This approach is exemplified by the EC Toy Safety Directive 1988. The general requirement of the directive is that toys may only be placed on the market where they do not jeopardise the safety or health of users.[9] The essential safety requirements to which all toys are expected to comply are set out considerable detail in Annex II of the Directive. However the Directive anticipates that more specific requirements in relation to particular types of toy may be set down either in other EC or legislative instruments or in voluntary standards. Producers are required either to check the conformity of their products with the applicable standards (eg CEN standards) or to secure type approval for the product from a standardisation body. All toys are required to bear a mark (the CE mark) indicating that the producer has checked for such conformity (Article 8). Since 1993 the placing of the CE mark on goods has provided an indication that the product is in conformity with all essential requirements, not just those in respect of safety.[10] Thus self-certification is a central aspect of the regime. Manufacturers are required to maintain records of processes of manufacture, test certificates, etc. The Directive is implemented in the UK by the Toys (Safety) Regulations 1995.[11]

Secondly, both EU and national authorities have placed greater reliance on non-binding instruments to stimulate behaviour modification by

---

7   N Reich 'Diverse Approaches to Consumer Protection Philosophy' (1992) 14 Journal of Consumer Policy 257.
8   This approach was not entirely new—the UK had been making reference to BSI standards in safety regulation prior to the 1980s. On soft law see G Howells '"Soft Law" in EC Consumer Law' in P Craig and C Harlow *Lawmaking in the European Union* (Kluwer, 1998).
9   Council Directive 88/378/EEC, Article 2(1).
10 EC Directive 93/68/EEC. For toys the 1995 regulations implement this requirement.
11 The 1995 Regulations (SI 1995/204) consolidate and replace earlier regulations. See Weatherill 'Toy Safety' in Daintith (ed) *Implementing EC Law in the United Kingdom: Structures for Indirect Rule* (Wiley, 1995).

industry. Thirdly, both UK and EC legislators have developed statutory standards of more general application. The creation of and adherence to voluntary standards are encouraged by the fact that such practices will often be sufficient to demonstrate compliance with general safety standards. Fourthly, the traditional due diligence defences have been used to encourage producers to adopt voluntary production standards which, if implemented properly, may provide the basis for establishing the statutory defence. We now look in turn at voluntary standards, general safety standards and statutory defences.

4   ALTERNATIVES TO CLASSICAL REGULATION: VOLUNTARY STANDARDS AND SOFT LAW

Disenchantment with the capacity of governments to regulate effectively through traditional 'command and control' methods has led both the UK and EC authorities to place greater emphasis on alternatives to classical regulation. The Consumer Affairs minister has noted in recent report on the use of statutory consumer safety powers in the UK:

> Whilst this report is specifically about the application of consumer safety legislation, the other tools which Government has used during this period include the promotion of industry codes of practice and voluntary safety standards, the provision of accident statistics, the publication of product safety research, and a rolling programme of consumer safety education.[12]

Chief among these alternative techniques has been a greater reliance on voluntary standards, set by private standardisation bodies or industry groups, and on governmental instruments which promote or encourage particular forms of conduct by producers distributors and retailers, but without the force of law behind them ('soft law'—codes of practice and guidance are classic examples).

Standardisation bodies such as the German DIN, the French AFNOR and the British Standards Institution (BSI) emerged in Europe in a number of countries in the early part of the twentieth century. The BSI remains a private body providing a service to industry through the creation of standards for a wide variety of products and processes. But provided there is general public confidence in the BSI then its standards can also be used as the basis for public regulation, either by specifically referring to requirements of compliance with BSI standards in statutory rules, or through a more general conception that compliance with BSI standards

---

[12]   DTI *Consumer Safety: Report by the Secretary of State for Trade and Industry for the Period 1 April 1993–31 March 1998* (1998) foreword.

should be deemed to be in compliance with general safety requirements. The financing of the BSI by sales of its standards, industry subscriptions and government grant reflects this multiple function.

Voluntary standards may also be set by trade associations. In two recent cases national industry groups have responded to pressure from the DTI to establish industry codes to address serious safety concerns about injuries caused by the caps of fizzy drinks bottles and solvent abuse. In respect of fizzy drinks the DTI had discovered that caps were often placed so tightly that consumers injured themselves after resorting to inappropriate tools (such as nutcrackers) to get the caps off. A new industry code was produced which encouraged manufacturers to provide clear instructions on opening of bottles, to reduce the torque applied to the caps, and to require undertaking of tests on caps. In the case of solvents a new warning *Solvent Abuse Can Kill Instantly*, was adopted by an industry forum.[13]

National voluntary standards of the sort created by the BSI create risks of fragmentation of international markets, either because regulators fail to recognise equivalent standards from other jurisdictions, or because businesses themselves believe that regulatory requirements downstream require them to ensure that components or processes supplied by others should meet national standards. A response to these concerns has been the creation of international standardisation bodies such as the International Standardisation Organisation (ISO) and various European bodies including the European Committee for Standardisation (CEN), CENELEC and ETSI (dealing with general standards, electrical products and telecommunications respectively). The European standardisation bodies comprise representatives of the national standardisation bodies of the EC and EFTA countries.[14] These organisations, in which national standardisation bodies participate, promote the harmonisation of voluntary standards internationally.

Whilst voluntary standard setting is central to contemporary product safety standards, these processes are not without their critics. Criticisms include suggestions that voluntary standard setting might too readily serve industry interests at the expense of consumers. This fear is fed by the limited opportunities for participation in standard setting by consumer representatives, although consumer representation is part of the structure of the BSI. Because of the importance of voluntary standard setting to EC product safety measures the European Commission has sought to counter

---

[13]   DTI *Consumer Safety: Report by the Secretary of State for Trade and Industry for the Period 1 April 1993–31 March 1998* (1998) paras 29–30.

[14]   G Howells '"Soft Law" in EC Consumer Law' in P Craig and C Harlow *Lawmaking in the European Union* (1998) p 322.

some of these difficulties by creating and financing the European Association for the Co-ordination of Consumer Representation in Standardisation (ANEC) an organisation representative of consumers to participate in the activities of CEN and CENELEC.[15]

Voluntary standards are incorporated into the legal regime for the regulation of product safety by a number of routes. First, the general safety standards created by the Consumer Protection Act 1987 and the General Product Safety Regulations 1994 (and discussed more extensively in the next section) explicitly refer to voluntary safety standards as factors to be considered in determining whether the general safety standard has been breached.[16] Thus under the 1987 Act it is relevant to consider 'any standards of safety published by any person' in determining whether there has been compliance with the general duty.[17] An attempt in Parliament to restrict the relevant safety standards to those put forward by the BSI or CEN was defeated.[18] Interpreting this provision, it appears that a producer who complies with a credible, published safety standard in respect of a product will be entitled to escape liability for breach of the general safety requirement in respect of matters covered by that standard. At a minimum there would be a strong prima facie case that no offence had been committed (see discussion of the *Whirlpool* case below).

A second, and more certain route to the effective incorporation of voluntary standards into legal requirements is the explicit reference to such voluntary standards in regulations. For example the current statutory instrument for the regulation of pushchairs and prams contains no substantive standards of its own, but rather requires compliance with either relevant BSI standards or standards of other EC Member States offering equivalent levels of safety.[19]

Instruments of soft law have long been recognised as providing an important technique for encouraging both government and industry to modify behaviour in the EU. Though the term is sometimes equated with self-regulation, it is helpful to think of it has having a slightly different meaning, as referring to officially mandated decisions, guidance, codes,

---

[15]   G Howells '"Soft Law" in EC Consumer Law' in P Craig and C Harlow *Lawmaking in the European Union* (1998) p 323.

[16]   However, the regime under which the Secretary of State formally approved voluntary standards as showing compliance with the general safety requirement under the 1987 Act was revoked by the General Product Safety Regulations 1994, SI 1994/2328, reg 6: Consumer Protection Act 1987, s 10(3)(b)(ii); Approval of Safety Standards Regulations 1987, SI 1987/1911.

[17]   Consumer Protection Act 1987, s 10(2)(b).

[18]   Hansard, Vol 116, cols 345–346.

[19]   Wheeled Child Conveyances (Safety) Regulations 1997, SI 1997/2294.

etc, intended to induce behavioural modification, but without the force of law.[20] Such soft law instruments have the advantage that they can be produced without legislative authority, and without the burden of following procedural requirements, while they also operate more flexibly than binding law, giving those to whom they are addressed more choices about how to respond. The DTI has been very active in producing soft law instruments in the consumer safety field. Examples of soft law instruments developed by or with the encouragement of the DTI include guidance notes, recommendations, codes of practice and even a humble press release.

Guidance may be issued to enforcement authorities, and the DTI can expect this to have knock-on effects on the behaviour of businesses. When the DTI was alerted to risks to eyesight associated with over-powerful laser pointing devices in Autumn 1997 it issued guidance to enforcement authorities that such devices were unsafe in the hands of consumers and that enforcement authorities should use their powers under the General Product Safety Regulations 1994 (discussed below) to remove the products from the market as quickly as possible.[1] The DTI has issued more general guidance on product recalls, which is intended to modify behaviour in the absence of any statutory power to require recalls of faulty goods (discussed below).[2] Whereas such guidance issued by the DTI is non-statutory, there is a statutory power for ministers to issue codes on enforcement of the Food Safety Act 1990 and associated regulations (s 40(1)). This power was introduced in order to satisfy the requirement of an EC Directive to the effect that there must be effective national co-ordination for control of foodstuffs.[3] The power has been widely used, giving ministers a more formal role in overseeing food safety enforcement than is true of product safety.

Recommendations to industry are commonly used as a means of dealing with a safety problem. Finding that a batch of 13 amp fuse links imported from China posed a possible safety risk, the DTI recommended that businesses replace the suspect devices, while the DTI carried out a risk analysis of the problem. Formal powers, for example enforcement of the Plugs and Sockets etc (Safety) Regulations 1994[4] were not invoked, because

---

[20]   F Beveridge and S Nott 'A Hard Look at Soft Law' in P Craig and C Harlow (eds) *Lawmaking in the European Union* (1998) pp 288–290; cf G Howells '"Soft Law" in EC Consumer Law' in P Craig and C Harlow (eds) *Lawmaking in the European Union* pp 310–311.

[1]   DTI *Consumer Safety: Report by the Secretary of State for Trade and Industry for the Period 1 April 1993–31 March 1998* (1998) para 35.

[2]   DTI *Consumer Product Recall: A Good Practice Guide* (1999).

[3]   C Scott 'Continuity and Change in British Food Law' (1990) 53 MLR 785.

[4]   SI 1994/1768.

the advice was deemed sufficient.[5] A press release was used by the DTI in response to a problem where tubes of paint were found to have a high lead content. Though intended for professional use the paint was inexpensive and widely available. Consequently it was bought for and used by children. A DTI press release was issued warning of the risk and advising anyone using the paint to wash their hands after use.[6] Publication of information for consumers is commonly used as a means to try to increase safety by modifying consumer behaviour, both directly by the DTI, and through grants to other organisations such as the Royal Society for the Prevention of Accidents (RoSPA).

5   GENERAL STANDARDS

For a long period both UK and EC legislators eschewed the use of general standards of safety. However, the corollary to placing greater reliance on voluntary standards has been a recognition that the development of general safety standards may be effective in bolstering compliance with voluntary standards, thereby enhancing the legitimacy and effectiveness of the entire regime. General standards have a much longer history in UK food legislation (discussed in Chapter 8 above). The current position is that detailed legislative standards generally take precedence, such that the general norms are only applicable in the absence of such detailed rules. The mechanisms for the creation of this 'hierarchy of norms' are discussed below.

The proposal to create a general safety duty in respect of consumer products emerged in a government White Paper in 1984.[7] Such a general safety duty was already owed by manufacturers in respect of products designed, manufactured, imported or supplied for use at work.[8] A new general safety requirement in respect of consumer goods[9] supplied in the UK market was introduced by Part II of the Consumer Protection Act 1987.

---

[5]   DTI *Consumer Safety: Report by the Secretary of State for Trade and Industry for the Period 1 April 1993–31 March 1998* (1998) para 35.

[6]   DTI *Consumer Safety: Report by the Secretary of State for Trade and Industry for the Period 1 April 1993–31 March 1998* (1998) para 35.

[7]   *The Safety of Goods* (Cmnd 9302 (1984)).

[8]   Health and Safety at Work Act 1974, s 6; *Miller: Product Liability and Safety Encyclopedia* para **IV [10]**.

[9]   Various classes of goods are excluded from the ambit of the new safety requirement on the grounds that they are regulated by more specific legislative provisions. The exclusion include growing crops, food, gas, aircraft, controlled drugs and licensed medicinal products and tobacco: Consumer Protection Act 1987, s 10(7); similar provision is made in respect of safety regulations made under s 11 (noted above), s 11(7).

The chief objective of the new provision in s 10 of the Act was to criminalise the supply of unsafe goods which were not caught by specific safety regulation made under what is now s 11 of the Act or the European Communities Act 1972. Prior to the introduction of the general safety requirement the only mechanism for removing unsafe goods not caught by specific rules from the market was through the cumbersome process under which the Secretary of State issues a prohibition order (noted below).

The general safety requirement which currently applies in most situations is contained in the General Product Safety Regulations 1994, which substantially displace the earlier provision of s 10 of the Consumer Protection Act 1987.[10] The 1994 Regulations apply to all consumer products (including foodstuffs and medicines, which are excluded from the 1987 Act) and thus are wider in scope than the 1987 Act.[11] The Regulations apply chiefly to producers, defined as being manufacturers (where based in the EC), importers into the EC or manufacturers' representative (where production occurs outside the EC) or others in the supply chain whose actions affect the safety of the product (such as a retailer who carries out some processing of the product, as with a car dealer carrying out safety checks before delivery of a new car) (reg 2). Thus the chief duty contained in the Regulations apply to producers who are not to place products on the market unless they are safe (reg 7). Producers owe a secondary duty to provide information to consumers about risks inherent to a product and to monitor the safety of their products so as to facilitate appropriate responses (including product recalls) should risks be discovered (reg 8(1)). These measures include the investigation of complaints and communications with distributors (reg 8(2)). Whereas breach of the requirements of reg 7 is an offence (reg 12) there is no direct sanction created for breach of reg 8.

More limited obligations are placed on distributors (defined as any professional in the supply chain whose activities do not affect the safety of the product—thus including wholesalers and retailers in most cases (reg 2)). The main duty on a distributor is subject to a *mens rea*

---

[10]   Council Directive 92/59/EC; General Product Safety Regulations 1994, SI 1994/2328. The European Commission has recently announced a review of the 1992 Directive with a view to strengthening the coordination and enforcement aspects: A proposal for a directive has been published: COM (2000) 139 final/2. The manner of implementation, under regulations issued under the European Communities Act 1972 was a recipe for confusion. Good legislative practice would suggest that the 1987 Act should have been amended to incorporate the new EC requirements. However, as with implementation of the EC Directive on Unfair Terms in Consumer Contract (discussed above Chapter 3) it was perceived by government that parliamentary time did not permit a full legislative revision, and so instead we have a highly unsatisfactory dual set of provisions in the 1987 Act and the 1994 Regulations.

[11]   The very limited list of products not covered are secondhand products which are antiques and products supplied for repair or reconditioning before use: reg 3.

requirement—the duty not to distribute products which it knows or ought to know are unsafe (reg 9(a)). Breach of this requirement is an offence (reg 12). Secondary duties owed by distributors to monitor the safety of products, pass on information and generally co-operate on the avoidance of risk (reg 9(b)) carry no direct penalties for breach. The only sanctions available in respect of these secondary duties appear to be the issue of prohibition notices and suspension orders (discussed below). Both producers and distributors can commit the offences of offering or agreeing to place on the market or supplying any dangerous product or exposing or possessing such products for placing on the market or for supply (reg 13).

Under the 1994 Regulations a 'safe product' is defined as:

> any product which, under normal or reasonably foreseeable conditions of use, including duration, does not present any risk or only the minimum risk compatible with the product's use, considered as acceptable and consistent with a high level of protection for the safety and health of persons... (reg 2(2)).

The concept of 'minimum risk compatible with the product's use' is important in providing a definition under which products which have dangers inherent to their function (eg knives, steam irons, etc) can nevertheless be regarded as safe.[12] In evaluating whether a product is safe in this sense various matters are to be taken into account, including the characteristics of the product, its effects on other products, the presentation of the product (including labelling, instructions, etc) and 'the categories of consumers at serious risk when using the product, in particular children'. The 1994 Regulations appear to set a similar standard of safety to that envisaged by the general safety requirement of the 1987 Act.

The Regulations create a hierarchy of norms, under which specific safety standards trump general requirements. The logic lying behind this is that the general safety requirement is intended to fill the gaps left by more specific regimes, and that where more specific rules exist then those rules should govern the situation, because a standard setting body (whether public or private) has explicitly considered what a producer should be require to do to make a product safe. Specifically the products for which all aspects of safety are governed by Community law rules are excluded completely from the ambit of the Regulations (reg 3(c)),[13] and otherwise the Regulations only apply to a product to the extent that safety matters are not addressed by such specific rules (reg 4)). Compliance with

---

UK statutory rules creates a rebuttable presumption that the product is safe (reg 10(1)). Where there are no EC or UK statutory rules, then any UK or EC standards are to be taken into account in considering whether a product is safe, but they are not said to be definitive on the question whether the product is safe.[14] In practice enforcement officers and courts are likely to evaluate the quality of the source of the standards—a CEN or BSI standard is likely to be accorded higher respect than one put out by trade association. But it is clear from UK case law that compliance with such a standard may not prevent a successful prosecution.[15]

The 1994 Regulations disapply s 10 of the 1987 Act to the extent that the 1994 Regulations impose general safety requirements on producers and distributors. Put another way, there is to be no overlap between the provisions. The search for theoretical examples of conduct which continues to be regulated by s 10 of the 1987 Act (discussed below) has not yielded many results. One possible case relates to products where the producer's conduct is regulated by specific Community requirements (and thus excluded from the ambit of the 1994 Regulations—see below), but the distributor's conduct is not caught by such specific requirements. As this falls outside the Regulations, then the 1987 Act may continue to apply.[16] It should be noted that although the 1994 Regulations apply to food stuffs the food safety requirement (introduced by s 8 of the Food Safety Act 1990) prohibiting the selling, offering, advertising, exposing, possession or preparation for sale of food which is injurious to health remains in place.[17] Thus the Regulations operate in parallel to, rather than to the exclusion of, the food safety requirement. Though s 10 of the 1987 Act is left little scope for application, it is helpful to consider the earlier approach taken in domestic legislation and by the courts in prosecutions, as the courts are likely to approach issues under the 1994 Regulations in a similar fashion to approach taken under the 1987 Act.

The general safety requirement applied to any person who, in the course of business (s 46(5)), supplied (whether by sale or otherwise) consumer

---

[14]   Prior to the implementation of the 1994 Regulations standards approved by the Secretary of State had acted as a completed defence under Consumer Protection Act 1987, s 10(3)(b)(ii); Approval of Safety Standards Regulations 1987, SI 1987/1911. The approved standards regime was revoked in order to comply with the General Product Safety Directive: General Product Safety Regulations 1994, SI 1994/2328, reg 6.

[15]   *Whirlpool (UK) Ltd and Magnet Ltd v Gloucestershire County Council* (1993) 159 JP 123, discussed at p 399 below; *Balding v Lew-Ways Ltd* (1995) 159 JP 541.

[16]   DTI *The General Product Safety Regulations: Guidance for Business, Consumers and Enforcement Authorities* (1995); DTI *Guide to the Consumer Protection Act 1987* (amended version, February 1999) para 21.

[17]   General Product Safety Regulations, reg 11(c)(ii)(bb); P Cartwright 'Product Safety and Consumer Protection' (1995) 58 MLR 222, 229–230.

goods or offered or agreed to supply such goods, or exposed or possessed such goods for supply (s 10(1)). The safety standard set by s 10 is one of reasonable safety (s 10(2)). A variety of factors may be considered in determining whether goods meet the standard. Thus it is relevant to consider whether goods which might otherwise be considered safe were rendered unsafe because of some aspect of their marketing or get-up or associated instructions (s 10(2)(a)). Equally such factors might render goods safe which would otherwise be unsafe. So, clear instructions or warnings about some risky factor inherent to the goods could make them safe. An example is prominent warning notices that the blades on a hover-mower continue to rotate for a period after the power has been disconnected. In *Coventry City Council v Ackerman*[18] it was held that a microwave egg boiler which failed to provide instructions that eggs were to be removed from their shells was unsafe, as eggs microwaved without being removed from their shells tended to explode. In this case it is clear that proper instructions would have rendered the product safe. The intended use may also be gleaned from manufacturers' instructions. In *Whirlpool (UK) Ltd v Gloucestershire County Council*,[19] it was held that a cooker hood which melted, causing exposure of electrical wires when placed at the recommended height from the gas cooker beneath, could not be regarded in isolation from the other products with which it was used, and that 'in the circumstances' in which it was intended to be used it was clearly unsafe, notwithstanding the fact that it had certification indicating it complied with CENELEC requirements. A similar standard would be applied under the 1994 Regulations which would now apply to these cases.

It is also relevant to consider whether there were 'any means by which it would have been reasonable (taking into account the cost, likelihood and extent of any improvement) for the goods to have been made safer' (s 10(2)(c)). This provision clearly imports a cost-benefit test into the determination of whether goods are safe in respect of possible safety improvements—albeit one conducted informally by enforcement officers or by the courts, rather than in the manner of more scientific public policy making. Thus where a producer fails to incorporate a relatively inexpensive improvement with a high potential to improve safety the application of this test would tend to suggest that the standard had been breached. Conversely a relatively expensive improvement with little potential for improving safety would not be required to comply with the test.

As with the 1994 Regulations the provisions of the 1987 Act general safety requirement effectively creates a hierarchy of standards, within which specific statutory and voluntary standards take precedence. The mechanisms through which this hierarchy of norms is created are somewhat

---

[18]   [1995] Crim LR 140.
[19]   (1993) 159 JP 123.

complex. As noted above compliance with a voluntary safety standard is a relevant factor, and may provide a prima facie case for compliance with the general safety requirement (s 10(2)(b)). In the case of detailed statutory standards (for example regulations made under s 11 of the 1987 Act or under s 2 of the European Communities Act 1972) the ousting of the general safety requirement is more or less absolute. Thus a producer who complies with the requirements of such specific regulations shall not be regarded as breaching the general safety requirement in respect of those matters covered by the regulations, and cannot be required to do more than the regulations require (s 10(3)).

6   DEFENCES TO PRODUCT STANDARDS OFFENCES

The various product and foods safety statutes and regulations offer a number of defences to those accused of offences. Of most general application is the due diligence defence (discussed more fully in Chapter 8 above). The defence is available, in rather similar form, in respect of breach of either of the general safety requirements (under the 1987 Act or 1994 Regulations) and for breach of regulations made under s 11 of the 1987 Act (reg 4). The limited evidence available from prosecutions in which the defence has been raised suggests that the courts require both a high standard of care and considerable evidence for the defence to be made out. Thus it has been held that a wholesaler cannot rely on a blanket condition in an order form that all goods supplied shall comply with statutory regulations. It was suggested that a specific assurance in relation to the particular goods or compliance with the particular regulations breached should have been sought.[20] Where importers engage in sampling of the goods (ie checking a certain proportion) it has been held that a sample of 1 in 10,000 was not adequate.[1]

There are also available defences of less general application. For example, the 1987 Act offers a defence to retailers in respect of the general safety requirement where the retailer 'neither knew nor had reasonable grounds for believing that the goods failed to comply with the general safety requirement' (s 10(4)(c)(ii)). The defence may be criticised on the ground that it gives to retailers incentives not to investigate the safety of goods which they supply. Small retailers might lack the capacity to investigate or test products for safety, but larger retailers frequently do

[20]   *Riley v Webb* (1987) 151 JP 372, [1987] BTLC 65.
[1]   *Rotherham Metropolitan Borough Council v Raysun (UK) Ltd* (1988) 153 JP 37. See also *P & M Supplies (Essex) Ltd v Devon County Council* (1991) 156 JP 328, QBD; *Sutton London Borough Council v David Halsall plc* (1994) 159 JP 431, QBD.

have such capacity, but the availability of the defence might make it rational for such retailers to abandon safety testing programmes in order to have the defence available to them. Thus a possible source of additional safety checks might be removed. In effect the defence allows retailers to rely on their suppliers for ensuring compliance with the general safety requirement. This objection to the defence is addressed to some extent by its non-availability in respect of goods which have not previously been supplied in the UK. Thus retailers of products of a type which are new to the UK market cannot deny a duty to take their own steps to ensure such products are safe. Notice that the Product Safety Regulations (1994) also treat retailers and other distributors differently from producers, but by creating lesser obligations rather than by making defences available. Defences can also be made out where the goods were possessed for export only and where the goods were secondhand or not supplied as new (except where the consumer obtains no interest in the goods, as with the hire of equipment or cars) (Consumer Protection Act 1987 s 10(4)(a), (c)(i), respectively).

7   MONITORING, ENFORCEMENT AND SANCTIONS

Responsibilities for monitoring and enforcement of product safety and food safety rules are split between the ministers, local authority trading standards departments and (in respect of food safety) local authority environmental health departments. For enforcement of hygiene rules in abattoirs there is a specialised enforcement agency, the Meat Hygiene Service (MHS) (an executive agency of the Ministry of Agriculture, Fisheries and Food (MAFF)). The MHS's unusually comprehensive on-site inspection regime was introduced in 1995 as a response to the BSE crisis, after it was discovered that regulations introduced in 1989 to address the problem of infected nerve tissues in cattle were not being effectively enforced by local authorities. There is also considerable European Commission involvement, both in co-ordinating information exchanges between the Member States and the substantive application of prohibitions in respect of particular products.

The European Commission has exercised a co-ordinating role in respect of product safety since the establishment of the system for rapid exchange of information (RAPEX) in 1984.[2] Under this regime Member States have a duty to inform the Commission of measures taken to address dangerous products, and the Commission then informs the other Member States. 204 such notifications were made in the five-year period up to the end of

---

[2]   Council Decision 84/133 EEC, OJ 1984 L 70/16.

March 1998, including 32 by the UK government.[3] The other States then provide information to the Commission on the steps they have taken. This regime has been incorporated within and considerably enhanced by the provisions of the General Product Safety Directive (Article 8). Where the European Commission has been notified of action by a Member State in respect of particular products and judges that action by the Member States will be ineffective to protect the safety of consumers, and that Community level action will be effective, then it may issue a decision requiring Member States to take temporary measures, including the prohibition of the supply of the product and the organisation of its withdrawal from the market (Articles 9, 6). The unusual and contentious nature of the powers given to the Commission is illustrated by the challenge made by the German government to the validity of this aspect of the General Product Safety Directive before the European Court of Justice.[4] Though the court upheld the provisions of the Directive, the Commission has been cautious in using the power, only putting them into play for the first time in 1999 to ban toys containing phthalates (pvc).[5] In the UK the Local Authority Co-ordinating Body on Trading Standards (LACOTS) was established in 1978 in part to facilitate co-ordination both within the UK and within the EC more generally.

Ministers have powers to issue prohibition notices prohibiting particular individuals from supplying unsafe products (to include foodstuffs by virtue of the 1994 Regulations[6]) and to require producers and others to publish notices where goods have been found to be unsafe in use.[7] In the last five year reporting period (up the end of March 1998) these powers were never invoked. The DTI has explained this non-use of the power to publish notices to warn by stating that 'the Department has often been

---

3   DTI *Consumer Safety: Report by the Secretary of State for Trade and Industry for the Period 1 April 1993–31 March 1998* (1998) para 43.

4   *Germany v Council* Case C-359/92 [1994] ECR I-3681; see also S Weatherill *EC Consumer Law and Policy* (1997) pp 129–137.

5   European Commission Press Release, 2/12/99. Cf S Weatherill *EC Consumer Law and Policy* (1997) pp 129–130 who thought it unlikely that the stringent conditions set by the Council of Ministers before the Commission could act would ever be met.

6   Ministers already had powers, which they retain, under ss 1, 2 of the Food and Environment Protection Act 1985 and s 13 of the Food Safety Act 1990, to issue emergency orders to take contaminated foodstuffs off the market and to close premises which are the source of food-borne inspection. Under the Food Standards Act 1999 these powers are to be shared with the Food Standards Agency, though ministers are expected to exercise the powers in most cases.

7   Consumer Protection Act 1987, s 13; General Product Safety Regulations 1994, reg 11. Detailed requirements for the content for such notices and procedures for issuing them are set out in Sch 2. The minister also has a duty to report to Parliament every five years on the exercise of these powers: s 42.

able to secure the necessary co-operation of suppliers without the necessity of exercising the power'. On other occasions the publication of a carefully considered press notice has been deemed to be more effective.[8] In one case, where the DTI discovered that a consignment of faulty 13 amp fuses had been imported into the UK installed in 13 amp plugs, it considered the use of powers to require issuance of notices to warn consumers and other related information measures but concluded that the risks associated with the faulty product remaining in use were less than the risk that consumers would bungle the changing of fuses, and decided to take no action.[9] Thus it appears the DTI gives due consideration to the exercise of its formal enforcement powers, but finds that it can achieve the objectives by other, less interventionist means, or that intervention is not merited on risk grounds. It is nonetheless possible that the credible threat that it will exercise its powers is important in securing the co-operation of business. Prior to the implementation of the 1987 Act the Secretary of State possessed more extensive powers to issue general orders prohibiting the supply of particular goods,[10] but the emphasis of enforcement in the 1987 Act (in provisions originally introduced by the Consumer Safety (Amendment) Act 1986) is on local enforcement by trading standards officers and by customs officers who are perceived to be in a better position to act quickly to address dangerous products.

Any enforcement authority (which technically includes both ministers and local authorities (Consumer Protection Act 1987, s 45(1)), but in practice will usually mean local authorities[11]) can issue notices suspending the supply of goods for up to six months where they suspect breach of relevant safety legislation (s 14).[12] This includes both breach of the general safety requirement (s 10) and of safety regulations (made under s 11). The provisional character of suspension notices is demonstrated by the fact that where a court determines that there was no breach then compensation is payable by the local authority. Though this appears to be a powerful disincentive against the application of the powers, there is little evidence that in fact enforcement officers are discouraged from taking action and

---

8   DTI *Consumer Safety: Report by the Secretary of State for Trade and Industry for the Period 1 April 1993–31 March 1998* (1998) paras 7–9.

9   DTI *Consumer Safety: Report by the Secretary of State for Trade and Industry for the Period 1 April 1993–31 March 1998* (1998) para 35.

10   Though the Secretary of State does retain the power to issue general prohibitions in the form of regulations made under s 11 of the 1987 Act. See, for example, Tobacco for Oral Use (Safety) Regulations 1992, SI 1992/2134.

11   In the five-year period up to the end of March 1998 the DTI did not exercise any of the powers also held by local authorities: DTI *Consumer Safety: Report by the Secretary of State for Trade and Industry for the Period 1 April 1993–31 March 1998* (1998) para 14.

12   *R v Birmingham County Council, ex p Ferrero Ltd* [1993] 1 All ER 530.

there have been few cases where compensation has been payable. As a more final measure enforcement authorities may apply to the magistrates' court to order the forfeiture and destruction of goods in breach of statutory safety requirements (s 16) (whether the breach is under s 10 of the 1987 Act, the 1994 Regulations or regulations made under s 11).[13] It is additionally possible for regulations implementing EC Directives, adopted under the European Communities Act 1972, to specifically state that they are enforceable in some or all respects as if they were regulations made under s 11 of the 1987 Act.[14] In support of their responsibilities, enforcement authorities have powers to inspect or seize goods and to carry out testing for products (s 29). Customs officers have powers to seize goods and detain them for up to 72 hours where they are imported from outside the EC.[15] Similar powers are held by enforcement officers in respect of food intended for human consumption under the Food Safety Act 1990 (s 9).

Breaches of either the general or specific safety requirements of the legislation and 1994 Regulations and of prohibition notices and notices to warn are criminal offences.[16] Responsibility for enforcement generally falls to local authorities (though, as noted above, the DTI is also an enforcement authority under the 1987 Act). Similarly, enforcement of the Food Safety Act 1990 generally falls to local authorities. Whereas under the 1990 Act there is a formal power conferred on ministers to issue codes of practice on the enforcement by local authorities of the legislation, there is no similar provision in respect of the 1987 Act. Nevertheless the DTI does issue informal guidance on enforcement under this latter provision. In the five year period up to the end of March 1998 the DTI reported 1,640 prosecutions under the 1987 Act, of which 1,588 led to convictions. Fines totalled £939,000.[17] Of prosecutions under regulations the largest categories were in respect of toys, electrical equipment, furniture and

[13] Consumer Protection Act 1987, s 16.
[14] Eg Chemical (Hazards Information etc) Regulations 1994, SI 1994/3247 (as amended). It should be noted, however, that the maximum penalty for regulations made under the 1972 Act is three months' imprisonment, and consequently all regulations made under that Act, including the General Product Safety Regulations 1994, restrict the penalty. Under the Consumer Protection Act 1987 the maximum penalty for breach of safety regulations is six months' imprisonment.
[15] EC Regulation 339/93, Article 5 (which effectively displaces s 31 of the 1987 Act which had given customs officers a right to detain all imports for up to 48 hours: DTI *Guide the Consumer Protection Act 1987* (as amended, February 1999) para 33).
[16] Consumer Protection Act 1987, ss 10(1), 12; General Product Safety Regulations 1994, reg 12.
[17] DTI *Consumer Safety: Report by the Secretary of State for Trade and Industry for the Period 1 April 1993–31 March 1998* (1998) para 14. A detailed breakdown of prosecutions is produced in Appendix 3 to the report. Annual data on

furnishings. Over 200 prosecutions were made for breach of the general safety requirements (87 were made under s 10 of the 1987 Act and 124 under the 1994 Regulations.)[18] During 1998 547 prosecutions were made under the Food Safety Act 1990, with fines of £706,873 being levied (though not all these cases would have related to safety).[19]

There is additionally limited potential for private civil enforcement as breach of safety regulations (made under s 11 of the 1987 Act) is actionable as a matter of civil laws (s 41(1)). Thus consumers injured by a product in breach of such regulations may enforce the rules. This provision does not apply in respect of the s 10 offence, nor to breach of prohibition notices, for which the common law action of breach of statutory duty would probably not be available (s 41(2)).

There are no powers under the 1987 Act to require producers to recall products which are found to be unsafe for the purpose of securing modifications. The DTI has published a soft law instrument—a guide to effective product recalls[20] but has no plans to introduce any legislative power to require recalls. As noted above the Secretary of State has powers to require producers and others to publish warning notices, and this power may create incentives on producers to publish such information voluntarily and follow this up with the recall of the products.[1] It has been held *ultra vires* for a local authority to publish a press release declaring certain products to be in breach of safety standards where the publication was designed to require the producers to recall the products. The press release evaded the statutory protections associated with the statutory duty held by the Secretary of State alone to publish warnings about the safety of products.[2] The EC General Product Safety Directive requires Member States to have the necessary powers to 'organise the effective and immediate withdrawal of a dangerous product or product batch already on the market…'.[3] The European Commission has apparently accepted the UK government's position that the requirement is met by having the power to withdraw products from the market (which can be achieved by using the suspension powers noted above) and does not require Member States to

---

prosecutions under the Consumer Protection Act 1987 can be found in the *Annual Report of the Office of Fair Trading*. For the 1998 Report (HC 524, 1999) see pp 80–81.

[18] DTI *Consumer Safety: Report by the Secretary of State for Trade and Industry for the Period 1 April 1993–31 March 1998* (1998) Appendix 3.

[19] *Annual Report of the Office of Fair Trading* HC 524, 1999, p 83.

[20] DTI *Consumer Product Recalls: A Good Practice Guide* (1999).

[1] See *Miller: Product Liability and Safety Encyclopedia* para **IV [7]**.

[2] *R v Liverpool City, ex p the Baby Products Association* QBD Crown Office List (Bingham LCJ) (23 November 1999, unreported).

[3] General Product Safety Directive, Article 6(1)(h).

be able to require producers to recall products which have already reached consumers. Enforcement officers do not have the power directly to require such steps to be taken and the statutory enforcement powers generally do not apply to products which are already in consumers' hands.[4]

If the Directive were interpreted to require Member States to take a power to require recalls from consumers then the UK government would be in breach. This position may be contrasted with that of other jurisdictions, such as the United States, where the Consumer Product Safety Commission has the power to demand corrective action in the event of a 'substantial product hazard' including recalls and refunds to consumers.[5] This is supplemented by a provision obliging businesses to report to the Commission immediately the existence of any substantial product hazard.

It is increasingly common for producers and retailers to decide to recall products when they discover faults which have the potential to affect safety. There was an average of 46 consumer product recalls each year between 1990 and 1996.[6] In the absence of regulatory coercion businesses make decisions to recall products on the basis that such measures are the responsible thing to do or, more cynically, will enhance their reputation, or prevent further damage to it. However there is no information available in the UK to indicate to what extent businesses decide to leave unsafe products in circulation, and how such calculations are made. There is some evidence from the United States. In a famous case involving the Ford Pinto car it emerged that there was a design fault associated with the location of the car's fuel tank which created a high risk that in high impact collisions the cars would burn creating the risk of death to the occupants. Having discovered the design fault the Ford Corporation carried out cost benefit analysis in order to decide whether to recall the cars. The necessary repair was comparatively cheap to carry out, but there were many cars in circulation. The corporation concluded that having regard to their likely liability for injury and death to consumers, it would be more cost effective not to recall the cars but to wait to be sued in private law.[7] No legislative development of a duty to recall is anticipated in the UK notwithstanding the apparently serious approach to the issue taken by the government.[8] It is arguable, however, that a duty to recall arises under negligence doctrines.[9]

---

[4]   The arguments for creating recall powers are set out in T Watt 'Improving Recalls of Unsafe Products' (1993) 3 Consumer Policy Review 204.

[5]   15 USC §2064 (b) (d).

[6]   *Product Recall Research* (DTI, 2000) p 6.

[7]   I Ramsay *Consumer Protection: Text and Materials* p 474.

[8]   DTI *Modern Markets, Confident Consumers* (Cm 4410 (1999)).

[9]   *Walton v British Leyland* (1978) Times, 13 July, QBD, extracted in Miller, Harvey and Parry *Consumer and Trading Law: Text, Cases and Materials* pp 208–213.

8   CONCLUSION

From the discussion in this chapter it will be clear that the pattern of standard setting, monitoring and enforcement in respect of consumer products is highly fragmented. The central issues relating to effectiveness relate to the extent to which this fragmented regime is effective in promoting consumer safety. In this context safety is not an absolute concept, but a relative one, referring to some conception of acceptable risk having regard to the utility of a product and the costs and benefits associated with making it safer. Examination of standard setting processes reveals the existence of a symbiotic relationship between voluntary and public standards. The comparatively recent development of general standards serves the function both of filling the gaps left in statutory vertical standards and encouraging compliance with voluntary standards. It is for this reason that the standards are ordered hierarchically, with precedence given to specific, rather than general standards.

A curious gap in provision for consumer safety is that there is no general provision for statutory regulation of the safety of services. Service sectors which involve substantial risk frequently have their own statutory safety regimes (for example with the provision of gas, transport, etc) and voluntary standards exist in many service sectors and are supplemented by more general process standards such as BS 5750 and ISO 9000. The introduction of general liability for unsafe services is to encourage maximum adoption of voluntary standards and to permit targeted enforcement action against service sectors or particular service providers where safety records are poor.

Chapter 11

Control of trade practices

In the past governments were reluctant to control trade practices other than by private law or by broad criminal prohibitions if this would interfere with the substance of consumer transactions. Apart from the administrative costs of further legal requirements, it was assumed that trade practices were so varied that widespread control was impracticable. A major assumption was that the great majority of consumers were sensible enough to protect themselves and that their range of choice would be restricted if controls were introduced for the benefit of the minority. It was said, on the rare occasions when difficulties arose, that consumers had certain rights at civil law and there might even be a criminal offence involved. The great majority of businesses were assumed to be reputable, one piece of evidence being that many had agreed to codes of practice setting acceptable standards of behaviour.

The 1970s witnessed a change in this attitude and a growth in public control. Consumers had failed to institute civil proceedings against businesses under the private law to secure redress for their grievances, and many prejudicial trade practices were recognisably not caught by the broad criminal prohibitions on the statute book penalising fraud or false trade descriptions. The very complexity and range of trade practices, and the need for considerable resources of investigation and detection, were seen as positive arguments for preferring public control in particular instances to other methods like voluntary codes of practice.[1] While voluntary codes are observed by many businesses, it was recognised that others ignored them so that overall effect was patchy and that areas of trade most in need of reform were usually the least likely to subscribe to

---

[1] *Seeking to Sell Goods Without Revealing that they are being Sold in the Course of a Business* (OFT, 1975) p 29.

them.[2] It was even said that public control stimulates efficiency and removes enterprises from the market which survive only through prejudicial practices.[3] The costs incurred by government and business in enforcing and complying with additional legal requirements were balanced against the economic advantages which accrue to consumers as a result. In some cases policy-makers conclude that such costs are small in relation to turnover and in any event can be minimised by businesses if they adopt better procedures.

Then in the 1980s competition emerged as a lodestar guiding public policy. This led to a questioning of the further regulation of trade practices. Regulatory costs, both the direct costs and the costs imposed on business, were often regarded as the determining counterweight to further regulation.[4] In most extreme form this movement led to deregulation, or at least to the privatisation of regulation in that regulation was to be carried out by non-governmental bodies.[5] In Britain regulatory proposals affecting business could not be entertained without both a compliance cost assessment and risk assessment, so that the burdens on business would be minimised.[6] Despite the predisposition against further regulation, a number of trade practices were brought within the regulatory net as a result of Britain's membership of the European Union. Before the introduction of a consumer protection title into the Treaty on the European Union at Maastricht (1993), these measures had to be based on single market grounds, which to an extent limited the subject matter covered.

Now the political change in Britain in 1997 means that the regulation of trade practices is back on the agenda. The Better Regulation Task Force recognises that the regulation of trading standards may be necessary to protect consumers from abuses or failures in the market. Nonetheless, the Task Force believes that good regulation and its enforcement must measure up to five principles—transparency, accountability, targeting, consistency and proportionality. This more subtle approach to regulation compared with the 1970s recognises that regulation must be easily understood and enforceable, that unintended consequences must be examined, that risk, cost and practical benefit must all be balanced, and that it will often be necessary to reconcile contradictory policy objectives.[7] The need for

2   *Prepayment for Goods* HC Paper 285 (HMSO, 1976) p 12.
3   *Prepayment in Mail Order Transactions and in Shops* (OFT, 1974) p 20.
4   Eg *Lifting the Burden* (Cmnd 9571 (1985)) p 24. See from a pro-consumer perspective: M Pertschuk *Revolt Against Regulation: The Rise and Pause of the Consumer Movement* (University of California Press, 1982).
5   Eg Deregulation and Contracting Out Act 1994.
6   J Froud, R Boden, A Ogus and P Stubbs *Controlling the Regulators* (Macmillan, 1998).
7   *Consumer Affairs* (Better Regulation Task Force, 1998) p 2. See also the DTI White Paper *Modern Markets: Confident Consumers* (Cm 4410 (1999)) especially Chapter 7.

regulation of trade practices to be back on the political agenda is underlined by the potential for abuse through the commercial exploitation of telecommunications and online services. Along with the explosion of telecommunications services have come new ways of misleading consumers about what they will get, overcharging, and the promotion of old deceptions such as pyramid schemes.[8]

I   THE FORMULATION OF CONTROLS

Over the years a number of statutes were enacted to control specific marketing and promotional practices which were particularly obnoxious from the point of view of consumers. Recent examples include the Timeshare Act 1992 and the Trading Schemes Act 1996. Controlling prejudicial trade practices through legislation has the self-evident disadvantage that trade practices change and new ones develop, yet legislative time is precious and the legislative machinery ponderous, so that measures may be delayed or in some cases never enacted. With this in mind special procedures have been introduced in several countries designed to permit more frequent and flexible regulatory action to be taken against prejudicial trade practices. In Britain the special procedures operate under the Fair Trading Act 1973, although they have not been used extensively.[9] There is a separate regime for financial services (examined in Chapter 12). In addition an important source of UK consumer protection law in the last decade has been European Directives. These are often implemented by regulations under the European Communities Act 1972.

---

[8]   For the US reaction: I Gotts and S Berg 'Developments in Consumer Protection: Enforcers Get Tough on Fraudulent and Deceptive Practices in Telecommunications Services' (1997) Antitrust, vol 11, Summer 1997, p 39; R Starck and L Rozell 'The Federal Trade Commission's Commitment to On-Line Consumer Protection' (1997) 15 Journal Marshall J Computer & Info L 679.

[9]   Since 1975 the Federal Trade Commission in the United States has had an explicit rule-making power to 'define with specificity acts or practices which are unfair or deceptive': 15 USC §2301–2312. The FTC must give public notice and conduct hearings in relation to proposed trade regulation rules. If promulgated trade regulation rules have the force of law: violation constitutes an unfair or deceptive act or practice in breach of s 5(a) of the Federal Trade Commission Act. Knowing violations enable the FTC to seek civil penalties. Yet as in Britain few rules have been issued because of the complexity of the procedure: L Parnes and C Jennings 'Through the Looking Glass: A Perspective on Regulatory Reform at the Federal Trade Commission' (1997) 49 Admin LR 989, 995. The FTC prefers 'industry guides' containing its interpretation of the law, which are intended to provide a basis of voluntary abandonment of unlawful practices. The guides do not have the direct force of law, but failure to comply might result in legal action.

The justification for the Fair Trading Act 1973 was that new machinery was needed in the face of rapidly changing trade practices. The Act establishes the Office of Fair Trading to exercise continual surveillance of commercial activities.[10] Under the Act the Office of Fair Trading is intended to act quickly and effectively against practices prejudicial to consumers as their effects become manifest, to collate information on matters affecting consumer interests, and to inform and educate consumers about their legal rights. In the event of a prejudicial trade practice becoming evident, the government has powers under Part II of the Fair Trading Act 1973 to prohibit or regulate it to protect consumers. The procedure is that the Director General of Fair Trading makes a recommendation to the Consumer Protection Advisory Committee that action be taken against a practice. The Consumer Protection Advisory Committee comprises independent persons appointed by the government, drawn from those with a variety of experience.[11] In considering the proposal, the Committee receives representations from interested parties and can either agree with the recommendations of the Director General, suggest modifications or disagree entirely. The government can then promulgate a statutory order unless the Committee adopts the last of these three courses.[12] Breach of an order is an offence; however, a contract is not void or unenforceable by reasons only of a contravention of an order, and no civil cause of action arises for breach of statutory duty.[13]

In general terms, the ambit of Part II of the Act extends to trade practices which relate to the terms and conditions on which goods and services are marketed, the manner in which those terms and conditions are communicated to consumers and the methods of promoting, selling and paying for the sale of goods and services.[14] Many provisions of existing consumer protection legislation fall within these heads. Under the legislation, objectionable trade practices may be completely prohibited or permitted subject to modification. The full range of control techniques available is contained in Sch 6 to the Act:

1   Prohibition of the specified consumer trade practice either generally or in relation to specified consumer transactions.
2   Prohibition of specified consumer transactions unless carried out at specified times or at a place of a specified description.

---

[10]   See Lord Howe 'The Birth of an Office: A Midwife's View' in *Fair Trading Past and Future* (OFT, 1992).
[11]   Fair Trading Act 1973, s 3. Membership was allowed to lapse in the 1980s, rendering the procedure moribund.
[12]   Sections 17, 18, 22.
[13]   Sections 23, 26.
[14]   Section 13.

3   Prohibition of the inclusion in specified consumer transactions of terms or conditions purporting to exclude or limit the liability of a party to such a transaction in respect of specified matters.
4   A requirement that contracts relating to specified consumer transactions shall include specified terms or conditions.
5   A requirement that contracts or other documents relating to specified consumer transactions shall comply with specified provisions as to lettering (whether as to size, type, colouring or otherwise).
6   A requirement that specified information shall be given to parties to specified consumer transactions.

To be considered for a statutory order under Part II of the Act, a business practice must have certain specified undesirable effects on consumers. First, it must adversely affect their *economic* interests as distinct from their other interests, such as in safety or health.[15] In addition, a practice must have one or more of the effects mentioned in s 17(2), which refers to matters such as whether a practice misleads consumers, pressurises them into transactions, or involves them in contracts which include inequitable terms. These requirements, especially economic detriment, are difficult to satisfy even though once the effects are demonstrated there is no need to examine whether or not they are intended. In addition, the procedures have proved time-consuming and inflexible. While the various points at which representations can be made about proposed controls ensure that there are consultative processes comparable to those operating in the legislative sphere, they can prolong the law-making process considerably.[16] More importantly, following the Committee's report the government's discretion is confined for it must implement either the original proposal of the Director General as agreed to by the Committee or the proposal as modified or reject the initiative altogether.

For these reasons, and through a lack of political will, the order-making power of the Fair Trading Act 1973 has not proved as effective as was expected. Only a limited number of trade practices have been regulated as a result.

(a)   Statements as to consumers' rights

The first Order concerns two practices related to the passage of the Supply of Goods (Implied Terms) Act 1973. That Act rendered void exemption

---

15   Sections 14, 19, 21.
16   I Ramsay 'The Office of Fair Trading: Policing the Market-Place' in R Baldwin and C McCrudden (eds) *Regulation and Public Law* (Weidenfeld & Nicolson, 1987) pp 189–190.

clauses purporting to deprive consumers of the benefit of the statutory terms implied in contacts of sale and hire purchase regarding title, correspondence with description, merchantable quality and fitness for purpose. (The Act's provisions in this regard have been replaced by s 6 of the Unfair Contract Terms Act 1977.) After passage of the 1973 legislation businesses continued to display noticed in shops or to give documents such as receipts which purported to restrict certain rights of consumers (eg statements like 'No money refunded'; 'No articles exchanged'; 'Money will not be refunded, credit notes will be given'). Moreover, consumers continued to receive documents such as guarantees which referred to rights and liabilities in connection with goods being sold, but which did not make clear the existence of inalienable rights against the retailer. The Office of Fair Trading took the view that these practices adversely affected consumers' economic interests. For example, they misled consumers as to their rights under a transaction so that they did not press a claim for redress in a situation where this was justified.[17] The Consumer Protection Advisory Committee agreed, but concluded that the proposed regulation by the Office of Fair Trading to ban the use in notices and documents of wording *likely* to suggest that the consumer's inalienable rights were restricted, went further than the practice.[18] Thus a notice 'No money refunded', while void in relation to a complaint about faulty goods, is perfectly valid regarding consumers who desire a refund simply because they have changed their minds. The government accepted the qualification suggested by the Consumer Protection Advisory Committee.

The Consumer Transactions (Restrictions on Statements) Order 1976[19] prohibits certain statements which would be void by virtue of the Unfair Contract Terms Act 1977 (article 3).[20] Unfortunately there is now the unsatisfactory situation where statements such as 'No money refunded except as required by the Unfair Contract Terms Act 1977' are legal, although quite unintelligible to many consumers. The Order also requires retailers' and manufacturers' guarantees to include a clear and conspicuous statement that they have no effect upon consumers' statutory rights (articles 4–5). The Order does not apply to terms and notices made void by the Unfair Contract Terms Act 1977, ss 2 and 7, which purport to exclude or restrict liability for death or personal injury resulting from negligence, or for the fitness of goods hired, exchanged or supplied as part of a service. The Office of Fair Trading has taken steps to eliminate the use of these

---

[17]   *The Purported Exclusion of Inalienable Rights* (OFT, 1974).
[18]   *Rights of Consumers* HC Paper No 6 (HMSO, 1974).
[19]   SI 1976/1813 as amended by SI 1978/127.
[20]   See *Hughes v Hall* [1981] RTR 430, 125 Sol Jo 255; *Cavendish-Woodhouse Ltd v Manley* (1984) 148 JP 299.

terms in the course of its consumer credit licensing activities and in evaluating agreements under restrictive trade practices legislation. Yet there continues to be a problem. In 1998 there were 16 prosecutions for breach of the Order, seven of which involved secondhand cars. Fines amounted to £9,000 and compensation ordered was £4,120.[1]

(b)   The identity of mail order advertisers

The second Order covers the practice of businesses taking prepayment for goods without any undertaking to return the money if the goods are not delivered in reasonable time. Associated with this in the case of some mail order transactions has been another practice, of not identifying the business's real name or giving its proper address. The argument was that these practices adversely affected consumers' economic interests, because once they had parted with their money they were largely at the mercy of such traders.[2] Evidence was available that some mail order companies, from which consumers had ordered goods and paid in advance, had gone into liquidation leaving consumers without a remedy. An Order was promulgated that mail order advertisements directed at consumers which suggest that prepayment has to be made should state the name and address of the business.[3] The Order is more limited than that proposed by the Director General, who thought that mail order companies should also state a delivery date in their advertisements and should be obliged to refund the payment if the specified date were not met.

Following the Order complaints by consumers who experienced delayed deliveries or the loss of their money because of fraud or insolvency continued at high levels. The Office of Fair Trading issued a Consultative Paper proposing that traders (other than mail order advertisers) who accepted prepayments from consumers should provide information about delivery times in a standard, written form. As a result of opposition to the proposal, the Office of Fair Trading abandoned its intention to seek changes in the law and instead sought a solution in self-regulation.[4]

---

[1]   *Annual Report of the Director General of Fair Trading, 1998* (HMSO, 1999) p 80.

[2]   *Prepayment in Mail Order Transactions and in Shops* (OFT, 1974). See also *Prepayment for Goods* HC No 285 (HMSO, 1976).

[3]   Mail Order Transactions (Information) Order 1976, SI 1976/1812. Advertisements by radio, television or film are excluded. The 1976 Order is to be repealed when the EC Distance Selling Directive 1997 is implemented by the Consumer Protection (Contracts Concluded By Means of Distance Communication) Regulations 2000. Implementation is not now expected before the Autumn of 2000, in breach of the terms of the Directive, which set a date of 4 June 2000.

[4]   *Annual Report of the Director General of Fair Trading 1979* (HMSO, 1980) p 21.

Self-regulation also goes beyond the provisions of the Order in relation to mail order advertisers. Under the Mail Order Protection Scheme, formed in consultation with the Office of Fair Trading and under an agreement between the national newspapers, the Institute of Practitioners in Advertising and the Incorporated Society of British Advertisers, readers are reimbursed if products which have been ordered fail to be delivered as a result of an advertiser going into liquidation or bankruptcy or ceasing to trade. It also covers readers who have returned goods but not received a refund from a failed advertiser. The scheme also vets each new mail order advertiser.[5]

(c) Disclosure of business character

In 1975 the OFT recommended, and the Consumer Protection Advisory Committee concurred, that it be made an offence for a trader to advertise goods for sale to the public without making it reasonably obvious that the goods were being sold in the course of a business.[6] Concern was expressed that consumers were prejudiced by advertisements in the classified columns of newspapers offering goods, creating the impression a private seller was involved, whereas they were being sold by a trader. An Order was made.[7] In 1999 there were 18 prosecutions for breach of the Order, 14 involving secondhand cars.[8]

(d) Other matters

At one time the Office of Fair Trading was considering possible Orders under Part II of the Fair Trading Act 1973 for door-to-door selling, one-day sales and party-plan selling (where persons invite friends and neighbours to their home so that a representative from a selling company may demonstrate to the group and take orders for items for future delivery). Nothing resulted, although some of these matters have been regulated in different ways. Because of the difficulties thought to be associated with Order making under Part II, regulation regarding bargain offer pricing was

---

[5]   The National Newspapers' Mail Order Protection Scheme (1996).
[6]   *Seeking to Sell Goods Without Revealing that they are being Sold in the Course of a Business* (OFT, 1975); *Disguised Business Sales* HC Paper No 355 (HMSO, 1976).
[7]   Business Advertisements (Disclosure) Order 1977, SI 1977/1918. Agents are covered by the Order whether or not they are acting in the course of a business: article 2(2). Disguised trade sales are extensive and are sometimes associated with other serious offences.
[8]   *Annual Report of the Director General of Fair Trading* (HMSO, 2000) p 91.

effected by statutory instrument under the Prices Act 1974.[9] Little was done following the report of the Consumer Protection Advisory Committee on VAT exclusive pricing.[10] As we have seen in Chapter 8, however, as a result of an EC Directive the Price Marking Order 1999[11] requires that price indications to consumers be VAT inclusive.

The DTI is consulting on reform of the rule-making powers under Part II of the Fair Trading Act 1973. It is proposed to give the Secretary of State the power to make new orders concerning trade practices on the advice of the Director General of Fair Trading. Breach of the new orders will continue to be a criminal offence. The Consumer Protection Advisory Committee will be abolished, creating a much more streamlined rule-making procedure.[12] However the new procedure will continue to be dependent on the actions of the Secretary of State, and does not go as far as giving the Office of Fair Trading independent rule-making powers.

2   TECHNIQUES OF CONTROL

Certain trade practices prejudicial to consumers have a long pedigree while others demonstrate the ingenuity of unscrupulous business people in uncovering loopholes in new law in order to fleece customers. A major concern in regulating prejudicial trade practices has been to prevent consumers being precipitated into transactions which they may regret on reflection. Since manipulation sometimes takes the form of subtle psychological pressure the freedom to choose is effectively reduced. Policy-makers have found difficulties in devising appropriate legal machinery to control prejudicial practices. One difficulty has been to eliminate consumer manipulation without infringing on the useful side, if there is any, of a trade practice. Another problem is that some trade practices are quite complex and it is not easy to devise forms of legislative drafting to encompass them. To some extent this simply illustrates the general difficulty of expressing the complex aspects of modern society in simple language. The following discussion focuses on several prejudicial trade practices and the legal techniques adopted to deal with them.

---

[9]   Price Marking (Bargain Offers) Order 1979, SI 1979/364, as amended. See now p 306 above.

[10]   OFT *Pricing Goods and Services Exclusive of Tax Payable on Retail Sale* (1975); *VAT Exclusive Prices* HC No 416 (HMSO, 1977). See Price Marking (Food and Drink on Premises) Order 1979, SI 1979/361.

[11]   SI 1999/3042, Articles 1(2), 9, implementing EC Directive 98/6/EC on Consumer Protection in the Indication of the Prices of Products Offered to Consumers OJ L 80, 27.

[12]   *Reform of Part II of the Fair Trading Act 1973* (DTI, 2000).

(a)   Banning or severely limiting a prejudicial practice

It would be of benefit on the grounds of convenience and public enlightenment if the provisions scattered through legislation which ban or severely limit trade practices prejudicial to consumers were gathered together into an omnibus consumer protection statute, like those enacted in other Commonwealth jurisdictions. For example, the Australian Trade Practices Act 1974 prohibits outright a number of prejudicial trade practices including false representations (not all of which are dealt with in the Trade Descriptions Act 1968); free gimmick promotions (offering gifts, etc with no intention of providing them as offered); referral selling (inducing consumers to acquire goods and services by representing that they will receive a benefit after a contract in return for introducing other consumers to the corporation); accepting payment without intending to supply as ordered; and using coercion at a consumer's place of residence.[13]

In the absence of such a measure, it requires a careful consideration of a wide range of statutory materials to determine the relevant provisions in Britain Moreover, the relevant legislation was sometimes drawn up in previous times and possibly also in a non-consumer protection context so that its application now involves fine distinctions. For example, so called free prize draws are a popular marketing tool, where consumers are invited to participate to win a car, holiday or whatever. These schemes, if lotteries, are largely illegal under the Lotteries and Amusements Act 1976, but are lawful if they can be categorised as competitions outside its ambit.[14] There is consumer dissatisfaction with certain free prize draws and the Director General of Fair Trading has recommended that for all competitions, in order not to mislead consumers, there should be a stronger obligation to publish the names of major winners, it should be clear at the outset that some prizes may not be awarded, and entry into a draw should not be described as a prize. In his view, however, these changes could be effected by amending the relevant paragraphs of the British Code of Sales Promotion, which is administered by the Advertising Standards Authority.[15]

(i)   Mock auctions

Sometimes known as one-day sales, mock auctions are normally conducted on premises not associated with retail trade, such as a public hall or hotel. The aim of a mock auction is to sell things to gullible purchasers at highly

---

[13]   Sections 54, 57, 58, 60.

[14]   Section 1. See R Bagehot *Sales Promotion and Advertising* (Sweet & Maxwell, 1993); *Re Vanilla Accumulation Ltd* (1998) Times, 24 February (winding-up of unlawful lottery on petition of DTI).

[15]   *Gambling, Competitions and Prize Draws* (OFT, 1996) pp 4–5.

inflated prices. Usually, the organiser first attracts attention by distributing free or selling at 'give-away' prices or with refunds. Having thus gained the confidence of those present, the auctioneer then offers unopened parcels for sale at set prices well above their true value. Complaints about mock auctions are usually that the trader has left the district and that consumers are unable to obtain redress for shoddy merchandise. Items are stated to be worth far more than the price at which they could be purchased in retail shops; they are presented in lavish boxes and packaging more in keeping with goods of higher value; and consumers are generally unable to inspect them prior to sale. Objection is also taken to the psychological techniques used in running mock auctions, whereby an artificial atmosphere of excitement is created and to the strategic placement of colleagues of the auctioneer (unidentified as such) around the hall to bid.

Legislation in Britain makes it unlawful to conduct a mock auction. A mock auction is defined as the sale of goods by way of competitive bidding if, during the course of the sale: (a) items are sold to persons at a price lower than the amount of his highest bid or part of the price is repaid or credited; (b) the right to bid is restricted to persons who have previously purchased articles; or (c) articles are given away or offered as gifts.[16] Competitive bidding is defined widely and includes any mode of sale in which prospective purchasers are enabled to compete for the purchase of articles in any way. Thus it covers situations where purchasers are asked who will pay a specified amount for a particular item and a number raise their hand to be first or to be chosen by the auctioneer, even though there is no competitive bidding as to price.[17] The mock auctions legislation is enforced spasmodically and is not wide enough to cover all types of one-day sales. The legislation is confined to sales involving a limited number of prescribed items including crockery, linen, furniture, jewellery and musical or scientific instruments. Certain techniques would appear not to be caught by the legislation such as secret bidding, the use of mystery boxes and the creation of a general atmosphere of frenzy and excitement to encourage spending. Moreover, in one decision the Court of Appeal has taken an unduly lenient view of mock auctions, comparing them to a form of entertainment where consumers must expect to be caught.[18]

---

[16]   Mock Auctions Act 1961, s 1(3).
[17]   *Allen v Simmons* [1978] 3 All ER 662, [1978] 1 WLR 879.
[18]   *R v Ingram* (1976) 64 Cr App Rep 119, 121. Cf *R v Pollard* (1983) 148 JPN 683. Other breaches of criminal law might be committed; in particular under the Theft   .
Act 1968. See ATH Smith 'Mock Auctions' (1981) 131 NLJ 49. With the cooperation of the national associations of bodies likely to hire premises for mock auctions apparently local codes of practice have been concluded. Under these trading standards departments are notified in advance that mock auctions

(ii)   Pyramid schemes

Pyramid schemes take a number of forms and have caused untold hardship to consumers in many countries. In the 1920s in the United States there were the so-called Ponzi schemes, named after Charles Ponzi. In 1934, the English Court of Appeal directed a conviction under the Lotteries Act 1816 on the basis that a pyramid scheme involved the sale of chances. (Participants, who were promised as much as £20,000 for a few hours work, had to buy one note case for £1 and recruit at least four friends to buy note cases. Nothing was received for the first three orders, but 10 shillings was paid on other orders).[19] More recently in Russia, Romania and especially Albania and China, thousands of consumers, especially vulnerable after decades of communism to the dream of getting rich quick, have lost enormous amounts in collapsed pyramid schemes.[20] In 1996 the Federal Trade Commission in the United States notified the operators of over 500 websites on the Internet that they may be promoting illegal pyramid schemes. The mathematics of pyramid schemes means that while those involved at the outset will reap considerable profits, the majority of participants will inevitably lose their money when a scheme collapses, as collapse it will. One writer outlines the mathematics:

> Subscribers are asked to pay an entry fee—£3,000 is typical in the UK—and are promised unrivalled rates of return, with the money being paid from the subscriptions of new people recruited to the venture. The rules are fairly straightforward: each new member is typically required to recruit a further six people. But for the first member to get a good return from the scheme they will need the three levels of the pyramid beneath them to be filled. This requires the recruitment of 216 people (6 x 6 x 6).
>
> While this may not be beyond an enthusiastic pyramid salesman, the mathematics are more daunting for those who are subsequently recruited to the scheme. For the six people on the second rung to fill the necessary three levels beneath them, each must find a further 216 people—a total of 1,296. When those 1,296 come to recruit, they will require 279,936 people. For these to get their reward, 60 million participants are required.[1]

---

are to be held and those conducting mock auctions undertake to comply with legal requirements and principles of fair trading. Breach of an undertaking would not of itself give rise to legal action; at most it might as a practical matter deter one day sellers from using certain venues.

19   *DPP v Phillips* [1935] 1 KB 391. See also *Atkinson v Murrell* [1973] AC 289.

20   In Russia, many lost money in the MMM bank; in Romania investors thought that the Caritas scheme was underwritten by the Roman Catholic Church; in Albania, thousands rioted following the collapse of pyramid schemes; and in China there were riots when pyramid selling was banned.

1   I Burrell 'Sold: A Pyramid of Greed' (1997) Independent, 27 January, p 15. In the United States the Federal Trade Commission uses the mathematics of pyramid

Pyramid selling involves participants buying products or services from promoters. Once a member of the scheme, the participant earns commission by selling the promoter's products or services and bonuses by attracting new members. Each distributor pays less for the product than the price received from the public and from those at lower levels in the distribution chain to whom they sell. Since one profits merely by being a link in the distribution chain, the emphasis is on recruiting more distributors rather than on retailing.[2] The essence of a pyramid scheme is the right to receive rewards for recruiting other participants, unrelated to the sale of products or services to end users.[3]

This type of pyramid selling must be distinguished from legitimate direct or network selling schemes, where individuals sell a wide range of products from their own or a customer's home. Such people are largely self-employed. Legitimate direct selling in Britain generates over £1 billion of retail trade a year. It is important that those participating in legitimate direct selling are not misled when recruited, so the controls discussed below may apply (controls on advertising, warnings, contracts and the cooling-off period). The Direct Selling Association operates a code of practice governing the relationship between promoters and participants and promoters and ultimate consumers.[4]

In addition to pyramid selling schemes are money circulation or snowball schemes. Under these participants may make regular payments to a promoter and encourage others to do the same. The false promise is that they will eventually receive a large return. The well publicised Titan Business Club involved members of the public being invited by pre-existing members to become a junior partner on payment of a fee of £2,500 (later £3,000). Prospective members were invited to recruitment meetings. In order to recoup their money members had to introduce other individuals to join the scheme. If the junior partner introduced two further junior partners he or she became a senior partner. The joining fee was distributed in an ascending scale amongst the recruiting junior partner and the senior partner who recruited him or her. The Court of Appeal had no difficulty in holding the

---

schemes to demonstrate that investors are precluded from recovering their return: R Bundy 'Federal Securities Regulations: Do They adequately Serve Their Prescribed Purpose of Protecting Investors from Pyramid Schemes?' (1990) 21 Mem St UL Rev 123, 142. See also E Witiw 'Selling the Right to Sell the Same Right to Sell' (1996) 26 Seton Hall LRev 1635.

2   See D Prosser 'How the Pyramids are Built' (1996) Investors Chronicle, 10 May, p 13.

3   *Webster v Omnitrition International Inc* 79 F 3d 776, 788 (1996).

4   DSA Code of Practice, 1987; Code of Business Conduct, 1991. See also *Direct Selling in the United Kingdom. 1997 Survey—An Overview of the Industry* (Direct Selling Association, 1997).

scheme to be an unlawful lottery under the Lotteries and Amusements Act 1976:

> Those who joined the present scheme pay their money for one reason only, to gain the chance, and it was only a chance, of reaping rewards from those who in turn paid and joined for the same reason. One source at least of the potential rewards came from those over whom the participant had no control and it followed as a matter of ordinary language and common sense that in that respect at least the participant was taking part in a scheme properly described as the distribution of prizes or rewards entirely by chance. Looked at as a whole the scheme had the word 'lottery' written all over it.[5]

Pyramid schemes are inherently unstable with the emphasis on selling participations rather than a product, service or genuine investment. Eventually growth must come to a halt as the market is saturated with participants. A scheme yields quick profits for promoters, who may recruit members by high pressure salesmanship at 'opportunity' meetings or parties where false enthusiasm and an evangelical air are generated. Pyramid schemes are aimed at individuals with little business experience and those most susceptible to the lure of get-rich-quick schemes. To participate, owner-occupiers may be persuaded to take out second mortgages on their homes. Those receiving redundancy payments have also been victims.

When the abuses associated with pyramid selling schemes became apparent in the late 1960s/early 1970s, it was clear that existing laws were inadequate. Fraudulent misstatement was generally avoided and there was doubt whether pyramid selling fell within laws such as those prohibiting lotteries. Statutory provisions were thus enacted in various countries—including Britain with Part XI of the Fair Trading Act 1973—to make illegal certain pyramid selling schemes.[6] However, the Fair Trading Act in its original form proved deficient,[7] notably because it applied only where schemes contained all the elements specified—a clear failure of legislative technique, since promoters needed simply to design a scheme without one of them. Indeed, some promoters gave respectability to their frauds by claiming, correctly, that they were in compliance with the Act and

---

[5]   *Re Senator Hanseatische Verwaltungsgesellschaft mbH* [1996] 4 All ER 933. One estimate was that 17,000 consumers lost £10m through Titan schemes. See also *One Life Ltd (In Liquidation) v Roy* [1996] 2 BCLC 608; *Re Vanilla Accumulation Ltd* (1998) Times, 24 February, Ch D.

[6]   JL Goldring and LW Maher *Consumer Protection Law in Australia* (Butterworths, 2nd edn, 1983) pp 399–408; B Dahl *Consumer Legislation in Denmark* (Van Nostrand Reinhold, 1981) pp 54–55.

[7]   R Sarker 'Pyramid Selling' (1995) 16 Co Lawyer 278. See also DTI *Review of Legislation on Pyramid Selling* (1986); DTI *Pyramid Selling and Similar Trading Schemes* (1995).

containing the statutory warning required under the regulations. Money circulation schemes fell outside the Act. Amendments were made to Part XI by the Trading Schemes Act 1996, a Private Member's Bill, and new regulations have also been promulgated.

Part XI of the Fair Trading Act 1973, as amended, applies to trading schemes meeting two criteria: first, participants expect to benefit from their participation in the scheme in respect of any of the specified matters; and second, goods or services are provided by the promoter to the participants for them either to supply to someone else or are supplied by the promoter to third parties introduced by participants.[8] In summary the specified matters from which benefit results are recruitment, loyalty or continuity, changing position within the scheme and selling or acquiring products or services. 'Goods' is now defined to include rights to property, so bringing money (and thus money circulation schemes) within the regulatory framework. Under s 120(1) of the Act it is an offence to be involved in issuing or distributing advertisements or notices in breach of the regulations. More importantly, some trading schemes are banned completely. Sections 120(3)–(4) create the offences of promoters or participants receiving or soliciting payment from participants in a trading scheme, if the payment is induced by the prospect of benefiting from the recruitment of further participants.

The Fair Trading Act 1973 contains regulation-making power to create new offences in respect of the issue of advertising to potential participants and of the operation of trading schemes.[9] The Trading Schemes Regulations 1997[10] require advertisements about such schemes to include certain information, such as the identity of the promoters and the products or services covered by the scheme's operation. Advertisements must also contain a bold warning, in particular: 'Do not be misled by claims that high earnings can be easily achieved.' Participants must be provided with written contracts, and there is a cooling-off period of 14 days within which they can generally withdraw without loss. Participants with participants below them in the network have the same obligations to the latter as the promoters have to them.[11]

As well as the regulatory controls of the Fair Trading Act 1973, the government has been successful over the years in obtaining winding-up

---

[8]   Section 118.
[9]   Section 119.
[10] SI 1997/30. See also Trading Schemes (Exclusion) Regulations 1997, SI 1997/32, as amended, which disapplies Part XI to certain single tier trading schemes, trading schemes in which the promoters and all participants are registered for VAT, and chain letters.
[11] See DTI *The Trading Schemes Guide* (1997).

orders against companies engaging in pyramid schemes. Application has been made under what is now s 124A of the Insolvency Act 1986 that they have operated against the public interest.[12] However, winding-up only operates *ex post facto*—after a considerable number of consumers may have suffered loss. No provision is available for compensating those who have been ensnared by a pyramid scheme, except what might be available in an insolvency. Government compensation is not available to compensate victims of pyramid schemes, on the basis that this would assist those who lose money through foolishness or in quasi business ventures.

(b)   Creating new consumer remedies

Another method of discouraging an objectionable trade practice, or the objectionable aspects of a trade practice, has been to create certain remedies for consumers which are such that abuse ought to be unprofitable. The effect is that the civil law is being used not only to provide a remedy for those adversely affected, but also as a deterrent device to those tempted to engage in undesirable trade practices. Three techniques are examined— setting compensation levels, creating new property rights and enabling the cancellation of consumer contracts during a 'cooling off' period.

(i)   Compensation levels

Under the general law, consumers can obtain compensation when products and services are not of adequate standard (see Chapters 4–6). First, however, consumers must establish a breach of the civil law. Moreover, the level of compensation once that is done is not immediately apparent, but must be calculated according to the different, and sometimes difficult, rules obtaining in the law of contract, tort, equity and restitution. In a limited number of areas legislation has intervened to set compensation levels. Relatively well known are the provisions of the Warsaw Convention of 1929 (as amended at Hague in 1955), which deal with an airline's liability for death or injury to passengers and for loss and delay in respect of their baggage.[13] The Warsaw provisions are in the main adopted both by IATA (International Air Transport Association) and non-IATA airlines in their

---

[12]   Eg *Re Golden Chemicals Products Ltd* [1976] Ch 300, [1976] 2 All ER 543; *Re Senator Hanseatische Verwaltungsgesellschaft mbH* [1996] 4 All ER 933.

[13]   N Taylor 'Limitation of Liability of Aircarriers to Aircrash Victims—Has the Warsaw Convention Reached Its Retirement Age?' [1994] Journal of Personal Injury Law 113.

standard conditions of carriage.[14] However, the levels set for compensation in the Convention are in need of up-rating: they are a very low ceiling but generally cannot be altered unless special arrangements are made by passengers beforehand.[15]

The compensation levels set for passengers with valid tickets on schedule flights, who are denied boarding ('bumped') because the airline has overbooked, are more realistic and thus more likely to act as an incentive for airlines to minimise the practice. It is uneconomic to eliminate bumping completely. Airlines regularly take more bookings than there are seats, on the valid assumption that some passengers with bookings will not appear. Maximising capacity in this way benefits consumers indirectly through lower fares. What airlines need to do, however, is to undertake the analysis so that the level of overbooking is estimated as accurately as possible for each flight.

Consumers denied boarding probably have a claim for breach of contract, although in the absence of economic loss English law has been reluctant to award damages for inconvenience alone.[16] Consumer pressure in the United States led to legal requirements for compensation for passengers denied boarding.[17] Indeed, some United States airlines are especially generous and avoid bumping passengers against their will: for example, some operate auctions, in which they offer progressively higher amounts of compensation until all the overbooked passengers have voluntarily agreed to take a later flight. The European Union followed the United States' lead in 1991. Council Regulation 295/91 sets minimum levels of cash compensation for passengers with confirmed reservations who, having presented themselves at the check in desk as stipulated, are denied boarding to scheduled services departing from any airport in a Member State.[18] It applies to all airlines operating international or domestic

---

[14] Frere Cholmeley Bischoff and International Institute of Air and Space Law, University of Leiden *A Study of the Legal Position of Air Transport Users Under the Contractual Terms Applying to Carriage by Air of Passengers and Baggage* (unpublished, 1997) (kindly provided by John Balfour, one of the authors).

[15] IATA has promoted waiver of the Warsaw limits through an Inter-Carrier Agreement, but few airlines have actually waived the limits.

[16] See, eg, *Farley v Skinner* [2000] EGCS 52.

[17] A leading case involved consumer advocate, Ralph Nader *Ralph Nader v Allengheny Airlines* 416 US 290 (1978). The federal oversales regulations are at 14 CFR §250 (payment, up to $400 if no alternative transport provided). See S Mirmina 'Overbooking and Denied Boarding Compensation: The Approaches of the European Union and United States' (1996) Air and Space Law, vol 11, Summer 1996, p 1.

[18] [1991] OJ L 36, 5. The Regulation also covers other expenses arising as the result of denied boarding, such as free telephone calls, meals, transport and where necessary accommodation. An announcement of proposals for the reform of the Regulation is noted at p 218 above.

scheduled services from these airports, including non-EC operators. The compensation levels were specifically set at a level intended to encourage airlines to avoid excessive overbooking, while not penalising them unduly so that they take an over-cautious approach, leading to reduced capacity and higher fares. The Commission has recently proposed that the minimum compensation levels be increased, and that the Regulation be extended, for example beyond scheduled passengers and to ticketless travel.[19] At present, while the Regulation has direct effect, there are no national legal remedies for infringement in Britain. The Commission proposal would also require Member States to determine effective, proportionate and dissuasive penalties for infringements of the Regulation.

(ii)   New property rights

An example of creating new property rights concerns inertia selling, whereby businesses send or provide unsolicited goods and services to consumers in the hope that they will feel obliged to buy them or at least do something to create a contractual obligation. The legislative technique in Britain has not been to prohibit the practice outright, perhaps because it might be difficult to draft a statute which distinguishes between inertia selling and the provision of unsolicited goods and services in other situations; eg a doctor giving assistance in an emergency.[20] Instead, consumers who receive unsolicited goods are made the unconditional owners of them after expiration of six months if the business has not reclaimed them.[1] The period can be shortened to 30 days if the business fails to collect the goods after being notified that they are unsolicited and the address where they can be collected. Further, unless a business has reasonable cause to believe that it has a right to payment for unsolicited goods, it is an offence for it to demand payment, to threaten any legal proceedings or to invoke any collection procedure such as placing the

---

[19]   Proposal for a Council Regulation (EC), COM (1998) 41 final. Passengers denied boarding on charter flights which form part of a package holiday are already covered by the Package Travel Directive (90/314/EEC).

[20]   In Britain it is illegal to send unsolicited sexual materials: Obscene Publications Act 1959, ss 1(3)(a), 2(1). Cf *DPP v Beate Uhse (UK) Ltd* [1974] QB 158.

[1]   Unsolicited Goods and Services Acts 1971 and 1975, s 1. The background to the Act is discussed in J Gray 'The Unsolicited Goods and Services Acts 1971 and 1975' [1978] Pub Law 242. Modest reform of the 1971 Act is under way at the time of writing: *Simplification of the Unsolicited Goods and Services Act 1971* (DTI, 2000). For elsewhere 'Unsolicited Merchandise: State and Federal Remedies for a Consumer Problem' [1970] Duke LJ 991; N Reich and Micklitz *Consumer Legislation in the EC Countries* (Van Nostrand Reinhold, 1980) pp 70–71.

name of a consumer on a list of defaulters.[2] In *Readers' Digest Association Ltd v Pirie*[3] a former subscriber was sent copies of a magazine and requests for payment. This was done at the direction of the company computer, which junior officials had failed to reprogramme on notice of cancellation. The court held, on the basis of *Tesco Supermarkets Ltd v Nattrass*,[4] that the knowledge of the junior officials could not be imputed to the company and that it could not be said that the company did not have reasonable cause to believe it had a right to payment. Associated with the provisions on unsolicited goods are controls designed to protect businesses from the practice engaged in by a few unscrupulous firms of demanding a substantial payment for unsolicited entries in business directories which they could publish.

(iii)   Cooling-off periods

Doorstep selling provides a service for a number of consumers who, for a variety of reasons such as age, illness or geographic location, cannot shop in the ordinary way. Credit trading done at home has been engaged in by some British householders for generations.[5] But doorstep selling has led to considerable abuse since it has been used to unload products and services which would not be sold at such high prices in shops and to induce consumers to sign contracts committing them to substantial payments for things which, on reflection, they do not want. Unlike retail outlets, which rely to varying extends on consumer goodwill, doorstep sellers can ignore consumer dissatisfaction if they are geographically mobile, and some have taken advantage of this to make quick profits. Quite apart from other factors, the presence of a seller in the home makes consumers particularly vulnerable to a sales pitch. Doorstep sellers are notorious for utilising deceptive ploys of various kinds; these are by no means new[6] and are fairly well known because of the considerable adverse publicity they have attracted. Claims that a seller is engaged in educational research, is a student working to win a travel scholarship, or represents a company which has chosen the consumer's house to be a showhouse,

---

[2]   Section 2. See also s 3A. Unsolicited Goods and Services (Invoices etc) Regulations 1975, SI 1975/732 (invoice etc to be regarded as asserting right to payment unless conspicuous statement to contrary).

[3]   1973 SLT 170. See also the poorly reasoned *Corfield v World Records Ltd* (1980) ITSA 88 MR 88.

[4]   [1972] AC 153.

[5]   M Tebbutt *Making Ends Meet. Pawnbroking and Working-Class Credit* (Leicester University Press, 1983) pp 178 (credit drapers), 180 (tallymen).

[6]   For example *Report of Select Committee on Patent Medicines* (1914) Parl Pap 414, ix, I, p xxii.

have all been exposed time and again as blatantly untrue. In 1962 the Molony Report commented on the more extreme psychological and other pressures used in some doorstep selling:

> We have received numerous and lurid accounts of the lengths to which some of these men are prepared to go in order to secure an order. We are told that they are known literally to force their way over the doorstep, to remain in the house for as long as six hours at a time—sometimes until midnight or later—keeping up a hypnotic flow of persuasive sales talk. It is alleged that their attitude and behaviour is sometimes such as to reduce households —in particular women— to a state of acute physical fear...By whatever proportion of door-to-door salesmen such practices are followed, and with whatever frequency, a considerable volume of evidence insisted that they are widespread (and successful) enough to amount to a serious social evil; resulting in homes labouring under an excessive burden of debt and sometimes torn by consequential domestic disharmony.[7]

In a number of cases over the years doorstep sellers have been prosecuted for fraud. *Potger*[8] was a prosecution of a doorstep seller for obtaining money by deception, by falsely claiming that he was a student taking part in a competition. Interestingly, the defence was partly the contention that any lies told were not dishonest, it being common for fellow sellers to tell lies of this nature! But fraud is absent in most cases where consumers are prejudiced because unscrupulous doorstep sellers know an overt lie is too risky and that a highly developed sales pitch is just as effective.

Legislation has been enacted in many jurisdictions in an attempt to curb abuses by doorstep sellers. Some have prohibited the practice unless there is a prior request by the consumer.[9] In other jurisdictions doorstep sellers have been obliged to reveal their purpose on arrival by means of an identification card.[10] Elsewhere doorstep sellers, as in Italy, have required a licence.[11] Hawkers and pedlars have long needed licences in Britain but the requirements are confined to doorstep sellers actually carrying goods

---

7   *Final Report on the Committee on Consumer Protection* (Cmnd 1781 (1962)) p 243.

8   *R v Potger* (1970) 55 Cr App Rep 42. See also House to House Collections Act 1939.

9   B Dahl *Consumer Legislation in Denmark* (Van Nostrand Reinhold, 1981) p 50. Doorstep credit sales are forbidden in Holland: E Hondius *Consumer Legislation in the Netherlands* (Van Nostrand Reinhold, 1980) p 87. On prohibiting doorstep selling completely, see P Schrag *Counsel for the Deceived* (Pantheon, 1972) p 195; T Ison *Credit Marketing and Consumer Protection* (Croom Helm, 1979) pp 197–221. Cf D Cayne and MJ Trebilcock 'Marketing Considerations in the Formulation of Consumer Protection Policy' (1973) 23 U Tor LJ 396, 423.

10   For example, Consumer Affairs Act 1972 (Victoria), s 20A.

11   G Ghidini *Consumer Legislation in Italy* (Van Nostrand Reinhold, 1980) p 37.

with them.[12] In some United States jurisdictions doorstep sellers have not only had to obtain a licence, but in a few areas have had to deposit a bond with enforcement authorities. Examples of supplementary restrictions in these jurisdictions have been limited selling hours and a prohibition on calling on residences displaying signs such as 'No Hawkers'. Britain has rejected a general scheme of licensing for doorstep selling on the grounds that it would create a considerable administrative burden and that there were doubts about its effect on unscrupulous sellers who moved rapidly throughout the country, often under aliases.[13] Under the Consumer Credit Act 1974 doorstep sellers selling on credit must obtain a licence.[14] Indeed, there is a limited prohibition on doorstep selling in the Consumer Credit Act 1974 in that doorstep canvassing by those offering money loans not associated with the purchase of goods or services is forbidden.[15] This should avoid the situation where agents have been engaged to peddle loans door-to-door, in particular on council housing estates. Legislation also makes it unlawful for anyone except a local authority or charities, etc employing the blind or disabled to represent that such persons are employed in the making of a product or benefit from its sale.[16] The legislation covers the situation where doorstep sellers might make representations along these lines and blind or disabled persons, if involved at all, are employed at a minimal wage on insignificant tasks.[17]

The major legislative technique to control malpractices in doorstep selling has been to create a 'cooling-off' period within which consumers may cancel a transaction resulting from a doorstep sale. The main provision in Britain is contained in the Consumer Protection (Cancellation of Contracts Concluded Away from Business Premises) Regulations 1987.[18] The regulations were introduced as a result of an EC Directive.[19] As the name suggests they apply to contracts resulting from unsolicited visits not only to consumers' homes but also to their place of work and during excursions organised by traders away from their business premises.[20]

---

[12] Pedlars Act 1871, as amended.
[13] Molony Report, p 264.
[14] Sections 21, 145(1)(a), (2).
[15] Section 49(1). See also s 154 (canvassing of services of credit-brokerage, debt-adjusting and debt-counselling—also banned).
[16] Trading Representatives (Disabled Persons) Acts 1958 as amended.
[17] Cf *Kent County Council v Portland House Stationers Ltd* (1974) 82 Monthly Review 2123 (Crown Court).
[18] SI 1987/2117 as amended by SIs 1998/3050 and 1988/958.
[19] Council Directive 85/577/EEC [1985] OJ No L 372. See *Faccini Dori v Recreb Srl* Case C-91/92 [1995] All ER (ECJ) 1, [1994] ECR I-3325 (on direct effect of this Directive).
[20] Certain types of contracts are exempted from the application of the Regulations. Some traders have sought to avoid the protection given by the Regulations by getting consumers to sign a paper on the doorstep signifying willingness to be

Contracts for both products and services are covered, as are guarantees given by consumers and ancillary to such contracts.[1] The cooling off provision is contained in reg 4:

> (5) If within the period of 7 days following the making of the contract the consumer serves a notice in writing (a 'notice of cancellation') on the trader or any other person specified in a notice referred to in paragraph (1) above as a person to whom notice of cancellation may be given which, however expressed and whether or not conforming to the cancellation form set out in Part II of the Schedule to these Regulations, indicates the intention of the consumer to cancel the contract, the notice of cancellation shall operate to cancel the contract.
>
> (6) Except as otherwise provided under these Regulations, a contract cancelled under paragraph (5) above shall be treated as if it had never been entered into by the consumer.

The Regulations provide that if consumers do not receive a written notice informing them of this right of cancellation and the cooling off period, any contract is unenforceable against them. Amendments to the Regulations make it a criminal offence to fail to supply a notice of the right to cancel in a relevant contract (reg 4A, as inserted by SI 1998/2050). The Regulations also deal with the consequences of cancellation of contracts such as the repayment of payments for products and services and of credit provided and the return of products received. They apply to cash transactions and to credit transactions not already cancellable under the Consumer Credit Act 1974. Where that Act applies, cancellation of contracts and the consequences of cancellation are governed by its provisions.[2]

A cooling off period operates at two levels. Firstly, it provides individual consumers with a remedy if they feel they have been prejudiced by a doorstep transactions. Secondly, doorstep sellers ought to take a greater interest in consumer satisfaction, and be less concerned with making a sale by whatever methods can be deployed, if they know that consumers can rescind a transaction. However, under the Regulations the period for cancellation is relatively short. The assumption is that consumers can quickly assess the wisdom of a transaction since 'decompression' normally occurs once the person departs. The assumption is questionable, however, where the complaint is about faulty products or about substandard services like, say, poor installation, for it will only be much later that the inadequacies are discovered. The effectiveness of written notice of cancellation must

---

visited before they open the negotiation leading to a contract. They rely upon this changing their subsequent visit from being unsolicited to solicited. See *Doorstep Selling. Improving the Protection of Consumers. A Consultation Paper* (DTI, 1998). SI 1998/3050 amends the Regulations (reg 3(3)) to close the loophole.

[1]   *Bayerische Hypotheken-und Wechselbank AG v Dietzinger* Case C-45/96 [1998] All ER (EC) 332.

[2]   Page 246 above.

also be questioned since the notice can be incorporated in the contract: will consumers read and understand their right in time? Perhaps the detachable cancellation form, which must be included, focuses the mind.

Sales pressure can be exercised just as much in a shop or showroom as on the doorstep. The argument against extending any cooling-off provision to shops is because abusive practices are not as prevalent there, and because in the case of shops it is more a 'self-inspired interest' in the articles on display and not sales pressure that motivates consumers. Another objection raised is that the finality of consumer transactions would be continually threatened and business would be placed under severe strain if consumers could change their mind simply because they found a shop a little further down the road offering more attractive terms. But the proposal to universalise the cooling-off period is not as radical as it seems at first, since the current practice of many retailers is to offer a refund without question if goods are returned unused within a reasonable time after purchase. The methods of selling of those businesses which do not give a refund are thus called into question. Their response might be that it is the larger businesses, with a high turnover, which can afford to refund. Extending cooling-off to general retail sales would provide consumers with a simple, inexpensive and speedy remedy in all cases when they have been victimised by defective products, dilatory delivery, deception, high pressure sales practices or even by their own stupidity. In other words, it would act as a useful supplement to existing remedies in the private law which, as we have seen, are deficient in many respects.

The other side of the coin to doorstep selling is *distance selling*. Distance selling is effected through direct mail and through modern technologies such as the telephone, fax, cable television, email and the Internet (on-line selling). Again the policy of the law must be to preserve free choice by consumers, their right to privacy and ready redress in the event of non-performance by the supplier. One difference from sales through retail outlets is that consumers are not able to see the product or as readily to ascertain the nature of the service; another is that information disseminated by certain technologies is ephemeral in nature, which means a potential for dispute as to what was said. Distance selling is a growing phenomenon, but especially well developed in Britain, Germany, France, Switzerland, Australia and North America.[3] Its growing popularity is attributable to its convenience, in enabling consumers to purchase from home, the price advantage, and the wider choice available.

---

[3]   Distance sales per capita in 1995 in US dollars in one survey were UK $169; Germany $345; France $162; Switzerland $231; United States $328; Canada $237; Australia $189. Scandinavian countries were also high. Etude Marketing Logistics Inc. USA, quoted in European Commission, Press Release IP/97/495 of 5 June 1997.

As in other areas, the problems for consumers of modern forms of distance selling were first recognised in the United States. Under the Telemarketing and Consumer Fraud Abuse and Prevention Act,[4] the Federal Trade Commission has promulgated a rule prohibiting certain deceptive and abusive telemarketing practices. Applicable to all goods and services sold over the telephone, the rule includes provisions on disclosure, misrepresentation, credit card laundering, privacy and record keeping.[5] There are calling time restrictions and restrictions on calls to consumers who ask not to be called by a specific seller.

In 1992 the European Commission published a recommendation that businesses engaged in distance selling adopt codes of practice so as to offer consumers some protection.[6] Then in 1997 the European Parliament and Council finally adopted a Directive on distance selling. There had been a fierce debate and much lobbying on its content, in particular whether it should be more extensive than its final form: for example, extending to financial services, and requiring prior consent from consumers before being contacted by telephone, email and so on[7] by salespersons identifying themselves and explaining the reason for their call. There is now a separate proposal for a Directive on distance selling of financial services, although it is unlikely to receive early approval.[8] As to cold calling, that is permitted under the Directive if there is no clear objection from the consumer.[9] The preamble to the Directive suggests that this imposes an

---

[4]   15 USC §§6101–6108; See R Pitofsky 'Telemarketing Scams' US Congressional Testimony, 5 February 1998.

[5]   16 CFR §310. In 'Project Telesweep' the FTC has taken over 100 enforcement actions against business opportunity fraud.

[6]   Directive 97/7/EC [1997] OJ No L 144 p 19. R Bradgate 'The EU Directive on Distance Selling' [1997] Web JCLI. For UK implementation see *Distance Selling. A Consultation Paper* (DTI, 1998); *Distance Selling Directive—Implementation in the UK* (DTI, 1999) which includes a draft text for the Consumer Protection (Contracts Concluded By Means of Distance Communication) Regulations 2000.

[7]   Commission Recommendation 92/295/EEC, [1992] OJ No L 156.

[8]   In March 1998 the Commission produced a preliminary draft of a Directive: most important for present purposes it would allow consumers to withdraw during a seven-day period, free of charge, without any penalty and without providing a reason. The 'financial services' industry takes the view that an absolute right to withdraw in the case of a high value loan or mortgage would expose lenders to unpredictable and irrecoverable costs. At present some countries such as the Netherlands ban the cold-calling of financial services, which is permissible under European Union law and the Investment Services Directive: *Alpine Investments BV v Minister van Financien* Case C-384/93 [1995] All ER (EC) 543. Note that the Distance Selling Directive also excludes distance selling of land and buildings and some other contracts: Article 3.

[9]   Article 10. Cold calling by automatic calling machines and fax requires prior consent of the consumer.

obligation on sellers to provide enough information at the beginning of the conversation so consumers can decide whether or not to continue.

The Distance Selling Directive applies to contracts formed after consumers have been contacted by a means of communication at a distance and the two parties are never present together.[10] The Directive requires consumers to be provided with certain information relating to the contract before it is concluded and requires confirmation to be provided in writing.[11] Once an order has been placed, a supplier has 30 days in which to provide the goods or services, unless the parties agree otherwise.[12] Most important for present purposes, and possibly the key provision in the Directive, is the cooling-off provision. Article 6 means that a consumer can choose to withdraw from the contract within seven working days, without penalty, and need not give a reason. The cooling-off period runs from when a product is received or, in the case of services, from the day the contract was concluded or the written confirmation given. Where written confirmation is not given, the cooling-off period expands to three months. If a consumer does not withdraw, the supplier must repay any sums paid in advance as soon as possible and in any case within 30 days. The failure of the UK government to implement the Directive by 4 June 2000 creates the possibility of liability of the government to consumers who are adversely affected under the principles of EC law.

Doorstep and distance selling are marketing techniques to which cooling-off applies. As indicated, there are particular contracts, such as consumer credit contracts, where the technique also operates. Another example involves timeshare contracts which, in brief, confer a right to spend a set period ever year in a holiday property. Timeshare has grown over the last 30 years to an industry with over 4,000 participating resorts and over 3.1 million owning families. Most timeshare resorts are affiliated to one of the two major exchange companies, which enable timeshare owners to exchange their holidays all over the world.[13] Complaints have concentrated not on the concept but on its marketing. In 1996 the Office of Fair Trading reported 4,941 complaints about timesharing, 3,814 of which involved selling techniques (misleading claims, representations and advertisements and lack of information).[14]

[10]   Article 2. An indicative list of the means of communication is contained as an Annex to the Directive, including printed matters, standard letters, press advertising with order form, catalogue, telephone with and without human intervention, radio, video phone, video text, electronic mail, facsimile machine and television.

[11]   Articles 4, 5. Tourist and reservable services such as hotels and taxis are exempt: many of these services are ordered at short notice, so information requirements would be impractical.

[12]   Article 7.

[13]   T Bourne 'Time for a Change' (1997) 147 NLJ 594.

[14]   Annual Report of the Director General of Fair Trading (HMSO, 1996) p 73. There are particular problems when consumers attend timeshare presentations: DTI *The Timeshare Guide* (1997) pp 3–5.

Following a considerable number of complaints, the Director General of Fair Trading reported on timeshare in 1990. He found 'unethical and wholly' unacceptable selling methods, with the result that timeshare was not being sold on its merits.[15] As well as various ways to provide prospective purchasers with more and better information, and to ensure the integrity of advance payments, management fees and money received on resale or through rental, the Director General recommended that prospective purchasers be given a period of reflection through a cooling-off period. It is worth quoting his reasoning at some length, since it neatly encapsulates the value and character of a cooling-off period:

7.17 A cooling-off period serves two purposes. First, it allows the purchaser to reflect. Timeshare is to some extent an emotional purchase, especially when it is sold on site, because the developer is selling something that aspires to be the perfect holiday. After a sales presentation which has relied heavily on unfamiliar financial arguments the purchase could well be left with a false impression of the value of the timeshare. Either way timeshare is not cheap and, unless purchasers have thought carefully about buying it beforehand, it is reasonable for them to pause to consider the arguments and whether they really wish to be committed.

7.18 The other purpose of a cooling-off period is to allow purchasers to consult their solicitor or financial adviser, or make any other checks they choose. Although expert advice may be expensive it could be needed in some cases and it is essential that purchasers have sufficient time to consult. When the purchase has been made in the United Kingdom two weeks are probably sufficient. When the property is situated abroad these checks are much more difficult to make, especially if the purchaser is reluctant to trust any documents to the post. It seems to follow that there should be a longer cooling-off period there …

7.19 In determining a reasonable length for a cooling-off period some account must be taken of the problems of developers. From the moment that a sale is agreed they begin to incur costs because of the need to process the sale, arrange for exchange membership and pass any loan application to the finance house. For developers these initial costs are probably the same whether the cooling-off period lasts two days or two weeks. But during a cooling-off period developers also lose the opportunity to sell the unit to someone else.

7.20 I have two further observations. The right to withdraw should be without cost to the consumer. Many developers make a charge to cover 'administrative costs' and the Office has heard of cases where customers have been told there is a cooling-off period only to find this may mean forfeiting a deposit of several hundred pounds. The second point is that a cooling-off period is useless if the purchaser does not know about it.[16]

[15] *Timeshare. A Report by the Director General of Fair Trading under Section 2(3) of the Fair Trading Act 1973* (HMSO, 1990) pp 4–5.
[16] *Timeshare. A Report by the Director General of Fair Trading under Section 2(3) of the Fair Trading Act 1973* (HMSO, 1990) pp 103–104.

Much narrower than the Director General's recommendations, the Timeshare Act 1992 had as its main provision a 14 day cooling-off period for purchasers of timeshares, during which they can cancel the purchase contract and any associated credit agreement.[17] Subsequently, the European Community adopted a Timeshare Directive in 1994,[18] both because the problems identified by the Director General were replicated in other European countries and because this genuinely is an area where many cross-border purchases are made. Since the Timeshare Directive is a minimum Directive, Member States can confer additional protection on consumers. While most Member States have adopted the 10-day cooling-off period mentioned in the Directive, Britain has retained its 14-day period.

The Timeshare Directive has been implemented in Britain by the Timeshare Regulations 1997,[19] which amend the 1992 Act —a rather inelegant solution but, given the pressure on parliamentary time, understandable.[20] The Timeshare Act 1992, as amended, now extends to insurance, share and points based timeshares, which fell outside the scope of the original Act. It gives consumers further rights, particularly to information prior to contract, and in their timeshare contracts, as well as prohibiting advance payments during the cooling-off period.[1] As to the cooling off provision, this in the amended Act is along the lines already sketched in relation to the Distance Selling Directive: for timeshares involving accommodation in a building, the 14-day cancellation period is extended up to three months and ten days if certain of the requisite information has not been provided to the purchaser.[2] The amended Act extends the existing provisions making it an offence not to issue notice of the right to cancel.[3]

Subsequent to the passage of the 1997 Regulations the maket has developed a variety of new products, similar in character to timeshare, but which fall outside the scope of the current legal regime. In each case there is the suggestion that the new product has been designed to evade the controls of the legislative regime. These new products include holiday/vacation clubs (where the seller agrees to provide holidays in future years, but not linked to particular properties), timeshare in floating vessels such

---

[17]   Sections 5–6. See also Timeshare (Cancellation Notices) Order 1992, SI 1992/1942; Timeshare (Repayment of Credit on Cancellation) Order 1992, SI 1992/1943. The provisions of the 1992 Act and associated regulations are currently under review by the DTI *Timeshare Sales: Improving the Protection of Consumers* (2000).
[18]   Directive 94/47/EC [1994] OJ No L 280.
[19]   SI 1997/1081.
[20]   There is a consolidated text, available from the DTI.
[1]   Sections 1A–1E, 5B.
[2]   Section 5A.
[3]   Section 2(3).

as narrowboats and timeshare of less than three years' duration (which falls outside the legislative regime). The DTI is considering three options in the light of these new problem areas: continuing to rely on existing controls; increasing publicity on timeshare issues (to encourage consumers to protect themselves) and extending the legislation to cover some or all of the new practices.[4] The DTI has indicated that the first option is not attractive, and that a mixture of the second and third options is its favoured response.

(iv) Protecting prepayments

Consumers sometimes make prepayments for products or services. This may constitute a deposit, or it may follow from the way a product or service is marketed (eg mail order) or the nature of the business involved (eg some builders may use prepayments as working capital). Prepayments have inherent risks, such as the forfeiture of a deposit if consumers change their mind, and a subtraction from their bargaining power when consumers experience delays or receive poor quality products or services. The ultimate risk, and the one addressed in this section, is when consumers make a prepayment and then the supplier becomes insolvent before it performs its part of the contract. A consumer is then in the unfortunate position of being an unsecured creditor of the supplier, along with trade creditors, and may receive little if anything by way of repayment.

Private law contains the first possible solution. Moneys subject to trust are taken outside an insolvency so the consumer will be fully repaid. There are creative decisions imposing a trust over consumer prepayments. *Re Kayford Ltd*[5] is a seminal case, where Megarry J held that by paying consumer moneys into a special account (eventually labelled 'customer trust deposit account') they were subject to a trust. It is clear that Megarry J was motivated by public policy considerations—'[consumers] can ill afford to exchange their money for a claim to a dividend in the liquidation'—and the decision has troubled doctrinal purists. Certainly if the business has mixed consumer prepayments with other moneys and there is nothing in the contract which requires the prepayments to be held on trust, a court will give the notion of trust short shrift and characterise the relationship as nothing more than that of debtor-creditor.[6] Even if a trust is imposed over the prepayments, they may have been disposed of and not be traceable in law.

---

[4]   *Timeshare Sales: Improving the Protection of Consumers* (DTI, 2000).
[5]   [1975] 1 WLR 279. See also *Re Lewis's of Leicester* [1995] 1 BCLC 428.
[6]   *Re Holiday Promotions (Europe) Ltd* [1996] 2 BCLC 618. See also *Re Goldcorp Exchange Ltd* [1995] 1 AC 74 at 102–104; *Westdeutsche Landesbank Girocentrale v Islington London Borough Council* [1996] AC 669, per Lord Browne-Wilkinson.

The majority decision of the High Court of Australia in *Hewett v Court*[7] has raised another possibility, that a consumer may have priority in a business insolvency as a result of a security interest over property specifically allocated to the performance of the contract. In the particular circumstances a builder agreed to construct a mobile home for a consumer, the price being payable by instalments, and title to the house passing only on payment of the last instalment and the house being transported to the consumer's land. It was held that the consumer had an equitable lien over the mobile home securing the deposit and instalments. The decision may not be followed in other common law jurisdictions,[8] based as it is on the notion that it would be unconscionable or unfair for the owner not to discharge its indebtedness to the consumer from the property. Moreover, it will be appreciated that only in special circumstances do businesses identify and appropriate specific property to a consumer contract over which such a security interest can operate.

A second possible source of solutions lies in public law. For example, insolvency law might be amended so that consumer prepayments are ring-fenced in a business insolvency. However, this runs counter to current thinking which is against extending, in fact favours a reduction in, the number of priority creditors in an insolvency. Nonetheless, the idea has found some favour in Canada. A report of the Law Reform Commission of British Columbia starts with the premise that consumer creditors are in a different position from trade creditors: consumer creditors do not expect to make a profit from extending the credit; they are not as readily able to ascertain a business's credit standing; they cannot spread their risks as can a business creditor; and they cannot protect themselves in the same way as businesses might do (eg by retention of title clauses). It recommended that consumers have a lien over either the property the subject of the contract, or the prepayments.[9] The recommendation was enacted in British Columbia in 1993, so that consumers making prepayments for unascertained products have a lien over the business's stock of products of that type and over the account into which the prepayments are deposited.[10]

Outside insolvency law, there have been proposals that businesses taking deposits or advance prepayments should place these into a separate account, which would be held on trust. The idea has merit, although monitoring arrangements need to be in place to ensure that moneys are actually paid in and subsequently not wrongly paid away (for if so, they

---

[7]   (1983) 149 CLR 639.
[8]   Cf *British Columbia v National Bank of Canada* (1994) 119 DLR (4th) 669.
[9]   *The Buyer's Lien: A New Consumer Remedy* LRC No 93, 1987.
[10] Consumer Protection Statutes Amendment Act 1993.

may not be legally traceable). For example, the Office of Fair Trading recommended statutory regulation, along the lines in some states in the United States, whereby all funds in relation to prepaid funerals (payments, earnings and so on) would be put into trusts or similar arrangements. Prepayments for funerals are at risk through business failure and fraud over several years, by comparison with other areas such as holidays where the period is weeks. The trust would be run by independent trustees, their names and the trust deeds would be published, and there would be set time limits within which payment in had to be made.[11]

Another approach lies in the creation of bonding or guarantee schemes. Earlier in the chapter the Mail Order Protection Scheme was referred to, which protects readers who send moneys in advance on the basis of advertisements.[12] There are other voluntary schemes along these lines, as well as insurance arrangements.

For present purposes, however, it is the statutory bonding and guarantee schemes which are especially relevant. The best example is in the travel industry,[13] where bonding schemes have been introduced to repatriate and compensate stranded and disappointed holiday makers. Since 1973 the Civil Aviation Authority has operated the Air Travel Organisers' Licensing system (ATOL), which licenses air travel organisers and obliges them to maintain a bond with the CAA should they become insolvent.[14] An Air Travel Trust has been available should individual bonds prove inadequate, funded by a levy on passenger tickets. These arrangements have been elaborated as a result of the Package Travel, Package Holidays and Package Tours Regulations 1992,[15] introduced to implement an EC

---

[11]   OFT *Pre-paid Funeral Plans* (1995). At the time the DTI preferred self-regulation (*Pre-Paid Funerals* (1996)), but the OFT pointed out that there was little consensus among plan providers about the nature of any organisation which would have the independence, authority and strength necessary to police the area and reiterated its call for statutory regulation.

[12]   Page 416 above.

[13]   See also the Policyholders Protection Act 1975 (as amended by the Policyholders Protection Act 1997), which through a levy system creates a fund to assist policyholders of insolvent insurers.

[14]   Civil Aviation (Air Travel Organisers' Licensing) Regulations 1972, SI 1972/223, as amended. *Barclays Bank Ltd v TOSG Trust Fund Ltd* [1984] 1 All ER 1060. See now Civil Aviation (Air Travel Organisers' Licensing) Regulations 1995, SI 1995/1054. A tour organiser must also satisfy financial criteria (reg 6(2)(b)). Bonds must be provided by banks which are members of the British Bankers' Association or authorised insurance companies: B Bedford 'United Kingdom' in Z Yaqub and B Bedford (eds) *European Travel Law* (John Wiley & Son, 1997) p 536.

[15]   SI 1992/3288 as amended by SI 1998/1208. See D Grant and S Mason *Holiday Law* (Sweet & Maxwell, 1995); J Downes and T Paton *Travel Agency Law* (Longman, 1993); J Nelson-Jones and P Stewart *A Practical Guide to Package Holidays: Law and Contracts* (Tolley, 4th edn, 1997).

Directive.[16] Sellers of holidays must provide a bond to a body approved by the DTI, or provide protection to consumers through insurance cover or a trust account.[17] Effectively the ATOL regulations cover tour operators and those selling charter or discounted scheduled airlines on a flight-only basis, whereas the 1992 regulations extend to the whole package holiday, including non-travel elements such as accommodation and travel other than ATOL regulated air travel.

(v)   'Cease and desist' orders

A concern that existing legislation was inadequate in deterring business malpractices has led various jurisdictions to emulate the United States by introducing a 'cease and desist' power whereby orders can be obtained against businesses to prevent them engaging in conduct detrimental to consumers. Particularly with respect to breaches of the private law it is recognised that consumers fail to institute legal proceedings even when they have a good case. When criminal convictions are obtained or favourable civil judgments rendered, some businesses are observed to continue their objectionable behaviour because it is more profitable simply to pay the fine or the damages awarded than to change their modes of behaviour. The technique of the 'cease and desist' order is designed to avoid this situation by ordering a business to desist from certain practices on pain of substantial penalties, including imprisonment. In this way the 'cease and desist' power is a supplement in securing compliance with existing legal provisions. An alternative mechanism for their enforcement is provided and the sanctions underlying them are strengthened.

In the United States the Federal Trade commission is empowered to act against unfair or deceptive trade practices. As a quasi-judicial body it can issue 'cease and desist' orders itself against businesses engaging in such practices, and if the orders are not obeyed civil penalties can be imposed.[18] 'Cease and desist' orders have prospective force but the FTC has sometimes incorporated in its orders restitution to compensate those injured by an offender.[19] Critics of the operation of the 'cease and desist' power point out that an order can be postponed for substantial periods by the delaying

---

[16]   Directive 90/314/EEC [1990] OJ No L 158. See *Dillenkofer v Germany* Cases C-178–190/94 [1996] All ER (EC) 917.

[17]   SI 1992/3288, reg 16(2). Approved organisations for bonds include the Association of British Travel Agents (ABTA), the Association of Independent Tour Operators (AITO), and the Federation of Tour Operators (FTO). Note that reg 16(1) contains a general obligation—irrespective of the steps required by reg 16(2)—on package sellers to have in place measures to protect consumers on insolvency.

[18]   15 USC §45(b), (1).

[19]   Possibly because of *Heater v FTC* 503 F 2d 321 (1974).

tactics of businesses. Violation of the order has to be proved in new and separate proceedings. Apparently in the past the Federal Trade Commission monitored 'cease and desist' orders on a haphazard basis and in many cases has been unaware whether its orders were obeyed.[20] In some cases the Federal Trade Commission did not react sufficiently speedily to halt unscrupulous businesses before they had victimised consumers and accumulated substantial profits.[1]

Under Part III of the Fair Trading Act 1973, the Director General of Fair Trading is empowered to obtain 'cease and desist' orders against businesses engaging in a persistent course of conduct detrimental to consumers which is in breach of criminal or civil law. The persistence requirement has been interpreted in a demanding manner to mean several breaches of the civil or criminal law having a common thread, and sufficient in number to be significant in relation to the size of the business. 'Its practical consequence has been that action usually cannot be taken until there has been a record of substantiated complaints stretching over several months.'[2] In 1990 the Director General of Fair Trading recommended that the requirement for a business to have 'persisted' in a course of conduct before assurances could be sought should be modified to a requirement that a trader has simply 'carried on a course of conduct which is detrimental to consumers' interests and is unfair to consumers'.[3] The interests of consumers which must be jeopardised before the Office of Fair Trading can act include economic, health and safety interests.[4] The ambit of the legislation means that breaches of law need not have been the subject of court proceedings. Thus action can be taken against a business if complaints from consumers establish that it was in breach of contract, even though no civil judgments to this effect have been obtained against it. In fact most Part III action stems from breach of the civil law, since trading standards departments take the view that a breach of the criminal law can be dealt with more promptly through an ordinary prosecution. There is a strong case for extending the cease and desist power further, beyond breaches of the criminal and civil law, to misleading, deceptive and unfair practices which, while sailing close to the wind, do not constitute a breach of the civil law.

---

[20] E Cox et al *The Nader Report on the Federal Trade Commission* (Baron, 1969) p 61.

[1] H Wellford 'The Federal Trade Commission's New Look: A Case Study of Regulatory Revival' in S Epstein and R Grundy (eds) *Consumer Health and Product Hazards* (MIT Press, 1974) pp 335–337.

[2] DTI *Reform of Part III of the Fair Trading Act 1973. A Consultation Paper* (1994) p 4.

[3] Director General of Fair Trading *Trading Malpractices* (1990) p 31.

[4] Fair Trading Act 1973, s 34(1).

Unfortunately the procedure for obtaining a 'cease and desist' order is convoluted and businesses can string it out. Firstly, enforcement is confined to the Office of Fair Trading and local trading standards departments are excluded. Yet the information which the Office needs for Part III action comes largely from trading standards departments, since the Office has no power to search, inspect or seize. Secondly, the Office of Fair Trading must jump various hoops. Initially the Office of Fair Trading must use its 'best endeavours' to seek a written assurance from a business that it will refrain from its objectionable or similar conduct. In favourable circumstances this can take a number of months; in unfavourable circumstances 'extracting promises from rogues can be a pointless exercise'.[5] Only if an assurance is refused or broken can the Office of Fair Trading seek a 'cease and desist' order from a court. Even here the Office of Fair Trading acts on legal advice that it cannot simply rely on the giving of the assurance as evidence that a course of conduct has been persisted in, but must assemble sufficient evidence to show that a trader has failed to observe assurances and has, after giving those assurances, persisted in a course of conduct.[6] A court may accept an undertaking from the business, but if it refuses, or if the court thinks an undertaking is unacceptable, it can issue a 'cease and desist' order forbidding the business to engage in the objectionable or similar practice.[7]

The procedure in Part III is largely replicated in other legislation conferring a cease and desist power. For example, under the Control of Misleading Advertisements Regulations the Director General of Fair Trading may bring proceedings for an injunction against a person concerned with the publication of a misleading advertisement, but may require that the complainant has first proceeded through the self-regulatory procedures and those procedures have not dealt with the matter adequately.[8]

Consistent with arguments that public interest groups should have a greater role in regulatory enforcement[9] the injunctive powers under the Unfair Terms in Consumer Contracts Regulations 1999[10] are shared between the Director General, other regulators and the Consumers' Association. Previously the Director General exercised these powers alone. The Director General, other regulators, or Consumers' Association, acting on a

---

5   *Unfair Trading. Recommendations for Reform of Part III of the Fair Trading Act* (NCC, 1997) p 1.

6   DTI *Reform of Part III of the Fair Trading Act 1973. A Consultation Paper* (1994).

7   Fair Trading Act 1973, s 37. See *Director General of Fair Trading v Smiths Bakeries (Westfield) Ltd* (1978) Times, 12 May.

8   SI 1988/915, regs 4–5. See Chapter 2 above.

9   I Ayres and J Braithwaite *Responsive Regulation* (OUP, 1992).

10 SI 1999/2083 (replacing SI 1994/3159). See Chapter 3 above. See also Estate Agents Act 1979. See p 448 below.

complaint about an unfair term in a consumer contract, may apply for an injunction (regs 10, 11) but if the Director General considers it appropriate to do so he may have regard to any undertakings given by those using the term (reg 10(3). In practice, what the Director General does, if his initial assessment is that terms are unfair, is to require the business to justify its approach. Where a business accepts that its terms are unfair, and wants to revise them, it is normally allowed a reasonable time to redraft and reprint them, subject to its giving undertakings not to rely on the objectionable terms or take advantage of them, and to end their use permanently by withdrawing them within an agreed timetable. Where it appears that a business is not pursuing discussions in good faith, or where there is a difference of view that cannot be reconciled, the Director General will seek the assistance of the courts.[11] New injunctive powers will be introduced by the implementation in the UK of the EC Injunctions Directive.[12] The qualifying bodies entitled to pursue the injunctive power to prevent breach of listed EC consumer protection Directives[13] are likely to be the same as for the Unfair Term in Consumer Contracts Regulations 1999 (Article 4), though the DTI is apparently considering extending the range of qualifying bodies to include other consumer organisations.[14]

What is needed is a more streamlined procedure. In 1990 the Director General of Fair Trading proposed in relation to Part III that both he and the local authority trading standards departments should be empowered to issue 'cautions' to businesses requiring them to stop an objectionable course of conduct, in place of the need first to seek assurances. A business would be able to challenge such a caution in court, but if it did not do so and subsequently ignored the caution it could then be taken to court. Moreover, an enforcement authority could apply to the court if it considered that there was a risk of the continuation or repetition of malpractice, and it would be able to by-pass the caution procedure altogether in cases where there was a likelihood of substantial detriment to the health, safety or economic interests of consumers.[15] In addition to the 'cease and desist' power, the National Consumer Council has recommended that:

---

[11] See *Director General of Fair Trading v First National Bank* [2000] 1 All ER (Comm) 371, [2000] 07 LS Gaz R 39, CA.

[12] Directive 98/27/EC of the European Parliament and of the Council of 19 May 1998 on injunctions for the protection of consumers' interests, OJ L 166 11.06.98 p 51.

[13] See the Annex to the Directive as amended by the Consumer Guarantees Directive 1999 (99/44/EC).

[14] UK implementation is required by January 2001: See *Injunctions Directive: Implementation in the UK* (DTI, 2000).

[15] Director General of Fair Trading *Trading Malpractices* (1990) p 33. See also DTI *Reform of Part III of the Fair Trading Act 1973. A Consultation Paper* (1994) Annex B, p 7.

the court should be given the power to ban a trader from running or participating in the running of the business, for up to a maximum of five years. Clearly this would be a severe penalty, intended only for flagrant and deliberate conduct. In deciding whether to impose such a ban the court would have to consider the frequency or persistence of the conduct, how many people were affected, the loss of consumers in general (not individual consumers), whether the acts were deliberate, breach of stop orders, failure to co-operate with the OFT, the size of the concern and failure to control the trader in any other way. It would also have to be able to consider earlier breaches of Part III relating to other trading activities, as some traders move from one 'scam' to another. Where a trader had been the subject of several banning orders it should be possible to prohibit him from running any business.[16]

Such a power would not be novel in principle, since the courts can disqualify a director of a company for between 2 and 15 years for unfit conduct as a director.[17] (By late 1997 some 4,800 directors had been subject to court order.) An assurance, undertaking or order obtained under Part III has prospective force only and neither punishes a business for past behaviour nor expropriates any illegal profits that it has accrued. Moreover, disadvantaged consumers are not compensated as a result of an undertaking or order and they must bring individual civil claims. 'Cease and desist' orders are therefore oriented towards the general public interest rather than the individual interests of consumers in transactions.[18]

To prevent the possibility that sole traders will evade the legislation by incorporating, or by engaging in a different sphere of commercial activity, changes are necessary in s 34 of the Fair Trading Act 1973. Under s 38, by contrast, company directors can be required to give life-long assurances, irrespective of their business. Directors, managers, secretaries etc, who can be shown to have consented to or connived at the detrimental course of conduct of a company might be required to give a threefold assurance that they will refrain: (a) from continuing to consent to or connive at the course of conduct in question; (b) from carrying on any similar conduct in the course of any business which may at any time be carried on by them; and (c) from consenting to or conniving at the carrying on of any such course of conduct by any other body corporate in relation to which they are a director or similar officer.[19] There is also power to proceed against persons controlling more than 50% of the voting shares in a particular

---

[16]   *Unfair Trading. Recommendations for Reform of Part III of the Fair Trading Act* (NCC, 1997) pp 24–25.

[17]   Company Directors Disqualification Act 1986. Note that under that Act there is no obligation on the government to accept an undertaking in lieu of applying for disqualification: *Re Blackspur Group plc* [1998] 1 WLR 422.

[18]   Cf *Mid Kent Holdings plc v General Utilities plc* [1996] 3 All ER 132, [1996] 1 WLR 14.

[19]   Section 38.

company. The courts can act against interconnected companies, including companies formed after the making of the original order, which prevents evasion by the creation of a new subsidiary.[20] However, there is the issue of businesses using agents and other intermediaries, where the business may be able to avoid responsibility for the intermediaries' malpractices. Breach of a court order constitutes contempt of court and exposes a business to an unlimited fine or a businessman to imprisonment.

The Office of Fair Trading relies importantly on the work of trading standards departments to obtain information relevant to the exercise of its power. (At one time the Director General of Fair Trading proposed that he should share enforcement powers with trading standards departments but the current view is that this would lead to undesirable inconsistencies.) A central registry of convictions is maintained which has enabled the OFT to identify a number of businesses for possible action. Other sources of information have been solicited for details of relevant convictions or complaints including consumer organisations, the mass media and the courts. A difficulty in relying on the past record of a business, as contained in the register of convictions or in the complaints received by the OFT, is that some current perpetrators of prejudicial trade practices will not have a record. Thus they may be able to avoid undertakings or an order, unless by fortuitous circumstances the Office of Fair Trading hears about them and takes action despite the fact that they have no record.

The Office of Fair Trading has investigated a number of sole traders and companies, some of which have subsequently gone into liquidation. At the end of December 1996, 826 assurances, undertakings or orders had been obtained since Part III came into effect. The number of cases per annum has fluctuated although there has been some increase in activity in recent times. To December 1996, nine undertakings had been given in lieu of court action under the Unfair Terms in Consumer Contracts Regulations 1994, and 28 court orders and undertakings obtained under the Control of Misleading Advertisements Regulations 1988.[1] While the matters are not

---

[20] Section 40.

[1] From *Annual Reports of the Director General of Fair Trading 1988–1996*. The assurances, undertakings and orders in any particular year are set out in Appendices to the Director General's annual report. See also David Hope 'Fair Trading Assurances' (1981) 78 MR 180. In *R v Director General of Fair Trading, ex p FH Taylor & Co Ltd* [1981] ICR 292, Donaldson LJ commented in relation to the Director General's seeking an assurance against a business with 13 convictions over three years under the Consumer Protection Act 1961: '[T]he only matter for surprise is that he [the Director General] refrained from doing so before April 1979' (at p 295).

strictly comparable, the much higher figure for disqualifications obtained under the Company Directors Disqualification Act 1986, mentioned above, is salutary. The businesses against which assurances, undertakings and orders have been obtained under Part III have been mainly small or middle-sized traders. Quite apart from the comparatively large number of such businesses, another factor might be the difficulty of relating the record of a large business to size: are ten convictions for a national business equivalent to two convictions for a local firm? Businesses have given assurances to comply with the terms of the contracts they enter, to supply goods which are of satisfactory quality and fit for the purpose, to perform work in a proper and workmanlike manner, to carry out work in a safe manner, not to make false statements about the products or services they market, and not to be in breach of duty in failing to return money paid in advance. Action can thus be finely tuned to the details of the particular products or services involved. The policy of the Office of Fair Trading has been to release to the press the text of all assurances, undertakings and orders, together with some background information. The power to publicise has been upheld judicially as an essential monitoring device, ensuring that breaches of assurances, undertakings or orders are reported.[2]

The 'cease and desist' power in the Fair Trading Act 1973 is a most important legal technique in furthering consumer protection, but it could be further improved in the ways touched on. Persistence should not be a prerequisite. The ambit of the 'cease and desist' power could be widened beyond the requirement that there be a breach of civil or criminal law. The objection to this may be that the law has always demanded clear standards of behaviour before imposing sanctions, but this overlooks a number of points. Firstly, there are widely-accepted standards among businesses for dealing with consumers, many of which are embodied in codes of practice but not necessarily in law. Secondly, the 'cease and desist' power does not constitute the imposition of criminal sanctions, although these may follow if an order is breached. Thirdly, there is a fundamental difference between provisions which can lead to the loss of liberty on the part of a subject and those where any sanction will almost invariably be the imposition of a monetary penalty. Fourthly, there could be a truncation of the procedures so that the Director General has the power to issue a caution or 'stop order' in relation to an objectionable course of conduct.

---

[2] *R v Director General of Fair Trading, ex p FH Taylor & Co Ltd* [1981] ICR 292. Apart from the law of defamation and statutory restrictions, a qualification might be that if the trader's convictions are publicised so too must its 'reasonable explanations' for these. The power of publicity should be used fairly; Part III of the Act is not for driving traders out of business (at pp 297–298).

A final reform would be to enable the Office of Fair Trading to obtain redress on behalf of consumers from those against whom it acts.[3]

The DTI is consulting on reform of Part III of the 1973 Act, and proposing to replace the current mechanisms with a 'course of conduct' injunction. The power to seek the new injunction will be shared between the OFT, the Secretary of State and local trading standards departments. The exercise of the new power will not require the authority seeking it to demonstrate that they have sought assurances before applying for the injunction (though the DTI anticipates that the Enforcement Concordat principles of seeking voluntary compliance before pursuing statutory action will generally be followed). The persistence test is to be dropped. The enforcing authority will simply have to show that the trader engaged in an unfair course of conduct. Separate from the injunctive power will be a power for the OFT, Secretary of State and local trading standards departments to seek new banning orders against both individuals and firms, ranging from a prohibition of the pursuit of certain types of business to an outright ban on dealing with consumers.[4] These proposed new measures, if implemented, will considerably enhance the capacity of enforcement authorities to act against unfair trading practices.

---

[3] Cf Trade Practices Act (Australia), ss 80, 87; W Neilson, 'Administrative Remedies: The Canadian Experience with Assurances of Voluntary Compliance in Provincial Trade Practices Legislation' (1981) Os HLJ 153, 154, 172; P Ward 'Restitution for Consumers Under the Federal Trade Commission Act: Good Intentions or Congressional Intentions?' (1992) 41 Am ULR 1139.

[4] *Reform of Part III of the Fair Trading Act 1973* (DTI, 2000).

Chapter 12

Prior approval by licensing

The hallmark of prior approval by licensing is that businesses must satisfy certain prerequisites before engaging in specified commercial activity. The theory is that licensing permits beneficial activity but at the same time prevents its harmful consequences. Licensing varies in the ambit of its control. Approval may have to be sought if a business is to engage in trade, but it may also be needed for more specific activity, for example, for each product marketed.[1] The former is far more common, but the case study on drugs demonstrates that licensing of products also has a role.

The present chapter considers licensing of consumer services and products. It opens with some general remarks on licensing, briefly examines occupational licensing, utilities licensing and consumer credit licensing (the most far-reaching type of licensing in Britain today) and concludes with a case study of one of the most significant examples of product licensing, the prior approval for drugs and drug manufacturing. At the outset it should be emphasised that the focus of the chapter is on licensing with the aim of controlling business behaviour in the public interest. Governments also use licensing to develop natural resources (eg oil and petroleum licensing) or to allocate scarce resources (eg airline routes, television transmission bands). This type of licensing has repercussions for consumers—it impinges on competition and involves the government in distributing wealth to particular groups in the community[2]—but these are rather indirect and not necessarily adverse to their interests.

---

[1] Ernst Freund *Administrative Powers Over Persons and Property* (Chicago University Press, 1928) Chapter 8.
[2] Cf Charles Reich 'The New Property' (1964) Yale LJ 733, 741.

I   THE TECHNIQUE OF LICENSING

Licensing is a powerful tool of control. Instead of the occasional private law proceeding or prosecution if it breaches the law, a business is faced with the possibility of being denied the right to continue an activity altogether. The Crowther Committee advanced this as a leading argument for licensing institutions granting consumer credit:

> The protective measures [in existence] are all concerned with individual transactions...The more unscrupulous type of credit grantor may well take the view that the occasional check on his malpractices by a determined consumer in an isolated transaction is not a serious deterrent, and is outweighed by the financial advantages he may derive from evading the law. There is thus a need for an agency entrusted with the continuing supervision of consumer credit grantors, with power to investigate trading practices, require production of accounts and records and, in the case of serious malpractices, suspend or revoke the offender's licence.[3]

Licensing can also give a state agency wide access to knowledge about an area of business through ancillary requirements relating to the supply of information. It may also be useful where a business engages in objectionable behaviour which does not fall exactly within any criminal prohibition; the business can be threatened with the loss of its licence if it does not desist.[4]

There are two main types of licensing schemes, negative and positive.[5] Under a negative licensing scheme, traders do not need a licence before setting up in business, but can be banned if they breach defined codes of conduct. An example of a negative licensing scheme is that established under the Estate Agents Act 1979.[6] Any person can establish themselves as an estate agent, but may be barred from acting as one if their conduct is not in accordance with certain standards.[7] By contrast, under a scheme of positive licensing, traders are not allowed to trade without a licence, and in order to obtain one have to demonstrate their 'fitness' to carry on that trade or occupation. An example is the licensing scheme under the Consumer Credit Act, discussed further below.

Positive licensing schemes offer the advantage that they identify in advance those who seek to operate in a particular area of business, and

[3]   *Crowther Committee* p 255.
[4]   See OFT *Consumer Credit Deregulation* (June 1994) Chapter 9.
[5]   Licensing may also be contrasted with registration and certification: see below pp 460–462.
[6]   Estate Agents Act 1979, s 3. M Clarke, D Smith and M McConville *Slippery Customers: Estate Agents, the Public and Regulation* (Blackstone Press, 1994).
[7]   *Antonelli v Secretary of State for Trade and Industry* [1998] 1 All ER 997.

enable their fitness to be assessed before they can start business. It enables the enforcement agency to seek information about a firm when the licence is applied for, or to visit premises, and provides an opportunity for the agency to explain to the applicant what standards of conduct are required and offer advice about how to comply with them and other relevant areas of law. As the OFT has stated, there is thus an element of 'preventive medicine' in positive licensing. Positive licensing schemes may be more costly to administer than negative ones, however, as a substantial bureaucracy may be necessary to approve individual businesses or particular activities. The cost of positive licensing schemes is often borne by the licence holder, who pays a fee for the licence, as under the Consumer Credit Act 1974 and utilities legislation. However, flat rate fees for licenses are sometimes opposed as they fall disproportionately on small firms; for that reason the government's initial proposals to introduce flat rate fees for licensing of food businesses was opposed, and the proposal dropped from the Food Standards Bill 1999.[8]

The scope for controlling business through either technique of licensing can be limited because of the cost of administering and enforcing it. Should insufficient resources be allocated to the administrative side of licensing, experience suggests either that there will be a delay in issuing licences or that the vetting procedure will be perfunctory with only a cursory check of applications. Likewise, licensing can become futile where it is not supported by adequate machinery to ensure that businesses adhere to the standards set. In this respect both negative and positive schemes may involve similar costs, as both require intensive enforcement processes if they are to be effective. However, licensing can be self supporting financially if the fees charged for licences are high enough to cover the administrative costs.

When first introduced licensing, particularly positive schemes of licensing, can have a powerful weeding out effect on business (and in this respect positive licensing may require less resources in its enforcement than negative licensing). After licensing of moneylenders was introduced in Britain in 1927, some 60% of existing moneylenders did not apply for a licence—no doubt they would have been denied one on the basis of their past behaviour.[9] It was for this reason that the OFT considered introducing a system of positive licensing for secondhand car dealers.[10] When a system

---

[8]   *Food Standards Agency: A force for change* (HMSO, 1998); *Food Standards Agency: Consultation on Draft Legislation* (January 1999); MAFF *Food Standards Bill: Summary of Responses to Consultation* (June 1999).
[9]   Information from the Office of Fair Trading.
[10] *Selling Second Hand Cars, A Report by the Office of Fair Trading* (OFT, October 1997).

of positive licensing for secondhand car dealers was introduced in New South Wales, the consumer protection administration refused several hundred early applications for dealer licences. Almost half of the eight thousand dealers then operating in the state went out of business because they realised that they would not obtain a licence.[11] However, the OFT rejected the idea of positive licensing for secondhand car dealers on a number of grounds. Firstly, the existence of a licence may lull customers into a false sense of security about the risks they face. Secondly, a system of positive licensing acts as a barrier to entry and can reduce competition. Thirdly, it can be difficult to define who should be licensed. If drawn too narrowly it would be easy to avoid (eg dealers could just redefine themselves as mechanics who sold cars as a sideline); if drawn too widely, however, for example to include everyone who had any connection with the motor trade, it would be a large and costly system to administer and enforce.

Ensuring that there is an effective system of enforcement in place is vital for any system of regulation, including licensing. Once established, a licensing system is deficient if it does not contain a gradation of sanctions ranging from the mild to the severe. This illustrates a general point about sanctions, that enforcement agencies are handicapped if there is a discrepancy between the sanctions they can initiate and the objectionable behaviour they are charged with eliminating.[12] If a sanction is too mild it will not deter, an illustration being a low fine; while if a sanction is too severe the agency will be reluctant to have it imposed. For example, variation, suspension or revocation are the only penalties for non-compliance with a consumer credit licence in Britain. It seems that licensees can commit minor transgressions with impunity because such severe sanctions cannot be justified. Suspension or revocation are especially out of the question with larger firms because innocent employees would be out of a job. In cases such as this the hope of policymakers must be that there will be a deterrent effect because of the possibility, albeit remote, that the licence can be suspended or revoked. In addition it might be thought that the threat that a licence can be suspended or cancelled will encourage informal resolution of disputes to the satisfaction of consumers.[13] But there is a danger that firms will realise that the regulator is unlikely to impose the sanction, depriving it of its deterrent effect. Much more sensible than simply having the sanctions of suspension or revocation is to have varied disciplinary powers. This enables a 'pyramid'

---

[11]   Many dealers in Britain have to be licensed as credit brokers under the Consumer Credit Act 1974.
[12]   Richard Arens and Harold D Lasswell *In Defence of Public Order* (Columbia University Press, 1961) pp 224–225; I Ayres and J Braithwaite *Responsive Regulation: Transcending the Deregulation Debate* (OUP, 1992).
[13]   Cf Macaulay *Law and the Balance of Power* (Russell Sage, 1966) p 140.

of enforcement strategies to be employed, ranging for example from a caution, through a fine, to suspension or revocation.[14] Enforcement officers can then better match the sanction to the scale and frequency of the breach. A good example of regulators who possess a wide range of enforcement powers are the financial services regulators who licence and regulate those who conduct investment business. The self-regulatory bodies that operated under the Financial Services Act 1986 had the power to suspend, vary and revoke licences, to levy fines, require the costs of investigation to be paid, and to issue a public reprimand. These powers have also been given to the new regulator, the Financial Services Authority (FSA), under the Financial Services and Markets Act 2000 (FSMA). The FSA also has the power (without going through the court) to issue a public censure, impose an injunction on a person from carrying on business, impose fines, order restitution of profits, disqualify individuals, withdraw authorisation, take disciplinary action against approved persons, compel information and conduct investigations.

2   OCCUPATIONAL LICENSING

The requirement to be licensed before a person can carry on a particular trade or business is used to determine who should be permitted to engage in that activity and who should not. Three main types may be distinguished: professional licensing, other occupational licensing, and the particular regime of utilities licensing introduced in the 1980s post-privatisation.

Professional and other occupational licensing have much in common. Defining a 'profession' is not easy, but one commonly accepted definition is that the task performed requires specialised skill acquired through intellectual or practical training, a high degree of detachment and integrity, and involves direct, personal and fiduciary relations with clients.[15] Often before a person can offer such services they have to be a member of a professional body, which in imposing conditions on membership effectively acts as a licensing body. Licensing of other occupations is far less systematic and countries vary in the extent to which licensing requirements are imposed on non-professional commercial activities.[16] Taken together,

---

[14]   I Ayres and J Braithwaite *Responsive Regulation: Transcending the Deregulation Debate* (OUP, 1992).

[15]   Monopolies Commission *Report on the General Effect on the Public Interest of Certain Restrictive Practices... in relation to the Supply of Professional Services* (Cmnd 4463 (1970)); A Ogus *Regulation: Legal Form and Economic Theory* (OUP, 1994).

[16]   See CH Fulda 'Controls of Entry into Businesses and Professions—A Comparative Analysis' (1973) 8 Texas Int LJ 109; see also RD Young *The Rule of Experts:*

states in the US require licences for over 400 occupations, ranging from tree surgeons, guide-dog trainers and pest controllers on the one hand, to cosmetologists, funeral directors and hairdressers.[17] In Britain licences are required for, amongst other things, selling alcohol,[18] firearms,[19] offering taxis for hire,[20] operating sex shops,[1] betting and gaming premises,[2] riding centres,[3] slaughterhouses,[4] nurseries,[5] residential care homes,[6] felling trees,[7] operating nuclear installations,[8] carrying out research or treatment on human embryos,[9] or carrying on business as a butcher.[10]

The strange occupations to which licensing applies, its tenuous connection with consumer welfare and the fact that business often advocates its adoption can lead strongly to the inference that occupational licensing acts against the public interest by restricting entry and raising prices.[11] The justification for occupational licensing is first that the consumer has insufficient information to assess the quality of service being offered, and/or that the occupation has potentially adverse effects that need to be mitigated.[12] Information deficits play a strong role in arguments for licensing of the professions. The service being demanded (eg legal advice, getting health care, buying an investment product) by

---

Occupational Licensing in America (1987) Chapter 12; G Williams 'Control by Licensing' [1967] Current Legal Problems 81; AJ Duggan 'Occupational Licensing and the Consumer Interest' in AJ Duggan and LW Darvall (eds) *Consumer Protection Law and Theory* (1980) pp 163–181.

[17] RD Young *The Rule of Experts: Occupational Licensing in America* (1987); A Ogus *Regulation: Legal Form and Economic Theory* (OUP, 1994) p 226.

[18] Licensing Act 1964 (as amended).

[19] Firearms Act 1968 (as amended).

[20] Town and Police Clauses Act 1847. A Fisher 'The Licensing of Taxis and Minicabs' (1997) 7 Consumer Policy Review 158.

[1] Local Government (Miscellaneous Provisions) Act 1982.

[2] Betting, Gaming and Lotteries Act 1963 (as amended); Gaming Act 1968.

[3] Riding Establishments Act 1964.

[4] Slaughterhouses Act 1974 (as amended).

[5] Nurseries and Childminding Registration Act 1945.

[6] Registered Homes Act 1984 (as amended).

[7] Forestry Act 1967.

[8] Nuclear Installations Act 1965.

[9] Human Fertilisation and Embryology Act 1990.

[10] Food Safety (General Food Hygiene) Regulations 1995, SI 1995/1763, Sch 1A (inserted by the Food Safety (General Food Hygiene) (Butchers' Shops) Amendment Regulations 2000, SI 2000/930).

[11] See W Gellhorn 'The Abuse of Occupational Licensing' (1976) 44 U Chi LR 6.

[12] For further discussion see A Ogus *Regulation: Legal Form and Economic Theory* (OUP, 1994) p 216; T Moore 'The Purpose of Licensing' (1961) 4 J Law and Econ 93; AD Wolfson, MJ Trebilcock and CJ Touhy 'Regulating the Professions: A Theoretical Framework' and HE Leland 'Minimum-Quality Standards and Licensing in Markets with Asymmetric Information' in S Rottenberg (ed) *Occupational Licensing and Regulation* (1980).

their nature require specialist knowledge that the consumer will not have. In the absence of this knowledge it is difficult for the consumer to assess the level of service given. Information (or perhaps more accurately, capability) deficits can also be justifications for licensing other occupations where consumers are in a particularly vulnerable position: consumer credit licensing, or licensing of residential homes, for example.[13] Alternatively, the consequences of a poor standard of service could be severe, or only be recognised too late: the wrong medicine prescribed, a 25 year investment plan bought that turns out to be worth less than has been paid in, a routine operation rendered fatal. Further, the consumer usually has to spend substantial sums of money engaging in a transaction before they can even receive the service.

Lack of information as to the quality of the service being offered by an individual business can also damage the quality of the business sector as a whole. If consumers cannot differentiate between providers on the basis of quality, then they are likely to buy the cheapest available: why spend more when everyone seems to be offering the same? Offering a higher quality service usually costs more, however, than offering a low-quality one. But those high-quality service providers will not be able to set their prices higher to recover those costs, as consumers will simply buy the cheapest available. The low-quality service then drives out the high-quality one.[14] It is for this reason that licensing tends to be demanded by those firms who regard themselves as being at the better end of the market; licensing enables them to drive out low quality but low-cost competitors.

The second justification for professional and other occupational licensing is what economists term externalities. Externalities are effects that are felt by those who are neither producing nor consuming the service. So subsequent buyers of a house suffer if the house is poorly built; we all suffer if there is an accident at a nuclear installation, or if guns are held by those who are not responsible in using them. But the adverse effects on third parties, even if they can be found, often seem flimsy justifications (what are the externalities to hairdressing, astrology?), or the reasons seem now to be lost in the mists of time.

Licensing may however be a way of achieving other ends: revenue raising, for example, in the case of dog licences[15] or gambling.[16] Or it could be a means of achieving wider social goals (the original goal of liquor

[13]   See A Ogus *Regulation: Legal Form and Economic Theory* (OUP, 1994) p 227.
[14]   G Akerlof 'The Market for "Lemons": Qualitative Uncertainty and the Market Mechanism' (1970) 84 Qly J of Economics 488.
[15]   Dog Licences Act 1959; A Ogus *Regulation: Legal Form and Economic Theory* (OUP, 1994) p 231.
[16]   D Dixon *From Prohibition to Regulation: Bookmaking, Anti-Gambling, and the Law* (Clarendon Press, 1990).

licensing was to ensure a sober workforce during the war) or of preserving or rationing natural resources: fishing licences, tree-felling.[17] The licensing process also enables public authorities to gain information about who is conducting particular types of business, and the threat of losing the licence can act as a powerful sanction, encouraging compliance with the licence conditions or other requirements. Licensing may also simply be a way of raising the standards of service in a particular area where those standards are hard to define or set down in a code of conduct. A person may be assessed according to vague and ill-defined criteria, eg 'fit and proper', and judgments then made about fitness and propriety that authorities are unwilling or unable to set down in codes of conduct.

Finally, licensing authorities can ensure that those in a licensed occupation furnish consumers with a simple and inexpensive avenue for redress of their complaints. Over the last 10–15 years there has been a marked trend in the UK to establish Ombudsmen to deal with customer complaints, particularly in the financial sector, also for estate agents, legal services, and insurance. Ombudsmen vary in their operation; some adopt an investigative role, actively investigating the consumer's complaint (eg the Pensions Ombudsman), others act simply as cheaper, faster and specialist alternatives to courts. There are sometimes rights of appeal to the courts on points of law (for example from the Pensions Ombudsmen, the Financial Services Ombudsman), and their decisions may or may not be binding on the parties (for example the decisions of the Financial Services Ombudsmen are binding on the firm but not the complainant; the decisions of the Estate Agents Ombudsman are binding on the firm only when accepted by the complainant; the Banking Ombudsmen has the power to make decisions which are binding on both parties but usually tries to seek a settlement between them). The maximum award that can be made is usually in the region of £100,000.[18]

(a)   Monopoly effects

Critics have argued that occupational licensing frequently acts against the consumer interest because it restricts competition and inhibits innovation. Sometimes the attack is by anti-collectivists who believe that the individual can decide matters for himself and that the market offers the best guarantee for consumer protection.[19] The view taken in this book is

---

[17]   Forestry Act 1967.
[18]   See further R James *Private Ombudsmen and Public Law* (Dartmouth, 1997) and Chapter 3 above.
[19]   Milton Friedman *Capitalism and Freedom* (University of Chicago Press, 1962) p 137.

that the consumer frequently needs government protection, but the point must be conceded that some licensing has monopoly effects and can operate as a cartel, in the interests of the members of an occupation.

In 1970 the Monopolies Commission tried to characterise situations where occupational licensing of the professions perpetuated undesirable monopoly practices.[20] It accepted that sometimes licensing was necessary to protect consumers because of the special nature of the skills required for professional practice or the peculiar fiduciary or personal character of the services involved. Risks to health, safety, property and so on lent support to licensing, particularly where consumers were bad judges of their own interests. Rather than identifying particular occupations where collective restrictions on competition were against the public interest, the Commission concluded that the best approach was to examine particular criteria for licensing. It concluded that education and training prerequisites were generally unobjectionable, although they could increase the cost of entry and thus benefit those already in a profession. Character tests could usually be justified, because the public interest was endangered if the whole structure or machinery of a profession was brought into disrepute. By contrast, the Commission thought collective restrictions on price competition were most likely undesirable, because they raised prices unnecessarily. It also said that complete freedom to advertise might involve the danger of consumers falling into the trap of the incompetent, but to prevent dissemination of price information was almost invariably adverse to consumers' welfare.

The adverse monopoly effects of occupational licensing are most pronounced where the state hands over its administration to the occupation itself, which often occurs in professional licensing. Particular reasons may dictate this decision, such as the government's lack of expertise or resources, or that state administration would meet strong political resistance.[1]

Clear examples of state backed self-regulation are law and medicine. Dentists, opticians, veterinary surgeons, chiropractors, solicitors and barristers must all be approved by their own professional body before they can practise. The Law Society has wide control over solicitors by virtue of the Solicitors Act 1974. Its regulations on the education and training of solicitors are given statutory force. Practising solicitors must hold a certificate issued by the Society which can only be obtained if they have complied with the training regulations and the Society is satisfied as to their character and suitability. The Society must formulate rules of

---

[20] Monopolies Commission *Report on [the] Public Interest [and] Certain Restrictive Practices... Professional Services* (Cmnd 4463 (1970)).

[1] Cf Thomas G Thomas 'The Purpose of Licensing' (1961) 4 J of Law and Econ 93.

conduct for solicitors and a Tribunal of the Society can suspend or strike off solicitors from practice if they are in breach of these or other provisions.[2] The Law Society also operates a complaints service which since 1996 has been provided through the Office of Supervision of Solicitors (OSS). The OSS deals only with complaints of poor service and misconduct, not negligence. It may reduce a solicitor's bill in part or in whole, award compensation of up to £1,000, require the solicitor to correct the mistake at his or her own expense, or discipline a solicitor for misconduct.[3] If the complainant is still not satisfied, she may go to the Legal Services Ombudsman who deals with complaints against solicitors and barristers as well as licensed conveyancers. The Ombudsman has the power to make recommendations to the relevant professional body and to issue orders.[4] There has been much recent criticism of the operation of the OSS. In 1999 there was a backlog of 17,000 cases, and following threats from the government that an independent complaints scheme would be established, the Law Society agreed to invest £10 million to improve the process.[5]

In the past, there is little doubt that occupational licensing of both solicitors and barristers served to preserve a monopoly for them over the provision of certain legal services.[6] Until 1990 solicitors had a monopoly on paid conveyancing work.[7] This enabled solicitors to charge fees that were out of proportion to the amount of work involved and the skill necessary to perform it. Barristers' monopoly on rights of audience in court has also been progressively eroded. In 1990 solicitors were given rights of audience in courts, subject to certain conditions.[8] These rights have been extended to all courts.[9] The prohibition on employed lawyers (ie qualified solicitors who do not work in law firms but work in the legal departments of companies or local government) has also been lifted, again subject to certain conditions on qualifications.[10]

Occupational licensing can have monopoly effects, especially if the government abnegates its responsibility and hands over control of a

[2]   Solicitors Act 1974.
[3]   Details of the operation of the OSS can be found at http://www.lawsociety.org.uk.
[4]   Courts and Legal Services Act 1990, ss 21–26 (as amended).
[5]   Law Society, Press Release, 14 April 1999, see p 138 above.
[6]   For discussion see R Abel *The Legal Profession in England and Wales* (Blackwell, 1988); R Kerridge and G Davis 'Reform of the Legal Profession: The Way Ahead' (1999) 62 MLR 807.
[7]   Removed under Courts and Legal Services Act 1990, s 36.
[8]   Courts and Legal Services Act 1990, ss 27–28, 33; Higher Courts Regulations Act 1992.
[9]   Lord Chancellor's Department *Rights of Audience and Rights to Conduct Litigation in England and Wales: The Way Ahead* (June 1998); Access to Justice Act 1999, s 36.
[10] Access to Justice Act 1999, s 37.

scheme to the occupation itself, as is common with professional licensing. But occupational licensing may be imposed for good reason, and its adverse monopoly effects are not inevitable. Guidelines like those drawn up by the Monopolies Commission in 1970 could do much to ensure that restrictions are only employed when the benefit to consumers outweighs the cost. A further way to ensure that consumers are not disadvantaged by occupational licensing is to ensure that they are adequately represented on the agencies or boards that are issuing the licenses. This may require government funding but would help to prevent licensing from degenerating into a successful effort by the members of the occupation to exclude competition. Finally the agency itself may be subjected to competition law. Under the Financial Services and Markets Act 2000, the financial services regulators themselves are subjected to scrutiny by the Office of Fair Trading and the Secretary of State to ensure that their rules are not anti-competitive to a significant extent.[11] Subjecting other occupational licensing bodies to competition law could be an effective way to avoid the adverse effects of monopoly licensing whilst preserving its benefits. However, under the Competition Act 1998 the rules of certain professions (including lawyers, engineers, surveyors and health professionals) may be excluded from the prohibition on anti-competitive agreements.[12] In November 1999 the government has asked the Office of Fair Trading to review the effect of these provisions.[13]

(b)   The standards required of licensees

Schemes of occupational licensing vary in the standards which they require of potential business licensees, depending on what reasons underlie the decision to adopt this particular method of legal control. The idea of professional licensing is to ensure adequate knowledge and standards on the part of those engaged in an occupation by defining the conditions of admission to and continuance in it. The standards required by the professions therefore stipulate levels of education, training and practical experience that the applicant has to have before he or she can be licensed to practice as a member of that profession: solicitor, doctor, architect, accountant and so on. Thus the Law Society requires that before a person can be admitted as a solicitor they have to have completed at least two years of graduate level legal education comprising the study of stipulated

---

[11]   FSMA 2000, Chapter II.
[12]   Competition Act 1998, Chapter I and Sch 4.
[13]   OFT *Review of Professional Rules* (April 2000).

core subjects, and two years of practical experience.[14] Areas of business which are not always thought of as professions may also stipulate minimum standards of education and training: life assurance salesmen, for example, have to satisfy the regulators that they have certain minimum qualifications.[15]

Other common requirements for both professional and other occupational licensing are as to a person's good character, with details of criminal offences, bankruptcies, or directors' disqualification orders having to be provided.[16] A common requirement in the area of financial services is that persons must show that they are 'fit and proper' to carry on the business for which licensing is sought.[17] The criteria used to assess fitness and properness have not always been made clear. However the FSA has indicated that it will take into consideration a number of factors including the extent to which the firm shows that it is committed to conducting its business with integrity and high standards, which will involve consideration of any criminal convictions, disqualifications, insolvency, and disciplinary proceedings taken against the firm or its directors or connected persons; whether the board of the company has sufficient skills and experience to understand the firm's activities; whether the Board has put in place adequate systems of internal control to ensure compliance with the rules and whether the firm approaches the control of risk in a prudent manner.[18]

A final requirement which is frequently imposed is that the firm must have a certain level of solvency or otherwise provide protection to consumers if it should become insolvent or otherwise be unable to meet its liabilities. Insurance companies, banks, building societies, and those investment businesses that handle client money are all required to show that they have a certain level of solvency. With regard to insurance companies, for example, they are required (in broad terms) to prepare accounts and balance sheets in the prescribed form, undergo regular auditing and actuarial investigations and handle their assets in the required manner (eg separate those attributable to long-term business).[19] The

[14] Solicitors Act 1974, s 2 (in conjunction with the Lord Chancellor, Lord Chief Justice and Master of the Rolls). In addition, the Advisory Committee on Legal Education and Conduct (ACLEC) was established under the Courts and Legal Services Act 1990, s 19) to make recommendations on training and education. It issued a report in 1998 which was implemented from 1 November 1999. ACLEC itself, however, has been abolished as part of the Woolf reforms.
[15] PIA and FIMBRA Rules; FSA Handbook.
[16] For example Consumer Credit Act, s 25.
[17] FSMA 2000, s 31.
[18] FSA *The Qualifying Conditions for Authorization* CP 20 (March 1999).
[19] Insurance Companies Act 1974, Pt 11. See *MacGillivray & Parkington on Insurance Law* (Sweet and Maxwell, 6th edn, 1975).

Department of Trade, now the FSA, has wide powers of intervention if it considers this desirable for protecting policyholders against the risk that a company may not be able to meet its liabilities or, in the case of long-term business like life assurance, fulfil consumers reasonable expectations.[20] Intervention takes the form of a 'stop order', whereby the company must not take on new business, realise its investments or allow its premium income to exceed a certain amount.[1]

Alternatively or in addition, firms may be required to contribute to a compensation scheme. Under the Financial Services Act 1986 and the Financial Services and Markets Act 2000, an Investors Compensation Scheme (ICS) was established, funded by a levy imposed on all firms who are licensed to engage in investment business. The scheme will compensate private (ie non-professional) investors should the firm against which they have a claim be insolvent, to a maximum of £48,000.[2] The Policyholders Protection Act 1975 established a similar scheme for general insurance business. The Board established by the Act is financed by levies on insurance companies. It may perform its functions by making arrangements for the transfer of a company's business to other firms or for the issue of substitute policies. If either of these fail it may pay consumers 90% (100% in the case of compulsory insurance) of the value of their policies. This scheme is transferred to the ICS under the FSMA 2000.

A final example is the requirement that a business take professional indemnity insurance, or some other form of bond with a bank or insurance company so that, in the event of financial failure, a specified sum will become available. Solicitors, for example, are required to contribute to a professional indemnity fund which will cover liabilities in negligence of those firms which have become insolvent.[3] Such requirements are not confined to occupations which require a licence, however.[4] Businesses that offer package holidays have to conform to statutory standards of conduct, and in addition are required to protect the consumer's money by making appropriate insurance or bonding arrangements.[5] A package holiday is defined broadly as a pre-arranged combination of at least two of transport, accommodation or other tourist services. The regulations require that the

---

[20]   See s 38. These powers are transferred to the FSA under the FSMA.
[1]   Sections 29, 37.
[2]   Investors Compensation Scheme Rules.
[3]   Solicitors Act 1974, s 37; the Solicitors Indemnity Fund was established in 1987.
[4]   See the discussion on p 436.
[5]   Package Travel, Package Holidays and Package Tours Regulations 1992, SI 1992/3288, regs 16–18.

tour operator offering a package holiday must at all times be able to provide sufficient evidence of security for the refund of money paid over and for the repatriation of the consumer in the case of insolvency.[6] This may be achieved either through a bonding arrangement supported by a reserve fund or additional insurance provision,[7] or the with an institution that will pay such sum as may be reasonably required to cover all moneys paid out by consumers in respect of package holiday contracts that have not been fully performed.[8]

(c) Licensing, certification and registration

Friedman draws the distinction within occupational licensing between registration, certification and licensing proper.[9] Licensing proper is the most restrictive, for once individuals meet certain criteria they are given the exclusive right to engage in a particular occupation. At the other end of the spectrum is registration, where individuals simply must list their names in an official register. The purpose of this type of registration is usually to provide information to enforcement authorities as to the identity and location of certain types of business. An example is the requirement under the Food Safety Act 1990 for the registration with local authorities of all premises that are used or proposed to be used for a food business.[10] Further, under the Poisons Act 1972, local authorities are to maintain a register of those persons entitled to sell non-medical poisons.[11] Certification lies in between the two, for an individual must demonstrate that he has reached a certain standard, but the government does not prevent the practice of skills by those who have not obtained a certificate.

Certification may serve to raise standards, but whether it does so is largely dependent on whether consumers and other people who may deal with the firm (suppliers, contractors) see certification as an advantage. One example of an unsuccessful system of certification in Britain was the

[6] Package Travel, Package Holidays and Package Tours Regulations 1992, reg 16.
[7] Package Travel, Package Holidays and Package Tours Regulations 1992, reg 18.
[8] Package Travel, Package Holidays and Package Tours Regulations 1992, reg 17.
[9] Milton Friedman *Capitalism and Freedom* (University of Chicago Press, 1962) p 137.
[10] Food Safety Act 1990, s 19.
[11] Poisons Act 1972, s 5.

regulation of insurance brokers introduced in 1981 under the Insurance Brokers (Registration) Act 1977. Considerable criticism had surrounded their activities. It was felt that some were incompetent or dishonest and that others were not acting as the independent advisers which consumers assumed them to be because many were really agents of insurance companies. A survey by the Consumers' Association in 1975 among more than 500 of its members revealed that two-thirds buying a common type of insurance policy were being sold a more expensive one than was needed.[12] The government at the time rejected state licensing because of the cost and because it did not have civil servants with the requisite expertise.[13] Instead, it opted for a scheme of certification, administered mainly by the British Insurance Brokers' Council (BIBC)—a body created by the four insurance broking trade associations. Brokers had to meet certain standards of independence, good character and either experience or professional qualification (new entrants), and be willing and able to adhere to the BIBC's code of conduct. Legislation reserved the title 'insurance broker' to those certified.[14] However, many consumers failed to make the distinction between certified and non certified advisers, and only one-third of brokers became certified.

A more successful example of certification is provided by the role of the British Standards Institute (BSI).[15] The BSI was founded in 1901 to co-ordinate the development of national standards. It is independent of the Government (although was incorporated by Royal Charter in 1929), and issues certificates of quality, or 'kitemarks', to firms which have attained its specified standards. It has specified standards for quality of products and services in a wide range of industry sectors, including building and civil engineering, healthcare and environment, chemicals, and has developed a specialised set of standards for consumer products and services. Its kitemark can also be awarded to firms who have met its standards on their internal management systems: the ISO 9000. Firms to whom certification has been awarded are assessed regularly to ensure that they are still meeting the requirements. Firms who do not meet the specified standards are free to enter into business. However, certification that a firm or product meets the BSI standards is an indication that its quality has been independently assessed, and is thus one that consumers may rely on and indeed may seek out.

---

[12] 'Life Insurance Selling Methods' (1975) *Money Which?* December, p 204.
[13] DTI *Insurance Intermediaries* (Cmnd 6715 (1977)) p 4.
[14] Insurance Brokers (Registration) Act 1977, s 22.
[15] For information on the BSI and requirements of certification see the BSI web page: http://www.bsi.org.uk

Certification may also be used as a way of indicating quality not to consumers of services as such, but to those who fund services that may be used by others. An example is provided by the recent reforms of the legal service and courts. As part of those reforms a Legal Services Commission has been established to co-ordinate the funding and provision of legal services by law firms, law centres, Citizens Advice Bureaux and independent advice centres. It is proposed that the Commission will develop core quality criteria for the provision of legal advice. These criteria will form the basis of a common accreditation scheme or 'kitemark', on which all potential funders of legal services (government, local authorities, charities etc) will be able to rely. In particular, those who provide legal services which are paid for by the government will have to obtain the kitemark as a condition of obtaining a contract from the Legal Services Commission, and other funders will be able to impose a similar condition.[16]

The requirements of registration, certification and licensing, although analytically distinct, may in practice often merge. So although certification may be optional in the sense that there is no legal requirement to be certified in order to carry on a particular business, in practice certification of a recognised level of quality may be a prerequisite for trading: consumers or suppliers may prefer not to deal with someone who is not certified. Certification thus becomes de facto licensing. Registration and licensing may also merge. Registration may in practice require far more than simply entering a name on a register. For example, under the Medical Act 1983 the General Medical Council is given the monopoly right to register persons as medical practitioners. However, in order to become registered, a person has to satisfy certain education and training requirements.[17] Further, only registered medical practitioners can recover fees for giving health treatment, or be employed in a hospital, prison, the army or any other public body or institution, and there are penalties for not being registered.[18] 'Registration' in the case of doctors is thus in reality licensing.

(d)   Utilities licensing

In the 1980s the Thatcher government undertook a programme of privatisation, transferring the ownership of the utility companies, those providing telecommunications, electricity, water and gas, into private

---

[16]   Lord Chancellor's Department *Modernising Justice* (December 1998) paras 2.6–2.21; Legal Aid Board *The Community Legal Service Quality Mark* Consultation Paper (August 1999).

[17]   Medical Act 1983, Pts II–IV.

[18]   Medical Act 1983, ss 46–48.

hands.[19] Public limited companies replaced the public corporations and shares were sold to private investors. The public corporations of British Gas and British Telecom were not broken up but given monopoly or near monopoly positions. The water authorities of England and Wales were privatised on a regional basis as virtual monopolies. The electricity industry in England and Wales was divided up so that electricity generators were owned by three companies, National Power, Power Gen and Nuclear Electric (the last is still publicly owned); transmission was owned by the National Grid plc, and supply and distribution split between 12 area regional electricity companies (RECs). In Scotland and Northern Ireland integrated electricity companies were created (Scottish Power, Scottish Hydro-Electric and Northern Ireland Electricity).

Those public limited companies were then given licences (or the functional equivalents) to provide those utility services, with the conditions under which they were to do so set out in the licence. Since privatisation the number of licence holders has increased to varying degrees in the different industries. The greatest increase in licence holders has been in the area of telecommunications, where competition, initially in international and mobile phone services, has increased. In March 1998 there were over 200 licensed public telecommunications operators.[1]

Licences are issued by the Secretary of State, with powers to delegate licensing to a separate, individual regulator called a Director General for each utility sector. The Directors General are supported by regulatory offices and have a range of powers, including powers to enforce and modify the licence conditions, obtain information from the licensed companies, set or oversee quality of service standards and monitor compliance with them, determine certain disputes, set prices, and investigate complaints.[2] Whilst the relevant statutes[3] set out the broad

[19] The literature is vast. See generally CD Foster *Privatisation, Public Ownership and the Regulation of Natural Monopoly* (OUP, 1992); J Vickers and G Yarrow *Privatisation: An Economic Analysis* (1988); T Prosser *Law and the Regulators* (1997); R Baldwin and M Cave *Understanding Regulation* (OUP, 1999) Chapter 14; C Graham *Regulating Public Utilities* (Hart Publishing, 2000). See also the discussion of regulation of utility services in Chapter 6.

[1] http://www.oftel.gov.uk

[2] See generally National Audit Office *Report by the Comptroller and Auditor General: The Work of the Directors General of Telecommunications, Gas Supply, Water Services and Electricity Supply* (HC 645, Session 1995–6, London, July 1996); Hansard Society and European Policy Forum, *Report of the Commission on the Regulation of Privatised Utilities* (London, 1996); Prosser, op cit.; *A Fair Deal for Consumers: Modernising the Framework for Utility Regulation* (Cm 3898 (March 1998)).

[3] Telecommunications Act 1984; Gas Act 1986; Electricity Act 1989; Water Act 1989; Water Industry Act 1991; Water Resources Act 1991; Competition and Service (Utilities) Act 1992; Environment Act 1995; Gas Act 1995.

institutional framework of regulation, it is the individual licenses issued to operators that contain the detailed terms on which services are provided, including the setting of prices. The system differs from other statutory licensing systems in that the Directors General are restricted in their ability to amend the licence provisions, including any price controls. Directors General may only amend licence conditions with the consent of the licensee concerned or following a relevant finding by the Competition Commission,[4] to whom the Directors General may refer the issue.

The restricted powers of the Director Generals to amend licences have a number of implications. For these purposes, the principal one is that it means that licences are a problematic technique of regulation where they are used to impose standard conditions across a number of licence holders. All licence holders have to agree to a change before it can be implemented. In the case of gas, there is a separate set of standard conditions. However these can only be amended if they are deregulatory in their effect or if 90% of licence holders agree.[5] A system of individual licences is appropriate where the differences between licence holders is such that they require individual regulation. However in some sectors, particularly telecommunications, this is not generally the case, and a rule based system using a range of rule types would arguably be more effective.[6] OFTEL has recently argued that the structure of telecommunications regulation should move from a system of regulation through individual licences to a system based on general authorisations backed by rules.[7]

(e)   Consumer credit licensing

A major area of licensing in Britain is of businesses involved with consumer credit. The OFT estimates that there are around 150,000 business licensed, from retailers selling on credit at one extreme to debt collectors at the other, with the majority engaging in credit brokerage.[8] Applications have been rising steadily in recent years, from 17,202 in 1996 to 21,443 in 1998, a

---

[4]   Competition Act 1998.

[5]   Gas Act 1995, s 23. Reform of the licence modification rules for telecommunications to enable modicication of conditions found in many licences is introduced by the Electronic Communications Act 2000, s 12.

[6]   See generally J Black 'Using Rules Effectively' in C McCrudden (ed) *Regulation and Deregulation in the Utilities and Financial Services Industries* (OUP, 1999).

[7]   OFTEL *Beyond the Telephone, the Television and the PC III* (March 1998) section 4, Appendix B. See Electronic Communications Act 2000, s 12.

[8]   *Consumer Credit Deregulation* (OFT 1994) para 9.2; OFT *Annual Report 1998* Appendix C, Table C.9.

rise of 25%.[9] The scheme is administered by the Office of Fair Trading although it draws on assistance from a number of sources including local consumer protection departments.

Licensing in the consumer credit area took modern shape in the Moneylenders Acts 1900 and 1927 and the Pawnbrokers Act 1872, which required those engaged in these activities to hold a licence. The impetus for licensing was that many moneylenders and pawnbrokers were guilty of manifest abuses, inducing fraudulent misrepresentation, and it was thought licensing would raise standards by excluding the unscrupulous.[10] Applicants for licences were required to demonstrate that they were of good character and suitable to carry on business and the licences could be suspended or revoked if the trader was convicted of certain offences. The Moneylenders Acts extended to commercial as well as consumer transactions, but important categories of lenders, notably banks and certain finance companies, were exempt.[11] Besides their limited application, the provisions were never adequately enforced.

The rationale of the Consumer Credit Act 1974 is to protect the consumer across the whole spectrum of credit transactions and to release the credit industry from outdated restrictions which varied according to the legal form of a transaction rather than its underlying nature. On this basis, licensing is extended to the whole credit industry so that all businesses are subject to the same licensing requirements.[12] The justification for selecting consumer credit for special treatment over other areas of consumer protection is said to be that it is particularly prone to abuses from which consumers can do little to protect themselves.[13] It also provides an effective means of enforcing the CCA provisions.

Licences are required by all firms offering consumer credit or hiring facilities, as well as by those acting as intermediaries or debt adjusters, debt counsellors, debt collectors and credit reference agencies.[14] The licensing requirement extends to those who carry on a business of a particular type, but the Act makes it clear that this does not cover those who occasionally enter into transactions of a particular type.[15] A retailer who occasionally supplies goods on credit does therefore not need to be licensed, although the other provisions of the Act will apply.[16] Businesses

---

[9]   OFT *Annual Report 1998*, Table C.8.
[10] For example, Report from the Select Committee on Money Lending (1898) 260, x, 101, p iii.
[11] Moneylenders Act 1900, s 6.
[12] Reform of the Law on Consumer Credit (Cmnd 5427 (1973)) p 6.
[13] *Crowther Committee* pp 329–334; Molony Committee, para 3.5.1; I Ramsay *Consumer Protection and the Law* (Weidenfeld and Nicolson, 1989).
[14] Sections 21, 145. See *Do You Need a Licence?* (OFT, 1975).
[15] Section 189(2).
[16] *R v Marshall* (1989) 90 Cr App Rep 73; *Hare v Schurek* [1993] CCLR 47.

must obtain separate authorisation for each activity. Generally speaking, all those holding a particular type of licence are subject to the same restrictions. However, there is power for the Office of Fair Trading to circumscribe the scope of individual licences, for example, by authorising a consumer credit business to enter into only certain types of agreements.[17] In 1994 the Director General of Fair Trading considered simplifying the licensing process by issuing one general licence that would cover all types of business, although the applicant could request a limited licence. In either event the Director General would retain the right, with good reason, to refuse to issue a licence covering particular types of business.[18]

Specific authorisation is needed if a business canvasses consumer credit or consumer hire agreements covered by the legislation off trade premises.[19] Group licences (as opposed to standard licences) can be issued covering those in a particular field if the public interest is better served than by requiring each to apply separately.[20] Solicitors, the main accountancy bodies, business advisers and Citizens Advice Bureaux are examples of categories for which group licences have been granted. In the main they act as credit brokers, debt adjusters or debt counsellors under the Act. In 1999 the OFT took the unprecedented step of granting the Law Society a group credit licence for one year only, instead of the usual five, so concerned was it at the failures of the solicitors' complaints scheme to handle complaints effectively.[1]

The wide ambit of licensing is illustrated by reference to retailers. Many retailers need a licence as a consumer credit business (if they provide credit themselves), as a credit broker (if they introduce their customers to independent finance houses to provide credit), as a debt collector (if they collect instalments and follow up arrears either on their own account or on behalf of a finance company) or as a debt adjuster (if they accept goods in part exchange, where the goods are on hire-purchase and negotiate a settlement figure from the finance company).[2] Businesses commit a criminal offence if they engage in activities controlled by the Act without a licence. In addition, a credit or hire agreement regulated by the Act cannot be enforced against the consumer without an order of the Office of Fair Trading if it was made by an unlicensed business or if an unlicensed credit broker was involved.[3]

---

[17] Consumer Credit Act 1974, s 23(2).
[18] *Consumer Credit Deregulation,* para 9.26.
[19] Section 23(3). Canvassing cash loans off trade premises is banned completely (s 49).
[20] Section 22.
[1] See (1999) Law Society Gazette, 9 August.
[2] 'Licensing under the Consumer Credit Business' *Hire Trading*, vol 29, Sprint 1976, p 6.
[3] Sections 39–40.

To obtain or renew a licence, a firm has to demonstrate to the Office of Fair Trading that it is fit to carry on business and that its name is not misleading or undesirable.[4] Factors which are taken into account are whether the firm or persons associated with it have committed any relevant offence (involving fraud, dishonesty, violence or breach of consumer law); practised discrimination on sex, colour, racial or ethnic grounds, or engaged in deceitful, oppressive, unfair or improper business practices. A misleading or otherwise undesirable business name is one too similar to an existing name, one which is misleading because it suggests that the organisation is larger than it really is or has connections (in fact non-existent) with other organisations or gives a misleading impression as to the cost or ease of borrowing.

In deciding whether to grant a licence, the Office of Fair Trading places heavy emphasis on information provided by the applicant, supplemented by that received from other sources, such as local authority consumer protection departments.[5] The form to accompany a standard licence application asks whether an applicant has been involved in a bankruptcy, scheme of arrangement or liquidation, has been convicted on certain types of criminal offence, has been adjudged in breach of the Race Relations Act 1976 or the Sex Discrimination Act 1975, or has been refused a licence under existing legislation. In the case of a company, information on these matters must also be supplied for its directors, company secretary, chief executive and controlling shareholders, and for other persons in a position to control the company. Information about the spouse and other close relatives of each of these persons is also required if relevant.

Consumer credit licensing in Britain is a social and not an economic tool. Licences cannot be refused on grounds of economic policy, for example to regulate competition, or because of the financial instability of a firm. Further, the purpose of licensing is to control the credit industry in relation to the loan aspect of its business, not in relation to the sale aspect. Therefore, control does not extend to the quality of products and services supplied; under a credit transaction and these matters continue to be regulated by the general law.

Licences were initially issued for a renewable period of three years, increased to ten in 1979 and 15 in 1986. In 1991 the period was substantially reduced to the current five years. Although the five year limit imposes an administrative burden on both the OFT and the licence holder, the previous period of 15 years was seen to be too long to enable effective monitoring

---

4   Section 25.
5   National Audit Office *The Office of Fair Trading: Protecting the Consumer From Unfair Trading Practices* HC 57 Session 1999–2000 (The Stationery Office, 1999) pp 38–40.

and control of businesses to be exercised.[6] In particular, the Director General of Fair Trading has no powers to request information from a business except on an application for a licence or its renewal, so reducing the licence period effectively enables the Director General of Fair Trading to obtain more information about the business than he would otherwise. In 1994 the Director General sought the power to request information from the licence holder during the period of the licence, but this has not been granted. Indeed the government is now considering abandoning the renewal requirement, but introducing more onerous application requirements combined with a power for the OFT to review the licence during its life.[7]

Licences may be granted with or without conditions being imposed, or refused. During the course of the licence the OFT may vary, suspend or revoke the licence.[8] In the year to March 2000 the OFT issued 124 notices to applicants and existing licence holders questioning their fitness to hold or be granted a licence. In respect of these cases 32 applications were refused, 13 were withdrawn and 21 licences were revoked.[9] Flexibility is limited, however, as there are no additional sanctions such as the imposition of monetary penalties if a licensee engages in objectionable activities which are not serious enough to justify revoking a licence.[10] The government is considering the introduction of some intermediate sanctions such as imposition of fines and partial suspensions.[11] Further it is questionable how effective revocation is. It is an offence punishable by £5,000 on summary trial or a fine or up to two years' imprisonment if convicted on indictment to carry on unlicensed business,[12] but this requires enforcement officers to be aware that unlicensed business is being conducted. Potentially more significant could be the provision that agreements entered into by unlicensed traders are unenforceable without a validating order from the Director General of Fair Trading.[13] This covers both agreements for which a licence is required and all related agreements, except those of a non-commercial nature. This places an incentive on creditors and owners to monitor their brokers, for agreements entered into as a result of any introduction made by the unlicensed broker will not be enforceable. However, a validating order is only necessary if the agreement

---

6   See further OFT *Consumer Credit Deregulation* para 9.31.
7   *Discussion Paper on Consumer Credit Licensing* (DTI, 2000).
8   Sections 31–32. See also Consumer Credit (Termination of Licences) Regulations 1976, SI 1976/1002.
9   *Discussion Paper on Consumer Credit Licensing* (DTI, 2000).
10   *Discussion Paper on Consumer Credit Licensing* (DTI, 2000).
11   *Discussion Paper on Consumer Credit Licensing* (DTI, 2000).
12   Consumer Credit Act 1974, s 39.
13   Consumer Credit Act 1974, s 40(1).

has to be enforced through the courts. It is not necessary to request or take payments under the terms of the agreement or to accept the voluntary surrender of goods. Consumers who are ignorant of the legal position are thus prejudiced.[14]

Those refused a licence in the terms applied for, or who have their licence suspended or revoked, can appeal to the Secretary of State for Trade and Industry.[15] The appeal is heard by an 'approved person' belonging to a panel of persons appointed by the Secretary of State. Those persons must either be legally qualified, or have special knowledge or expertise in the area, or be representative of the group to which the applicant belongs.[16] Hearings are public, and the approved person then makes a recommendation, with reasons, to the Secretary of State. The Secretary of State's decision has to be published, and appeal may be made to the High Court on a point of law.[17] There is a public register of licence applications and licences granted, but the public has no right to be heard when a business applies for a licence (except with the approval of the Director General of Fair Trading), or to challenge the Director General's decision to grant a licence. These are serious deficiencies in the legislation.

The government has initiated a consultation on reform of the consumer credit licensing regime, hinting that too many resources are devoted to the regulation of rather low risk activities, which tend to inhibit businesses from developing new areas of lending for which regulatory approval is then required.[18] Additionally it is argued that initial checks on licensees are insufficiently rigorous and that there is insufficient co-operation between local authorities and the Office of Fair Trading in linking the local monitoring of business behaviour with the capacity to apply licence based sanctions.[19] Possible solutions to perceived problems include abandoning licensing altogether, to replace it with compulsory registration and tougher enforcement powers.

3   PRODUCT LICENSING, A CASE STUDY: DRUGS

An alternative form of licensing is product licensing. Product licensing is not widely used and may be criticised on the grounds that it impedes

---

[14]   *Consumer Credit Deregulation*, para 9.23.
[15]   Consumer Credit Licensing (Appeals) Regulations 1998, SI 1998/1203.
[16]   Consumer Credit Licensing (Appeals) Regulations 1998, reg 24.
[17]   Consumer Credit Licensing (Appeals) Regulations 1998, regs 22, 23.
[18]   *Discussion Paper on Consumer Credit Licensing* (DTI, 2000).
[19]   National Audit Office *The Office of Fair Trading: Protecting the Consumer From Unfair Trading Practices* HC 57 Session 1999–00 (The Stationery Office, 1999) pp 45–48.

innovation and competition. Where there is the risk of dangerous consequences arising from the use of a product, however, licensing may be justified. A key example of the use of product licensing is in the licensing of medicines. The EU is the largest consumer of pharmaceuticals, consuming 46 billion ECU's worth in 1993, 30.8% of the world market.[20] Consumers are however in a very peculiar, and vulnerable, position in the pharmaceuticals market. They often do not choose which drugs to take, but have them prescribed by a doctor and largely paid for by the state. Even if the choice were available to them, however, consumers could not exercise it effectively. Consumers cannot always turn information into knowledge. Consumers cannot assess the risks and benefits of drugs, but adverse effects may be fatal, and may not become apparent for years. The products are highly technical, and there are few consumers who could 'prescribe' themselves drugs without becoming doctors.[1] Manufacturers of drugs are of course subject to product liability rules,[2] but relying on private civil action alone as a means of redress for unsafe drugs, and thus of indirect regulation, is inadequate. The information costs in bringing an action are high: the consumer may not know that the drug caused the illness, and causation may be difficult to show without extensive expert knowledge. But perhaps more significantly, civil actions are only brought after the harm has been caused; they cannot prevent it occurring in the first place.

Concern about abuses in the preparation of drugs, their poor quality, the incompetence of many pharmacists and the insufficiency of powers given to the authorities to authorise the destruction of adulterated drugs was raised in Parliament as early as 1747.[3] In 1856 another Select Committee remarked of patent medicines that 'there can be no doubt that the public health is endangered by the use of several of these compounds', and it recommended the registration of chemists and druggists.[4] In 1921 recommendations were made for the establishment of a special commission to authorise drugs for marketing.[5] Drug manufacturers should be registered

---

[20] European Parliament, Directorate General for Research *American and Japanese (Bio)Pharmaceutical Presence in Europe*, Working Paper, Environment, Public Health and Consumer Protection Series, E-2, 3-1996, 2.

[1] E Mossialos and B Abel-Smith 'The Regulation of the European Pharmaceutical Industry' in S Stavridis, R Morgan, E Mossialos and H Macrum (eds) *New Challenges to the EU: Policies and Policy Making at the End of the Century* (Dartmouth, 1996) p 358.

[2] See Chapter 5.

[3] Report from the Select Committee [on] Examination of Drugs to Prevent Adulteration (1747) Journals (HC) vol 25, p 592.

[4] Report from the Select Committee on Adulteration of Food etc (1856) Parl Pap 379, viii, I, at p ix.

[5] *Report of the Departmental Committee on Therapeutic Substances* (Cmnd 1156 (1921)), xiii, 331.

and required to submit a statement of the composition and therapeutical claims of their products to a government chemist for verification. For 50 years such suggestions went unheeded, and it required the Thalidomide tragedy to galvanise the government into action.[6]

(a) The aftermath of Thalidomide: prior approval for drugs

Thalidomide was discovered in the 1950s by the German company Chemie Grunenthal. It came on to the German market in 1957 and was sold without prescription; by 1960 one million people in Germany were taking it regularly as a sedative and it accounted for nearly 50% of Grunenthal's profits.[7] It was marketed around the world under over 50 different names, a factor which significantly impeded an immediate halt being put to sales.[8] It was introduced into Britain by the food and drinks conglomerate Distillers in 1961. It was advertised as a completely safe, non-toxic sedative with no side-effects whatsoever, a revolutionary claim for a sedative, and as being completely safe for pregnant women and nursing mothers. However, the conduct of early clinical trials had been highly unsatisfactory, and Grunenthal (and Distillers) ignored early reports from doctors and sales representatives of severe side-effects. Indeed Grunenthal went so far as to delay publication of adverse reports in medical journals and harassed clinicians who produced unfavourable reports on the effects of the drug.[9] These effects included severe foetal abnormalities, with foetuses being born with severe internal and external deformities. The final total of thalidomide children was 10,000 worldwide, with another 40% being stillborn or dying at or shortly after birth.[10]

The Thalidomide tragedy focused attention on the absence of legal safeguards for drugs in nearly all countries, except perhaps the United

---

[6] A fuller history of the development of medicines regulation can be found in the earlier editions of this book.

[7] J Crawford *Kill or Cure? The Role of the Pharmaceutical Industry in Society* (Arc Print, 1988) p 37.

[8] The drug was still on sale in Italy ten months after it was withdrawn from the UK; and doctors continued to prescribe it in Sweden after adverse reports in Germany, for an intesive study of the literature failed to identify the different brand names in the two countries was Thalidomide. J Braithwaite *Corporate Crime in the Pharmaceutical Industry* (Routledge, 1986) p 66; H Sjostrom and R Nilsson *Thalidomide and the Power of the Drug Companies* (Penguin, 1972) p 132.

[9] J Braithwaite *Corporate Crime in the Pharmaceutical Industry* (Routledge, 1986) pp 67–75, J Crawford *Kill or Cure? The Role of the Pharmaceutical Industry in Society* (Arc Print, 1988) pp 35–43. See also Chapter 5 above.

[10] J Crawford *Kill or Cure? The Role of the Pharmaceutical Industry in Society* (Arc Print, 1988) p 43.

States where it was not authorised.[11] The disaster showed all too tragically that new drugs were marketed without any official inquiry into their safety, their unrevealed dangerous properties or their harmful side-effects. Consumers relied entirely on the reputations of the drug manufacturers and of their prescribing doctors. As was said in the House of Commons at the time: 'The House and the public suddenly woke up to the fact that any drug manufacturer could market any product, however inadequately tested, however dangerous, without having to satisfy any independent body as to its efficiency or its safety.'[12]

The Thalidomide disaster had a number of affects on aspects of the legal regimes affecting consumer protection. The reforms to product liability law which ensued are discussed in Chapter 5. But perhaps more marked was the focus on the need for testing and licensing of medicinal products, as already occurred in the United States. A government-appointed committee in Britain (the Cohen Committee) accepted that the pharmaceutical industry as a whole discharged its responsibilities under the Food and Drugs Act 1955 of ensuring that drugs were safe, but concluded that no matter how meticulous the preparatory work, ultimately there was no substitute for the prolonged experience of the use of a drug in practice. The Committee felt that public and professional opinion demanded formal machinery, independent of drug manufacturers, to assess the safety of drugs.[13] An independent body should be satisfied that before a drug was submitted for clinical trial it had been subject to suitable tests on animals. On the basis of these clinical trials it should then decide whether a drug could be safely released for general use. Safety testing would remain the responsibility of individual pharmaceutical manufacturers with the independent authority simply evaluating its results.

Following the Committee's report and pending legislation, Britain introduced a voluntary approval scheme administered by the Committee on the Safety of Drugs, which operated between 1963 and 1971.[14] The pharmaceutical industry agreed to submit details of new drugs to the scrutiny of the Committee before they were released for clinical trials or placed on the market. Under its terms of reference the Committee also established a register to record any adverse reactions to drugs already in

[11] The scientist at the Federal Drugs Agency who resisted its approval, Dr Frances Kelsey, was honoured by President Kennedy for saving the nation from disaster: J Braithwaite *Corporate Crime in the Pharmaceutical Industry* (Routledge, 1986) p 71. The drug was also not authorised in France and Israel.

[12] Parl Deb HC, vol 677, 8 May 1963, 448.

[13] Ministry of Health *Safety of Drugs, Final Report of Joint Sun-Committee of the Medical Advisory Committeee* (HMSO, 1963).

[14] See further J Abraham *Science, Politics and the Pharmaceutical Industry: Controversy and Bias in Drug Regulation* (UCL Press, 1995) pp 66–74.

use. Not all products were submitted, however, and the only sanction available to the Committee was to recommend to the government that it publicly advise doctors, hospitals and pharmacists against using a product.

The Medicines Act 1968 put the licensing of medicines on a statutory footing. It firmly rejected the premise 'that drugs are ordinary commodities whose sale can take place anywhere and be left to the ordinary commercial pressures of the market'.[15] Reliance on broad criminal provisions has been greatly curtailed, although it remains an offence to supply a drug which is either harmful or not of the nature, substance or quality the ordinary consumer would expect.[16] Retention of this provision means checks will continue to be made by sampling to ensure that drugs actually conform to recognised standards of purity and potency. The general framework for controlling safety, efficacy and quality, however, is a system of statutory licensing, administered by an independent expert body, the Committee on the Safety of Medicines.

Although the voluntary system was supplanted, the hope of the government was that licensing would not operate in a rigid manner and that legal proceedings would be exceptional. There has in fact been an increasing incidence of litigation over the MCA's decisions.[17] The justification for singling out drugs for licensing was that special care was needed with the revolutionary changes in modern drugs because of the possibility, made real in the Thalidomide tragedy, that they could have dangerous properties or dangerous side-effects.[18] In addition, the White Paper argued that consumers could not assess the risks and benefits of drugs, and that private markets had clearly failed to protect them. This market failure had been reflected in inadequate testing, inadequate quality control, and deficiencies in information, including misleading claims. Further, the risks associated with a drug could arise at any stage in its life cycle, so licensing must be comprehensive. Thus licences are necessary for clinical trials, marketing, manufacturing, and the importation and wholesaling of drugs.[19] The government has regulatory power to bring within the scope of the Act substances marketed for non-medicinal purposes, which can be put to medicinal use, such as certain toilet articles,

---

[15] Forthcoming Legislation on the Safety, Quality and Description of Drugs and Medicines 1966–7, Cmnd 3395, lviii, 505, p 9.

[16] Medicines Act 1968, ss 104, 129.

[17] See for example Re Smith Kline & French Laboratories Ltd [1990] 1 AC 64; R v Licensing Authority, ex p Monsanto plc [1997] Eu LR 42.

[18] Parl Deb, HC, vol 758, 15 February 1968, 1602. See also Parl Deb, HC Standing Committee D. Medicines Bill 1968, Session 1967–8, vol 5.

[19] Forthcoming Legislation on the Safety, Quality and Description of Drugs and Medicines (Cmnd 3395 (1967)).

cosmetics and household disinfectants.[20] In the United States, for example, cosmetics are closely regulated.

The Medicines Commission was established in accordance with s 2 of the Medicines Act 1968 with the general duty to advise the government on matters relating to the execution of the legislation or otherwise relating to drugs. In particular the Commission supervises the other committees which administer the details of the legislation, advises the government regarding licensing where there is an appeal against the advice of the Committee on the Safety of Medicines, considers representations against an order prohibiting the sale of a drug and supervises the body which draws up the British Pharmacopoeia, responsibility for the preparation of which has now been assumed by the government.[1] The Committee on the Safety of Medicines administers the licensing provisions of the Act, as well as promoting the collection and investigation of information relating to adverse reactions to drugs in use.

The licensing scheme of the Medicines Act 1968 operates at three different levels. Firstly, manufacturers, assemblers or wholesalers of drugs must obtain a licence by demonstrating that their facilities are suitable.[2] For instance, a manufacturer has to show that it has the capacity, staff and equipment (including the arrangements as to quality control) to carry out the drug manufacturing operations specified in its licence.[3] Secondly, to guarantee that appropriate toxicity testing has taken place on animals, a new drug cannot be clinically tested on humans unless a certificate has been obtained from the Committee on the Safety of Medicines.[4] Thirdly, a manufacturer must obtain a product licence before marketing any particular drug.[5] To issue a product licence the Committee must be satisfied that there are no considerations affecting the safety, efficacy and quality of a drug which would justify withholding it from sale in the light of current medical or scientific knowledge and that the proposed methods securing its specified quality are adequate.[6] Manufacturing and product licences are normally issued for five years but they may be renewed.[7] When the licensing of drugs began, product licences of right were granted automatically for some 36,000 drugs shown to be already on the market, but in 1974 the Medicines Commission began a review of these products

---

[20]   Medicines Act 1968, s 64.
[1]   See generally Sir Derrick Dunlop 'The Work of the Medicines Commission' (1971) 91 Royal Soc Of Health J 141.
[2]   Medicines Act 1968, s 8.
[3]   Medicines Act 1968, s 19(5)–(6).
[4]   Medicines Act 1968, s 31.
[5]   Medicines Act 1968, s 7.
[6]   Medicines Act 1968, s 19(1).
[7]   Medicines Act 1968, s 24.

to ensure that they reached the standards of safety, efficacy and quality required for new drugs.[8]

An important element of the regulation introduced under the Medicines Act was that it demanded proof of the efficacy of drugs. The voluntary system which preceded it had ignored the efficacy of drugs unless it related to safety. Inefficacious drugs were only prohibited where they might have been prescribed for a serious illness for which there was already a satisfactory treatment, where they carried the slightest risk to the patient in the treatment of diseases for which they might have been recommended, or where they did not live up to the claims made for them. As a result of this approach a number of relatively worthless though innocuous drugs were cleared for the market. When in 1970 the Food and Drugs Administration in the United States issued a list of drugs which it classified as dangerous or ineffective, the Committee conceded that about 90 were available in Britain but said that the dangerous drugs in the list were available on prescription only and their hazards well-known to the medical and pharmaceutical professions.[9] An indication of the total number of ineffective drugs on the market in the mid-1960s emerged when two groups of experts set up by the Sainsbury Committee concluded that just over a third of 2,657 proprietary drugs then available on the National Health Service were undesirable because they were ineffective, obsolete or in unsuitable combinations.[10] Similarly, a review of drugs for effectiveness in the United States after the 1962 Kefauver-Harris Act carried out by the National Academy of Sciences led to the withdrawal of some 1,300 out of the 4,000 drugs examined.[11]

The Medicines Act 1968 directs the Committee on the Safety of Medicines, in considering an application for a product licence, to leave out of account whether other drugs are more efficacious unless they may also be as safe or safer.[12] In implementing the statutory mandate, the Committee initially adopted the criteria of its predecessor. In 1972 the Committee changed its policy and with respect to products which are of doubtful efficacy, although harmless, it will not now grant a product licence unless some positive evidence of efficacy is forthcoming.[13] This policy can be justified in terms of the statutory language on the basis that an inefficacious drug, although harmless in one sense, may still have adverse results. For example, it may fail to cure a disease, albeit minor, for which a

---

[8]   *Medicines Commission, Annual Report* 1974 HC Paper 442, 1975, p 11.
[9]   *Committee on Safety of Medicines* First Report, 1971 (HMSO, 1972) p 8.
[10]   *Report of the Committee of Enquiry into the Relationship of the Pharmaceutical Industry with the National Health Service* (Cmnd 3410 (1965–7)) pp 208–209.
[11]   FDA at Law, Nature, 19 January 1973, p 159.
[12]   Section 19(2).
[13]   *Committee on the Safety of Medicines, Second Report, 1972* (HMSO, 1973) p 6.

remedy is available, or it may relieve a symptom, the natural danger-signal, without affecting the disease which causes it. The change in policy by the Committee brought the practice into line with the law in the United States, where the 1962 Kefauver-Harris amendments to the Food, Drugs and Cosmetic Act added proof of efficacy to proof of safety as a prerequisite for drug marketing.[14] Critics have said that not only should safety and efficacy be taken into account, but that consideration should also be given to whether a drug is a therapeutic advance. The concern is with drugs which are simply variations of those already on the market, but which are developed to avoid patent restrictions or to improve the sales position of a manufacturer who can promote them with suggestions that they are newly formulated, so called 'me-too' drugs.

Decisions about licences are made by the Committee on the Safety of Medicines on the basis of information submitted by the drug companies. The Committee neither conducts research nor specifies designs for either toxicity or clinical trials. Regulations simply require that an application for a product licence set out, inter alia, the name of the drug, its constituents and their chemical formulae, certain details about the method of manufacture and the way the drug is to be used, and any experimental and biological results which 'in the view of the proposed licensee' are relevant to the assessment of the production.[15] It seems unlikely that the Committee will adopt a more activist stance. It has been suggested that the government actually regulate the way clinical trials are conducted to eliminate unethical practices. Another reform suggested is that information submitted by the drug companies in their licence applications should be available to the public for critical evaluation, subject to a protection for trade secrets.[16]

It seems accepted that complete safety in drugs cannot be guaranteed before they have been used on a widespread basis for a substantial period. Neither may it always be desirable that drugs be absolutely safe; for example, a considerable degree of toxicity might be tolerated in a drug which stayed the progress of cancer, although not in one used for the treatment of trivial conditions. To monitor the safety of drugs after they have received a product licence and are on the market the Committee on the Safety of Medicines issues standard cards on which doctors can report adverse reactions. Additional to this voluntary scheme is the

[14]   76 Stat 780, 21 USC s 355(b) (1964).
[15]   Medicines (Applications for Product Licences etc) Regulations, 1971, SI 1971/1973. See also DHSS *Guide to Good Pharmaceutical Manufacturing Practice* (HMSO, 1971) p 4.
[16]   'Human Experimentation and Medical Ethics' Nature, vol 242, 16 March 1973, p 152; *Consumer Council: Fifth Annual Report* 1967–8, p 4 and more recently NCC *Secrecy and Medicines in Europe* (1994).

statutory obligation on drug companies to keep records of adverse reports they learn about, to include warnings in advertisements if directed and to institute suitable procedures in case a drug must be recalled from the market.[17] When the evidence warrants it, the Committee communicates information on adverse reactions to the profession at large, for example, warning them about the prescription or dispensing of particular drugs in certain circumstances.[18]

The Medicines Act 1968 actually empowers the Committee to suspend, revoke or vary a licence, inter alia, where a drug fails to a material extent to correspond to its characteristics as licensed, where it can no longer be safely administered for the purposes indicated in the licence or where the specification to which it is administered can no longer be regarded as satisfactory.[19] In practice the Committee has usually been able to convince manufacturers to withdraw drugs where serious adverse reactions have been reported without legal moves being necessary. A particular problem has been to induce the medical profession to report adverse reactions. Following publicity of the matter the number of reports has increased but there remains concern that many adverse reactions may be unreported.[1] One reason is that an individual doctor may not realise the connection between a symptom and the use of a particular drug.

(b)   Licensing: the European regime

European legislation aimed at harmonising regulation of the licensing of medicines was first introduced in 1965,[2] and various, largely unsuccessful,

---

[17] Medicines (Standard Provisions for Licences and Certficates) Regulations 1971, SI 1971/972 as amended.

[18] For example *Committee on the Safety of Medicines, Second Report, 1972* (HMSO, 1973) p 6.

[19] Section 28.

[1] The number of reports has increased steadily from an average of just under 4,000 per year in 1971–1975 (for details see earlier editions of this book) to an average of 17,550 per year in 1995/4–1998/9: figures compiled from MCA Annual Report 1998/9, 21. The MCA has recently begun to implement focused schemes to stimulating reporting in areas where it has been poor (eg in relation to children and AIDs) and is to extend the yellow card scheme to community pharmacists in 2000: MCA Annual Report 1998/9.

[2] Council Directive 65/65/EEC of 26 January 1965 on the approximation of provisions laid down by Law, Regulation or Administrative Action relating to proprietary medicinal products introduced a requirement that no medicinal product could be marketed in a Member State unless it had been authorised, that authorisation process to accord to the minimum requirements set out in the Directive.

attempts had been made to facilitate an internal market in pharmaceuticals through the establishment of mutual recognition procedures. In 1975 the European Commission established a committee of representatives of national authorisation authorities, the Committee for Proprietary Medicinal Products (CPMP), and set up a mutual recognition procedure for medicines approval.[3] Applicants who had obtained authorisation to market a drug in one Member State could apply for extension of that authorisation to the authorities of five or more other Member States via the CPMP.[4] The CPMP had no decision-making powers, however; it would give its opinion on whether authorisation should be granted under European provisions,[5] but the decision was left to Member States.[6]

The procedure was not extensively used, and between 1976 and 1985 only 41 applications were submitted.[7] The Commission therefore introduced an amended procedure in 1983. The minimum number of states that could be approached for authorisation was reduced to two, and companies were given access to CPMP hearings to present their application.[8] The procedure was more successful: between January 1991 and December 1992, for example, 119 applications were submitted to the CPMP.[9] The CPMP still lacked any decision-making powers, however, and decisions on authorisation continued to be made at the national level.

This position has changed significantly with the establishment in 1995 of the European Medicines Evaluation Agency (EMEA), based in London.[10] For the first time, there is now a European agency responsible for licensing of medicines for marketing throughout Europe, and in addition

---

[3]   Second Council Directive 75/319/EEC of 20 May 1975 on the approximation of provisions laid down by Law, Regulation or Administrative Action relating to proprietary medicinal products, Chapter III.

[4]   Directive 75/319, Article 9(1).

[5]   Directive 65/65/EEC.

[6]   Directive 75/319, Article 11(3), Article 12(4).

[7]   E Mossialos and B Abel-Smith 'The Regulation of the European Pharmaceutical Industry' in S Stavridis, R Morgan, E Mossialos and H Macrum (eds) *New Challenges to the EU: Policies and Policy Making at the End of the Century* (Dartmouth, 1996) p 364.

[8]   Council Directive 83/570 of 1983 amending Directives 65/65/EEC, 75/318/EEC and 75/319/EEC on the approximation of provisions laid down by law, regulation or administrative action relating to proprietary medicinal products.

[9]   Commission of the European Communities, *Report on the Operation of the Committee for Proprietary Medicinal Products in 1991 and 1992* (Brussels, 12 May, 1993).

[10]   Council Regulation (EEC) No 2309/93 of 22 July 1993 laying down Community procedures for the authorisation and supervision of medicinal products for human and veterinary use and establishing a European Agency for the Evaluation of Medicinal Products. The EMEA is established under Article 49 of the Regulation.

new mutual recognition procedures have been established.[11] The task of the Agency is to co-ordinate scientific evaluation of the quality, safety and efficacy of medicinal products, transmit assessment reports and details of products, and co-ordinate the supervision of medicines authorised in the EU, in particular by establishing a database of adverse reactions to the product.[12] The EMEA is comprised essentially of the CPMP and its counterpart for veterinary medicines, the Committee for Veterinary Medical Products (CVMP), supported by a central secretariat and headed by a single management board.[13] The Committees are each composed of one expert from each Member State appointed on renewable three-year fixed terms,[14] and liaise closely with experts in the different Member States. It is funded largely through fees payable by those seeking authorisations, and its budget for 1999 is ECU 41.35 million (approximately £69 million).[15]

Since 1995 there are now two routes for authorisation for medicinal products marketed within the EU: the centralised procedure, and the decentralised or mutual recognition procedure. The centralised procedure is compulsory for all medicinal and veterinary products derived from biotechnology and optional for other innovative medical products. Under the centralised procedure applications are made directly to the EMEA and may lead to the granting of a European marketing authorisation. Authorisation is valid for five years and is renewable for further five-year periods.[16] Authorisation will be refused if it appears that the quality, safety or efficacy of the product has not been adequately or sufficiently demonstrated by the applicant.[17] It will also be refused if the particulars and documents provided are incorrect or if the labelling or package leaflets proposed are not in accordance with EU labelling requirements.[18]

The work of the EMEA in authorising human medicines is carried out by the CPMP. The Committee considers all applications made to the EMEA, and can require supplementary information, including oral or written explanations.[19] It can also require that the product to be independently

---

[11]   Council Directive 93/39/EEC of 14 June 1993 amending Directives 65/65/EEC, 75/318/EEC and 75/319/EEC in respect of medicinal products.
[12]   Regulation 2903/93, Article 51.
[13]   Regulation 2093/93, Article 50.
[14]   Regulation 2903/93, Article 52.
[15]   EMEA, Fourth General Report (EMEA 1998); Council Regulation (EC) No 2743/98 of 14 December 1998 amending the Regulation (EC) No 297/95 on fees payable to the European Agency for the Evaluation of Medicinal Products.
[16]   Regulation 2903/93, Article 13; Directive 93/39/EEC, Article 2.
[17]   Regulation 2093/93, Article 11.
[18]   Regulation 2903/93 Article 11; the labelling requirements are set out in Council Directive 92/27/EEC of 31 March 1992 on the labelling of medicinal products for human use and on package leaflets.
[19]   Regulation 2309/93, Article 6.

tested in a designated laboratory, and/or that manufacturing sites be inspected by appropriately qualified inspectors from a Member State, accompanied if necessary by a rapporteur or expert appointed by the Committee.[20] Where the CPMP considers that authorisation should not be granted, the applicant is informed and has a right to appeal. The Committee is then required to consider whether it should revise its opinion.[1] Once it has reached a final opinion, whether in favour of authorisation or not, that opinion is forwarded to the Commission, the Member States and the applicant together with an assessment report, a statement of reasons for the Committee's conclusions and, if the opinion is favourable, a summary of the product's characteristics and draft labelling and package information. The Committee may also impose conditions or restrictions on the supply or use of the product, and whether it should be available by prescription only or over the counter.[2]

The Commission then prepares a draft decision which is forwarded to the Member States and the applicant. Member States can forward written observations to the Commission and can require that it is discussed by the Standing Committee. The Commission may remit the decision to the EMEA if it considers that the Member State has raised 'important new questions of a scientific or technical nature' which have not been addressed in the opinion of the Agency.[3] If there are no objections, the Commission consults the Standing Commitee on Medical Products for Human Use. If there is a qualified majority in favour, the licence is granted and the decision published in the Official Journal. If there is no qualified majority in favour, then the decision goes to the Council of Ministers who may approve it by a qualified majority. If they do not, the final decision rests with the Commission unless it has been rejected by the Council by a simple majority.[4]

Since its establishment in 1995, the EMEA has received 177 applications, two-thirds of which have been optional applications for innovative products, and the remaining one-third compulsory applications for biotechnological products. In 1998, authorisation was refused in three cases, and between 1995 and 1998, in 30 cases the application has been withdrawn prior to an opinion being given.[5] The EMEA notes that most of these withdrawals were linked to specific clinical problems that may have

---

[20]   Regulation 2309/93, Articles 6 and 8.
[1]   Regulation 2309/93, Article 9(1).
[2]   Regulation 2309/93, Article 9(2)–(3).
[3]   Regulation 2309/93, Article 10.
[4]   Regulation 2903/93, Article 73.
[5]   EMEA, *First General Report* (1995); *Second General Report* (1996); *Third General Report* (1997) *Fourth General Report* (1998). The level of authorisations refused in previous years is not available.

led to authorisation being refused.[6] On average, it takes 180 days for an application to be assessed by the CPMP, and a further 35–50 days for it to go through the remaining procedures.[7] This compares with 40 days for the MCA.[8] The CPMP has also been increasingly involved in giving scientific advice to potential applicants at the developmental stage of the drug prior to an application being made. The CPMP has created a network of experts and involved its own working parties on biotechnology, efficacy, safety and quality more closely in the advice process. In 1998, for example, it had 70 such pre-submission meetings. It has also developed pre-submission guidance for the centralised procedure,[9] and for those seeking advice provides a list of specific issues relating to different requests that the applicant should address before an oral presentation to the CPMP consultation group.[10]

After authorisation, there is a requirement that the person who places the product on the market must amend methods and controls of manufacture in accordance with scientific progress and apply for approval of amendments following the same procedures as for authorisation. It must notify the Member States, the EMEA and the Commission of new information which might entail amendment of the relevant particulars and documents, or which would influence the evaluation of risks or benefits of product, and of any prohibition or restriction imposed by the authorities of any country (in or outside the EU) in which the product is marketed.[11] In the case of any amendments to the product characteristics, the person must apply for a variation to the authorisation, except where that variation is minor.[12] If the authorisation has been granted under the centralised procedure, application must be made to the EMEA. Between 1995 and 1998 a total of 424 applications for variation have been made.

Although authorisations granted under the centralised procedure are awarded by the Community institutions, there is no central European enforcement agency. Instead, reliance is placed on the competent authorities of the Member States to ensure those who have been granted a European wide licence comply with the regulations. In the UK, this responsibility falls to the MCA. The decision whether or not to sanction any breach,

---

6   *Fourth General Report* (EMEA, 1998) p 23.
7   Figures taken from *Fourth General Report* (EMEA, 1998) p 20.
8   *Medicines Control Agency Annual Report and Accounts 1998/9* (HMSO, 1998) pp 13–14.
9   EMEA/H/38179/1998.
10   *Fourth General Report* (EMEA, 1998) pp 25–26.
11   Regulation 2309/93, Article 15.
12   Regulation (EC) No 542/95 concerning the examination of variations to the terms of a marketing authorisation falling within the scope of Council Regulation (EEC) No 2309/93, as amended by Regulation EC No 1069/98 of 26 May 1998.

however, lies with the EU institutions. So if supervisory authorities in a Member State consider that manufacturer or importer is no longer fulfilling its obligations then it has to inform the CPMP and the Commission, indicating the course of action proposed. The Commission and the EMEA/CPMP examine this proposal and reasons, and where practicable invite the person to make oral or written representations. The Committee produces an opinion which it sends to the Commission, which in turn produces a draft decision. That decision is then adopted under the procedures for authorisation.[13] This can take some time. So where urgent action is essential to protect human or animal health or the environment, the Member State may suspend the use in the territory of an authorised product. It must then inform the Commission and other Member States no later than following working day of its reasons for action, and the above procedures are then set in motion. The product may remain suspended until a final decision has been reached.[14]

There is also a system of pharmacovigilance in place which provides that the EMEA is to receive all relevant information about adverse reactions to medicinal products it has authorised from person who placed them on the market.[15] The person who places the drug on the market has to have a nominated person responsible for pharmacovigilance and systems to ensure that all instances of adverse reactions are collected, evaluated and collated at a single point within the company in the EU, and reported to Member States the EMEA within 15 days.[16] The CPMP may formulate opinions on the measures necesary to ensure their safe and effective use. In 1998 the EMEA received a total of 8,933 reports of suspected serious adverse drug reactions occurring for centrally authorised products, of which 4,417 reports were received from outside the EU.[17]

The second procedure is the decentralised or mutual recognition procedure, which was amended further in 1995. This is applicable to the majority of conventional medical products and since 1998 all those who wish to market their products in more than one Member State must use the procedure. Applicants apply to the licensing authorities of one Member State, and the procedure operates by mutual recognition of national marketing authorisations. Applicants may either apply to a licensing authority in one Member State or make a parallel application to more than one Member State, in which case other Member States may wait for the application in the first to be processed before considering it. The Member

---

[13]   Regulation 2309/93, Article 18(1)–(3).
[14]   Regulation 2903/93, Article 18(4)–(5).
[15]   Regulation 2903/03, Articles 18–23.
[16]   Regulation 2093/93, Articles 22 and 23.
[17]   *Fourth General Report* (EMEA, 1998) p 29.

State's licensing authority prepares an assessment report and has to reach a decision within 210 days. The application and assessment report are then sent to other Member States for recognition within 90 days. If a Member State objects to authorisation, then the EMEA (acting through the Mutual Recognition Facilitation Group) is called upon to arbitrate. If that opinion is unfavourable to the applicant, there is a right of appeal and the CPMP considers whether it should revise its opinion. In either case, the CPMP's opinion then sent with an assessment report and summary of product characteristics to the Commission who prepares a draft decision. The procedure is then as for the centralised procedure, described above.

The mutual recognition procedure got off to a shaky start, but the number of applications has been increasing. In 1998 180 applications were submitted and completed, with only one going to arbitration; this compares with 10 in 1995, 84 in 1996 and 147 in 1997.[18] Attempts have been made to streamline the procedure, for example by adopting an automatic validation procedure from May 1998. There is also concern to improve the visibility of the process through the publication of increased statistical information and feedback in the press and on the internet, and a summary of products that have been through the procedure. Use of the procedure remains low, however; in 1998 the procedure attracted only just over 10% of the applications made to the UK alone (1,700).[19]

(c)   Restrictions on sales and promotions

The Medicines Act 1968 marked a change in the status of drugs in relation to retail sales, for until then they could be sold from any shop unless specifically restricted as poisons, narcotics or therapeutic substances. Drugs are now divided into three categories for the purposes of retail supply: prescription only medicines (POMs), which are only available on prescription by a doctor or dentist; medicines available to a consumer without prescription but only at a pharmacy (P); and general sale list, available to consumers generally, eg at a supermarket. As drugs are authorised, they are classified into one of the three groups by the Post-Licensing division of the MCA, on advice from the Committee on the Safety of Medicines. The classification is made taking into account the product's possible use, any side-effects that it may have, and the risk of its misuse.

Advertising for drugs occurs at two levels: the ordinary consumer is the target of advertising for P medicines and general sale list drugs, but

[18]   *Fourth General Report* (EMEA, 1998) pp 37–39.
[19]   MCA Annual Report and Accounts 1988/89.

POMs and certain P medicines for serious diseases (eg tuberculosis, diabetes, chronic insomnia) may only be promoted to medical practitioners. Because of the particular structure of the pharmaceutical industry, especially in the area of POMs, those who are demanding the drug are not paying for it. Competition is thus based primarily on product differentiation rather than price[20] (although this may change with the introduction of the National Centre for Clinical Excellence (NICE), discussed below). As noted above, whilst the MCA has to assess the comparative safety of drugs, it does not have the power to assess the comparative efficacy of drugs, nor does it have the power to require that the drug should represent a therapeutic advance. Drugs can therefore be licensed which have very similar therapeutic value, so-called 'me too' drugs. Given the high costs of developing new drugs, most of the drugs licensed are in fact 'me too' drugs, and many of these are directed to the alleviation of common but minor problems, as this is the biggest market: of the 1,655 licence applications considered by the MCA in 1997 only 45 contained new active substances, and that was the highest number ever.[1]

Competition in the pharmaceutical industry is based on product rather than price, although price competition can be important in the case of 'me too' drugs which provide therapeutic alternatives. Advertising and marketing are nonetheless key tools in enabling companies to increase their market share. In particular, as the patent protection on a drug (and thus the monopoly on production that it gives the patent holder) nears the ends of its term the role of marketing increases in significance, as the pharmaceutical company wants to preserve its position through its brand name when other competing products enter the market.[2] Under the price regulation scheme agreed between the government and the pharmaceutical industry, the amount that pharmaceutical companies can spend on promotional activities (principally medical sales representatives, medical press advertising and literature) is limited to 9% of sales income (which still allows for expenditure of £1bn). This compares with a ceiling of 20% of sales income for research and development (£2.5bn spent in 1998).[3]

There has been long-standing concern at the practices used by pharmaceutical companies to promote their products. These concerns relate both to advertising to the general public, and the practices used by companies to promote their products to medical practitioners. The potential

[20]   See L Hancher *Regulating for Competition: Government, Law and the Pharmaceutical Industry in the United Kingdom and France* (Clarendon Press, 1990) Chapter 2.
[1]   MCA Annual Report and Accounts 1997/98.
[2]   B Abel-Smith and E Mossialos 'The Pharmaceutical Industry' in R Baldwin et al *Regulation in Question: The Growing Agenda* (LSE, 1995) p 89.
[3]   ABPI, Pharmaceutical Fact Sheet, 1998.

scope for making false and misleading claims in promoting a drug is significant, and the consequences could range from the serious or fatal through to the consumer simply wasting their money on a product that was in fact ineffective for them. Alternatively, doctors could be induced to prescribe medicines to patients not because they were the best treatment for the patient, but because the doctor would receive considerable inducements or kickbacks from the producer. Successive studies done in Britain in the late 1960s and early 1970s found that the majority of advertisements made unwarranted claims, and that it was common for adverse effects to be omitted or glossed over.[4] This led to a tightening of the relevant regulations, but in the early 1980s the Opren scandal drew further attention to the need to control marketing.[5] Opren was claimed as a major breakthrough in the treatment of arthritis, claiming to prevent the spread of the disease, not simply to relieve pain. Although it was a POM, and thus could not be advertised to the general public, internal documents of the US company that developed the drug, Eli Lilly, stated that the company had initiated a public relations programme aimed at the general public as well as at medical practitioners, and articles about a new 'wonder drug' appeared in the press.[6] One of the major selling points of Opren was that it had few side-effects, which was simply untrue. It could result in phototoxicity, an acute and painful reaction to sunlight, loosening of fingernails, and liver, bowel and skin disorders. Most seriously, it was discovered that it could be lethal to the elderly. These side-effects were suppressed by Eli Lilly, who reported their incidence to be far lower than was in fact the case. Its data sheet (product summary) also played down the side-effects, stating for example that the reactions to phototoxicity were 'generally mild'.[7] Moreover, subsequent investigations found that the drug had absolutely no effect in stopping the disease.[8] The drug's authorisation was suspended in the UK in 1982 after 62 deaths had been attributed to it; and the company was found guilty in the US of breaching the Federal Drugs Agency's rules and fined $25,000.

---

4   *Sainsbury Report* (Cmnd 3410 (1967)) p 66; *Which?* report 1974.
5   For discussion, see J Crawford *Kill or Cure? The Role of the Pharmaceutical Industry in Society* (Arc Print, 1988) pp 45–47; J Abraham *Science, Politics and the Pharmaceutical Industry: Controversy and Bias in Drug Regulation* (UCL Press, 1995) Chapter 4.
6   J Crawford *Kill or Cure? The Role of the Pharmaceutical Industry in Society* (Arc Print, 1988) pp 45–46.
7   J Crawford *Kill or Cure? The Role of the Pharmaceutical Industry in Society* (Arc Print, 1988) p 46.
8   J Crawford *Kill or Cure? The Role of the Pharmaceutical Industry in Society* (Arc Print, 1988) p 45.

In 1994 the regulation of advertising and promotion was considerably enhanced. The policy is currently implemented through statutory provisions,[9] enforced by the MCA, and self-regulatory codes administered by the Association of British Pharmaceutical Industry and the Advertising Standards Authority. In addition, the Office of Fair Trading recently participated in an international 'sweep' of the Internet led by the Australian Competition and Consumer Commission for potentially misleading health claims and medical cures.[10] The Medicines Act 1968 prohibits false and misleading advertisements, and provides wide regulatory powers to control the form and content of drug advertisements in the interests of securing adequate information, preventing misleading claims and promoting safety.[11] In particular, advertisements directed to consumers must not indicate that the effects of taking the medicine are guaranteed or unaccompanied by side-effects, that the product is equivalent to or better than any other, that a person's health could be enhanced by taking it or harmed by not taking it (with the exception of vaccinations), refer to recommendations by scientists, health professionals or celebrities, or suggest that its safety or efficacy is due to the fact that it is natural.[12] However, a report by the National Consumer's Council in 1993 expressed concern that the function of ensuring compliance with the regulations had not been pursued with sufficient diligence, and recommended that the staffing capacity of the MCA be enhanced to ensure that it could adequately monitor and vet advertising by pharmaceutical companies.[13]

Advertising to medical practitioners is not as constrained,[14] but the regulations do require the advertisement to accord with the product summary and cover the practices that pharmaceutical companies use to encourage medical practitioners to prescribe their drugs rather than another

---

[9]   The Medicines (Advertising) Regulations 1994, SI 1994/1932 and the Medicines (Monitoring of Advertising) Regulations 1994, SI 1994/1933 (as amended), implementing Council Directive 92/28/EEC of 31 March 1992 on the advertising of medicinal products for human use. Further the Food Labelling Regulations 1994, SI 1994/1305 make it an offence for a medicinal claim to be made in respect of a product unless a product licence under the Medicines Act 1968 has been issued.

[10]   OFT Press Release 38/98.

[11]   Medicines Act 1968, ss 93, 95.

[12]   SI 1994/1932, Part III; Directive 92/27, Article 5.

[13]   *Balancing Acts: Conflicts of Interest in the Regulation of Medicine* (NCC, 1993) pp 8, 57. The Department of Health now has power to require companies to furnish it with samples of actual or proposed advertisements and to prevent publication and require corrective statements to be published: the Medicines (Advertising and Monitoring of Advertising Amendment) Regulations 1999, SI 1999/267, reg 13.

[14]   Further, the ASA Code does not apply to health related claims and promotions addressed only to the medical professions: ASA Code para 1.2.

similar one.[15] Drugs are promoted to medical practitioners in three main ways: through advertising in medical journals, direct mailing of product literature, and through the sales representatives of pharmaceutical companies (called 'medical representatives' by the industry). The industry as a whole employs over 6,000 representatives who visit more than 30,000 GPs, 30,000 hospital doctors and several thousand more pharmacists.[16] Because, as noted above, many drugs perform the same or similar functions ('me-too' drugs), practitioners have to be persuaded to prescribe one company's product over another. A study done in the US by the Kennedy Sub-Committee on Health in 1974 revealed that during 1973 20 pharmaceutical companies gave 12.8 million gifts to members of the health-care professions and over two billion samples of free drugs.[17] Regulations are now in place to limit the inducements and hospitality that can be given by salesmen to doctors to induce them to prescribe medicines.[18] The statutory scheme of regulation is echoed in the APBI's Code of Practice for the Pharmaceutical Industry, drawn up in consultation with the British Medical Association, the Royal Pharmaceutical Society and the MCA. The ABPI's code of practice provides that no gift, benefit in kind or money may be given as an inducement to prescribe, supply, administer or buy any medicine, although relevant inexpensive promotional items may be provided, and there are restrictions on the provision of hospitality.[19] In addition, representatives (who are usually science graduates or nurses) have to be given adequate training, and since 1994 have to pass examinations set by the ABPI within two years of starting their employment.[20]

Problems remain, however. Following a series of publicised breaches, where companies were offering mountain bikes, air miles, electrical goods, prize draws, among other things, to medical practitioners and pharmacists the MCA in 1997 wrote to pharmaceutical companies and professional bodies reminding them that it was a criminal offence to offer inducements to prescribe their medicines and for the person to accept them.[1] There remains concern however that enforcement of the restrictions on advertisements and promotions remains inadequate. As noted above, the effectiveness of the MCA in enforcement has been questioned. Criticism has also been levelled at the self-regulatory role of the ABPI and at the low

---

[15] SI 1994/1932 and SI 1994/1933 as amended.
[16] ABPI *Marketing and Medicines* (1998).
[17] Cited in J Braithwaite *Corporate Crime in the Pharmaceutical Industry* (Routledge, 1986) p 211.
[18] SI 1994/1932, Pt IV; Directive 92/28, Article 9.
[19] ABPI Code of Practice for the Pharmaceutical Industry, cl 18.
[20] The syllabus was revised and extended in 1998, and introduced in 1999; copies available from the ABPI.
[1] Department of Health, Press Release 97/128.

levels of sanctions imposed for breach of its Code.[2] In 1993 significant changes were made by the ABPI to the system for dealing with complaints and the Prescription Medicines Code of Practice Authority (PMCPA) was established. The Authority is independent of the ABPI and since 1996 has been self-financing.[3] In 1997 a formal Protocol was agreed between the Authority and the ABPI setting out the terms of their relationship.[4]

Enforcement both of the rules on advertisements for prescription medicines and on inducements is principally the preserve of the PMCPA. The PMCPA has jurisdiction over the 80 members of the ABPI and an additional 50 companies who have agreed to abide by the Code. Complaints under the Code against companies and their sales representatives are considered by the PMCPA Panel, set up in 1993. Appeals are heard by a Code of Practice Appeal Board, chaired by a legally qualified chairman. The level of complaints under the Code has increased steadily from its introduction. Complaints averaged just under ten per annum in 1973–1975,[5] but in 1998 there were 144. The main sources of complaints are normally health professionals and secondarily other pharmaceutical companies. In addition, the PMCPA scrutinises on average 1,500 advertisements a year for compliance with the code.[6]

Table 12.1 Sources of complaints to the PMCPA 1993–1997*

Source of complaints	1993	1994	1995	1996	1997
Health professionals	59	86	62	38	76
Other companies	13	41	26	48	48
PMCPA director	14	12	6	7	11
Local ethics committees	—	1	2	4	3
Organisations	3	4	5	4	2
Others	1	1	3	1	5

* Figures compiled from PMCPA Annual Reports 1993–1997

Initially the only sanction that could be imposed was to seek an undertaking from the company that the breach would cease immediately and that it would take reasonable steps to ensure it did not recur. In 1993 further sanctions were introduced, although they are rarely used. These

2   See *Balancing Acts: Conflicts of Interest in the Regulation of Medicine* (NCC, 1993).
3   PMCPA Annual Reports, 1996 and 1997.
4   ABPI Annual Report 1997.
5   See the second edition of this book, p 400.
6   Figures compiled from PMCPA Annual Reports 1993–1997.

include the reporting of the company to the APBI Board of Management, (six companies between 1993–1997)[7] which may publicly reprimand the company (once between 1993–1997), require an audit of the company (four times between 1993–1997),[8] require a corrective statement to be published, require products distributed in breach of the Code to be returned, and/or suspend or expel a company from its membership (once, in 1994).[9] In 1995 the constitution of the PMCPA was amended to give it the power to require an audit itself, although again this power is rarely used.[10] Details of cases considered are published, but only since 1996 are the companies named in all cases, not just those where a breach has been found.[11]

Table 12.2 Complaints to the PMCPA 1993–1997*

	1993	1994	1995	1996	1997
Complaints received	87	145	104	102	145
Complaints considered	79	140	95	87	136
Cases arising from complaints	87	159	112	88	165
Cases where breach found	54	80	51	65	94
Cases where no breach found	33	79	61	23	71

* Figures compiled from PMCPA Annual Reports 1993–1997

In its 1993 report the National Consumer Council recommended a tightening of sanctions for breach of the code, and cited as an example the sanctions imposed by the US FDA on the multinational Syntex for breaching US advertising regulations for the anti-arthritis drug Naproxen (naprosyn). Syntex was ordered to clear in advance all subsequent advertisements with the FDA for two years, to pay FDA costs, and to set up an account of $2 million to fund corrective information for one year in every journal that had carried the offending advertisement. The company also had to show that the new information really did correct the impression of the original advertisements.[12] In contrast, the sanction normally imposed

---

[7]   Figures compiled from PMCPA Annual Reports 1993–1997.

[8]   Three in 1994 and one in 1995; two voluntary audits were completed in 1994 and one in 1996: PMCPA Annual Reports 1993–1997.

[9]   Between 1993–1997, two companies have been suspended, both in 1994. PMCPA Annual Reports 1993–1997.

[10] It was not used at all in the years for which information is currently available, 1996 and 1997. PMCPA Annual Reports 1996 and 1997.

[11] The cases are reported in the Code of Practice Review, issued quarterly and available from the PMCPA.

[12] *Balancing Acts: Conflicts of Interest in the Regulation of Medicine* (NCC, 1993) p 8.

by the ABPI is to require the company to cease to publish the offending material and undertake not to do so again; however, as noted, it rarely requires any further action to be taken, and has no powers to fine.

A key way in which statutory control is exercised post-licensing is through regulation of the information that must be supplied to those prescribing drugs, and in particular the requirement that all companies must provide the medical practitioner with a Summary of Product Characteristics (which used to be called data sheets), compiled by the firm and approved by the MCA on authorisation. The Medicines Act 1968 provides prior to the delivery of publication of any promotional literature, or prior to a visit by a sales representative, a medical practitioner must receive a summary of the product's characteristics.[13] This must contain information relating to side-effects, precautions, relevant contra-indications and conditions of use. Again, however, doubts have been cast over the efficacy of the product summaries in giving full information about a drug, and studies in the UK show that there can be considerable variations in the product summaries prepared by different companies for substantially similar products, or those prepared by the same company for different national markets.[14]

Although relying on consumer choice alone has limitations, there has been an important move to improve the information available to consumers about the medicines that they are taking. Since 1994, draft labelling and package leaflets have to be submitted with the application for authorisation or renewal of an authorisation to market the drug, and authorisation (or renewal) can be refused if they do not comply with the regulations.[15] The packaging of the drug must be labelled with specified information in a clear and legible manner. This information includes the name of the drug, its pharmaceutical strength (if it can appear in more than one, eg baby, child, adult), a statement of the active ingredients expressed qualitatively or quantatively per dose, the pharmaceutical form and contents by weight, volume or number of doses, instructions on use of the drug, a special warning that it must be stored out of the reach of children, the expiry date, any special precautions for storage and disposal of unused products or waste materials, the name and address of the holder of the marketing authorisation, the number of the authorisation and the batch number.[16]

---

[13]   Medicines Act 1968, s 95.
[14]   L Hancher *Regulating for Competition: Government, Law and the Pharmaceutical Industry in the United Kingdom and France* (Clarendon Press, 1990) pp 274–275; C Medawar *The Wrong Kind of Medicine* (Consumers' Association, 1984).
[15]   Regulation 2093/93, Article 11; Council Directive 92/27/EEC of 31 March 1992 on the labelling of medicinal leaflets for human use and on package leaflets, Article 10.
[16]   Directive 92/27, Article 2.

Some of the information can be omitted from small packets, which need indicate only the name of the product, its strength, how it should be taken, the expiry date, the batch number and the contents by weight, volume or unit. Blister packs that are contained in fully labelled packets need only state the name of the product, the name of the holder of authorisation, the expiry date and the batch number.[17]

Further information has to be set out in a package leaflet that has to be included with the drug. That information has to be written clearly and legibly and in terms that are understandable for the patient.[18] It has to contain further information on the method, frequency and appropriate time of use (eg before or after meals), what the drug can be used to treat, possible side-effects, the nature of interaction with other substances such as alcohol, tobacco, or foodstuffs, special precautions, actions that should be taken in the event of an overdose, and has to take into account the particular condition of certain types of patient (pregnant women, children, the elderly), and mention any potential effects on the ability to drive vehicles or operate machinery.[19] Package leaflets are always included in medicines that consumers buy over the counter. However, prescribed medicines have historically often been dispensed from bulk, and the label need not show directions for use, side-effects and so on. The possibility thus arises of the drugs being accumulated around the house and consumers being unaware of the drugs they are taking. In order to improve the information available to patients, in 1994 the Department of Health in consultation with the BMA, ABPI and others introduced an iniative on patient packs. From January 1999 all medicines should be dispensed in a pack containing a patient information leaflet.

The potential for abuses in drug advertising and information provision led the Sainsbury Committee in 1967 to recommend that the Medicines Committee (the MCA's predecessor) should become the sole source of information on all matters concerning drugs,[20] a recommendation that has also been made by the World Health Organisation.[1] The MCA publishes the British Pharmacopoeia which provides a comprehensive reference source of published standards and test methods on medicinal materials, but the industry is also a key source of information on products. The ABPI is introducing an Electronic Medicines Compendium (EMC) which

---

[17] Directive 92/27, Article 3.
[18] Directive 92/27, Article 8.
[19] Directive 92/27, Article 7.
[20] *Sainsbury Report* (Cmnd 3410 (1967)) p 97.
[1]   WHO, *Drug Information* (WHO Regional Office for Europe, EUR/ICP/DSE 168, 1992), cited in *Balancing Acts: Conflicts of Interest in the Regulation of Medicine* (NCC, 1993).

will make available in electronic form the summaries of product characteristics and patient leaflets for all the drugs authorised on the market, information which it currently provides in printed form.[2] Whilst doctors could gain all the information they need on a drug from reading medical journals and other sources, pressures of time and resources mean they rarely do. Instead, successive surveys of medical practitioners, particularly GPs, show that company representatives are seen as the most important sources of information about new drugs.[3]

Decisions on which medicines should be prescribed to patients has traditionally been the preserve of the medical profession. Pharmaceutical companies had to negotiate prices with the government, but dealt principally with medical practitioners on the question of treatments. However, prompted by concerns at the ever-rising NHS bill, the government is beginning to become more actively involved in the decisions on which treatments should be given, which has upset the industry. The Department of Health is planning to introduce a computerised decision support system for GPs, PRODIGY. A GP can type in a diagnosis and be given medical advice and specific recommendations about which medicines to prescribe. The scheme has been criticised by the industry, who argue that the system favours older, cheaper medicines, gives only a limited number of choices, that the information is in some cases supported by inadequate evidence, or is misleading or open to question. Further, they argue that it is not clear how new medicines will be included speedily on the system, and how decisions about which medicines and treatments included on the system are made.[4] PRODIGY is not binding on GPs, but the Department of Health says that it will be used as a basis for auditing GPs' budgets. This leads the industry to claim that unless it is modified substantially, PRODIGY is simply a form of rationing health care in disguise, an issue to which we will return below.[5]

(d)   An evaluation of present controls

One of the central issues in the operation of the licensing regime concerns the accuracy of the information that product companies submit to the regulatory authorities, and the level of assurance that regulators require that the drug is safe and efficacious before allowing a licence to be granted.

---

2   ABPI, press release, March 26, 1998.
3   *Sainsbury Report* (Cmnd 3410 (1967)) p 132; B Abel-Smith *Value for Money in the Health Services: a Comparative Study* (Heinemann, 1976); APBI, *Medicines and Marketing* (1998) p 2.
4   *PRODIGY Computer Prescribing of Medicines* (APBI, 1999).
5   *PRODIGY Computer Prescribing of Medicines* (APBI, 1999).

But just what the 'right' level of risk should be is disputed. Successive studies have shown that individuals vary widely in the levels of risk that they deem to be acceptable, and that the views of lay persons and scientists may differ significantly.[6]

It is often said that no medicine is completely safe: adverse drug reactions (ADRs), including fatalities, are an inevitable consequence of modern drug therapy. But as one commentator has noted, 'whatever the validity of that general claim, it should not be used as an excuse for complacency about specific adverse drug reactions and investigations into how they could have been prevented'.[7] Further, this view could favour lax regulation on the grounds that as no drug is completely safe, a certain level of toxicity is to be expected. In this context there is scope for significant bias in regulatory decision-making.

In a detailed study of the approval of five different anti-inflammatory drugs for marketing in the UK and US, Abraham concluded that the regulation is indeed biased in favour of the pharmaceutical industry. This bias is revealed both in the scientific studies which are carried out prior to licensing to test the drug's safety and efficacy, and in the level of evidence that the regulators will require before approving a drug or removing it from the market.[8] Rather than evaluating the therapeutic value of new drugs 'objectively', ie in terms of their logical consistency and consonancy with the facts, Abraham argued, many industrial scientists have put forward self-contradictory arguments or made claims that were logically inconsistent with the established scientific standards of drug testing and medication at the time.[9] Further, those technical inconsistencies coincided with the commercial interests of the pharmaceutical company involved. One example is the drug Zomax, which scientists recommended for chronic use in the UK but cautioned against such a use in US.[10] Moreover, senior industrial scientists have an instrumentalist view of their science as a means primarily to produce data that will demonstrate product safety and efficacy in order to overcome regulatory hurdles; and other research suggests that such a view is quickly adopted by graduates who enter

[6]   B Fischoff, S Lichtenstein, P Slovic, D Derby and R Keeney *Acceptable Risk* (Cambridge University Press, 1981); HJ Otway and D von Winterfeldt 'Beyond Acceptable Risk: On the Social Acceptability of Technologies' (1982) 14 Policy Sciences 247; *Risk: Analysis, Perception, Management* (Royal Society, 1992).

[7]   J Abraham *Science, Politics and the Pharmaceutical Industry: Controversy and Bias in Drug Regulation* (UCL Press, 1995) p 152,

[8]   *Science, Politics and the Pharmaceutical Industry: Controversy and Bias in Drug Regulation.*

[9]   *Science, Politics and the Pharmaceutical Industry: Controversy and Bias in Drug Regulation* p 242.

[10] *Science, Politics and the Pharmaceutical Industry: Controversy and Bias in Drug Regulation* p 229.

industry.[11] The case studies undertaken by Abraham show that industrial scientists may expend considerable efforts to attempt to produce evidence that a drug is exceptionally effective, but only undertake toxicity checks if required to do so by regulators.[12]

The evidence of industrial scientists is open to challenge and check by independent scientists. This could counteract bias, although there remain concerns that given the sponsorship of academic research by the industry and the increasing commercialisation of academic science that there is no such thing as an 'independent' scientist.[13] However, faced with uncertainties or dispute as to a drug's quality, safety and effectiveness, Abraham's studies suggested regulators consistently give the benefit of scientific doubt to the drug manufacturer, and indeed that regulators have become increasingly permissive during the 1980s, at least with respect to the types of drugs studied.[14] In the Opren case, for example, the FDA in the US approved the marketing of the drug there (under the name Oraflex) despite the unsatisfactory nature of the drug's carcinogenicity testing by reference to the agency's own standards, and despite lack of evidence of the drug's efficacy to outweigh the risks of phototoxicity.[15] The CSM in the UK approved Opren without requiring experimental phototesting on humans and after the completion of only one, unsatisfactory, carcinogenicity testing in animals.[16] The FDA appears to treat the evidence put forward by manufacturers with more circumspection than the UK regulatory authorities, although given the lack of transparency of the UK regulatory process this is difficult to assess.[17] Nevertheless, in the case of Feldene and Zomax the FDA overrode the doubts of its own scientists and approved the drug for marketing,[18] and in the case of Suprol the FDA effectively re-wrote the statistical rules to represent a clear cut statistically siginficant result as a marginal one.[19]

[11] J Abraham *Science, Politics and the Pharmaceutical Industry: Controversy and Bias in Drug Regulation.*

[12] *Science, Politics and the Pharmaceutical Industry: Controversy and Bias in Drug Regulation* p 243.

[13] T Barlow 'Science plc' Prospect, August/September 1999, 36.

[14] *Science, Politics and the Pharmaceutical Industry: Controversy and Bias in Drug Regulation* p 249.

[15] *Science, Politics and the Pharmaceutical Industry: Controversy and Bias in Drug Regulation* p 177.

[16] *Science, Politics and the Pharmaceutical Industry: Controversy and Bias in Drug Regulation* p 177.

[17] *Science, Politics and the Pharmaceutical Industry: Controversy and Bias in Drug Regulation* p 246.

[18] *Science, Politics and the Pharmaceutical Industry: Controversy and Bias in Drug Regulation* Chapters 5 and 6.

[19] *Science, Politics and the Pharmaceutical Industry: Controversy and Bias in Drug Regulation* p 240.

Abraham's evidence goes to support the arguments of other commentators on risk regulation, that regulators routinely opt for 'consumer risk', putting the risk onto the consumer, rather than 'producer risk'.[20] This bias is evidenced both in the initial decision to grant a licence for marketing and in the subsequent decision to withdraw a product. The result of giving the benefit of the doubt to the producer is that regulators require a lower standard of evidence of safety and efficacy to be proved in licensing decisions, and a far higher standard of evidence of harm to be shown before a drug will be withdrawn from the market.[1] Further, Abraham's case studies show that the regulators have preferred to require companies to disclose the evidence of risks rather than to withdraw the product from the market. The preferred strategy is to require companies to alter their product summaries and labelling, and to send 'Dear Doctor' letters informing practitioners of adverse reactions or the results of further trials. This effectively shifts the decision to the practitioner, and exposes the consumer to the risk of poor prescribing.

In making assessments on a drug's efficacy and safety, regulators are engaged in decisions that extend well beyond science, and concerns about ensuring the drug's safety and efficacy have to be balanced against the impact of costs of the regulatory requirements on bringing drugs to the market, on innovation and also on the delay that regulation imposes. One of the common criticisms of the regulation is that the clinical trials and testing that have to be done to satisfy the regulation create a 'drug lag', inhibiting the speed with which drugs can be put on the market and so used to treat patients. The pharmaceutical industry estimates that it takes 10–12 years and costs £350 million to develop a new medicine.[2] It has been argued that the regulatory requirements inhibit innovation, discourage the development of new drugs for the treatment of rare diseases, 'orphan drugs', and encourage, or at least do not discourage, the development of 'me too' drugs, which have no additional therapeutic value.[3] A recent report for the European Commission recommended that the regulators should facilitate experimentation and earlier controlled dissemination of new medicines coupled with more stringent post-marketing evaluation

[20] KS Shrader-Frechette *Risk and Rationality: Philosophical Foundations for Populist Reforms* (University of California Press, 1991) pp 131–145. See also the discussion in Chapter 10 above in respect of risk and product standards.

[1] *Science, Politics and the Pharmaceutical Industry: Controversy and Bias in Drug Regulation* p 249.

[2] ABPI, Pharmaceutical Fact Sheet, 1998.

[3] See for example M Weatherall *In Search of a Cure: A History of Pharmaceutical Discovery* (OUP, 1990) p 278. The concern that 'me too' drugs are poor value for money has been countered by H Kettler *Competition through Innovation, Innovation through Competition* (Office of Health Economics, 1998).

involving post marketing surveillance, post marketing clinical trials and prescription event monitoring. Such a policy, the authors argued, could accelerate the pace of innovation whilst steering health care system to cost effective and genuinely advantageous technology.[4]

Some question whether existing systems of post-licensing monitoring are sufficiently robust to justify a relaxation of controls at the pre-licensing stage, however. At present companies are required to have pharmacovigilance systems in place to monitor the effect of the drug in use, and there is a system for reporting adverse drug reactions, the 'yellow card' system. However, Abraham's study found that regulators do not always take ADRs as seriously as some might like. Abraham observed a bias in regulators' appraisals of ADRs, with regulators assuming that new drugs will have higher ADRs than older drugs simply because the incidence of reporting is higher. It is assumed that because in the past reporting on drugs has decreased over time, then this must follow for any new drug. Higher rates of ADR tend therefore to be seen as to be due to the drug's newness rather than its exceptional toxicity.[5]

A further criticism that can be made of the current regulatory system is its lack of transparency. It is possible to gain far more information about the licensing process and the drugs available in the US under US freedom of information laws than is possible for the same drugs marketed in the UK. There are no consumer or patient representatives on the boards of the licensing authorities; authorities do not have to give reasons for their decisions either to refuse a licence or withdraw medicines from sale, and indeed are inhibited by the requirement to observe commercial confidentiality. The only exception is drugs licensed under the centralised procedure, for the CPMP is required to issue an assessment report and give reasons for its decision to grant a licence which are then available to any person on request.[6] In a report into drug regulation in 1993 the Consumers' Association found that key information was barred from disclosure. This included the safety data on which decisions to license drugs are taken, the advice of expert committees on issues of safety, the categorisation of medicines and the list of approved medicines for the NHS, official reports on inspections of manufacturing sites, and data on adverse drug reactions, particularly newly marketed medicines.[7] In 1993

---

[4]   E Mossialos, C Ranos and B Abel-Smith *Cost Containment, Pricing and Financing of Pharmaceuticals in the European Community: A Policy Makers View* (LSE Health and Pharmetrica SA, 1994).

[5]   J Abraham *Science, Politics and the Pharmaceutical Industry: Controversy and Bias in Drug Regulation* p 201.

[6]   Regulation 2903/93, Article 12(4).

[7]   *Balancing Acts: Conflicts of Interest in the Regulation of Medicine* (NCC, 1993) p 5. See also *Secrecy and Medicines in Europe* (NCC, 1994).

the NCC joined forces with the Campaign for Freedom of Information to draft a bill that would give consumers access to information on drug safety. The Medicines Information Bill was accepted by Giles Radice MP, but failed to get through the report stage in the House of Commons.[8]

One of the central characteristics of pharmaceutical regulation is complex nature of the relationship that the pharmaceutical companies have with the government. The government is at once the pharmaceutical industry's sponsor, regulator and principal customer.[9] The pharmaceutical industry is a significant contributor to the UK's balance of trade in visibles (after North Sea oil), with a trade surplus in 1998 of over £2.1 billion, and directly employs approximately 75,000 people.[10] Successive governments have undertaken a number of initiatives to assist the industry in improving its competitiveness, particularly in biotechnology.[11] The government's role as sponsor is in potential conflict with its role as regulator,[12] and is in constant conflict with its position as customer. For whilst on the one hand the government may want to ensure the profitability and success of the pharmaceutical industry, as the principal consumer of its products the government simultaneously wants to ensure that it does not pay an excessive price for its products.

A constant concern over the years has thus been the price of drugs, both prescription medicines and over the counter (OTC) drugs. As noted above, competition in the pharmaceutical industry is largely product based, not price based. With product competition there is little incentive to reduce prices. Further, medicines are seen as essential in the ways that other goods are not. This prompts some to fear that there is no effective limit on the price that pharmaceutical companies can charge.[13] For many OTC drugs, which have very similar therapeutic effects, price competition is theoretically possible. However OTC drugs have been subject to a retail

8   *The Medicines Information Bill: A Guide to the Bill* (NCC, 1993).
9   For discussion of this relationship, see in particular L Hancher *Regulating for Competition: Government, Law and the Pharmaceutical Industry in the United Kingdom and France* (Clarendon Press, 1990).
10   *Pharmaceutical Fact Sheet* (ABPI, 1998); *The Value of Medicines* (ABPI, 1998).
11   In 1992 the Biotechnology Industry Regulatory Advisory Group was set up by government to discuss the regulation of biotechnology, and in 1995 a £17 million awareness programme, 'Biotechnology Means Business', was launched. The programme includes funding for small companies and for joint ventures between academia and industry, funding for academia to encourage it to develop patenable products, the creation of business 'mentoring and incubation' services, and a finance advisory service. For details see the DTI's Bioguide at: http:www.dti.gov.uk/bioguide.htm#contents
12   See J Abraham *Science, Politics and the Pharmaceutical Industry: Controversy and Bias in Drug Regulation* Chapter 2.
13   D Taylor and A Maynard *Medicines, Europe and the NHS* (King's Fund Institute, 1990).

price maintenance scheme since 1970, which allows manufacturers to set and enforce minimum prices on branded OTC medications such as painkillers, cold and cough remedies, vitamins and anti-smoking products. In March 1999 the Director General of Fair Trading was given leave to apply to the Restrictive Practices Court to remove RPM, arguing that the structure of the OTC market had changed significantly in the last 29 years. Traditionally it had been argued that RPM was essential to ensure that small chemists did not go out of business. However the Director General of Fair Trading argued that as pharmacists get over 70% of their turnover from dispensing prescriptions, allowing large retailers to reduce prices in OTC drugs would not be such a threat to the existence of smaller chemists. The case is due to be heard at the end of 2000.

It is on the cost of prescription medicines that government attention has traditionally focused. Pharmaceuticals absorb just under 11% of the NHS budget, a total cost in 1994 of £4.3 billion.[14] The legislative controls exclude economic considerations of price or cost effectiveness from consideration when drugs are being approved, and prices are not directly set by the government in the UK, in contrast to most other EU countries.[15] Instead, a voluntary pharmaceutical price regulation scheme (PPRS) has been negotiated between the Department of Health and the ABPI since 1958 regarding the price of drugs which is based on the level of profits that companies can make. The scheme is voluntary, but the Department of Health does have statutory powers to set prices if companies do not comply.[16] These powers have never been used.

The initial aim of the PPRS was to ensure that the drug bill for the NHS was fair and reasonable. Social policy was combined with industrial policy when the objectives were broadened in 1969 to include that of securing the strength, competitiveness and innovativeness of the UK pharmaceutical industry.[17] Initially the scheme related price to what was paid in other countries, a system in place in several other EU countries including Italy, the Netherlands, Ireland and Portugal.[18] It moved to a

---

[14] B Abel-Smith and E Mossialos 'The Pharmaceutical Industry' in R Baldwin et al *Regulation in Question: The Growing Agenda* p 87.

[15] E Mossialos and B Abel-Smith 'The Regulation of the European Pharmaceutical Industry' in S Stavridis, R Morgan, E Mossialos and H Macrum (eds) *New Challenges to the EU: Policies and Policy Making at the End of the Century* (Dartmouth, 1996) p 379.

[16] NHS Act 1977, s 57; Health Act 1999, ss 33–38.

[17] J Sergeant 'The Politics of the Pharmaceutical Price Regulation Scheme' in W Streeck and P Schmitter (eds) *Private Interest Government: Beyond Market and State* (Sage Publications, 1985).

[18] E Mossialos and B Abel-Smith 'The Regulation of the European Pharmaceutical Industry' in S Stavridis, R Morgan, E Mossialos and H Macrum (eds) *New*

profit based system in 1967 following the report of the Sainsbury committee, and was successively tightened during the 1970s.[19] The PPRS regulates the profits which companies can make from their sales to the NHS. The general agreement is negotiated every five years between the Department of Health and the ABPI, and individual company details are negotiated between the Department of Health and that company. The scheme covers all branded pharmaceutical products sold to the NHS. It does not operate with respect to each individual drug, but rather on the companies' business with the NHS overall. It restricts the levels of profit that companies can make on their total business with the NHS, measuring profitability in terms of the return on capital employed.

A new PPRS was agreed in 1999 to commence in October 1999 to run for five years. All companies are to be allowed a profit level of 21% on capital employed, reduced to 17% for assessing price increases. There is a margin of tolerance. Companies can retain additional profit of up to 40% over the target however where this is based on innovation, efficiency and competitiveness (raised from 25% in the 1993 agreement). If profits fall below 50% of target companies may ask for a price rise to take them to 80% of target. In addition all suppliers will be required to reduce the prices of products covered by the scheme by 4.5%, thereafter no price may increase before January 2001. If profits exceed the margin, the company may repay the excess profit or the company can reduce the price of some of its products to a level which will ensure it will not exceed the target in the coming year.

Those in favour of the PPRS argue that its five-year life span gives stability and certainty, that it regulates allowable expenditure on promotion and research and development, that the industry participates in negotiating the regulation, it is not imposed upon it, thus it is argued improving compliance with it, and finally, the freedom for the company to choose how to price individual products enables companies to export drugs profitably. In order to prevent parallel imports (drugs being bought by wholesalers cheap in one country where the price is regulated by the state and sold on at a higher price in another where prices are not regulated) many countries specify that the price of the drug in their country cannot

---

Challenges to the EU: Policies and Policy Making at the End of the Century (Dartmouth, 1996) p 379; and see further E Mossialos, C Ranos and B Abel-Smith Cost Containment, Pricing and Financing of Pharmaceuticals in the European Community: A Policy Makers View (LSE Health and Pharmetrica SA, 1994).

[19] See generally L Hancher Regulating for Competition: Government, Law and the Pharmaceutical Industry in the United Kingdom and France (Clarendon Press, 1990) Chapters 3 and 5.

exceed the price in the country of origin. Companies can thus load their profit on the product they are trying to push onto the export markets.[20]

The PPRS has also been criticised on a number of grounds, however.[1] Firstly, it has been argued that it is unnecessary: the market for branded and patented drugs is competitive, or at least would be in the absence of price controls. Price controls, even in the form of profit control, are unnecessary and counterproductive.[2] Secondly, establishing what is a 'fair' profit is difficult in most industries, and particularly hard in the pharmaceutical sector where the costs of research and development are so high (only two out of ten products which enter the market cover their research and development costs), where only one product in every 5,000 evaluated at the clinical stage will reach the market, where it is difficult to predict competition, there is uncertainty about future market conditions, and where so little is known of the cost effectiveness or outcomes of different therapies.[3] Thirdly, the profits of the pharmaceutical companies are linked with the average profits of the FTSE 500 companies, which overlooks the peculiarities of the market. Fourthly, the system suffers the same limitations as any system of rate of return regulation. The informational demands on the regulator are high; creating incentives to efficiency is difficult; there is a bias to capital-intensive modes of production; and linking the price structure to the rate of return is complex. Further, as only part of the company's products may be regulated, there may be an incentive to shift part of the unregulated costs to the regulated part of the business.[4] Fifthly, companies may seek to recover profits on unregulated products, in this case generic drugs. As the government encourages the prescribing of generic drugs, this will in fact enable companies to recover profits in any event. Sixthly, the system does not provide incentives for the development of orphan drugs, nor indeed establish any priorities regarding

---

[20] See B Abel-Smith and E Mossialos 'The Pharmaceutical Industry' in R Baldwin et al *Regulation in Question: The Growing Agenda* p 99.

[1] For more detailed discussion of the politics of the PPRS see L Hancher *Regulating for Competition: Government, Law and the Pharmaceutical Industry in the United Kingdom and France* (Clarendon Press, 1990).

[2] W Duncan Reekie 'The PPRS: Regulations without a Cause?' and P Brown 'The Increasing Irrelevance of the PPRS' in D Green (ed) *Should Pharmaceutical Prices be Regulated?* (IEA, 1997); W Duncan Reekie *Medicine Prices and Innovations: An International Survey* (IEA, 1996); P Danzon *Pharmaceutical Price Regulation: National Policies versus Global Interests* (AEI Press, 1997).

[3] B Abel-Smith and E Mossialos 'The Pharmaceutical Industry' in R Baldwin et al *Regulation in Question: The Growing Agenda*; E Mossialos 'An Evaluation of the PPRS: Is There A Need for Reform?' in D Green (ed) *Should Pharmaceutical Prices be Regulated?* (IEA, 1997).

[4] See R Baldwin *Regulation in Question* (LSE 1995) p 37; R Baldwin and M Cave *Understanding Regulation* (1999) Chapter 17.

health targets or outcomes. The same ranking is given to every innovation.[5] Seventhly, price regulation is very hard to police and the system is not heavily enforced. In 1994 the Department of Health employed only 14 officials, including administrative staff, plus four accountants to audit 60 companies. In 1988–1991, 38 of the 60 companies exceeded their targets, but only one a year was required to repay anything.[6] Finally, the system is not transparent: negotiations with each company are confidential and the outcomes known only to that company and the DoH.[7]

PPRS operates to control the supply side of the pharmaceutical market. There are also a number of other strategies which have been adopted to contain the cost of drugs which apply to the demand side. The first is a requirement that the consumer pay part of the cost of the drug. In most EU countries the patient has to pay a proportion of the cost. In the UK this is £5.25 for each item prescribed, which represents about 60% of the average cost. Exemptions and provisions mean that only about 15% of patients pay this charge.[8] The government also operates a negative list, a list of drugs which will not be paid for by the NHS. Further, as patients do not choose which prescription drugs to take, this has a limited impact. The government has thus increasingly tried to influence doctors' prescribing. It has promoted the use of generic drugs, that is drugs that contain the same active ingredient as a prescription medicine that is no longer protected by a patent. The manufacturer simply copies the original product, and so does not have to incur the risks and costs of development. Generic medicines are therefore significantly cheaper. Generic prescribing is where a doctor prescribes a medicine using the generic name of its active ingredient. Over 55% of all prescriptions for NHS medicines are written generically (accounting for 20% of the drugs bill),[9] and in some surgeries

---

5   E Mossialos 'An Evaluation of the PPRS: Is There A Need for Reform?' in D Green (ed) *Should Pharmaceutical Prices be Regulated?* (IEA, 1997).

6   E Mossialos 'An Evaluation of the PPRS: Is There A Need for Reform?' in D Green (ed) *Should Pharmaceutical Prices be Regulated?* (IEA, 1997). For companies with NHS sales of over £20 million per year (which is around 85% of sales to the NHS), full financial returns are negotiated every year. For companies with NHS sales of between £1 million and £20 million full financial information is not required on an annual basis, and companies with sales of under £1 million are not normally regulated.

7   *Balancing Acts: Conflicts of Interest in the Regulation of Medicine* (NCC, 1993); L Hancher *Regulating for Competition: Government, Law and the Pharmaceutical Industry in the United Kingdom and France* (Clarendon Press, 1990); E Mossialos 'An Evaluation of the PPRS: Is There A Need for Reform?' in D Green (ed) *Should Pharmaceutical Prices be Regulated?* (IEA, 1997); B Abel-Smith and E Mossialos 'The Pharmaceutical Industry' in R Baldwin et al *Regulation in Question: The Growing Agenda.*

8   B Abel-Smith and E Mossialos 'The Pharmaceutical Industry' in R Baldwin et al *Regulation in Question: The Growing Agenda* pp 92–93.

9   W Duncan Reekie *Medicine Prices and Innovations: An International Survey* (IEA, 1996).

(principally fund holding ones) the rate is over 90%.[10] Some have argued that to encourage the use of generic drugs where the doctor has not prescribed a generic drug, but rather a brand name, the pharmacist should have the power to override the prescription and dispense a generic drug instead. Such a practice, known as generic substitution, is currently prohibited in the UK except in emergencies and under strict hospital control. Opponents argue that this would enable the pharmacist to override the doctor's judgements on an individual patient, and that there may be good reason why the doctor has prescribed a brand rather than a generic. Changes of drugs, even minor ones, can be harmful in the course of some treatments, and further elderly patients in particular who are on a long course of drugs are likely to become confused or not take the drug if the packaging or dosages change. It could be argued that there are other methods than generic substitution that can contain the drugs bill, and further that it does not get to the heart of the problem, which is the need to ensure that drugs are only prescribed where they are necessary and that those which are prescribed are the most effective.

It is ostensibly to address both these issues and that of rationing of health care in the NHS that in August 1999 the National Institute for Clinical Excellence came into operation, surrounded by a certain degree of controversy. The role of NICE is to act as a central point of appraisal of new medicines and other medical technologies and to produce and disseminate clinical guidelines for the NHS on ways of treating clinical conditions and diseases. It is estimated that it will assess between 30 and 50 treatments a year, selected on the basis of their intrinsic siginficance to the NHS, either in cost terms or in terms of potential health gain and benefit, or where there is considerable variation in their use in practice.[11] At present, any appraisal of a new medicine that comes on to the market is normally done by district health authorities acting independently. The concern was that there was no agreed criteria for assessment, many health authorities did not have the resources and expertise to make an assessment, it was a huge duplication of effort, and authorities could ultimately reach different conclusions.[12] NICE will act as a central point of appraisal of new medicines and technologies for England and Wales, and provide an assessment of their clinical and cost effectiveness. It will categorise the medicine into one of three groups: those that should be available for routine use in NHS, those that should be subject to further research, or

---

[10]   ABPI *Generic Medicines* (1998).

[11]   Select Committee on Health, Minutes of Evidence (Thursday 4 February 1999) Q15 (Dr Radford, DoH).

[12]   Select Committee on Health, Minutes of Evidence (Thursday 4 February 1999) Q5 (Sir Michael Rawlins (chairman of NICE)); C Mihil, *Hard Rations: Getting the Right Treatment on the NHS* (ABPI, 1999).

and those that for reasons of clinical ineffectiveness or lack of evidence should not be in routine use.[13] It will then disseminate clinical guidelines to doctors. Compliance with the guidelines will be audited by a new Committee on Health Improvement.

It is the central focus on the criteria of cost effectiveness which has prompted concerns that NICE is essentially a way to reduce the NHS budget and introduce more systematic rationing. Exactly what the relationship between NICE and the DoH will be remains to be seen. There are fears that the DoH will simply tell NICE that a particular treatment is too expensive and should not be permitted for routine use. Others argue that NICE will be able to put forward stronger arguments for the use of apparently expensive treatments based on full and systematic assessment.[14] Further, there are concerns at how clinical effectiveness will be measured, whether it will include the views of patients on their treatment or whether it will be left to the preserve of the medical and scientific professions. There are also concerns that in measuring cost effectiveness, zero or inadequate account will be taken of the costs that may be incurred by sectors other than the NHS if treatment is not given. An example is treatment of mental health, where the costs of failure to treat would fall on social services, prisons or other sectors of the community and other Departments. Thus the treatment may be costly for the NHS, but confer large potential savings for society as a whole, to say nothing of the patient's own situation. The position at the moment is not reassuring, for the Department of Health has admitted that such costs are not necessarily considered in current programmes, and there is no system envisaged for including them in the cost effectiveness appraisals performed by NICE.[15] Finally, the industry in particular is concerned at the introduction of a fourth, economic, criteria, which is in addition to those of safety, quality and efficacy required for licensing. They argue that the pre-licence development of a drug does not include such criteria, and that its introduction at the post-licensing stage will act as a chokepoint for innovative new therapies, delaying their introduction further. Moreover, the cost effectiveness of a drug is not always apparent until it has been in use for several years. Opponents argue that there will thus be insufficient evidence on which NICE could make a decision, and assessments made too early could exclude potentially cost-effective treatments from being used.[16] Whether NICE will meet these objections remains to be seen.

[13] Select Committee on Health, Minutes of Evidence (Thursday 4 February 1999) Q6.
[14] Select Committee on Health, Minutes of Evidence (Thursday 4 February 1999) Q37 (Sir Michael Rawlins).
[15] Select Committee on Health, Minutes of Evidence (Thursday 4 February 1999) Qq24 and 25, Dr Radford (DoH).
[16] *NICE and Medicines* (ABPI, 1999).

PART IV

Conclusion

Conclusion

Chapter 13

Conclusion

The techniques of consumer protection considered in this book range from self-regulation by business, through the use of private law, to the regulatory activities of bodies of central and local government. The reasons why consumers need protection, why the free operation of the markets will usually operate to their disadvantage, were considered in Chapter 1. It is important to note that in deciding whether and how consumer protection can be achieved, two considerations need to be borne in mind. The first is that in choosing between courses of action to adopt we need to recognise that the comparison should be made between solutions which are themselves imperfect. Markets do not operate in accordance with the model of the perfectly competitive market; regulation does not operate in accordance with the model of an accurately designed set of regulatory techniques that matches perfectly the problems they aim to correct and which are seamlessly and fully implemented by both regulators and firms alike. The second is that markets themselves are not 'free'. The opposition, frequently made, between regulation and the 'free' market is deeply misleading. Markets are constituted by rules, by laws. Laws of contract, of property, make it possible for a market to function. In the absence of those laws, and institutions for their enforcement and implementation, transactions could not occur with any certainty for it would always be open to either side to step aside from the transaction.[1] Now there are distinctions to be made between law and regulation that these arguments often fail to recognise. But nonetheless the central point is clear: that in

---

[1]   See further C Sunstein *Free Markets and Social Justice* (OUP, 1997); C Shearing 'A Constitutive Conception of Regulation' in P Grabovsky and J Braithwaite *Business Regulation and Australia's Future* (Australian Institute of Criminology, 1993).

determining whether consumers are better protected by the market or in
some other way the choice is not one of 'free markets' as opposed to
'unfree markets', but of particular states of ordering.

Each of the different techniques adopted to achieve the goal of
consumer protection which have been considered in this book has its own
strengths and limitations, which the preceding discussions have
highlighted. The strategies have been broadly grouped into those which
are self-regulatory, and those which operate in private and in public law.
The next section will consider at a more general level the relative advantages
and weaknesses of theses broad categories of techniques, before making
some suggestions as to the future direction of consumer law and regulation.

I   SURVEYING THE TECHNIQUES OF CONSUMER PROTECTION

(a)   Self-regulation

Relying on self-regulation of business to protect the consumer, as we
have seen, has several potential advantages. It can provide regulation
which is based on sounder knowledge of the area being regulated,
particularly important in complex areas such as technical standard setting,
and a greater sensitivity to and awareness of what forms of regulation will
be appropriate and effective. As it is meant to be developed by firms
themselves, it is argued that there will be greater compliance as firms will
feel more committed to the rules that they themselves have written.
Enforcement of the regulation will be undertaken with greater flexibility—
'technical' rule breaches, ie breaches that have not in fact resulted in any
harm occurring, will not be punished at all or as onerously as those that
have resulted in some substantive damage. The costs of the regulation fall
on the firms themselves, and their customers to the extent firms can pass
those costs on, but there is no cost to the state. Finally, the regulation is
likely to be perceived to be more legitimate by those it is regulating than
regulation imposed by the state. There will be a sense of ownership and
thus acceptance of the regulation, again improving compliance.

However as was discussed in Chapter 2, self-regulation can often fail
to deliver these advantages for a number of reasons. The first, and one of
the most important, is that self-regulation is voluntary. In its purest form,[2]
there is no requirement, direct or indirect, for a firm to subscribe to a

---

[2]   For discussion of the different types of self-regulation see J Black
'Constitutionalising Self-Regulation (1996) 59 MLR 24; A Ogus 'Rethinking Self
Regulation' (1995) 15 OJLS 97.

system of self-regulation. Firms can be discouraged from joining self-regulatory organisations because they may see that not joining confers a competitive advantage: they do not have to incur the costs of complying with the self-regulatory rules or code. Alternatively, or in addition, some firms who have taken the trouble to build an individual brand reputation may not want to be associated with other, less reputable firms who may be members of the association. The voluntary nature of self-regulation also means that no one self-regulatory body necessarily has a monopoly. There may be several self-regulatory associations whose membership covers firms in the same area of business. Those associations may compete for members (members pay fees which provide the income for such associations), and so to make themselves more attractive to potential members they may well lower the standards they require of member firms. The self-regulatory rules, rather than being standards to which firms should aspire are instead simply confirmatory of the lowest existing standards of behaviour. If any one organisation does try to raise its standards then it risks losing members, and those who remain are unlikely to accept them if they feel that those outside the organisation can get away with lower standards (a version of the adverse selection problem discussed in Chapter 1).[3]

Voluntary membership also poses problems when it comes to enforcement. Self-regulatory bodies are unlikely to want to impose onerous sanctions on firms for fear that they will leave the organisation either before they are disciplined or after. This will have the effect of reducing their membership (and income) base. But it also has the paradoxical effect that those firms who are perhaps in most need of regulation are then subject to none at all.

Self-regulatory associations are also likely to be beset with chronic conflicts of interest. They are likely to be acting both as trade associations and as regulators. In their guise as trade associations they will be actively representing and promoting interests of their members. However in their guise as regulators they are meant to be imposing requirements on those firms, that are meant to require those firms to act in a way other than they otherwise would to further a broader public interest. In addition, those rules will impose costs of complying with the regulation. Associations may themselves seek to avoid costs associated with implementing regulation—not enforcing the regulation, or by discouraging consumers from using their arbitration service, both of which would impose costs on the association itself. While it might be that in the long run regulation is actually in the self-interest of the firm as it may result in greater consumer confidence and recognition of quality and thus in increased business, not

---

[3]   See above p 31.

all firms or associations may be able to see that far ahead. Firms, like individuals, are not the all-seeing, all-knowing rational actors that economists think them to be.

None of the above means that self-regulation will always be ineffective. It does mean, however, that there are very particular conditions that have to be met before any self-regulatory system will in fact deliver the advantages that are so often claimed for it by its proponents. Those conditions are firstly, that there has to be sufficient incentive for firms to join the association, either imposed by the state or the market. Incentives imposed or provided by the state could simply be the threat of statutory regulation. They could also be the conferral of monopoly status on the association (eg the professions) or other form of requirement for membership before a person can engage in a certain type of business, although this represents a modification to the 'pure' model of self-regulation. For the incentive to be imposed by the market consumers have to be aware that those firms who are members of the association will offer better quality services or products than those that are not. However, as we have seen, consumers are often not in a position to make this assessment, and so market incentives may well fail. Secondly, there have to be pressures to minimise the tendency of self-regulatory bodies to dilute standards. These could again be provided by the market, but only if consumers really can assess the difference in quality between different firms, which they only can in limited circumstances. Alternatively, benchmarks have to be set by other bodies, but again this is contradictory to the model of 'pure' self-regulation. Thirdly, there has to be a system of effective sanctions, and no place for firms to hide if they want to avoid the sanction. This could be achieved by the strong incentives to stay a member of the association noted above, or by the agreement of all other firms that they will not, for example, do business with the infractor (an example is the effectiveness of the 'cold shoulder' given by banks and other firms to companies who do not comply with the rulings of the Panel on Takeovers and Mergers). Finally, in order to resolve the issue of conflicts of interest, the association has to establish a separate disciplinary body that is, and is accepted by consumers and others to be, truly independent from the association.

These conditions are necessary to ensure the effectiveness of self-regulation, but they can rarely be met. Indeed, as the OFT concluded in its assessment of self-regulatory systems encouraged under the Fair Trading Act:

> Trade associations, set up for the benefit of members, will frequently be neither comfortable nor effective in the role of sectoral regulator. The inherent conflict between the tasks of a regulator and their representational and promotional duties, as well as their lack of necessary power over their

membership, militate against choosing this route, save in exceptional circumstances.[4]

Instead of self-regulation, the OFT is proposing a voluntary system of accreditation. A firm will be accredited by the OFT as a 'better business' if it complies with a core standard. That core standard covers four issues: pre-sale relationships, terms of contract, complaints, and dispute resolution, and is based on three principles. Firstly, a firm is not to exploit its greater knowledge and understanding of a product to effect a sale against the consumer's best interests. Secondly, a firm is to take all possible steps to improve the customer's knowledge of the product and the market. Thirdly, having made the sale the firm is to provide prompt after sales service and resolve complaints speedily and equitably. There will then be sector-specific standards for each business area. The argument for a voluntary system is that it enables standards to be maintained, and the hope is that those who are accredited will in turn only deal with other accredited firms.

Another alternative to the pure model of self-regulation (in which firms voluntarily agree to organise themselves to develop standards of conduct which all agree to abide by and to accept some form of sanction for their breach) is 'enforced self-regulation'.[5] Developed principally by Ayres and Braithwaite, the idea is that firms should be encouraged to write their own rules, subject to regulatory approval, and should introduce their own systems for monitoring and compliance. Regulators should adopt an enforcement strategy that is co-operative as long as the firm is behaving co-operatively; it should however then become increasingly coercive should the firm begin to exploit the co-operative stance or cheat on compliance. This, Ayres and Braithwaite argue, combines the advantages of self-regulation (expertise, flexibility, adaptability, commitment, increased compliance) whilst avoiding the disadvantages (standards are maintained, enforcement is not left solely to the firms, conflicts of interest are mitigated, costs of rule formation are placed on firms).

There are limitations to the model as a regulatory strategy, however. It is highly resource intensive, both for the firm and for the regulator. Firms would have to be well resourced to have the time and personnel to commit to such an exercise, and the regulation would probably have to be central to their business operations for them to be willing to do so. Regulators also have to have the resources to examine individually each set of rules. These resource requirements cannot satisfactorily be reduced by making the process of approval routine and carried out by low-level officials acting

4   *Raising Standards of Concumer Care* (OFT, 1998) para 2.23.
5   I Ayres and J Braithwaite *Responsive Regulation: Transcending the Deregulation Debate* (Clarendon Press, 1992) Chapter 4.

in accordance with internal guidelines. This would defeat the reasons why the technique was adopted, and provide a sure way for it to mutate into simply another form of bureaucratic regulation. The approach can only work effectively if the agency engages in the process, and really does treat each individual set of rules individually, and not in accordance with internally set general guidelines applied either by rote or out of a concern to exercise as much control as possible over the regulated firms.[6] Further, to the extent that the technique involves reliance on internal models or audits in the hope that these will reveal the true state of affairs within a firm, then this hope could be misplaced. For as soon as it becomes known that they are to be used for regulatory purposes then those documents will come to be written in a way that is formalistic and defensive.[7]

(b)   Private law as a technique of consumer protection

The second main set of techniques explored which provide consumers with protection are those requirements imposed by law which affect the rights and duties of producers, suppliers and consumers, and which consumers are required to enforce themselves through the courts. Often described as private law systems of regulation, it is not the nature of the law which differentiates private law from regulatory law in this context, but the fact that private individuals have a right to bring a legal action if the requirement has been breached, and the right to receive a remedy. Indeed the primary responsibility for enforcing the standard may lie with the individual, although in some cases, for example competition law, the state also has a responsibility for enforcement.

A hallmark of the views which society has about consumer protection is that it is still seen largely as a collection of individual problems which individual consumers must attempt to solve by taking individual action. Much of consumer protection law is private law, which consumers must initiate by themselves if they are to benefit. Consumers who receive a faulty product or sub-standard service, for example—the most common consumer complaints—must seek redress on their own, and if a business should refuse a reasonable settlement, consumers are expected to enforce their private law remedies by taking court action. Professor John Western has contrasted this perception with that towards similar issues in society:

---

[6]   See further J Black 'Talking about Regulation' [1998] Public Law 77; R Baldwin and M Cave *Understanding Regulation* (Clarendon Press, 1999).
[7]   M Power *The Audit Society* (Clarendon Press, 1997); F Haines *Corporate Regulation: Beyond Punish or Persuade* (Clarendon Press, 1998).

[Consumer] problems are still seen as very much an individual affair which the citizen must attempt to solve on his own. The contrast was made with other situations he might confront: a burglary, a major breakdown in services such as a massive power failure or interruption to the water supply. In these situations societal resources would immediately be called upon to assist.[8]

The assumption is that consumers know their rights and are sufficiently motivated to press them. If they are harmed because a business infringes their rights, economic self interest will impel them to take action, including court action if a settlement cannot be achieved. The advantages of private law, or more specifically private enforcement, are said to be that it can provide a deterrent effect on firms through the threat of civil damages, and that it has inherent advantages over enforcement by government regulators.[9] Firstly, it can overcome failures in government enforcement arising from lack of resources or capture. Secondly, individuals have an incentive and personal motivation to bring actions to enforce the law that public bodies do not have—it is the individual who has suffered harm or loss. Thirdly, individuals will have first hand knowledge of the fact that they have been harmed: the costs of detection can be much lower. The fourth and fifth reasons are less instrumental. They are, fourthly, that there is an intrinsic benefit to ensuring that those who harm others by their conduct should be obliged legally to compensate those persons (an idea that underlies the current developments for 'restorative justice' in criminal law).[10] Fifthly and finally, enforcement can be seen as a participatory activity which allows individuals to air their grievance and to assert their understanding of the public interest (although it will be the court that makes the final determination).

There are however limitations to the effectiveness of private enforcement, and thus to relying on private law to implement much consumer protection regulation. Firstly, the incentive to bring an action will only operate where the harm is significant for that individual, and in particular is greater than the time and money needed to bring litigation. Where a harm is widely distributed then the free rider problem will mean that there will be under enforcement. The harm suffered by society as a whole may be significant, but that suffered by each individual may be small. A single individual is unlikely to bring an action in a situation where

---

[8]   Philip G Schrag 'Bleak House 1968: A Report on Consumer Test Litigation' (1969) 44 NYU LR 115, 116; cf Andrew Nichol 'Outflanking Protective Legislation—Shams and Beyond' (1981) 44 MLR 21.

[9]   On the relative merits of public and private enforcement see further S Shavell 'The Optimal Structure of Law Enforcement' (1993) J Law and Econ 270; G Calabresi 'Transaction Costs, Resource Allocation and Liability Rules—A Comment' (1968) J of Law and Econ 67, 69.

[10]   See, for example, W Cragg *The Practice of Punishment: Towards a Theory of Restorative Justice* (Routledge, 1992); T Marshall *Restorative Justice: An Overview* (Home Office, 1999).

the harm to that individual is not great, and where others will benefit from any action that individual does take. The person will instead hope that someone else goes to the trouble and expense of bringing litigation, from which that person will then benefit without having to have taken any action at all. The outcome in such a case is that the enterprise will continue committing the harm, despite the fact that there will be an inefficient utilisation of resources, if the value of the harm to the enterprise is less than its total cost to individuals. Rosenfield gives this example of 10,000 individuals illegally harmed by a large enterprise:

> Let the economic harm to each be relatively small—say $1,000. Assume also that by causing the harm, the enterprise benefits by $8,000,000. Then if the cost of joining the claims of the harmed individuals is great, and if the cost of bringing an individual action for damages is greater than $1,000, it will pay no one to litigate the issue. The enterprise will have an incentive to commit the harm, and the result will be an inefficient utilisation of scarce resources (the harm is worth $8,000,000 to the firm but imposes costs of $10,000,000 on the harmed individuals) and a clandestine redistribution of wealth from the harmed individuals to the firm.[11]

Secondly, there is the issue of the relationship of the remedy (damages) to the deterrent effect that such damages are meant to provide. The remedy of damages is primarily concerned with compensating individuals who have been harmed rather than with operating in a preventive way against wrongdoing. If damages were to act as a deterrent, however, they would need to be fixed at a level which is greater than the benefit to the firm for breaching the rule, taking into account the probability of detection.[12] This is likely to be higher than the individual harm suffered in any one instance, but may serve as an incentive to individuals to bring actions in which they will receive over-compensation. Some economists argue that this will lead to over-enforcement: the amount paid out by businesses will be greater than the social harm inflicted. The way to avoid such over-enforcement is to ensure that damages are set in relation to the harm suffered, as at present, but the deterrent effect may then be reduced. Businesses can still be in a better position and can profit by wrongdoing after paying compensatory damages to the few consumers who complain and incurring other amounts such as opportunity costs. Damages will only have a deterrent effect if it is less expensive for a business to alter its behaviour than to give relief to consumers who complain or who are likely to complain

---

[11] A Rosenfeld 'An Empirical Test of Class Action Settlement' (1976) 5 J of Leg Stud 113.

[12] E Allan Farnsworth 'Legal Remedies for Breach of Contract' (1970) 70 Col LR 1145, 1147–1148.

in the future. The award of punitive damages might have a deterrent effect, but the courts are reluctant to award them because, it is said, they involve a windfall for plaintiffs and a punishment of defendants without the protection of the criminal law. If private law has a modifying effect on business behaviour, this should be evident following the huge volume of product liability litigation in the United States, yet the evidence is that this has not effected the safety of consumer products in that country.

The third disadvantage of private enforcement is that the costs and responsibility of detecting the harm, and of proving that it was caused by the defendant's actions, fall on the individual. Many consumers fail to complain, and those who do and face business resistance rarely have the knowledge or incentive to take the matter further. Not only is cost likely to serve as a disincentive to bringing an action, but where the harm is being suffered by a whole sector of consumers, in the absence of the ability to bring a class action, valuable economies of scale are lost as each individual has to bring a separate action. Moreover, detecting harm and proving causation may in some cases be quite straightforward, but very complex in others. A characteristic of certain consumer offences is that they are complex, diffused over time and unpublicised. Consumers may not recognise that they have been adversely affected by a trade practice or lack sufficient incentive to complain. In many cases where the impact of wrong doing occurs in the future, there are no victims to complain in the present. The adverse effects of some food additives and drugs are cases in point, for their effects are not manifest until after use over a period. The further related point is that regulation which is designed to prevent harm occurring cannot effectively be implemented by private regulation which requires consumers to wait until the harm has occurred before an action can be brought.

Furthermore, consumers may not be cognisant of their legal rights and the remedies by means of which their grievances can be redressed. They may not connect their problems with a legal obligation on the part of businesses to provide a solution. Thus a number of surveys indicate that consumers who in their own view have cause to complain do not do so, that consumers mistakenly think that manufacturers and not retailers are liable for defective products and that few consumers know whom to contact when they strike difficulties.

The problem is especially acute with poorer consumers, a fact which reflects their general inequality in society. Poorer consumers are more likely to pay higher prices for what they buy and to be exposed to unscrupulous marketing techniques, but are less likely to complain when things go wrong or to know about official consumer protection agencies. The class action or the mass restitution suit, in which consumer protection agencies or consumer protection organisations can seek redress on behalf of the many consumers adversely affected by an unlawful trade practice, even if they have not complained, was suggested in Chapter 3 as the main way of overcoming the drawbacks to the private law as an instrument of consumer protection. There have been some recent developments which have made some limited moves in the latter direction which could be built on. One good example is the ability of the Consumers' Association to bring actions for unfair terms under the Unfair Terms in Consumer Contracts Regulations 1994.[13] The Consumers' Association has recently threatened to use such powers to proceed against some of the major mortgage lenders, who the Association argue have included unfair terms in their mortgage contracts.[14]

Apart from the procedural deficiencies of the private law, we saw the doctrinal inadequacies as well.[15] The notion of freedom of contract, for example, explains many of the defects of the private law in practice, because it has been used by the more powerful party in the market place, business, to the detriment of the less powerful, the consumer. Some legal doctrines directly protect business from consumer claims. For every *Farnworth Finance Facilities Ltd v Attryde*,[16] there is a *United Dominions Trust Ltd v Western*;[17] for every *Donoghue v Stevenson*,[18] a *Daniels v R White & Sons Ltd*;[19] and for every *Financings Ltd v Baldock*,[20] a *Galbraith v Mitchenhall Estates Ltd*.[1] However, some commentators think that the common law underwent an important shift in the twentieth century away from the values of market individualism towards a system more informed by consumer welfarism.[2] This shift has been supported by important legislative reform, for example over the control of unfair terms. However, perhaps the most radical change in structures of contract law as they affect consumers is not doctrinal, but rather the introduction of *administrative* controls over the use of unfair terms, which effectively combines contract law doctrine with more pro-active regulatory controls than the private law itself can offer.

Finally, there is the separate issue of whether the courts are competent consciously to give judgment with a view to improving consumer standards. One line of thought is that it is beyond the limits of adjudication,

---

13   SI 1999/2083.
14   Http://www.whichnetcampaigns
15   See also for example SM Waddams 'Legislation and Contract Law' (1979) 17 UWO LR 185; Barry J Reiter 'The Control of Contract Power' (1981) 1 OJLS 347. Cf Edward P Belobaba 'The Resolution of Common Law Contract Doctrinal Problems through Legislative and Administrative Intervention' in Barry J Reiter and John Swan (eds) *Studies in Contract Law* (Butterworths, 1980) pp 432–435.
16   [1970] 2 All ER 774, [1970] 1 WLR 1053.
17   [1976] QB 513.
18   [1932] AC 562.
19   [1938] 4 All ER 258.
20   [1963] 2 QB 104.
1   [1965] 2 QB 473.
2   H Collins *The Law of Contract* (Butterworths, 3rd edn, 1997).

because the courts can only manage separable issues, which can be isolated analytically at one time, as opposed to 'polycentric' questions, where a litigant's argument relating to any matter changes depending on how the court reacts to any other issue.[3] In this view courts which attempt to set standards are engaged in polycentric balancing—they have to place values on factors such as functional ability, aesthetics and safety—but they have neither the knowledge nor expertise to do this. In rebuttal, other commentators argue that standard setting is not necessarily highly polycentric and that courts are capable of investigating, understanding and evaluating evidence of a scientific or technical nature if the adversary process is improved with more sophisticated trial methods. The debate seems peculiarly American, for there the courts take an active role in standard setting in the consumer area. In Britain there seems little possibility that the courts will be bold enough to engage in setting consumer standards, and in any event the matter can be more efficiently dealt with by government regulation.

Perhaps the fundamental problem of private law, at least as a means of influencing the behaviour of businesses, is that its impact is interstitial rather than comprehensive.[4] Courts are primarily concerned with settling concrete disputes on a case by case basis rather than with the long-term social implications of their decisions. Judicial decision-making is incremental, and an overall policy must be derived inductively from a succession of separate decisions, each based on its own facts. The nature of a seminal case can influence the entire trend of the law, but in many cases the courts will not be aware of the drift of legal change. The courts are subject to procedural and evidentiary limitations which make a full examination of the relevant facts impossible, with judicial notice expanding the scope of the investigation only slightly. Courts cannot enforce their decisions, oversee the consequences of make adjustments in the event that these are unforeseen.

(c) Public regulation

Public regulation in the area of consumer protection became important in the nineteenth century when it was realised that the courts were not a

---

[3] AD Twerski et al 'The Use and Abuse of Warnings in Product Liability—Design Defect Litigation Comes of Age' (1976) 61 Cornell LR 495.

[4] M Shapiro 'Stability and Change in Judicial Decision Making' (1965) 2 Law in Transition Q 134; Paul J Mishkin and Clarence Morris *On Law in Courts* (Foundation Press, 1965) p 124; Edward P Belobaba 'The Resolution of Common Law Contract Doctrinal Problems through Legislative and Administrative Intervention' in Barry J Reiter and John Swan (eds) *Studies in Contract Law* (Butterworths, 1980).

suitable vehicle for consumer protection measures. Reformers quite rightly recognised that the costs of litigation meant that change through the courts would come slowly, if at all; as Hurst notes of developments in the United States:[5]

> Slowest to develop was a third great field of public responsibility for the social environment—the protection of the ultimate consumer, now reduced to individual insignificance in the mass markets the law had helped to form. One set of problems had to do with sales of goods. Here common-law remedies by actions for damage negligently inflicted or for fraud and deceit or breach of warranty were expensive; the complaining party carried a difficult burden of proof against remote sellers or manufacturers, and the law was liberal in defenses offered the entrepreneur; the loss in the particular instance often was not big enough to warrant the trouble and cost of suit, though the aggregate of individual losses might represent a substantial total waste or oppression. From about 1881 the states began to legislate to protect consumers of food.

At the same time reformers also had a healthy suspicion of the political philosophy underlying judicial doctrines. It is clear from the courts' decisions earlier in the century that the adoption of negligence in place of strict liability was to assist industrial growth by insulating businesses from liability and imposing the social cost on workers and consumers.[6] This is not to say that judicial doctrines were unaffected by the dominant morality and the notions of individual responsibility prevalent at the time, or that the doctrines, in the interests of consistency, did not apply equally to all. But the reality of formal equality was substantive inequality in practice, because businesses were responsible for the great bulk of the activities causing harm to others, in particular in the industrial sphere. Likewise, 'freedom of contract' meant that entrepreneurs could use their power to force contracts onto consumers to the latter's disadvantage.[7] A true concern on the part of the courts with equality in practice would have seen them develop further the notions of unconscionability and contracting in good faith. Doctrinally, the courts have taken some steps to further consumer protection in the twentieth century, but the main advances have passed the courts by; for example, there is still no common law doctrine of product liability as in the United States and statute has been necessary to overturn some of the worst excesses of standard form contracts.[8]

It has been against this background—the lamentable inadequacy of private law remedies—that public law has assumed such an importance in

---

[5]   James Willard Hurst *Law and the Conditions of Freedom* (University of Wisconsin Press, 1956) p 97; C Sunstein *After the Rights Revolution* (Yale UP, 1990).

[6]   See Chapter 5.

[7]   Grant Gilmore 'Products Liability: A Commentary' (1970) 38 U Chi LR 103, 113.

[8]   Consumer Protection Act 1987, Pt I; Unfair Contract Terms Act 1977; Unfair Terms in Consumer Contracts Regulations 1999, SI 1999/2083.

the field of consumer protection. The general favour with which the present work views public law is not, however, a completely uncritical acceptance. One of the reasons for the categorisation of public law adopted above was to bring out the advantages and disadvantages of the different techniques. For example, broad criminal prohibitions are relatively simple to formulate and, in the main, to enforce. On the other hand, they are not always diligently enforced in practice, and when legal proceedings are taken the courts tend to impose minor penalties which businesses can treat as an ordinary expense. Successive studies of the enforcement techniques adopted by regulatory agencies emphasise the importance of 'compliance' as opposed to 'deterrence' models of enforcement.[9] The latter places strong emphasis on criminal prosecution. But bringing prosecutions is fraught with difficulties. Not only is it highly costly for the regulatory agency, involving a significant commitment of financial resources, time and personnel, but it is often fraught with frustration and delays. For example, Professor Philip G Schrag, who was for a time head of the enforcement division of the New York City Department of Consumer Affairs, tells how initially under his leadership the division began with a 'judicial model' of action: it interviewed witnesses, gathered facts and then went to court to prosecute.[10] But in doing so it encountered numerous frustrations, in particular delays and an unsympathetic judiciary who regarded crime in the streets as much more important than consumer fraud. As a reaction, the department evolved what Schrag calls a 'direct action' model, or what is generally termed a 'compliance' model of enforcement. In addition to prosecution, agencies seek out non-litigious methods of pressuring disreputable companies into changing their practices.

Techniques used can range from using the threat of action as a tool in negotiating compliance with the firm through to publicity of the breach— 'naming and shaming', mass restitution suits (in the US), revocation of licences, taking advantage of technical breaches of legislation and putting pressure on reputable financial institutions and suppliers to withdraw support.

One suggestion to improve the threat of criminal law is that civil consequences should attach to violations of criminal provisions so that contracts are automatically unenforceable when criminal provisions have been breached. Coupled with the power of consumer protection agencies to seek compensation for individual consumers adversely affected through mass restitution suits, this would greatly increase the deterrent effect of

---

[9]   K Hawkins *Environment and Enforcement* (Clarendon Press, 1984); B Hutter *Compliance* (OUP, 1997).
[10]   Philip G Schrag 'On Her Majesty's Secret Service: Protecting the Consumer in New York City' (1971) 80 Yale LJ 1529.

criminal provisions. There seems no reason whatever—apart from the political power of organised business—for a provision like s 35 of the Trade Descriptions Act 1968, which provides that contracts are not void simply by reason of breach of the Act.

Another suggestion, based on North American experience, is that criminal penalties should be converted into civil penalties. The argument is that the courts are more prepared to impose civil penalties because of the lower standard of proof and because offenders are not stigmatised.[11] Clearly if civil penalties imposed are equal to or greater than any profits accruing as a result of unlawful activity, they would affect the behaviour of rational businesses. But courts are in no position to know this under present judicial procedures, and consequently it seems premature to abandon the uncertain but real stigmatisation associated with the imposition of criminal penalties.

What is really needed is a completely different approach by the courts to criminal offences like violations of consumer law. One possible way of achieving this is the establishment of a separate court for considering consumer protection offences, like the Market Court in Sweden. Such a body could be expected to treat consumer offences with greater severity, because it would get to know their adverse consequences for ordinary citizens, and at the same time have a bureaucratic desire to demonstrate output. The establishment of a consumer court is only a first step, however, and there needs to be a much more fundamental reshaping of opinion in the community towards violations of consumer law.

Public enforcement of consumer law and regulation has the advantage that it can provide economies of scale in detecting breaches and bringing actions against businesses. However, it has the difficulty that the vigour of its implementation is often compromised by the paucity of resources allocated to enforcement. Enforcement agencies are thus limited in what they can do, and tend to rely on public complaint or public outcry to determine their priorities. As a result objectionable behaviour, whose adverse effects are not immediately obvious to ordinary consumers, may be overlooked.

Another major defect with public control is that enforcement agencies may become closely identified with those they are supposed to regulate. It has been observed how enforcement agencies go through a degenerative life-cycle, starting it as vigorous protagonists of the public interest, then gradually becoming bureaucratised and more increasingly solicitous of those they are regulating. To the Marxist, this is a logical development of monopoly capitalism: economic power is in the hands of private capital and subject only to nominal control by a government, which itself is in the

[11] David Tench *Toward a Middle System of Law* (Consumers' Association, 1981).

hands of private capital. As Marx put it in the Communist Manifesto: 'The executive power of the…state is simply a committee for managing the common affairs of the entire bourgeois class.' In other words, the Marxist argues that government regulation is a sham to assuage public opinion, while in fact it leaves quite undisturbed the real focus of power. Baran and Sweezy, two Marxist economists, argue that the main reason for government regulation is to ensure that industries are neither too profitable nor too unprofitable, for extra large profits are gained at the expense of both consumers and other capitalists, while extra low profits damage elements of the capitalist class.

> It therefore becomes a state responsibility under monopoly capitalism to ensure, as far as possible, that prices and profit margins in the deviant industries are brought within the range prevailing among the general run of giant corporations…In each course some worthy purpose is supposed to be served— to protect consumers, to conserve natural resources, to save the family-size firm—but only the naïve believe that these fine-sounding aims have any more to do with the case than the flowers that bloom in the spring.[12]

Such analysis may be over-fatalistic, however. Whatever the motives, there have been significant advances in consumer protection over the last few decades, although there is still much that could be done. Nevertheless, it is the case that ultimately the question of whether enforcement agencies can exercise sufficient control over businesses is a question of whether these agencies have political support for their tasks. Political support at the level of party politics is of obvious importance, for while an enforcement agency can attain a degree of autonomy from its political masters, that will be fairly short-lived if its behaviour is diametrically opposed to their interests. Direct political support from the community on a day-to-day basis gives a clout to enforcement agencies enabling them to ignore to some extent political forces. Consumer protection has moved further onto government agendas, and it is now common in new regulatory agencies to have some form of consumer representation. Nevertheless this has its own difficulties. The person or persons appointed to perform this role may not be representative of all consumers, they may not be sufficiently familiar with the area of business being regulated to be able to have an effective impact on decision making, and they may themselves be co-opted into adopting the dominant perspective of business or the regulator.[13]

12 Paul A Baran and Paul M Sweezy *Monopoly Capital* (Penguin, 1966) p 74. For a similar view of the practice of 'compliance' models of enforcement see F Pierce and S Tombs *Toxic Capitalism: Corporate Crime and the Chemical Industry* (Dartmouth/Ashgate, 1998).
13 MJ Trebilcock 'Winners and Losers in the Modern Regulatory System: Must the Consumer Always Lose?' (1975) 13 Os HLJ 619, 641–643.

2   THE FUTURE REGULATION OF CONSUMER MARKETS

It is a challenging but interesting time to write of the future regulation of consumer markets. Within the highest level debates the old tensions between interventionist public regulation and laissez-faire and deregulatory approaches have to some extent been displaced a new approach variously described as 'transcending the deregulation debate'[14] developing 'smart regulation'[15] or offering a 'third way' for the state to promote social welfare.[16] The ambition lying behind these debates is to develop mechanisms which are effective at delivering social policy outcomes, such as a high level of consumer protection, but in ways that involve less direct control via costly public regulation. The successful pursuit of this agenda is likely to involve subtle mixtures of instruments and techniques. However, the problem of government control (the limited capacity of the state both to develop knowledge and to direct others what to do) is equally present in attempting to develop these new solutions. A central characteristic of the contemporary consumer law scene is the fragmentation of authority between local, national and supranational authorities and non-government organisations over both standard-setting and enforcement. Programmatic action by any particular public authority is likely to be at its most effective when using indirect interventions to shift the balance between these fragmented groups, rather than when seeking to impose some overall system of control.[17] An equally intriguing prospect is that perceptions of failure by both consumers and industry will lead them to bypass government altogether to forge consensus on self-regulation for certain products, such as genetically modified organisms.[18]

How does the current programme of reform of British consumer policy shape up against these considerations? What are the main themes? Firstly, there have been a number of major institutional reforms. Financial services regulation has been consolidated and strengthened in a new Financial Services Authority. The utilities regulators are being reformed with consumer protection functions substantially transferred to independent consumer councils. The advisory function on food standards has been moved outside ministerial departments to a new Food Standards Agency. New standards and mechanisms for setting standards are being developed. The discretionary system of competition regulation has been substantially

---

[14]   I Ayres and J Braithwaite *Responsive Regulation* (OUP, 1992).
[15]   N Gunningham and P Grabosky *Smart Regulation* (OUP, 1997).
[16]   A Giddens *The Third Way and its Critics* (Polity, 2000).
[17]   A Dunsire 'Tipping the Balance: Autopoiesis and Governance' (1996) 28 Administration and Society 299.
[18]   D Campbell 'Of Coase and Corn: A (Sort of) Defence of Private Nuisance' (2000) 63 MLR 197.

displaced by a system of prohibitions over anti-competitive conduct. The precautionary principle is to receive greater prominence in the work of standard-setting bodies in areas such as food and product safety. The system of rule-making to address unfair trade practices under the Fair Trading Act, moribund for 20 years, is to be revived and simplified. Linked to this enforcement is to be reformed by simplifying the mechanisms by which the OFT can issue cease and desist orders against unfair trade practices, and extending the enforcement capacity to local authorities. The co-ordination of enforcement has been promoted through soft law, in the form of the Better Regulation Task Force Enforcement Concordat.[19] A key plank of government policy is providing better information to consumers, through disclosure requirements and better education. The approach to EC norms has softened with the development of a principle that EC and domestic rules should be consolidated (to be applied first to the relationship between the Unfair Contract Terms Act 1977 and the Unfair Terms in Consumer Contracts Regulations 1999).

The ambition of these reforms does appear to be linked to the objective of shifting power to those with the greatest capacity to secure the achievement of consumer policy outcomes and developing mixed patterns for standard-setting and enforcement by involving consumers, businesses and state bodies at all levels.

In some cases it is hard to evaluate the effectiveness of the current reforms. The tightening of regulatory enforcement powers, for example for the Financial Services Authority and the Office of Fair Trading, may be part of a strategy for using the *potential* of tougher regulatory intervention to promote more responsible self-regulation by firms and trade associations. However there is no institutionalised requirement of this kind of responsiveness in regulation, and consequently the risk that a pattern of heavy-handed and ineffective regulatory interventions might develop.

Some measures cut in two directions. Thus the empowerment of third parties to take regulatory enforcement action under the Competition Act 1998, the Unfair Terms in Consumer Contracts Regulations 1999 and the instrument to implement the EC Injunctions Directive of 1998 simultaneously bring power to those who may have a greater interest and capacity to enforce the law than state bodies, but who may, thereby interfere with any responsive approach through over-zealous regulatory enforcement. The government is taking steps to address the problem of over-zealous enforcement generally by taking powers under the Regulatory Reform Bill 2000 to issue enforcement codes, which will provide more

---

[19]   See also Better Regulation Task Force *Consumer Affairs* (The Stationery Office, 1998).

formal rules than the current Enforcement Concordat (noted above).[20] Though such codes, where issued, will not be binding, a court will be able to take them into account in determining remedies for breach of regulatory standards. There is a further general problem that flexible or responsive enforcement practices may be inadequate to satisfy the European Commission that effective and uniform enforcement of EC measures is being pursued.[1]

In other policy areas there is clear resistance to the logic of the new approach. In some policy areas the government is resisting calls to replace ineffective standards with new ones—for example control over extortionate credit bargains under the Consumer Credit Act 1974. Institutional reforms have been criticised for being insufficiently radical, for example failing to fully recognise the distrust of government in food safety policy, and retaining key powers in the Department of Health and Ministry of Agriculture Fisheries and Food.

Overall, the espousal by the government of a new commitment to the rhetoric of consumer protection, exemplified by the 1999 White Paper and subsequent action plan, represents the most significant reform of consumer law since the early 1960s. But there is no measure within the programme as radical as the Trade Descriptions Act 1968, Fair Trading Act 1973 or Consumer Credit Act 1974, and no institutional reform as important as the creation of the Office of Fair Trading (1973). The reform programme is more modest, and falls to be evaluated against the standard of how well it remedies defects in the operation of existing standards and enforcement mechanisms.

The future prospects for consumer markets do not, of course, depend on the conduct of national governments alone. Measures introduced into UK law because of EC legislation already have a central position in understanding UK consumer law, and further supranational initiative is likely, though perhaps at a slowing pace. The changing practices of firms both in terms of methods of production and for transacting business, together with consumer responses to such change are also of central importance. Two areas of rapid change demonstrate this wider point. New methods of transacting business associated with electronic commerce are already beginning to profoundly affect the ways that consumers buy goods and services, throwing up novel problems. New methods of producing foodstuffs by genetic modification, for example of cereals and fruits, have caused considerable controversy and consumer resistance.

---

[20] Cabinet Office *Publication of Draft Regulatory Reform Bill* (Cm 4713 (2000)) clause 9.

[1] European Commission 'Enforcement of European Consumer Legislation' SEC (1998) 527 Final.

With electronic commerce the UK government has legislated to facilitate transactions by making electronic signatures as legally valid as conventional signatures.[2] An EC measure is passing through the legislative process with a view to harmonising such facilitative rules in the EU. The Organisation for Economic Co-operation and Development is attempting international consumer protection through soft law in the form of guidelines. But fundamental to the shift in practices, and thus the regulatory issues, is the conduct of firms and consumers. There is, as yet, considerable uncertainty as to what will make trading by e-commerce successful, and the extent to which consumers will take up new forms of transaction. The UK's leading supermarket has become the UK's leading 'e-tailer' (retailer trading by electronic commerce) with a system for ordering groceries on the Internet and a fleet of delivery vans. New companies, for example selling books at a discount, have also had considerable success. The continuing evidence of wide disparities in car prices between the UK and other EC countries[3] has encouraged the Consumers' Association to establish its own business importing cars bought in other Member States for UK consumers—a market-based example of 'direct action'.

But many consumers are likely to be wary of developing considerable dependence on internet shopping as it can be much more difficult to be certain who the retailer is, where they are located and what remedies might be available if things go wrong. The implementation of the EC Distance Selling Directive provides some protection, in the form of cooling-off periods of similar standard across the EU. However some novel problems have yet to be addressed. For example, though the information which consumers give to businesses about themselves is protected by data protection legislation[4] these measures do not control the use of 'footprints' left by consumers on the internet. Thus it is possible to build a profile of the kind of sites which particular consumers visit and what kind of things they look at or buy from them, and to use or sell that information for further marketing. Other more prominent concerns have related to access by children to unsuitable internet sites. We might conclude that governments, business and consumers are collectively creating cultural changes in shopping habits, but that considerable uncertainty as to the future remains, and major regulatory problems are likely to emerge. The responses to these problems are as likely to be self-regulatory, coming from the industry, as they are to be derived from governmental action at national or supranational level.

---

[2]   Electronic Communications Act 2000, s 7.
[3]   Competition Commission *New Cars: A Report on the Supply of New Motor Cars within the United Kingdom* (2000).
[4]   Data Protection Act 1998.

Linked to changing technologies of communication, the success of the liberalisation of the EC market in telecommunications has led the European Commission to initiate liberalisation measures in postal services in the EU. Before the initial liberalisation measures have been fully implemented in the Member States,[5] the European Commission is proposing further measures of liberalisation. Accompanying these initiatives have been new regulatory rules, forcing the UK government to establish for the first time an independent regulator of postal services and to introduce statutory service quality standards, similar to those applying to other utility services (discussed in Chapter 5 above). A possible further consequence of the introduction of new firms into the basic letter market is that the Royal Mail will lose its exemption from VAT, with the consequence that consumers will be required to pay an additional 17.5% for stamps. What is interesting about the developments in postal services is the perception that changes in the market—growing competition in parcel services, and the growing importance of alternatives to postal services such as fax and email—are stimulating supranational regulatory initiatives to open up and re-regulate domestic postal services.

With genetic modification of foodstuffs major international firms have rapidly been developing the technology to improve crop yields or improve shelf life of fruits. Much of this development has occurred in the United States where government adopted a fairly minimal approach to regulation of these new production techniques and consumers appeared unconcerned. However in Europe in general and in the UK in particular governments have been cautious and consumers have been even more concerned about the new development. Consumer groups have been particularly vigorous in arguing for the application of the 'precautionary principle' (discussed in Chapter 10) to regulation of genetically modified foods. A key aspect of the EU and UK approach has been the use of the compulsory disclosure technique (discussed in Chapter 9 above) for genetically modified elements in food, which enables consumers to make a choice. An international regulatory battle over this regulatory requirement led a reluctant United States to agree that US products marketed in Europe would comply with these labelling requirements. Perhaps the most interesting and important aspect of this story is that consumer anxieties have led retailers to believe that the disclosure-based approach to regulation is inadequate. Consequently many big retailers have gone to extraordinary lengths to remove genetically modified elements from the foodstuffs which they sell. In this way the new regulatory regime established by government has been by-passed by the practices of consumers and businesses.

---

[5]   A Postal Services Bill which implements an EC Directive on Postal Services 97/67/EC is before Parliament at the time of writing.

Overall we can conclude that it is important to recognise the capacities not just of national and supranational governments, but also of businesses and consumers in shaping the future regulation of consumer markets. When coupled with an appreciation of the wide range of possible techniques for addressing both old and new regulatory problems we have the basis for a critique of the current pattern of consumer law measures and for developing alternative and perhaps more effective forms of control. However, the fullest understanding of the operation of existing laws and regulatory regimes and prospects for new measures is hampered by the absence of systematic research on the origins, effects and effectiveness of law in consumer markets. The development of such research by academia, government, business and consumer groups remains a central challenge.

Index